1968

SOCIAL AND CULTURAL DYNAMICS

Volume One: Fluctuation of Forms of Art

*Volume Two: Fluctuation of Systems of Truth,
Ethics, and Law*

*Volume Three: Fluctuation of Social Relationships,
War, and Revolution*

Volume Four: Basic Problems, Principles, and Methods

Social and Cultural Dynamics

VOLUME THREE

Fluctuation of Social Relationships,
War, and Revolution

BY PITIRIM A. SOROKIN

The Bedminster Press

New York

1962

This book was printed in 1962 in the United
States of America. The text is identical with
that of the original edition in 1937.

PREFACE

Whereas Volumes One and Two deal mainly with fluctuations in the field of cultural processes, this volume concentrates on those in the field of social phenomena. Cultural and social are two aspects of a single, indivisible reality; but for the purposes of analysis they may be conditionally divorced and studied separately.

This volume opens in Part One with a definition of a real social group and indicates its modalities. This leads to a classification of all social relationships and groups into three basic classes: Familistic, Contractual, and Compulsory. With these three providing a foundation, we proceed to study qualitative and quantitative changes in the network of social relationships of the main social groups of European peoples — the State, the Church, the family, guilds, rural and urban communities, and others — from about the eighth to the twentieth century. Part One is primarily concerned with the following problems. Out of what strands — familistic, contractual, or compulsory — and with what proportion of each strand, have the various networks of social relationships been woven? Has the proportion of these different threads been changing for all these groups in the course of time? Which of the groups has been predominantly familistic, or contractual, or compulsory, and at what times? What have been the main changes in this respect in each group during these centuries? What was their "spectrum" in the prewar period and how has it changed since? Wherein does the contemporary social transformation consist from this standpoint? Finally, how are these qualitative transformations in the threads of the network of social groups related to the fluctuation of the main types of culture?

No doubt this brief formulation of problems sounds somewhat abstract. But when the individual chapters have been read carefully, the reader will probably see that the abstractions have become very concrete. These chapters offer a penetrating portrait of social groups, making clear the profoundest transformations. The nature of these transformations once grasped, it is easy to understand that many changes in the political, economic, and other spheres of social organization are merely the by-product of deeper fluctuations. This becomes quite evident in the sections devoted to the study of the fluctuation of the theocratic-Ideational and secular-Sensate forms of political regime and of social leadership, of Ideational and Sensate liberty, and of economic conditions.

After the *qualitative* fluctuations have been studied, we turn to a concise investigation of the *quantitative* fluctuations in the various social relationships of which the network of organized groups is made up. This leads to an investigation of the fluctuation of social groups between totalitarianism and *laissez faire*, between expansion of governmental regimentation and its contraction, and to the consideration of the migration of social relationships from group to group. Hitherto these problems have been largely neglected. They are especially important at the present time when most Western societies are undergoing one of the sharpest "swings" of this kind. In the light of such an analysis, the contemporary changes assume a definite meaning, a significance very different from that of the usual popular interpretations.

Parts Two and Three of the present volume are devoted to a study of the phenomena accompanying sudden and catastrophic breakdowns in a system of organized intergroup and intragroup relationships. These breakdowns lead to war and to internal disturbances (disorders, riots, revolts, revolutions). Part Two attempts to study systematically the movement of war, its increase and decrease, in the history of Greece and of Rome and of Europe. Part Three does the same with regard to the fluctuation of internal disturbances in the same countries during the same twenty-five hundred years. However imperfect may be the investigations in these parts (and the nature of their limitations is clearly indicated), they yet represent what is probably a more adequate, more systematic, and more impartial study of the movement of war and internal disturbances than any other hitherto undertaken. Both the theoretical and the practical importance of these problems is evident and need not be argued.

Finally, Part Four of the volume offers a concise study of the connection between the dominant type of culture and mentality, on the one hand, and the dominant type of culture and conduct, on the other. It closes with a Postscript in which, less formally than in all the previous chapters of the three volumes, I attempt to diagnose the contemporary cultural and social situation and indulge in a kind of guess as to what awaits Western culture at the other end of the crisis in which it now is.

Volumes One, Two, and Three, taken together, constitute a preliminary study of cultural and social dynamics. In Volume Four I will present in a more finished and more fully analytical form, a systematic theory of social and cultural changes, as well as a formulation of the guiding principles of sociological methodology.

The faults of these volumes as they now stand are undoubtedly many, but they do not spring from lack of sufficient preparation or of careful consideration on my part. Nor do they include thinness of substance, shallowness of penetration, incoherence of thought, or pseudo-scientific sentimentalism. Considering the days of responsible but free social investigation to be numbered for the present, I have taken the opportunity, while it yet remains, to follow exclusively the testimony of the facts and evidence, regardless of whether the results are pleasant or unpleasant to this or that group. In justification of such a course I can say, without malice to anybody, "*Amico Plato sed veritas amicissima.*"

PITIRIM A. SOROKIN

Cambridge — Winchester

CONTENTS

PART ONE

TYPES AND FLUCTUATION OF THE SYSTEMS OF SOCIAL RELATIONSHIPS

Chapter One. FAMILISTIC, CONTRACTUAL, AND COMPULSORY RELATIONSHIPS AND SYSTEMS OF INTERACTION (GROUPS) 3

I. Introductory. This volume deals with the fluctuations in the *social* aspect of sociocultural phenomena. Though social and cultural are interlocked elements of an indivisible sociocultural world, theoretically, for the purposes of analysis, they can be studied separately. II. Social interaction and its modalities. Interaction as the generic trait of social phenomena in the real group or real social system as contrasted with the nominal. Main modalities of social interaction: (1) one-sidedness or two-sidedness; (2) extensity of interaction; (3) intensity of interaction; (4) duration and continuity of interaction; (5) direction of interaction (solidary, antagonistic, and neutral); (6) organized and unorganized interaction — the symptoms of organization. Main forms of social systems of interaction (groups). III. Familistic, contractual, and compulsory types of social relationships: these are the result of combining in a certain way the main modalities of social interaction. Analysis of each type.

Chapter Two. FLUCTUATION OF THE FAMILISTIC, CONTRACTUAL, AND COMPULSORY RELATIONSHIPS IN THE LIFE PROCESS OF THE MAIN EUROPEAN SOCIAL GROUPS: I. FROM THE CAROLINGIAN SOCIETY TO THE FOURTEENTH CENTURY 43

I. Introductory remarks. The essential nature of any given social system (group) depends upon the part played in its network of social relationships by the familistic, or contractual, or compulsory type. A knowledge of these elements is more important than that of purely political or economic or other relationships, which are, comparatively, surface phenomena. The purpose of the present chapter is to study the fluctuations of the proportion of familistic, contractual, and compulsory relationships in the network of the main social systems into which the population of Europe was organized during these centuries. II. Predominant sociorelational "spectrum" of the important social groups of the Franco-Germanic human universe in the Carolingian and feudal periods: from the eighth to the thirteenth century. *Fidelitas* as the central form of the period. The Carolingian State. The Feudal State. The Church. The family. Guilds, *Bruderschaften, Bundbruderschaften, Schwurbruderschaften,* corporations, and other associations. Village communities and the urban communes. Feudal hierarchical bonds between the freemen and free social strata. Bonds of serfdom. General summary.

Chapter Three. FLUCTUATION OF THE FAMILISTIC, CONTRACTUAL, AND COMPULSORY RELATIONSHIPS IN THE LIFE PROCESS OF THE MAIN EUROPEAN SOCIAL GROUPS: II. FROM THE FOURTEENTH TO THE TWENTIETH CENTURY 81

I. Main changes. II. The spectrum of the systems of social relationships in the centuries from the end of the thirteenth to the end of the sixteenth. The State. The Church. The family. Village and urban communities. Corporations, guilds, crafts, confraternities. Hierarchical bonds between the free strata of society. Bonds between the free and unfree strata. III. The centuries from the sixteenth to the second part of the eighteenth. Main changes in the chief groups. IV. From the end of the eighteenth to the twentieth century. Main changes. The nineteenth century as the golden age of contractualism. The so-called capitalist system as a contractual system. Summary. V. The Postwar period. Decline and degeneration of contractual systems. Rise of compulsory, familistic, and pseudo-familistic systems (Communist, Fascist, National-Socialist, and others).

Chapter Four. GENERAL CONCLUSIONS CONCERNING THE FLUCTUATION OF THE FORMS OF SOCIAL RELATIONSHIPS IN WESTERN SOCIETY . 123

Summary of the main fluctuations from the eighth to the twentieth century. The reasons for or causes of (*ratio sive causa*) the fluctuations. Internal and external factors. Contemporary degeneration of contractualism. Contemporary governments and statesmen as potent agencies of this degeneration. Sequence of the rise and decline of the main forms of relationships. Association of the main forms of social relationship with Ideational, Idealistic, and Sensate types of culture.

Chapter Five. FLUCTUATION OF THEOCRATIC (IDEATIONAL) AND SECULAR (SENSATE) FORMS OF GOVERNMENT AND LEADERSHIP . . 139

I. Preliminaries. Connection between theocratic and secular forms of political regime and leadership, and the predominant forms of social relationships and types of culture. II. Pulsation of Ideational and Sensate sociopolitical regimes: India, Tibet, China. Greece and Rome. Western society. The contemporary situation. III. Fluctuation of other forms of sociopolitical organizations and processes.

Chapter Six. FLUCTUATION OF IDEATIONAL AND SENSATE LIBERTY . . 161

I. Ideational, Mixed, and Sensate liberty. The nature of liberty and its main forms. II. Fluctuation of Ideational, Mixed, and Sensate forms of freedom in time and space. Connection of this fluctuation with that of the dominant types of culture. Which forms of liberty have been dominant in the various periods of the Graeco-Roman and Western cultures? Rise of Sensate liberty with the rise of Sensate culture. The contemporary situation. III. Why the fluctuation of the Sensate and Ideational forms of freedom? IV. Transition from the one form of freedom to the other,

and the movement of internal disturbances: riots, revolts, revolutions.
v. General conclusions on qualitative fluctuations of social relationships.

Chapter Seven. FLUCTUATION OF SYSTEMS OF SOCIAL RELATIONSHIPS IN THEIR
QUANTITATIVE ASPECTS. ("Rarefaction" and "Condensa-
tion" of the Network of Organized Social Groups. Their
Oscillations between Totalitarianism and the *Laissez Faire.*
Expansion and Contraction of Government Control and Regu-
lation. Migration of Social Relationships) 181

I. Preliminaries. The preceding chapters studied the *qualitative* transformations and fluctuations of social relationships. This chapter inquires
into the *quantitative* aspect, that is, increase and decrease of the *number* of
social relationships that compose the network of a given system or group.
Such a process is styled "rarefaction" and "condensation." "Rarefaction"
means a decrease, condensation an increase, of government control and
regimentation in a group. It means also the fluctuation of the group's
structure between the extreme poles of absolute totalitarianism and *laissez
faire.* II. Rhythm of "rarefaction" and condensation of the net words of
the state system: contemporary expansion of government control and regimentation is not new; it is a recurrence of what has happened many times
before in the history of many state systems, from the remotest past to the
present time. There are, in these fluctuations, long-time and short-time
waves. The state system and its government's functions now swing toward
totalitarianism, now toward *laissez faire.* Outline of these swings in the history of Egypt, Greece, Rome, and the European States. III. Reasons
for and factors of the long-time fluctuations. IV. Factors of short-time
fluctuations: war, impoverishment, and social emergency of whatever
kind. Contemporary expansion of government regimentation and the
trend toward the totalitarian state (Communist, Fascist, Nazi, New
Deal, and others) in the light of the theory advanced. v. Liberty in
its relationship to totalitarianism and the *laissez faire* in the state system.
VI. Transfer and migration of social relationships from one social system
to others.

Chapter Eight. FLUCTUATION OF ECONOMIC CONDITIONS 217

I. Preliminaries. Long-time waves in this field. II. Relationship between
the main types of culture and economic conditions. Reservations. Specifications of economic well-being and its different types. Long-time fluctuations of economic well-being (viewed sensately) in the history of Greece,
Rome, France, and Germany. III. Main conclusions as to the chief
fluctuations in the economic situation of these countries in general and
in the conditions of the leading social classes. Association of long-time
economic waves with rise and decline of the main types of culture, though
not very close, does exist.

PART TWO

FLUCTUATION OF WAR IN INTERGROUP RELATIONSHIPS

Chapter Nine. FLUCTUATION OF WAR IN THE HISTORY OF GREECE, ROME, AND EUROPE: I. METHODOLOGICAL 259

I. Introduction. Organized intragroup and intergroup relationships incessantly change. The changes proceed often gradually and in orderly fashion, in conformity with the rules of change provided for in the constitution of the groups. Such changes do not lead to disorganization and breakdown of the organized network of the social relationships of the groups. Once in a while change is sudden, abrupt, and leads to a collapse of the existing network before the new one is crystallized and established. When this happens in intragroup relationship, the result is internal disturbance (disorders, riots, revolts, revolutions); when it occurs in intergroup relationship, the result is intergroup disturbance which oftens becomes war. Internal disturbances and wars are the sharpest forms of disorganization of the crystallized system of social relationships; hence they must be studied in a work dealing with sociocultural fluctuations. II. Methodological explanations and reservations. The difficulties in the way of a satisfactory study of the movement of war in the course of time. III. The materials of the study: almost all the recorded wars in the history of Greece, Rome, and of nine European countries considered from the standpoint of their duration, the strength of the armies involved, and the casualties.

Chapter Ten. FLUCTUATION OF THE MAGNITUDE OF WAR IN THE HISTORY OF GREECE, ROME, AND EUROPE: II. ABSOLUTE FIGURES . . 289

Total measurements of war in duration, size of the armies, and casualties, by quarter centuries and centuries in the history of Ancient Greece, Ancient Rome, France, Russia, England, Austria-Hungary, Germany, Italy, Spain, Holland, and Poland and Lithuania.

Chapter Eleven. SUMMARY AND MAIN RESULTS 335

I. Absolute figures for four and then nine European countries. Faster increase of casualties compared with the strength of the army in the course of time. Why absolute figures are misleading. II. Relative indicators of the movement of war (per million of population) from the twelfth to the twentieth century. The twentieth century as the bloodiest century of all the twenty-five hundred centuries studied. III. The absolute and relative magnitude of war activities of the various countries studied. IV. The percentages of years with and without war. V. The problem of periodicity in the fluctuation of war magnitude. VI. The "evolution and progress" of war movements. Theories neither of the disappearance nor of the steady growth of war in the course of time are valid. The curve of war movement fluctuates, without any steady trend of whatever kind. The future of war. VII. The curve of war in the life history of a nation. Contrary to the popular opinion the maximum of war activities in the history of a nation falls more frequently within the periods of cultural and social (political, economic) blossoming than within those of cultural and social decline. The reason for this. VIII. War movement and fluctuation of the Ideational and Sensate types of culture. Factors making for war and peace.

PART THREE

FLUCTUATION OF INTERNAL DISTURBANCES IN INTRAGROUP RELATIONSHIPS

Chapter Twelve. FLUCTUATION OF INTERNAL DISTURBANCES IN THE HISTORY OF GREECE, ROME, AND EUROPE: METHODOLOGICAL . . 383
Methodological explanation of the difficulties, uncertainties, and deficiencies of a systematic study of the movement of internal disturbances in the course of time. The materials: most of the recorded important internal disturbances in the history of Greece and Rome, and of nine European countries. Each disturbance is studied from five standpoints. I. As to the social area of the disturbance. II. As to the duration of the disturbance. III–IV. As to the intensity of the disturbance and the masses actively involved in it. Proportional indicator of the magnitude of a disturbance. V. As to the predominant qualitative nature and the main objective of the disturbances.

Chapter Thirteen. MOVEMENT OF INTERNAL DISTURBANCES BY COUNTRIES . 409
The total geometric averages of internal disturbances by quarter centuries and centuries in the history of Ancient Greece, Ancient Rome, Byzantium, France, Germany and Austria, England, Italy, Spain, the Netherlands, Russia, Poland and Lithuania, and Europe. Which centuries and quarter centuries in the history of each country have been most turbulent, which most orderly? Which disturbances have been of the greatest magnitude? The movement of disturbances in Europe as a whole.

Chapter Fourteen. SUMMARY AND MAIN RESULTS 473
Average frequency of important internal disturbances in the history of the countries studied. Number of years with and without disturbances in their history. Evidence that there are no particularly orderly or disorderly nations: the comparative indicators of their disturbances do not differ essentially. The same is true of the comparative violence of their disturbances. Duration of disturbances. Varying configurations, rhythms, and tempo of disturbances. "Action and reaction" in the movement of disturbances. There is no steady trend in the movement of disturbances in the course of time. Neither the partisans of the theory of an increasing orderly progress, nor those of the opposite theory are right: the movement of disturbances fluctuates without any steady trend toward increase or decrease. There is no regular periodicity in the rhythm of order and disorder. Increase of disturbances in the twentieth century: this century has been, so far, the bloodiest in war and one of the most turbulent in regard to internal disturbances. The movements of war and internal disturbances do not show any close and direct interconnection. Disturbances occur in the periods of blossoming of a nation as well as in the period of decline. Current theories

of the factors leading to disturbances — economic, geographic, political, educational, and others — do not account for most of the ups and downs of the curve. Status of the system of cultural values and of the network of social relationships of a group is the decisive factor. Relationship of the movement of the disturbances to the types of culture and to their transformations.

PART FOUR

CULTURE, PERSONALITY, AND CONDUCT

Chapter Fifteen. RELATIONSHIP BETWEEN TYPES OF CULTURE AND TYPES OF PERSONALITY AND BEHAVIOR 509
I. Preliminaries. II. Main propositions. Relationship between the dominant type of culture and actual conduct cannot be expected to be as close as that between the dominant type of culture and mentality. The reasons for this. But in a looser fashion the relationship between the type of culture and that of conduct does exist and is measurable. The reasons. Verification of the propositions in four sets of relevant data. Frequency of the Ideational and Sensate types of personality among all historical persons as listed in the *Encyclopaedia Britannica* by fifty-year periods from 950 B.C. to A.D. 1849; among all the Roman Catholic Popes from 42 to 1937; among the French, Russian, Hapsburg, and English kings. The proportion of historical persons who became historical through religious and business activities from 900 B.C. to A.D. 1849. Conclusions.

Chapter Sixteen. POSTSCRIPT 531
An informal diagnosis of the contemporary crisis. It is infinitely deeper than it is generally understood to be. It is the crisis of our whole over-Sensate culture and society. The Western world is passing through one of its greatest transformations. The Philistinism of the utopia of "orderly progress"; of the cyclical conceptions and diagnoses of decline; of the revolutionary schemes. Western society and culture seem to have entered the stage of transition from an overripe Sensate to a coming Ideational form. The transitory period already is and will continue to be painful, cruel, and bloody, having nothing in common with the popular after-dinner cloud-cuckoo lands of milk rivers with ice-cream shores, of guns turned into golf clubs, and so on. Beyond the grim transitory period there loom not the decline and end of Western culture, but the magnificent peaks of a new Ideational society.

APPENDIXES 541
    APPENDIX TO PART TWO 543
    APPENDIX TO PART THREE 578

INDEXES 621
    INDEX OF AUTHORS 623
    INDEX OF SUBJECTS 627

LIST OF TABLES

1. Total Measures of War for Ancient Greece from 500 to 126 B.C. by Quarter
   Centuries and Centuries 293
2. Relative Indicators of War Magnitude for Ancient Greece Measured by
   Casualties and by Army's Strength 295
3. Total Measures of War for Rome from 400 B.C. to A.D. 476 by Quarter
   Centuries and Centuries 301
4. Relative Indicators of War Magnitude for Ancient Rome Measured by
   Casualties 303
5. Relative Indicators of War Magnitude for Ancient Rome Measured by
   Army's Strength 304
6. Total Measures of War for France from 976 to 1925 by Quarter Centuries
   and Centuries 306
7. Total Measures of War for Russia from 901 to 1925 by Quarter Centuries
   and Centuries 311
8. Total Measures of War for England from 1051 to 1925 by Quarter Centuries
   and Centuries 315
9. Total Measures of War for Austria-Hungary from 1101 to 1925 by Quarter
   Centuries and Centuries 319
10. Total Measures of War for Germany from 1651 to 1925 by Quarter Centuries
    and Centuries 322
11. Total Measures of War for Italy from 1551 to 1925 by Quarter Centuries
    and Centuries 325
12. Total Measures of War for Spain from 1476 to 1925 by Quarter Centuries
    and Centuries 328
13. Total Measures of War for Holland from 1551 to 1925 by Quarter Centuries
    and Centuries 331
14. Total Measures of War for Poland and Lithuania from 1386 to 1800 by
    Quarter Centuries and Centuries 333
15. Summary Figures by Century Periods for France, England, Austria-
    Hungary, and Russia from 1101 to 1925 335
16. Summary Figures by Century Periods for Nine European Countries from
    1101 to 1925 336
17. Percentage of Casualties in Four Countries from the Twelfth to the
    Twentieth Century 337
18. Relative Indicators of War Activities by Century Periods for Nine
    European Countries 341
19. Relative Indicators of War Activities by Century Periods for France,
    Great Britain, Austria-Hungary, and Russia 345
20. Relative Indicators of the Casualty Burden of the Specified Country (per
    Unit of Population) 349
21. Percentage of Years with War 352
22. Comparison of Mewes's and Sorokin's Studies 356

23. Values Given to Internal Disturbances 396
24. Total of the Geometric Average of Internal Disturbances of Ancient Greece from 600 to 126 B.C. by Quarter Centuries 409
25. Total of the Geometric Average of Internal Disturbances of Ancient Greece by Centuries 411
26. Total of the Geometric Average of Internal Disturbances of Ancient Rome from 525 B.C. to A.D. 500 by Quarter Centuries 414
27. Total of the Geometric Average of Internal Disturbances of Ancient Rome by Centuries 418
28. Total of the Geometric Average of Internal Disturbances of Byzantium from A.D. 526 to 1400 by Quarter Centuries 420
29. Total of the Geometric Average of Internal Disturbances of Byzantium by Centuries 421
30. Total of the Geometric Average of Internal Disturbances of France from 526 to 1925 by Quarter Centuries 423
31. Total of the Geometric Average of Internal Disturbances of France by Centuries 427
32. Total of the Geometric Average of Internal Disturbances of Germany and Austria from 701 to 1925 by Quarter Centuries 430
33. Total of the Geometric Average of Internal Disturbances of Germany and Austria by Centuries 433
34. Total of the Geometric Average of Internal Disturbances of England from 651 to 1925 by Quarter Centuries 435
35. Total of the Geometric Average of Internal Disturbances of England by Centuries 439
36. Total of the Geometric Average of Internal Disturbances of Italy from 526 to 1925 by Quarter Centuries 441
37. Total of the Geometric Average of Internal Disturbances of Italy by Centuries 447
38. Total of the Geometric Average of Internal Disturbances of Spain from 526 to 1925 by Quarter Centuries 448
39. Total of the Geometric Average of Internal Disturbances of Spain by Centuries 454
40. Total of the Geometric Average of Internal Disturbances of the Netherlands from 676 to 1925 by Quarter Centuries 456
41. Total of the Geometric Average of Internal Disturbances of the Netherlands by Centuries 459
42. Total of the Geometric Average of Internal Disturbances of Russia from 926 to 1925 by Quarter Centuries 460
43. Total of the Geometric Average of Internal Disturbances of Russia by Centuries 464
44. Total of the Geometric Average of Internal Disturbances of Poland and Lithuania from 951 to 1800 by Quarter Centuries 466
45. Total of the Geometric Average of Internal Disturbances of Poland and Lithuania by Centuries 468
46. Total Measure of Internal Disturbances of Europe from 525 to 1925 by Quarter Centuries 470

47. Total Measure of Internal Disturbances of Europe by Centuries . . . 471
48. Frequency of Important Social Disturbances 474
49. Intensity of Revolutions by Countries — by Class 476
50. Duration of Revolutions by Countries — by Class 478
51. Types of Historical Persons from 950 B.C. to A.D. 1849 Included in *Encyclopaedia Britannica* 519
52. Types of Roman Catholic Popes 522
53. Types of Monarchs 524
54. Geometric Averages for Historical Persons Engaged in Religious and Business Activity Included in *Encyclopaedia Britannica* . . . 527

LIST OF FIGURES

1. Extensity of Interaction 8
2. Feudal Structure 72
3. General Economic Situation in the Ancient World, 600 B.C. to A.D. 400 . 231
4. General Economic Situation in France from 800 to 1926 236
5. General Economic Situation in Germany from 700 to 1932 . . . 242
6. Relative War Magnitude by Casualties and Internal Disturbances for Greece, Rome, the Roman Empire, and Europe 297
7. Relative War Magnitude by Army's Strength and Internal Disturbances for Greece, Rome, the Roman Empire, and Europe 298
8. Periodic Recurrence of Internal Disturbances in China 358
9. Fluctuation of Internal Disturbances in Europe from 500 B.C. to A.D. 1900 Shown by Three Curves 391
10. Movement of Internal Disturbances in Ancient Greece 412
11. Movement of Internal Disturbances in Ancient Rome 418
12. Movement of Internal Disturbances in Byzantium 422
13. Movement of Internal Disturbances in France 428
14. Movement of Internal Disturbances in Germany and Austria . . . 434
15. Movement of Internal Disturbances in England 440
16. Movement of Internal Disturbances in Italy 447
17. Movement of Internal Disturbances in Spain 455
18. Movement of Internal Disturbances in the Netherlands . . . 459
19. Movement of Internal Disturbances in Russia 465
20. Movement of Internal Disturbances in Poland and Lithuania . . . 469
21. Movement of Internal Disturbances in Europe 472

PART ONE

Types and Fluctuation of the Systems of Social Relationships

Chapter One

FAMILISTIC, CONTRACTUAL, AND COMPULSORY RELATION-SHIPS AND SYSTEMS OF INTERACTION (GROUPS)

I. INTRODUCTORY

From the study of the forms and fluctuations of aesthetic, scientific, philosophical, religious, and moral culture mentality, we now pass to the study of the *social* phase of the sociocultural phenomena. The preceding parts dealt mainly with what are often styled culture and cultural values; all the parts of this volume will deal mainly with what are called "*social* phenomena*," in the sense of the interindividual and intergroup relationships of which any social system or group, any organization or institution, is made up, which compose their "texture" and their "structure." The difference between the categories "cultural" and "social" is very conditional and relative: any culture exists through and is objectivized by some social group; and any social group has this or that kind of culture. Nevertheless, technically they can be studied separately, and for the sake of analysis can be isolated from each other, as different aspects of the same one and indivisible "sociocultural world." This conditional "social world" embraces what the partisans of the Formal School in Sociology (Tönnies, Simmel, L. von Wiese, A. Vierkandt, and others)[1] call "the forms of social relationships," interindividual and intergroup. This class of sociocultural phenomena is again double in its nature: on the one hand it consists of the "objectively" existing network of social relationships among the interacting and contacting individuals and groups; on the other, the nature of these relationships, their "color," "qualification," and "evaluation," depends most closely upon the mentality of those who are involved in them or who deal with them (observers, investigators, etc.).

Without this mentality these relationships do not and cannot have any social meaning or sense. Without it the relationships between the patient and the surgeon operating on him and between a knifer and his victim look alike. In their sociocultural sense, these two relationships

[1] See my *Contemporary Sociological Theories* (New York, 1928), chap. ix.

3

are as different as they can be. "Pure behavior" divorced from the
mentality becomes a mere "reaction" or "motion," devoid of any sociocultural meaning. The same can be said of all social relationships. For
this evident reason, the phenomena of social relationships are always the
phenomena of "mentality." They cannot be studied apart from it,
whether it be the mentality of the persons involved in the relationship —
what they think and how they qualify the social relationships — or the
mentality of other persons — observers, onlookers, investigators — and
their qualifications of the phenomena. Therefore, we shall study the
world of social relationships and their fluctuations as the phenomena of
culture mentality also. On the other hand, we all know that the mentality of this or that person (whether involved in the relationships or outside them) qualifies the given relationship in one way; meanwhile the
"objective nature" of the relationship viewed from the standpoint
of the logico-meaningful mentality contradicts this qualification most
sharply. Who does not know of many a master who considered the
relationship of slave and master as most sacred and beneficial, not only to
the master but to the slave also? Who does not know of various religious
or political fanatics who have sent to death thousands, either *ad majorem
gloriam Dei* or for the glory of the "Proletariat," or "Communism," or
"Nationalism," or any other purpose? We may grant their sincerity;
but in many cases we may question the identity of their qualifications of
the relationship with its nature, considered impartially, from the logico-
meaningful standpoint. These two aspects often contradict each other.
Hence the necessity of keeping in mind these two aspects of the social
relationship: the aspect of the mentality of the persons who qualify
them; and the objective logico-meaningful aspect inherent in the nature
of the relationships themselves. This aspect is also the aspect of mentality; but it is logico-meaningful mentality in contradistinction to the
mere factual psychology — with its biases, emotions, passions, "residues,"
"derivations," and the like — of the persons swayed by their qualifications. A dictator may sincerely think he is doing everything for the
benefit of mankind; a serious and competent investigator, after having
examined the logico-meaningful nature and "causal" effects of his activities, may qualify them differently. A master who whips a slave to death
may style his relationship "fatherly"; a logico-meaningful study of it
may give it quite the opposite qualification.

These remarks show that the nature of all social relationships has
two aspects, psychological and logico-meaningful (including the "causal-
functional" traits). Any social relationship has to be studied from both

standpoints. If such a study is made competently, it completely dissects the social relationship until, from the standpoint of its social nature, there remains nothing in it except millions of physical, chemical, or other properties which hardly concern it.

After these introductory remarks we can start with our study of the world of social relationships, their forms, and their fluctuations. By definition, the study will be also a study of the texture and structure of the main types of social systems of interaction, or groups. Let us begin with the study of the most general and most fundamental forms of social relationship. After that we can pass to more specific — economic, political, and other — forms of social relationship and their systems. In view of the lack of any unanimously accepted system of classification of social relationships, and because of the great diversity of meanings given to the same terms by different authors,[2] it is advisable to start with a brief systematic outline of the main concepts involved.

II. SOCIAL INTERACTION AND ITS MODALITIES

Any real social group differs from a mere nominal conglomeration of individuals [3] by the fact that its members are in the process of inter-action, in the sense that the behavior and psychological status of a member are conditioned by the activities or even by the mere existence of other members to a tangible degree.[4] Without such a tangible interdependence

---

[2] *Ibid.*, chap. ix.

[3] Quite intentionally I start the analysis of a social group or social system from a mild nominalistic standpoint. This is done for pedagogical reasons. Eventually this standpoint imperceptibly passes into an organically united nominalism-realism, or singularism-universalism, proper for the idealistic standpoint assumed in this work.

[4] To a tangible degree, because theoretically everything is bound together in this world and nothing is lost in it. Therefore, theoretically the existence and behavior of any individual influences to some infinitesimal degree those of all other individuals. However, this admission does not hinder the existence of different degrees of functional dependence between various individuals, beginning with the closest dependence, in which two or more individuals are bound by such a short "rope" that every action of one of them affects the actions of the others (for instance, between the members of an ideally integrated family), and ending with such a remote and intangible dependence that it cannot be noticed and therefore is practically non-existent. Cournot's brilliant lines express this excellently. In spite of the possibility that "*tout se lie, tout s'enchaîne dans ce monde,*" "nobody would seriously think that by stamping the ground with one's foot one can derange the navigators of the other hemisphere from their course or shake the system of Jupiter's satellites; at any rate the derangement would be of such an infinitesimal order that it cannot be manifest through any effect noticeable for us and therefore we are perfectly authorized to disregard it. It is not impossible that an event occurring in China or Japan has some influence upon the happenings in Paris or London; but generally it is quite certain that the manner in which a Parisian *bourgeois* arranges his day is not influenced by what is happening actually in a Chinese city which

of the existence, behavior, and psychology of the members, there is no real social group. What exists instead is a merely "statistical" or nominal or fictitious collection of individuals.

This tangible interdependence of the actions and psychology of individuals is the *conditio sine qua non* of any real social group or socially interactive system.

A. *Modalities of Social Systems of Interaction.* Such being the general basis of a real social unity, the modalities of the interdependence lead to various forms of social groups or social systems of interaction. Of these modalities the following are important : *one- or two-sidedness of interaction; its extensity, intensity, duration, and continuity; its direction and its organization.*

(1) *One-sidedness and Two-sidedness of Interaction.* First of all, the interdependence of the parties in the process of interaction — and for the sake of simplicity of analysis let us take only two parties — may be more or less equal or it may be such that one party strongly conditions the other.   The executioner conditions the behavior of the victim much more than the victim affects the executioner.   A person who has another person in his complete power can condition his behavior and psychology more than the controlled person can influence his master.   From this standpoint, in a relative way, we may talk of *two-sided* or *mutual*, and *one-sided conditioning*.   The first type is what can properly be styled "interaction" or "interdependence," while the second is one-sided dependence or one-sided conditioning.   Both forms, however, are varieties of the real social group.

(2) *Extensity of Interaction.* Second, we must distinguish the extensity of interaction.

By extensity of interaction is meant *the proportion of the activities and psychological experiences involved in interaction out of the total sum of the activities and psychological experiences of which the person's whole life process consists.*   Let us say that 100, or a circle, is the symbol of the total sum of activities and psychological experiences which compose the whole life process of a given person.   Theoretically we can imagine so complete an interaction that it would condition to some extent all the 100

---

has never been penetrated by a European. These are like two little worlds, in each of which one can observe the chain of cause and effects which develop simultaneously but without a mutual connection and without exerting any influence one upon each other." A. Cournot, *Essai sur les fondements de nos connaissances et sur les caractères de la critique philosophique* (Paris, 1851), Vol. I, pp. 51–52. Compare A. A. Tschuproff, *Ocherki po teorii statistiki* (St. Petersburg, 1909), pp. 99 ff. See a detailed treatment of these and subsequent problems in my *Sistema Soziologii* (in Russian) (St. Petersburg, 1920), Vol. I, chaps. i-iv.

activities and psychological experiences of that person. In the circle there is no sector exempt from conditioning by interaction. This means that none of a person's activities and psychological experiences is independent of the other person; that the whole life of the person, without any exception whatsoever, is conditioned by the process of interaction and is fused with the life of the other person. He cannot do anything without influencing and being influenced by the interacting party. Interaction covers all the fields of his existence and experiences. The extensity of the interaction is complete, unlimited, universal, or *totalitarian*.

In the real processes of interaction hardly a case can be given coinciding with this supposititious case of absolutely unlimited — *totalitarian* — *extensity* of the interaction, but various forms of interdependence give an imperfect approach to it. The interaction of a baby and his mother, who alone takes care of the child, is an approximation to that kind of interaction: sleep, feeding, clothing, bedding, most of the baby's actions and feelings, are dependent upon the mother. Interaction of the members of the closely integrated family is another approach to it: most of their important activities throughout every twenty-four hours are conditioned by the existence and activities of the other members: the time of their rising, the time and the character of their breakfast; what they do, how much, where, and when; their dinner and evening recreation; their tastes, their beliefs, their political attitudes, their occupations, their visits, their clothing; and so on. The joy or sorrow of one member influences the psychology of the others; a change in the activity or psychology of one member reflects upon those of the others. None of their spheres of activity and experience is exempt from conditioning by the others.

If not 100 but only a part of it is conditioned by the interaction with another person, we have a *limited — not universal, not complete — extensity of interaction.* Not the whole circle but only a sector may be involved in the interaction, and is dependent upon the other party. And the less the figure, in comparison with 100, or the narrower the sector, the more limited is the extensity of the interaction, the less universal and complete it is in covering the total field of man's activities and experiences. This means that the remainder of them are independent and unconditioned tangibly by a given process of interaction. Most of the contemporary interaction processes between employer and employee, housewife and grocer, house owner and plumber or carpenter, even a contemporary teacher and pupil, minister and parishioner, doctor and patient, political boss and his henchman, owner and tenant, and so on, are cases of such a *limited extensity* of interaction. In all of these the interacting parties have a specific sector of life, and sometimes — for instance, in purchasing a package of favorite cigarettes at a drugstore — a very narrow, small, and limited one. Interaction between the house owner and plumber concerns only the matter of plumbing and nothing else. The employee-employer interaction concerns only the matter of doing stipulated work for so many hours for such and such remuneration, and that is all. All the other infinitely great number of life activities and experiences of one party — religion, political activity, family, education; aesthetic, scientific, moral, and other activities; opinions, convictions, experiences — normally do not concern the other party. "They are not his business." Thus, from the standpoint of the extensity of the interaction, it may range from 100 — the total circle of human activities and experiences — down to 0.0000001 or the smallest line of the circle; *from an unlimited and universal or all-embracing totalitarian extensity, to the most narrowly specified and limited.*[5]

Diagrammatically this can be depicted as follows.

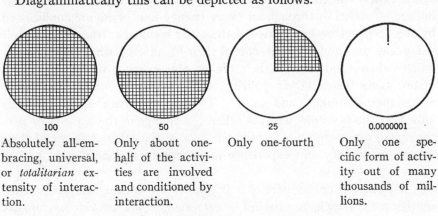

100	50	25	0.0000001
Absolutely all-embracing, universal, or *totalitarian* extensity of interaction.	Only about one-half of the activities are involved and conditioned by interaction.	Only one-fourth	Only one specific form of activity out of many thousands of millions.

FIG. 1.   EXTENSITY OF INTERACTION

[5] I expressed the same idea in my previous works, in the form of distinguishing the "cumulative" and "simple" systems of interaction. In the all-embracing interaction the parties are bound together by the maximum bonds, by all 100 ties. In a theoretically most limited interaction system, they are bound together only by one relationship or bond. Between this maximum and minimum are situated all the other more and less complex cumulative groups, bound together by 100–1 bonds, 100–2, 100–3 . . . until we come to parties bound together only by 5, 4, 3, 2, 1, ties. Here the idea is the same as in my previous theory, only it is put in other terms and without details. We shall see that an increasing cumulativeness does not mean at all an increasing solidarity between the parties, and vice versa. See the same theory developed much more comprehensively in P. Sorokin, *Sistema Soziologii*, Vol. II, *passim*. A simplified exposition of it is given in Sorokin, Zimmerman, and Galpin, *A Systematic Source Book in Rural Sociology* (Minneapolis, 1930), Vol. I, chap. vi.

In the interactions which approach the unlimited, universal, and all-embracing type, the total life of the one (in the one-sided interactions) or of both parties (in the two-sided ones) is made dependent upon, conditioned by, and bound to, the life of the other party, for good or bad. One party cannot perform any important activity, cannot have any deep psychological experiences — ideas, convictions, opinions, feelings, emotions — without influencing in some way and to some tangible extent the activities and experiences of the other party. Their total life processes — either one-sidedly or mutually — are bound to one another by thousands and millions of ties.

In the limited and narrowly specified forms of interaction, only within the sector specified are the activities and experiences conditioned and bound together. Outside it, they are "independent." In these independent sectors the parties can do many things without influencing, conditioning, or determining the activities of the other. It is not my concern to what church or movie my plumber goes; it does not concern me whether he is married and has children or not; it is not my business to know that he has the right kind of friends and the right manner of living — these and millions of other things he does and experiences do not concern me; do not influence me; do not condition my own beliefs, tastes, convictions, activities, and experiences. The same is his attitude in regard to most of my activities and experiences. His interest in my person, activity, and experiences is limited to my payment of the agreed wage for the work done by him. The infinitely greater part of our lives moves in independent spheres, without any noticeable mutual or one-sided conditioning. We are independent of each other in the greater part of the life circle, and can do many things without disturbing the greater part of the life circle of the other.

These lines make clear what is meant by the completeness, all-embracing universality of the extensity of the interaction process, and by its limited, narrow, specified extensity.

(3) *Intensity of Interaction.* Quite different from that is *the intensity* of the interaction process. Within the same "sector" of interaction — for instance, in the interaction between the religious teacher and the religious pupil — the intensity may be such that every word of the teacher will be accepted as the Gospel, and everything that he advises will be followed by the pupil. In other cases, the words and teachings of the preacher will be of little influence; most of them will be given no attention and will be ignored in practice. Likewise the interaction of a child and a parent in a specific sector of life — for instance, in the field of

their mutual help in a given work or in financial aid when needed — can have such an intensity of devotion and desire to help that one party or the other is ready to exert himself to the utmost, to the point of exhaustion; or give all the money he has, and even go into debt, in order to help the other. In other cases they may help each other only slightly, give only a little amount, covering only a portion of the money needed. Two criminals chained to each other would mutually condition their movements with quite different intensity when the chain is two feet long and when it is two hundred yards long. Two enemies can fight a duel to the death or only until the first light wound. And so in any other field of activity and interaction. The intensities may vary greatly from the possible maximum to the possible minimum.

The same is true of the intensity of an interaction involving not one but many sectors of activity and experience. The parent-child or husband-wife interaction in some cases displays an unlimited devotion, love, affection, so that anything happening to one party is reflected upon the other: the slightest joy or sorrow of one becomes a joy or sorrow of the other; and so with other experiences. In other cases only the most important actions and happenings that affect one party influence the other, and even then the influence is less deep and intense. Theoretically, here again we have a scale of intensity of the dependence or conditioning (mutual or one-sided) in the same field or sector of activity and experience, ranging from the theoretical maximum, say 100, to the theoretical minimum, slightly above zero. All the intensities will be situated on this scale between these values.[6] Theoretically, combining the extensity

---

[6] The problem of intensity involves several other problems which I do not want to discuss here. Main among these are: first, the *criteria* of intensity. Shall it be purely "behavioristic," based entirely upon the dependent variation of the overt actions of the parties; or shall it be "internal," judged by the intensity of the respective feelings of the parties, for instance, their devotion, or hatred, or wish to help? Separately taken, each of these *criteria* is inadequate and may be misleading: overt actions in many cases are meaningless if the inner motives and psychology of the person are not considered; in other cases they will be misleading, especially in the cases involving lying, hypocrisy, and the like; or in the cases where several external-internal conditions hinder the person from performing overtly what he would like to do and would have done if the conditions (*vis absoluta*, for instance, in criminal law) would have permitted. The purely inner motives and desires and their intensity in the psychology of the others we can hardly read without their external manifestations by overt actions. Therefore the internal *criterion* per se is also inadequate. The conclusion is that here as in almost any other field of the social phenomena, we have to use a combined *external-internal criterion*. Only it can give us a more or less satisfactory basis. And only it can prevent us from many blunders. This is particularly necessary in a special type of the influences exerted by one party upon the other. We know many cases when an action of one party seemingly did not immediately have any important effect on the overt behavior of the other party: perhaps only a slight blush or paleness of the face, or little quivering of

and intensity of the interaction, we can say that *the more extensive it is and the more intensive are the sectors of the interaction, the more conditioned and bound together (for good or bad) are the life, behavior, and psychology of the interacting parties.*

(4) *Duration and Continuity of Interaction.* Each of us knows that some of the interactions arise, exist a few moments, and end. Others are continued for years, or even for life. A tourist steps into a drugstore on the road, buys a few things, pays for them, says "Good-by" and is gone, forgetting the druggist as the druggist forgets the tourist. *Duration* of the interaction existed a few moments only. On the other hand are the interactions of parents and children, of husband and wife, which are continued — even now when the family ties are broken more often — for life, unto death, and even beyond it, because the memory of the dead and the social conditions which often perpetuate this memory (a prohibition to remarry, or a transmission of the rights and the liability of the deceased to the consort or children, and so on) affect the behavior and experience of the surviving party even after the death of the other. In such cases the duration of the interaction is a life duration, and sometimes lasts even beyond death.

A definite answer to the problem of the duration of the interaction process, however, depends upon what we regard as the beginning and the end of it and what we consider respectively as a *continuous* or *discontinuous* or *intermittent* interaction. Shall we regard in each case as the beginning and the end of the interaction process the moments when the parties meet face to face and when they separate or end this face-to-face interaction?

Or shall such moments occur when one party, separated from the other by some space, begins and ends a letter, telegram, cable, radiogram ; or loads a gun to shoot at the other party ; or prepares some gift to be

---

the hand. But in spite of that, the internal effect may be enormous, planting an unquench-able hatred or love in the other party ; and sometimes this enormous internal revolution only after a long time shows itself eventually in a series of the most striking actions directed toward the other party. Purely "behavioristic" observation has to miss and underestimate most of such cases. And vice versa : a violent reaction of one party to the actions or the words of the other party — for instance, strong words used, a blow, or perhaps something trivial, like breaking a glass — would appear a very intensive form of reaction from the behavioristic standpoint. And yet, often the whole reaction is limited and exhausted by such momentary reactions, leaving little force or effect for the future. A behavioristic standpoint would lead almost always to overestimation of such explosions and underestimation of the deepest, but mainly internal, effects, with long and far-reaching and almost ineffaceable manifestations in a long series of overt actions postponed until "the moment comes," which moment sometimes does not come until many weeks, months, or years after the time when the interaction took place.

sent? Or shall the beginning of the process of this indirect interaction be regarded as the moment when the party starts an activity which results in a good or bad message, or object, being sent to the other party, in order to influence its behavior and experience; and the end of such interaction the moment when such an activity is ended — the message is sent, the bullet is fired, the gift is mailed? In all these cases the beginning and the end of the interaction process and, respectively, its duration will evidently be different from one another.

Shall the beginning and the end of the process of interaction be the moment when one party begins to influence the other party and the moment when the influence evaporates, regardless of when the face-to-face or the overt activity of indirect interaction begins and ends?

The above shows that the duration of the process of interaction, as well as its continuity or intermittency, may mean very different things, or nothing, if the *criteria* are not agreed upon or outlined clearly.

I am inclined to think that, from many standpoints, the first and the second of the above *criteria* are unacceptable, or anyhow less convenient than the third solution. If we accept the first solution, then all the indirect interactions — through letters, radiograms, bullets, money, and gifts sent — would have no duration, because there was neither a beginning nor an end of the face-to-face interaction. *Process with no duration is nonsense.* The partisans of this idea can get out of the difficulty by declaring that there is no duration because there is no interaction. But, by definition, the presence of interdependence, or the conditioning of the conduct or psychology of one party by another, is interaction; in the indirect interactions such a conditioning is given, and sometimes, as in the case of the other party being struck by the bullet or receiving the $100,000 sent, it is enormous. The presence of the interaction process is certain; since it exists, it has a duration; therefore, the partisans of the first method are wrong.

The second method is also unsatisfactory. First of all, it is exceedingly difficult in many cases to determine when the activity of an indirect interaction begins and ends. Does it begin with the moment when a man steps out and walks to a store to buy paper and stamps for a letter, or when he starts to write, or when he does some work with the idea of earning money to buy the paper or stamps or some gift? Likewise, does the activity end when the letter is sealed, or when it is dropped into the mailbox, or when? These questions show the nature of the difficulty and at the same time the irrelevancy of any of these moments of beginning or ending for one of these overt activities. Why shall we take any of these moments as the first and last points of the interactional activity? Per se they are meaningless. As a sign of whether a person thinks and is thought of, influences and is influenced by, conditions and is conditioned by, the other party, these moments do not mean much. Before writing his letter or buying his gift or preparing his ammunition, he thought of and remembered and was influenced by the actions and experiences of the other party perhaps for weeks and weeks. Perhaps during all this time most of his own important actions were performed with the idea of earning enough money to return a favor or to help the other party; or with the idea of making the other party proud of him and his activities, or perhaps with the hope the action would harm the other party. Likewise, after sending the letter, the gift, the bullet, he may think of the other party with particular intensity, and be influenced by his remembrances very tangibly. On the other hand, the addressed party would receive the letter or gift or the bullet not exactly at the moment when they are sent or prepared or written, but sometimes moments or weeks later. He is not conditioned exactly during the period between the beginning and ending of the overt activity of the sender. These considerations show why such points are inadequate to determine the beginning and ending and, respectively, the continuity or intermittency of the indirect interaction process.

To make a long story short, the best way for that purpose seems to consist in taking the beginning of the influencing of the behavior and psychology of one party by the other as the beginning of the interaction, and to consider it continued as long as the influence exists, no matter whether the persons meet face to face, or how often they exchange their letters, gifts, bullets, and what not. Respectively, only when the very memory and idea of the existence of one party ceases to influence in a tangible way the psychology or the behavior of the other party — only then is the process to be regarded as ended. If, after that moment, some time elapses and the contact is renewed again and begins again to exert an influence, then a new process of interaction is started and it will again exist continuously as long as the influence exists.

This means that throughout its existence any process of interaction tends to be continuous, though its stimulants and agencies — like the face-to-face meeting, the exchange of letters or gifts or bullets — may occur only from time to time, intermittently. The clock hand moves, so to speak, continuously, though the clock winding takes place only intermittently, once in several hours or days. Similar is the situation here. This means that we have to distinguish clearly the continuity of the process of interaction from the occasions and factors which start,

reinforce, or weaken it. The first is continuous, the second are intermittent. Admission of the continuity does not preclude a possibility and
probability of fluctuation of the *intensity* of interaction during the continuous process. It may go up and down at various moments.

The continuity of the process itself is due partly to *physical*, partly to
biological, partly to *psychological*, and finally and especially to *social
conditions*. First, some of the actions and interactions between two
people may be of such a nature that they leave ineffaceable or long-lived
consequences. A wound by the bullet or knife takes only a few moments
to inflict; the consequences of that wound sometimes remain for the
lifetime of the party who received it. Since they remain, he can hardly
help being influenced all the time by the other party through these
"ineffaceable" consequences. The "old wound" not only reminds its
bearer of that, but stirs many emotions, feelings, and conditions, and
many actions, a long time after its infliction.

Similar is the situation between parties who have had a love affair
resulting in the birth of a child. Love may be over long before; the
lovers may long ago have ceased to meet each other. And yet, the
pregnancy, then the existence of the child which is born, can condition
the behavior and psychology of one or both parties for many years,
sometimes for a lifetime. There are many other actions whose consequences last long years after the interactions which involved them were
ended.

Human memory likewise leads to similar results: it helps the continuation of the process of interaction after the cessation of the overt activities and thus fills the hiatuses between the intermittent occurrences of
the stimulants of interaction. Finally, the social conditions are particularly important in this respect. They are a sort of track which determines
the direction of the movement of the human train which happened to
take the track. The ceremony of marriage occupies only a few moments.
After that the married people may be separated and may never see each
other or exchange any communication. And yet, the marriage ceremony
conditions the life of each party up to death, in many important ways.
A crime perpetrated may take only a few minutes of interaction between
the criminal and the victim. And yet, these few moments often land the
criminal in prison for life. The same can be said of thousands of short-
time interactions with continuous consequences or continued existence
for a long time after the "winding" action is ended. The whole social
order is a kind of system which makes continuous an enormous number
of interactional reactions after they overtly are ended.

It makes them continuous through, first, the existence of a set of conductors of interaction (letters, books, pictures, language, music, radio, telephone, telegraph, etc.) ;[7] second, through involving other individuals and groups in a given interaction between the parties. For instance, marriage involves not only the bride and bridegroom, but also their relatives and many other people. Besides direct interaction between the parties concerned, there always are the complementary interactions between both parties and other persons and groups. Through these two factors social life facilitates and maintains the continuity of interaction between the parties, when the "winding" actions are intermittent.[8] A judge of the Supreme Court, appointed to his office through his interaction with others ; or the president of a huge corporation ; or a professor with a life tenure — all continue to "move" along the existing rails of social order, sometimes for the rest of their lives.

These considerations explain why and how the process of interaction is continuous and exists as long as the conditioning of the one party's behavior and psychology by the existence or actions of the other party remains and functions. Respectively, the beginning and ending of this conditioning are the terminal points for the duration of the process. No doubt, from this standpoint, there are the interaction processes with the shortest duration and those with the duration for life and even beyond death. Plato, Caesar, Kant, Beethoven, are dead long ago. And yet, they still influence many of us, and, sometimes, quite intensely.

(5) *Direction of Interaction.* As to *the direction* of the interacting process, it may be either *solidary* or *antagonistic* or *mixed.* The interaction is *solidary* when the aspirations and respective efforts [9] of one party concur with the aspirations and efforts of the other party. In such cases the direction of the aspirations and efforts of both parties is the same or similar. When the desires and efforts of one party clash with those of the other party and meet resistance or hindrance from it, the interaction is mutually *antagonistic.* The direction of aspirations and efforts of the two parties is contrary.

Finally, there may be an interaction in which the parties concur in only part of their aspirations and efforts, while in another part they are antagonistic to each other. Such direction of the interaction is

---

[7] See about the conductors of interaction in my *Sistema Soziologii*, Vol. I, chap. iii.

[8] See about this point in E. Dupréel, *Le rapport social. Essai sur l'objet et la méthode de la sociologie* (Paris, 1912), pp. 33 ff.; also my *Sistema Soziologii*, Vol. I, pp. 202–206.

[9] Here again the solidary or antagonistic nature of the interaction is determined by the combined internal and behavioristic data. Either one of these alone is insufficient to diagnose the direction of the interaction process.

styled *mixed*, partly antagonistic and partly solidary. Such are the main types of interaction from the standpoint of its direction.

Since the interaction may be either all-embracing or limited and specific, from the standpoint of the extensity; more or less intensive, from the standpoint of intensity; more or less durable and continuous, from the standpoint of duration and continuity, *the antagonisms and solidarities of the interacting parties may be either universal and all-embracing or only limited by the specific "sector" of interaction relationship; more or less intensive; more or less durable and continuous.*

Of these modalities of antagonisms and solidarities, the universally all-embracing antagonistic or solidary interaction, and the limited form of these, needs a little more elucidation. As explained above, from the standpoint of the extensity of the field of interaction, the interaction processes range from the all-embracing interaction (symbolized by 100 or a full circle, which covers all the field of man's activity) to a very narrow sector of this whole field (somewhat above zero). Combining this range of the extensity of interaction with its antagonistic or solidary direction, and assuming for a moment that all the other conditions of intensity, duration, etc., are equal, we have the following scale of the antagonistic and solidary interrelations of the interacting parties.

(*a*) *1a*. The maximum of solidarity is given when the interaction is all-embracing and all its numerous sectors are solidary. This means that the lives of the two parties are completely fused into one unity in all the fields of life and experience. They are represented by the circle, and the whole of the circle field is white — not marred by any black line of antagonistic relationship. The parties in such an interaction give a real "*consortium omnis vitae, divini et humani juris communicatio*" (co-unification of the whole life and fulfillment of human and divine law), speaking in the terms of Modestinus, who excellently defined the essence of marriage as it should be. Though empirically *two* bodies, socially, psychologically, and morally, such interacting parties have an indivisible oneness.[10]

(*b*) *1b, 1c, 1d*, etc. As the sectors of the interaction field (in the circle) become more and more narrow, more and more limited, the solidarities among the interacting parties become also narrower and more and more limited. The parties may be solidary with no antagonism to mar their relations, but as the field of the interaction covers a smaller and smaller portion of the total life activities of the parties, their solidarity becomes also more and more narrow, until it is reduced to the solidary

[10] In my previous terminology this is the maximal cumulative solidary system of interaction.

interaction of the tourist buying his package of cigarettes in a corner drugstore and his casual exchange of "How do you do?" and "Good-by" with the druggist. This means that interaction can have quite different extents or amplitudes of solidarity free from any infusion of antagonism. The narrower the field of the interaction (other conditions being equal), the less and less important it becomes, of less and less account, less and less binding the parties into one harmonious unity, until it drops practically to zero.[11]

(c) 2a. The maximum of antagonism is given when (other conditions being equal) the interaction between the parties is all-embracing and universal, and all its sectors are antagonistic — without any white line breaking the black field of the circle of the life activities. It means that the life and all the actions of the interacting parties are an incessant mutual struggle; an incessant effort to defeat everything that the other party tries to achieve. (The case 2a is the direct opposite of case 1a.)

(d) 2b, 2c, 2d. These are the limited antagonisms, similar but opposite to the limited solidarities of the types 1b, 1c, 1d. With the narrowing of the sectors of interaction, the purely antagonistic interactions of the parties become also narrower and narrower until they come to a superficial and unimportant antagonism of two stranger-tourists who at an oil station begin mildly to argue as to which of two varieties of oil or gas is better. With "You are wrong," they depart, each in the opposite direction. Their antagonism covers only a negligible part of their life activities and does not mean anything.[12]

(e) 3. Finally, between these purely solidary and purely antagonistic interactions there lie the "mixed" interactions, some of which are nearer to solidary, some to antagonistic. In a social reality the above pure types 1a and 2a are rarely if ever found. Even the best friends or the members of the most exemplary family have a few discords among the enormous majority of the solidary sectors. Even the worst enemies have usually a few points where they agree and are solidary, whether in rendering a mutual service to a third party, or mutually hating the *tertius gaudens*, or in something else. More frequent are the limited solidary and the antagonistic interactions (1b, c, d, and 2b, c, d) or the mixed interactions.[13] By these are meant all the cases where the whole

[11] In my previous terminology these are less and less complex systems of cumulative solidary interactions.

[12] 2a and 2b, c, d are the maximal and decreasingly complex cumulatively antagonistic systems of interaction.

[13] Mixed cumulative systems of interaction in my previous terms.

circle or a sector of the interaction consists partly of solidary, partly of antagonistic, relationships, or where one part of it is white and the other is black. Considering our interaction with many persons, we find that in some matters we agree with each of them; in other matters we disagree. With individual A we may agree in our attitude in regard to communism and the gold standard but disagree in regard to a certain movie, play, Gertrude Stein, Wagner, unemployment policy, or prohibition. In different forms, the same takes place in regard to B, C, D, and other interacting parties.

The mixed interactions may contain different proportions of the solidary and antagonistic relationships. Therefore, some of them are nearer to solidary, others to antagonistic relationships. Again, besides proportions of solidary and antagonistic relationships in the total interaction, *the extent of the sector of the interaction* has a considerable significance. If the sector of the interaction of the parties is, say, 50 per cent of the whole circle, and the relationship of the antagonistic and solidary parts in the interaction is 25 and 75 per cent, the mixed interaction here will be different in many respects from the interaction which covers only 5 per cent of the circle, though the relationship of the antagonistic and solidary parts in it will also be that of 25 to 75 per cent. In the first case, the lives of the parties are much more interwoven than in the second case; therefore, the mixed relationships are likely to be different — deeper — than in the second case.

These remarks outline the main types of interactions and the antagonisms and solidarities, so far as they are determined by the extent of the interaction, in the above sense of the word.

(6) *Organized and Unorganized Interaction.* Finally we must distinguish the *organized and unorganized* forms of interaction, as the last modality important for our purposes. The interaction is *organized* when the relationship of the parties, their actions and functions, are *crystallized* into certain patterns and have as a basis a certain *crystallized* system of values. It is *unorganized* when the relationships and values are in an amorphous state, having no crystallization and no established patterns.[14] This is an important point and therefore needs at least a brief commentary.

(a) A crystallized system of social relationships and values means that within an interacting group, or between interacting parties, there is a *definite system of distribution of the rights and duties, functions (conduct), and social position for each member.* The system defines point-

[14] Here the "social" comes into contact with the "cultural."

edly what are the rights and duties of each member; what, under what conditions, when, and how much each member is entitled to do or not to do, to tolerate, or not to tolerate in regard to each member and outsider.[15] Such a clear distribution of rights and duties means a definite assignment of the *functions* (and *conduct*) to each member of the system of interaction. The clear-cut delineation of the rights, duties, and functions of each member perfectly defines his *social status* or *social position* within the system of interaction. X, assigned the rights, duties, and functions of a slave or of the president of a state, has respectively the social position of a slave or of the president. Thus the crystallized system of relationships and values is a map indicating the conduct and the relationship of the interacting members with one another and with outsiders under all the important configurations of social circumstances.

(*b*) As a result, the crystallized system of social relationships and values means further that such an interacting group has a definite system of values divided into three classes: *lawful, recommended,* and *prohibited* (see Chapters Thirteen and Fifteen of Volume Two). When each member's conduct corresponds to the sum total of the specific rights, duties, and functions assigned to him by the crystallized system, his conduct is regarded as lawful. He is behaving as he is expected, is entitled and obliged to behave. When he transgresses the norms he commits a sin, a crime, or an action which he should not, which contradicts the total sum of rights and duties ascribed or assigned to him, and which thus violates the system. In this way, the class of negative values is always present in any organized group, whether it is styled by the term of sin, sacrilege, crime, unlawful action, or "maladjustment." When finally a member discharges not alone his duty but something which is beyond it, which is not required but which is a further extension of conduct along the line of duty, he is performing a "heroic," "saintly," "virtuous" action, far above the minimum prescribed for him by the system of the rights and duties. In this way the category of the recommended actions is given in any organized group, no matter what its concrete content is.

(*c*) As a mere consequence of the above, the crystallized system of social relationship in a group or between the interacting parties means further the existence of *social differentiation and stratification* in any organized group or system of interaction. The fact of a definite distribution

[15] See here the profound analysis of law phenomena in the works of Leo Petrajitzky, *Introduction to the Theory of Law and Ethics* (in Russian) (St. Petersburg, 1907) and *Theory of Law and Ethics*, 2 vols. (St. Petersburg, 1908–1909).

of the rights, duties, functions, and social positions among the members of a group (or interacting parties) means that the functions of each are specified, therefore differentiated. Even in such a small group as the family, the rights, duties, and functions of the father, the mother, the younger child, and the older child are not the same and cannot be the same on account of the age, sex, and other biosocial differences : they are specified sharply even in the most democratic and equalitarian and contractual family. And there is no large organized group, including the groups of the levelers and equalitarians, where such a differentiation does not exist in this or that form and to this or that degree. This means also that such a group is *stratified*, because in any organized group there is and has to be the ruler or manager or director or the boss — or generally the governing and the governed members. As soon as this is given, no matter whether in its most democratic form where the boss or the manager is just *primus inter pares*, or in an autocratic form, social stratification is given. It is an inseparable part, inalienable from the very concept of social organization.[16]

All these traits — (a), (b), (c) — of the organized system of interaction are but different aspects of the same phenomenon — the existence of the crystallized system of social relationships and values — but each of them stresses its specific aspect and as such needs to be mentioned.

The unorganized system of interaction does not have these characteristics. It is amorphous in all these respects : the rights, duties, functions, social position of its members are undetermined and undefined either in broad outlines or in meticulous details ; so are its categories of the lawful, recommended, and prohibited forms of conduct and relationship ; so its structure of social differentiation and stratification. They all remain respectively uncrystallized. The whole system of social relationships and values is confused and vague. Therefore, the parties do not know who is the ruler and who is to be ruled ; what are the rights and duties of each ; what is the proper form of social relationship between them ; what actions and conduct are recommended, lawful, and prohibited for each party. All this remains amorphous and "messy," in an unorganized system of interaction.

No doubt that the passage from the absolutely unorganized to the perfectly organized groups or social systems of interaction in reality is

---

[16] P. Sorokin, *Social Mobility* (New York, 1927), chaps. ii–vi, and xiv. From this one can see the extreme narrowness and vagueness of E. Durkheim's characteristics ("exteriority and constraint") of social phenomenon and social category generally.

gradual : we have a gradation from the unorganized social groups through the better organized to the perfectly organized social bodies, where practically all the actions of the members and all their relationships are crystallized clearly, where each member has a definite norm for each configuration of circumstances.

The organized and unorganized modality of a system of interaction should not be mixed with the solidary and antagonistic modality. Though they are almost always interlinked by most of the social scientists, nevertheless they are different modalities. A system of interaction can be organized and yet the interacting parties can have antagonistic directions. A model prison can serve as an example of that : it is an organized system of interaction, with a clearly defined system of the rights, duties, functions, social position of each prisoner and each member of the guard. And yet, in most cases, we can hardly qualify the relationship between the prisoners and the guard as solidary : the first party endeavors to escape ; the other hinders it. In many other respects their relationship is antagonistic. The relationships of the Belgians and the Germans who occupied Belgium during the war were crystallized ; and yet they hardly were solidary. And vice versa. There are many systems of interaction with the solidary good will of the parties involved, yet remaining often unorganized, without a clear-cut distribution of the rights, duties, functions, and positions of each person concerned. This means that combining the organized-unorganized and antagonistic-solidary modalities, we can have the following types of social systems of interaction.

(1) *Organized-antagonistic System of Interaction Based on Coercion and Compulsion.* The group has all the above traits of the organized system of interaction, but the distribution of rights, duties, functions, and positions of its members is maintained by force or compulsion of the weaker part by the stronger part. The prison system gives an example of that type. The systems of interaction imposed by conquerors upon the conquered ; by masters upon slaves and serfs ; by a gangster upon his victim ; by an executioner upon his "patient," and hundreds of other — interindividual and intergroup — systems of interaction belong to this type It is the system of interaction organized but innerly antagonistic.

(ii) *Organized-solidary System of Interaction.* It has all the earmarks of the organized system and of the solidary direction of the efforts and wishes of the parties involved. Many free associations, with voluntary membership ; a good family ; devoted religious, political, economic, and other co-operative associations belong to this type.

(iii) *Organized Mixed: Solidary-antagonistic System of Inter-action.* It is maintained partly by compulsory enforcement, partly by voluntary support of the crystallized system of relationships and values, with its rights, duties, functions, social positions, assigned to each member. Probably most of the organized social systems of interaction, from the family to the Church, the State, the occupational union, and so on, belong to this type, some having the compulsory factor more greatly developed, some less. Most of the citizens of a given state would probably wish to belong to it voluntarily and voluntarily would support many of its laws. And yet, many of these same citizens would hardly pay their taxes, go into battle, or perform many other disagreeable duties if they were not forced to do so. Such "burdensome" duties exist in almost all organized systems of interaction, even in the universities and colleges: numbers of professors would prefer to be free from too many lectures, recitations, blue-book readings, if the choice depended entirely upon them, and if such omissions would not lead to a loss of their positions.

The same varieties exist among the unorganized groups: (1) *Unorganized-antagonistic*, (2) *Unorganized-solidary*, (3) *Unorganized-mixed.* So much about this modality.

Besides the above modalities, the social systems of interaction have many others. Respectively, they can be classified differently. However, the above modalities seem to embrace those most important, in the sense that any systematic investigation and classification of social groups can hardly avoid them and because they are sufficient for the basic classification and analysis of the empirically given systems of interaction.

Since each process of interaction between two or more parties is but another name for a real social group, in accordance with the modalities of the interaction process we can distinguish the following modalities of social groups.

B. *Social Groups or Systems of Interaction.* These range as follows.

(1) From the standpoint of the extensity of the interaction process, they range from the all-embracing unlimited totalitarian (maximally cumulative) to the slightest, where the interacting relationship is limited to one unimportant "interest."

(2) From the standpoint of intensity, from the most intensive to the barely tangible.

(3) From the standpoint of duration, from the most durable and continuous to the groups existing only a short moment, sometimes a few seconds.

(4) From the standpoint of the direction of the interaction, from the maximally and relatively solidary through the mixed groups, to the limited and all-embracingly antagonistic.

(5) From the standpoint of organization, from the highly organized to the barely organized and unorganized groups.

Each of these modalities is irreducible entirely to any other. It is especially necessary to stress again that the solidary-antagonistic modality is neither identical nor similar to the organized-unorganized modality, though this identification is almost always made. A great many sociologists introduce the concept of solidarity even into the generic definition of a social group, saying that any real social group is a solidary union of its members, created by common will and for common welfare. A nice definition, repeating Cicero's statement of what the good State or Society should be; but what is excusable to Cicero, who delineated the matter from the standpoint of what "should be," is inexcusable to the theorizers who define what a social group really is.[17]

III. FAMILISTIC, CONTRACTUAL, AND COMPULSORY TYPES OF SOCIAL RELATIONSHIPS

Let us leave out of consideration all the systems of interaction or groups which are unorganized, short lived, small, and with low intensity of interaction. These, anyhow, count for comparatively little in the total social world. Let us concentrate on the organized groups which are relatively long lived, large in membership, and with a tangible and high intensity of interaction among their members. Like chemical elements which do not always exist in isolated, pure forms in the chemical world, and ordinarily are found in certain combinations with other elements, the above modalities, or types of social relationships, in the

---

[17] One can enumerate hundreds and hundreds of sociologists and social scientists who are guilty in this respect and who introduce the concept of solidarity, common will, and common welfare in various terms (community of purpose, co-operation, unity of aims, common welfare, etc.) as a fundamental characteristic of a social group generally. After the above analysis it is hardly necessary to show that such definitions are replicas of the following definition of plant organism: plants are the organisms which bear beautiful and fragrant flowers, enjoyable and beneficial to everybody. Yes, some plants are such; the others — and such is the majority — are not; and some are harmful and poisonous. Nevertheless, they remain plants. Here, as in the above case of identification of the total class of social groups with a specific — "beautiful and fragrant" — variety of the class, the properties of the variety are ascribed to the whole class; as a result, the concepts of the class, as well as of the variety, are disfigured. The majority of social groups are either mixed or limitedly antagonistic; nevertheless they are real social groups and cannot be thrown out of the social reality or ignored by an investigator.

organized systems of interaction also rarely exist in an isolated form, but ordinarily are combined with one another, thus producing a few types of social groups or systems of interaction, which occur frequently and are met in any human universe. Of these "combined" types, three appear to me particularly important from many standpoints. They are met in almost any human universe, past, present, and probably future; primitive and modern; Oriental and Occidental. They are the Familistic, the Contractual, and the Compulsory types. Each of them is, in a sense, a complex form of social relationship, because each is produced by a combination of two or more of the above modalities. On the other hand, each of them is irreducible to any other, and is itself a real type in the sense that the modalities are combined not purely mechanically, but organically. You cannot remove one of the modalities without destroying the type itself.

Besides these three real types which cannot be reduced to one another, there is a multitude of the mixed forms composed of various combinations or mixtures of these three types. As such, they need no special treatment, though in social reality the totality of the relationship within any organized group — the family, the State, the labor union, the religious association, the political party, the literary, artistic, scientific, philanthropic association, and what not — represents usually a mixture of these types in various proportions and degrees. Let us now define concisely what is meant by each of the real types of social relationship.

A. *The Familistic Type.* If we select from the above modalities of social relationships in the interaction system the following ones: (1) *universal totalitarian or all-embracing in extensity*, (2) *high in intensity*, (3) *purely solidary in direction*, (4) *durable* — then a combination of all the four modalities gives us what I style the familistic system of interaction or social relationship. It may have different amplitudes of extensity — more and less all-embracing — different degrees of intensity, and different potentials of solidarity, and thus may be more or less pure; but all these four modalities are present to a tangible degree in any pure or diluted familistic system of interaction or social relationship. Such is its "chemical formula." Now upon this basic frame we can depict its living physiognomy. A concrete example is given by the relationship between a loving mother and her baby; between the mutually devoted members of the family; between true friends, in the Aristotelian sense of real friendship.[18] In these systems of interaction almost the whole circle of life activities of the parties is involved in the process of interaction, and

---

[18] See Aristotle, *Nicomachean Ethics* (Everyman's Library ed.), Bks. VIII and IX, particularly pp. 201–216; also A. Menzel, *Griechische Soziologie* (Wien, 1936), chap. iv.

certainly all the most important life relationships. In this sense, their whole lives are thrown together and organically united into one "we." There is almost nothing of the "it does not concern me," "it is none of my business," "mind your own affairs" attitude. On the contrary, what concerns one party concerns the other: joy and sorrow; failure and success; sickness and recovery; food, clothing, shelter; comfort, mental peace, beliefs, convictions, tastes of one party — all these concern most vitally the other, and meet concurrence, care, approval, aid, and sympathy.

Not only does the extensity of their interaction cover all the important activities and experiences of their lives, but the interaction is most intensive: what happens to one party affects the other, and sometimes quite as strongly.

It is as though they are bound by so short a rope that one party cannot make a step without pulling the other. Not only is the interaction all-embracingly extensive and highly intensive, but it is solidary par excellence. This solidarity comes out in millions of forms and continuously. It is as close as, sometimes even closer than, the mutual well-being of the various parts of one organism. The sorrow, joy, misfortune, success, of one becomes that of the other party. Their lives are fused together; their personalities are merged into one "we." The individuals here need one another, seek one another, and are bound into one unity, neither by compulsion, nor by considerations of profit, nor by contract; but spontaneously, for the sake of "being together," for the sake of the other party itself, regardless of pleasure, profit, compulsion, or contract. All these are unnecessary and superfluous in such forms of interaction, because isolation and separation are felt painfully by both members.

Coercion is necessary here not to keep them together but to keep them apart. Likewise the bond is not a contract or covenant. To say that a loving mother seeks to be with her baby because of an implicit or explicit contract between herself and the baby, or even between herself and society, is nonsense. Most mothers do not have even an idea of contract. They want to be with their children spontaneously, organically, regardless of any contract or duty. The same is true of real friends. If a man is a "friend" of another man by mere contract, this means he is a pseudo friend. The real friend is, as Aristotle says rightly, "one who intends and does what is good (or what he believes to be good) to another for that other's sake; or one who wishes his friend to be and to live for that friend's own sake," [19] and not because the friend gives pleasure or is useful.

[19] *Ibid.*, Bk. IX, 1166*a*. See generally his analysis of the three fundamental forms of friendship: the real friendship, where the motive is the friendship itself as an absolute end;

Or as Cicero more flatly puts it :

[In] that genuine and perfect friendship [the friends] are so intimately one that no advantage can attend either which does not equally communicate itself to both; they are strong in the strength, rich in the opulence, and powerful in the power of each other. They can scarcely indeed be considered in any respects as separate individuals and wherever the one appears the other is virtually present.[20]

In other words, in such a relationship there is a spontaneous internal unity between the individuals; their spontaneous gravitation to one another; the deepest solidarity of the merging of their "selves" in one collective "we." And this "we" or social group is here more real than the individuals involved. Such a relationship may give and usually results in some utility or pleasure for the parties, but neither one of these factors is the reason for the existence of such a tie; on the contrary, it is a mere result or by-product. Side by side with pleasure and utility, there is also sorrow and sacrifice in such a relationship, because any sorrow of one party becomes that of the other; the oneness of the parties leads each of them to offer or to render — again spontaneously — to the other any service or any sacrifice that is needed. Therefore, the utilitarian or hedonistic motives are neither the only ones existing in such a relationship nor the main ones. So far as they exist, they are a by-product but not the essence of such bonds. A good mother loves her sick or helpless child perhaps even more than the healthy one, in spite of the fact that she may be forced to pass sleepless nights at its side, has to exert herself physically and mentally to the point of exhaustion, has to make many a vital sacrifice, and is full of grief on account of the sickness or defectiveness of the child. Such is the essential nature of the familistic bond or relationship.

The contractual principle and psychology are heterogeneous to the familistic. In a collective oneness of the "we" of the familistic group, there is no place for a contractualism with its "so much, no more and no less" —

---

the pseudo friendships, where the motive is either pleasure or utility rendered by the partners. "They whose motive is utility have no friendship for one another really, but only in so far as some good arises to them from one another. And they whose motive is pleasure are in like case" . . . they love the friend "not in so far as the friend beloved *is* but in so far as he is useful or pleasurable. . . . Such friendships are of course very liable to dissolution . . . when they are no longer pleasurable. It is the nature of utility not to be permanent but constantly varying : so, of course, when the motive which made them friends is vanished, the friendship likewise dissolves: since it existed only relatively to those circumstances." The same is true of pleasure as the motive of friendship. *Ibid.*, Bk. VIII, 1156a; pp. 185–186 in the mentioned edition.

[20] Cicero, "On Friendship," in *The Offices* (Everyman's Library ed.), p. 179.

just as it would be silly if the organs of one body were in contractual relationship, serving one another only "so much, no more and no less," each organ caring egotistically about itself and not caring at all, or only within the limits of the contract, about the others or about the whole organism. Likewise in the familistic collective unity, with the spontaneous and internal "we," in which the "I"s of each member are merged, any contractualism is superfluous. It is superfluous also because where the lives are merged together it is unnecessary and impossible to specify a few relationships "agreed upon" and accepted "so far, no more and no less." The mother does not have any contract to get up during the night four times, no more and no less, to help the baby. A real mother would get up as many times as necessary. The same can be said of any familistic relationship. It differs profoundly from the contractual in that it is in a sense an unbounded, *"blank," all-embracing relationship*, without any definite limited sector or amount of mutual or one-sided services or sacrifices or actions. Any "no more and no less" is superfluous for a unity of the "we," where each individual, like an organ in a body, is a part of the whole and as such spontaneously does and is expected to do his best, up to the ultimate sacrifice of his life for the "we" or its parts. But again, any such "sacrifice" in the ideally pure familistic relationship is not felt as a "sacrifice," as a personal disadvantage or painful loss. It is rendered not because there is any physical coercion or "contract" or some externally felt "obligation and duty." "Sacrifice" is offered gladly and is not felt as depriving oneself of something valuable in favor of the other; it suggests itself spontaneously and is made spontaneously without any such feeling. "Sacrifice" here is felt as a privilege of free gift of a part to the whole. And the more is given, the more sublime is the "gladness" that flows from it.

As a consequence of that, no detailed *external* delineation of the duties and rights, of the "how much" and "under which circumstances," and other specifications and limitations of an *external* nature imposed by society are necessary for that kind of relationship. They become superfluous too.

The next point to be mentioned in regard to these relationships is the specific coexistence of *internal freedom of individuals with the external appearance of its limitation*. Considered outwardly, from a behavioristic standpoint, the familistic relationship may often appear as a great limitation of the freedom of the parties. From the standpoint of a contractual "flapper," the fact that the mother stays with the children, instead of going places and having parties, passes many a sleepless night instead of comfortably resting, spends her money buying necessities instead of purchasing a new dress for herself; "slaves" for them and sacrifices pleasures and even health, instead of freely enjoying her own life; and so on — for such a "flapper" all this is a "frightful" slavery or serfdom, a great limitation of freedom. Likewise, when a loving father inflicts some "pedagogical" punishment upon a child (spanks him, puts him to bed, etc.); prohibits his children from doing various things; deprives them sometimes of this or that pleasure; tries to impose upon them a discipline; to inculcate various good habits; and all this for their own good, even perhaps with some painful feelings to himself — such actions again appear, from the standpoint of a contractualist, a limitation of the freedom of the children. And so in other familistic relationships. However, when one puts himself in the position of the familistic party, most of these "limitations of freedom" of an individual are not such at all. The mother or the father do not feel at all that their "slaving" for the children is a limitation of their freedom; on the contrary, they are glad to do it and prefer it to the freedom of the flapper. Even children, when they become older and wiser, do not feel the punishment imposed upon them by their parents as something given with inimical intentions, intended to pain them or to hurt them. On the contrary, they often realize its "loving nature" and therefore very quickly forget it and in no way hold a resentful attitude toward the parents because they were punished or limited in their desire to do something they wished. The same is to be said of the relationship of friends and other familistic cases. One may reprimand his friend most severely; and yet it is absolutely different from a reprimand by an outsider or by a "contractual" partner. In brief, the familistic relationship permits us to reconcile duty and discipline with freedom; sacrifice with liberty; many an external inhibition of the actions of the members with their internal feeling of freedom.

In this respect again the familistic relationship differs greatly from the compulsory as well as the contractual bonds. In the compulsory bonds there is no freedom for the subjugated party; in the contractual relationship, rarely and within much more narrow limits can it be reconciled with discipline, sacrifice, order, "common interests," and the like.

To sum up, the familistic relationship *eliminates or reduces* to the minimum the feeling of being a "stranger" or "outsider" among its members. It is the relationship in which the *whole life* of each member in all its important aspects and interests tends to be merged into the collective "we." Using again the definition of marriage by Modestinus, it is the "*consortium omnis vitae, divini et humani juris communicatio.*" All aspects and spheres of life of the members are dissolved into oneness. All become known to one another and understandable, up to all and the most intimate spheres of life. Nothing "private," which is kept by the individual apart from the other members, in which he does not want and does not permit the others to meddle, as a matter which does not concern them ; nothing of "this does not concern me," "mind your own business" quality can exist in the extreme type of the familistic relationship. The members are merged together for life and death ; for the *consortium omnis vitae*, and not for merely one temporary specific aspect, as is the situation in the contractual relationship. The ideal familistic relationship is the opposite pole to "the stranger," to "the outsider," to "the private" as the sociological category.[21]

Such in the ideal form is the nature of the familistic relationship or social bond. I style it familistic because most often, and in the purest form, it is met in the relationship between the members of the good and harmonious family.[22] In a more diluted form it exists, of course, in many other nonfamilistic groups : between devoted and close friends ; between the members of a religious organization ; even between the members of the State, and of many other groups, as will be shown further. On the other hand, the term familistic must not lead to the conclusion that all or even the majority of the social relationships among members of the family are familistic. We shall see that it is not so, especially in application to the modern family, where, besides the familistic, the contractual form composes a considerable part of its total system of relationship. Such is

---

[21] See M. M. Wood, *The Stranger* (New York, 1934), chaps. i, ii, *et passim*. The author sums up the literature on the Stranger; grasps the essence of the problem; and gives a fairly thoughtful analysis of it; unfortunately, it is not pushed deep and far enough by the author, or by Simmel and several others who have studied it.

[22] The familistic relationship in the above sense is similar to the general nature of the five fundamental relationships of Confucius, whose entire social and political system is built upon this principle; also to the concept of real friendship of Aristotle and Cicero. In more recent times, the type of social relationship in the patriarchal family analyzed by Le Play; the type of the *Gemeinschaft* relationship of Tönnies, Makarewicz, Kistiakowsky, and (partly) G. Richard is also near to — though far from being identical with — the familistic relationship in the above sense. See besides the quoted works of Aristotle and Cicero, the *Hsiao King* and *The Li-Ki*, among the texts of Confucianism, in the *Sacred Books of the East*, Vols. III and XXVII (Oxford, 1885); F. Tönnies, *Gemeinschaft und Gesellschaft*, 3d ed. (Leipzig, 1920); Makarewicz, *Einführung in die Philosophie des Strafrechts* (Stuttgart, 1906), pp. 36 ff. ; B. Kistiakowsky, *Gesellschaft und Enzelwesen* (Berlin, 1899); G. Richard, *La sociologie générale et les lois sociologiques* (Paris, 1912). About Le Play's works, see P. Sorokin, *Contemporary Sociological Theories*, chap. ii; C. Zimmerman and M. Frampton, *Family and Society* (New York, 1935). See a summary of other theories (of M. Scheler, Durkheim, etc.) in G. Gurvitch, "*Remarques sur la classification des formes de la sociabilité*," in *Archives de philosophie du droit* (1935), nos. 3-4, pp. 43-91.

the first fundamental form of social relationship and of the social bond in the organized groups.

B. *The Contractual Type.* In the terms of the modalities, its "chemical formula" is as follows.

(1) *It is limited definitely in the extensity* of the life activities involved in the interaction; there is always only one, or a few, interests or matters involved in the interaction and never the whole life or even the greater part of it. Only within a small sector of the life circle do the parties come in touch with one another.

(2) *As to the intensity*, it may be high or low, depending upon the nature of the "contracted sector" of activities, but this sector is always limited; therefore the high intensity is limited by this sector and never extends over the whole life circle.

(3) It is limited in its duration; even when it is durable, the duration is again specified by the contract.

(4) Within the contract sector it is *solidary* (in a contract which the parties freely enter into and which fairly distributes their rights and duties). But this solidarity is in a sense egotistic, directed to getting either mutually some pleasure or service or profit or utility from the other party, or even to getting "as much as possible for as little as possible." It is egotistic-bargaining solidarity of rationalistically computed profit. The other party is important, not so much as an associate, and is not sought for itself, but as an agency or instrumentality which may render some service, enjoyment, utility, or profit.[23] Besides the limited sector of the contracted interaction, the parties may remain either total strangers to one another in their "private life," or even be inimical and antagonistic to one another. Such, in brief, is the formula of the contractual relationship in the terms of the above modalities. On this skeleton framework we can now paint the living picture of contractual relationship. It is a well-known picture. "I agree to do so and so for you, and you agree to do so and so for me. If you do not discharge your obligation, I am freed from mine and, besides, you will have to bear some unpleasant consequences of your breaking the contract." The parties may agree according to the classic Roman formula: "*Do ut does, facie ut facies, do ut facies, facie ut does*" ("Give to be given, serve to be served, give to be served, serve

---

[23] It is the solidarity which Aristotle styles as not a real friendship but a pseudo friendship, motivated by the intention of getting from the other party either pleasure or utility. See his *Nicomachean Ethics*, quoted. *Cf.* G. Davy, *La Foi jurée; étude sociologique du problème du contrat* (Paris, 1921). One of the best analyses of contractual relationships in its ideal form is given by M. de la Rivière in his *L'ordre naturel et essentiel des sociétés politiques* (Paris, 1846). See also A. Menzel, *op. cit.*, chap. iv.

to be given.") Here parties do not merge into one "we," but each feels and acts as an independent party not concerned with any interests but its own. It is not merged in the partner with whom the contract is made. It is even not concerned with his welfare. So far as the party is an individual, the contractualism presupposes the existence of an independent individual, free to enter or not to enter into the contractual relationship. If he enters, he is free to stipulate all the conditions which he wants to specify. If he enters and stays in the contractual group, it is because such a connection is, repeating Aristotle, either enjoyable or useful. Whether in the relationship of "buying and selling," or "employing and rendering service," or "renting a house and paying rent," or "contractually governing and obeying" — in these and thousands of other contractual relationships the real motive for entering into the contract is because it is a kind of utility, or because pleasure is to be derived or expected from such an association by the contracting parties. Each member in such a group is, first of all and most of all, conscious of his own interests and is not merged into one collective "we." In this sense, the contractual group is more nominalistic and singularistic and less universalistic than the familistic group. Respectively, the place of sacrifice or dissolving of the individual interests in the collective "we," in contractual relationship, is taken by the bond of mutual *bargaining*. Each party to the contract tries to secure from the other party as much as possible for as little as possible. The result of such a mutual bargaining may be and often is a fair exchange of goods or services. Nevertheless, such a fairness is not the result of a spontaneous sacrifice, like that of the mother for the welfare of her child, but of sensible and reasonable *bargaining*, profitable to both parties.

This means that the explicit or implicit attitude of the contracting parties toward each other is a *sensible egotism*, moderate or extreme, reasonable or unreasonable, but egotistic in the sense that each party tries to pursue its own interests most of all and first of all ; and only in so far as they coincide with, and can be facilitated through, the contractual agreement with the other party are the interests of that party considered. Otherwise, per se they are of little importance and can be neglected. This standpoint is radically different from the principle of real devotion and sacrifice in the familistic relationship.

As a result of such an egotism, *the real contractual relationship cannot be blank, unlimited, or undefined meticulously.* As each party is pursuing in it its own interests, there cannot be, as a rule, a faith, a confidence, or a trust that one party will not try to take advantage of the other if their

III — 4

covenant is not specified and definitely agreed upon.   More than that: there is often even no confidence that the other party will not try to twist the contract to the disadvantage of his partner.   Therefore, a fixed or written contract, witnesses, and the notary to certify to its authenticity are a usual part of such an agreement.   Since a definite distrust in regard to the sincerity and honesty of the other party is inherent in it, experts or experienced lawyers are hired to make the agreement clear and to leave no loophole through which the interests of a given party may be harmed by the other.   Contractual relationship is the lawyers' paradise, their "bread and butter," while the familistic relationships do not need them, or a public notary, or even a judge.   All this means that by their very nature the contractual relationships are *limited* and definitely "measured": "so much, no more and no less."   "Fifteen dollars a week for your honest work, eight hours a day."   "Fifteen cents for a package of cigarettes." This "exactly so much, no more and no less" appears in any contractual relationship, beginning with that of the Merchant of Venice and ending with the "so much, no more and no less" in the covenants of the state constitutions, between the rulers and the ruled; in the "covenant between Jehovah and His people," and in a contractual agreement of any kind.   The rights, the duties, the functions, the services, the remunerations — in a word, the social relationships of the contracting parties — are ordinarily specified as fully as possible.   They are rarely omitted, or unlimited, or not followed by reservations, specifications, clauses, comments, which outline meticulously what each party has the right to claim from the other and what it is obliged to do in regard to the other participants in the contract.   If such omissions happen it is usually the result of technical inability to specify them, rather than an intention to leave them out.

Therefore, the members of the contractual group *always remain to a considerable degree strangers and outsiders in regard to one another*.   They are "fused" and bound together only in that specific respect which is covered by the contract.   In all other respects, they do not concern one another; do not know one another; and do not want to be known. One calls his plumber, carpenter, or painter; agrees about the job to be done and the price to be paid for it — so far the parties cease to be complete strangers.   But in all other aspects of which the life relationships are made up, they remain strangers.   Only a small part of the personality of the contractual group is "fused" together and becomes "open" to the other members.   All the other aspects of the personality, life, mentality, interests, of each remain "private" for each member; and normally it is regarded in such a group as bad taste to try to violate this "privacy" and to ask the other to "open up" and to make their lives a *consortium omnis vitae*. Member remains to member a kind of "closed monad" of Leibnitz, in all respects except the little window unshuttered by the contract.

Of course, in accordance with the nature of the contract, the amount and the degree of "mutual fusion" may fluctuate. In the marriage contract of a modern couple (at the beginning of the marriage) the husband and wife cannot help but learn a great deal about each other; the fusion into "oneness" reaches a considerable degree; "privacy" of life and the status of the stranger are reduced greatly. In the buying-selling contractual unions, the buyer and seller "touch" one another most superficially and only in one very narrow respect. There they remain strangers in 99.99 out of 100 aspects of their personalities. Their short-lived fusion concerns only the exchange of money and goods, plus, perhaps, some meaningless phrase about the weather. This shows the different degrees of the strangeness and privacy and nonfusion into one "we" of the parties in contractual relationships. But this difference being given, the fact that the members always remain "strangers" to one another applies to the contractual group. Pure contractualism and some degree of strangeness are inseparable from each other, as snow and white are inseparable. If the members of the contractual association cease to be strangers, this means that the relationship itself is transformed from its previous contractual form into the familistic — a fact which happens not rarely.

It follows from the above that, compared with the familistic relationships, the contractual relationships bind the party not only by fewer bonds (only by those which constitute the contract), but these bonds are, as a rule, also shorter, so far as their duration in time is concerned. Most contracts have a definite time limit — a day, a week, a month, a year, and so on. A great part of the contracts, as a matter of fact, are of very short duration. Very few are for life, unto death, like a marriage contract, which is rather a pseudo contract; it is, or usually becomes, familistic in its nature. As soon as the time span of the contract elapses, or its essence is fulfilled (plumbing is repaired, house is built, cigarettes are bought, etc.), the bond between the parties ends; their very superficial and short-time "fusion" in a thin "we" disappears; and they are again strangers to each other, and, as it usually happens in our contractual world, quickly forget each other's very existence.

Generally, the more contractual the relationship, the more limited in time it tends to be. Like a telephone call to a stranger, the light flashes, the connection is made for a minute or two, and then is discontinued.

In contrast to that, most of the familistic relationships are more durable; the real familistic relationships are for life, even beyond it.

Finally, it follows that *the contractual relationship is inseparable from a great degree of freedom of each party from the other.*   Since to enter or not to enter the contract (in real contractual relationships — not in pseudo-contractual, which are but a variety of the compulsory relationships) depends upon the choice of an individual; since the conditions upon which he enters depend upon him also, he is free to a great degree, at least outwardly.   And since in the real contracts his precontractual position is such that he can afford to choose, the individual in a contractual group is indeed given a large opportunity for display of his singularistic freedom. Contrary to the freedom of the familistic type, here the freedom of an individual manifests itself clearly in the form of explicit choice by an individual, in the form of his recognized right to enter or not to enter the contractual alliance; to stay or not to stay in it; to prefer this or that; to approve or disapprove various values and groups; to have the liberties and "the inviolable rights of a man and individual."   In the familistic relationship the interests of individual freedom and of the group rarely come to a collision; they ordinarily coincide and manifest themselves in the form of "what is good for the group is good for me," "what makes the group free makes me free also."   Here, in the contractual relationships, such a coincidence is not so frequent.   Here the individual declares: "What is good for me, must be good for the group; if not, so much the worse for the group; at the best, I can sacrifice somewhat my inalienable rights if the others are willing to do the same, and if in that way the rest of my freedom can be secured and guaranteed.   Otherwise, it is my right and duty to fight any unjustifiable tyranny of society and other individuals."   All this is fundamentally different from the freedom of the familistic relationship.

Again, in various forms and proportions, *the contractual relationships compose a considerable part of the network of the social relationships of many and various social groups, beginning with the "employers and the employees," "buyers and sellers," "owners and tenants," and ending with many a religious, political, state, occupational, educational, artistic, scientific, and even family groups and associations.*   So it was in the past and so it is in the present.

Such are the essential traits of this type of social relationship and bond. The contractually organized groups are limitedly and conditionally solidary groups, but with a solidarity which ordinarily does not involve the greater part of the personality of the members and which is limited in time and does not appear unbreakable.   It is neither a solidarity for the whole of life and death, nor for the *consortium omnis vitae* unto death.   It is based upon utilitarian and hedonistic considerations, often carefully calculated, artificially established, and rationalistically bargained.   As such it is variable, elastic, in most cases temporary, conditional, and short lived.

C. *The Compulsory Type*.   Its main trait is that it is *antagonistic* in its nature.   Being such, it gives many varieties.   It may be most intensive, seeking extermination of the party, and less intensive, seeking to inflict some pain, damage, or fines upon it.   Again, its area can cover the whole circle of life or only a small sector.   Respectively, there may be, like the familistic relationship, an all-embracing compulsory relationship, and one very limited, confined to one narrow sector of the interacting activities. The living picture of the compulsory relationship can be drawn up as follows.

When one of the interacting parties imposes upon the other certain forms of conduct, certain duties and functions — *contrary to the desire and inclination of that party*, and subjectively and objectively not for its welfare — and forces their realization exclusively by application of various forms of physical and psychophysical coercion, the social interrelation is compulsory in its nature.   The bond which unites the parties and hinders its rupture is this coercion.   It may have various forms, from a purely physical compulsion, infliction of various physical harms, tortures, and pains, up to the more complex psychosocial coercion, assuming now the form of depriving the party of necessities, like food, shelter, freedom of movement, and so on ; now the form of threat to inflict injury upon other persons dear to the party : wife, husband, children, friends, and so forth.

In brief, the compulsion and coercion can assume most different forms, quantitatively as well as qualitatively.   But wherever it is given, and especially when applied not so much for the good of the party — like a loving and moderate spanking of a child by the parent — but just for the sake of the stronger party, the relationship becomes in part or in whole compulsory.   The relationships of the master and slave and serf ; of the executioner and the executed ; of the conqueror and the conquered ; of the despotic government and the governed ; of the extortionist and the victim ; of the ravisher and the ravished ; kidnaper and the kidnaped — and many others — are rich in this type of relationship (though not always, and not entirely, consisting of them : in the relationship of many a master and slave, the lord of the manor and the villeins, and so on, there often were present the familistic and partly even contractual relationships).   As a specific case come the pseudo-familistic and the pseudo-contractual relationships. By pseudo-familistic is meant a relationship where the stronger party takes over the similitude of the familistic relationship — its terminology, its "clothing," as "this is done with fatherly feelings," "for your own good," and so on — while factually the interests and the welfare of the weaker party under coercion are not considered at all, and the compulsion or pains imposed do not serve its welfare in any way. By the pseudo-contractual is meant a relationship where the weaker party enters into the contract seemingly by its own will, but in fact does not have any choice, and the "free agreement" is but a simulacrum of a really free decision. A man or woman dying from starvation and suffering from lack of other necessities is often forced to make such a contract : to accept a job for evidently inadequate remuneration; to take upon himself or herself some service which in normal conditions would not have been taken; for instance, to become a mistress, a hired murderer, and the like, or to serve in a most infamous role. All such relationships and contracts are in fact purely fictitious. They are but a disguised form of compulsory relationship. This is important to keep in mind because many compulsory relationships, especially in recent times, manifest themselves in this pseudo-contractual form, just as many of such relationships in the medieval and other past societies tended to assume the pseudo-familistic forms. Only a study of the real character of the relationship in each specific case permits one to state what kind it is in reality.

In contradistinction to the familistic and contractual relationships, the compulsory relationships are marked by the following traits.

(1) They are internally *antagonistic*. If they were not, the amount and the cruelty of compulsion applied would have been unnecessary. This explains that they have to be present in any interindividual and intergroup relationships which are antagonistic. And vice versa, with the exception of the "pseudo-punitive familistic coercion," the presence of a large amount and a high intensity and rudeness of coercion is one of the best symptoms that the relationship is antagonistic; no matter what are the "clothes" in which it is wrapped.

(2) *It does not give any freedom to the coerced party, while to the coercing party it gives a freedom* (in the sense of doing what one pleases) sometimes much greater than that *given by the contractual relationships to both parties.* Here their liberty to do whatever they please is limited mutually; while in the compulsory relationship the stronger party is limited much less by the weaker party, whose interests do not exist for the stronger party — it does not want to consider them. Therefore, it

tends to do anything that it physically can do and that is dictated by its own wishes.

(3) Respectively, in the *pure compulsory* relationship, the parties remain to each other total strangers and outsiders, much more so than in any of the preceding relationships. And not only a stranger and outsider, but often a negative value, worse than a mere stranger. A slave to a cruel master is but a mere instrument, something even more "unhuman" than his cattle; at the best, he is but a species of animal. On the other hand, the coercing party remains also a stranger to the coerced. It is felt and perceived not as a human personality capable of understanding, feeling, being united by a psychosocial *rapport;* it is perceived merely as an instrument of oppression — cruel, inhuman, perverse, unjust, a kind of "whip" which only hurts, tortures, and oppresses. There is no bridge of real mutual understanding between the parties as human beings and personalities; there is no mutual fusion and no "we" feeling except the purely external, mechanical, like that between a cruel driver and his horse. The inner world of each party is mutually closed to the other; often there is not even a desire to open it. This explains why in such relationships there always are present various "ideologies," especially on the part of the oppressor, that they are fundamentally different in nature ("pure" and "impure" race, "blue" and "poor" blood, "twice-born caste" and "outcast," "chosen" people and "unchosen," "saintly" and "sinful," "bearer of culture" and "hopelessly backward," "proletarian" and "bourgeois," and so on in hundreds of forms); why the masters display often an unbelievable cruelty to the coerced group or party, sometimes styling them "dogs" and the like [24] and treating them worse than

---

[24] A few examples out of the infinitely great number of such cases of remaining strangers are :

"The feudal literature, which was addressed to the privileged classes only, gives only a caricature of the peasant.

"Disdain was general in regard to him; brute force was regarded the only method fit in dealing with him: 'Oignez vilain, il vous poindra; poignez vilain, il vous oindra.'" J. Calmette, *La société féodale* (Paris, 1932), pp. 166–167. Characterizations of that kind were general throughout the whole medieval literature in regard to the unfree and semifree classes, on the part of the privileged classes with which the former were connected by the compulsory ties mainly.

"The literature of the Middle Ages is not favorable to the peasants. . . . Where we meet the peasant, he is first of all depicted as the coarse and clumsy yokel." See P. Meissner, *Der Bauer in der englischen Literatur* (Bonn, 1922), pp. 17 ff. See also G. von Below, *Probleme der Wirtschaftsgeschichte* (Tübingen, 1926), p. 94.

Similar mentality is found in practically all the purely compulsory relationships on the part of the masters toward the slaves, serfs, victims, and so on.

On the other hand, a study of the mottoes, songs, and other "speech reactions" of the coerced groups in the times of their revolts discloses an analogous mentality on their part toward their masters. "Kill the priests, kill these dogs, kill the wealthy, kill that wretched

dogs; why, in the period of the revolts of the oppressed, they show also an inhuman delight in killing and torturing their masters; why in their mutual relationship the other party is looked upon and interpreted always in the most debased, most contemptuous, or hateful form.   Remaining total strangers, they speak different languages and rarely can grasp and understand the real personality and nature and the mentality of one another.   They are more remote from one another than a cultured European who for the first time visits a primitive tribe.   Such are the main characteristics of this type of relationship.

(4) After this typological characterization of the main types of social relationship, it is hardly necessary to say that in the real social world, there is a *gradation and scale to the relationships*.   The passage from one type to another is not abrupt in the sense that there are no inter-mediary — more or less familistic, more or less contractual, more or less compulsory — grades between the main forms.   As in almost every field of phenomena these "more or less" are given and imperceptibly and gradually pass from the pure compulsory through less and less compul-sory forms to something in between the compulsory and the contractual, or compulsory and familistic relationships.   Such intermediary forms are undoubtedly present, and some of them are "intermediary" to such an extent that one has a difficulty in deciding to which of these three "pure" types a given form is nearest.   For evident purposes here, as in many other fields of classification, we have to select and stress a few main forms as typically "pure," while in reality what we have is a gradual scale of many forms passing from one class to another step by step.

D. *Mixed Forms*.   These three forms seem to embrace almost all the pure forms of social relationship.   The numerous concrete forms represent mostly their combination.   Through a combination of various modifica-tions of each of these three forms, it is possible to obtain most of the forms of social relationship given in the interaction of individuals and groups.   As a matter of fact, the totality of interrelations within practically all the social groups represents usually a combination of these main forms: they are partly familistic, partly contractual, and partly compulsory.   But the proportion of each type in the totality of the net-

---

vampire — the Czar; kill all these scoundrels" — such is the Russian revolutionary hymn. Similar are the characteristics of the privileged classes in the "*Carmagnole*," "*Ça ira*," and other revolutionary hymns of the French Revolution.   There these classes are styled also as "the impure blood" which had to be shed.   See many examples of that in P. Sorokin, *The Sociology of Revolution* (Philadelphia, 1925), pp. 149 ff.

In many variations the same phenomenon appears always in any social relationship of purely compulsory type.

work of social relationships of various groups is not the same. It varies from group to group; and, in the course of time, changes even within the same group.

(1) If we select various social groups, we can easily see that some of them at all times have had *one of these types more predominant than the others*. If we take such groups as *the family, the Church, the association of real friends*, we find they almost always had an abundant portion of the familistic relationship in the network of their relationship system. Beginning with the "primitive family" (no matter what its form) and ending with the most modern, the relationship of the family members has always been familistic, either in a relatively rough, or a refined and tender form. There (pathological cases excluded) is always present the family "we," the fusion of the members into one team, their freedom from strangeness to one another; their mutual help, solidarity, altruism, and collective interests, as well as responsibilities. The proportion of this "familism" certainly varies from family to family; but as a rule it is considerable and in most cases is the dominant form of relationship. The others, the compulsory and the contractual relationships, are certainly present but, with few exceptions, they are hardly the main forms. Likewise, the *religious groups* have nearly always been built along the pattern of the familistic group. This is shown clearly in the terminology of such a group. "Our Father" (God), "we are children, sons and daughters of God," "God the Father," "God the Son," "Mother of God," "Mother Church," "Holy Father," "Sisters in Christ," "Brethren," "Spouse of Christ," and so on. Whether one takes the Bible, the Gospel, or the writings of the Church Fathers, or the prayers, sermons, and letters, the terminology used in religious services and talks everywhere is full of the familistic terms like the above. Even the church sacraments are full of them also — "rites of passage," from a "stranger," "gentile," to the "Brotherhood in God." The same is true of practically any real religion. Religious associations have been formed mainly along the line of familism in the above sense.

The same is true of real friends. Here again, as indicated, the relationship by definition is familistic and always assumes this type. This is shown again by such terms and "rites of passage" as mixing of blood, as drinking *Bruderschaft*, and the like.

If now we take such groups as the compulsory military group — the army as such (with the exception of groups like early medieval "companions in arms," which were modeled along the familistic pattern) — there compulsory relationships are always present to a considerable degree, especially where the army is large and recruited from all kinds of people. Likewise, in the state network of social relationships, especially in a despotic, dictatorial, or tyrannic State, a great portion of relationship is compulsory, as is manifest in the mechanism of the coercion of the State: its police, its army, its jails, its courts, its punishments, and other coercive forces.

Finally, when we turn to the commercial and trade organizations, they always had, to a considerable degree, a developed system of contractual relationship. Trade is ordinarily a "bargaining," the exchange of something for something. Beginning with a trade between the newcomers, the Europeans, and the primitive peoples — where the exchanged objects were left at a certain place by one party in order that the other party could see them and exchange them for the objects which it had — and ending with the contemporary exchange by purchase and sale, trade and commerce have always consisted greatly of contractual relationships.

These examples give an idea that some of the organized groups by their very nature are "destined" to have one of the main types more preponderant than the others and that there are several types of social groups which at all times have tended to build their network of social relationships predominantly either out of the familistic, or the contractual, or the compulsory relationships.

(2) *Warning: Do not confuse the existing nature of the relationship with how it originated or was established.* One must not mix these two different things. A given interaction and relationship may originate in a contractual form — for instance, the relationship between married parties or the relationship of the *fidelitas* in the Middle Ages. But in the course of time it may turn into either the familistic or compulsory type. The marriage contract even nowadays often turns into a real and pure familistic relationship between the husband and wife, parents and children. A business contract and subsequent meetings of the parties often lead to an establishment of true friendship between the contracting parties. Even many relationships compulsory in their origin turn into the familistic (for instance, in the past, in many marriages imposed upon one or both parties by others) or contractual form. On the other hand, a diluted familistic relationship, in the course of time, sometimes degenerates either into a contractual or even a compulsory one; or a contractual relationship degenerates into a compulsory one. In other words, one thing is *the way in which the relationship originated* (contractually or compulsorily or familistically); and quite another thing is *what it is in its nature* (familistic or contractual or compulsory). A certain form of origin

does not always mean that its nature is the same as the form of origin, and vice versa.   This is particularly important for a proper understanding of the nature of relationships in many cases and especially such medieval relationships as are styled by the term *fidelity*. According to the manner of establishment, the relationships of fidelity seem to be contractual. As we shall see, they were, especially before the fourteenth century, predominantly familistic.

This difference is the more true : the established relationship does not always remain the same in the course of time.   It often changes its nature, passing from one form into another.   Still more easily it can differ in its nature from the external form of its establishment.   This is to be kept in mind if one does not want to commit grave errors in analyzing the real nature of many social relationships and systems of interaction, interindividual as well as intergroup relationships.

The above concise but sufficiently precise characterization of the process of social interactions, of the modalities, of the types of social systems of interaction, and then of the familistic, contractual, and compulsory relationships with the respective systems of interactions, is sufficient to permit us to pass to a study of the fluctuation of the proportion and the quality of each of these relationships in the main social systems of the European population, from the beginning of the Middle Ages up to the present time.   The subsequent chapters show the scientific and practical importance of such a study.

Chapter Two

FLUCTUATION OF THE FAMILISTIC, CONTRACTUAL, AND
COMPULSORY RELATIONSHIPS IN THE LIFE PROCESS OF
THE MAIN EUROPEAN SOCIAL GROUPS: I. FROM THE
CAROLINGIAN SOCIETY TO THE FOURTEENTH CENTURY [1]

I. INTRODUCTORY REMARKS

The direct object of this part is : first, to find out whether, in the course
of existence of the main social groups of the European population, the
proportion of the relationship of each type within the structure of the
same group, as well as the totality of these groups, has been fluctuating,
and if so, how and when ; second, to inquire whether these fluctuations
have been correlated with those of the main types of cultures studied
(Ideational and Sensate), and if so, which of these types of social relationship is positively associated with each type of culture and what are the
reasons for such an association. Such are the main problems to be studied
now. For a thoughtful person the importance of the inquiry is evident.
For a less thoughtful reader it is enough to say that a change in the
proportions of the familistic, contractual, and compulsory relationships
that make up the "texture" of a group or social system of interaction is
much more important, and indicates a much greater revolution, than any
change of its political or economic structure. The first is fundamental
and alters the very nature of the group ; the second is only a partial and
much more superficial change. Even this can amount to something only
when it involves a quantitative-qualitative alteration of the main forms
of social relationship. A political or economic revolution that does not
involve a change of the proportions and quality of the familistic-contractual-compulsory relationship in a group amounts only to a change in
the positions of its members, without any serious effect on the constitution or structure of the society itself. The so-called "Industrial
Revolution" was an important change only because it meant a serious
decrease of the familistic and compulsory relationships in the structure of
Western society in favor of the contractual relationship. The so-called

[1] In co-operation with N. S. Timasheff.

43

" Overripe Capitalist Regime," as an economic regime, means mainly a social structure composed primarily of contractual relationships. These taken away, the capitalist regime is destroyed. The contemporary crisis of capitalism is first of all the crisis of the contractual relations. The "to be or not to be" of the capitalist regime means the "to be or not to be" of the contractual society. If contractual relations continue to decrease quantitatively and degenerate qualitatively, the days of the capitalist regime are numbered. If the former are going to exist and grow, capitalism will become bigger and stronger. These remarks are sufficient, for the present, to enable us to understand the fundamental importance of the change in the proportions and quality of the main social relationships in the structure of any group.

A systematic study of the problem meets enormous difficulties. Without entering into their discussion, it is enough to say that the most careful study can yield, at the best, only roughly reliable results. But such rough approximation seems to be possible.

It appears quite possible indeed, so far as the character of the mentality in the field is concerned — that is, how and along which of the main types the relationships were thought of and understood by the contemporaries, and how and in which way this mentality changed in the course of time, and in which form the relationships began to be comprehended later. There are, for most of the periods, a number of formulas, statements, theories, opinions, rites, ceremonies, and other manifestations of the mentality to permit the investigator to see whether the relationships were thought of as familistic, contractual, or compulsory.

Much less certain is the situation so far as behavior is concerned. As mentioned, man's "speech reactions" and mentality may seem perfectly familistic, while his actions may be very different from that type, being either coercive or pseudo-contractual or purely contractual. However, in the groups whose relationships were stamped for a long period by the same verbal characteristics, e.g., familistic, there is strong reason to believe that these verbal characteristics corresponded, to a considerable degree, to the real, actional relationships — that these were probably familistic, indeed, to a considerable degree; but one can never be sure in that assumption. As we are preoccupied with mentality no less than with actional behavior, a study of the mentality fluctuations in this field is important, even if its forms do not correspond to the "actions" of the members. If some degree of correspondence is found, the study becomes an investigation of mentality as well as of conduct.

The study of the problem can be carried on in two different ways:

the simpler and the more complex.   By the simpler way I mean a study of the fluctuation of the proportions of each of these types in the total network of only *one* important organized social system in the history of one or more European country, such as the State or the Church or the family, or some other important group.   Such a method is simpler, permits us to study the fluctuations more carefully, and has several other advantages. It is the method usually pursued by most political scientists and jurists who often seriously think that the State is the all-embracing group and that if one knows what changes take place within it, one knows all the changes within all the other — nonpolitical — groups of a given population.[2]   The fallacy and the shortcoming of such an approach must be evident, however, to everybody who has studied the problems of social structure and social organization.   The point is that the state group or the religious organization or the family or the political party or the labor union or the "language-grouping" (nationality)   each of these groups is only one among many into which the population of a given territory or country is differentiated and integrated.   In other words, the population has not only one group — the State, or the Church, or the family — but several, each being different from the others and each functioning in its own way and with its own totality of membership not coinciding exactly with that of the other groups.   The line of social differentiation and integration of a given population into a social organized group is not unilinear and monistic but multilinear and pluralistic.[3]   Therefore, what happens in one of the systems into which a part of the population of a given area is integrated — for instance, in the State — does not necessarily happen in the other groups (the family, the Church, the labor union, etc.) which include a part of the same population.   The structure of the state network of relationship may change from the familistic to the contractual ; that of the religious association from the contractual to the familistic ; and so on.

For this reason the more complex method is much more adequate, the more so that it gives all that the simpler method does.   The essence of this more complex method in the study of our problem lies in the fact that we shall take at least most, if not all, of the diverse and important organized social groups into which the population of the given territory was integrated at a given period, and study what changes in regard to the pro-

---

[2] See my criticism of it in *Sistema Soziologii* (St. Petersburg, 1920), Vol. II, pp. 125–145.

[3] See the pluralistic theory of social differentiation developed in my *Sistema Soziologii*, Vols. I and II.   See a brief and simplified skeleton of it in Sorokin, Zimmerman, and Galpin, *A Systematic Source Book in Rural Sociology* (Minneapolis, 1930–1931), Vols. I, II, and particularly chaps. vi and vii.

portions and the quality of the main types of social relationship have taken place within each of them in the course of time; and then within their totality. Knowing that, we can grasp, at least roughly, which of the types of bonds studied in the total population has been growing at a given period and which declining. Such a knowledge concerning most of the important social groups guarantees us against the mistake of generalization upon the basis of only one group. In other words, in conformity with the multilinear and pluralistic theory of social differentiation and integration of the population of a given territory into many diverse social systems, the adequate theory of the fluctuation requires that the inquiry be carried along the lines of at least several of the most important groups which existed during the period studied.[4]

The main groups whose structural changes, from the standpoint of the kind and the proportion of their social "fibers," are to be studied here, mainly within the French and the Germanic areas of Europe [5] from the Carolingian even to the present time, are as follows: *the State, the Church, the occupational groups* (the guilds, labor unions, etc.), *the family, the military groups, the communes*, plus the *main organized social classes* (the orders, the seigniors, vassals, serfs) which united the free or unfree population into real collective bodies. To be sure, these do not exhaust all the important groupings into which the population of this main area of Europe

---

[4] I cannot enter here into an analysis of which of the organized social groups are important and which not, and why. It is enough to say that the criteria of being important may be many and various, in accordance with the objective of the study. For our purposes those groups are important which are comparatively the most powerful, that is, condition most effectively the multitude of the individuals, the other groups, and through them the whole given population and eventually the course of social events and historical destiny of the population. From this standpoint, other conditions being equal, the greater the group's membership, the better it is organized technically, the less are its internal antagonisms, and the greater and more perfect are the values around which the group is organized, and the total means of influencing human behavior by the group (army, arms, weapons, jails, money and wealth, technical knowledge, scientists, preachers, propagandists, etc., etc.), the more powerful — ergo, more important — is its role among the other groups in the process of history. See the details developed in my *Sistema Soziologii*, Vol. II, pp. 45 ff.

[5] Besides the French and the Germanic area of the population of Europe, more cursorily are touched the Russian and the Italian populations. An investigation of all other European countries and their population would require enormous additional energy and time. The novelty and the difficulty of the problem required the investigators to spend a great amount of time and effort to study even the few countries mentioned. For the purposes of this work it is enough to show that there is a big problem, and that it has to be studied; and that the essential results obtained for these countries can, with some modifications, be extended over the rest of the European population; and that, finally, the material demonstrates the existence of a relationship between the structural changes of the main social group and the changes in the type of the cultures. These considerations show why it is not necessary, for this work, to study all the other countries.

was integrated in the course of the centuries studied; but they embrace at least the majority of them. For this reason, the results obtained in regard to all these groups are indicative of the main changes which have been occurring in the total social organization of the population.

II. Predominant Sociorelational "Spectrum" of the Important Social Groups of the Franco-Germanic Human Universe in the Carolingian and Feudal Periods: from the Eighth to the Thirteenth Century

If by the term *sociorelational "spectrum"* we style the predominant nature of the social relationships (bonds) in a given group — predominantly familistic, or contractual, or compulsory, or mixed — the problem studied can be set forth in the following way: What was the predominant spectrum of each of the important groups and of the totality of such groups in the French and Germanic population during the centuries from about the eighth to the thirteenth? Has the spectrum of each of these groups been changing, or has it remained constant? If changing, how, from which spectrum to which, and when? Do we move, in the course of time, more and more to the contractual, or to the familistic, or to the compulsory type; or is no such trend shown and, instead, do the types of these bonds just fluctuate, now giving victory to one, now to the other?

In order to elucidate this difficult question adequately, a special monograph, even a series of volumes, needs to be written. This being impossible, a short cut is taken in as concise a form as possible, and as well documented as possible in the way of references to sources and texts, to the characterization of the most fundamental and conspicuous changes which took place.

If one asks which type of bond was predominant in that period, the answer seems to be the *familistic*. This type seems to have been the main "fiber" of which the network of most of the important social groups was composed. It permeates most of them. It is the dominant "color" or, if one prefers, "pattern" of social relationships. The other two, the contractual, and the compulsory "fibers," not to mention the mixed ones, are not lacking. They are present, and in some groups one of these is prevalent. Nevertheless, the mentality of the period felt and viewed the most frequent relationship as nearest to the familistic type. It was dominant in the Church, the State, the family, the occupational, the "feudal," and other groups.

As we move from the eighth and the ninth centuries to the twelfth and thirteenth, this form shows a notable weakening, though it still remains throughout the period as strong as the others, while they — especially the contractual — show definite signs of growth : many a familistic relationship is replaced by contractual toward the twelfth and the thirteenth centuries. Such is the central shift in this field. Such, further, is the dominant "spectrum" of the social structures of the period.

Let us now substantiate these two claims. What are the evidences that make the claims probable ? In the briefest form, they are as follows : The Carolingian and the post-Carolingian *state system* (so far as it still existed with the shrinking of many state organs and functions) has been woven mainly along the familistic pattern : in the relationship of the monarch and the subjects ; of the monarch and the notables and officials ; and of the subjects and the notables to one another. The familistic principle dominated the association of companions in arms or the *military* relationship ; it dominated the *family;* it was the main pattern in the dealings of the *Church*, as possibly the most powerful group in the period ; it controlled various *guilds, "companionships," "Bruderschaften,"* and similar organizations ; it played a most important part in the bonds between *the lord and the vassal; even the relationships of *the seigniors and their peasants, tenants, and serfs* were not entirely devoid of it. This means that it was present in all groups, and in most of the important ones it was the predominant pattern. The other two types were also present in many groups, practically in all, but hardly played as important a part as the familistic pattern.

In order to prove the validity of this claim it is enough to point to the *fidelitas*, as *the fundamental category of social bonds of the period.* The *fidelitas* was the central axis around which were built the State, the feudal and religious systems, the army, the family, the guilds, and other relationships. It is in all these different groups ; and it unites and keeps together their members in one organization ; it ties them to one another ; it is the heart and the soul, the controlling and the formative principle of the structure of the social organized groups of the period.

The *fidelitas* in its nature (not in its external form or the form of its establishment between the parties) is neither contractual nor compulsory, but mainly familistic.[6]

---

[6] M. Granet depicts well the nature of vassaldom in China, based also upon fidelity, as identical with the familistic bonds. "The bond of vassaldom . . . does not differ at all from the bond of parenthood, existing at the same epoch between father and son. The vassal wears mourning for the overlord with the same strictness with which he wears mourning for his own father. The feudal group is a species of family. Like the domestic group, the feudal group is a communal unity. The members of the group are possessed by the same genius, all sharing in it, but all sharing unequally, for the group is in the nature of a hierarchy."

Let us take the State of the period and analyze in some detail its structure from this standpoint. Such an analysis would make clearer the essence of fidelity as the dominant tie, as well as many related problems. After such a somewhat detailed analysis it would be possible to characterize the ties or the fibers of other important social groupings of the period more briefly, without the risk of being either unclear, or incomprehensible, or shallowly superficial.

The state structure of the period had two phases, the Carolingian and the post-Carolingian, or feudal, which differed from each other considerably. Therefore it is advisable to investigate the structure of the State separately in these two periods.

A. *The Carolingian State.* How were the social ties or relationships between the monarch and his subjects, between the monarch and his officials, and between the subjects themselves thought of by the contemporaries of this state?

(1) So far as the relationship between *the monarch and the people* is concerned, its main form seems to have been thought of along the pattern nearest to the *familistic* type. This can be stated with a reasonable degree of certainty. The main evidences in brief are as follows.

(a) The power of the monarch was regarded as that of the head of a tribe, which was near to that of the *pater familias;* the tribe was a union of kinship; its members were the related members of a big family; its head, the head of the family. The head of the tribe, the head of the big family, and the monarch, these three aspects of the Carolingian monarch were closely interwoven.[7]

(b) The sources style this authority by the term *mundium.*[8] *Mundium* means hand, which reminds us of the Roman *manus* — the term meaning the authority of the *pater familias.*

He stresses further that the oath of fidelity in marriage and in brotherhood in arms is the same — unreserved fusion of the contracting parties. "In death, in life, in sorrow — I take thee for my partner! I take thy hands in mine: I hope to grow old with thee!" "We divine in this vow a sort of heroic resolve: as a matter of fact, soldiers on a campaign vowed the same vow as husband and wife, taking each other by the hand. The vocabulary makes no distinction between conjugal fidelity and brotherhood in arms. Both have their origin in the same covenant of friendship." M. Granet, *Chinese Civilization* (London, 1930), pp. 308 and 158. This means that any vassaldom based upon the real principle of *fidelitas* is a species of familistic relationship.

[7] See P. Viollet, *Histoire des institutions politiques et administratives de la France* (Paris, 1890), Vol. I, p. 218.

[8] *Marculfi Formulae*, I, 24, in *Monumenta Germaniae historica : Formulae* (Hannover, 1886), p. 58. Further on, the *Monumenta Germaniae historica* are quoted as *Monumenta*, with an indication of the series, the volume, and page, but not the number of the document.

(c) The subjects are termed the *fideles*, the faithful bound to loyalty by oath.[9] Again the term, as well as the meaning given to it, is a variety of the familistic term. The oath itself (*sacramentum fidelitatis*) is a variety of the act of adoption or the "rite of passage" of all the subjects into the membership of the same big family, loyal to its head.[10] As such it has to be and was a personal bond binding every subject directly to the monarch, as a member of the family to its head.

(d) Like the head of the family, the monarch was considered as acting in harmony with the people represented by their elders, the notables, at the *placita*.

(e) The monarch was looked upon as acting not for the sake of his own interests but, as a good *pater familias*, for the welfare of the people, for their common good, motivated by spontaneous and religiously felt good will.

(f) As such, his power and authority were derived neither from a contract directly, nor from force, but from God Himself, with the approval of the notables, as the power of the *pater familias* is derived. Therefore, he was thought of as a leader in social service to the people, but not as an egotist using his possibilities for his own aggrandizement.

(g) The monarch looked on the state territory as that of a bona fide *pater familias*. The separation of the personal estate of the monarch and that of the State was practically nonexistent.

(h) The subjects were thought of as devoted to the monarch, not for the sake of fear or profit, but spontaneously and unlimitedly for their whole lives, even beyond. Their "duty" was represented exactly as the unlimited and spontaneous devotion of the members of the family to its head. Such an unlimited devotion is manifested in the oath of fidelity which is introduced now.

[9] *Marculfi Formulae*, I, 40; *Monumenta*, p. 68.

[10] I am using the term "the rites of passage" in the sense of extension of the familistic bond to a newcomer, whether he be a newly born baby in the family, or an adopted member, or a member taken into the family under other conditions. The term is coined by A. van Gennep, in his *Les rites de passage* (Paris, 1909), p. 27. This familistic rite of passage is practiced in various forms by families, by tribes, by the Masonic organization, by various brotherhoods, and other organizations when adopting a new member. It always has a familistic pattern, no matter whether it assumes the form of various rites of adoption, of mixture of blood, of oath of fidelity and loyalty, of drinking the *Bruderschaft* cup, or other forms. See the details in the work of Van Gennep, mentioned. See also a good summary in M. M. Wood, *The Stranger* (New York, 1934), chaps. ii, iii, and iv. As we shall see, the oath of fidelity in the Middle Ages was generally familistic in its meaning and character, whether it was between the companions in arms, vassal and suzerain, king and subject, master and apprentice in a guild, and so on.

All these characteristics are nearer to the familistic type than to the others.

When one reads the contemporary sources, this familistic conception of the relationship in the mentality and the writings of the contemporaries becomes clear.

First of all, the ascendance to the throne, the appointment of the heir and successor, the choice of the wife, the division of the kingdom among several inheritors, generally the decision of an important question, all these transactions were carried on as though by the family council, where the head consults with the elder members of the family, the notables, and, with their consent and approval, decides matters. The whole character of these transactions is not a contractual bargaining between the king and the notables or the people, but just a large family council, because the *placita* neither limited the power of the monarch nor had any definite and clearly outlined rights and authority, which would be the case if they were contractual institutions. The time and the place of summoning the *placita* were determined by the king; their competence remained indefinite; they gave advice but the decision depended entirely upon the king. Only when the king was weak and a poor ruler, then, naturally, as the case of Lothaire shows, was he reproached for his inability to rule and, as sometimes happens in the family, he could be replaced by another head or king.

Here are a few out of many texts which well sustain the above characterization.

About the ascendance to the throne :

Quo tempore una cum consilio et consensu omnium Francorum missa relatione.[11]

About the consent of the notables in the appointment of the heir of the kingdom and its division :

Conventum habuit imperator cum primoribus et optimatibus Francorum de . . . divisione regni faciendo. . . . De hoc partitione et testamentum factum et jurejurando ab optimatibus Francorum confirmandum.[12]

About the marriage of the king or the heir. Lothaire II took his wife, " *cum consensu et voluntate fidelium suorum.*" [13]

---

[11] *Fredegarii chronicarum continuatio*, c. 117. *Monumenta : Scriptores rerum Merovingiarum* (Hannover, 1888), Vol. II, pp. 181–182.

[12] *Annales Einhardi anno 806, Monumenta*, in-F (Hannover, 1826), Vol. I, p. 193.

[13] Hincmar, I, 373. See G. Waitz, *Deutsche Verfassungsgeschichte* (Berlin, 1882), Vol. III, p. 274.

About the consultation and deliberation of important state affairs Hincmar states:

Consuetudo erat ut . . . in anno placita duo tenentur. [In the first of the annual] placita, seniores propter consilium ordinandum, minores propter idem consilium suscipiendum, et interdum pariter tractandum, et non ex potestate, sed ex proprio mentis intellectu vel sententia confirmandum.[14]

On the other hand, Alcuin explicitly states that these *placita* and deliberations were not contractual in their character and that the people did not have any rights which limited or opposed the authority of the monarch.

Populus juxta sanctiones divinas ducendus est, non sequendus, et ad testimonium personae magis eliguntur honestae.[15]

Farther on, when one studies the formulas and the expressions with which the relationship of the monarch and the people is characterized by contemporaries, the familistic mode of thinking about it becomes especially conspicuous. Here are a few examples.

Thus the summoning of the *placita* and the deliberation they characterize:

Pro salute patria et utilitate Francorum tractando. . . . Ad honorem regni et communem utilitatem. . . . Propter vestram salutem ac totius populi utilitatem et regni honorem et stabilitatem.[16]

An Anglo-Saxon monk writes to Charlemagne a whole treatise about the eight main duties of the monarch as the protector and promoter of the common good.

Sunt autem octo columnae regis justi propriae. . . . Prima est veritas in rebus regalibus, secunda patientia in omni negotio, tertia largitas in muneribus, quarta persuadibilitas in verbis, quinta malorum correctio et constrictio, sexta bonorum elevatio et exaltatio, septima levitio tributi in populo, octava aequitas judicii inter divitem et pauperem.[17]

These eight categories of the duties are but those of a careful family head. They sound quite domestic and fatherly.

---

[14] Hincmar, *De ordine palatii*, c. 29, *Monumenta : Capitularia* (Hannover, 1897), Vol. II, p. 524. See many other details in G. Waitz, *op. cit.*, Vol. III, p. 596; R. Schröder, *Lehrbuch der deutschen Rechtsgeschichte* (Berlin, 1922), pp. 120–122; *Capitula cum primis constituta*, c. 12. *Monumenta: Capitularia*, Vol. I, p. 139; *Annales Einhardi anno 822*, *Monumenta*, in-F, Vol. I, p. 209.

[15] Alcuin, *Epistola*, 253; quoted by Waitz, *op. cit.*, Vol. III, p. 234.

[16] *Fredegarii continuatio*, c. 125, *Monumenta*, Vol. II, pp. 186–187. Capitulare 825, c. 15, quoted by Waitz, Vol. III, p. 234. Capitulare 829, c. 4, *Monumenta : Capitularia* (Hannover, 1897), Vol. II, p. 10.

[17] Waitz, *op. cit.*, Vol. III, p. 231.

This *pater familias* attitude is, in addition, penetrated by the religious principle of social service imposed by God upon the monarch and therefore felt still more urgently.

Nostrum est secundum auxilium divine pietatis [writes Charles the Great to Leo III] sanctam ubique Christi Ecclesiam ab incursu paganorum et ab infidelium devastatione armis defendere et indices catholice fidei agnitione munire.[18]

The divine source of the monarch's authority is taken for granted and regularly mentioned in various forms, like "*regnum a Deo nobis concessum; ministerium a Deo impositum*" and so on.[19]

These formulas indicate also that the duty of the monarch was regarded as a duty to God, and not only to the people.

In complete conformity with such a "patriarchal-familistic" conception stands the fact that the territory of the State is regarded as the familistic estate divided, if need be, by the *pater familias* between his heirs — the division quite common in the Merovingian and Carolingian kingdoms. Especially typically familistic were the Merovingian partitions: like the father giving to each son lots in both the near and far field, the king divided the central part of the state territory among his sons, and in addition, each son received a part in the remote, newly conquered territories. Generally, the law of inheritance was understood as the private law, as a familistic affair. Only, due to purely incidental circumstances — namely, the early death of the brother of Charlemagne and the brothers of Louis the Pious — the Frankish monarchy remained undivided during almost a century.[20]

Still more familistic sounds the term *fideles* for the subjects and the detailed characterization of the rights, duties, and the relationship between the monarch and the *fideles*. Of these the oath of *fidelity* (*sacramentum fidelitatis*) given before the *missi dominici* in a sacred place, sometimes on the relics of a saint, has all the earmarks of a religious and familistic sacrament. Such an oath established a direct personal bond for life between the king and the subject. It is not a contract but, so to speak, a confirmation of the natural, familistic bond. Even more than in an old-fashioned marriage vow — outwardly contractual, in fact an establishment of union into "one body and soul for life, unto death," of an all-

[18] Quoted by E. Chénon, *Histoire générale du droit français public et privé* (Paris, 1925), Vol. I, p. 343.

[19] Waitz, *op. cit.*, Vol. III, pp. 232–233.

[20] See E. D. Glasson, *Précis d'histoire de droit français* (Paris, 1904), p. 83; Waitz, *op. cit.*, Vol. III, p. 274; J. Calmette, *La société féodale* (Paris, 1932), chaps. i and ii.

embracing *consortium omnis vitae* — the *sacramentum fidelitatis* was but a pseudo-contractual clothing for a familistic (and partly compulsory) union for life and death. "The Carolingian State was based upon fidelity, *fidelitas*. The oath of fidelity was required from every subject. Thus a personal bond was created from the subject to the king." [21]

This bond of *personal devotion*, on the one hand, and bona fide *social service*, on the other, looks familistic in all its essential traits. An element of compulsion was certainly present, but it was not the only element and hardly the main one.

It is comprehensible that since it played the role of "the rite of passage" through which a "stranger" becomes one of the family and a group of persons becomes a closely tied familistic union, the oath of fidelity was given an exceptionally important significance and was styled "*sacramentum*," and often required to be made personally, either by all the people above a certain age, or in their behalf by their notables and representatives. [22]

To sum up, so far as the relationship between the monarch and the people is concerned, it was thought of mainly along the line of the familistic type. The term "the patriarchal monarchy" is therefore quite properly applied to it. It has a much deeper meaning than many of its users have possibly thought.

(2) In the relationships between *the monarch and the state officials* as such, in the total structure of the state system, the "*contractual fibers*" are quite noticeable, side by side with the familistic. As one of the *fideles*, the official is bound to the monarch by the familistic tie; as an official (count) appointed by the king, with a certain salary, and with definite, specified, and limited rights and duties beyond which, without the king's permission, he was not entitled to trespass, he stood to his sovereign in a relationship similar to the *contractual* type. Hence, the double or dualistic character of the position of the official in regard to the king and of the king to the official.

However, even the contractual ties were of such a nature that they approach the familistic one in their total configuration. First of all, the

---

[21] Calmette, *op. cit.*, pp. 18–19.

[22] See, for instance, capitularies 802, 806, and others. Praecepit ut omnis homo in toto regno suo, sive ecclesiasticus sive laicus, uniusquisque secundum votum et propositum suum, qui antea fidelitate sibi regis nomine promisserunt, nunc ipsum promissum nominis caesaris faciat. . . . Et ut omnes traderetur publice . . . quam magna in isto sacramento et quam multa comprehensa sunt. See *Marculfi Formulae*, I, 40, in *Monumenta*, p. 68. Capitulare 802, c. 2, *Monumenta: Capitularia*, Vol. I, pp. 92 and 131. See also G. von Below, *Der deutsche Staat des Mittelalters* (Leipzig, 1925), pp. 234–235 and 214.

position of the official to his king was a continuation and modification of the position of the German *comitatus* or the companionship; partly that of the members of the late Roman *scholae* or the troupes of the personal pretorians and companions. It was also termed by the Romans *obsequium*. As such, it meant an unlimited, almost unbreakable, tie of personal devotion for life and death between the leader and the follower. Such a tie, though contractual in its origin and appearance, in its nature is as familistic as the tie uniting bride and bridegroom in their marriage oath of fidelity. It is a union for the *consortium omnis vitae*, not temporary and conditional, and limited by one or more "interests," specified in the contract. The *sacramentum fidelitatis* brought by the *comitatus* to his leader created "the almost indissoluble tie which united the 'companion' to his chief in faith and loyalty." . . . The relationship which ensued "was not one of mere dependence, or of mere advantage, but one of faith and loyal service." [23]

Even in the terminology and in many empirical characteristics, it bears out the familistic traits. Such companions are styled often "*domestici*," "*milites in privato obsequio*"; younger men admitted to the band — the "*globus*" — are termed "*adulescentuli*," "*pueri vel vassali*"; others, "*antrustions*" or "*scholares*" — the terms taken mainly from the circle of the family and kinship, and all stressing personal devotion.[24]

Teutonic society had recognized very definitely a personal tie, quite apart from family ties or state ties, between man and man. Young men would attach themselves to some great warrior to eat at his table and to fight his battles, and this companionship or vassalage was recognized as a bond even stronger than that of son to father, or of subject to sovereign. Roman society also, from very early times, had recognized voluntary ties of this kind, under the title of *patrocinium*, or patronage.[25]

When the duties of these vassals or, in this case, the king's officials, are taken, they can be characterized by the same terms by which Fulbert de Chartres, in his famous letter of A.D. 1020, specified the duties of a vassal

[23] R. W. Carlyle and A. J. Carlyle, *A History of Mediaeval Political Theory in the West* (New York, 1916), Vol. III, pp. 20 ff.

[24] See J. Calmette, *op. cit.*, pp. 9–19.

[25] G. G. Coulton, *The Medieval Scene* (Cambridge, 1930), pp. 4–5. The Roman patronage or the early relationship between the patron and the client was of the same familistic nature. It was also an intimate and durable relationship, so close and many-sided that Virgil put in the nether world the patron who neglected the interests of the client side by side with those who, during their lives, betrayed their brothers or maltreated their fathers; an identification of this kind shows especially clearly the familistic nature of the relationship discussed. See Virgil, *Aeneid*, VI, 609.

— negative duties expressed in his six adjectives : *incolume, tutum, honestum, utile, facile, possibile*, which meant in their totality to do nothing to the detriment of the suzerain ; and the positive duties : *consilium et auxilium*, to do almost everything that he can to help his chief.[26]   On the other hand, the king was bound to do the same in regard to his official or *fideles. "Dominus quoque fideli suo in omnibus vicem reddere debet,"* as Fulbert puts it.

Such a relationship, in spite of the contractual form of the establishment of the bond between the king and the official, shows itself in fact much nearer to the familistic than to the contractual type. It was dominated by the same principle of personal devotion of an almost indissoluble character signified by the same *sacramentum fidelitatis.*

Hence it is comprehensible why the official position is styled *honor* or *dignitas;* why the services of the count were regarded not merely as those of a private salaried employee but mainly as a social service for the common good of the people.[27]

Side by side with this familistic (plus some contractual and pseudo-contractual) nature, the relationship of the monarch and his officials — as well as the monarch and the *fideles* generally — had, in the Carolingian monarchy, some compulsory elements also, especially in military matters. Capitulary 802, as well as 807 — to mention only two — imposed upon the free subjects a certain minimum of obligatory duties.   If they were not discharged, severe fines were imposed upon the guilty.   These are the manifestations of the presence of compulsory relationships.   Contractual elements crop up also in several other forms, first, that a *beneficium* is now granted under the condition of fulfillment of the military duty, for which before a *beneficium* was not necessary.[28]

To sum up, the total network of the State of the Carolingian period was woven mainly out of the familistic fibers, and then out of the compulsory

[26] As it is known even in vassalage relationship, the limitation of the positive duties of vassal, or the limited vassalage, *hominium planum*, appeared only after the tenth century, especially in the twelfth and later.   Up to that time, homage was unlimited or *hominium ligium* in the later terminology, as opposed to the limited *hominium planum*.   See Calmette, *op. cit.*, pp. 33 ff. and 41–43.

[27] This is shown even by the formula of an appointment of such an official.   Ergo dum et fidem et utilitatem tuam videmur habere compertam, ideo actionem comitiae in pago illo . . . tibi ad agendum regundumque committimus, ita ut semper ergo regimine nostro fidem inlibatam custodias.   *Marculfi Formulae*, I, 8, in *Monumenta : Formulae*, pp. 47–48.   See about the position of the count and the official in Waitz, *op. cit.*, Vol. III, p. 438 ; Schröder, *op. cit.*, p. 136 ; Capitulare 802, c. 19.

[28] See Capitulare 802, c. 2 and 7 ; Capitulare 807, c. 2, in *Monumenta : Capitularia*, Vol. I, pp. 92–93 and 134 ; Chénon, *op. cit.*, Vol. I, pp. 288–289 and 293 ; Schröder, *op. cit.*, pp. 120 and 164 ; Glasson, *op. cit.*, p. 82.

and contractual ones. This is true in regard to the totality of the relationship between the monarch and the people, the monarch and the officials, and finally the relationship between the *fideles* themselves. So far as the principle of personal devotion and fidelity was the main animating idea which permeated the whole structure of state relationship, so far the state system has to be considered as made up of the familistic (or near to this form) relationships mainly.

If, however, the unfree classes which were living in the State but were not part of it in the sense of being active and full-pledged participants are considered, they remained to a considerable degree "strangers" to it rather than subjects. Therefore a considerable part of their relationship with the State and its government was compulsory, mitigated by a sort of familistic relationship which existed between the masters and the serfs.

B. *The Feudal State* (particularly of the twelfth and the thirteenth centuries). If we pass now from the Carolingian State to the feudal State as it existed in France around the eleventh, the twelfth, and partly the thirteenth century, and in the twelfth and thirteenth centuries in Germany, the main changes in its structure, from the standpoint investigated, can be summed up as follows: first, the purely "external" (for our purposes) shrinking and atrophying of the network of social relationships of the state system. As is well known, the State was "swallowed" by the feudal social bodies, and an enormous number of relationships just dropped out of the state system.[29]

[29] The quantity and the quality of the relationship, which in their totality compose the network of social relationships of a given organized group, are not constant in the course of time. At one time many new relationships are included and therefore controlled by a given group; at another time many relationships are dropped out of it. For instance, most of the economic relationships in the field of production, distribution, and even consumption are not internal "fibers" of the state system in so-called "capitalist societies." They are part of other organized groups than the State and therefore the State does not control them. When, however, a Communist and a Fascist or a Nazi state system appears, most of these relationships are included in the state system and therefore are controlled by the State. The same can be said of other groups. Their network of social relationship fluctuates — quantitatively and qualitatively — all the time, now becoming "thicker" and consisting of more numerous strands, now becoming thinner. This is a process which takes place in the life history of practically any organized group, if such a group exists a sufficiently long time. By itself it is one of the universal forms of fluctuation of the sociocultural processes. As such it can be, and should be, carefully studied in a special monograph. In Chapter Seven I am giving a concise analysis of these fluctuations. For the present, these explanatory remarks must suffice. In the light of the above it must be clear that in the period studied we have an example, especially in France, of an enormous "thinning" of the network of the relationships of the state social system. An enormous part of them just dropped out of the state system and were included and controlled by the other organized social systems — the Church, the family, the guild, the commune, the feudal estate, and so on.

Respectively, the rights of the king as king, his functions, his officials —
a considerable part of these were taken out of the hands of the monarch
as monarch, and of the State as State, and passed into the hands of other
bodies social : the Church, the seigniors, the communes, the guilds, and
so on. The *rapport* of the central seat of the State with the subjects,
carried usually through the powerful hierarchy of the state officials,
disappears ; the authority of the seigniors (feudal lords) isolates them from
the central state authority, creates an unbreakable wall which separates
their subordinated vassals from the Crown ; disrupts the administrative
relations of the king with the provinces, and in this way leaves only a few
rights to the king as king. If he sometimes has many of these, he has
them not as a king, but as a great seignior and great suzerain.[30]

This change is merely mentioned here and is left without further
analysis because it does not concern our problem directly. (See
Chapter Seven of this volume.)

Second, the internal change in the relationships which remained still
the fibers of the state system consisted mainly, compared with the
Carolingian State, in *a reinforcement of the contractual relationships*
(especially in Germany) and in *quantitative-qualitative weakening of the
familistic relationships*. This weakening did not, however, go so far as to
make them either unimportant or unnoticeable. In comparison with
the preceding period, the contractual relationships grew, the familistic
weakened ; that is all that can be said. No further statement as to how
much they increased or weakened can be made.

Third, as to the compulsory relationships in the state system, no definite
answer can be given. In all probability they remained about the same
(proportionally) as in the previous period. Such, roughly, were the main
changes in the field studied. The main categories of the facts which
substantiate the propositions are as follows.

That the familistic type of relationship is still quite conspicuous in the
state system, so far as the relationship of the king and the subjects is
concerned, is witnessed by the fact that : (1) the universal bond of
fidelity to the monarch manifested by the oath of fidelity still remains ;
(2) the source of his authority (in France) is still believed to be based
on the divine law ; (3) he is still regarded as the supreme judge, responsible to God alone ; (4) there are no limitations of his power except his
conscience and those which are imposed by the nature of his mission.

[30] See A. Luchaire, *Manuel des institutions françaises* (Paris, 1892), p. 243 ; A. Luchaire,
Histoire des institutions monarchiques en France sous les premiers Capétiens (Paris, 1896),
Vol. I, p. 206 ; G. von Below, *op. cit.*, p. 279.

In all these traits, there is still little of the contractual type of bond.   The monarch still is a figure similar to a *pater familias*.[31]

In all these respects the contemporary formulas are about the same as in the preceding period.

As an example, the text of the oath of fidelity to Henry V resembles the earlier oaths :

Ab hoc ora fidelis ero imperatori per rectam fidem secundum meum scire et posse.   Non ero in consilio, ut vitam aut membra perdeat [and so on].[32]

In the diploma of Hugh Capet stands :

Nostrae sublimitatis pietatis non aliter recto stare valet ordine, nisi omnibus et per omnia justitiam operando de justo priorum sectanto mentaliter decreta regum, Deique ecclesias sublimando.[33]

Louis IX preaches to his son :

Care fili, si contingat quod tu venias ad regnum, provideas quod tu habes ea quae pertinent ad regem, hoc est dicere quod tu sis justus quod non declives a justitia pro aliquod quod aleat evenire.[34]

While Widukind straightly says that *"imperium non a patribus sibi relictum, sed per semet ipsum acquisitum et a solo Deo concessum."* [35]

In spite of the continuation of the familistic form, the contractual form, especially in Germany, makes notable progress in the system of the state network of social relationships.   It begins to occupy a greater portion in this "spectrum."

First, the bonds between the king and the officials, now much fewer in number, tend to become more contractual than before.   In Germany this is manifested by the fact that, beginning with 887 factually and with 1077 juridically, the monarchy becomes elective, elected up to 1257 by all the grand seigniors, and after that by seven great electors.[36]   In election, a preference is often given to the sons and relatives of the preceding monarch, in which fact the familistic principle shows itself; [37] nevertheless, the fact that there is an election is an evident sign of the introduction of the contractual form.

[31] See A. Luchaire, *Histoire*, Vol. I, pp. 41 and 48; G. von Below, *op. cit.*, p. 236.
[32] Quoted by Waitz, *op. cit.*, Vol. VI, 1st ed. (Kiel, 1875), p. 383.
[33] Chénon, *op. cit.*, Vol. II, p. 567.
[34] *Ibid.*, Vol. III, pp. 435–436.
[35] *Vidukindi res gestae saxonicae*, I, 41, in *Monumenta*, in-F (Hannover, 1839), Vol. III·
[36] K. von Amira, *Grundriss des deutschen Rechts* (Strassburg, 1913), p. 156.
[37] For instance, the chronicler says about the election of Otto I : *"jure hereditario paternio eligitur succedere regnis."*   Annal. Quedlingburg, *Monumenta*, in-F, Vol. III, p. 54.

As a result of this, the king is now obliged to take the oath of obedience
to the feudal law; to consult the opinion of the notables in issuing any
law; to introduce the electoral capitularies, or contracts; to hold the
rights of the seigniors inviolable; even the dethronement of the king for
violation of the laws becomes possible.[38]   The act of the dethronement of
Adolphus contains a whole dissertation about the right of dethronement
of a king.[39]

These contractual rights of the seigniors continued after the election
and led to the transformation of the preceding *placita* into the Reichstag,
with its rights, shown clearly, for instance, by the rule of 1231.

Ut neque principes neque aliquilibet constitutiones vel nova jura facere
possint, nisi meliorum et maiorum terrae consensus . . . habeatur.[40]

Here before us is a genuine constitutional and contractual monarchy.

However, as mentioned, the familistic principle remains still, especially
in France.   Even the summons of the king to the Reichstag bears a mark
of this familistic pattern.[41]

So far as the bonds between the king and his officials are concerned,
though such officials remained in a greatly diminished number, they
had a similar familistic-contractual nature.[42]

As for the military bonds, they practically ceased to exist as state
bonds (dropped out of the state system of social relationship) and became
purely feudal bonds.   The king controlled as a seignior whatever military
contingents and vassals he had.   Thus the bond was mixed: contractual-
compulsory, and partly familistic in its nature.   Contractual, because

---

[38] See Von Amira, *op. cit.*, p. 156. Here, for instance, is the electoral capitulary of Adolphus
of Nassau (April 26, 1292): "Eligimus et arbitramus quod si contra premissa vel aliquod
premissorum fidem nostram (quod absit) infringendo deveniremus . . . ipso facto cademus a
jure electionis et jure regni nobis per electio non acquisito. . . . Item habemus quod principes
. . . ad electionem alterius regis procedant, si hoc archiepiscopo videbitur expedire."
K. Zeumer, *Quellensammlung zur Geschichte der deutschen Verfassung* (Berlin, 1900), pp. 132–
135.

See also the contracts of Frederic II with the ecclesiastic (1220) and the secular lords (1232)
where he agrees to respect a large number of important prerogatives of these princes: not to
appropriate the income of a deceased bishop, not to put into circulation a new money over
their territories, not to accept the fugitives from their territories, not to build fortresses,
not to open new fairs, not to build new roads, etc., etc.   See *Privilegium in favorem principum
ecclesiasticorum, 1220,* and *Constitutio in favorem principum, 1232* in *Monumenta: Constitutiones* (Hannover, 1896), Vol. II, pp. 86 and 211–213.

[39] See its text in Zeumer, *op. cit.*, p. 138.

[40] *Monumenta: Constitutiones*, Vol. II, p. 420.

[41] See, for instance, its typical form in *Monumenta: Constitutiones*, Vol. I, p. 120.

[42] See the details in A. Luchaire, *Manuel*, pp. 519–520; Waitz, *op. cit.*, Vol. VI, 2d ed.
(Berlin, 1896), pp. 354–359.

there were definite norms which indicated the size and the duration of service of the military force, to be supplied by a vassal. Compulsory, because the duty was obligatory as *allgemeines Aufgebot* and because its nonfulfillment led to a loss of the feod and other fines; familistic, because there still remained a great deal from the previous German-Roman companionship (*comitatus, obsequio*) or brotherhood in arms, in the relationship of the military chief (monarch) and vassal.[43]

To sum up : the main transformation of the state system of social relationships or bonds in the period considered consisted, in comparison with the preceding period, in a notable increase of the contractual relationships at the cost mainly of the familistic bonds, the compulsory bonds remaining possibly about the same as before, though these shifted from the state system to other feudal systems of social bodies. This net result is to be noted because, as we shall see, about this same time these other social groups show a similar trend in the transformation of the "fibers" of their structures and because, as we have seen, the twelfth and the thirteenth centuries were the centuries of mixture and balance of, and transition from, the Ideational to the Sensate forms of culture. This is the first suggestion of a possible association of the predominantly Ideational with the familistic, and of the Sensate with the contractual kind of social relationship.

C. *The Church.* The system of social relationship which composes a religious organized group tends generally to be familistic, regardless of the time and place of such a religious society. The Christian Church was such from the moment of its emergence. Beginning with the writings of the apostles and the Church Fathers of the first period of the existence of the Christian Church, and ending with those of later times, the social relationships of the members of the Christian Church were conceived and thought of almost entirely along the familistic type.

"Thou shalt share all things with thy brothers." . . . "Christ is our true father and faith in him is our mother." "Spouse of Christ" (Church). Christ as a "bridegroom" of many virgins.[44] These and similar, purely familistic terms are incessantly used by practically all the Church Fathers. "Brethren," "Sisters," "Our Holy Father," and the

[43] See, for instance, the description of the military inspection by the king of the army given by Otto von Freising, in Waitz, *op. cit.*, Vol. VIII, p. 108; Schröder, *op. cit.*, p. 563. See in these volumes a detailed characterization of the organization, composition, and functioning of the military forces of the period. See also Luchaire, *Manuel*, p. 487.

[44] "The Didache or the Teaching of the Lord through Twelve Apostles to the Gentiles" (*c.* A.D. 100), pp. 4–6; in B. J. Kidd, *Documents Illustrative of the History of the Church*, Vol. I, pp. 31 ff.

like, are the usual forms of characterization of the comembers of the Church, its priests, its dignitaries, and also God.[45]   Even the Trinity itself is characterized in familistic terms: "God the Father," "the Son of God."

More than that. In so far as the social organization of the early Christian Church is concerned, it was in a sense *familistic* par excellence. The members composed one *"corpus mysticum,"* one "we," with *communis omnium possessio et omnium una libertas*, with a really familistic community of property (for instance, in the Jerusalem Community), with respectively strong anti-individualistic and "private-property" tendencies.   They all were "brethren in Christ," and tried to carry out this deep and fundamental unity of the Christian "we" in their beliefs as well as actions.

In brief, the engulfment of every individual "I" by the group's "we" was so complete, many sided, unlimited, and spontaneous, and the fact of it is so well known, that there is no need to quote various documents and evidences in verification. The whole system of the relationships of the Christian Church in its earliest period was familistic par excellence.[46]

Beginning with the end of the fourth century, this familism expressed itself, among other ways, in the organization of the Christian monasticism, with the regime of the monasteries where the members were fused into one "we," where individualism and any form of private property were most vigorously extirpated by a prohibition to own anything, even a book or pen or blackboard (*sed nihil omnino*).[47]

[45] See in Kidd's work the documents and writings of the Church Fathers.   They all are full of similar terms and expressions.

[46] As mentioned, among other things it is manifest in a familistic community of property (quite different from communism, which is a system of a mechanistic — through the machinery of the State and by the means of compulsion — annihilation of private property).   Writings of the majority of the Church Fathers, like the Didache, the Epistles of Barnabas, of Justin Martyr, of St. Cyprian, St. Jerome, St. Augustine, St. John Chrysostom, St. Basil, St. Gregory, and others, are samples of such an attitude.   Likewise, the Church affairs were managed by "the family gathering" of all the "brethren" in the councils.   These and practically the whole system of the social organization of the early Christian communities show conspicuous familism, unmistakably and unquestionably.   See R. W. Carlyle and A. J. Carlyle, *op. cit.*, Vol. I, chap. xii; O. von Gierke, *Genossenschaftsrecht* (Berlin, 1881), Vol. III, pp. 510–644, *et passim;* J. O. Hannay, *The Spirit and Origin of Christian Monasticism* (London, 1903), pp. 39–40; R. Pöhlmann, *Geschichte der socialen Frage, und des Sozialismus in der antiken Welt* (München, 1912), chapters on the Early Christian Communism.

[47] See F. J. Foakes Jackson, *An Introduction to the History of Christianity* (New York, 1921), p. 5 ff.; Msgr. L. Duchesne, *Early History of Christian Church*, 3 vols. (New York, 1924); I. C. Hannan, *Christian Monasticism* (New York, 1925); A. Harnack, *Monasticism* (New York, 1895).

In the essentials this domination of the familistic type of social bonds continued during the subsequent centuries, in the Carolingian and later period. The network of the Church system of relationship was still thought of along the same familistic lines. However, considerable changes in the factual organization of the Christian Church took place.

As before, the terminology remains almost purely familistic. For example, Teodulf addresses comembers: "Beloved Brethren," [48] as do practically all Christians. The religious association remains an all-embracing fusion into one "we" of all members, without any "contractual" limitations and reservations.[49] *Vita communis* of the communities persists not only in the monasteries but also outside them.[50] The familistic management of religious and community affairs continues also in the form of meetings of the members, and common participation in the discussions and decisions, in a direct or indirect election of the bishops and other dignitaries by the believers, and in many other forms.[51]

As an illustration of this a few lines from the letters of Gregory VII can serve. He addresses the kings as "dearly beloved sons," "good children," "the best beloved son of St. Peter," "beloved daughter," and so on. Church is "Your true mother"; God is "Our Father"; Christians are "brethren," and so on and so forth. Practically, the whole system of relationship, even where he threatens to apply punishment, is unmistakably familistic.[52]

When from these centuries we pass to the twelfth, the thirteenth, and the fourteenth, the familistic form remains dominant. Its role in the whole social life even grows, through a growth of the role of the religious ties in the whole social life, especially in the eleventh century; but within the religious network itself the contractual elements show the first signs of increase.

The religious tie indeed plays now an exceptionally important role — the role of a cement binding together the other social ties. On it are based the king's power itself, to a considerable degree;[53] it permeates and

---

[48] R. F. W. Guéttée, *Histoire de l'église de France* (Paris, 1848), Vol. III, p. 139.

[49] Shown clearly in the petition of the notables to Charlemagne, *ibid.*, pp. 135-137.

[50] See P. Hinschius, *System des katolischen Kirchenrechts* (Berlin, 1879), Vol. II, p. 613.

[51] The capitulary of 817 says: Adsensum ordinis ecclesiastico praebuimus, ut scilicet episcopi per electionem cleri et populi secundum statuta canonum de proprio diocesi . . . ob vitae meritum et sapientiae donum eligantur. Capitulare ecclesiasticum 818-819, c. 2, in *Monumenta : Capitularia*, Vol. II, p. 276. See about the organization of the Church, besides the works quoted in this chapter. Chénon, *op. cit.*, Vol. I, pp. 310, 314, and 336; Waitz, *op. cit.* Vol. III, pp. 423-424.

[52] See *The Correspondence of Pope Gregory VII*, trans. by E. Emerton (New York, 1932), pp. 20, 55, 64, 66, 67, *et passim*.　　　　[53] Luchaire, *Manuel*, p. 487.

"glues" together the communal, the corporative, the family, and other collective unities. The village community emerged from the parish community;[54] the city communities are also bound together through the Church as one of the main uniting centers.[55] Religion reinforces the ties of various free associations: brotherhoods, free corporations, guilds, and so on.[56] It cements in its own way the members of the family, through purifying it of the previous compulsory elements and through suppression of divorce and other forms of family disintegration.[57] Finally, the whole system of the religious groupings enters the feudal system and becomes a part of it: bishops become suzerains of some seigniors and vassals of others; the church patrons begin to view the priests as vassals, who have pledged their oath of fidelity.[58]

All this means that the role and the weight of the Church as such increased among other forms of social groupings; and in so far as the religious system was still mainly familistic, the permeation of other social groups by religious ties meant a spread of the familistic ties through those groups.

But in the system of the social relationships of the Church itself, the contractual, and partly even the compulsory, elements seem to show the first signs of growth, though the familistic principle remains still dominant; the parishioners still manage collectively the affairs of the parish;[59] very numerous are the religious "brotherhoods";[60] the Church *capitularia* (chapters) continue to have *vita communis* (up to the end of the eleventh century) with renunciation of individualism in favor of the whole group.[61]

The differentiation between the clergy and the parishioners now becomes conspicuous; election of the Church dignitaries by the parishioners and the clergy together ceases and becomes mere fiction; the "*communis omnium possessio*" ceases; the expenses of the Church for its poor members decrease greatly, in spite of an enormous enrichment of the Church. The Church as one *corpus mysticum* undergoes the first important split — into the Eastern and the Western — and within each, the "heretics" and sects and factions appear: with the resulting persecution of the "heretics" and the "politics of the dissident minority" (even in the monasteries). At the same time, the enmeshment of the Church into the feudal system introduces more and more the contractual elements into

---

[54] *Ibid.*, p. 377.
[55] See C. de Ribbe, *La société provençale à la fin du Moyen Âge* (Paris, 1898), p. 430.
[56] *Ibid.*, p. 380.   [57] *Ibid.*, p. 95.   [58] Luchaire, *Manuel*, pp. 8–12, 31, and 46.
[59] *Ibid.*, p. 5.   [60] *Ibid.*, p. 366.   [61] *Ibid.*, p. 57.

the network of social relationship of the Church. In these and similar ways the contractual and the compulsory elements enter more and more the structure of the Church; at the same time, the familistic principle becomes less and less spontaneous, intensive, and sincere.[62] To sum up, like the system of the State, the Church shows also, though in a smaller degree, the first signs of the growing infiltration of the contractual and compulsory elements into the Church system of social relationships.

D. *The Family*. The Germanic family as a union of kinship was a union of equals, so far as the grown-up male members were concerned; the women and children were under the *Munt* of the head of the family. The central and predominant part of its bonds was familistic. This is manifest in that the family, not the individual, was the social unit for the purposes of taxation, of discharge of the duties, of responsibility. The family was responsible for the crime of its member; the family was the subject which was honored by some heroic action of its member; the family sought to carry out justice, if one of its members became a victim of crime. Each member of the family was obliged to appear as a codefendant, cojuryman, corevenger.[63] Its members had the right of mutual inheritance. The will of the testator was not free and was limited by the law and tradition.[64]

---

[62] *Ibid.*, pp. 31, 55 ff., and 75–76. G. Ratzinger, *Geschichte der kirchlichen Armenpflege* (Freiburg, 1881), pp. 66 ff. and 236. E. Munsterberg, "*Geschichte der öffentlichen Armenpflege*" in *Handwörterbuch der Staatswissenschaften* (1909), Vol. II, pp. 7–8. In passing, it can be noted that parallel with the weakening of the familistic principle in the system of the official Church, it becomes strongly stressed in various sects and heretic groups, like the Cathari — with their principle : *omnem nostram possessionem cum omnibus hominibus communem habemus*, the Pathareni, the Arnoldians, the Waldenses, the Humiliats, the Lyon Poors, the Moravian Brothers, and other sects which emerged at the end of the eleventh century and continued to appear in the centuries from the twelfth to the fourteenth. Most of them professed and were organized along the line of the familistic principle, with common property and *vita communis*. See especially L. Karsavin, *Ocherki religioznoi jizni v Italii v XII–XIII vekakh* (St. Petersburg, 1912); B. Jarrett, *Mediaeval Socialism* (London, n. d.), and *Social Theories of the Middle Ages* (London, 1926).

[63] See Chénon, *op. cit.*, Vol. I, pp. 314, 378, and 395; Von Amira, *op. cit.*, pp. 171–172; J. Brissaud, *Manuel d'histoire du droit privé* (Paris, 1908).

[64] *Deus non homo facit heredes*. The will of the testator is not free and is limited: absolutely, as far as the family property is concerned, and greatly, as far as the property acquired by the testator himself is concerned. With slight variation, this is true of the early Germanic, Frankish, and Slavic (Russian) family and law. See *Lex Romana Burgundiorum*, X, 4; XLV, 5 : *testamenta vero quibus filiis aut nepotibus faleidia (legitima) non dimittitur, nullo jure subsistunt;* see also about *quarta legitima* in *Lex Romana Wisigothorum:* Codex Theodosianus, I, c. 4, § 3. Even in regard to the other part of the property the consent of the relatives (*laudatio parentum*) is necessary in order that the testament be valid. See the details, E. Chénon, *op. cit.*, Vol. I, p. 457. For Russia see M. Vladimirsky-Budanoff, *Obzor istorii Russkago prava*, 5th ed. (Kiev, 1904), p. 484. The same is true of the common law (*pays de coutumes*) where inheritance was mostly *ab intestat*, where the relatives were the inheritors, where the *réserve*

The marriage or the choice of the mate of the member was not only — and perhaps even not so much — the member's affair as that of the family as a whole.   Likewise, the divorce depended only in part upon the husband's volition ;   in part, it depended upon the family group as such.[65]   All this means that the family was a strongly integrated and all-embracing collective unity, with a deep and spontaneous solidarity leaving to an individual no "private sphere," and no compartment of life where he remains a "stranger."

This, however, does not hinder the presence of the contractual and the compulsory relationships in the family network, as secondary to some extent and degree.   As already mentioned, the consent of the married persons began, at least from the seventh century, to be required.   So far the marriage had a contractual aspect.   Likewise, the contractual aspect was present in the agreement, partly of the family groups as such and partly of the married persons, concerning the dowry which the bridegroom should give to his bride (or the bridegroom's family should give the bride's family) and about the property relationships between the husband and wife.   Likewise, divorce was not prohibited entirely and the husband could obtain it, which again points to the presence of the contractual element.[66]   Finally, a grown-up son could, by publicly breaking over his head four branches and throwing them in four directions, declare himself free from his family duties and rights, and in this way break his family bonds by his own volition.   Though this custom began

---

coutumière was the right not only of the nearest relatives but of the remote ones also.   Only in the form of donation to the Church (the *Seelgeräthe, Seeldinge*) were deviations from that permitted.   Generally, roughly up to the reception of the Roman law and factually up to the fourteenth century, the real freedom of testamentary disposal of one's property hardly existed in any important sense.   This means again that even economically the family was a strongly integrated solidary unit.

[65] The consent of the bride is either not required or is required rarely.   As a rule, in the ancient Germanic and Slavic law, the choice of the mate is made by the parents; and their consent to the marriage is quite necessary.   *Lex Wisigothorum*, III, 1, art. 2, forbids *puella sponsata* to contradict the decision of the parents and relatives.   Later on, the edict of Clotaire (584–628), art. 7, prohibited the marriage of women against their will (" *nullus per auctoritatem nostram matrimonium viduae vel puellae sine ipsarum voluntate presumat, expedire* ") ; likewise the Canon law definitely required the consent of the married to the marriage.   (Pope Nicolas I, *Resp. ad Bulgaras*, in 866 : " *Sed post sponsalia . . . federa quoque consensu eorum qui hic contrahunt . . . et eorum in quorum potestate sunt celebrantur.*" *Grat. Decret.* II, 30, qq. 5 and 3.   But as is seen from this quotation, side by side with the consent of the married, the consent and approval of the parents and the relatives were invariably required, signifying thus that here we have a harmony of the will of the married individual with that of the family group.   See Brissaud, *op. cit.*, p. 38, notes 2, 3, 4, and 5.   For the Russian law, see Vladimirsky-Budanoff, *op. cit.*, p. 434.

[66] See Chénon, *op. cit.*, Vol. I, pp. 388–390.

to disappear, it again shows contractual implications in the family structure.[67]

As to the compulsory elements surviving from the previous period, there still remained the unlimited *Munt* of the head of the family over the members: several strong disciplinary rights which in a few specific cases gave to the head the right of life and death over a guilty member, the right of selling him into slavery, and so on. Though in most cases such rights were probably used with the agreement of the whole family, nevertheless we can hardly assume that in all cases they were also welcomed by the "disciplined member." The presence of such a relationship indicates the compulsory elements. However, they were rare even before, and were dying out now, and the conception of the head of the family as its protector and defender, serving to the best of his ability the interests of the family, becomes stronger and more dominant.[68]

Thus in the earlier centuries of the period studied the family appears as a predominantly familistic system; only in part was the network of this system woven of contractual and compulsory elements, and these played a comparatively unimportant part.

If we take the family of the centuries from the ninth to the twelfth, the thirteenth, and partly the fourteenth centuries, we notice that all in all its structure remained about the same, from the standpoint studied. The main change seems to have consisted in a further mitigation and elimination of the compulsory elements, and perhaps of a slightly more pronounced contractual form in the system of the family; but these changes seem to have made the familistic elements only purer and more clarified than before the ninth century.

The decrease of the compulsory elements shows itself in a further reduction of the disciplinary power of the head over the members and of the husband over the wife especially in France: the parent's power over the children now lasts only up to the moment of their maturity, while his right to sell them into slavery is entirely eliminated. In Germany the compulsory *Munt* remains still somewhat sterner than in France; but it also is mitigated in comparison with the previous period. Likewise, now the consent of the party to marry is stressed and required more and more, and compulsory marriage is largely prohibited.[69] These and similar

---

[67] *Lex Salica*, 63; Chénon, *op. cit.*, Vol. I, p. 380; Von Amira, *op. cit.*, p. 175.

[68] See A. Heussler, *Institutionen des deutschen Privatrechts* (Leipzig, 1885), Vol. I, pp. 106–108; Chénon, *op. cit.*, Vol. I, p. 395; Schröder, *op. cit.*, p. 357; see especially H. Fehr, *Die Rechtsstellung der Frau und Kinder in den Weistümern* (Jena, 1912), p. 60.

[69] See Chénon, *op. cit.*, Vol. II, p. 135; *Schwabenspiegel*, art. 291; Schröder, *op. cit.*, pp. 237 and 251; H. Fehr, *op. cit.*, p. 100.

symptoms seem to indicate definitely the mitigation of the compulsory elements in the family system of relationship.

A slight increase of the contractual relationships shows itself in the fact that marriage and many family relationships begin to assume more and more the character of a free contract of the parties, at least, in the fields where the compulsory relationships are now eliminated, as indicated above. Divorce is still permitted on the declaration of the husband, for the special reasons indicated in the Canon law. Even when the reason is illegal, his refusal to continue the union with the wife still leads to the annulment of the marriage.[70]

All in all, according to the common law (*coutumes*) the mutual *fidelitas* and union of the parties now is stressed more. The family, around the eleventh to the thirteenth century, still remains a familistic union but purified in its familism through the decrease of the compulsory relationship.

E. *Guilds, Bruderschaften, Bundbruderschaften, Schwurbruderschaften, Corporations, and Other Associations.* Various *fraternities* and *confrèries* or voluntary associations for mutual help existed before the ninth century. In their nature, they were familistic organizations, in spite of the quasi-contractual form of their origin. Whether they originated under the influence of the ideas of Christian charity, or were a continuation of the Roman guilds and corporations, or were formed in the early periods of the Germanic tribes, does not concern us here.[71] What does concern us is that such associations sprang up and multiplied enormously during the period studied, and that beginning roughly with the centuries seventh to ninth the guilds — in the narrow sense of the word — appeared and developed into one of the most important social institutions of the period analyzed.[72] Though most associations of that kind seem to be contractual in their origin, the bond uniting their members was in its inner nature mainly familistic: in many of these "confraternities," as the term itself indicates (also the *conviviums, Bruderschaften, affrairements*, etc.), the bond established was not limited either in time or in duties; sometimes, as in the arm companionships, it was a union for life and death. The rites with which such a contract was sealed were a clear indication of the fact that the bond was regarded as strong and of the same nature as that between brothers by blood : the predominant rite of the mixture of blood,

[70] See Chénon, *op. cit.*, Vol. II, pp. 94–99; Schröder, *op. cit.*, p. 336.
[71] See about that in E. Martin Saint-Leon, *Histoire de corporations de métiers* (Paris, 1922), chap. ii.
[72] *Ibid.*, pp. 38 ff. and chap. iii.

of walking along the same path together, of the oath of fidelity and so on.[73] The same is true of the early guilds. Whether we agree with Wilda that the earliest function of the guilds was retribution, *Vergeltung*, and that they were a substitute for the family in many respects,[74] or with other investigators who submitted different theories of their origin, it must be admitted that in their nature the guild's bonds were much nearer to the familistic than to the contractual or compulsory bonds. Even later, when the occupational guilds emerged and crystallized (in the twelfth and the thirteenth centuries), the relationships between the master and the valets and the apprentices were more similar to that between the head of the family and his children, than to the purely formal, limited, and cold contractual form. And this in spite of the fact that primarily the bonds in a given guild between its main strata and members originated usually in a contractual form.[75] The great contemporaries like Hincmar show this also in their definition of guilds: " *de collectis, quas geldonias vel confratrias vulgo vocant.*" [76] The very fact that the State and the Church often found it necessary to prohibit such confraternities, companionships, and guilds [77] is one of the indications of the closeness and strength of the fellowship which bound together their members. The contractual element, especially in the establishment or origin of a confraternity, was not absent ; nevertheless in its inner nature the bond was not so much contractual as familistic. The same seems to be true of the comparative importance of the familistic and compulsory bonds in such associations. The latter were, of course, also present : the various stages and the length of each stage in the guild were obligatory; an apprentice who left his master could be brought back by force ; and so on. But the familistic principle was the foundation, the heart, the soul, and the cement which bound together the members, which permeated the organizations, and which gave them power, strength, and unity.

This is true of the eighth and ninth centuries as well as of the eleventh, the twelfth, and the thirteenth centuries. In this later period, we have guilds, corporations, and various confraternities in a perfected form, especially the guilds and the corporations. The guild and corporative bonds tied together, on the one hand, the members of the same artisan

---

[73] See Von Amira, *op. cit.*, pp. 185 ff.; Saint-Leon, *op. cit.*, chap. ii.

[74] See W. E. Wilda, *Das Gildenwesen im Mittelalter* (Halle, 1831), pp. 1–25.

[75] See the details in Saint-Leon, *op. cit.*, Bk. II; Von Amira, *op. cit.*, pp. 186 ff.

[76] Hincmar, *De ordine palatii*, c. 16, in *Monumenta : Capitularia*, Vol. II, p. 523.

[77] See, for instance, the capitularies of A.D. 789 and 884 in *Monumenta : Capitularia*, Vol. I, pp. 81 and 64 and Vol. II, p. 375. See also E. Hegel, *Städte und Gilden der germanischen Völker* (Leipzig, 1891), Vol. I, p. 4, *et passim*.

establishment — the master, the valets, and the apprentices; on the other hand, the various establishments were represented by the union of the masters. Contractual in its origin, the bond was familistic in all its essential traits. It is useless to attempt to enumerate these traits, but any serious investigator of these organizations can hardly fail to see and to feel them, when he enters their atmosphere.[78]

The same is to be said of other brotherhoods (*affrairements*) and associations of persons in the same occupational group. Their familistic nature is well expressed, even in the usual reason given for their organization: *propter sanguinitatis et fraternitatis et benevolentiam.*[79] Often their members pooled their property and work and profits. Their other motives were religious — work *ad majorem gloriam Dei* — or a totalitarian protection of their interests, as in the association of the *institutiones pacis* of the rural people against brigandage, or the urban people for the maintenance of order, protection against a seignior, and the like. To sum up: an enormous majority of these numerous and important organizations were familistic in their nature; the contractual and compulsory elements were present, but they played a much less important role in the structure of these groups.

F. *Village Communities and the Urban Communes.* What is said of the guilds and corporations can be said, to a considerable degree, of the territorial urban and rural communities. The network of the relationships of the members of the urban communes or the rural or village community was also woven mainly out of familistic fibers, though perhaps of not particularly great intensity. Whether the village community was composed of the free or unfree individuals, it was the *familia*[80] either of closely integrated land tillers or the *familia* of serfs of the same master, living together and bound together by many ties other than the compulsory ones.

The village community was not only a union for guaranteeing to each one his fair share in the common land, but also a union for common culture, for mutual support in all possible forms, for protection from violence, and for a further development of knowledge, national bonds, and moral conceptions. . . .

---

[78] See besides the works quoted, P. Boissonade, *Essai sur l'organisation du travail en Poitou depuis le XI siècle jusqu'à la révolution*, 2 vols. (Paris, 1900); Boissonade, *Life and Work in Medieval Europe* (New York, 1927); R. Eberstadt, *Der Ursprung des Zunftwesens* (Leipzig, 1900), pp. 11 and 20 ff.

[79] See C. de Ribbe, *op. cit.*, pp. 388–389; Chénon, *op. cit.*, Vol. II, p. 632; Hegel, *op. cit.*, p. 14.

[80] Heussler, *op. cit.*, p. 135; Luchaire, *op. cit.*, p. 412; De Ribbe, *op. cit.*, p. 230.

The community being a continuation of the *gens*, it inherited all its functions. It was the *universitas*, the *mir* — a world in itself.[81]

Since the detailed analysis of the village communities of the European Middle Ages as well as those of the Chinese, the Hindu, and other peoples has been presented elsewhere [82] by the author; and since the familistic nature of the bonds which united the members is reasonably certain, there is no need to repeat the study in detail here, and the above statements may suffice.

The urban communes of the free citizens did not appear until after the development of urban life in the Middle Ages. And we can talk of only those city communes which received special charters for such a privilege. The other — unchartered — cities represented the totality of the persons united by general subjection to the seignior, and by various other ties, but these inner ties were possibly less familistic than in the "free city communes." A mere study of the charters granted to such cities, in spite of the fact that they enumerate but fragmentarily the rights and duties, plus a study of the common law which supplemented them, [83] shows that their network of social relationships and their bonds were mainly of the familistic type. This is shown first of all by the *oath of fidelity* to advise and aid in various forms one another, which the members of such communes had to give. Such *sacramentum fidelitatis* was often the very foundation of the city commune. This can be seen from the following chronicle, which tells of the foundation of the commune in Cambrai in 1076.

Cives Cameraci male consulti conspirationem multo tempore susuratam et diu desideratam *juraverunt* communiam. Adeo sunt inter se *sacramento* coniuncti, quod, nisi factam concederet coniurationem, denegarent . . . introitum Cameracum . . . pontifici.[84]

The familistic character of the bonds manifests itself also in the public and solemn ceremony of the admission of a person to citizenship in the commune — the ceremony which is a variation of the "rite of passage" so typical of the establishment of the familistic bonds; [85] in the

---

[81] P. Kropotkin, *Mutual Aid* (New York, 1902), pp. 119-152. See the details and the selected readings about that in Sorokin, Zimmerman, and Galpin, *op. cit.*, Vol. I, chap. vi, and Vol. II, chap. x. See there a systematic analysis of the "cumulative rural community," the readings from M. Kovalevsky, F. Le Play, Altekar, R. Maunier, H. Douglas-Irvine, and others; see there also detailed bibliography.

[82] See Sorokin, Zimmerman, and Galpin, *op. cit.*

[83] See about that in Hegel, *op. cit.*, Vol. I, p. 112.

[84] Quoted by Waitz, *op. cit.*, Vol. VI, p. 396. [85] See Luchaire, *op. cit.*, pp. 390 ff.

association of the high bourgeois families into a kind of superfamily union, which managed the affairs of the city and from which, often in a hereditary form, the syndics and other officials of the municipality were elected by the upper class of the city commune; [86] and other characteristics. Perhaps the intensity of the familistic tie was not so great as in the relationship of the members of the Church, of the confraternities, of the family, but it seems to have been the predominant form of relationship from which the communes were made.

Again the contractual and compulsory relationships were not absent in the network of the communes. Before being granted citizenship, a man had to agree to pay his share of taxes and levies in the commune and to carry on certain duties. Several other conditions were stipulated. Likewise, the relationship of the commune to the outside world was in several respects contractual [87] (the commune's feudal rights and duties). It goes without saying that the compulsory elements were also noticeable. If, in the interrelationship of the "full-pledged" citizens, they did not occupy a conspicuous place, they were considerably in evidence in the relationships between the stratum of the full-pledged *bourgeoisie* and the other classes of the commune which lived in it but were not a part of it. But this was the result of an existence of such relationships in the feudal world (to be analyzed further) and as these elements were not a part of the commune, they do not enter directly into the structure of the commune per se: they are the strangers, the means and the instruments of it, but not members of it.

Thus, these important associations, the village and the city communities, were built along the pattern of the familistic type; and the vital bond uniting their members into a solidary unity was also mainly familistic.

G. *Feudal Hierarchical Bonds between the Free Men and Free Social Strata* (from king to villein). Possibly the most general ties of the period,

which shot through the system of the State, the Church, the corporations, the communes and communities, and which linked together into much larger social systems multitudes of men and of families, and which bound into an interdependent vast body the upper and the lower classes among the free men, especially after the tenth century, was the feudal bond of the sacred *fidelity*. It was the bond which united the vassals and the seigniors, the lower and the upper strata. The figure of the feudal structure is a bunch.

FIG. 2.   FEUDAL STRUCTURE

86 *Ibid.*, pp. 418 and 440.   87 Luchaire, *Manuel*, pp. 388–390.

Each of the subordinated vassals can be a seignior in regard to other vassals, until we come to the lowest stratum of vassals, who are not seigniors of any vassals, and, at least theoretically, to the king, who is a suzerain and is no vassal of any seignior. But in this "many-storied" [88] social structure the direct relationships were limited to those of the seignior and his immediate vassals; the vassals of these vassals were "screened" from the seignior and had no direct personal relationship with him. In this sense, the feudal bond was personal, face to face, or, as Cooley says, a primary relationship.[89]

The weaker party vowed its fidelity to the other, the more powerful one returned for that its protection and *beneficium*. Though the bond is contractual, according to the mode of its establishment, in its nature, especially in the earlier ages of feudalism, it was much nearer to the familistic type. First came the terms themselves: the *antrustiones*, who are "*truste regi*," according to the expression of Marculf; the Frankish *trustes*, from which came the English trustee; the *Degen* and *pueri*, which mean children; and somewhat similar terms: *adolescentuli*, *custodes*, *satellites*, *vassali* — these words, side by side with "brothers," point out definitely the familistic nature of these relationships, as they were conceived by contemporaries.[90] Second, the ceremony of establishment of the bond, which consisted in the vassal's kneeling and putting his hands into those of the seignior while the latter raised him up and kissed him; the earlier varieties of the ceremony of establishment of companionship and brotherhood, which consisted of mixing the blood, and similar obvious "rites of passage," all indicate the same character of these bonds. Even the earlier ceremony of putting the patron's hand upon the subservient person, the *manus immixtio*, or the Germanic *Munt*, is taken from the family, as a replica of the *manus* of the *pater familias* and of the husband over a member of the family or over the wife.[91]

---

[88] The number and the names of these strata, though not quite crystallized in the first period considered, in the later period, about the twelfth and the thirteenth centuries, fluctuated from five to eight main ranks, according to the country. The *Livre de justice et de plet*, edited at the time of Louis the Pious, gives the following pyramid: "Duke is the first dignity, then marquis, then count, then vice count, then baron, then chatelain, then vavassor, then citadin and then villein." Somewhat similar is the pyramid of feudal Germany, given in *Heerschilder*, and of Italy. See Calmette, *op. cit.*, p. 72; Schröder, *op. cit.*, pp. 431–432.

[89] See the details in A. Luchaire, *Manuel*, pp. 159, 243, and 462; De Ribbe, *op. cit.*, p. 460.

[90] See the details in Schröder, *op. cit.*, pp. 37 ff.; Chénon, *op. cit.*, Vol. I, pp. 351 ff.; *Marculfi formularia*, in *Monumenta*, Vol. I, p. 55; Calmette, *op. cit.*, pp. 16 ff.

[91] See the details in the quoted works of Chénon, Vol. I, p. 481; Waitz, Vol. IV, pp. 245–246; De Ribbe, pp. 460 and 488; Luchaire, *Manuel*, p. 186; Schröder, p. 434.

Here are a few descriptions of the oath of fidelity.

Domino manibus coniunctis suum praebeat hominium et aggrediatur illum tam prope quod dominus manus eius suis manibus comprehendere valeat. Si autem dominus sedeat, homo genus flectat ante illum pro praebendo hominium.[92]

Da osculum mihi in conditione servandae . . . tunc fidei et promissionis. . . .[93] Se in militem dedit fidenque sibi servaturam iuramento affirmavit . . . .[94] Comes inquisivit si integre vellit homo suus fieri; et ille respondit: volo; et junctis manibus amplexatis a manibus comitis osculo confederati sunt. Secondo loco fidem dedit in iis verbis: spondeo in fide mea me fidelem fero comiti W. et sibihominium integritatis contra omnes observaturum fide bono et sine dolo.[95]

These formulas sound far from merely cold and bargaining contracts, in their insistence upon *fidelitas*, integrity, *contra omnes* and so on, the words denoting the union for life and death. Third, the oath of fidelity, or the *sacramentum fidelitatis*, was again familistic in its content. The totality of the rights and duties of both parties was, up to the later period of declining feudalism, all-embracing, universal, unlimited, and as broad as that among the members of the family. The vassal agreed to love and to hate what his seignior loved and hated; the patron's friends and enemies became his friends and enemies.

Si aliquis homo seniori suo vel domino fidelis et amator existat, et quempiam hominum senserit illi inimicum, detractatorem et comminatorem, non vult ei esse amicus nec socius messae nec particeps ciborum.[96]

The same universality of the bond is well stressed in the famous letter of Fulbert of Chartres, A.D. 1020:

Qui domino suo fidelitatem iurat sex in memoria semper habere debet; incolume, tutum, honestum, utile, facile, possibile . . . ut autem fidelis haec nocumenta caveat iustum est; sed non ideo casamentum meretur; non enim sufficit abstinere a malo, nisi fiat quod bonum est. Restat ergo ut in eiusdem sex supradictis consilium et auxilium domino suo fideliter praestat, si beneficii dignus videri velit.[97]

---

[92] "Auctor Vetus," quoted by Waitz, *op. cit.*, Vol. VI, p. 47.

[93] Chronicon St. Huberti, c. 23, in *Monumenta*, in-F. (Hannover, 1848), Vol. VIII, pp. 580–581.

[94] *Monumenta*, in-F. (Hannover, 1839), Vol. III, p. 341.

[95] *Monumenta*, in-F. (Hannover, 1856), Vol. XII, p. 591.

[96] *Agobardi libri duo*, in *Monumenta*, in-F. (1887), Vol. XV, pp. 276–277 (Hannover, 1887). See also Von Amira, *op. cit.*, p. 188; Chénon, *op. cit.*, Vol. I, p. 481; Luchaire, *Manuel*, p. 186. See further the text of the oath given August 4, 1274, in *Monumenta : Constitutiones* (Hannover, 1904), Vol. III, p. 57.   [97] Fulbert, *Epistola*, 38.

On his part the seignior must reciprocate fully : *"Dominus quoque fideli suo in his omnibus vicem reddere debet."* [98]

The descriptions and the formulas of these mutual duties and rights are so all-embracing, universal, unlimited, that even the strictly familistic bonds can hardly be more all-embracing than these bonds of fidelity.

This mutual bond of fidelity was, as mentioned, unlimited in the first period of feudalism. Only in its later part, beginning with the eleventh century, arose the distinction between *hominium ligium* or simply *hominium* and *hominium planum*. The first was unlimited and unrestricted ; the second was limited and restricted in its character, in the sense that the duties and the rights of both parties were now specified and limited.

Up to the eleventh century the expression is almost always *hominium* and almost never *hominium planum*. When there appeared the expression *hominium ligium* [German : *ledig*, unreserved], it was opposed either by *hominium* or *hominium planum*. Finally in the twelfth century every hommage which was not *ligium* was *planum*. This history of the terminology is extremely suggestive. . . . The letter of Fulbert confirms this . . . and shows that the military duty was unlimited, just as that which followed from the *obsequium* of the time of Charlemagne. . . . Etymologically then the hommage "lige" is that which was made without reservation of any other engagement." [99]

The very nature of a real contractualism, with its "measured and limited and bargained" mutual services, excludes such an unlimited unity for death and life, as close and intimate as that between the members of the family. Shall we wonder that a multitude of other traits of this feudal relationship show the same familistic traits : the elder children of the vassals went to and were brought up and educated at the court, or in the castle of the lord, being treated as *"pueri"* of the lord himself ; the suzerain took part, like a parent, in the approval or disapproval of the marriage of his vassals, in the choice of his heirs. The vassal received *beneficium* and arms and other means for the fulfillment of his duties from the seignior, as a member of the family receives them from the father. On the other hand, like that member, who is equipped by his family and returns to it the money and wealth earned, the vassal returned them to his lord.[100]

[98] See the details in Calmette, *op. cit.*, pp. 40 ff.

[99] Calmette, *op. cit.*, pp. 33–34.

[100] See the quoted works of Von Amira, p. 188 ; Chénon, Vol. I, p. 481 ; Schröder, p. 39 ; also Luchaire, *Manuel*, pp. 186, 295, and 203.

In brief, there can be hardly any doubt that the nature of this feudal tie of fidelity was familistic mainly. Only in part was it contractual in the form of origin and disruption; and in a still lesser part was it compulsory. The appearance of the *hominium planum*, after the eleventh century, with its "measured" service and contract, was a sign of contractualism. Instead of unlimited and "unmeasured" mutual service, the duties of the vassal were limited to only forty days in a year, in military service; by only three *plaids* a year, so far as the duty of giving council is concerned, and so on. Likewise the duties of the seignior or suzerain began to be limited and measured.[101] In brief, *the real contractualism in the content of the bond became definitely noticeable only after the eleventh century.* Before that, it was present mainly in the form of the establishment and disruption of the feudal tie of fidelity, and but little in the content of the fidelity itself. Even the manner and the reasons for the disruption of this tie are like those which sometimes take place in a family, where the relationship of its members is far from being familistic.[102]

The compulsory elements were also present in the feudal bond. One of the reasons of the feudal commendation on the part of the vassal was insecurity and fear of the weaker before the stronger; a direct or indirect use of force to get submission; and also the role of force in maintaining the inviolability of the oath of fidelity of the vassals: it is not rare that as soon as the power of the seignior began to crumble, the vassals exhibit a violation of the fidelity *en masse*.[103] However, this coercion played a secondary role, and the feudal bond, as it was understood by the contemporaries, was thought of as mainly along the familistic pattern.

H. *Bonds of Serfdom.* If the bonds between the free men and the free strata of the feudal society were predominantly familistic, predominantly compulsory seem to have been the links between the free, the semi-free, and the unfree classes. The relationship between the master and his serfs — and especially his slaves — is mainly compulsory. To a smaller degree the same sort of connection exists between the upper strata and

---

[101] See the details in the quoted works of Calmette, *op. cit.*, pp. 34–35 and 40 ff.; Luchaire, *Manuel*, pp. 195 and 202. Therefore the elements of the contract in the establishment of this bond of fidelity in these later centuries are already more stressed than before. See for instance the *Constitutio ducatus Brunswicensis* about the establishment of this feudal State, August 15, 1235. *Monumenta : Constitutiones* (Hannover, 1896), Vol. II, pp. 263–266.

[102] See about the forms and the reasons for annulment of the tie of fidelity in Calmette, *op. cit.*, pp. 46–47; Schröder, *op. cit.*, pp. 452; see the law of Frederic, November of 1158, *Constitutio Frederici*, in *Monumenta : Constitutiones* (Hannover, 1893), Vol. I, p. 248; and a similar law in the *Constitutio Heinrici de causis amittendi feudi*, in *Monumenta, ibid.*, p. 104. See also Luchaire, *Manuel*, p. 216.

[103] See Luchaire, *Manuel*, p. 219; Waitz, *op. cit.*, Vol. VI, p. 73.

the semifree villeins. The serf, and especially the slave, is rather a chattel than a subject of law. He is a mere addition to the land owned. He can be sold, presented as a gift, exchanged. The disciplinary authority of his master is practically unlimited.[104] This is so well known and generally recognized that there is no reason to insist upon it at length.

It is more important, perhaps, to point out that even this relationship was not entirely compulsory and contained, partly *de jure* — and especially *de facto* — some familistic and contractual elements. The contractual streak comes out juridically in that a certain minimum of rights was recognized, even for a serf. He had definite rights of possession to his land; he could acquire property and could even have his own serfs; his marriage and his family rights were recognized by law, and he had some other rights [105] which limited the power of the lord. Still greater were the rights of the free villeins. The familistic relationship shows itself in the paternal attitude of the master toward his serfs, which was not especially rare, and, *de jure*, in the prohibition, under the influence of the Church, to separate the family of the serf by selling any member, and in other "business transactions." [106]

As we pass from the eighth and ninth centuries to the eleventh and succeeding ones, we have the beginning and growth of the movement in regard to the emancipation of the serfs. The process is only in its initial stage,[107] but it led to a reinforcement of the contractual elements in the bonds between the upper and the semiservile and servile classes at the cost of the compulsory ones. The change is hardly radical, but it is tangible. In several respects the compulsory relationships are mitigated; the number of the freed or semifreed men seems to have steadily increased; the rights of the lowest class were also somewhat enlarged, while the unlimited power of the masters began to be curbed.[108]

In the course of the Middle Ages, the servile class decreases in many ways. Emancipations are the one open door to liberty; admission to the citizenship of a chartered town is another; marriage with a free villein is the third. The *taille abonnée* aids much a serf who wants to escape his condition of serfdom. . . . The fixed *taille* is, in fact, the condition of a villein. It is determined

---

[104] See H. Sée, *Les classes rurales et le régime domanial en France au Moyen Âge* (Paris, 1901), pp. 69 ff.; Schröder, *op. cit.*, p. 237; Chénon, *op. cit.*, Vol. I, pp. 364 ff.

[105] H. Sée, *op. cit.*, p. 70; Calmette, *op. cit.*, pp. 108 ff.

[106] Chénon, *op. cit.*, Vol. I, pp. 371 ff.; Glasson, p. 99, also 70.

[107] See Von Below, *op. cit.*, p. 125; Calmette, *op. cit.*, p. 112; H. Sée, *op. cit.*, p. 201.

[108] See the details in the quoted works of H. Sée, pp. 162, 201, and 275; Von Below, p. 125; Schröder, pp. 240 and 493; Von Amira, pp. 127 and 143; also Heussler, *Institutionen des deutschen Privatrechts* (Leipzig, 1885), p. 143.

by custom.   The unfixed *taille* at the mercy of the lord becomes more and more
rare in the thirteenth century. . . .   Economic evolution tends to an ameliora-
tion of the conditions of the rural classes.   The flourishing status of agriculture
on the eve of the Hundred Years' War is a conspicuous sign of that.[109]

Such is the main difference in that field at the end of the period considered in comparison with its first half.

I.   *General Summary*.   We have concisely analyzed the spectrum of
the social relationships and bonds of all the most important groups of the
Middle Ages, from about the seventh and eighth centuries to the thirteenth and fourteenth.   The results can be summed up in the following
propositions.

(1) The predominant type of social relationships and bonds which
shot through all the important groups of medieval society, and out of
which the texture of their social life is woven, is familistic, of various
degrees of intensity and purity.   It is the main thread running through
all the social relationships of the Church, of the family, of the guilds,
the corporations, the fraternal associations.   It is also the main fiber in
the texture of the system of state relationships — of the king and the
fideles (subjects); of the king and his officials; and, to a smaller degree, of
the military forces of the State.   Likewise, the familistic is the predominant pattern among the members of the village community and the city
communes.   Finally, the feudal *fidelitas*, as the most general bond which
binds together the free men and the free classes or strata of medieval
society, is also predominantly familistic in its inner nature, in spite of the
semicontractual form of the establishment of this bond in certain given
cases.   When properly analyzed, the *fidelitas* can be taken as the most
common and universal form of social relationship in the Middle Ages.
All this means that the "style" of the society considered is conspicuously
familistic, or, as it sometimes used to be called, patriarchal.   The last
term is quite accurate, though many of those who used it were not aware
of its deep meaning.

(2) Side by side with this predominant type, the other main forms
are also present.   The contractual type of bond is evident in almost all
the groups.   It plays a particularly important part in the initiation and
establishment of relationships between the members of each of these
groups, as well as between the groups themselves.   The *fidelitas* almost
always originated in the contractual solemn form.   If one pays attention
not to the inner nature of the bonds established but to the *mode* of their

[109] Calmette, *op. cit.*, p. 112.

establishment, then the medieval society is to be regarded as predominantly contractual. But for reasons given above, we must clearly distinguish between two things: the manner in which this or that bond is established and the nature of the relationship itself. When this latter aspect is considered, there can hardly be a doubt that the main fiber of the texture of medieval society was familistic.

Likewise, the compulsory relations had their share in the structure of the social life of the period. They seem to have formed the main "rope" with which the upper, free strata of society were bound to the semifree and unfree classes. The "junction" where these two great sections of medieval society touch each other consists mainly of this kind of bond. The familistic and contractual "ropes" are also noticeable, binding together the foundation and the upper stories of the medieval building, but their role at this specific junction is quite secondary. On the other hand, it is to be emphasized that in cementing together the sections, either of the "foundation" or the "upper floors," the familistic rope plays a more important part than the compulsory one; as we have seen, the relationships of the members of the semifree and unfree classes toward one another were built mainly on the familistic pattern.

Besides the specific "junction" mentioned, the compulsory relationship played an important part in the binding together of various groups and persons around the *military* activity. It was also present — but in a secondary role — in the texture of all the medieval organizations. Such is the brief characterization of the "social texture" of medieval society.

(3) Passing from the earliest period of the Middle Ages to the twelfth and thirteenth centuries, we notice changes in this social texture. The main one seems to be that the threads of the contractual type become more and more frequent, more and more used in making the texture of this social fabric. Roughly, beginning with the end of the eleventh and with the twelfth century, the contractual character enters more and more the feudal relationships of *fidelitas*, the state system, the family system, the guilds and corporations and brotherhood systems, the urban communes, the military groups, even the bonds between the free and unfree classes. The familistic relationship begins to weaken slightly — quantitatively and qualitatively. The same is perhaps true also of the compulsory relationship. In other words, the *medieval society begins to move toward the contractual type of society.* The move is only in its initial stages, but it is tangible and fairly certain.

Such is the net result of the preceding analysis. Its meaning for our main topic, its relationship to the Ideational and Sensate cultures, will be discussed later.   Here it is only to be noted that the period of the domination of the Ideational culture coincides with that of the familistic type of social texture.   The period of the domination of the Idealistic culture (twelfth and thirteenth centuries) is marked by some weakening of the familistic and, partly, of the compulsory, and by reinforcement of the contractual relationships.   This is shown here by a sort of synthesis and a more even distribution of all the main forms of social bonds, under the domination of the familistic type.   It represents an interesting replica of the very essence of the Idealistic culture as an "organic culture" uniting the purely Ideational and Sensate elements under the domination of the Ideational form.

We shall now continue our analysis of the social texture of European society during the subsequent centuries.

Chapter Three

FLUCTUATION OF THE FAMILISTIC, CONTRACTUAL, AND COM-
PULSORY RELATIONSHIPS IN THE LIFE PROCESS OF THE MAIN
EUROPEAN SOCIAL GROUPS: II. FROM THE FOURTEENTH
TO THE TWENTIETH CENTURY [1]

I. Main Changes

If we omit many secondary fluctuations of the total network of social
groups in the French and German areas of Europe; if we disregard
intentionally the enormous number of local deviations and differences;
if we grant in advance that the results given can be but a rough approximation to the reality — with these reservations the main transformations
in the field studied during the centuries from the fourteenth to the twentieth can be summed up in the following propositions.

A. The thirteenth, fourteenth, fifteenth, and partly sixteenth
centuries give an exceedingly complex, somewhat contradictory picture
of a transitional period, differing in important details in France and
Germany. Of the changes, the most important seems to have been a
continuation of the growth of the contractual relationships started at
the end of the preceding period and especially of the growth of the
compulsory relationships. Both grew at the cost of the familistic
relationships.

B. The period beginning with the end of the sixteenth century
and continuing up to the last quarter of the eighteenth century is marked
— in addition to many other changes — mainly by an increase of the
compulsory relationships at the cost of the familistic and, partly, contractual, and by a compensatory growth of some of the contractual
relationships at the cost of the familistic. The main loser here was
again the familistic category.

C. The nineteenth century and the prewar period of the twentieth
century show a great and notable triumph of the contractual relationships at the cost of the compulsory and, in a smaller degree, of the
familistic relationships.

[1] In co-operation with N. S. Timasheff.

D. The present period of the twentieth century reveals a convulsive weakening of the contractual relationships in favor mainly of the compulsory and partly of the pseudo-familistic and familistic relationship.

Such are the main changes when numerous important fluctuations and changes are intentionally omitted; when the complex and often self-contradictory social reality is divested of an enormous number of important — but not the most important — details and variations; and when it is schematized and typologically simplified.

Let us now briefly enumerate at least some of the many evidences upon which these propositions are based.

II. The Spectrum of the Systems of Social Relationships in the Centuries from the End of the Thirteenth to the End of the Sixteenth

A. *The State.* So far as the State is concerned, the period is marked by a decay of feudal relationships and the reinforcement of the state system of relationships: many social relationships, which in the period of feudalism dropped out of the state system, now were reintroduced into it. As a result, quantitatively the network of the State became closer, which means that the interference and control of the State and its government expanded. This process is opposite to what occurred after the decay of the Carolingian State and growth of feudalism. (See the footnote on page 57.) However, this is, so to speak, a quantitative change which does not directly concern us. What does concern us are the following new symptoms.

(1) The beginning of the growth in strength and absolute power of the position of the king in France; especially after Philip the Fair; though in formulas and statements the relationship between the king and the people sounds still somewhat familistic. Nevertheless, the vastness of the empire prohibited these relationships factually. The very reality of the growth of the power of the king tended to render the relationship more and more autocratic, a paternalism with ever-increasing compulsory powers and demands. Neither oath of fidelity nor the direct personal pledge of every subject was required. They became unnecessary and even meaningless under the new government.

Perhaps more than ever before the king's authority was now regarded as based upon the will of God. Here is a typical formula given in a petition of the people to Philip the Fair, in 1302.

A vous très noble prince par la grâce de Dieu roi de France supplie et requiert le peuple de votre royaume . . . que vous ne reconnaissiez de votre temporel souverain en terre fors que Dieu.[2]

Similar was the claim of Philip the Fair in his address to the General States of 1302.[3]   It is true that the king is expected to use this authority, as the famous Beaumanoir puts it, "*por le commun profit et par grand conseil.*" [4]   This shows the remnants of the familism and, as we shall see, the elements of contractualism; but it does not contradict the ever-increasing compulsory paternalism in which, in the seventeenth and the eighteenth centuries, real paternalism almost evaporated, leaving but the compulsory character of the relationship.   Here we have at least a slight encroachment of the compulsory elements at the cost of the familistic. The growth of contractualism shows itself, aside from several other symptoms, in the organization of the summons to the General States, as well as the provincial States.   The latter began to be summoned by Louis IX, while the General States were summoned for the first time in 1302 and functioned up to 1614.[5]

This fact is one of the evidences of an infiltration of the contractual relationship into the central kernel of the state system of relationships. The rights of the General and the provincial States, composed of the representatives of the main estates and of communes, seem to have been modest *de jure*.   But still, without their approval, no extraordinary subsidies and levies could be ordered by the king.   *De facto* at some periods their functions were important.[6]   At others, as in 1356, they even for-

---

[2] See E. Boutaric, *La France sous Philippe le Bel* (Paris, 1861), pp. 24 and 2–23.   The legists and the theorizers of the time stressed, especially in connection with the sharpness of the struggle between the spiritual and temporal powers, more and more this aspect of the king's power and contributed greatly to the molding of this mentality.   On the other hand, these theories themselves were but a reflection of the objective social process of the decline of the papacy, and of the growth of the national State and the power of the king.   See for the theories, C. H. McIlwain, *The Growth of Political Thought in the West* (New York, 1932), chap. vi; see here the main literature and sources; also English translation of O. von Gierke's *Genossenschaftsrecht, Political Theories of the Middle Age* (Cambridge, 1900); A. C. Flick, *The Decline of the Medieval Church* (London, 1930), especially about the theories of John of Paris, Peter Flotte, William Nogaret, Dante, Peter du Bois, pp. 13 ff., 31 ff., 54–56, and 170–171; B. Jarrett, *Social Theories of the Middle Ages* (London, 1926); R. W. and A. J. Carlyle, *A History of Medieval Political Theory in the West* (New York, 1916–1922), Vols. III and IV.

[3] See Boutaric, *op. cit.*, p. 24.

[4] P. de Beaumanoir, *Coutûme de Beauvoisis*, ed. by Beugnot (Paris, 1842), chap. 49, § 6.

[5] See Boutaric, *op. cit.*, pp. 19–21; E. D. Glasson, *Histoire du droit et des institutions de France* (Paris, 1893), Vol. V, p. 485.

[6] See the details in the quoted works of Beaumanoir; Glasson, Vol. V, pp. 340–380, 427, 437, *et passim;* Boutaric, pp. 31 ff. *et passim.*

mally tried to limit the power of the king.   The establishment of this institution is a manifestation of a modest but an evident growth of the contractual elements in the state system.[7]

In Germany, the change assumed somewhat different forms, but resulted in an even greater growth of the contractual elements in the state system.   So far as the Holy Roman Empire is concerned, the power of the emperor at this time is limited by the Reichstag even more than before.   Without the approval of the Reichstag, he cannot decide any important issue.   If he does, he is liable to be dethroned.   The resolution of the Reichstag, August 20, 1440, about the dethronement of Wenceslaus opens with a statement that he did not fulfill his promises and duties : in spite of his promises, he did not maintain peace ; he permitted a part of its territory to be cut from the empire ; and so on — explicitly contractual motivation.   And further, the text of the resolution stresses this contractualism still more.[8]   The same is to be said of the relationship of the local states newly emerging from the highest seignorial dominion : their kings are also limited contractually in their power by the *landtags* of these kingdoms.   The approval of the *landtag* is necessary for the issuance of any important ordinance or measure, be it the establishment of new taxes, a declaration of war, the enactment of laws of the type of the *Landfrieden*, when a question of an heir to the throne is involved, and so on.[9]

(2) A growth of contractual relationships in the French and German state systems is manifest also in the trend of the replacement of the previous feudal relationships by the "bureaucracy" of the king, by his officials (*bailli et prévôt* in France and *Fögte* in Germany), who are appointed and discharged by the king, paid by him, responsible only to him, and who, especially in France, systematically are shifted from one place to another in order to prevent their intimate closeness with the population.   Though the elements of the familistic relationship remain between the king and his officials — they have to take the oath of fidelity, etc. — nevertheless, it has now a much more conspicuous quality of contractualism, so far as the king-official relationship is concerned, and becomes

[7] This process began also to be reflected in the social thought in the form of the first appearance of the germs of the later contractual theories.   Manegold of Lautenbach and a few others set forth the essentials of the social compact theory in regard to the origin of the State as well as the source of the ruler's power.

[8] *Deutsche Reichstagsakte* (Berlin, 1877), Vol. III, pp. 254 ff.   About the whole character of the rights of the emperor and the Reichstag see R. Schröder, *Lehrbuch der deutschen Rechtsgeschichte* (Berlin, 1922), pp. 511 ff.

[9] See about these points in Schröder, *op. cit.*, pp. 642–670.

compulsory in a considerable degree, so far as the relationship between the official and the administered population is concerned.[10]

(3) When we consider the military service in the state system — and now the State is the main system which discharges these functions, compared with the previous period — we find again an increase of the compulsory and contractual relationships at the cost of the familistic. An increase of compulsory relationship is witnessed by the attempt of Philip the Fair and later kings to reintroduce universal military duty as obligatory — the institution which did not exist for a long time after the Carolingian monarchy. Similar attempts were started in Germany. The *ordonnance* of 1315 by Louis X reads:

Nisi in casu retrobanni; in quo casu quilibet de regno nostro tenetur, tunc tamen de mandato nostro per totum regnum . . . fiat.[11]

Though the possibility of replacing the personal discharge of this duty by payment of a certain amount of money was allowed, this substitute was also compulsory.

On the other hand, with this money and funds from other sources, the kings began to hire military forces — from knights to ordinary soldiers. The relationship between the king and many of these hired military men assumed thus the character of a contractual relationship, instead of the previous relationship of *fidelitas* as between the seignior and his vassal.

These and many other "novelties" seem to indicate definitely that the main change which took place in the *state system* of the period considered, in comparison with the previous period, consisted mainly in the *increase of the contractual, and partly compulsory, at the cost of the familistic relationships.*

B. *The Church.* Up to the moment of the Reformation and the great split of the Church, its system of social relationship experienced little change from the standpoint studied. The main form still is the familistic, though more and more diluted and more and more waning.[12] However, due to the appearance of various sects and schisms, the element of compulsion, which had begun to grow at the end of the previous period and

---

[10] See the details in A. Luchaire, *Manuel des institutions françaises* (Paris, 1892), pp. 544 ff.; Glasson, *op. cit.*, Vol. V, pp. 475 ff.; Boutaric, *op. cit.*, pp. 173 ff.; Schröder, *op. cit.*, p. 662; G.,Waitz, *Deutsche Verfassungsgeschichte* (Berlin, 1882), Vol. VI, pp. 325 ff.

[11] *Ordonnances des rois de France de la 3-me race* (Paris, 1723), Vol. I, no. 569. See the details in Luchaire, *Histoire des institutions monarchiques en France sous les premiers Capétiens* (Paris, 1896), Vol. II, p. 82; Boutaric, *op. cit.*, pp. 367 ff.; Schröder, *op. cit.*, pp. 565 ff.

[12] See Glasson, *op. cit.*, Vol. V, pp. 208 ff.

had resulted in the establishment and growth of the Inquisition in the thirteenth century and in increasing persecution of the heretics, was greatly reinforced by the grave split of the Church introduced by the Reformation. Persecution of the "dissidents," whether in the Catholic or the Protestant countries, assumed an extraordinarily large scope and resulted in the religious wars of the sixteenth and seventeenth centuries. All this means a compulsory imposition of the dominant creed, whether in Protestant or Catholic countries. The same is the meaning of the famous *Cujus regio ejus religio* of the Augsburg Peace, 1555. In other words the period marks a growth of the compulsory elements within the Christian Church.[13] This growth took place mainly at the cost of the familistic relationship, because the same period gave, at least in theory, a growth of the contractual elements through the proclamation of the principle of religious liberty already proclaimed by Luther. If given little choice in practice, in theory the individual was granted the right to choose his religion, especially in the Protestant doctrine, and in this way was placed theoretically in a contractual relationship with his church and religious association. The period saw little of that in realization, but its mentality introduced and stressed this contractualism of man in regard to his God as well as to his congregation. Therefore the net result of the change in the system of the Christian Church was a weakening of the familistic relationship, a notable reinforcement of the compulsory relationship (which progressed still more in the subsequent period), and a slight trend toward contractualism in theory but not in the social reality.

C. *The Family.* Up to the sixteenth century and the Reformation, the family system did not experience any radical change in the field studied. Perhaps the amplitude of the compulsion on the part of the head of the family was limited *de jure;* but *de facto,* even in the previous period, the right of life and death was rarely exercised. Now, especially in Germany, definite limits were put to the power of the parents over the

---

[13] "It is mockery to describe the principle which underlay the Peace of Augsburg as one of toleration. *Cujus regio ejus religio* is a maxim fatal . . . to freedom of conscience; it is the creed of Erastian despotism. . . . Even for Princes, religious liberty was limited to the choice of one out of two alternatives, the dogmas of Rome or those of Wittenberg. . . . But even this meagre liberty of choice between two exclusive communions was denied to the mass of the German people. For them the change consisted in this, that instead of having their faith determined for them by the Church, it was settled by their territorial Princes; instead of a clerical, there was a lay persecution; for the tyranny of Wittenberg, if it was less than that of Rome after the Council of Trent, was certainly greater than that of the Catholic Church before the appearance of Luther." *The Cambridge Modern History* (New York, 1934), Vol. II, p. 278.

children.[14] The main change seems to have consisted in a development of the contractual "fibers" in the texture of the family system. This is true especially of the Protestant countries after the Reformation. But the trend is found also in France. It manifested itself by several facts.

(1) After the death of the parents, the children remained together, either by tradition or by a special contract, sometimes even for a definite period of twenty years. This gave to the family bond a definite contractual nature ("contractual family").[15]

(2) By a contract, the grown-up children could emancipate themselves from the family and sever their connection with it, with certain and defined consequences of such a contractual emancipation.[16]

(3) The divorce, which before the Reformation was impossible (only a separation from board and bed was recognized by the Church), now was admitted on the basis of the cases enumerated by law. And the very fact of proclamation of marriage as a private or civil affair by Luther is a symptom of the same nature. This change means again an introduction of the contractual element in marriage and the family system. The continuation of the bond, whose severance had previously depended little upon the will and contract of the parties, can now be broken at their will.[17]

(4) The consent of the parents likewise becomes less and less necessary to the legality of a marriage. At the best, it is required up to the age of twenty-five for women and thirty for men, after which age it is unnecessary (the *sommation respectueuse*).[18] This again means an increase of the contractual element in it.

(5) The same is shown by the tendency to give more and more right to the will of the testator, to dispose of the property of his family. After the reception of the Roman law — that is, about the fourteenth and the fifteenth centuries — the testament acquires the character of a civil act, instead of the previous *Deus non homo facit heredes*. In this way the element of contract is reinforced in the family system.[19]

---

[14] See the details in the quoted works of C. de Ribbe, *La société provençale à la fin du Moyen Âge* (Paris, 1898), pp. 138 ff.; H. Fehr, *Die Rechtstellung der Frau und Kinder in der Weistümern* (Jena, 1912).

[15] See De Ribbe, *op. cit.*, pp. 386–389.

[16] See Fehr, *op. cit.*, pp. 99–112.

[17] See Glasson, *op. cit.*, Vol. V, pp. 425 ff.

[18] Édit February 15, 1556; *Ordonnance de Blois*, 1579. See E. Roguin, *Traité de droit civil comparé. Le mariage* (Paris, 1904).

[19] See the details in E. Roguin, *op. cit.* (Paris, 1912), Vols. III and IV.

Without an enumeration of other similar symptoms these seem to warrant the conclusion that the main change of the period consisted in the reinforcement — however slight it appears — of the contractual relationship in the whole texture of the relationship of the family.

D. *Village and Urban Communities.* (1) So far as the village territorial communities are concerned, the changes in the period considered are somewhat different in France and Germany. As it will be noted later, in France the emancipation of the peasants from serfdom made great progress in the period considered, while in Germany, in the fifteenth century, the proportion of the unfree rural population was rather larger than in the thirteenth century. For this reason, it is probable that the contractual relationships made somewhat greater progress in the mutual relations of the members of the village community in France than in Germany, because the relationships of free men are likely to be more contractual than those of the unfree ones. At least, we see it in the beginnings of the rural self-government in France, in the emergence of a kind of "rural patriciate" there, a fact which results in the establishment of certain contractual relationships between the members of the rural population itself.[20]

All in all, however, so far as the mutual relationships of the rural population are concerned, they seem to have remained a mixture of the mainly familistic and compulsory types, without any radical change. If such a change occurred, it consisted mainly in some increase of the contractual elements in France and of the compulsory ones in Germany.

(2) So far as the city communes are concerned, the situation is different in France and Germany. In France, we are at the period of decline of the free city communes and their subjugation to the power of the king. This means an extension of the compulsory relationships in the system of these organized groups. On the other hand, as a result of many convulsions and revolutions, and the civil struggle between the rich and the poor, the upper and the lower classes, within the commune itself, the contractual relationships and agreements between various members of the commune seem also to have progressed. In addition, the compulsory relationships expanded also, as a result of the expansion of the regulation by the city authorities of many aspects of the life and work of the city population: the prices, the work of the guilds, crafts, corporations,

[20] See Glasson, Vol. V, pp. 163 and 440; A. Heussler, *Institutionen des deutschen Privatrechts* (Leipzig, 1885), p. 300; also P. Boissonade, *Life and Work in Medieval Europe* (New York, 1927), *passim;* J. L. Loutchisky, *L'état des classes agricoles en France à la veille de la Révolution,* (Paris, 1911), chaps. i and ii; H. Sée, *Esquisse d'une histoire de régime agraire en Europe* (Paris, 1921).

and so on. All this means the decay of a portion of the familistic relationship in favor of the compulsory and, partly, of the contractual elements.[21]

Somewhat similar is the situation in Germany, with the difference that during this period their city communes continue to develop, instead of declining, as in France.[22] Many of them, like Isny, now buy their freedom from the seignior and become independent. Such a development was likely to increase the proportion of contractual relationships among the members and groups of the communes, partly at the cost of the compulsory and partly at the cost of the familistic. This is evidenced by the decline of the monopoly of the previous city aristocracy, by the beginning of the participation in city management by the representatives of various guilds and crafts; by many mutual "bargainings" between various classes of the communes and the like.[23] On the other hand, here also the city government begins to interfere in and to regulate many aspects of the city life which were unregulated before by the city authorities.[24] To sum up, here the main change seems also to have consisted in a growth of the contractual relationships at the cost of the familistic.

E. *Corporations, Guilds, Crafts, Confraternities.* If up to the second part of the fifteenth century the "spectrum" of the social system of the corporations, crafts, guilds, and free occupational associations did not undergo any notable changes in comparison with the previous period,[25] from the standpoint studied, beginning with the second part of the fifteenth century, some change is noticeable. It manifested itself in two main tendencies.

(1) In France, due to the greater and greater interference of the king in the control and regulation of the corporations, many compulsory rules were imposed upon them which led to a weakening and degeneration of the familistic relationships among their members (substitution of money for the *chef d'œuvre* in 1461 to increase the revenue of the *fisc;* increasing number of *les lettres de maîtrise*, and grants of privileges *par l'octroi*, etc.).

[21] See the quoted works of Boutaric, pp. 147–153; E. Hegel, *Städte und Gilden der germanischen Völker* (Leipzig, 1891), p. 112; Beaumanoir, chap. 50; Schröder, p. 696; G. von Below, *Der deutsche Staat des Mittelalters* (Leipzig, 1925), pp. 270 ff.

[22] See Von Below, *op. cit.*, pp. 264 ff.; Hegel, *op. cit.*, pp. 385 ff.; E. M. Saint-Léon, *Histoire de corporations de métiers* (Paris, 1922), pp. 148 ff., 178–179, and 250 ff.

[23] See the quoted works of Von Below, pp. 264 ff.; Hegel, pp. 385 ff.; Schröder, pp. 690 ff.

[24] Schröder, *op. cit.*, p. 696.

[25] "The period (1328 to 1461) does not differ much from the preceding one. The corporations did not have any fundamental changes." The structure remains as before. Saint-Léon, *op. cit.*, p. 260.

All this weakened the familistic morale of the corporations and crafts, and led to its replacement by the compulsory and contractual rules and agreements.[26]

(2) The internal relationship of the strata of the guilds — master, valet, apprentice — as well as of various guilds to one another, lost a great deal of the previous familistic relationship and was replaced partly by "bargaining" of contractual nature, partly by compulsory bonds imposed by the stronger, privileged corporations (which now emerged) upon the weaker ones, and by the stronger stratum within the corporation upon the subordinated. Around the middle of the fifteenth century, "artisans continue to obey their masters, but the previous trust and devotion to them are already lacking; likewise the masters do not have any more their good will and protection towards the artisans as before." [27]

At the beginning of the sixteenth century, the corporations and crafts and guilds continue to degenerate. Now we see "a decline of benevolence and justice on the part of the masters and of respect and obedience on the part of the artisans." [28]

In brief, in many ways the previous familistic relationship declined and was replaced, partly by compulsory, partly by egotistically contractual forms.[29]

F. *Hierarchical Bonds between the Free Strata of the Society.* So far as the free classes are concerned, the main change in the tying together of their hierarchical strata consisted in the weakening of the familistic bond in favor mainly of the contractual bond. The decline of feudalism meant a decline of the bond of the all-embracing and unlimited *fidelitas* in favor of the limited and restricted *fidelitas*, around the twelfth and the thirteenth centuries; and then a progressive replacement of this limited *fidelitas* in favor of the contractual and commercial bond of the employed chivalry and knights to their employer — their contractual "boss" and seignior. A knight became a vassal in so far that he was granted a "feud" or salary, contractually agreed upon and accepted by both parties. In this way, already in the thirteenth century in France and somewhat later in Germany, there had appeared the class of hired and paid vassal knights. The very nature of such a relationship has little in common with the old-time *fidelitas* and is contractual in its greater part.[30] In Germany, likewise, the pyramid of the *Heerschilder* disintegrates and is replaced by a simplified, three-story structure of the strata — king, great princes, and

---

[26] *Ibid.*, pp. 265–266, 289, and 376.   [27] *Ibid.*, pp. 260–261.
[28] *Ibid.*, p. 280.   [29] See the details in *ibid.*, Bks. III, IV, and V.
[30] See the details in Luchaire, *Manuel*, pp. 198 ff.

knights.[31] In brief, *fidelitas* tends to be replaced more and more by contractual relationships between these strata.

The stratum of the knights becomes more and more consolidated as a separate estate with its own *esprit de corps*. So far, within this stratum there appears some similitude of the familistic bond and spirit. This is manifest in the ceremony of the initiation into knighthood, which somewhat resembles the *sacramentum fidelitatis*.[32]

To sum up, this bond, through which different strata are tied to one another, shows also a weakening of the familistic threads and their replacement by the contractual fiber.

G. *Bonds between the Free and Unfree Strata*. We have seen that even in the preceding period this bond was woven mainly out of the compulsory fiber. A considerable part of the unfree class was chained to the upper and middle classes, either directly, or through the land, *ad glebae adscripti sunt*, like the late Roman *colons*. During the period considered, in France the process of emancipation of the serfs progressed a great deal, especially through the institution of the *désaveu:* by giving up the land a serf could obtain his personal liberty. But the main way consisted in the liberation of the serfs from above. Following the kings who, like Philip the Fair and Louis X, began to emancipate the serfs on a large scale in their royal domains, the great feudal lords did the same.[33] Serfdom begins to be thought of as something incompatible with the spirit of the time.[34] This process meant a weakening of the compulsory bond and its replacement more and more by the half or contractual relationship.

In Germany, the situation was different. If anything, up to the sixteenth century, there was no decrease of serfdom. In the fifteenth century the proportion of the unfree among the rural classes was hardly less than in the thirteenth.[35] Therefore, the increase of the contractual

---

[31] Schröder, *op. cit.*, pp. 433 ff.   [32] *Ibid.*, pp. 481 ff. and 502 ff.

[33] See the details in H. Sée, *Les classes rurales et le régime domenial en France au Moyen Age* (Paris, 1901), pp. 171 ff.; also his *Esquisse d'une histoire*, quoted; P. Boissonade's and J. Loutchisky's quoted works; Boutaric, *op. cit.*, pp. 153 ff.

[34] Here is an example of this mentality as it is given in the *ordonnance* of the Count of Valois, April 19, 1311:

"Comme créature humaine qui est formée à l'image nostre Seigneur, doit généralement estre franche par droit naturel et . . . ceste liberté ou franchise par le jou de servitude soit si effacée et occurcie que les homes et fames en leur vivant sont réputés ains comme morts. . . . Nous muez de pitié pour le remède et salut de nostre âme et pour consideration de humanité et commun profit dounons et octroions très plénière franchise et liberté perpétuel à toutes personnes . . . de nostre conté de Valois." Likewise in the *ordonnance* of 1315 it is said: "Chacun par droit de nature doit être franc." *Ordonnances*, quoted, Vol. I, p. 583; Boutaric, *op. cit.*, p. 161.

[35] Schröder, *op. cit.*, p. 499.

relationships, similar to that in France, at the cost of the compulsory ones hardly took place to any tangible amount and degree.

Summing up the totality of the changes in the main organized social groups of the French and German populations of the centuries considered, we have to conclude that the main change consisted in *a weakening of the familistic bond in favor of partly the compulsory and partly contractual relationships*. Both of these seem to have grown in practically all the important horizontal and vertical intragroup and intergroup bonds except only (in France) the bond which roped together the free and unfree classes : here in France the compulsory threads were replaced in a notable degree by the contractual ones.

In passing, it is interesting to note that the centuries from the twelfth to the sixteenth inclusive appear in many other respects as the centuries of transition from the Ideational to the Sensate culture. In a very erratic way, the elements of the Ideational culture tended, with most irregular fluctuations, to decrease ; those of the Sensate, to increase. The former were not erased as yet, neither were they reduced to an insignificant proportion ; likewise, the Sensate culture did not become overwhelmingly dominant. Both fluctuated, as though measuring their strength, not being sure of their power.

We see that such a transition in the culture is followed by a decrease of the familistic relationships and by an increase, also erratic, of the compulsory and contractual relationships. Such a "correlation" may be incidental ; it may also be, as we shall show later, not incidental, but organically connected with these types of culture.

Another thing to be noted is this. A study of the movement of the internal disturbances given in Part Three of this volume shows that the twelfth, thirteenth, fourteenth, and fifteenth centuries give the peak of the disturbances. So far as they are conditioned greatly by the strong or disorganized system of the social relationships, the above suggests that these centuries were indeed the period of a deep transformation with an unsettled condition in the social relationships which existed before : the waning and weakening of the familistic relationships of the previous period resulted in the disintegration, unsettling, and shattering of the whole system of social relationships. Hence, the amorphic status of the network and hence the growth of the disturbances of the period. Thus one part supports the other. One induction corroborates the others. Such a corroboration is a sign of some validity of each and of all the conclusions reached.

III. The Centuries from the Sixteenth to the Second Part of the Eighteenth

This period is especially complex, contradictory, and full of the most whimsical short-time turns of the most contrasting nature.[36] When, however, all the secondary short-time turns and swings are disregarded, its main feature, from the standpoint of this inquiry, stands out as a *notable increase of the compulsory relationships at the cost of the familistic and partly even contractual forms of the previous period; a secondary feature is the maintenance of their position by the contractual relationships; if they were driven by the compulsory from many places, they obtained new ones, snatched from the familistic bonds. The net loser here, as in the previous period, happened to be again the familistic bond of social relationship.* Here are the summarized and greatly schematized reasons for such a conclusion.

A. *The State.* So far as the number of the relationships included in the state system is concerned, the period continues the trend of the preceding one; an enormous number of relationships which hitherto were not included in the state system, and were not controlled or regulated by the State, now are included and have become a part of it. In France, as well as in Germany (so far as the local kingdoms are concerned), the network of the state system becomes ever wider and "thicker"; more and more relationships are included in it. Control and regulation by the state government both expand enormously. The State begins to regulate most of the relationships of the population within its territory. We are in an age of "enlightened absolutism"; "police state," or the "totalitarian" age. The reverse side of the situation is that the network of social relationships of other, nonstate social groups — be they Church, the corporation, the municipality, the feudal class, or what not — becomes thinner and thinner; the relationships which before were a part of these systems and were regulated by the nonstate organizations now drop out of the systems of these groups and pass into the state system. What the State gains, the other groups lose. In other words, the State swells, while the other groups shrink and decline in their power and vigor. The State in France swallows the Church, crushes and disintegrates

---

[36] "He who would decide to study the structure of the period on the basis of the law codes only would have fallen into many ridiculous errors," says Tocqueville. A. de Tocqueville, *L'ancien régime et la révolution* (Paris, 1860), p. 121. Glasson adds: "Monarchy, which so jealously guarded its legislative monopoly, failed to make us respect its laws. They are little enforced and even are not applied at all." Glasson, *op. cit.* (Paris, 1903), Vol. VIII, p. 319. See also M. Marion, *Dictionnaire des institutions de la France au 17 et 18 siècles* (Paris, 1923), p. 123. In Germany the discrepancy between the law and the reality was much less than in France.

corporations, communes, feudal hierarchies, and orders.[37] A similar picture is presented in Germany, with the exception of the religious associations, which in a subordinated form exist without a formal affiliation with the State. This describes the purely quantitative aspect of the state system of relationships in this period. One who lives in the postwar period of the twentieth century can witness in a somewhat different form a similar "swelling" of the state system and a similar expansion of state control and interference, as exemplified by Communist Russia, Hitlerite Germany, Fascist Italy, and other "totalitarian" dictatorships. However unlike are the concrete "trappings" of the monarchy of Frederic the Great, or of Louis XIV or Louis XV, the totalitarian nature of the State of their times and of our own is about the same.

Turning now to the direct object of our study, we find that *the main change in the state system of relationships studied consisted in a further development of the compulsory relationships at the cost of the familistic and partly contractual.*

In France, the monarchy becomes absolute, unlimited, and, as some legists claimed, *legibus solutus est*, not bound even by its own laws. The traces of patriarchalism and familism greatly decline. Likewise, almost all the contractual limitations evaporate.[38] The situation is well summed up in the famous answer of Louis XV to the Parliament, May 3, 1766:

C'est en ma personne que réside l'autorité souveraine. Mon peuple n'est qu'un avec moi; les droits et les intérêts de la nation sont nécessairement unis avec les miens et ne reposent qu'entre mes mains.[39]

L'état c'est moi is only an abbreviation of this statement.

It is true that even in this formulation some familistic notes can be heard. We know also that up to the moment of the Revolution the people regarded the king as their protector against injustice, as guardian of the law, and defender of the weaker against the stronger.[40] However, all this was more a façade than a reality. Elevated to an extraordinary position, separated from the people by a huge and stratified body of nobility and officials, the monarchy could not factually maintain the ancient patriarchalism and familism. Instead, only in so far as the people sponsored every whim and measure of the king were they considered. Otherwise, their will and wishes were given little, if any, attention.

[37] See Glasson, *op. cit.*, Vol. VIII, p. 218.
[38] Chénon, *Histoire générale du droit français public et privé* (Paris, 1927), Vol. II, pp. 385 ff.; Glasson, *op. cit.*, Vol. VIII, pp. 317 ff.
[39] H. Taine, *L'ancien régime* (Paris, 1909), Vol. I, pp. 134 ff.
[40] *Ibid.*, Vol. I, pp. 18–19.

Whether they approved or not, the rules imposed by the State had to be obeyed. This means that the compulsory relationships replaced more and more the familistic ones which were left from the previous period.

Similar is the relationship of the aristocracy, the officials, and the army to the king. Notwithstanding some elements of familism and contractualism present in these relationships, they play quite a small role in comparison with the compulsory ones. The nobility is turned into mere courtiers and officials. As courtiers they just "represent," as Taine says, or as La Bruyère puts it: *Qui considère que le visage du prince fait toute la felicité du courtisan qu'il s'occupe et se remplit toute sa vie de le voir et d'en être vu."* [41]

As officials they are entirely dependent upon the king. The local seigniors were removed from administration after the time of Richelieu. Now administrators are appointed, discharged, promoted, demoted, increased, decreased, entirely by the king's power. Such are the *intendants* and the *subdélégués* who control the police, trade and commerce, public works, justice, finances; watch and ward all the classes, the religious life, the city communes. Their competence is unlimited, except by the central seat of the state's power — the king.[42]

The *intendants*, in their turn, considered their service in a somewhat familistic light; [43] likewise, since they were paid a certain salary, their relationship to the king contained some contractual elements; nevertheless, all this was quite secondary in comparison with their complete dependence upon the king's power, duplicated by the dependence of the subjects on their own discretional power.

Likewise, the military service, which in the preceding period became contractual to a considerable degree, now tends to become compulsory; a kind of obligatory military duty is introduced, especially in regard to

[41] *Ibid.*, Vol. 1, pp. 69, 134, and 156.

[42] See the quoted words of Tocqueville, p. 60; Taine, Vol. I, p. 68; Chénon, Vol. II, pp. 385 ff.; Glasson, Vol. VIII, pp. 347 ff. Though the provincial estates still dragged out an existence, their role became insignificant. Their rights were reduced to mere "petitioning," and their members were also appointed by the king. *L'états généraux* ceased to be summoned after 1614. The attempt of the Fronde to force the king to respect personal freedom failed. See about that in Glasson, *op. cit.*, pp. 317 ff. and 352 ff. Here is an example of the jurisdiction of the *intendants* as given in the king's appointment in 1754: "Surveiller justice, police, finances, entendre les plaintes de nos sujets, entrer et présider aux assemblées des villes, aux bureaux de nos finances, se faire représenter les chefs de recettes et de dépenses de nos deniers, informer des exactions, violences, concussions et malversations, procéder par jugement en dernière ressort contre ceux qui s'en trouveraient coupables, empêcher toutes foules, oppression et desordre et généralement faire et ordonner tout ce qu'il verra nécessaire et à propos pour notre service." Marion, *op. cit.*, pp. 294–295.

[43] See, for instance, the documents given in Marion, *op. cit.*, pp. 297–298.

III — 8

the rural population. Draft tends to become a fixed rule. A limited possibility to pay a certain amount of money instead of giving personal service still remains; remains also the institution of hired soldiers, mainly from foreigners; this, however, does not obliterate the main tendency toward compulsory military service.[44]

Thus, whatever aspect of the French state system of social relationships we take, in all of them an increase of the compulsory form at the cost of the familistic and partly of the contractual seems to have taken place.

With few differences, consisting mainly in a further decline of the empire in Germany, the situation in the recently emerged local States, beginning with Prussia, is similar to the above change in France. The system of the declining empire displays an increasing element of contractualism — the electoral capitularies now become the official contract of the emperor with the empire's electors; [45] but the real power shifts to Prussia and to other local states.

Prussia enacts its *Allgemeines Landrecht*, which gives a fairly good reflection of the social reality. The code testifies that the power of the king is unlimited. The king is the embodiment of the State.[46] No traces of contractualism or familism can be found in these formulations. The enactments of the king are obligatory upon the subjects, and do not need the approval or consent of any social body. The general *landtag* was absent in Prussia; the provincial *landtags* lost their importance and are mentioned but once in the *Landrecht*. The relationship of the king and his agents — the officials, the administrators — shows the same obligation to and complete dependence upon the central power. Only in a very limited way is the element of contractualism noticeable. The officials have a right not to be discharged discretionally, without a proper cause; without proper explanation on their part and proper consideration of the case by the State Council; in some cases even the sanction of the king is needed for such a discharge.[47] But these elements of contractualism are very slight and hardly important.

The army of Frederic the Great is organized, like the French army, upon the same compulsory principle of draft, seconded by a hired and contractual army recruited mainly from foreigners.[48] In application to the subjects of Prussia, this means a growth of compulsory relationship in that field.

---

[44] See Taine, *op. cit.*, Vol. II, pp. 301 ff.; Marion, *op. cit.*, pp. 473–474.

[45] Schröder, *op. cit.*, pp. 896 ff.

[46] Part ii, Title 13, §§ 1, 2, 3, and 6 of the *Landrecht*.

[47] §§ 98, 99, and 100 of Title 10 of the second part of the *Landrecht*.

[48] F. Meinecke, *Das Zeitalter der deutschen Auferstehung* (Leipzig, 1906), pp. 11–12.

In other respects, the spectrum of the Prussian state system is about the same as that of the French State. The governmental control expanded greatly; the State absorbed and subjugated to itself most of the nonstate organizations. The main difference is, as mentioned, the relationship of the State to the Church. In France the State subordinated the Church to itself, and established a kind of official state or national religion. In Prussia, religious particularism, within certain limits, was admitted under state control; religion was declared a private affair and thus did not enter into any close official affiliation with the State, as a religion *ex officio*.

Otherwise, in French and Germanic States, the main change consisted in a growth of the compulsory relationships at the cost mainly of the familistic and partly of the contractual bonds.

B. *The Church*. So far as France is concerned, a further weakening of the familistic relationship in the Church system in favor of a growth of the compulsory relationship seems to have been the essential change during the period. The monarchy established definitely its domination over the Church, included it in the state system, gave to it public rights and privileges, and at the same time subordinated it completely to the state laws.[49] In the monarchy, as well as in the Church, the compulsory rules grew at the cost of the familistic bonds. The other side of this change, and at the same time its manifestation among the common people, was an increase of animosity toward the clergy and the monastic orders;[50] among the upper classes a diffusion of free thinking and irreligiosity. Already at the end of the seventeenth century the mother of the regent wrote that there were no more young men who would not try to show themselves atheists.[51] Another contemporary says, in 1783, that during the last ten years, it had become a fashion of the high society not to attend Mass or church services.[52] A similar mentality was diffused also among the prelates themselves.[53] As a result, the Church tended to turn into a compulsory association, with obligatory rules imposed, with increasingly harsh measures against nonconformists and dissidents. The provincial Church conclaves ceased to function. The Church hierarchy itself considerably disintegrated, since various ranks of its dignitaries were equally subjected to the king.[54] This does not mean

[49] Glasson, *op. cit.*, Vol. VIII, pp. 218 ff.
[50] See Taine, *op. cit.*, Vol. II, pp. 134 ff.; Glasson, *op. cit.*, Vol. VIII, p. 230.
[51] Taine, *op. cit.*, Vol. II, pp. 133–134.
[52] *Ibid.*, Vol. II, p. 140.
[53] *Ibid.*, p. 141.
[54] Glasson, *op. cit.*, Vol. VIII, pp. 227 and 562 ff.

that the familistic elements in the texture of the Church system disappeared; [55] they continued to exist there, but notably weakened. Such is the main change in France.

In regard to the German Church associations, particularly Prussian, the main change consisted in a growth of the contractual elements, sowed, at least ideologically, after the beginning of the Reformation. Only now its "liberty of religion," little realized during the previous period, begins to become a fact. Belonging or not belonging to this or that church group is left entirely to the decision of the individual. A considerable amount of freedom — and consequently of contractualism — is given to many important aspects of religious relationship. The *Allgemeines Landrecht* states that a belief in God and in divine subjects cannot be prescribed to the population by compulsion. Everyone is granted full liberty of belief and conscience. Nobody can be persecuted for his religious convictions.[56] Everyone is entitled to choose the religious denomination to which he wishes to belong. A shift from one denomination to another is made through a mere declaration.[57] These and several other declarations of law show the growth of the contractual elements in the Church social body clearly.[58]

The other change, also at the cost of the familistic relationship, was a growth of the compulsory regulations side by side with that of the contractual elements. The State demands that every religious society teach its members loyalty to the State. The permission of the state government is required either to summon Catholic meetings, or to accept an invitation to religious meetings abroad. Likewise, the permission of the State is necessary for the organization of a new parish.[59] Other compulsory measures are not lacking, and all this means the growth of some of the compulsory relationships within the Church body.

C. *The Family*. It continues to be familistic mainly; but partly juridically, partly factually, familism somewhat loses ground. In the French upper classes, the familistic "we" and the intimate fusion of the

---

[55] *Ibid.*, pp. 568 ff.   [56] Part ii, Title 11, §§ 1–3.   [57] §§ 40–41.

[58] Partly as a reflection of the growth of contractualism in social life, partly as a protest against the increased compulsory relationships in the State and other social organizations, the period is marked by a great development of various contractual theories in France and in Germany, not to mention England and other countries. Marsiglio of Padua, N. Cusanus, and others in the preceding period; Francis Hotman, Hubert Languet, Duplessis-Mornay, Althusius, Suarez, and the monarchomachs; Pufendorff, Grotius, Hobbes, J. Locke, J. J. Rousseau, and others are but a few of many who appear to be the partisans of contractualism in some form or another. See P. Janet, *Histoire de la science politique* (Paris, 1887), Vol. II, pp. 82 ff.

[59] *Allgemeines Landrecht*, pt. ii, Title 11, §§ 13, 141–142, and 238.

members weakens. The children are brought to the parents only in the morning, merely to kiss their hands while the parents are making their toilets. Caresses become infrequent. Daughters are sent to convents for education and to get them out of the way. Conjugal fidelity seems to be broken more and more often. Scandals and love affairs become fashionable.[60] In law there begins the process of return to the pre-Christian doctrine that marriage is a private contract.[61] Consent of the parents and relatives is demanded less than before. Divorce or separation from bed and board (in Catholic countries) becomes easier and the legitimate causes for it multiply.[62] Thus the contractual elements tend to increase here also.

Somewhat similar is the situation in Prussia.[63] The familistic relationships still remain predominant in both countries, in Prussia possibly stronger than in France, though the contractual elements gain. The compulsory elements remain without a notable change.

D. *Municipalities and Village Communities*. Municipal bonds in this period greatly weakened and became more and more compulsory. Municipalities lost most of their rights and autonomy and became subordinated entirely to the *intendant* of the State. Their relationship to him is that of complete submission. This is typically reflected in the following address of the municipal officials to a newly appointed *intendant*.

Nous vous prions très humblement, monsieur, de nous accorder votre bienveillance et votre protection. Nous tâcherons de ne pas nous en rendre indignes par notre soumission à tous les ordres de votre grandeur.[64]

This evidently is not a contractual tone ; neither is it familistic, because no familism toward officials who are all the time being changed can be expected. It is the tone of compulsory relationship.

On the other hand, municipalities ceased to be democracies where the executives were elected in fact by the population. They turned into oligarchies of a few families or persons who could buy, even for the posterity of their families (after 1692), the municipal position.[65]

Under these circumstances the oligarchy treats the population bureaucratically ; and the population considers the oligarchy and municipal

---

[60] Taine, *op. cit.*, Vol. I, pp. 209 ff.
[61] Glasson, *op. cit.*, Vol. VIII, pp. 425 ff.
[62] *Ibid.*, pp. 497 ff.
[63] See *Allgemeines Landrecht*, pt. ii, Title 1, §§ 174–183 and 669.
[64] Tocqueville, *op. cit.*, p. 90.
[65] *Ibid.*, pp. 83–84 and 88; Glasson, *op. cit.*, Vol. VIII, pp. 367–374; Marion, *op. cit.*, p. 388.

affairs as none of its concern, and as persons and affairs with whom it is not bound into any familistic "we." Perhaps a little more familism existed in the village communities, and between neighbors. The village tax collectors and syndics were elected, under the supervision of the delegates of the *intendant*, in the open meeting of the villagers, which usually took place near or in the church. However, here also the compulsion and imposition of the rules of the state officials were dominant.[66]

Probably still weaker became the municipal bond in Prussia. The *Allgemeines Landrecht* devotes only one article to the election of the municipal official.[67] Concerning the village community, the code says that its syndic is appointed by the lord.[68]

Due to natural conditions of neighborliness, there is hardly a doubt that the familistic relationships existed, but they seem to have been somewhat on the wane.

E. *Corporations and Guilds.* There is hardly any question but that the period was one of a slow decline of the corporations and guilds as such in France, and the decline of the familistic bonds in those organizations. The decline of the corporations manifested itself first in an ever-increasing control by the State (edicts of 1673 and 1691); in the fact that positions began to be more and more for sale (in the fiscal interests of the State); that the stratum of the masters tended to become more and more an oligarchy, not so much masterful as of a commercial character; in the appointment of the syndics as state officials; in the decay of the autonomy and self-government of the corporations; in the appearance and growth of the freedom of the apprentices and valets to leave; and, finally, in the closing or liquidation of the corporations and guilds in 1776 by Turgot. Though they were reopened in the same year, their subsequent short existence was an agony and had little in common with the nature of the corporations of the previous period.[69]

The quoted historian of the corporations well sums up the main changes by saying that though in the seventeenth century they preserved the traits of the thirteenth, the solidarity of the masters and workers weakened, as did mutual sympathy also, and the "corporations which before were autonomous now became a mere institution of the State."[70]

Likewise the familism within the corporations evaporated still more.

---

[66] *Ibid.*, pp. 93–96; Marion, *op. cit.*, p. 390.   [67] Part ii, Title 8, § 112.
[68] Part ii, Title 7, § 47.
[69] See the details in the quoted work of M. Saint-Léon, Bks. V and VI.
[70] *Ibid.*, pp. 501–502.

Instead, partly contractual — but mainly compulsory — relationships gained.

Creation of the state offices in the corporations was a hard blow which transformed them into something opposite to what they were in their traditions and reglementations. Besides, the fiscal measures developed in them a greedy corruption which gradually changed deeply the character of these institutions and led to a new type of organization, where the title, rank and rights became the result not of merit and achievement, but of money.[71]

Finally, the law of 1776, which closed them (temporarily)

violently disrupted the centuries-old bonds. . . . It was for the corporation a death, silent and irrevocable. . . . It abandoned the handicraft men to the influence of harmful suggestions of social isolation and individualism.[72]

When they were reopened they were organized differently. They became free corporations, contractual by their very nature. The "organized" corporations were also infused with a great deal of contractualism, which after 1791[73] became the normal and main fiber of the social texture of the nineteenth-century corporations and labor associations. A few fraternal — mainly Masonic — organizations existed, with the familistic bond evident to a considerable degree (Les Enfants de Salomon, de Hiram, etc.) but they were secret and as such limited, and embraced a small minority of the artisans and handicraftsmen.[74]

In Prussia the situation was somewhat better and the corporations preserved more from the familistic relationships, but even there the tendencies were about the same. The *Allgemeines Landrecht* prescribes that a master should give to the apprentice the necessary knowledge, should educate him in good mores, stimulate him to attendance of religious services, keep him away from vice and indecency, give him the possibility of attending school, etc. The apprentice should obey his master, and so on.[75] However, here also the compulsory state reglementation increases, and imposes many obligatory rules, limiting their self-government.[76] Likewise, contractual elements manifest themselves in that the remuneration as well as the time of apprenticeship could be determined by agreement of the master with the parents of the apprentice; in that the

---

[71] *Ibid.*, p. 418. [72] *Ibid.*, p. 581.

[73] *Ibid.*, pp. 586 ff. and 615; Marion, *op. cit.*, p. 153; E. Levasseur, *Histoire des classes ouvrières* (Paris, 1901), Vol. II, pp. 646 ff. and 756 ff.

[74] Saint-Léon, *op. cit.*, pp. 557 ff.

[75] *Allgemeines Landrecht*, pt. ii, Title 8, §§ 292–298, 353, and 356.

[76] *Ibid.*, pt. ii, Title 8, §§ 181, 326, 341, 350–351, and 390–391.

valet can leave the master with fourteen days' notice.[77]   The code defines, admits, and sanctions a purely contractual agreement between the
employer and the employees or workers.   Here contractualism appears
in a pure form.[78]

The net result of these changes in the organizations, in France as well
as in Germany, was a decline of the familistic and an increase of the
compulsory and contractual relationships.

F. *Hierarchic Relationship of the Social Classes*.   So far as the relationship between the seignior and his vassals was concerned, it continued to exist by inertia, but lost its living content.   New *feods* were
not formed after the seventeenth century.   As a mere formality, with the
change of the persons in this relationship, there arose the purely formal
ceremony of *hommage*.   Personal relationships between these two strata
of society disappeared to a considerable degree.   As a result, social ties
turned into a mixture of the compulsory-contractual bonds, retaining
little of the familistic type.   The feudal privileges of the seignior assumed
the form of an eternal, unending claim which could neither be paid off,
nor terminated by a lapse of time, from the standpoint of the vassals.
Seigniors continued to demand privileges, but without the return service
or duty with which such privileges were formally connected.   Only a few
remnants of the previous mutual responsibility remained.   For the
insult of a seignior by a vassal the latter loses *feod* (so-called *commise* is the
consequence), while the dishonesty of the seignior frees his vassal from
his obligations.   The familism is dead in this "rope" tying together the
upper and lower free strata.   Its place is taken by compulsion and
contractualism.[79]

In Germany, the feudal relationship of fidelity also disintegrates.[80]
The feudal nobility is more and more displaced by the new state nobility.
This represents the totality of the families closely tied to the State, which
they served and for which service they were given special privileges and
honors.[81]   It is the nobility of the state bureaucracy rather than the
feudal nobility.

Among the members of this class there crystallized some sort of solidarity, but in view of the mobile and changing character of the membership,
the solidarity was very moderate and did not go very deep.   In its
relationship to the other classes, the new bureaucracy stood as the com-

[77] *Ibid.*, pt. ii, Title 8, §§ 290, 378, and 385.
[78] *Ibid.*, pt. ii, Title 8, § 895.
[79] See the details in the quoted works of Glasson, pp. 437 ff., and Taine, Vol. I, pp. 39 ff.
[80] See Schröder, *op. cit.*, pp. 879 ff.
[81] See the *Allgemeines Landrecht*, pt. ii, Title 9, §§ 1, 35, 37, 76, and 79.

pulsory agent of the State, plus some familistic relationships which survived from the previous period and were possibly established in the course of time around the estates of the members.

As to the relation of the free classes to the unfree, in France at the end of this period, serfdom, as such, practically disappeared and was replaced by milder forms of feudal relationships. This means a decrease of the compulsory elements and the growth of the contractual ties in their place.[82]

In Germany, on the contrary, the period is marked rather by a further diffusion of serfdom, especially in the eastern section, where free peasants become exceptions. Though the serfdom may have been milder, nevertheless it included many compulsory duties of the serfs to their lord — in labor, in service, etc. Such a diffusion means a diffusion of the compulsory relationships, too. But side by side with serfdom, the contractual elements also begin to grow : the serf has a right to purchase his freedom, for instance.[83] The familistic relationship still remains and the *Allgemeines Landrecht* indicates several forms : a lord is obliged to help his serfs, to secure work for those who do not have it, to provide for the education of their children, to protect them from usurers, etc., while the serfs are bound to be obedient and loyal to their masters and the like.[84] However, the very fact of the diffusion of serfdom compensates amply for any increase of familism in their relationships, if such an increase took place.

G. *Summary.* Summing up the totality of integral changes in all important groups studied for the period under investigation, one has to note that the main change evidently consisted in an increase of the compulsory form of relationship at the cost of the familistic, in most of the social organizations. It increased in the State, in the corporations and guilds, in the municipalities and village communities, in the French Church organization, in the relationships of military character. The contractual type seems at least to have held its own ; driven out of several fields of relationships, it conquered new ones — in the family, in the German religious organizations, in the relations of the lowest classes in France to their previous masters, and in some others. The familistic relationship seems to have been the net loser. Increase of compulsory relationships in the State was followed by that of totalitarianism in the State system, by expansion of its interference and regimentation.

[82] See Marion, *op. cit.*, pp. 507 ff.
[83] See Schröder, *op. cit.*, pp. 890 ff.
[84] See pt. ii, Title 7, §§ 122–135 and 227.

IV. From the End of the Eighteenth to the Twentieth Century

The changes in the texture of the social relationships of various organized groups of the French and German population during this period were so numerous, so complex, so fanciful, so contrasting, that it is absolutely impossible to analyze them, in a brief chapter or paragraph. Even a special monographic study would require several volumes, if the study were to give a comprehensive picture of all the most important transformations and modifications of the spectrum of social relationships in the main social groupings. All that can be done, therefore, is to point out the principal change which marks the period, omitting all the others, however important they are, per se. What is this main change? With a reasonable degree of certainty it can be claimed that it consisted of a *most conspicuous growth of the contractual relationships at the cost partly of the compulsory, and partly of the familistic relationships.* All in all, the nineteenth century and the prewar period of the twentieth century were the golden age of contractual relationships. Throughout all the centuries studied, there hardly was one which could rival the nineteenth century in this respect.

A. *The State.* In France, after the turbulent period of the Revolution and the Napoleonic Empire, with the effusion of the revolutionary "derivations" of contractual and even of the familistic type,[85] and the

[85] The manifestations of contractualism in the Revolution are: the Declaration of the Rights of Man and Citizen with its inalienable liberties, which put a demarcation between the rights of the State and those of a citizen. The place of an unlimited subordination of a subject to the State was replaced by it with a limited citizenship, beyond which the State did not have the right to go. From that the so-called subjective public claims of a citizen to the State followed, and many other contractual relationships. See G. Jellineck, *Le déclaration des droits de l'homme* (French translation, Paris, 1912), pp. 2–3 and 13 ff. Another evidence of contractualism was the accepted theory that law is a manifestation of the common will of the people. As Robespierre put it in his address, April 21, 1793: "The people are sovereign; the officials are their employees; they can change their government when they please." Hence the democratic and elective (in theory) character of the state officials. See E. Lavisse, *Histoire de la France contemporaine. La révolution* (Paris, 1920), pp. 21, 78–80, and 177; Taine, *op. cit.*, Vol. I, p. 4. Familistic ideas and phraseology were also conspicuous, especially in the first part of the Revolution. Having become free, the people thought they became brothers. In the address of June 5, 1791, it is said: "From everywhere is heard a touching call: Frenchmen, we all are brothers. Yes, we are indeed, because we are free." The king uses also the same phraseology: "Tell to all that I am their father, their brother, their friend," he says in July, 1790, to the delegates from Bretagne. Thousands of persons solemnly give public oath to remain always faithful to one another or to remain brothers. See Taine, *La révolution. La conquête Jacobin* (Paris, 1909), Vol. II, pp. 50–51; L. Madelin, *La révolution* (Paris, 1911), pp. 130 ff.

In reading the addresses, the speeches, the plays, the articles of the period, the familistic terminology and conceptions are met very often, especially in the speech reactions of the members of the same party or faction.

most compulsory relationship imposed by the Jacobin terror and dictator-ship,[86] the net result of the change was a steady increase of contrac-tualism between the citizen and the State; the State and the officials; the State and other nonstate organizations.

It is unimportant for our purposes whether various rights of citizens in regard to the State were achieved through a struggle, as in France, or were granted (juridically) by the monarch, as in Germany; whether the mutual limitations of the rights and duties of the State and the citizens were between the nation and the head of the State, or between every citizen and the State as such — these and many other points, very im-portant from other standpoints,[87] make little difference for our purpose.

The important point is that the relationships of the State and the citizen were definitely specified; quite definite limitations to their mutual

---

[86] Though the relationship of the members of the Jacobin and other political clubs of the period was somewhat familistic at the beginning, soon they turned into the compulsory dictatorship of a few leaders over the other members, and, in relation to the population, they were most compulsory throughout practically all the period of their dictatorship and control and terror. See Taine, *La révolution*, Vol. I, pp. 66 ff., 79 ff., and 99–102. There was no contractualism and but little familism in their factual treatment of the people, and indeed of all who were not their comembers.

[87] For instance, there is a profound difference, from a specific standpoint, between the relationship of the king and the people in France, according to the Constitution of August 7, 1830, and in Germany, according to the Empire's constitution of 1871. As one of the most prominent contemporary commentators on the French constitution (Gand) says: "When the people elected their head, and when the head accepted the conditions of election, a contract was established, a mutual obligation to follow the conditions of election, and a prohibition to both parties to deviate from them." N. Gand, *Traité de droit constitutionnel positif de la France* (Paris, 1842), p. 18.

In Germany, according to the most authoritative interpreters of the constitution men-tioned, Bornhak and Laband: "German constitutions were entirely the result of the will of the monarchs. Whether in the enactment of the constitutions there was an attempt to come to an agreement with the representatives of the people (as in Prussia) or it was even achieved (as in Württemberg) is unimportant. The only juridical basis of the constitutions was the decision of the monarchs. From this it follows that the rights of the monarch do not come from the constitution, but, on the contrary, the constitution comes from the will of the monarch. He is obliged to govern according to the constitution, but he rules not on its account. . . . Constitutional limitations of the monarch are thus only the self-limitations of the monarch. He is bound by them because he enacted them in juridically relevant forms." C. Bornhak, *Allgemeine Staatslehre* (Berlin, 1895), pp. 37–38. See also P. Laband, *Deutsches Reichstaatsrecht* (Tübingen, 1907), pp. 40 ff. Two conceptions are very different from the given standpoint, but the difference is unimportant to us. What is important is that what-ever, juridically, the pretexts, the basis, the circumstances, of the establishment of the broader or narrower contractual relationships in France as well as in Germany, the relationships remain contractual in both. The German monarch is "bound by them" and "is obliged to govern according to the constitution," no matter whether the limitations of his power were forced upon him, or granted freely by himself. In both cases, the established relationship is contractual.

rights and duties were established, and each party was mutually bound to follow the agreement or contract. The manifestations of this were: the Declaration of the Rights of Man and Citizen; several constitutions, all of which explicitly or implicitly recognized the limitations; the laws that definitely recognized political liberties; free movement from place to place, or the right to stay at will at a chosen place; inviolability of the dwelling place from the unlawful search and other intrusions of the state agents; protection from unlawful arrest and detention; liberty of choice of occupation and work; liberty of making contracts (within the limits established by law); liberty of religion; liberty of holding meetings; liberty of the press; liberty of associations (after the revolutionary law of 1791, which temporarily prohibited them). In different degrees and with some variations, most of these liberties were given in practically all the French constitutions from that of 1791 to the latest.

The same trend existed and was manifested in most of the Germanic States as well as in the Empire's constitution and special laws, up to the now eliminated Weimar Constitution.

All this means that "the State has duties in regard to the citizens," that "its functions are limited, positively and negatively, by law, and that there are things which it cannot do and things which it is obliged to do." [88]   *Pacta sunt servanda*, no matter how the compact originated.

As Hatschek says, "In democracies the catalog of the liberties is a kind of social pact which lies at the foundation of society." [89]

Other phenomena, like the introduction and universalization of the suffrage and the expansion of the elective character of most of the important positions in the State; in some periods, like that of the July Monarchy, a proclamation of the noninterference of the State in private contracts — these and many other phenomena are the manifestations of the growth of the contractual principle, so far as the relationships of the citizens and the State are concerned.

Fidelity and obedience, in the terms of Laband and Hatschek, are still the duties of the citizen, but both are only required within certain limits and on certain conditions which the State has to fulfill.

If we take the relationship between the *State and its officials*, there also the contractual elements show some gain. It is manifested first of all by the fact that a part of the officials of a certain category are elected, either

---

[88] See L. Duguit, *Traité de droit constitutionnel* (Paris, 1925), Vol. V, pp. 1 ff.; (Paris, 1924), Vol. IV, pp. 6 ff.   See in Vol. V, pp. 61 ff., an analysis of the liberties.   For Germany, see the short history and the Weimar Constitution in F. Stier-Somlo, *Die Reichsverfassung* (Bonn, 1919), pp. 73–83 ff.

[89] J. Hatschek, *Deutsches und Preussisches Staatsrechts* (Berlin, 1922), Vol. I, p. 133.

by the citizens or by special bodies (judges, jurymen, and others). The majority of the officials, however, are appointed by various state authorities. But the appointment is not entirely one sided; the consent of the individual is necessary, and, in so far, the relationship becomes — at least *de facto* — two sided.[90]

Further contractual traits in this relation are stated salaries for services, the definite outlining of the duties of each official and his rights also, indicating that he has not only duties to, but claims on, the State, that he is free to resign, that his disciplinary responsibility is definitely limited and fixed, and so on.

In the field of military relationship, the state system hardly shifted toward contractualism during the period considered; the compulsory-familistic principle held its own, especially the compulsory one. The main method of recruiting the army was by compulsory draft of a certain number of men of certain age and of specified qualifications (*e.g.*, 40,000 annually in France, according to the law of March 21, 1832; a varying number subsequently; universal draft in Germany according to the law on the organization of the army, 1874). But even here the contractual relationship crops out in many forms, especially in France. One could replace his personal military service by paying a certain amount of money; those who volunteered to enter the army were admitted; in the discharge of their duties there were many definite conditions as to the length, the kind, and other specifications of service beyond which the State could not press its demands. Then, in France, there was the National Guard (organized by the law of March 22, 1832), whose organization was different and contained still more contractual factors. In Germany, it was absent; the replacement of personal service by the payment of a certain amount of money was lacking; but the other contractual elements were present.[91] However, in this specific field one

---

[90] Bornhak and some others deny the presence of any contractual elements there, but they hardly succeed in proving their claim. See C. Bornhak, *Preussisches Staatsrecht* (Freiburg, 1889), Vol. II, p. 30; L. Duguit, *op. cit.*, Vol. III (Paris, 1923), pp. 111–118; Vol. IV, pp. 202 ff; 150, 165, and 169. The contractual elements in the relationships of the officials to the State increased especially in the twentieth century (before the establishment of the Third Reich) in both countries. See the above volumes of Duguit and Hatschek, *Lehrbuch des deutschen und preussischen Verwaltungsrechts* (Leipzig, 1927), pp. 311 ff.

[91] See the details and the laws of France in G. Weill, *La France sous la monarchie constitutionnelle* (Paris, 1912), pp. 79, 55, and 104; for Germany, P. Laband, *op. cit.*, p. 347; C. Bornhak, *Geschichte des preussischen Verwaltungsrecht* (Berlin, 1886), Vol. III, pp. 113 ff.

Temporarily, by Articles 173 and 174 of the Versailles Treaty, the universal draft in Germany was abolished and the army was made almost contractual. But at the present time the situation is changed in the direction of the re-establishment of the draft system.

cannot claim that the contractual relationships increased. In other fields such a claim is justifiable. This does not mean that the familistic and compulsory relationships in the state system disappeared; they continued to exist; the compulsory apparatus of the State in regard to its citizens, its officials, its military men, certainly lived and functioned. Likewise, the familistic elements, in the form of the willingness of the citizens to perform their duties to the country, up to readiness to fight for it and to die for it, were evident. But all in all, these elements seem to have somewhat decreased in favor of the contractual bonds, which fitted best and which were probably the most satisfactory under the circumstances. The system of state relationships of the nineteenth and twentieth centuries was made up of all the three main forms, but the contractual type occupied possibly a larger place than before.

B. *The Church*. At the beginning of the French Revolution, as the speech of Mirabeau on August 23, 1789, and the resolution of the National Assembly, February 12, 1790, show, it was planned to establish purely contractual relationships with the Church, in the sense that the individual could himself choose to what church — if any — he would belong.[92] These *desiderata* were not fulfilled and the law of August 24, 1790, on the civil organization of the Church, and the later dictatorship, introduced to a notable degree the compulsory relationship: the clergy, as well as the parishioners, had to conform to the conditions imposed by the State, and these conditions were enforced by the police and the compulsion of the State. Subsequent developments, with some deviations, have been steadily in the direction of the increase of the contractual relationship at the cost mainly of the compulsory and partly of the familistic elements. In France, these both remain: the familistic relationship is unavoidable to some extent in any really live religious organization; the compulsory relationship instituted by the Concordat of 1802 established the Catholic religion as the national or state religion of France; the head of the State appoints the dignitaries (selected from those who are eligible according to the Canonic norms of the Catholic Church); and so on.[93] However, due to the increase of religious liberty, the purely contractual relationship to the Church began to play a larger part than before. This became especially conspicuous after the separation of the Church from the State by the law of December 9, 1905, and the law of the congregations, July 1,

---

[92] See the details in J. N. Jager, *Histoire de l'église de France pendant la révolution* (Paris, 1860), Vol. I, pp. 392–403, 228, and 424 ff.

[93] See the juridical analysis of the situation in L. Duguit, *Droit constitutionnel* (Paris, 1925), Vol. I, pp. 479 ff.; F. D. Mathieu, *Le concordat de 1802* (Paris, 1902), pp. 101 ff.

1901, with subsequent modifications and enactments (especially after 1921 and 1924).

As a result of these laws, the compulsory element in Church associations almost entirely disappeared. Article 1, of the law of 1905, proclaimed a complete liberty of religion, of performance of religious rights and services (if they do not violate the public order). Everyone has the right to belong or not to belong to a religious association.[94] A few compulsions, imposed partly by the State, partly by the Pope (see the encyclicals *Immortale Dei, Vehementa, Gravissime*), remain, but they are insignificant. The bonds which unite the members of the religious associations, therefore, are partly familistic, partly contractual. To belong or not to belong is the prerogative of the individual; those who become Church members do so probably on their own volition. But once they enter the association, and as long as they remain in it, they have to comply with the basic conditions, duties, and obligations of the Church, many of which they cannot change or eliminate.

Similar was the trend in Germany, up to the Third Reich. There the leading principle during the nineteenth century was not a separation of the Church from the State, but one of mutual co-ordination. The Prussian Constitution of 1848,[95] then the law of May 13, 1873, and of May 14, 1873, and finally Article 137, d. 2, of the Weimar Constitution, all proclaimed complete liberty of religion in Germany. The compulsory elements were practically eliminated. The total network of the religious associations became partly familistic, partly contractual, as in France.[96]

C. *The Family*. The principal change in the social texture of the family for the period considered consisted also in an increase of the contractual elements at the expense mainly of the compulsory ones. In France the Revolution had already pushed the family in that direction. Marriage was declared a purely civil contract between the parties (*contrat solennel*, the Constitution of 1791, Law of September 20, 1792). Consequently, divorce, as the voluntary disruption of the contract, was greatly fostered by the law of September 20, 1792, and the causes for it were multiplied. The "family tyranny" was decreased, in the sense of equalizing the rights of the husband with those of the wife, and those of the children with those of their parents. The project of the Civil Code planned to establish the decision of family affairs by the council of the whole family, instead of by its head alone, and in several other respects

---

[94] See L. Duguit, *op. cit.*, Vol. I, pp. 508 ff., 556–566, and 635. [95] Articles 15, 16, and 18.
[96] See the details in Bornhak, *Preussisches Staatsrecht*, Vol. III, pp. 621 ff.

the Revolutionary legislation tried to abolish the compulsory elements and to increase at least the contractual bonds in the family organization.[97]

Later legislation, beginning with the Civil Code of 1810, with some regressive steps (*e.g.*, divorce was prohibited in 1816), as a whole, continued this trend. According to the Civil Code, the main form of family relationship is familistic,[98] with the contractual (*il n'y a pas de mariage lorsqu'il n'y a pas de consentement*) [99] reinforced, in comparison with the pre-Revolutionary period, and the compulsory weakened in comparison with the previous period. The net change consisted in some reinforcement of the contractual elements at the expense of the compulsory ones, in the relationship between husband and wife, as well as in that of the parents and children.[100] The subsequent laws of July 27, 1884; July 24, 1889; January, 1933, pushed the contractual principle still further, readmitting divorce, annulling the parents' authority for improper treatment of the children, and eliminating the necessity of their consent to the marriage of grown-up children. This meant also a further weakening of the compulsory principle in the family.[101]

In the German family, by the law of February 6, 1875, marriage was established as a civil contract, instead of a religious institution; the same was done in regard to divorce. Though the conditions were not changed radically, such a secularization emphasized more the contractual character of marriage and divorce. The main relationship was familistic; the compulsory tended to decrease, but the contractual gained.[102]   Essen-

---

[97] See the details in P. Sagnac, *La législation civile de la révolution française* (Paris, 1898), *passim* and pp. 277–284, 305–310, and 371. After twenty-one years of age the consent of the parents was made unnecessary. The marriage of the clergy was permitted. The laws of September 20, 1792, and December 3–14, 1791.

[98] The familistic character of the relationship in the French as well as in the German civil codes is stressed by many articles. In the Code Civil of France, Article 212 says that the husband and wife are bound to be loyal to one another, faithful, to help mutually, to care for one another, and so on. The same things are stressed in regard to the relationship of parents and children. In the German Civil Code of 1900, Article 1313 states that the married parties are obliged to help one another, not only in the matters which result from the marriage, but in all matters where their interests and welfare are involved. Article 1627 says that the parents' right and duty is to care for the persons and property of their children, their intellectual and moral education, their welfare and so on. The other articles define in details the mutual rights and duties of the husband and wife, and of the parents and children.

[99] Article 146 of the Code Civil.

[100] See G. Baudry-Lacantinière, *Traité de droit civil* (Paris, 1908), Vol. III, pp. 587 ff., 600 ff., 665 ff., and 701–713.

[101] See J. Bonnecasse's *Supplément au traité de droit civil* by Baudry-Lacantinière, quoted, pp. 638, 653, and 663.

[102] See the details in A. Englemann, *Das alte und das neue bürgerliche Recht Deutschlands* (Berlin, 1898), *passim* and pp. 638–683.

tially the same principles were continued in the Civil Code of 1900.[103] The increasing contractualism in both the German and the French family is shown not only by the changes in the law, but by increasing statistics of divorce in those countries, especially in the postwar period. Such a fact indicates that contractualism has been growing at the cost of both the familistic and compulsory relationships; if the family ties had been strong, they would not have been broken with such increasing frequency. The very fact of such an increase of divorces and separations is a symptom that the parties did not succeed in establishing strong familistic bonds.

The validity of these conclusions is well sustained also by the studies of Le Play's school.[104] Numerous and penetrating investigations of Le Play and his followers have shown in detail the decay of what they style the patriarchal family, and the ascendance, especially since the second part of the nineteenth century, of the unstable and the particularistic family type. Le Play's patriarchal family is akin to the familistic type of family, while his changeable and individualistic types resemble our contractual family. The data of the law, of statistics, and of detailed and searching investigations all concur in the results received. The contractual family has been in the ascendance during the nineteenth and twentieth centuries.

D. *Municipalities.* These organizations changed, during the period considered, mainly in the increase of contractualism and the compulsory relationships, with a waning of the familistic ones. In France, as well as in Germany, they became a subordinated agency of the State. In France, in the period of the Revolution, the municipal government was practically the government of the political club or party which governed the State. Therefore, in the relationship of the municipal authorities to the population, there was as much of the compulsory element as in the relationship of the Revolutionary state dictators to the population. On the other hand, the municipal authorities of the Revolution were chosen by election, at least in theory, and in this way the contractual element was introduced and, later, developed.[105]

The nineteenth and twentieth centuries continued this line of development. The laws of 1831 and 1833 re-established the elective character of the municipal officers (which character was lacking before in practice) but added that the mayors were to be appointed by the state govern-

---

[103] See Articles 1313, 1354 ff., 1399, 1565–1569, 1627, and 1632.

[104] See about Le Play and his school as well as their works in Sorokin, *Contemporary Sociological Theories*, chap. iii; Zimmermann and Frampton, *Family and Society* (New York, 1935), *passim.*

[105] See the details in Lavisse, *op. cit.*, Vol. I, pp. 174 ff.

ment from these elected officers. In this way, the contractual as well as the compulsory character of the relationship was stressed again. As the right to vote was limited to the wealthy classes of the citizens, from the standpoint of the large masses of the city population the municipal union was but the same compulsory power which imposed taxes and other regulations, in which the masses did not participate. So far it was but a compulsory agency in the feeling of the masses. Subsequently, the situation remained fundamentally the same. The municipal bond still appears as a mere emanation of the state authorities. It is obligatory for all who dwell or possess property in the municipal territory. On the other hand, the officers become elective entirely, the mayor is now elected by the officers, and the right to vote becomes universal for all classes of the citizenry. So far the municipal relationship remains contractual.[106] The community of interests of the people of a municipality imposes some "fraternal" ties upon it, but in the large cities this familistic bond is not felt deeply and the familistic feeling is probably much weaker than in the earlier centuries.

Somewhat similar was the trend in Germany. Here the state compulsory relationship was stressed by the juridical commentators rather more strongly than in France. According to Bornhak, "Municipal self-government realizes the state functions through special agents within the limits of their competence. Municipal unions use the same methods of government as are used by the State, namely: command, and if necessary, compulsion."[107] The contractual character is manifested in the elective appointment of the officers, in the right of a municipality to defend its lawful competence through the organs of administrative justice, and so on. In more recent time, the right to vote has been made universal (according to the Weimar Constitution), but the essentials of the structure remain about the same as in the nineteenth century. The net change, then, in this type of social organization was a weakening of the familistic principle and a reinforcement of the contractual and partly of the compulsory bonds.

E. *Labor Unions, Corporations, Associations.* Among these, the main change consisted also in an increase of the contractual relationship which, at the end of the nineteenth and in the twentieth century, was paralleled by an increase of the compulsory and partly the familistic bonds.

In France the famous — or infamous — law of the Revolution, June 14, 1791, prohibited a labor union, association, or corporation.

---

106 See H. Barthélémy, *Traité de droit administratif* (Paris, 1923), pp. 195 ff. and 207–208.
107 C. Bornhak, *Preussisches Staatsrecht*, Vol. II, pp. 101–105, 125, and 419.

The citizens of the same position (état) or occupation, workers and companions of a craft cannot, when they happen to be together, nominate or elect a president or secretary or syndic . . . and make any rules concerned with their alleged common interests.[108]

The law of Fructidor 3, the year third, declared "all kinds of associations styled club or people's society are dissolved." [109]

Through this, the relationships of laborer to laborer, and of laborers to their employers, were entirely atomized and turned into an almost entirely contractual or pseudo-contractual form. Hardly ever before, during all the centuries studied, had such an atomistic contractualism occurred.

This situation continued without essential change throughout the first half of the nineteenth century, almost up to 1848. Labor and professional organizations were still prohibited. The State did not interfere (in the name of preservation of liberty!) in the relationship of labor and employers.[110] A typical situation is shown by the statement of the prefect of police of Paris to the workers:

The State and law do not and will not interfere in the relationship between the employers and the workers concerning the wages, duration of labor day, or whom the employers employ. Respective petitions will not be accepted, as contrary to the laws which guarantee the liberty of industry.

Likewise, the Lyon textile workers who rioted in 1831 were told, "No tariffs which are contrary to the freedom." [111]

In spite of the law of March 12, 1841, which attempted to protect child labor from excesses and exploitation, practically all the first half of the nineteenth century shows almost purely contractual relations in this field. Beginning with the second half of the century, the compulsory, and partly the familistic, relationships enter into the unions of members of the same or similar occupations and into the relationship of the employers and the employed. The tie is still mainly contractual: nobody can be forced to make a labor or service contract with any person, or to terminate or not to terminate it. The matter depends upon the decision of each party involved.[112] But this contractualism becomes more and more limited by the compulsory interference of the State. Contracts between employers and workers are regulated and sometimes require the sanction of the State. In various forms and by a series of laws, this interference

[108] See the details in M. Saint-Léon, op. cit., Bk. VIII, pp. 622 ff.
[109] L. Duguit, op. cit., Vol. V, pp. 5 ff. and 194 ff.
[110] Ibid., Vol. V, p. 198.
[111] E. Lavisse, op. cit., Vol. V, p. 242.　　[112] Duguit, op. cit., Vol. V, pp. 164 ff.

of the State progressed.   Beginning with the laws of March 2 and September 3, 1848, down to the laws of May 19, 1874, November 2, 1892, then to the laws of July 13, 1907, and April 23, 1919, and ending with ever-increasing enactments in this field,[113] the compulsory state regulation of labor organizations and their relation to the employers' organizations (the length of the labor day, protection of children and women, the question of wages, and so on; likewise strikes and similar measures) has been constantly extending, limiting thus the unlimited contractual *laissez faire* of the first part of the nineteenth century.   Likewise the laws of 1864, 1884, and 1919 permitted labor organizations, collective contracts, and other similar proceedings.   All this means that though the condition between employees and employers is still contractual, the contractualism is notably and progressively limited by the compulsory regulation of the State.

If we consider the nature of the bonds which unite the members of the labor or employers' unions, or other occupational or professional organizations, it is partly contractual, partly familistic, and in cases where there is direct or indirect pressure and threat and compulsion, compulsory.   It is contractual because entrance into the membership and withdrawal from it are optional, because the duties and rights are limited, because the officers are elective, and so on.   It is partly familistic because the membership is prompted by the community of interests and because feelings of "brotherhood" (as even the names of some of these unions show), of "comradeship," and of familistic affiliations are certainly present to a noticeable extent.   It has also a compulsory tint because a vast set of pressures is brought to bear upon the members of the same occupation to conform to the decisions and verdicts of their unions, their leaders, and their bosses.   In the case of strikes, or competition among various unions, or between unionized members and nonunionized, the compulsion frequently assumes the forms of bombing, violence, murder, threats, and other of the sharpest types of violence.   In some cases there are present milder forms of pressure by the bosses upon the ordinary or the nonconformist members, by one faction upon another.   There are hardly any associations where one or another form of compulsion is not present.

To sum up: in France, during the period considered, these organizations moved toward contractualism; it was particularly strong in the first part of the nineteenth century; but in the second part, it began to be more and more limited by the compulsory and familistic elements. This limitation has been noticeably growing in the twentieth century.

[113] See the details in Duguit, *op. cit.*, Vol. V, pp. 156 ff., 176 ff., and 199 ff.

Prussia and Germany did not pass through the state of the *laissez faire* and atomistic contractualism through which the French organizations passed. There was no prohibition of labor and occupational organizations in these countries. With these differences, the situation was very similar to that in France. The nineteenth century, especially in its first part, was marked here also by an exceptional development of contractualism in the relationship of the employer and employee. Article 105 of the Industrial Code of June 21, 1869, states that the "establishment of the relationship between the employers on the one hand and the apprentices and workers on the other is a matter of their free agreement. But nobody can be forced to work on Sundays and holy days." Thus the main relationship is contractual, but with some modest compulsory regulation on the part of the State.[114] To this extent, the situation was similar to that in France in the first three quarters of the nineteenth century. In the latter part of the nineteenth and in the twentieth century, the contractualism became more and more limited by the interference of the compulsory and familistic relationships. The trend was the same as in France, but the compulsory — and possibly the familistic — elements were emphasized even more. The laws of June 21, 1869; July 17, 1878; and June 15, 1883, marked the beginning of strong regulation by the State; and subsequent laws up to those of the Republic (February 15, 1918; December 23, 1918; and others) [115] and ending with the enormous interference of the Third Reich indicate this tendency.

Finally, so far as the relationships studied in the Third Reich are concerned, there can hardly be any doubt that during the past few years the element of contractualism has notably decreased, while the element of compulsory regulation on the part of the State has notably increased. The change is already so great that at the present moment we have a situation fundamentally different from that which existed during the nineteenth century; the state obligatory regulation has become the main fiber in the system of relationships of labor unions to employers' unions, and of the members of the unions to one another. A considerable familism seems to be also present, but the contractual phase seems to be on a rapid and sharp decline.

[114] See further, Articles 128, 129, 134, and others of this code.

[115] See the details in G. Meyer and E. Löning, "*Gewerbegesetzgebung*," in *Handwörterbuch der Staatswissenschaften* (Jena, 1909), Vol. IV; C. G. Lamprecht, *Deutsche Geschichte der jüngster Vergangenheit* (Berlin, 1912), Vol. II, pp. 184 ff. W. Kulemann, "*Gewerkvereins*," in the *Handwörterbuch*, quoted, Vol. IV, pp. 1141–1166; H. Zeidler, *Geschichte der deutschen Genossenschaften der Neuzeit* (Leipzig, 1913), pp. 133 and 163 ff. W. Kaskel, *Arbeitsrecht* (Berlin, 1927), pp. 18 ff.

F. *Associations, Co-operative and Voluntary Organizations*. If a period has been marked by a conspicuous contractualism, one can expect to find a great development of various contractual associations in it. Not the familistic type, with its unlimited mutual responsibility and devotion; not the compulsory; but the contractual, in the sense that the relationships are voluntarily agreed to, freely organized, but in each case the "common interest" is specific and limited, is not universal, does not involve the whole personality, but just exists as "so much and so far in a specific field," "no more and no less."

The expectation is well corroborated by the facts. The nineteenth century and the twentieth, up to the latest years, were the age of enormous voluntary and — by definition — contractual organizations, associations, unions, clubs, societies, and other organized unities, "with a limited responsibility," in all fields of social life, from the society of the collectors of stamps, the "Mystic Knights of the Sea," or garden clubs, and ending with various ethical, scientific, philosophical, artistic, religious, philanthropic, political, technical, occupational, athletic, recreational, economic groups — with all possible kinds of interests and objectives. Their nature has been contractual in almost all cases.

In France, about 1830, the Revolutionary laws prohibiting associations began, partly *de jure* but mainly *de facto*, to be thrust aside. Partly through expansion of the "permissive" system, partly by other methods, political and other associations began to thrive. It is true that the Constitution of 1830 is silent concerning the liberty of meetings and unions; it is also true that the law of April 10, 1833, and the order of the prefect of Paris police of May 31, 1833, demanded that any union and any meeting, even balls and concerts, obtain permission in order to be legal.[116] However, the Constitution of 1848 [117] already recognized the liberty of associations and unions, and with a temporary setback under the Second Empire, it has continually grown since that time, being definitely elaborated by the law of July 1, 1901. At the present time, the law gives wide opportunity for such associations, and the result has been an innumerable number of them. In a sense, one can say that they compose the main part of the total set of social relationships of the French population.

With the difference that Prussia and Germany did not pass through the stage of prohibiting associations and unions in the nineteenth century, the situation and the trend there have been about the same as in France.

---

[116] See the details in L. Duguit, *op. cit.*, Vol. V, pp. 155 ff. and 342 ff; A. Nast, *Code de la co-operation* (Paris, 1928), pp. 5 ff.; D. G. Weil, *Le droit d'association et de réunion* (Paris, 1893), pp. 98 ff. and 136 ff.   [117] Article 8.

They were recognized in a limited form by the Prussian Constitution [118] and continued, with some fluctuations (like the prohibition of the Social-Democratic Party by the law of 1878) to grow, up to the time of the Third Reich. The period beginning with the second half of the nineteenth century witnessed an enormous development of associations, and organizations and unions of all kinds, and especially the co-operative associations. The Weimar Constitution reaffirmed and still more enlarged this liberty. Only with the beginning of the Third Reich appeared the first symptoms of the reverse movement, of the limitation of this as well as of many other liberties.

As mentioned, the number of such contractual associations in the nineteenth and twentieth centuries was enormous; they embraced in their totality an extensive membership; they were busy in all fields of sociocultural activity; they included definitely diverse interests; they served so many important social needs and purposes that in their totality they composed the basic "routine" texture of the entire set of social relationships. Most of these associations were small in themselves; but their number was so great that they were of the utmost consequence in their totality. In addition, a part of these associations were large in their membership and important in their functions.

This fact alone would be sufficient to validate the claim that the period considered was contractual par excellence, even if the other influential organizations had not shown a contractual trend. The enormous multiplication and flowering of the contractual associations discussed is more than sufficient evidence of the validity of the claim that the period was marked by an extraordinary development of contractualism.

G. *Bonds Uniting the Upper and Lower Social Strata.* The final elimination of serfdom and feudalism at the end of the eighteenth and in the nineteenth century put an end to a considerable part of the purely compulsory bonds which were the main ropes that tied together various strata of the social pyramid in previous periods. To be sure, these compulsory bonds did not disappear entirely with the elimination of serfdom and slavery; in a new and often masked form of pseudo-contractual or pseudo-familistic relationship, they continued to exist, to some extent. But it is to be admitted that only a part of them survived; another part was eliminated indeed.

What sort of bonds replaced them? Mainly and almost exclusively *contractual.* The relationships of the stratified social classes of the nineteenth and twentieth centuries (again up to the Third Reich) were largely

[118] Article 29.

contractual. Peasants, farmers, laborers were not obliged to give their services to the landlords, to the class of industrialists, to the rich people, and to the upper and middle classes by compulsion of either serfdom or slavery. Each of these classes exchanged its goods by mutual agreement or contract, and each was free to enter or to ignore such agreements. There were, of course, often various forms of pressure and explicit or implicit — mainly financial — compulsion. The existence of that, however, does not eliminate the profound difference between the compulsory relationship of serf and master and that of a worker or peasant and the employer or landlord. One is predominantly compulsory, the other contractual. Such a change testifies once again that contractualism was indeed the main gainer during the period considered.

H. *Summary.* The nineteenth and twentieth centuries, up to recent years, were marked by a decrease of the compulsory relationship and by an enormous increase of the contractual relationship in the totality of the organized social groups of the period, as well as in most of the groups taken separately. The familistic relationship possibly also lost to some extent to the contractual. This form was the main gainer, during the period; it was the most important characteristic of the social texture of the nineteenth century — its mark, its pride, its vice, and its source of "perdition." Such an element stamped with itself the entire social network; manifested itself in millions of daily phenomena; permeated the mentality and culture of the people. And when, as any other form, it began to degenerate and decline internally, its "pathologic transformation" conditioned a decline and transformation of the social and political organizations of European society, its mentality and its culture, as will be shown in the next portions of this analysis.

V. The Postwar Period

In France, in Germany of the Third Reich, and also in Italy, in Poland, in Hungary, in Austria, in Jugoslavia, and especially in Russia, the postwar period is marked by decisive and violent changes of the spectrum of the totality of social relationships. The essence of the change can be formulated as follows: a violent decrease of the contractual relationships in favor of compulsory (mainly) and (to a less degree) familistic forms. The contractual relationships, so successfully functioning in the preceding era, in the postwar period show themselves in a decisive and rapid decline. They begin to realize their own nemesis. Whether the decline is temporary or for a long time, its very fact can hardly be questioned in all of the above and in practically all other Western countries.

It follows from a conspicuous growth of state interference, which is transforming the state systems from the contractual-democratic form into the authoritarian, totalitarian state of the Communist, Fascist, Hitlerite, Pilsudskian, Hortian, and other varieties of this type. Such an authoritarian and totalitarian state greatly limits most of the previous contractual liberties, or destroys practically all of them, as does the Soviet State which declares they are mere "*bourgeois* prejudices," or partly eliminates them. (The "new" Soviet Constitution of 1936 changes the situation mainly in phraseology and little, if at all, in reality.) The elimination or abrogation of liberties means an enormous blow to contractualism. The State unhesitatingly imposes its own rules upon all its subjects, regardless of whether or not they are liked, approved, or disapproved. Contractualism is cut also by limitation or abrogation of the universal suffrage (*de facto*, at least) in many of these states, and it is limited further by the very increase of the state — and authoritative — regulation of an excessive number of the various relationships hitherto left to the agreement of the parties (see Chapters Six and Seven of this volume). The Communist State prescribes and controls practically all important social relationships in all the significant fields of social life and culture. In other states the compulsory prescription is more limited and administered somewhat more cautiously, but it also has increased astoundingly. The press, the associations, the meetings, the strikes, the lockouts, the religion, the education, the work, the salaries, the wages, the prices, the profits — all and everything no longer are left to the contractual decision of the parties involved; to their own agreement or to their mutual choice; it is authoritatively regulated, prescribed, imposed, under the severest penalty for disobedience. The sphere of liberty or choice or agreement in the lives of the subjects of these states is terrifically narrowed; in the Communist State almost eliminated entirely. An enormous number of relationships are "regimented," "coded," "ordered." And this trend is universal in all the Western countries, no matter what concrete forms it assumes in each — Communist, Fascist, Hitlerite, or Rooseveltian.

The result of such a change in the state system means a similar change in almost all the nonstate organizations. Through the imposition of the obligatory state rules, the contractual fibers are decreased in the municipalities and village communities, in the trade unions and corporations, guilds and associations (which in many states are transformed into the state or prescribed or governmental unions, guilds, associations). Likewise, the entrepreneurs' and the employers' organizations have suffered the same decrease of contractualism in their systems and in their relationships to the outside world; the control of their business is taken largely out of their own hands and contractual bargaining is notably reduced. In many states a similar atrophy of the contractual fibers has taken place in the religious organizations, where some forms of religion are proscribed under the penalty of death or imprisonment or fines (as in the Soviet State), or some types of religious organizations and their functions are persecuted and other types imposed. The same is true of the family to a lesser extent; and especially applies to the majority of contractual associations — political, scientific, philosophic, economic, philanthropic, artistic, and others. In many of the states, numbers of them have been disbanded; others are prohibited; some are forced to modify their organization and activities.

The fact of this sudden and enormous decline of contractualism throughout the Western World is so evident and so unquestionable that there is no need to insist upon it.

It is less certain which of the other two main forms — familism or coercion — of the social bond has profited at the expense of the declining contractualism. There is no doubt that in all these States a certain part of the population whole-heartedly approves of the elimination of contractualism and the establishment of authoritative regulation by the dictatorial State. For such a part, these measures will be familistic rather than compulsory. There is also no doubt that there is another part among the citizens or subjects of these states to whom all these measures of a dictatorial state are merely coercion and often of the rudest, most painful, and least excusable type. Which of these groups is the larger? One can hardly answer the question by a general formula. In all probability, the situation is different in different countries. In Russia, the majority is the victim, rather than the supporter of the new system. There a decline of the contractual relationship means its replacement by compulsory bonds. In other states — like the United States, or possibly Italy, or even Germany — the supporters of the new state are probably either a majority or at least numerically equal to their opponents. In such states the change means a replacement of the contractual measures partly by compulsory ones, partly by something approaching paternalism and familism. But even there it can hardly be expected that the familism, so far, is of a very fine or deep type. For that a long time is necessary, and long living, suffering, and sacrifice for one another. The dictatorial government may for a time find an emotional echo in that part of the population which sees its enemies attacked; but that is not enough for the establishment of the real familistic relationship. New rulers and their trains of followers in purely dictatorial countries soon begin to behave toward the masses of the population as conquerors, rather than as the careful, devoted, sacrificing parent. When such simple conditions are considered, it becomes rather probable that the gainer from the contractual decline has been principally a rude sort of compulsion, a coercion of the new dictators, but not a real familistic system. Such a conclusion is corroborated further by the general fact that compulsory relationships are usually the gainers during the periods of deep transition. We seem to be living in such a period now. Therefore, the new relationships can hardly be regarded as a further step toward higher and loftier forms of social relationships, or as the foundation of the new, large, and constructive civilization, in which to live humanly for a long time. They are the measures of a wrecking company, rather, which artlessly but energetically clears the ground of tumbledown, decaying, and more and more dangerous contractual buildings, beautiful in the past, but now rotten. The destruction of the contractual relationships being carried on by the various " dictatorial wrecking companies" is a manifestation of such a situation. They are not the builders of the future, but gravediggers of the past texture, which has degenerated and decayed enormously. Such is the time we live in. Why and how this degeneration of the contractual relationships happened, I shall discuss further in Chapters Four, Six, and Seven of this volume.

Chapter Four

GENERAL CONCLUSIONS CONCERNING THE FLUCTUATION OF
THE FORMS OF SOCIAL RELATIONSHIPS IN WESTERN SOCIETY

The preceding concise analysis of the fluctuations of the spectrum of
social relationships in France and Germany shows that within a specific
social system, as well as in the totality of the social systems of a given
population, the texture of the relationship is not constant but changes,
appearing now in one form, now in another. It shows, further, that in
spite of several important differences, the main waves of the changes in
both countries have been essentially similar. However considerable
may be the secondary differences in other European countries, we would
hardly err much in assuming that the texture of social relationships
among their populations has changed in a way essentially similar to that
in France and Germany. The analysis disclosed further that all the centuries considered can be divided into a few periods, with a typical predominant spectrum in each period. In a summary form, the picture is as
follows.

(1) The social texture of relationships in the period from the eighth to
the twelfth centuries appears to have been woven mainly out of *familistic
and in a smaller degree compulsory* fibers. The contractual relationship
played a relatively small role. The establishment of many familistic and
compulsory relationships had a contractual form ; but, as has been explained, the nature of the relationship was not contractual but familistic.
It is a familistic and patriarchal society in the first place ; compulsory in
the second ; and contractual in the third.

(2) Toward the thirteenth century the familistic forms show indications
of decline ; the contractual and the compulsory begin to multiply in their
place. This trend continues throughout the centuries from the thirteenth
to the sixteenth. It is a *period of a mixture of all three, with a slight domination of the familistic, and with the other two playing a more or less equal
role.*

(3) The centuries from the sixteenth to the middle of the eighteenth
are marked by a notable growth of the compulsory relationships at the

cost of the familistic — mainly — and the contractual — partly. Up to perhaps the postwar twentieth century, we have hardly a period in which compulsory fibers were so many and so strong in the total social texture of the societies studied.

(4) Beginning with the last part of the eighteenth century, the compulsory relationships rapidly decrease and the contractual relationships increase throughout the nineteenth and the prewar twentieth century to a proportion unknown before in the history of the Western society. Contractualism is the most typical mark of the European and the Western society of the nineteenth century.

(5) The postwar period marks a rapid decline of contractual relationships in favor of mainly compulsory ones.

Such in a schematized and somewhat simplified form is the course of the forms of social relationships in the Western World. The sequence of relative domination so far has been as follows:

(1) Familistic-compulsory-contractual (eighth to twelfth centuries).

(2) Weakened familistic-contractual-compulsory (thirteenth to sixteenth).

(3) Compulsory-familistic-contractual (sixteenth to eighteenth).

(4) Contractual-familistic-compulsory (nineteenth and twentieth, up to the war).

(5) Compulsory-familistic-contractual (the postwar period).

Thus the forms and combinations of the types fluctuate. Each form has had its heyday, and each has then declined. We see from this sequence that within the centuries studied there is no evidence that in the course of time one of these forms tends to grow steadily at the cost of others. Instead, they just fluctuate, without any clear indication that mankind proceeds steadily toward bigger and better familistic relationships, or toward bigger and better contractual relationships. Many theories which claim the existence of a certain perpetual trend of progress toward bigger and better sociality, solidarity, altruism (familism), or to the opposite, ever-increasing compulsoriness and antagonisms seem to be as unwarranted in this field as in many others.

This raises three important problems. What is the reason of this fluctuation? Why does not the texture of social systems remain constant, "eternally standardized" as to the quality and the proportion of the fibers from which it is woven? The second problem is: To what extent is the sequence of the domination of the forms of social relationship universal? Is this sequence something "incidental," in the sense that it happened thus in Western society but may be quite different in other societies? Or is the sequence typical and universal for all societies in the course of their existence? Is it something similar to what, for instance, Polybius claimed in regard to the sequence of the political regimes? The third problem is: Can these forms of social relationship be regarded as associated positively or negatively with the Ideational, Idealistic, and the Sensate types of culture?

Let us briefly take the problems. The general answer to the first problem is given by the "principle of limit" and "immanent change-ability" of any empirico-sensory object or process ("immanent causation"). The forms of social relationship are a part of the sensory world. If everything in it belongs to the world of Becoming, they have to belong to it too. More specifically, not only in a vast social system composed of a multitude of individuals, each of whom changes incessantly, but even in the much simpler case of two individuals, the relationship alters all the time. Each of these individuals incessantly changes — biologically, psychologically, and culturally; the concrete conditions in which they live, act, and feel also change continually; therefore their moods, emotions, feelings, ideas, desires, volitions generally, and in regard to one another, change all the time. As a result, their relationship cannot help changing incessantly also. In some cases the amplitude of the change may be enormous, transforming "true friendship into a hatred," affection into distaste, devotion into contempt, familism into contractualism or tyrannical compulsory exploitation. In other cases, the amplitude may be much narrower, changing, so to speak, not the nature of the relationship but just its shadings and modalities. Even most devoted and true friends, even the most mutually loving mother and child do not sustain the same intensity, tone, and timbre of their familistic bond all the time: it has its moments of highest pitch and its moments of weakened intensity. The same is true of the tempo of the change. Sometimes it is sudden, explosive, and surprises the parties themselves. Sometimes it is gradual and slow, imperceptibly growing for a long time before the parties become aware of the change.

Since such is the situation in the case of the social relationship of any two individuals, there is no doubt as well as no surprise that the relationships change in the vaster and more complex universe of large groups of individuals, with its everchanging intergroup and external conditions. It would be a real miracle if a social relationship remained constant and unchangeable. Such a constancy would indeed be contradictory to logic, and to observation, and to common sense. So much as to "why the social relationships change in their nature in the course of time in any social group."

Putting the same in more concrete form, I can say that in the course of time none of these forms of social relationship can really stay unchanged. Taking first the familistic and the contractual relationships and using Aristotelian-Polybian terminology, I can say that each of them is liable to degenerate into something which preserves only the external shell of the relationship without its inner content or with a content quite different from what it should be. Whether in the relationship of man to man, or of group to group, the initial form of the relationship — say familistic — established between a certain family A and the group of the families B, C, D, E, F, represents a real resultant of the qualities of A and of those of B, C, D, E, F. A consists of individuals highly gifted, strong in body and mind, capable of rendering important service to B, C, D, E, F. In this service A displays a real care of B, C, D, E, F, unselfish, paternal, wise, and felt respectively by B, C, D, E, F. Suppose that B, C, D, E, F also consist of persons who, at least, are neither ungrateful nor incapable of appreciating the services of A to them, nor of paying for them by their devotion and appreciation. The result is the establishment of a relationship of the familistic character between A and B, C, D, E, F, be A a warrior or king or lord or priest or artisan or merchant or farmer; be the others soldiers, subjects, citizens, neighbors, or what not. Now suppose that the next generation of group A happens to be quite different from the founders of group A. Suppose the members of A group now are stupid, weak, spoiled, in brief, devoid of the leadership qualities of the previous generation. If we even grant that the next generation of B, C, D, E, F is exactly the same as the preceding one, the mere change in A group is sufficient to lead to a deep inner transformation of the nature of the familistic relationship. The same is true if group A remains the same but the next generation of B, C, D, E, F is changed; the same is still more true if both groups A and B, C, D, E, F are changed. However, the external or objectivized relationships established by the initial A and B, C, D, E, F cannot be changed as quickly as the internal nature of the relationship. Many long-time obligations were made by the initial families; many other "shells" came into existence, which cannot be either destroyed at once or changed rapidly, or generally modified to conform to the new inner nature of the relationship. Hence, the phenomenon of the existence of the "shells" of the relationship for some time, while the inner content becomes empty or different. Hence, the degeneration of the familistic into a pseudo-familistic, with the external "shell" which looks like the previous one but with the content very different from familism.

The same is true of the contractual relationship. Real contractual relationship presupposes equally free parties with an equal freedom to "bargain" and to choose in accepting or not accepting the conditions of the other party. It presupposes also that a choice is generally possible. In these circumstances the contractual relationship seems to deserve all the praise that has been lavished upon it. It is a free bond willingly chosen by a free man for the mutual benefit of himself as well as of his free party. When, after the elimination of serfdom and unfree forms of relationship, such a freedom (if not absolutely, then at least relatively) was given to the previously unfree groups, the change was certainly great and noble : no wonder that it went to the heads of many of them like a wonderful wine. In this sense replacement of the previous compulsory relationships of the sixteenth to the eighteenth centuries by contractual ones was a great achievement. But now suppose that this freedom of bargaining and choice is greatly narrowed or eliminated. Suppose you have on the one side a hungry (but free!) worker with hungry members of his family ; on the other a "capitalist" who does not starve and has no need unsatisfied and no difficulty. In such a situation the freedom of one party is lacking. Therefore it is ready to accept any "contractual" condition which is offered : anything is better than nothing. The contractual form becomes compulsory in its nature. Suppose that the worker is glad to have any work on any conditions ; but there is no work at all, as is the case with millions of the unemployed. Juridically, man is still free to accept the contract or not ; but factually there is no contractualism any more ; what exists is something even worse than the compulsorily imposed work with a small compulsory remuneration. The shell stays, the content is changed.

The same can be said of an enormous number of the important contractual relationships of European society of the nineteenth century. Toward the end of the nineteenth and the twentieth centuries many of them preserved only the shell while the content of a real contractual relationship was gone. Most of the liberties of speech, press, meetings, unions, and so on, continued to exist in law and on paper ; but in fact they became inaccessible to an enormous section of the population : various private and public agencies monopolized them and created a situation in which the persons not belonging to the dominant factions, or unorganized, found themselves as speech-less, press-less, union-less, as the villeins and serfs of the previous period.

The universal suffrage was extended, and the governments became the mouthpiece of the people. But in fact the elections were monopolized by small factions, and the right of suffrage was reduced to the doubtful pleasure of checking on a piece of paper names chosen by one of the dominant parties regardless of whether the voter would have selected them personally or not.   And so in almost any field.

Through a complex interplay of many factors the contractual relationships lost, in the twentieth century, in many fields, their real and vital content and became almost empty shells.   As such they were deprived of a great deal of their value and service, and became in many cases mere "flattering and high-sounding" words without moral or material usefulness.   As a result, we can hardly wonder that the masses ceased to appreciate them; that they showed a readiness to flock to the standards which openly slandered them and their liberties and their whole social system.   Hence, the crises of parliamentarism, of democracy, of liberties, of liberalism, of democratic rugged individualism, of Adam Smith's "capitalism," of "liberal humanitarianism," and of hundreds of other manifestations of contractualism in the postwar period.   Hence the ascendance of Communism, Hitlerism, Fascism, and of many other — anticontractual — regimes in political, economic, and social life.

An additional sign of the degeneration of contractualism has been particularly conspicuous in the postwar period.   And, what is important, it has been displayed *urbi et orbi*, by the leading statesmen, financial and industrial leaders, and by moral, mental, religious, civic, and other leaders whose minds still run in the tenets of contractualism.   Perhaps the most important condition of a real contractualism is the old Roman *pacta sunt servanda* — a contract should be fulfilled, and the duties taken discharged. Meanwhile, in our courts, through the intricate nature of contemporary laws and the overdevelopment of lawyers' ingenuity, many weaker parties cannot enforce the fulfillment of the contract duties of the stronger party : with the aid of first-class lawyers, the stronger party often finds a hole which invalidates the bona fide claims of the weaker party.   The beginning of the war witnessed the invasion of Belgium and the "scrapping of a mere piece of paper," on which was written the solemn promise of the invading party to keep the neutrality of Belgium unimpaired.   This fact was a real symbol of what we have been witnessing.   After the war, beginning with the Versailles Treaty, which was in itself a breach of the promises of most of the statesmen of the Allies, who so many times and so solemnly promised many things which did not find any expression in the treaty, and promised not to do many things which they incorporated in the treaty — beginning with that, the subsequent years have been an almost incessant violation of the *pacta sunt servanda*.   One after another the governments began to break their contracts, sometimes even before their signatures had time to dry. Almost immediately after the signing of the Versailles Treaty part of the signatories began to repudiate their signature and clamor for a revision of the treaty. Revisions started : the Dawes Plan, the Young Plan, the other plans ; then followed one international conference after another, in which promises and previous contracts were broken, not two-sidedly but one-sidedly. The governments of the Western as well as the Eastern world (Russia, China, Japan, etc.) have mainly been busy with an incessant breach of their contracts of international character.

In brief, the international relationships of recent years have mainly been a demonstration that any solemn contract is something less than a piece of paper ; that it does not bind, or binds only up to the first convenient moment to break the agreement ; that the high signatories do not intend to stick and are not believed by their party to have any intention of sticking to the contract. The contract — even a solemn international pact between states or the members of the League of Nations — has been reduced to precisely nothing. A similar violation of agreement has been shown by practically most of the governments in their internal activities. Beginning with breach of duty to pay in gold the bearers of gold certificates and ending with endless "reforms," most of which broke some governmental contractual obligations, the *pacta sunt servanda* and the similar *dura lex sed lex* (stern law but law) have been more and more replaced by "expediency." The expedient is a fine thing for the moment and from the standpoint of the moment (just as the sensual wine, women, and song), but in the long course of time it leads to nihilism and cynicism ; to that "everything is permitted" for expediency, which ruins not only contractual duties but any duty, any obligation, any social and moral responsibility ; and makes parties untrustworthy and faithless to one another. In such deep demoralization nothing except a rude force counts ; neither the religious nor moral nor any other inhibitions and principles and values. If I have the power to impose my conditions upon all others, what shall stop me from this "expedient and profitable" operation ! That is exactly the situation we are now in. Therefore, we should not wonder that the contractual relationships in internal and international affairs have declined and been replaced by a stern force and rude compulsion. They are mere fruits "dialectically following" from the seeds sown before. Any shell, including the contractual shell, can last for some time without its vital content ; but not forever. The hour of reckoning always comes. And at the present time we are in such an hour, as far as contractual relationships are concerned. For the time being they have "immanently" outlived themselves.

This illustrates the meaning of the immanent change of each form of social relationship; and also the particular "why" of the present-day decline of contractualism.

With modifications, the same can be said of the respective familistic relationships in interindividual and intergroup action. Sooner or later they are bound to wither into either contractual or pseudo-familistic compulsory relationships, both on account of liability of internal change and of the play of external circumstances.

It is hardly probable that throughout the course of history there is a steady growth of familistic relationships at the cost of the others. However desirable and uplifting is such a belief, it is still mere belief and nothing more. The "ugly facts" contradict it.

Among the persons with whom each of us associates there are a few to whom we are bound familistically, usually the members of our own family and our closest friends. With the majority we are bound contractually. To some persons we are tied by the bond of coercion — psychologically we feel animosity, mild or sharp dislike, and sometimes even hatred. But in spite of that, many of us cannot sever the connection forced upon us by circumstances and have to endure the bond and relationship however antagonistic they are. So it is at the present; and so it was in the past.

Finally, the compulsory relationships are no exceptions to the above rule: they also cannot continue eternally without changing in their modality and without passing sooner or later into the contractual or even familistic form. Again in interindividual relationship, beginning with the old-fashioned compulsory marriages, where a party is married to the other, contrary to his or her will, by the coercion of parents or relatives or overlord, it has not been an exceedingly infrequent fact that the compulsory bond used to turn, after some time, into a real familistic or contractual one. The fact is noted even by a Russian untranslatable proverb: "*sterpitza-slubitsa*"; that is, in the course of time the party would come to love what has been imposed upon her. The same can be said concerning the passing of some other compulsory relationships into the contractual. Finally, in many cases, such relationships are ended by a disruption of the interaction and contact. The same can be said of the intergroup relationships. For some time a part of the members of one group may maintain a compulsory control over the other part, but not forever. Sooner or later the compulsory relationship will pass, at least in part, either into a contractual form, as we have seen in the case of the serfs liberated, or into the familistic; as we have seen in some cases, this has happened even in the relationships of masters and slaves, of conquerors and the conquered. Or, finally, the compulsory relationships, when they become too oppressive and too unbearable and when there is no other way out, lead either to disruption of the relationship and open conflict of the parties, or to the dying out of the oppressed party, or to some other form of their limitation, mitigation, termination, and transformation. No slavery is eternal; no serfdom; no tyrannical dictatorship; no other form of compulsion. For some time it may bind the group or groups together; but if, under this bondage, there is not forming a contractual or familistic bond to replace the chain of compulsion, the chain is bound to be rusted and decayed or violently broken, or it will kill the bearers of the chain and exhaust the masters who imposed it. In the next chapter we shall see in greater detail the reasons why some amount of freedom is biotically necessary and why if it is not given after a time the result is tragic: it kills the chained and it exhausts the chainers. For these reasons no compulsory tie is eternal; and it must pass, sooner or later, into a different form of bond, either contractual or even familistic.

So much about the first problem.

Passing to the second question, I do not think the sequence observed in the history of the Western society is universal or uniform for all societies and at all times. Only to minds somewhat obsessed by the idea of the universal uniformities will a claim to universality of the sequence here as well as in other questions appear plausible. As has been shown many times in this work, such an obsession is not shared by the writer. First of all, there are no logical reasons why the observed sequence shall be universal and not merely one of those possible. Second, an observation of the simpler interindividual social relationships shows that in some cases a friendship turns in the course of time into a cold, bargaining contractualism, egotistic but reasonable; in other cases it turns into a hatred and antagonism, where the bonds and relationships are continued by the sheer coercion of one party by the other. The same is to be said of the change from the contractual to the other forms or from the compulsory to the other two. In other words, we do not observe a uniform and universal sequence in the transformation of a given form of social bond into the others, but a variation of different sequences. If such is the case in the interindividual relationships, there is still more reason to expect it in the intergroup relationships. And a slight observation of the alliances and animosities of two or more groups in the course of time supports the claim.

Turning finally to the third problem, the results show that at least empirically there is some — purely incidental or deeper — association of the main type of cultures with the domination of the forms of bond studied.   From the above we see that the period of the domination of the Ideational culture, from the eighth to the twelfth century, is marked by a domination of the familistic relationships, plus the compulsory relationship as subsidiary.   The period of Idealistic culture — from the twelfth to the fifteenth centuries — is marked by a mixture of the familistic with a greater proportion of the contractual and the compulsory.   The period of a rapid ascendance of the Sensate culture — the sixteenth, seventeenth, and the first part of the eighteenth centuries — by a proportionate rise of the compulsory relationship with some increase of the contractual ones, at the cost of the familistic.   Finally, the period of the ripe and well-developed Sensate culture, the nineteenth century, is marked by an unusual increase of the contractual bonds.   The twentieth century, which, as we have seen, is marked in many compartments of culture by a sudden revolt against the Sensate forms, is also marked by a sudden decline of contractualism.   In other words, the more Ideational is the period, the more conspicuous are the familistic relationships; the more Sensate is the culture, the more either compulsory or especially contractual becomes the texture of the network of social relationships of a given society.   Such is the empirical result of the above analysis.

How shall these "associations" be interpreted?   As a mere coincidence in time and in space of the "relationship variables" and those of culture? Or is it deeper and has it either a functional or logical character?   A definite answer is hardly possible.   But with reservations, one seems to be entitled to claim that the "coincidence" is not purely incidental; that there are logico-functional reasons why Ideational culture would tend to be bound with the familistic and the rising Sensate with the compulsory; while the overripe Sensate culture coincides with the contractual form of relationships.   What are these reasons?   In concise form, they can be put in the following way.

Ideational culture has an affinity with the familistic type of social bonds first of all because it inhibits the sensual and carnal desires of its members; therefore it makes them less egotistic and less prone to exploit their fellow men, or to increase the total sum of pleasures at the cost of the individual, or to bargain with another to obtain as much as possible for as little as possible.   Whether the ideational man is an ascetic or an active ideationalist, he is much less interested in the acquisition and appropriation of the "commodities," "wealths," and "comforts" of this world for himself at the cost of the others than a purely sensate man, of a passive or active type of Sensatism. The whole mentality of the ideationalist is such that it does not value as highly as that of the sensatist the empirical values of this world. Therefore this mentality is reluctant to bargain in detail about the amount, the conditions, the proportions, the "no more and no less," so far as the empirical — especially the material and sensory — values are concerned. All this is superfluous to such a mentality, which is centered and posited in the superempirical world. For this reason the ideational man is less likely to enter into a contract to apportion these values advantageously for himself or to use a rude compulsion in order to secure for himself as large a portion of these values as possible, at the cost of others.

The ideational man is a man with the psychology of the absolute and religious principles. These principles command a fraternal relationship to other men who are "brothers in God" or in Spirit. As these principles are much less "expedient," they do not admit egotistic "expediency" as much as the utilitarian, or hedonistic, and very relative principles of Sensate mentality and ethics. So far the Ideational commands inhibit egotistic compulsion or bargaining more than the expediency of the relativistic, often cynical, and nihilistic Sensate morality and mentality.

But the most important reason is that the Ideational mentality does not regard any individual man as a single unit, as an ultimate reality, as the real center of the world. The ultimate or true reality is "the abstract and universal principles" hidden behind the empirical individual. Ontologically, psychologically, and socially, not the individual man is the reality in social phenomena but the group as such, or the Ideational principle (brotherhood in God, "identity of the eternal self," or other ideational entity), which permeates all the participants of the main Ideational values. We have seen this above, in the study of the problems of realism-nominalism and of sociological universalism-singularism. For such a mentality, the individual himself and his "self" and ego are a kind of illusion, a surface phenomenon. The reality is the total "we" of all the participants of the given Ideational culture. All are one, and one is a part of all. No individual exists as such and every individual, as a participant of a given culture, is a mere part inseparable from the other individuals, participants of the same culture. Therefore, if an individual tries to hurt the others, to cheat, to coerce, to exploit, to impose a harm upon them, he is cheating and harming himself as an inseparable part of the collective oneness.

In addition, the whole ideational psychology is such that there is a deep fusion of the individual "selves" into one "we." For an ideationalist, all the participants of the given system of Ideational culture are "one body and one mind." A kind of *corpus mysticum* is the only true reality.

Under such circumstances, with such a mentality, the relationships of the members of an Ideational culture tend to assume familistic character; sometimes, when the ideationalism is particularly intensive, as for instance among the early Christians, the familism is of the purest and all-embracing type. In other cases it is more diluted, but it still has much greater affinity to the familistic than to the compulsory or contractual form.

These are the reasons which elucidate somewhat the affinity of ideationalism and familism, and the internal unlikeness of ideationalism and contractualism.

From this standpoint it is not a mere incident that the medieval Ideational culture coexisted with a domination of the familistic relationships. It is rather what should be expected in this as well as in almost all the cases of a real Ideational culture.

But how then to explain that side by side with familistic relationship the same medieval period witnessed a considerable development of the compulsory form? In a sense it is due to the inheritance of slavery and serfdom, from the Graeco-Roman and partly from the "Barbaric" cultures, where among several tribes the unfree groups existed. Developing the Ideational culture of Christianity did not create these forms; neither did it aggravate them; if anything, after its inception it tended to mitigate and eliminate them. In the early Christian Church the slave members were not slaves at all; they were considered equal to the free members; even more, many of the early Christian leaders (preachers, priests, bishops) had been slaves. When the Church was legalized, the very entrance of a slave into the Christian Church often made him free. Subsequently, if the Christian Church did not eliminate serfdom entirely, it mitigated it and was the earliest and the main agent which fought for the freedom of slaves and their humane treatment.[1] If it did

---

[1] Even the most conservative Christian thinkers did not approve of slavery or serfdom. Even they styled it as a result of the Fall; the imperfect and negative value, the evil, perhaps less poisonous than other evils, but evil. Many among the Christian writers explicitly denounced it. See the respective theories of the Christian writers in R. W. and A. J. Carlyle, *A History of Mediaeval Political Theory in the West*, 4 vols. (New York, 1903–1922); O. von Gierke, *Das deutsche Genossenschaftsrecht*, 3 vols. (Berlin, 1868–1881); P. Janet, *Histoire de la science politique*, 2 vols. (Paris, 1887); W. A. Dunning, *A History of Political Theories* (New York, 1923), Vol. I; C. H. McIlwain, *The Growth of Political Thought in the West* (New York, 1932).

not succeed entirely in that program, the fault was not with it but lay in the fact that the social and cultural world was not purely Ideational. The Sensate aspect of it weighed heavily and required its "pound of flesh."

This combination of circumstances was one of the reasons. The other reason may be inherent in Ideational mentality. In the preceding pages I have several times stressed the phrase "in regard to all the participants of a given Ideational culture." By this I meant that the ontological and sociological "realism" of Ideational mentality, and its psychological fusion of the individual "selves" into one real "we," is limited to the participants of the Ideational culture. Only such participants are a part of this "we"; only they are the empirical embodiment of the ideational entity (children of Jesus, brothers in God, etc.) which makes all of them one real collective unity, inseparable and nonexisting in separateness from one another. The situation becomes quite different in regard to all who are not the participants in this "ideational entity" which is diffused in all the participants and of which every single participant is but an empirical form. Since the nonparticipants do not have it, they are not bearers of this "grace," this "brotherhood in Christ," this ultimate and supreme value. Being such, they are neither "sacred" nor "brothers" nor "children of God." They are just strangers, heretics, Gentiles, or a mere empirical instrumentality which can be used as any instrumentality. Hence, in regard to such "outsiders" the Ideational mentality, unless it is really universalist and cosmopolitan, does not have any inhibition against treating them rudely, imposing all kind of coercions, sometimes being even more cruel than the purely empirical mentality. This is one of the reasons why several Ideational cultures are followed by the coexistence of compulsory forms of social relationships in regard to the "outsiders" ("the outcasts, the Súdras, in India who were not "twice born"; the heretics and the pagans or "unbelievers," in other cases).

Such, in brief, are some of the reasons for a real affinity of Ideationalism with the familistic and partly the compulsory relationships.

Similar considerations explain the affinity of Sensate culture with the contractual and compulsory relationships. Sensate mentality is singularistic and individualistic. Only the separate individual is the true reality for it. Of these in the first place "myself." People are not regarded as a mere screen behind which there is one entity — living, vibrating, existing. Ontologically "group" as true reality does not exist for the Sensate mentality. It is a mere fiction. For this reason the human world appears to it as a mere sum of atomized individuals. Psychologically, in conformity with this singularistic outlook, a fusion into one "we" is more difficult. At the best, "we" is a co-ordinated, agreed upon, arranged, number of single individuals.   It cannot help seeing the individual and not the "we" as a true reality.   Therefore it cannot efface this "singularism" and "individualistic atomism" in its grasp of social relationships.   Such a mentality has much greater difficulty in merging the "ego," "the self," into the "we" than the Ideational mentality.   So far as the merging is absolutely necessary for the existence of the genuine familistic relationships, where "mine" and "thine" are obliterated, this "singularistic" mentality of sensate man is a great obstacle to the familistic bond. Either the contractual or the compulsory forms, with their "individual" centers as the "subjects" of agreement or coercion, are more congenial to such a mentality than familism.

Empirical mentality looks at man as a sensory creature.   It sees mainly his bodily and sensate needs.   Therefore it values the sensory and material values, commodities, objects, wealth, much more than the Ideational mentality.   Sensate men, each of whom is a true reality, strive to appropriate, each for himself, as much of these values as possible. They are more prone to "snatch" them from the others by force or acquire them from the others by a hard bargain.   As most of these individuals have the same attitude, the result is a much more intense struggle for these values than in the society of ideationalists.   Therefore, more antagonisms, more attempts either to "reasonably apportion the distribution to mutual benefit" through a fair or unfair contract, or to force the other party to concede them by force or by trickery.   The very fact that the Sensate culture is sensory and sensual, and looks at man first of all "carnally," is conducive to contractualism or to compulsory relationship.   To contractualism, because only men who highly value every bit of the "material values" are anxious to come to an agreement, and in detail to enumerate, to describe, to catalogue all the "ifs" and "whereas" and "A, B, C's," of the conditions and subconditions, and specifications and subspecifications of their contract.   For the "otherworldly" man, all such meticulousness is foolish.   When a contract fails, the Sensate mentality is ready to use force in order to "protect oneself" in the inexorable "struggle for existence."   Here are no inherent inhibitions against using force as the *ultima ratio* of expediency.   "Each man for himself," or "each sum of men, whose interests are the same, for themselves."   Neither absolute religious or moral or any other principles hinder the use of force if such a use is possible and expedient.   No *corpus mysticum* is hurt because no such *corpus* exists.   What exists is the empirical man or number of men; force hurts them, but does not hurt me or my partisans. This "carnalism," often "lust," religious and moral relativism, utilitarianism, and hedonism, or, what is the same, this relativistic "expediency," has much more affinity with contractualism and the compulsory form of social relationships than ideationalism with its "realism," "absolutism" and "universalism."

Finally, Idealistic culture, as a balanced synthesis of both, has to show, for reasons comprehensible from the above, a synthesis of the three forms, with some predominance of the familistic form.

It is thus comprehensible that the thirteenth, fourteenth, and fifteenth centuries show a mixture of all the three forms. When the Ideational culture began to decline, the sensate man began to awaken. The familistic form became insufficient; contractual and partly compulsory forms had to be increased. And we have seen that this period is marked by a weakening of familism and the first increase of contractualism and partly compulsory form.

Toward the sixteenth century the Ideational culture declined still more and the Sensate made an enormous progress. Now sensate man appeared. But this man, having lost his ideational bearings, did not acquire at once the reasonable and balanced sensate outlook: "to live and to let others live." He was violent and emotional and explosive and greedy. Being so, he was not educated to consider carefully his own interests and to come to agreement with others as to what was his and what he had to concede to others for the mutual benefit of all parties. But social existence is impossible without some sort of order. Mere contractual and similar preachings were not strong enough to "order such a man." Hence the appearance of physical compulsion as the most convincing method of training him and the growth of compulsory relationships in the sixteenth, the seventeenth, and the eighteenth centuries.

Drilled by this method, the sensate man was tamed and began to realize step by step that contractualism is perhaps the best and most comfortable way to arrange things.

The wild youth of sensate man was over; he was becoming more and more balanced, reasonable, and ready to settle down. After the explosion of the Revolution, in the nineteenth century he became a solid contractual citizen, who wanted to bargain, instead of fight; who wanted to live and let others live. We are in an age of contractualism, the mature form of the mature and balanced Sensate culture.

However, as any other form, the Sensate culture and contractualism bear in themselves the seeds of their own destruction. In the nineteenth century these seeds grew; and in the twentieth century they led to the degeneration of contractualism itself. It turned more and more into a pseudo contractualism. Parallel with a revolt against the extreme forms of Sensate culture which we noticed in many compartments of the Western culture, beginning with the end of the nineteenth century, a revolt against the depreciated and defrauded contractualism took place also in the post-war period. So far it has manifested itself mainly in an ascendance of the compulsory forms. But there is hardly any doubt that sooner or later these forms will subside and either contractual or — what appears to me more probable — familistic forms will take its place. Hitlerism, Communism, Fascism, Socialism, and many other "isms" of our days are groping and looking for these forms. But unfortunately, like the cubists in art, they are strong in their revolt against contractualism but perfectly helpless in their attempt to establish a new "collective" or "familistic" form, because, like cubists, their eyes and mentality are materialistic and sensate par excellence, and their collectivism is a mere mechanical manipulation of men and social forces. The result is not so much a familism or altruism or anything like that, as it is the "collectivism" of the hard-labor prison, with its hatred and its coercion — the regime fundamentally opposite to familism and its allies. They successfully destroyed contractualism, but replaced it mainly by compulsory and mechanical slavery: soulless, mirthless, compassionless, largely devoid of real altruism, real familism, real solidarity. It has created so far only the pseudo solidarity of the executioners among themselves and the alliance of the victims. Since their mentality is anti-Ideational and Sensate through and through, nothing else can be expected. For the creation of really familistic, and in this sense really collectivistic, bonds, an Ideational mentality is necessary. As long as it is absent, the work of these "wrecking companies" will be very successful in destruction but of little value in the construction of the familistic relationship and a really collectivistic society. However, they clear and prepare the room for it. This is the only excuse for their activity.

Chapter Five

FLUCTUATION OF THEOCRATIC (IDEATIONAL) AND SECULAR (SENSATE) FORMS OF GOVERNMENT AND LEADERSHIP

I. PRELIMINARIES

In the preceding four chapters the social relationships have been studied from the standpoint of their fundamental qualitative forms. Each of these forms is a complex of several more elementary characteristics integrated into one living unity and functioning as such. In tracing the fluctuation of these forms, here and there remarks have been made as to what happens to this or that more elementary constituent when these forms change; for instance, what happens to the liberty of the individual, or to the form of the political regime and leadership, when one of these forms declines and the other rises. These remarks were, however, in a sense casual, and their significance might easily escape the attention of the reader. For this reason, in this and the following chapter I am taking two or three classes of the sociopolitical phenomena and I intend to show concisely that these phenomena are greatly dependent, in their forms, as well as in the rise and decline of each form, upon the dominant type of culture and the respective forms of social relationship: familistic, contractual, and compulsory. The phenomena to be considered are: the Ideational and Sensate forms of government and sociopolitical leadership; the Ideational and Sensate forms of freedom. They compose one of the central problems of the political and ethicojuridical disciplines. If in regard to them it can be shown that neither an adequate grasp of their main forms nor of the rise and decline of either of them is possible without a preliminary understanding of the main forms of culture and of social relationships, such a demonstration entitles us to conclude that still greater must be the dependence of many other sociopolitical phenomena upon our fundamental "variables." In this way their importance will be vindicated once more. We turn now to the problem of forms of government and leadership.

II. Pulsation of Ideational and Sensate Sociopolitical Regimes

The concept of Ideational culture implies logically that, if no external circumstances hinder, the government and the intellectual, moral, and social leadership (aristocracy) in such a culture must belong to the persons and groups that incarnate, or are supposed to incarnate, in themselves the Ideational values.   Since the sensory-empirical values, whether wealth, physical might, sensory happiness, and the like, are only pseudo values to Ideational mentality, the rich, the physically mighty, the capable organizers of the economic, political, or other enterprises in such a society cannot be its recognized "aristocracy," its leaders, and its rulers, if they are not backed by the Ideational values, are not their upholders, or are not supported by the group that is thought to be the incarnation of these Ideational values par excellence.   The supreme prestige and authority — and respectively the governmental influence — must belong in such a society to theocracy, be it the group of priests and the sacerdotal class generally, be it the caste of Brahmins, the lamas, the shamans, the "elders," or any other group which is believed to be in closest contact with the supersensory power and values, their manager and delegate in the sensory world.

And vice versa.   In the Sensate culture, with its disbelief in Ideational reality and values, the leaders and rulers can be only those groups which are the bearers, the creators, the organizers, of the most important sensory values; physically powerful protectors of safety and security, organizers of prosperity of the given population.   The aristocracy of such a society has to be, therefore, either the military class; or the rich class; or the group that physically dominates the society — various dictatorial factions and their leaders; or the clever politicians and machinators; or the organizers of new economic and other empires; or the inventors and scientists who deal with the "material forces of nature" and discover ever new sources of human, sensate well-being; or various manipulators and "bosses," down to the powerful leaders of criminal gangs.

Finally, the Mixed or Idealistic society is to be expected to have a political regime and leadership of a Mixed nature, partly theocratic, partly Sensate secular.

These deductions are corroborated by the data of history so well that it is hardly necessary to enter here into a detailed verification of them. A mere reminder of the fundamental facts in the field is sufficient.

A. First, *the proposition is well corroborated in social space.*   The Brahmanic, Buddhist, Tibetan, and the Taoist part of the Chinese culture have been predominantly Ideational.   Their aristocracy and their socio-political regime have been theocratic in their essentials.   At least during two thousand years, the supremacy of the Brahman caste in India has never been questioned seriously.   It is probably the longest-lived aristocracy in the world and less disputed in its superiority by the population of India than any other aristocracy.   Even now, when the caste system seems to be weakened, the nearness of some three thousand other castes in India to the Brahmanic caste is the main criterion of their relative position in the hierarchical ladder of the social strata of India.   Who are the Brahmans?   Priests, without a church organization; religious and moral and spiritual leaders.   What is the basis of their prestige?   Only the belief that they are the bearers and representatives of the super-sensory Ideational values.   They are neither rich nor physically mighty; nor do they control the army; nor do they invent and create new sources of sensate well-being.   They are nothing of the kind, and do not have any of these means for the maintenance of their prestige and superiority. They formally do not rule; the kings and the princes of India are the rulers.   But if their power is not purely compulsory, its authority depends upon the attitude of the Brahmanic caste and its support.   In brief, India is the country whose sociopolitical regime and aristocracy have been the decentralized theocracy par excellence, no matter whether the rulers have been the members of the Brahman or the Kshattrya caste.[1]

The Tibetan regime is an explicit regime of the centralized theocracy. The Dalai Lama is its supreme ruler and the head of its aristocracy, consisting of the multitude of lamas and monks who act as his agents. Similar has been the situation in the countries with a dominant Buddhist culture.   The ruler himself may be the theocratic head of Buddhism, like the emperor Açoka, or he may not be such a head; but the power, the authority, the prestige of the government depends upon the approval of the theocratic authority.   Often the government has been but an instrument of the theocratic group and values.

Similar has been the situation with the Taoist theocracy and the government of China, when and where (especially in southern China in some periods) the Taoist mentality was dominant.[2]

[1] See C. Bouglé, *Essais sur le régime des castes* (Paris, 1908); E. J. Rapson (ed.), *Cambridge History of India* (New York, 1922), Vol. I; M. Sénart, *Les Castes dans l'Inde* (Paris, 1896); and other works quoted in three volumes of this work.

[2] The statement applies also to the political regime of ancient Egypt, Assyria, Carthage, the State of the Incas, and Mohammedanism, for the periods when their culture was predominantly Ideational.   The Egyptian Pharaoh was incarnated God; so was the Inca; likewise the supreme rulers of the Mohammedan countries, of Carthage, and several other

In all these and similar cases the government has been an explicit or implicit, centralized or decentralized, theocracy, with its authority derived from the Ideational source; with its policy permeated by Ideational mentality; with its dependence based upon the explicit theocratic groups in the society. The aristocracy of such cultures and societies likewise used to be the theocratic aristocracy, composed of the stratum regarded as the bearer and delegate and incarnation of the Ideational forces and values. Nearness to this source — and not wealth, or might, or sensate useful services, and other criteria — determined the hierarchical rank of the group and its aristocratic or nonaristocratic status.

The "objective fact" of such a situation is well reflected, in these cultures, in the respective sociopolitical and moral ideologies; in the social and political theories, opinions, convictions; in the literature and law of such cultures and periods. These ideologies and law provisions aimed to show the superiority of such an aristocracy, as well as the hierarchical rank of the main social classes on this Ideational scale. The Hindu ideology of the four castes can serve as an example of that. Here is one of its versions.

Now for the prosperity of the worlds, he (the self-existent Lord or Brahma) from his mouth, arms, thigh and feet, created the Brahman, Kṣatriya, Vaiçya, and Çūdra.

Now, for the sake of preserving all this creation, the most glorious (Being) ordained separate duties for those who sprang from (His) mouth, arm, thigh and feet.

For Brahmans he ordered teaching, study, sacrifice, and sacrificing (as priests); for others, also giving and receiving (gifts).

Defence of the people, giving alms, sacrifice, also study, and absence of attachment to objects of sense, in short, for Kṣatriya.

Tending cattle, giving alms, sacrifice, study, trade, usury, and also agriculture for a Vaiçya.

One duty the Lord assigned to a Çūdra — service to those (before mentioned) classes, without grudging.

Man is declared purer above the navel; therefore the purest part of him is said by the Self-Existent to be his mouth. Since he sprang from the most excellent part, since he was the first-born, and since he holds the Vedas, the Brahman is, by right, the lord of all this creation. What being is then superior to him, by whose mouth the gods eat oblations and the manes offerings? Of beings, the most excellent are said to be the animated; of the animated,

---

societies were, in the Ideational periods of these countries, either the sacerdotal kings — that is, the supreme bearers of the supreme Ideational value — or the secular rulers, as instrumentalities in the hands of the theocracies of these countries.

those which subsist by intelligence; of the intelligent, men; of men, the Brahmans. . . .   The birth of a Brahman is a perpetual incarnation of *dharma;* for he exists for the sake of *dharma,* and is for the existence of the Vedas. . . . When a Brahman is born, he is born above the world, the chief of all creatures, to guard the treasury of *dharma.* . . .   Thus, whatever exists in the universe is all the property of the Brahman. . . .[3]

These lines indicate clearly the Ideational basis of the superiority of the Brahman caste; as well as the various sources from which this superiority was derived; creation from the mouth, the Ideational function of maintenance of the *dharma* and the Vedas and, through that, of the existence and of the order of the whole Universe.[4]

With many a concrete variation, the same principles will be found in all the ideologies of the theocratic-Ideational aristocracy and regime, be it the Buddhist (the Dalai Lama as an incarnated Buddha), the Taoist,[5] or Egyptian, or Mohammedan, or the ancient Hebrew, or any other. In all such ideologies and provisions, the Ideational — and no other basis — is stressed as the source of this superiority. It is this basis that gives physical power and wealth into the hands of such theocratic groups, and not wealth and physical might that attracts the Ideational prestige and halo. The superiority itself, as well as the ranks of various social strata, is "measured" by the comparative nearness to, or the proportion and purity of, this Ideational value granted to these classes and borne by them. Any purely secular power, even that of the king, is declared to be subordinated to this Ideational power and its bearers, if the king himself does not happen to be the head of this theocracy (as in Tibet, or, up to recent times, in Mohammedan countries, beginning with Turkey, or in Ancient Egypt).

So far as contemporary knowledge concerning the "primitive peoples" is reliable, the proposition discussed seems to be supported also by these tribes. A study of the facts shows, first, that the culture of some primitive tribes, like the Zuñi and several Polynesian tribes, is more Ideational than the culture of many other primitive tribes; among the more Ideational tribes, the form of government and leadership respectively is much more theocratic than among the groups with a more Sensate culture. It is enough to study carefully the forms of government and leadership among

---

[3] *The Ordinances of Manu* (London, 1884), chap. i, 31 and 87–102. Quite similar are the provisions in other lawbooks of Ancient India, like the *Gautama, Narada, Brihaspati, the Instituts of Vishnu,* as well as in the whole Brahman literature.

[4] See other quotations in Chapter Three of Volume One of this work.

[5] See, for instance, the treatise the *Thâi-Shang,* in the Texts of Taoism, in *The Sacred Books of the East* (Oxford, 1891), Vol. XL, pp. 236 ff.

the Zuñi to see that it is a conspicuous theocracy.[6] Likewise theocratic is the regime and leadership of the Ideational tribes of Polynesia or Samoa. The ruling stratum, the aristocracy, and the chief there derive their power from "holiness" (*Heiligkeit*); are regarded as incarnated deities; are ascribed all the supersensory halo of power; in brief, the regime and leadership have the essential traits of theocracy.[7] In other tribes with more developed elements of Sensate culture, the political regime, leadership, aristocracy, are also Sensate, and often are characterized as a "secular aristocracy" or even "plutocracy," and their authority is based either upon mere inheritance of position, or physical power, or utilitarian services to the tribe and the like.[8]

Well corroborated by the data of various cultures and societies, the propositions are supported also by the historical data concerning the fluctuation of theocratic and secular (Sensate) political regimes and leadership, in time, in the history of the Graeco-Roman and the Western societies. Let us recall the main phases of this fluctuation.

In Greece, the earliest period was that of *sacerdotal monarchy*, with the king who was first of all and most of all the supreme priest, or *pontifex maximus*.

They [the kings] were their generals in war, and presided over their sacrifices. . . . The king was their general, their judge and their high priest.[9]

In the social system of the ancients, religion was absolute master; the State was a religious community, the king a pontiff, the magistrate a priest, and the law a sacred formula; patriotism was a piety; and exile, excommunication.[10]

In other words, here we have the king and supreme priest as the supreme bearer of the Ideational value united in one and the same person. The aristocracy and the leadership thus belonged to those who were the incarnation of the Ideational value par excellence. Without it, it would be hardly possible for the king and the leaders to be the king and the leaders.[11] This was before the sixth century, in the period which

---

[6] See a good characterization in R. Benedict, *Patterns of Culture* (Boston, 1934).

[7] See R. Thurnwald, *Die Menschliche Gesellschaft* (Berlin and Leipzig, 1935), Vol. IV, pp. 156–157 and 36 ff. See there literature.

[8] *Ibid.*, pp. 158 ff. *et passim*.

[9] Aristotle, *Politics* (Everyman's Library ed.), Bk. III, chap. xiv, pp. 96–97. About the sacred and religious nature of the early kingship and the Greek State see Gilbert Murray, *Rise of the Greek Epic* (Oxford, 1924), pp. 27–60; F. de Coulanges, *The Ancient City* (Boston, 1900), *passim*.

[10] F. de Coulanges, *op. cit.*, pp. 11 ff., 154–169, and 519 ff.

[11] Numerous statements of Herodotus make this clear. For instance, King Gyges became king only after confirmation by the Delphic oracle; and Herodotus cites many other cases

appeared in all the compartments of Greek culture as predominantly Ideational.

B. Then, as we approach the sixth century, the theocratic Ideational source of the government and sociopolitical leadership seems to have greatly weakened. Already in the time before Solon (c. 639–559 B.C.) in Athens, at least, we find the leadership and the domination of the rich and the physically powerful. Respectively, during the sixth and the subsequent centuries, we notice in most of the Greek states (except, perhaps, Sparta) a progressive de-Ideationalization or secularization of the government and the sociopolitical aristocracy. Throughout all this period, from the sixth century to the end of Greek independence in the second century B.C., the religious-theocratic basis of the government, aristocracy, prestige, and leadership played a progressively decreasing role, and wealth, military power, physical force, political cunning, "intellectualism," and other factors played the decisive role in these matters and in numerous upheavals of sociopolitical regimes: in tyrannies, oligarchies, timocracies, democracies, and, finally, monarchies of the Greek states. So far, this trend was in agreement with the trend of progressive sensatization of the Greek culture during these centuries.

This trend was naturally reflected in the respective ideologies. If, in the poetry ascribed to Solon, the Ideational motives are still conspicuous, in the political theories of the fifth century B.C. they play either no part (as in the theories of the Sophists like Georgias or Thrasymachus, where law and government and leadership were reduced either to a kind of compact among the people to safeguard their sensate interests, or to the mere power of the mighty and the cunning of the clever to exploit for their own interests the people, without any trace of an Ideational reason or principle) ; [12] or find only the Idealistic motives (in my sense of this term), as in the theories of Plato (with his Utopian kings-philosophers and aristocracy of the Idealistic philosophers and the guardians), or in the theories of Aristotle's three good forms of government (monarchy, aristocracy, and polity) in contradistinction to the three wrong or bad forms of government

---

where only through the sanction of the Delphic oracle, or Pythias, or other religious authorities could the position of a ruler or leader be obtained by secular rulers. *The History of Herodotus* (Everyman's Library ed.), Vol. I, pp. 7 ff. Plutarch stresses still more the religious nature of earliest Greek aristocracy. Theseus "divided the Commonwealth into three distinct ranks, the noblemen, the husbandmen, and artificers. To the nobility he committed the care of religion, the choice of magistrates, the teaching and dispensing of the laws, and interpretation and direction in all sacred matters." Plutarch's *Lives* (Everyman's Library ed.), Vol. I, p. 17.

[12] See on Thrasymachus, in Plato's *Republic*, pp. 338 ff. in Jowett's trans. On Georgias, see Plato's dialogue, *Georgias*.

and leadership, where these Idealistic values are absent (tyranny, oligarchy, and mob rule).[13] As we come to later centuries even these Idealistic motives are less and less noticeable. Their place is occupied by purely Sensate — eudaemonistic, utilitarian, hedonistic, or even cynical — considerations and justifications (or assailing) for wealth, might, physical power, organizing ability, and the like as the bases for leadership, superiority, and government. When it was declared that Alexander the Great was born from Zeus and a goddess, the ideology appealed possibly only to the subjugated Oriental countries, while in Greece, and especially in Athens, it was rather ridiculed and satirized. Besides, the very nature of this cult of the monarch, like a similar cult of the Caesars in the later Rome, was not so much a cult where the king or dictator was regarded as a delegate of the Ideational forces as a belief that supernatural forces and prestige were derived from the "deified empirical man," be he Alexander, Caesar, Augustus, or other king. In real theocracy, a given person is *sacrosanctus*, because he is a delegate of the super-sensate forces. In this cult of Alexander or Caesar or any man, an empirical man, in his own right, demands for himself the honor and rank of a superhuman deity. The two standpoints are at the opposite poles. One is Ideational ; the other Sensate.

C. The early — monarchical — period of Rome (before 510 B.C.) had also the regime of the sacerdotal government and aristocracy and leaders, where the king was simultaneously the secular ruler (*rex*) and the supreme priest (*pontifex maximus, rex sacrificulus*). "He held intercourse with the gods of the community, whom he consulted and appeased (*auspicia publica*), and he nominated all the priests and the priestesses." [14]

Even after the fall of the monarchy, in the early stages of the Republican regime, the sacral or Ideational elements were still strong in the Roman government, and in the leadership of the Roman aristocracy (the important roles of the *jus divinum, sacrum, fas,* sacral criminal law with its *sacer esto* and expiation ; the religious form of marriage, *confarreatio;* the role of the *dies nefasti;* of *jus pontificum* ; of augury ; of the pontifical college, and so forth). However, the secularization of the government and of the aristocracy progressed in the subsequent centuries, and especially after the penetration of the influence of Hellenistic Greece. The importance of the Ideational source in the prestige of the government

---

[13] See Aristotle, *Politics* (ed. cited), Bk. V, chaps. x, xi, xii, *et passim*.
[14] T. Mommsen, *The History of Rome* (Everyman's Library ed.), Vol. I, p. 63. See also F. de Coulanges, *op. cit.;* Danz, *Der sacrale Schutz im römischen Rechtsverkehr* (Jena, 1857).

and of the aristocracy or leadership tended to fade more and more, being replaced by the Sensate bases, like wealth, military services, political machinations, secular intellectualism, and simple physical force of the respective groups and persons. Toward the end of the Republic, there was little, if anything, left from the Ideational or theocratic bases in these fields. It is true, the position of the *pontifex maximus* still remained, had some prestige, and was often taken by the dictators, like Caesar, as an additional source of their claims and influence. But it lost its previous importance and became just a secular office without important functions and especially without any Ideational inner value. The decay of the traditional religion among the Roman aristocracy and intelligentsia signified a decay of Ideationalism and of the theocratic character of the government and leading and aristocratic groups. Only through that decay was it possible to proclaim the cult of the Caesars, where the Sensate man was elevated to the rank of the gods and demanded for himself the honor paid to deities (*divus, tamquam praesenti et corporali deo*). In a sense, as in the case of Alexander the Great, this was the extreme limit of the decline of the Ideational elements and the limit of the Sensate character of the government and leading groups. The factual history of the government, the Caesars, the aristocracy, and the leading groups of these centuries manifests this clearly. The incessant struggle for power, violence, capable adventurers seizing the position of the king when they can [15] — all this shows the rule, "Might is right." So far as these centuries, from the second B.C. to the first centuries of our era, were Sensate in all the main compartments of Roman culture, this secular character of the government and of sociopolitical leadership is in harmony with the character of the culture.

D. With the growth of Christianity and its power, a new Ideational force entered the scene and toward the end of the fourth century turned the direction of the culture from the Sensate to an increasingly Ideational form in all the main compartments of Roman culture. This enormously increased power of Christian Ideationalism was one of the reasons for the acceptance of Christianity by Constantine and his legalization of the Christian Church. After that time the Ideational source and sanction of secular power became necessary. Leaders of Christianity, like St. Ambrose and many others, did not hesitate to censor, sometimes even to excommunicate, to guide, and to control the emperors and the subordinate secular rulers and leaders. During the subsequent centuries, especially

---

[15] During these centuries 45.6 per cent of the Roman kings were "upstarts." See P. Sorokin, *Social Mobility* (New York, 1927), p. 143.

after Leo the Great and then Gregory the Great, the government and sociopolitical leadership became again predominantly Ideational or theocratic.   Either in the sense that the secular rulers were controlled by the Christian Church, and obliged to follow its guidance and to have its approval for obtaining and holding their positions,[16] or in the sense that the spiritual power held the supremacy over the secular one, the doctrine and the reality lasted up to about the end of the thirteenth century.   During these centuries Europe had a predominantly theocratic regime, with the Roman Catholic See as the supreme government and unquestioned power in spiritual matters, and as the great power in all secular matters, sometimes even greater than any secular king, and almost always indispensable for obtaining and holding power by any secular ruler.   The doctrine that God is the only source of any government and the prevailing doctrine of explicit or implicit supremacy of the spiritual power over the secular one are the manifestation of this change.[17]   For three or four centuries European history fluctuated between the course of secularization it later assumed and the explicitly theocratic culture analogous to the theocracy of Brahmanic India.   We know that these centuries from the fifth to the thirteenth were Ideational in the culture of Europe.   Now we see that this culture was, during the same centuries, theocratic or Ideational in its government, aristocracy, and sociopolitical leadership. Around the end of the twelfth and then in the thirteenth century the objective historical reality and then the ideologies begin to show the first signs of the coming turn from the theocratic constitution to the secular, in the field discussed.   Most of the political theories of the period try to reconcile the spiritual and secular power and in this way show their Idealistic character.[18]   But voices ascribing to the secular power supremacy over the spiritual appeared and began to multiply (John of Paris, Peter Flotte, W. Nogaret, Dante, Pierre du Bois, Marsilio of Padua, and others).   The *Unam Sanctam* of Pope Boniface VIII, who in 1300 declared, "I am Caesar, I am Emperor," may be taken as a landmark of the

[16] See above Chapter Two; Luchaire, *Manuel*, pp. 377 and 487; C. de Ribbe, *op. cit.*, pp. 95, 380, and 430.

[17] See the doctrines and ideologies and the whole struggle between the ideologies of the supremacy of the secular and spiritual power in the quoted works of O. von Gierke, pp. 13 ff.; E. Troeltsch, pp. 31 ff.; A. C. Flick, pp. 54–56 and 170 ff.; C. H. McIlwain, chap. v; R. W. and A. J. Carlyle, Vol. I, chaps. xiii and xxi, Vol. II, pp. 254 ff., and Vol. IV, *passim;* E. Chénon; also Imbart de la Tour, *L'évolution des idées sociales du XIe au XIIIe siècle* (Paris, 1907).

[18] See about this in the works quoted in the preceding footnotes of this chapter; also the essays on St. Thomas, Dante, Pierre du Bois, Marsilio of Padua, in F. J. C. Hearnshaw, *The Social and Political Ideas of Some Great Mediaeval Thinkers* (London, 1923), Vol. I.

beginning of the decline of theocracy and of the ascendance of secular power. The subsequent arrest of the pope by Guillaume de Nogaret, and the compulsory removal of the popes to Avignon, marked clearly this turn. In the political ideologies, the change was manifest in the ever-increasing theories which more and more clearly claimed the supremacy of the secular power over the spiritual. The center of the influence shifted to the emerging national monarchies and their new aristocracy and new leaders. In some cases, these secular governments did not hesitate to repudiate any claims of the Papal See and openly revolted against it; in others, they tried to be in good relationship with it, but only in so far as it did not hinder the realization of their aims. The new aristocracy and leadership became more and more secular, nonreligious, and sometimes even antireligious. From the previous theocratic regime there remained "the government by the Grace of God," but this as well as other survivals of Ideational-theocratic regimes tended to become more and more empty formulas or the formulas to be used merely for the aggrandizement of the new rulers or for showing the independence of their absolute power from any other group in the society. With several minor fluctuations, the trend continued to grow up to the beginning of the twentieth century and in many Western countries resulted in the formal separation of the State and the Church, and into partly juridical — and especially factual — subordination of the Church to the State; of the spiritual power to the secular or sensate; in other states, like Russia, Spain, Germany (partly), and a few others, the power as well as the Church itself was suppressed.

E. At the present time, most of the governments and the influential class of the people do not refer to God or to any other supersensory authority for "sanctification" of their power. An Ideational source is not mentioned. Instead, "the will of the people," or "of the proletarian class," or "of the nation," or of any other group, functions as the source of the power. The power itself is obtained and maintained either by the rich classes and financial magnates, or by the physically mighty, or by the clever political machinators, or lucky adventurers and gang leaders, with a sprinkling of various intellectuals, as the "brain trust" of each of such groups. The justifications used are the sensate services of the rulers to their faction or to the people: the promotion of welfare, prosperity, internal peace, order, happiness, and the other utilitarian and hedonistic values. Almost no trace of Ideationalism and theocracy exists. This is true even in regard to the priests and ministers, who replaced considerably the Gospel of God by "Social Gospel"; the Ideational values by the Sensate ones. This means again that the centuries after the fourteenth show a rise of the secularly Sensate political regime parallel with that of the Sensate culture.

Today we have all the signs of a superripe Sensate political regime and social leadership. In the sociocultural reality, the power belongs either to the rich classes, or to those groups which — no matter how — control the physical forces through which they can rule and coerce society. At the top of the social leadership and aristocracy are "society" — that is, a group of the rich — or the "proletarian" — "the fascist," the "Nazi," the "socialist," the "liberal" factions, sprinkled with the Sensate aristocracy of the previous regimes and various sensate intellectuals. They base their authority upon the possession of the power itself, and do not try to refer to any Ideational reason or value for its sanctification. Again, to keep it, they rely only upon holding the physical power and its substitutes in their control, and try to feed their partisans and followers (at the cost of the others), to eliminate and, if necessary, to exterminate dangerous rivals; to prevent any organization of the rival forces and to disorganize such an organization by any accessible means, from killing, persecuting, imprisoning, banishing, up to bribery, propaganda, machinations, and manipulations of the most diverse character. Anything that hinders their objective is eliminated and brushed aside, without any hesitation, be it religion, be it science, be it art, be it ethics, or law. If they do not suit the objective, they are suppressed, eliminated, prohibited, no matter how great is their value per se. One of the first actions of almost every faction that seizes (obtains) the power is (1) to eliminate all the *laws* that are inconvenient to it (including often the faction's own promises); (2) to prohibit any *religious* or *moral* or *scientific* beliefs, theories, opinions, convictions, that contradict it; (3) to try to create their own "ideologies" — proletarian, fascist, racial, national, socialist, "New Deal type" — which aim to replace the values eliminated; (4) to forcibly teach the youth, in the schools and outside them, mainly — and only — their hurriedly tailored doctrines; (5) to silence all opponents through imposition of penalties, censorship, through depriving them of all the means of communication, from printing press to radio and school and meetings; (6) to seize all the means of communication and to use them exclusively for the propaganda of the governmental doctrine. Then come other, still more "material," means for maintenance of the power: creation of special guards (with their secret police and terroristic "committees," G P U, O G P U, Gestapo, etc.); the strategic disposition of these forces, especially in strategically important places; the physical extermination of opponents; and so on and so forth.

In some countries all this is done openly and without any ceremony; in other countries it is done more mildly, with decorum and decency, and supposedly in accordance with law.   But everywhere the trend is the same.   Law does not bind contemporary governments much if it is inconvenient; if the government's own contract and solemn promise become inconvenient to it, they are broken unhesitatingly, as "a scrap of paper."   (See the preceding chapter.)   If the Supreme Court dares to decide anything in a way unpleasant to the government, the government is ready, even in the United States, to abolish or to "reform" the Court, in the way that suits it.   Likewise neither religion nor morals nor any value — scientific, aesthetic, or cultural — binds the government.   If this or that science or theory does not fit it, it is prohibited, suppressed, or deprived of support, together with its representatives.   On the other hand, any theory, however silly it may be, is elevated to the rank of the eternal truth when it glorifies the government.   The same in regard to art.   Any art value that does not suit the government is also penalized and prohibited; any rotten pseudo-artistic concoction that meets governmental approval is advertised and praised and put above Homer and Shakespeare and Phidias and Beethoven.   And so in any other field, with any other value.   All the values that do not serve the narrowest, immediate, utilitarian purpose of preservation and reinforcement of the power in the hands of the government are neglected and treated most unceremoniously.   We have gone in this respect so far that this is true not only of the Ideational, but even of the general Sensate values themselves.   Their value is narrowed to the smallest utilitarian demand of a given faction at a given moment.   Utilitarianism here is suffocating itself through sacrificing the more general and durable utilitarian values in favor of the narrowest that serve the immediate purpose.   Shall we wonder, therefore, that government and leadership have lost a great deal of their halo and are viewed as a game where one unceremonious faction tries to overcome another, as cynical and unscrupulous — just as in Sensate Hellenistic Greece and Sensate Rome, we observe endless riots, revolts, revolutions; most violent struggles for power among a multitude of factions, with a multitude of unceremonious adventurers trying to grab the power to which they have no right except the physical possibility of getting it through mere force?   "Might again has become right."   The whole matter is but a combat of physical force with physical force, without any Ideational or Idealistic or even decent Sensate reasons and justifications.

The political ideologies reflect, on their part, this reality.   The main ones stress the theory that government and leadership are nothing but a struggle of the classes or factions, where the victorious class or faction exploits the victim and all the subjects. The other current theories represent either a justification of the rule of the rich, or the "proletarians," or the group A or B to which the authors belong. The "ideologists" serve their respective Sensate masters, instead of serving the Ideational or eternal values, as they do in Ideational and Idealistic regimes or in the rising period of the Sensate culture. Hypocrisy, the conscientious lie, cynicism, partiality, factionalism, carelessness about the truth and the lasting values — these are the conspicuous traits of the present-day political ideologies, no matter whether they are communistic, socialistic, fascistic, Nazistic, conservative, liberal, New Deal, or old-deal type. In different degree and proportion, the traits are present in all of them. All claim "open-mindedness," "impartiality," "scientific validity," and, of course, "justice"; and all break these claims on the first pretext. For persons and groups who indeed try to be impartial, the situation is particularly painful. Not identifying themselves with any of these factions, they are not helped by any and, at the same time, are the recipients of blows from all.

Other ideologies are "cynical." They openly admit that their ideologies are but a mere means — "derivations and rationalizations" — to help the respective practices of their creators. Being cynical themselves, the authors of such "ideologies" view similarly all ideologies and ascribe the same cynicism to all, from Satan to Christ, from St. Paul and Augustine to St. Thomas and Hesoid.[19] All the teachings are but the same "derivations" for these authors. Born in the atmosphere of "social sewers," they are incapable of admitting that there is fresh air and that there are "ideologists" and "ideologies" aimed at something quite different from an increase of dividends or income, or the number of mistresses, or any other Sensate value.

Ideologies being "naked," the practices of the masters are also stripped of any decorum.

Rival factions do not make any secret of their preparation of physical force for their support. With a little modification, the Hobbesian motto can be used: faction to faction *lupus est* nowadays. As we have seen in preceding chapters, the compulsory relationships triumph everywhere,

---

[19] Read various contemporary "economic and class-struggle" interpretations of history and politics; various "psychoanalytical" and "debunking" biographies of prominent men; speeches and addresses of statesmen, politicians, reformers, intellectuals. Most of these exhibit this "mentality of social sewers" clearly.

and particularly in this field.   Here again we see the atomization of the values that finally grind them to dust.

It is hardly probable that such a trend and situation can continue forever or even for a long time.   Sooner or later a reaction against this overripe Sensatism in government and leadership is bound to come. The real reaction can be but a swing toward Ideationalism.   Some signs of the revolt against this overripe and cynical regime are already notice-able.   So far as the nineteenth century was the government of the rich (in alliance with Sensate aristocracy) this form of the overripe Sensate regime is already discredited and partly abolished.   Then, especially in the immediate postwar period, came the so-called labor-socialist-radical variety of the Sensate regime.   Within a short number of years it has lost its charm also, and in many countries is already superseded by either the Communist or Fascist or Nazi or other governments.   These still exist, but in their existence, by the inexorable immanent development, they have either undermined themselves and lost any prestige except that of pure physical coercion, or are changing before our eyes, rejecting what they approved yesterday and approving what they rejected a short time ago.   The cycle of the Sensate regime is approaching its end.   One faction after another has been tried : radical and conservative ; one class after another : rich and poor, aristocratic and democratic ; business-labor, peasant-farmer — all have been tried and found wanting.   We may continue for some time to drift in this Sensate current, changing one "sensate horse after another."   And the more we change, the more we shall have to change, until all Sensate groups pass this cycle of "being tried and found wanting."   The final result of this merry-go-round can be but Sensate dust : unrespected, incapable, impotent.   With dust society cannot live for a long time.   If it is going to live, it must begin to restore the sociopolitical values to their real level ; to make them less and less relative, more and more absolute.   Their absolutization will mean a shift toward Ideationalism in some form and to some degree.   In this way, the future may keep in store one more recurrence of a shift from the secular regime to Ideational theocracy.

In the preceding chapters, we found that Ideational culture is con-nected with the familistic form of relationship ; that the religious organ-izations are generally more familistic than many others ; and that the present time is marked by a revival of the compulsory relationships. All this tallies well with the findings of this chapter : that Ideational periods are marked by an Ideational-theocratic regime ; that theocracy is congenial to familism ; that the rise of the secular-Sensate government and leadership proceeds hand in hand with that of the Sensate culture, with its contractual and compulsory relationships; that, finally, the present time is marked also by the coercive variety of the Sensate regime and leadership. The findings thus reinforce one another.[20]

F. So far as the forms of government and leadership have theoretical and practical importance, the forms studied here are at least as important as any distinction of such forms of government as monarchy and republic, autocracy and democracy, and the like, given in most of the treatises on Constitutional Law. As a matter of fact, the forms of government and sociopolitical leadership: Ideational, Mixed (Idealistic), and Sensate, are possibly more important than the others.[21] The difference between monarchy and republic is mostly formal: there have been many monarchies, like the English, which were more "republican" than many autocratic and dictatorial republics. The distinction — monarchy-republic — hardly gives an idea of the inner, intimate nature of the political regime and social leadership that permeates the whole sociopolitical structure, government, law, and morals of society. The forms stressed here give, to a considerable extent, such an idea. When one understands that the sociopolitical regime of a given society is Ideational (or Sensate), from this major premise one can deduce, with a reasonable degree of certainty, a host of the characteristics that should be expected, and are usually contained, in such a regime. One can reasonably expect that the government of such an Ideational regime will be an implicit or explicit theocracy; that the laws will be regarded there as the absolute commandments or tabus of the supersensory power; that in the policy of the government and in the laws, the "supernatural sanctions" will play a considerable part (excommunication, *sacer esto*, deprivation of Christian burial, and the like); that as court evidence, various "supernatural techniques," like the ordeals and the "Judgment of God," will be used;

---

[20] So far here, as in many other points, the study vindicates G. B. Vico's theory of the fluctuation of the three forms of government and leadership: the Sacral, the Heroic, and the Human, corresponding somewhat to our Ideational, Idealistic, and Sensate.

"*L'Età degli Dei* nella quale gli uomini gentili credettero viver sotto divini governi, ed ogni cosa essere lor comandata con gli auspicj e con oracoli . . . l'*Età degli Eroi*, nella quale da per tutto essi regnarono in Republiche Aristocratiche, per una certa da essi riputata differenza di superior natura a quella de' lor plebei; e finalmente l'*Età degli Uomini*, nella quale tutti si riconobbero esser uguali in natura umana; e perció vi si celebrarono prima le Republiche populari, e finalmente le Monarchie, le quali entrambe sono forme di Governi Umani. Vico, *Principj di una Scienza Nuova, Opere* (Milano, 1854), Vol. V, p. 39. See the development of this theory, pp. 44–48 and 465–491.

[21] With perhaps the exception of the forms of government given by Plato and Aristotle. But their "typology" of the main forms is not formal, but intimate, sociopsychological, in the best sense of this term.

that the government and the law will protect many Ideational values having no direct utilitarian or hedonistic value; that in the penal system the principle of "expiation of a sin or crime" will play a conspicuous role; that the system of education, so far as it is controlled by the leaders and the government, will be "theological" to a considerable degree; that some institutions of "oracles," "Pythias," "prophets," "saints and seers," will be a part of the political structure; that the rulers themselves will be closely connected with the performance of sacral duties; that the laws, beginning with the criminal laws, will be of absolutistic nature, with little room left for the principle of "relativity" and "expediency"; that, consequently, the contractual relationships will be little developed in the sociopolitical system of relationships; that the rich as the rich, and the physically powerful groups as such, will have little chance to play a decisive part, at their own value, and can play it only as instruments subordinated to the bearers of the Ideational values; and hundreds of other traits and characteristics that give not only the external and formal silhouettes of the regime but its intimate and inner picture, its living portrait.

The same can be said of the Sensate or Idealistic sociopolitical regime. The validity of these "deductions" has been shown, to a considerable extent, in many previous chapters, particularly those that deal with ethical systems, with the criminal law, with the forms of social relationships. When one reads statements from the lawbooks like the following, one can be sure that they can be expected and found only in a society with a theocratic regime containing a great many of the Ideational elements.

Now therefore hearken, O Israel, unto the statutes and unto the judgments, which I teach you, for to do them, that ye may live, and go in and possess the land which the Lord God of your fathers giveth you. Ye shall not add unto the word which I command, neither shall ye diminish ought from it, that ye may keep the commandments of the Lord your God which I command you.[22]

Or

If a man weave a spell and put a ban upon a man, and has not justified himself, he that wove the spell upon him shall be put to death. . . . If a man has put a spell upon a man . . . he upon whom the spell is laid shall go to the holy river, and the holy river overcome him, he who wove the spell upon him shall take to himself his house. If the holy river makes man to be innocent, and has saved him, he who laid the spell upon him shall be put to death.[23]

[22] Deuteronomy iv. 1 and 2.
[23] *The Oldest Code of Laws in the World* (the Code of Hammurabi), trans. by C. H. W. Johns (Edinburgh, 1903), I. 2.

Or

Içvara created punishment, his son, as the protector of all beings, consisting of the glory of Brahma, criminal law.   From fear of him, all beings, immovable and movable, are fit for enjoyment, and wander not from their law. . . .   He, Punishment, is a royal person;   he is a guide and ruler. . . .   Punishment rules all men;   punishment alone protects them;   punishment is watchful while they sleep;   the wise know the punishment to be justice. . . .   The crow would eat the sacrificial cake, and the dog would likewise lick the offering; there would be no lordship in any one;   and all would be upside down.   The whole world is mastered by punishment;   a pure man is hard to find . . . gods, devils . . . birds, and snakes — even they, ruled by punishment, become fit for enjoyment. . . .   Where dark, red-eyed Punishment, destroying sin, advances, there the people are not confounded, if the leader discerns well.[24]

When properly understood, these and many similar statements are unthinkable and impossible for a Sensate regime and law; but they are in perfect accordance with the Ideational-theocratic regime and law.

This contrast and difference between these regimes comes out in thousands of other forms — in their mentality, in their law, in their mores, in their practice, in their political institutions, in the composition and change of their governments. In brief, here as in other divisions of culture, the categories of Ideational and Sensate political regimes and leadership are the "key principles"; once understood, they make comprehensible, even "predictable," hundreds of details of a given political regime, as soon as its Ideational or Sensate nature is defined. Heuristically, they are the "keys" that open a multitude of inner doors and hidden passages in history.

The above means that here again there is hardly any eternal trend toward a systematic growth of either Sensate or theocratic regimes and leadership in the course of time. Instead, each form grows, reaches its climax, and declines, giving way to the other form, which passes through the same cycle.

G. Neither the religious theory of origin and development of government and law, nor its opposite can be accepted as valid. According to the "religious theory," expounded particularly by such scholars as Sir Henry Maine, the ancient form of law and government was religious.

Quite enough remains of these collections [of ancient law codes] both in the East and in the West, to show that they mingled religious, civil, and merely moral ordinances, without any regard to differences in their essential character; and this is consistent with all we know of early thought from other sources,

24 *The Ordinances of Manu*, VII. 14–25 *et passim.*

the severance of law from morality, and of religion from law, belonging very distinctly to the later stages of mental progress.[25]

There is no system of recorded law which, when it first emerges, is not seen to be entangled with religious ritual and observance.[26]

If the religious theory is consistently developed, it means that the earliest form of law and government was religious or Ideational; that in the course of time both began to separate from this source and became more and more secular; that, therefore, the steady trend of history consists in a movement from the religious-theocratic to the secular-Sensate forms of law and government. Maine makes, though not always consistently, such a claim. A large number of other writers and popularizers take the theory for granted. In their belief, the age of theocracy is over, and "with the progress of mankind" this age, once and forever, is superseded by a government and law based upon the progress of science and intelligence and autonomous morality, independent of any supersensory authority.

Is such a theory acceptable? It is not. Why? Because it is contradicted by the relevant facts. Above, in this chapter, I indicated that the forms of government and leadership among so-called primitive tribes are not the same, some tribes having more theocratic, others more secular forms. Such appears the situation in the light of contemporary knowledge of the culture and social life of the "primitive peoples." [27] There is not a slightest reason to believe that all "primitive peoples" have the same culture, are equally religious or superstitious, equally given to magic, and to control over the supersensory forces believed in. As to the law and the codes of law, the claim is equally unwarranted. A serious investigation of the body of so-called earliest codes shows that many of them, especially the earliest, have little or no marks of a religious origin or religious character.[28] One of the most recent investigators of the problem concludes:

In the least advanced and in the most advanced of the Codes of primitive law there is never any trace of religious or moral rules, but there are Codes of an intermediate stage of legal development in which religious rules are to be

[25] H. S. Maine, *Ancient Law* (London, 1906), p. 14.

[26] H. S. Maine, *Dissertations on Early Law and Custom* (New York, 1886), p. 5.

[27] See the summary in the quoted work of R. Thurnwald. See there other references and literature.

[28] See A. S. Diamond, *Primitive Law* (London and New York, 1935), chaps. vii, viii, *et passim*. This careful study goes to the opposite extreme, claiming that almost none of the known earliest codes has a religious character. This unwarranted claim is partly due to the vagueness and too narrow meaning of "religious" in the work.

found. . . . After this examination of the written law of the past, it will be seen in regard to the unwritten law of the tribes that here, too, there is no evidence to support the theory under discussion, but that all the evidence is opposed to it.[29]

This claim, almost contrary to the "religious theory" of Maine and others, shows its one-sidedness and factual incorrectness.[30] Thus, there is no reason to accept the theory of a historical trend from the sacral (Ideational) to the secular (Sensate) regimes and leaderships. Neither is there any basis to claim the opposite trend in the course of time. The nearest approximation to the reality is the theory that these regimes and forms of leadership fluctuate in time and in space. So much about this point.

Now the question arises: *Why these fluctuations?* The answer is the same that has been given many times — namely the principle of limit, of the immanent self-regulation of sociocultural processes, according to which any concrete cultural form sooner or later wears itself out (not to mention the influence of the factors external to it). More specifically, these regimes are connected with the respective Ideational and Sensate forms of culture. If these fluctuate, the political regime must fluctuate also.

III. Fluctuation of Other Forms of Sociopolitical Organizations and Processes

So far as other forms of the political regime are concerned, such as monarchy and republic; autocracy and democracy; or aristocracy, timocracy, oligarchy, tyranny, and the like, they all trendlessly fluctuate. The still popular belief that with the "progress of culture and civilization" the monarchy is driven out by the republic; autocracy by democracy; leadership of the military, or the rich, or the physically powerful tyrants

---

[29] *Ibid.*, pp. 52-53.

[30] As mentioned, Diamond goes too far in the opposite direction. Even many of the ancient written codes, including the Hittite, Hammurabi, and others, where he does not find any trace of religious nature, have a large amount of it. His error is that, like Maine, he also assumes that all the primitive peoples are identical, in that case, secular in their law and codes; meanwhile, the real situation is different: various primitive peoples are different: some "Religious," some not. See also R. Thurnwald, *Werden, Wandel und Gestaltung des Rechtes* (Berlin and Leipzig, 1934), pp. 16 ff. Here Dr. Thurnwald seems to overstress the universality of the religious character of primitive law (*die religiöse Gebundenheit des primitiven Rechts*). However, he indicates clearly that the law has sacral character only in the matters that concern directly the whole community; in other spheres it does not have it; and he seems to be inclined not to assume that the proportion of the sacral law is the same among the law of all the primitive tribes. See also his review of Diamond's book in the *American Sociological Review* (1936), Vol. I, No. 1, pp. 150-151.

is more and more disappearing, being replaced by the "self-government for the people, by the people, and of the people"; or by the guidance of the highly scientific, highly moral, and highly rational and just groups and persons — all these and a host of similar theories and beliefs, so far as they mean something definite by the terms used, are but *pia desideria* — noble and commendable — and nothing more. The historicosocial reality does not give any support to such claims. Much nearer to the reality are the ancient "cyclical" theories of Plato, Aristotle, Polybius, and many other thinkers of the past, who claimed that the main forms of government just fluctuate and immanently pass into one another without any perpetual trend whatsoever. The only questionable point in these theories, especially of the type of Polybius, is their contention that the sequence of the forms of the political regime is definite and uniform: monarchy, according to Polybius, passing into tyranny; tyranny into aristocracy; aristocracy into oligarchy; oligarchy into democracy; democracy into mob rule; and then the mob rule again into monarchy, and a repetition of the same cycle.[31] However satisfying logically is such a theory, it is at the best but a local and special case, in no way universal.

The same is to be said of other theories claiming a definite and universal succession of forms of a certain cycle: be it the theory of Ibn-Khaldun, that in a political regime the first generation or the founder of a given aristocracy is the best; the second generation "usually keeps something from its glory," the third, "is already a mere imitator," while the fourth "is usually a nullity."[32] Or Campanella's or Botero's or Machiavelli's theories of the fluctuation of forms of government, taken from Aristotle and Polybius mainly and somewhat modified.[33] Or the theories of the type of Ferrero's and K. Mewes's, discussed in Parts Two and Three of this volume. All these theories — in so far as they claim a universal sequence of the order of the change of the forms of government

---

[31] See *The General History of Polybius*, trans. by Hampton (Oxford, 1823), Vol. II, pp. 124–131.

[32] Ibn-Khaldun, "*Prolégomènes historique*," in *Notices et extraits des manuscrits de Bibliothèque Imperial* (Paris, 1862), Vol. XIX, pp. 286 ff.

[33] See N. Machiavelli, *History of Florence* (The Colonial Press, with introd. by C. W. Colby), Bk. V, chap. i, p. 225; Campanella, "Aforismi politici," in *Opere di Tomaso Campanella* (Torino, 1854), Vol. II, pp. 25 ff.; Giovanni Botero, *Della ragion di stato, libri dieci* (Ferrara, 1590), pp. 3–8 and 328–334. Various forms of "cyclical" or erratically fluctuating theories of political and cultural changes have been set forth many times by many thinkers. See, for instance, J. Olorinus, *Ethnographia mundi*, 2d ed. (Magdeburg, 1614); D. Hume, "On the Populousness of Ancient Nations," in *Essays, Literary, Moral, Political* (London, 1870), pp. 222–223. See in one of the last parts of this work chapters devoted to a survey of these theories.

and political regimes, or also the definite periodicity in these changes —
can hardly be accepted.   They fail through the elevation of a special
and local case into a universal rule — the usual mistake of most general-
izers.   In fact, history here shows a great deal of variety, so far as the
sequence is concerned.   In one society or period, the form A is replaced
by B and then D ; in another the form of C is replaced by A and then by
D or M.   No uniform sequence can be claimed for all societies and for
all time.[34]   The only valid claim is that there is no perpetual trend in
the course of time from one form to another ; the forms just fluctuate.

Whether some of these forms are connected with the fluctuation of our
main variables — Ideational and Sensate forms of culture — and then with
the familistic, the contractual, the compulsory forms of social relationships, depends a great deal upon the meaning given to various terms
like monarchy and republic, autocracy and democracy, and the like.
Per se, these terms are very vague and indefinite.   If they are defined
better — if, for instance, the monarchy or aristocracy means the familistic
monarchy and familistic aristocracy — then clearly such regimes can be
found only in a society and culture of predominantly familistic type.
If they mean either the coercive absolute monarchy, and either the
exploitatory or parasitical aristocracy, then obviously such regimes can
exist only in a society and culture with greatly developed compulsory
relationships ; finally, if monarchy and aristocracy mean mainly the
contractual ("constitutional") monarchy and aristocracy, then evidently
such a regime normally can be expected to be developed only in the
society of predominantly contractual type.   The same can be said of
many other terms.   This means that the majority of the most essential
forms of political system are probably connected with the variables of our
types of culture and forms of social relationship.   Where they are not,
the forms are often purely "external" with a content different from the
form ; or are sometimes the "incidental" result of the special configuration of external circumstances.   As such, they are usually short-lived
and as quickly go as quickly come.   A few important forms may be
coming and going independently from our main variables.   But these
forms can hardly be numerous.   Finally, many secondary traits of the
political regime and leadership live their lives without any close connection
with our variables.   Being secondary, they generate and pass through the
play of other factors and forces.   All this will be shown, partly, in the
next part of this work.

[34] In Volume Four the respective theories will be analyzed and criticized, including
A. Weber's, R. McIver's, and other recent theories in the field.

Chapter Six

FLUCTUATION OF IDEATIONAL AND SENSATE LIBERTY

I. IDEATIONAL, MIXED, AND SENSATE LIBERTY

In the discussion of the main forms of social relationships (Chapter One) I indicated that in the familistic relationship the apparent external restraint of the parties (or party) is not a restraint at all, from their standpoint, but, on the contrary, a free realization of their wishes and desires. In the contractual relationships the external freedom of the parties, with their choice of entering or not entering into a contract, gives them a limited liberty, but it rarely is as deep and hearty as that of the familistic relationship. Finally, in the compulsory relationships, one party is deprived of freedom, while the other — the dominant — party seems to possess a sort of liberty to do with the suppressed party what it pleases. These remarks allude to one of the important elements of each form and to the existence of seemingly different qualitative forms of what is called liberty or freedom. But they neither go deep enough nor define precisely enough the elusive phenomenon of "liberty." Therefore they need to be developed more substantially.

In mechanics we read:

When a particle is perfectly free to move in any direction whatever, it can move in three and only in three directions.[1] . . . Like a particle, an unconstrained rigid body can have three possibilities, in the way of independent translation. But in addition to them, "the free rigid body has also three possibilities in the way of rotation, for it may be turned about any one of three rectangular axes. . . . A rigid body has therefore altogether six degrees of freedom, three of translation, and three of rotation; but by means of suitable constraint, the body may be deprived of any number of these six. [For instance, an elevator is deprived of five degrees (it can move in only one direction); a door swinging on its hinges is also robbed of five degrees of its freedom, though they are not the same as in the case of the elevator; a coin lying on the table has only three degrees of freedom: two of translation and one of rotation.] [2]

[1] H. Crew and K. K. Smith, *Mechanics for Students of Physics and Engineering* (New York, 1930), pp. 85 ff.   [2] *Ibid.*, p. 95.

Here we have a perfect "behavioristic" conception of freedom: no psychology, no inner subjective element, is involved in it. Human behaviorists can but envy such a definition.[3]

However, even to the most enthusiastic behaviorists it must be evident that such a "perfectly behavioristic" definition of freedom is inapplicable to a human being. Whether his overt actions are free or not, the decisive criterion is the "subjective" experience of the individual: his wishes, desires, aspirations, wants, and the like. Generally, it can be said that a human being is *free when he can do whatever he pleases, need not do anything he does not wish to do, and does not have to tolerate what he does not want to tolerate. Consequently, his freedom becomes restricted when he cannot do what he would like to do; has to do what he would prefer not to do; and is obliged to tolerate what he would like not to endure.*

The definition introduces a new element nonexistent in the freedom of mechanics, namely, the inner, psychological experience described by the words "whatever he pleases," "would like," "prefers," or "wants" to do or not to do, to tolerate or not to tolerate. Without them, the concept becomes void, because a human being, as long as he lives, and whether he is free or not, would always be either doing or not doing, tolerating or not tolerating something.

Without a knowledge of the individual's desires, and observing his overt activities only, we cannot pass any judgment as to whether or not he is free. A person with a limited set of wishes can feel himself free in the narrow limits of the available possibilities of satisfaction of his needs (an ascetic, a fakir, a good mother tied to her child — in her time and activities). And vice versa, a person with a seemingly wide range of possibilities of satisfaction of his wishes can be quite unfree, if the number, intensity, and character of his desires exceeds the possibility of their gratification.

Hence the formula of freedom of an individual $\dfrac{\text{Sum of Wishes}}{\text{Sum of the available Means or possibilities of their gratification}}$

In a shorter form it will be $\dfrac{\text{SW (wishes)}}{\text{SM (means)}}$

[3] The definition shows also that absolute freedom does not exist, even for a material particle. For such a freedom an absolute isolation is necessary and such an isolation is hardly to be found in the material world. Still less is an absolute material freedom or freedom of absolutely unrestrained action possible for a man as a material body. He is not absolutely isolated from the rest of the material world in which he lives, and ordinarily not from other men. His actions and motives always meet with some resistance or restraint on the part of the other individuals or other organisms or the external cosmic world.

If the total "Sum of Wishes" is greater than the "Sum of Means" of their satisfaction, the individual is not free, and he is the less free the more the numerator exceeds the denominator. If the denominator (SM) is greater than the numerator (SW) or equal to it, the individual is free. Consequently there are two forms of freedom, and two ways to preserve it, or even to increase it: first, the individual may minimize his wishes until they equal or are less than the available means of their gratification; or he may increase the available sum of the means of their satisfaction. The first is the inner Ideational way of being free; the second is the external Sensate way to be free. Thus, quite naturally, and somewhat unexpectedly, we are brought to two different (Ideational and Sensate) kinds of freedom. Both kinds are freedom in their generic trait (with SW not exceeding SM), but each is as different from the other as possible in their *differentia specifica*. One corresponds to our definition of Ideationalism; the other to that of Sensatism. Intermediary forms of freedom, where the SW is kept lower, or not greater, than the SM, partly through control of the wishes, partly through increase of the external means of their satisfaction, would fall into the Mixed type of freedom.

When this is understood, it becomes evident, first, that it is superficial to discuss freedom generally, without specifying the type involved (Ideational, Sensate, or Mixed); second, a usual mistake of all those who, consciously or not, assume there is only one kind of freedom, say, Sensate; and do not see any freedom where the SM is very modest, or the sum of wishes in regard to Sensate values is very limited. All such individuals or groups or cultures are identified by such Sensatists with the "unfree" conditions: slavery, serfdom, and the like.[4] And vice versa; for a partisan of Ideational freedom, the Sensate freedom is but a most foolish imprisonment in the clutches of external material conditions, which rob the individual of every freedom and make him a plaything in the hands of blind material forces. The above formula of freedom permits one to see freedom of both types, providing that in both — Sensate and Ideational — situations the SW does not exceed the SM. The most sensate multimillionaire may be free or not, as he can or cannot gratify his every whim through the vast external means in his possession; and the sternest ascetic, with only bread and water barely sufficient to keep his body and

---

[4] This is the most common mistake of almost all the works on history and the progress of civil and other liberties written in the nineteenth and twentieth (prewar) centuries. Explicitly or implicitly, they imply that liberty appeared in human history only with the "Declaration of the Rights of Man and Citizen," or the like. For their authors, there was hardly any freedom or liberty in the history of the Oriental and other countries, or in medieval Europe.

soul together, is free if his wishes do not go beyond these means, and if his other wishes, including his aspiration for union with God, are satisfied. Finally, a well-balanced man, who does not give free rein to his wishes and who at the same time possesses the means to satisfy a great many of them, may also be free in the condition of Mixed freedom.   In all such cases, the formula, freedom is $\dfrac{SW}{SM}$, where SW does not exceed SM, remains.[5]

II. Fluctuation of Ideational, Mixed, and Sensate Forms of Freedom in Time and Space

One of the great marvels of a number of human beings is their ability to shift from one form of freedom to another, when such a shift is desirable or necessary.   Through such a shift, they remain free, where otherwise they would be deprived of freedom and, as a result, would be miserable and unhappy.   During the last two decades, many a person who had been rich and powerful was thrown into poverty and external dependence upon others.   Not a few of these, deprived of the Sensate freedom which they had previously enjoyed, found, in their enormously reduced circumstances, an "inner" or Ideational freedom and remained in a sense happy and contented.   On the other hand, almost everyone knows persons who had contentedly lived in modest material and social circumstances and then became rich and powerful and climbed the Sensate ladder fast and high. Parallel with their new opportunities they began to expand their wants, and shifted to more extensive Sensate forms of freedom.   Some kept their balance and remained free in their new Mixed or Sensate freedom.   Others expanded their desires faster than their means of satisfaction ; therefore, they felt themselves no more, but less, free than before ; the more they had the more they wanted to have.   These individual cases are familiar enough and the shifts from one form of freedom to another are well known also.   Likewise, the ability of some individuals to make such a shift successfully, and the inability of others to do it, are routine phenomena. On this individual scale, these phenomena of the fluctuations of the forms of freedom in the life history of individuals are the possession of every careful observer.   Less known and less simple are the similar fluctuations that occur in the life history of an integrated culture mentality.   As in other aspects of the culture mentality, such fluctuations do occur in social space, from society to society, and in time from period to period.   Here

[5] Compare J. Maritain, *Freedom in the Modern World* (New York, 1936).

and now Ideational freedom is dominant; there and at another period, the Sensate form was the main one.

Generally, in the predominant Ideational cultures, whether the Brahman, the Taoist, the Buddhist, the medieval Christian, or in the smaller Ideational cultural circles, like the Cynics, the Stoics, the Ascetics, Ideational freedom is the prevalent form, which is possessed, thought of, and aspired to; while in the predominantly Sensate culture, the Sensate form becomes prevalent, is sought for, praised, and paraded. In the Mixed culture mentality, the Mixed or balanced form of freedom tends to become dominant.

Lack of space does not permit me to demonstrate the approximate validity of these propositions through the factual analysis of the historical material and the respective theories and concepts of the leading thinkers of various cultures and various periods. When, however, such a verification is made (it has been made, in fact, by the writer) the proposition is fairly well borne out by the relevant facts. The following general remarks will elucidate the logical and factual connection of the respective forms of culture mentality with their forms of freedom.

(1) That a consistent Ideational mentality stands for the Ideational form of freedom, and a Sensate mentality for the Sensate, is axiomatic and self-evident. One follows from another logically.

(2) That factually, the predominant freedom is Ideational in the Hindu, the Taoist, the Buddhist, the early and medieval Christian, the Stoic, the Cynic, and in many other ascetic and Ideational mentalities, is also evident to everybody who has studied these currents of thought from this standpoint. None of them pleads for a maximum expansion of the sensate wishes; on the contrary, they preach their inhibition. None of them blesses a particular care for material values and external means in order to satisfy sensual needs. If anything, they damn it. All of them talk, preach, plead for, and extol only the inner freedom of soul, the inner "self-sufficiency," freedom in God, in Nirvana, in mystic union with the Absolute, and the like. All of them expose the frailty, the illusiveness, and the foolishness of any other freedom than the Ideational one.

With a slight modification, the subsequent formulas of the Ideational freedom of Epictetus, Marcus Aurelius, and Seneca are shared by all Ideational mentalities.

Seek not that the things which happen should happen as you wish, but wish the things which happen to be as they are, and you will have an even flow of life.[6]

6 Epictetus, *Discourses*, III.

As Zeus dwells within himself and is tranquil by himself . . . so ought we to be able to talk with ourselves, not to feel the want of others also. When a man has this peace, not proclaimed by Caesar (for how should he be able to proclaim it) but by God through reason, is he not content he is alone? . . . No evil can happen to me.   For me there is no robber, no earthquake; everything is full of peace, full of tranquility; every way, every city, every meeting, neighbor, companion is harmless.[7]

Is it not better to use what thou hast, like a free man, than to long, like a slave, for what is not in thy power? [8]

Dig within! Within is the fountain of good; ever dig and it will ever well forth water.[9]

Either [in this universe] God works and then all is well; or, if all is random, be not thou a part of the random.[10]

To vicissitudes caused from without, be imperturbable; in actions whose cause lies with yourself, be just.[11]

Freedom is not gained by satisfying, but by restraining, our desires.[12]

Not only ambition and avarice, but even desire of ease, of quiet, of travel, or of learning, may make us base, and take away our liberty.[13]

Wherever I go, it will be well with me, as it has been here, and on account not of the place, but of the principles which I shall carry with me.   They are all my property, and they will be all I shall need, wherever I may be.[14]

Non qui parum habet, sed qui plus cupid, pauper est.[15]

He is king who fears nothing and longs for nothing.   Everyone may give himself the kingdom of noble thoughts.[16]

He is free who rises above all injuries, and finds all his joys within himself.[17]

In the lofty soul there is always peace.[18]

Very little can satisfy our necessities, but nothing our desires.[19]

Nothing is so honorable as a great soul; but that soul is not great which can be shaken by either fear or grief.[20]

[7] *Ibid.*
[8] Marcus Aurelius, *Meditations*, IX, 40.
[9] *Ibid.*, VII, 59.
[10] *Ibid.*, IX, 28.
[11] *Ibid.*, IX, 31.
[12] Epictetus, *Discourses*, IV, i, 175.
[13] *Ibid.*, IV, iv, 1.
[14] *Ibid.*, IV, vii, 14.
[15] Seneca, *Naturales Quaestiones*, III, pref. to 12.
[16] Seneca, *Thyestes*, 388.
[17] Seneca, *Dialogues*, II, ix, 2.
[18] *Ibid.*, V, vi, 1.
[19] Seneca, *Dialogues*, XII, x, 11.
[20] Seneca, *De clementia*, II, v, 4.

The wise man's joy is woven so well as not to be broken by any accident.[21]

The grandest of empires is to rule one's self.[22]

Who has most? He who desires least.[23]

And so on.[24]

In a similar vein, Christianity extols the same form of inner freedom. So do Hinduism, Taoism, and other Ideational culture mentalities.

The bondage is of the mind; freedom is also of the mind. If thou shouldst say, "I am a free soul, I am the son of God; who can bind me?" free thou shalt be.[25]

This formula of one of the modern Hindu thinkers (1836–1886) is but a variation of the old Hindu philosophy and of any other Ideational mentality. Since the Ideational ethics is, as we have seen, the ethics of absolute principles, it cannot be otherwise.[26]

In the Sensate mentality, the concept of freedom would be and factually is Sensate. For all such mentalities and cultures the Ideational freedom is not freedom at all. At the best it is self-illusion; at the worst an egotistic device for the exploitation and enslavement of the masses and the individuals generally. Such a mentality does not see any value, any utility, any pleasure, any benefit in this inner freedom which it does not have and cannot have. Freedom to their mind is the right and possibility to do whatever one pleases sensately; and the more one expands his wishes and the more he can satisfy them, the greater the freedom.

The Ideational mentality is little interested in political and civil rights and declarations, in various political devices to guarantee the liberty of speech, press, convictions, meetings, and overt actions; in the constitution, in "free government," and the like. For it, in the terminology of Taoism, "the best government is that which governs least"; and "the more mandates and laws are enacted, the more thieves and robbers will there be."[27] Or, "My kingdom is not of this world."

For the Sensate culture mentality, the Sensate freedom, with all these "guarantees," declarations, laws, and constitutions, the slogan "Give me

[21] Seneca, *Epistles*, lxxii, 4.   [22] Seneca, *Epistles*, cxiii, 30.   [23] Seneca, *De Moribus*, 46.

[24] See a good selection of the main moral and social maxims of the Roman Stoics in F. M. Holland's *The Reign of the Stoics* (New York, 1879).

[25] *The Teachings of Sri Ramakrishna* (Calcutta, 1934), No. 516. See also Benoy Kumar Sarkar, *The Might of Man in the Social Philosophy of Ramakrishna and Vivekananda* (Calcutta, 1936), p. 8.

[26] Compare Maritain, *op. cit.*

[27] Lao-tse's *Canon or Reason and Virtue*, 9, in W. S. A. Pott, *Chinese Political Philosophy* (New York, 1925), p. 106.

liberty or give me death," is its heart and soul and "ethos." Sensate relativistic ethics of utilitarianism, hedonism, and eudaemonism also demand such a Sensate freedom. It is but natural that in all Sensate cultures or periods, that form of freedom should be dominant. A concrete case is furnished by the Western culture. Here the Sensate freedom emerged and has grown parallel with the emergence and growth of Sensate culture. The first theories of it, especially in the field of political freedom, appeared in the twelfth and thirteenth centuries. The first laws that were aimed to guarantee the political freedom of the upper classes were made about the same time. The Magna Charta of 1215 is a sample. Similar charters aimed at guaranteeing the political rights and privileges of the upper classes and then of the middle class (*bourgeoisie*) of the "free cities," and the political struggles for "liberties" on the part of these classes and cities date from about the same time, with particularly intensive fights and struggles on the part of the cities at the end of the twelfth and in the thirteenth and fourteenth centuries. These internal disturbances, with all the phraseology extolling freedom and liberty, constitute one of the most important processes in the sociopolitical life of the Western countries during these centuries. (See further Part Three of this volume and the detailed enumeration of them in the appendix to that part.)

Subsequently, with minor setbacks, this growth of Sensate freedom, with its political charters, laws, constitutions, with the accompanying political activities, struggles, uprisings, and so on, continued in Western society. After the nobility and aristocracy, the middle class clamored for this Sensate freedom; the lower classes followed in their footsteps, until, toward the end of the eighteenth century, the process became universal and led to an enormous number of constitutional and statutory provisions, declarations, laws, and charters, all with a view to guaranteeing the liberty of speech, press, religion, associations, meetings, etc. In France, the Declaration of 1789, the law of December 14, 1789, the Constitution of 1791, the Declaration of 1793, the Constitution of 1793 (a temporary reaction resulted from the Constitution of 1799 and the Napoleonic Code of 1810); then the charters of May 17, 1819, of July 18, 1828, those of 1830 and 1835; the Constitution of 1848; then the laws of September 5, 1870, June 30, 1881, March 28, 1907, July 1, 1901, and the laws of 1901, 1903, 1914, and 1916 — to mention the most important enactments — are the objective manifestation of this trend.[28]

[28] See the details in L. Duguit, *Traité de droit constitutionnel* (Paris, 1925), Vol. V; De Nucé de Lamothe, *La liberté de réunion en France* (Toulouse, 1911); G. Jellineck, *Die Erklärung*

In Prussia and Germany, the *Allgemeines Landrecht* of 1794; the Constitution of July 8, 1815; the constitutions of 1848 and 1849 and 1850; the laws of May 7, 1874, December 11, 1899, April 19, 1908; and then the Weimar Constitution of 1919 are similar manifestations.[29]

In Italy, the Statute of 1848 of Sardinia; the law of March 26, 1848; the laws of June 30, 1889, of 1906, and the others are landmarks of the growth of this trend.[30]

A similar movement went on in other Western countries, in some at an earlier time, in others later; in some guaranteeing the greater, in others more modest liberties and "inalienable rights." Before the World War, there was not a single country on the European continent which was not involved in a similar movement toward a regime of Sensate liberty, with its satellites.

This brief sketch demonstrates the correlation of the movement of Sensate freedom with that of Sensate culture. The correlation holds, even for the postwar period. We have seen that the end of the nineteenth and the twentieth century are marked by a "revolt" against the overripe Sensate culture in almost all the other compartments of Western culture. We see the same here. The weakening of this culture is accompanied by a reaction against its Sensate sociopolitical liberties and laws. The Communist regime declared all these a mere "bourgeois prejudice" and abolished them entirely. Fascism, Hitlerism, and other dictatorial governments of the postwar period followed its example. The trend is universal for practically all the Western countries, in this respect. It is quite opposite to the trend that existed before the war. In Italy, besides the Fascist Criminal Code, the laws of July 22, 1923, January 24, 1924, July 10, 1924, January, 1925, December 31, 1925, March 4, 1926, November 26, 1926, January 9, 1927, February 26, 1928, and especially a series of new enactments during the Italo-Abyssinian War, abolished practically all the liberties and "inalienable rights" guaranteed (forever!) by the preceding constitutions and enactments.[31]

A similar trend is seen in Germany. The reaction began there even

---

der Menschen und Burgerrecht (Leipzig, 1895); M. Potulicki, *Le régime de la presse* (Paris, 1929).

[29] See the details in C. Bornhak, *Preussisches Staatsrecht* (Freiburg, 1888), Vol. III; O. Jöhlinger, *Pressfreiheit und Presspolitik*, in the *Handbuch der Politik* (Berlin, 1920), Vol. I; the works of Jellineck and Potulicki, quoted.

[30] See the details in V. Orlando, *Principes de droit public* (Paris, 1902); A. Brunialti, *Il diritto constitutionale é la politica* (Torino, 1900), Vol. II; J. Tombaro, *Diritto costituzionale* (Napoli, 1929).

[31] See J. Tombaro, *op. cit.;* F. L. Ferrari, *Le régime fasciste Italien* (Paris, 1928).

before the Third Reich, under the regime of the Weimar Republic (the laws of May 8, 1920, March 23, 1921, June 21, 1922, March 25, 1930; the decrees of the President of the German Republic of July 23 and September 6, 1920, August 29, 1921, August 10, September 26, November 8, and December 23, 1923; the edict of April 17, 1924, and others). Under the Third Reich, liquidation of the liberties in Germany has gone almost as far as in Italy, and at the present time there remains little of this inheritance from the nineteenth century.

In milder forms, similar changes have been going on in other lands, even in the Anglo-Saxon countries of the classical regime of liberty and liberalism.

The revolt discussed is unquestioned. Its existence demonstrates the association claimed still more convincingly; we observe and feel it directly, from day to day, being its victims or its administrators. It may be a short-time flurry; it may be the beginning of a long-time trend; whatever its duration, the fact of the reaction is certain. We are living, in this field (plus many other fields analyzed in the chapters in Volume Two devoted to the fluctuations of criminal law), in a period of limitation of Sensate freedom and liberty; in the period not of Sensate liberation, but of Sensate curbing of the individual. This does not mean that we are on an ascent to Ideational freedom. Here, as in other compartments of our culture, we are merely in a period of transition. From the shore of Sensate liberty we have departed; but we have not arrived at the Ideational port. As yet it is not even in sight. We are on a stormy sea, tossed aimlessly and roughly hither and thither; handled unceremoniously by the self-appointed, dictatorial "captains of the ship," suffering and stunned, demoralized and benumbed. A few of us perhaps have a glimmering of what is going to be the port of our destination. The majority, including the captains themselves, live from day to day, still permeated by the feelings of Sensate freedom only, but faded and superannuated, and therefore incapable of inspiring the old "Give me liberty or give me death" spirit. Hence all the unattractive characteristics of our times, in this field.

III. Why the Fluctuation of the Sensate and Ideational Forms of Freedom?

Why is either of the main forms of freedom not eternal, or why does not one perpetually grow at the cost of the other? Why their fluctuations? Why not a linear eternal trend? One of the reasons for minor and so to speak "incidental short-time" fluctuations is the external factors which

may reinforce one form of freedom and weaken the other. In Volumes
One and Two I have indicated several times that the periods of great
social calamities seem to reinforce the Epicureanism of despair when the
Sensate culture is rising, and the mysticism of despair when the Ideational culture is arriving. The Epicureanism of despair and the mysticism
of despair are the equivalents for the extreme Sensate and Ideational
freedom. In hundreds of forms, various external circumstances may
help to lead to the decline of one form of freedom and to the rise of the
other. However, the role of the external factors is, in a sense, incidental.
Regardless of any external forces, each form of freedom is bound to rise
and decline eventually, by virtue of its own development. In this development it generates the very forces that prepare its stagnation and decline.
How and why? Suppose we take the Sensate freedom. Let us grant
that it grows. Its growth means an expansion of wishes and an increase
of the means of their satisfaction. In this double process sooner or later
comes a point when something similar to the "law of diminishing returns,"
or to the so-called "Weber-Fechner law" takes place. Expansion of
our wishes is practically limitless. If a given set of needs, say hunger, can
physiologically be easily satisfied and has a narrow limit psychologically,
in the refined form of gluttony, it still does not have any exact limits.
If the old appetites are satisfied, a host of new ones appear, ravenously
waiting for their satisfaction. The more a sensate man has, the more he
desires to have, whether it be riches, popularity, or love experience; or
fame or power or charm; or anything else. Meanwhile, in any given
generation, there are always limits to the increase of the means for satisfying the ever-growing desires. Sooner or later there comes a moment
when the expansion of the wishes outruns the available means for their
satisfaction. In addition to this, sooner or later comes a moment when a
further increase of means begins to give less and less complete satisfaction,
or more and more diminishing returns. In the terminology of Weber-
Fechner's proposition, the satisfaction increases only as a logarithm of
the increase of the means of satisfaction. In both cases a discrepancy
appears between the SW and the SM. The latter begins to be outdis-
tanced more and more by the former. The result is dissatisfaction, a
growing thirst for more and more freedom, which is unquenched. Eventually the dissatisfaction and misery lead to a devaluation of the less and
less satisfying Sensate freedom; its charm fades; its value diminishes;
it becomes little cared for or sought. People are ready to say "good-by"
to it, as a pseudo value or of little account.

Overdevelopment of the Sensate freedom leads to the same result eventually through many other ways.   One of these is its demoralizing, devitalizing, and disintegrating effects upon its partisans as well as upon society as a whole.   The persons with an overdeveloped wish for Sensate freedom are likely to become the Dorian Greys — the oversensual seekers for perverse pleasures that soon debilitate both body and mind ; or erratic seekers for thrills and sensations, no matter what they are or what their results ; or the absolute anarchists, revolutionaries, and scandalmongers who do not want to reckon with or respect any value except their own wish, whim, fancy, or volition ; or the unbalanced and overexcited types ; or, at the other extreme, the ever-bored incarnations of spleen, and the like.   Through their scandals, indecencies, erratic exploits, their bomb throwing and killing for the sake of excitement or curiosity ; and through the actions of robbery, murder, sacrilege, and the like, they ruin themselves and ruin the society of which they are a part.   They become a real danger.   Likewise, when overdone, the positive value of the Sensate freedom itself evaporates.[32]

[32] For instance, the liberty of speech, of the press, of thought, is a great boon. But when it begins to be used for the printing and circulation of all kinds of valueless and indecent stories, purely sexual novels, or artistically rotten and otherwise sensational plays; or for calumny, discrediting, and undermining all the values; or for most irresponsible and socially dangerous fiery propaganda; all kinds of rotten things — then such liberty becomes a social liability rather than an asset.   It is like a gun given into the hands of a child or a moron or an imbecile. Its positive value is nil; its negative value is great.   The results are about the same as those from the gun.   Considering further the vast commercial interests served by printing, circulating, broadcasting, various rotten but scandalously sensational — and successful — plays, novels, movies, pamphlets, magazines, periodicals, newspapers, such a misuse of this boon of liberty usually assumes enormous proportions and becomes a most influential social force. To permit such a socially useless but dangerous force to operate freely means to set free for operation all the disintegrating social forces.   When the overdeveloped Sensate liberty reaches this stage — and we are living in exactly such a stage — one should expect one of two things : either a progress of social demoralization and disintegration, which would express itself in the growth of criminality, riots, revolts, sex scandals, and the like; or a reaction against it, either of a mild or severe form.   From this standpoint it is not incidental that during the last few years such a reaction has occurred in the United States against too indecent movies; once in a while against this or that scandalously sensational (mainly through some sex abnormality) play; or against this or that book.   When I hear and read and am even asked to sign a protest against a "despotic prohibition" of this or that play or movie or political oratory — the protest being in the name of liberty and other sonorous terms — I can but pity the protesters if they are sincere, or be sorry that they are not branded as vicious commercial disintegrators and demoralizers of the social values.   Among all the books and plays and speeches prohibited during the last few years in Massachusetts, I have not seen a single one whose artistic or other positive value amounted to anything.   In most cases, these "sensations" were a commercial exploitation of sex, especially in its pathological and perverse forms.   Why such rotten products have a sensational interest in our times, the preceding parts of this work have explained.   But apart from that, a protest against the prohibition of such things has less moral and social value than the sheet of paper upon which it is written.   If we are going to continue this kind of liberty and this kind of misuse of it,

A society with a considerable proportion of these overfree members cannot exist for a long time, with such lunatics at large. It will either disintegrate, or must take measures to bridle them; bridling them means a limitation, sometimes even an elimination, of the greater part of Sensate liberty. This puts before society the alternative: Sensate freedom eliminated, whether to become unfree in any sense, or try to be free in another form — innerly, through self-control and limitation of desires. This leads to Ideationalism. Hence, the immanent decline of the Sensate freedom and the rise of the Ideational.

In a similar way, the Ideational freedom, pushed too far, unfailingly prepares its own decline. It generates the consequences which sooner or later begin to defeat Ideational freedom itself, and also become socially and even biologically dangerous for society. When such a stage of Ideational freedom is reached, it, in turn, loses its charm, prestige, fascination, holiness, and begins to be replaced more and more by Sensate freedom. Here is one of the methods of this self-destruction of Ideational freedom. In minimizing the wishes, even the carnal wishes, there is a physiological limit, even for ascetics. For the mass of people this limit is much higher. Certain sets of wishes — physiological, psychological, and social — have to be satisfied and cannot be eliminated. Respectively, they have to possess the minimum of means for their satisfaction. If they do not have them, they will try to get them. If they cannot obtain them peacefully, they will try to obtain them by violence. The possible result is riots, disorders, revolts, etc., which place society in a dangerous situation. If they cannot obtain this minimum of means in any way whatever, the people may begin to die out, in the strict sense of the term. The process of depopulation and devitalization is likely to be the result of such conditions. This again puts society in a dangerous situation. It will become extinct, or weakened, or make a shift toward a greater Sensate freedom to save itself from the overstressed and over-developed Ideational ascetic freedom of mortification.

This last point — the social and biological harmfulness of a too greatly overdeveloped Ideational freedom — deserves special comment. It is manifest in the fairly common phenomenon of self-destruction of many Ideational groups, which prefer their Ideational — inner — freedom to life without it. The Russian "old believers" of the seventeenth and eighteenth centuries, who threw themselves into the fire and preferred to die

---

the "protesters" and the "liberty addicts" should not be surprised at its possible restriction or elimination in the future. The boon of liberty is a boon only when the privilege of its use is accompanied by a sense of responsibility.

in this dreadful way, rather than to change some of their religious beliefs under the pressure of the Czar and the Patriarch Nikon, are an example of this.

More important are those more common facts which in various ways show that a too limited Sensate freedom becomes biologically harmful. Here are a few evidences of that.

Pavlov says that there exists a special freedom reflex.

The freedom reflex is one of the most important reflexes, or, if we use a more general term, reactions, of living beings. . . . If the animal were not provided with the reflex of protest against boundaries set to its freedom, the smallest obstacle in its path would interfere with the proper fulfillment of its natural functions. Some animals, as we all know, have this freedom reflex to such a degree that when placed in captivity they refuse all food, sicken and die. [33]

(The dog experimented with by Pavlov starved for a long time before it began to take food, being bound to the cage.)

Whether or not such a reflex exists is unimportant. What is important is that a series of psychologists and physiologists have given evidences that one of the most important factors that cause the new-born baby, and young babies, to fall into a rage and make an audible protest is a severe limitation of the freedom of their movement.

Penology and criminology testify that confinement in a prison cell, even when the food and other conditions are satisfactory, undermines the health of a prisoner and has caused many of them since time immemorial, up to the present day, to attempt to break out of prison and regain their liberty, sometimes at the cost of their lives.[34]

Finally, history seems also to supply a series of evidences that for most of the people and races of the world a minimum of Sensate liberty is a biological necessity, and when it is lacking, the people begin to dwindle biologically and even to die out entirely.

Rivers, in regard to the decline of the Melanesians, says that the main factor in their depopulation is psychological: the loss of interest in life, due to the imposition upon them of many and new restraints (by mission-

[33] I. P. Pavlov, *Conditioned Reflexes*, trans. by G. V. Anrep (Oxford, 1927), p. 12.

[34] The literature is vast. It is to be mentioned that just as among Pavlov's dogs, among human beings the power of this "freedom reflex" is different: in some it is weak, in some strong, whether due to hereditary or acquired differences. Furthermore, like the "savagely free" dog of Pavlov, in whom finally, after a long struggle, the reflex was broken, even the strong reaction of freedom in men can be broken. After that the individual is like a tree which, until it is bent strongly, tends to straighten back, but when it is so bent that it becomes broken, loses its power to regain its "free posture," and withers. Long-applied and cruel measures seemingly can produce such effects, even in a large mass of the population.

aries, European "enlighteners"(?), rulers, traders, etc.) that reduce enormously their habitual Sensate freedom.

Interest in life is the primary factor in the welfare of people. The new diseases and poisons, the innovations in clothing, housing and feeding, are only the immediate causes of mortality. It is the loss of interest in life underlying these more objective causes which gives them potency for evil and allows them to work such ravages upon life and health.[35]

He and many others have shown that most of the declining primitive races (either through high mortality or low birth rate, or both) have been those on which were imposed, to the very core of their lives, prohibition of many of their ways of living and enforcement of many ways which were new to them and which were contradictory to their inclinations and mores. The Melanesians, the Tasmanians, the Polynesians, the Fijians, and other peoples of the Pacific give examples of this process.

The main reason for their decline is hardly the alleged diseases, previously unknown to them and to which they were not immune and which tended to be particularly disastrous to them. Such a theory is contradicted by the fact that among the primitive peoples there are several tribes which are not declining. And these are usually the ones whose lives have been disturbed least by foreign invaders — like the Javanese, whose exploitation was not followed by any deep interference into their lives, mores, and habits, or by a sudden and relentless suppression of the actions and behavior to which they were accustomed.[36] Several other primitive people in similar conditions did not die out.

The rude exploitation is sometimes more healthy than the best-intentioned "reforming," just as letting a person go barefoot is often much better than to force him to wear a pinching, fashionable shoe, which distorts and hurts his foot.

An irreducible minimum of freedom to follow our own path, no matter how mistaken it may be, is as necessary to the health as it is to the happiness of mankind. This minimum doubtless varies as widely as education and experience among individuals and races. The consequences of an attempt, even by entirely wise and unselfish rulers, to uproot all our manifold deficiencies and force on us against our will a better way of life, might be as ruinous as the devastations of a Genghis Khan.[37]

[35] W. H. R. Rivers, "The Psychological Factor," in *Essays on the Depopulation of Melanesia*, edited by him (Cambridge University Press, 1922), pp. 95–96. See there substantiation of this. The theory is a variation of the larger theory that the psychological factors are among the most potent factors of health and vitality.

[36] See a good summary of this and of many relevant facts in Louis Le Fevre's *Liberty and Restraint* (New York, 1931), chaps. i, ii, and iii.   [37] Le Fevre, *op. cit.*, p. 35.

The *virgin-soil* theory is unable to account for the comparative rarity of tuberculosis in tribes [Indian] which have clearly been exposed to infection, as long as they maintained their ancient ways of life, and for the extraordinary variations in mortality between different Indian tribes.[38]

According to Hrdlicka, the tuberculosis mortality among the children in the non-reservation schools is higher than among the children out of them, though to the governmental schools are admitted only the healthiest Indian children and their sanitary and other conditions are better.   The reason is the "depressing effect on the newly arrived child of a radically different environment.   A child taken from a reservation where it has become accustomed to almost unrestricted freedom of will and motion, is subjected to discipline for at least four fifths of its waking hours.[39]

Statistics of the mortality among the British Army during the World War give also instructive data (for 1918).[40]

The enormous mortality of negroes, in the time from capture to the vessel, from the vessel to America, and during the "seasoning" is further evidence of the same point.[41]

When, consequently, the restraint of the bodily needs and wishes and actions becomes too excessive, or lasts for some time, in severe forms, the vitality of the group tends to become impaired.   A series of diseases, including possibly also neuroses, psychoses, and other mental ailments,[42] begins to spread more and more widely.   If the group can help it, it will try, consciously or not, to resist such effects and the excessive restraint. In other words, it will tend to fight the complete lack of freedom or the too severe Ideational freedom which, for the masses, often amounts to the same thing.   If the resistance is successful, the group will shift toward Sensate freedom.   In this way, Ideational freedom will be weakened and Sensate freedom reinforced.   Hence the fluctuation.

[38] *Ibid.*, p. 38. See Ales Hrdlicka, "Tuberculosis among Certain Indian Tribes of the United States," in *Bureau of American Ethnology Bulletin, No. 42* (Washington, 1909), pp. 6–7 and 32.

[39] Hrdlicka, *op. cit.*, p. 32; Le Fevre, *op. cit.*, p. 50.

[40] See Great Britain: Imperial Defence Committee: *History of the Great War. Medical Services: Pathology*, ed. by W. G. Macpherson and others (London, 1923), p. 480; Le Fevre, *op. cit.*, p. 51.

[41] About forty millions perished in the slave trade. See Le Fevre, *op. cit.*, chap. iv.

[42] Le Fevre contends that there exists an association between liberty (he knows only Sensate liberty) and genius: free Athens was more creative than less free Sparta; the growth of freedom in the time of the Renaissance was followed by an overabundance of genius; and so on. "The people who have enjoyed an exceptional degree of freedom are those who have contributed most to the advancement and welfare of man." (*Op. cit.*, p. 206; see chap. vii.) This generalization seems to be overdrawn and remains uncertain, partly because of the subjectivity of what is meant by genius, and especially because it ascribed to liberty the effects which seem to be the resultant of many other factors.

The outlined way is but one of many which immanently generate from the overdeveloped Ideational freedom. Having once appeared, they begin to undermine it and prepare the way for Sensate freedom. Thus each form, when excessive, begins to destroy itself and to pave the way for the other. Hence their fluctuation and the alternation of their domination. Such, in brief, is the answer to the question: "Why the fluctuation of the forms of freedom?"[43]

IV. Transition from One Form of Freedom to the Other, and the Movement of Internal Disturbances: Riots, Revolts, Revolutions

If the above theory of "Why the Fluctuation" be correct, we can expect that the periods of transition from one form of freedom to the other — the periods when a hitherto dominant form is on the eve of decline, and the other form on the eve of ascendance — will be marked by a notable increase of internal disturbances in the respective social system or society. In a society with an overdeveloped Sensate freedom they must increase, on account of the weakening and annulment of all the values that control, restrain, and inhibit its members from the unrestricted following of their own wishes. If many members of a given society follow the maxim: "Everything is permitted that I please, and that I can do," and if they are particularly Sensate personalities, the result is, in a sense, "*Bellum omnium contra omnes*," each person, faction, group, and class trying to procure, by any means whatever, everything for which their sensate wishes clamor. Hence an increase of internal struggles, disorders, anarchy, revolts, riots, and revolutions. One faction will revolt because it is poorer than the other; another, because it does not have as much power and influence as the first faction; the third may revolt because it is excluded from "society" and has not the privilege of making love to and marrying its girls and women (*jus connubii*); the next, because its literary, artistic, or scientific creations are less appreci-

---

[43] In stressing these reasons for the fluctuation, I am not inventing anything new, but only reminding the reader of the old truth, so fundamentally forgotten nowadays, in our fashionable "externalistic explanation" of everything through the factors external to the subject. Plato's theory of the change of the political and social regimes: aristocracy, timocracy, oligarchy, democracy, and tyranny; the Aristotelian theory of the fluctuation of his main sociopolitical regimes: monarchy-tyranny, aristocracy-oligarchy, real democracy-mob rule, are the classical cases of such changes. According to both, each of these regimes generates forces which finally destroy it and lead to another regime. Their theories are theories of the immanent change in this field. In addition, their works give a wonderful amplification and detailization of the brief statements of this paragraph. See Plato, *Republic*, Bks. VIII and IX; Aristotle, *Politics, passim*, and particularly Bks. III, IV, and V.

ated than those of others; the next because it feels itself unfairly treated; and so on. Since there is no other command than "Follow your desire," everything and anything can serve as a pretext for getting what one does not have and what others do have.[44]

In the condition of such an overdeveloped thirst for Sensate freedom those who aim at equality will be ever ready for sedition, if they see those whom they esteem their equals possess more than they do, as well as those also who are not content with equality but aim at superiority; if they think that while they deserve more than, they have only equal with, or less than their inferior.[45]

The same, with respective changes, can be said of the overdevelopment of Ideational freedom, when it is pressed upon the masses. Few ascetics and individuals can go along this path very far — much farther than most scholars think — and be perfectly satisfied with their inner freedom and self-sufficiency, even though they amount, externally, often to a real self-mortification. But the masses of the people are not ascetics or excessive Ideationalists. They just cannot reach the heights of Ideationalism and especially they cannot live for a long time on these "superhuman summits." If they are forced to do so, they begin even to die out biologically. When the Ideational freedom is pressed upon them too strongly, and in too severe form, it amounts to them to a lack of any freedom. Before resigning themselves to their fate, they will try to resist it by all the means in their power. Styling it "tyranny," "despotism," "slavery," and the like, they cannot help but make efforts to free themselves from such intolerable and suffocating conditions. Hence revolts, riots, disorders — especially when the inner enthusiasms and *ethos* of Ideationalism are already spent, when it continues to exist merely by inertia, and mainly in its external form. For some time, in its ascending stage, Ideationalism can inspire and carry on, with its "divine madness," even the masses; for such a period even the sternest forms of Ideational freedom can be shared by the masses, and can keep them restful and quiet, without any attempt to free themselves from this "yoke of slavery." But the divine *élan* of Ideationalism does not last forever, and especially not for the masses. When it weakens and then dies and leaves only its

[44] See here the marvelous statements of Plato concerning the relationship between the "insatiable desire of liberty," the anarchy, and finally the tyranny. The eighth and the ninth books of Plato's *Republic* are as fresh as though written today for an interpretation of what is happening now with freedom as well as for the passage of democracy into tyranny. See also the no less remarkable fifth book of Aristotle's *Politics*.

[45] Aristotle, *Politics* (Everyman's Library ed.), p. 145. Again, Aristotle's theory of change of political regimes is an excellent case of an immanent theory of change.

mummy, Ideational freedom becomes, for the great majority of people, nothing but the lack of freedom. Hence their violent efforts to get rid of it, in the name of liberty.

These considerations explain why, in the decaying period of each of these forms of freedom (and their respective cultures), the curve of internal disturbances should be expected to rise notably. Let us mark this expectation. In Part Three of this volume, devoted to the study of the movement of internal disturbances, we shall see that the expectation is corroborated by the factual data: the tide of internal disturbances indeed rises greatly in the period of the transitions discussed.

V. General Conclusion on Qualitative Fluctuations of Social Relationships

The preceding chapters of this part have depicted the main qualitative forms of social relationships and respectively the main qualitative types of the network of social relationships of the social systems (organized social groups). Likewise, these chapters demonstrated the existence of the qualitative fluctuations of the social systems, so far as these qualitative types are concerned. The transformation of a social system from one of these types into another—for instance, from the contractual to the familistic — implies the transformation of a legion of other less general characteristics of the respective social system — its political regime, its liberty, its social differentiations, the stratification and relationships of the social classes; their hierarchy; the role of the masses; and many other structural and dynamic traits. This general idea has been demonstrated on two problems: the forms of political regime and liberty.

What has been found out about these can be found out about dozens of other important traits of the social systems. Their forms are also dependent upon our main variables: the two main types of culture. These subsidiary characteristics are "correlated" with these variables, not only logically but also causally, to a tangible degree; and they change with them.

The lack of space does not permit these "dozens of other important properties" of the social systems to be analyzed and to be shown that they, like the political regimes and freedom, have also Ideational and Sensate forms, and that each form rises and declines with the rise and decline of the respective culture. But after the foregoing, the thoughtful reader can easily do this by and for himself.

This does not imply that all the properties of a social system (organized group and its network of social relationships) are "functions" of our main variables. On the contrary, many traits seem to appear, grow, and decline, independently of these variables. But many others, besides those mentioned, are associated with the type of culture, and neither in their nature nor in their fluctuations can be properly understood without these variables.

In the next chapter particularly, and in some other subsequent chapters, these last two points will be given further corroboration.

For the present, these chapters may suffice to give an idea of the main qualitative types of social relationships and their fluctuations. Serving as algebraic formulas, they can easily be filled with many concrete arithmetical values — more specific and narrower traits of the social systems, which enter the formula and compose one of its constituent elements. We can turn our attention now to the quantitative aspect of the fluctuation of the network of social relationships and the respective social systems of interaction.

Chapter Seven

FLUCTUATION OF SYSTEMS OF SOCIAL RELATIONSHIPS IN THEIR QUANTITATIVE ASPECTS

("Rarefaction" and "Condensation" of the Network of Organized Social Groups. Their Oscillations between Totalitarianism and the *Laissez Faire*. Expansion and Contraction of Government Control and Regulation. Migration of Social Relationships.)

I. PRELIMINARIES

In the preceding chapters the systems of social relationships have been dealt with almost exclusively from the qualitative standpoint. In this chapter attention is concentrated on the types of systems of social relationships (the network of organized groups) and their changes, viewed from the quantitative standpoint. By this is meant the *number of social relationships that serve as the "fibers" of any given network*. In Chapter One it was pointed out that the *extensity* of interaction ranges from one hundred, or unlimited totalitarian, embracing all relationships between the parties, up to the most narrow, limited single link. In other terms, this means that the number of social relationships that compose the "fibers" in a system's network may range from the unlimited to one. If a given social system embraces all the relationships of its members, regulates their entire behavior and all their interrelations, the extensity of the social system is unlimited, or *totalitarian*. The number of social relationships involved in such a system is enormous. The network itself is thick and dense with its "wires." Almost any step of its member affects it and brings it into action. If its network is composed of only one social relationship (say, the co-operative activity of collectors of Nicaraguan stamps), the extensity of the network, or the number of the relationships that compose it, is only one. The "Association of the Collectors of the Nicaraguan Stamps" is a social system (group) that regulates only one relationship out of hundreds in the existence of its members. It covers such a small portion of their life and relationships that it amounts almost to the absolute *laissez-faire* system. The members can do anything, except co-operate in the collection of the stamps, without touching the network and its wires and bringing it into action.   Viewed from this standpoint, the social systems range from those of only one relationship, or two, or three, up to those whose network is made up of thousands and tens of thousands of relationships.   Other conditions being equal, the first type of social system influences, controls, and regulates very little the behavior and interrelationships of its members ;   the second, an enormous slice of them.   This gives a preliminary idea of what is meant by the *quantitative* aspect of the social system of interaction, by the *number* of social relationships that compose the network of a group, and by the fluctuation of the *number* of the relationships in social systems.

Let us consider now the series of processes that recur in an organized social group in this quantitative aspect of their network of social relationships.

Even the ordinary man talks now of the increase of governmental control and regimentation in the postwar period.   Intelligentsia use the term "totalitarian" to denote the Hitlerite, the Communist, the Fascist, and other state systems with an enormous expansion of governmental control and regimentation.   Some are much worried about this contemporary expansion.   Others welcome it, particularly the partisans of these governments.   Most of the worried as well as of the welcoming groups assure us that such an expansion of government regimentation is a novelty of history and is happening for the first time.   This is where they greatly err.   Leaving the worries and cheers to the respective parties, one can say that the contemporary expansion of governmental regimentation is an old, old story : in various state groups it has occurred many times in the past, is occurring now, and will probably occur in the future. More than that : *the fluctuation of an increase and expansion of the " magnitude" of governmental regulation and its decrease and contraction is a process common to all organized groups in the process of their life history.*   The regulatory functions of government in any organized group do not remain constant in the course of time ; but fluctuate, now expanding into greater numbers of relationships,[1] now contracting.   This is true of the family, of the religious group ; the occupational union, political party, business corporation, and various educational, scientific, artistic, and other organizations.   If they exist for any length of time, the regulatory and regimental functions of their respective governments (head, committee, bureau, chief, president, board of trustees, of directors, and what not) fluctuate, in some cases sharply, in others slightly.   As an example, take the

[1] Here we are interested only in the *number* of relationships controlled, but not in the *intensity* of the measures of control.

American family from this standpoint. The contemporary American family, compared with what it was some thirty or forty years ago, has lost many of its economic functions (preparation of various foods; laundry; sewing; and others; these are now taken over by the nonfamily agencies); of its educational functions (nursery schools, kindergarten, first-grade school, and others); nonfamily agencies have taken control of most of these, as well as its religious, recreational, protective, and other activities.[2] Since these functions were performed before by the family, the family and its government regulated them in the past. Since they are now considerably curtailed, the controlling and regimental functions of the family and of its government are curtailed also. In other terms, this fluctuation of the controlling and regulatory functions of a social group and its government means *"rarefaction" and "condensation" of its network of social relationships.* An increase of the number of the functions of an organized group means an increase of the "fibers" of social relationships in its network. It signifies an inclusion of many relationships that hitherto were not among its fibers and, therefore, were not discharged by the group and not controlled by its government. When the new relationships are included in the network of the group, as its "wires," the group and its government must naturally control and regulate them. Consequently, the controlling and regulatory functions of the government of the group expand and increase. And vice versa. When, as in the case of the contemporary American family, several functions or relationships hitherto included in the network of social relationships of a given group are now excluded from its network, and cease to be its concern, the regulatory and controlling functions of its government decrease and shrink in extensity; the network itself becomes thinner, or more rarefied, the number of "wire" relationships in it decreases. In other words, *the rarefaction of the network of social relationships of a given organized group; the contraction and decrease of its functions; and the decrease and shrinking of the extensity of regulative functions of its government — these three processes are three different aspects of the same process of "rarefaction" of the network of social relationships of a given social system (organized group). Likewise, condensation of the network of social relationships of a given social system through inclusion of many relationships which hitherto were not its "fibers," an increase of the number of its functions, and an expansion of its government's control are again three aspects of one process of "condensation" of its network of social relationships.*

[2] W. F. Ogburn, "Decline of the American Family," in *New York Times Magazine*, February 17, 1929.

As mentioned, every organized social group undergoes this process. Its network is experiencing almost all the time now inclusion of social relationships that before were outside it; now exclusion from its "wires" of some relationships that hitherto were its part; respectively, the functions of the social group increase or decrease in their *number* while its government's control and interference expand or contract in their extensity. The theoretical limits between which the process fluctuates are the absolute *totalitarianism*, where a given group and its government control and regulate all the behavior of its members, leaving nothing to their choice or to the regulation of other groups, and the absolute *laissez faire*, where the group does not regulate anything and its government's regulatory functions are at zero. Such a situation — an ideal anarchy — means practically the nonexistence of the group as well as of its government, while absolute totalitarianism of a group means that all its members belong only to that group and to none other and that this group absorbs and controls them completely, in all their relationships and behavior.

In actual reality there has hardly ever been a social group either of the absolutely totalitarian or absolutely *laissez-faire* type. But some of the real social groups in their system of social relationships have been nearer to the totalitarian, while some others have favored the "liberal" or "anarchistic" type. The same is true of the same group at different periods of its existence. At one period its network of social relationships swings toward the totalitarian pole, and the regulatory and regimental functions of its government increase and expand. At another period many "fibers" of its network drop from it; it swings toward the "rarefied" — liberal — anarchistic type, and its government's control and regulation decrease and contract in their extensity; its members now are given by the group government "liberty" and "choice" to manage the dropped relationships as they please (or their regulation is shifted to the government of different social groups, from the State to the Church; from the Church to the school; and so on).

This "swinging" between "totalitarianism" and the *laissez faire* may be styled as *the fluctuation of the quantitative aspect of the network of social relationships*.

This fluctuation is one of the processes that goes on *urbi et orbi* in the life history of any organized group. It has an important theoretical and practical significance.[3]

[3] To an intelligent reader it must be clear that the problems of "capitalism," "liberalism," "totalitarianism," "state socialism," "communism," and many others are in their essentials

Subsequently, we shall attempt to answer the following problems in this field, limiting our study to the state group (for the sake of brevity) : (1) Has this quantitative fluctuation occurred in the history of the Western (and partly Graeco-Roman) state? (2) Which periods have been the periods of rarefaction and condensation of the network of social relationships and respectively of contraction and expansion of the governmental control in the state system? (3) What is the situation at the present moment in this respect? (4) What relationship has this fluctuation to that of the main types of culture and of social relationships? (5) What are its bearings upon the liberty of the individual? (6) What, if any, are the other special factors (*ratio sive causa*) that facilitate either the expansion or contraction of the governmental "regimentation" in the state system? (7) In which way does the "rarefaction" or "condensation" of the network of the state system affect the networks of other than the state social groups or systems? (8) Do social relations migrate from group to group?

II. Rhythm of Rarefaction and Condensation of the Network of the State System

A. *Long-time Waves.* That some of the state systems have been nearer to the totalitarian type than others and that the totalitarian type is not a novelty of modern times but has occurred many times in the past is beyond doubt. Totalitarian were the state systems of ancient Egypt, especially in some periods like the Ptolemaic Egypt ; the state system of

a variety of this problem: the quantitative (plus qualitative) character of the network of social relationships of a given social system. When socialist, communist, fascist, Hitlerite, and other totalitarianists clamor for their system, they strive to replace the more "rarefied" and "liberal" social state system with the most "condensed" totalitarian system, where all the economic relationships have to be included in the state system of relationship and controlled by the government; so with all the education; all the beliefs; all the recreations; all the activities and relationships of the members of the "totalitarian state system." The partisans of capitalism and rugged individualism fight, on the contrary, for a state system from which the economic and many other relationships would be excluded : these respectively would be left to the "free choice" of the individual or, with his consent, would be controlled by social groups other than the state (the business corporation, the labor union, the Church, the free associations). This understood, one can but wonder at the thoughtlessness and superficiality of an enormous literature on socialism, communism, capitalism, syndicalism, liberalism, totalitarianism, and other related subjects. The majority of the writers rarely even mention the central point of the problem discussed, and talk on all kinds of irrelevant (but emotionally gratifying) points except the main ones. Only in a few old and contemporary works is the real issue recognized and properly analyzed. Even with these works, the problem of the quantitative-qualitative fluctuation of the networks of social relationships of various social systems, beginning with the State, has been remarkably little studied and its adequate investigation waits the attention of a group of first-class scholars.

ancient Peru, under the Incas; that of ancient Mexico; of ancient China especially in periods like that under the leadership of Wang-an-Shi, in the eleventh century; that of Japan under the Tokugava shogunate; the state network of relationships of Ancient Sparta, Lipara, and some other Greek states; of ancient Rome, especially after Diocletian; of ancient Byzantium; the State of the Taborites, in Bohemia of the fifteenth century; several state systems of ancient India; that of ancient Persia; then many short-lived state systems in revolutionary periods in the Islamic Empire (during the revolutions of Haradgits, Alides, Karmats, Ishmaelites, Kopts, Babekists, Vakhabits), the Persian Empire (during the Mazdakist Revolution, and those under Kobad and Hormuz III); in the European Middle Ages (in Münzer and Mulhausen). These and several other state systems were as "totalitarian" as the contemporary Communist, Fascist, Hitlerite state systems.[4] Likewise among some of the primitive tribes their state system is also "totalitarian," while in some tribes it is nearer to the *laissez-faire* type.[5]

[4] Of the enormous literature the following works give the necessary minimum of facts: Aristotle, *Politics;* M. I. Rostovtzeff, *The Social and Economic History of the Roman Empire* (Oxford, 1926), chaps. ix-x; Rostovtzeff, "Ptolemaic Egypt," in the *Cambridge Ancient History* (Cambridge, 1924), Vol. VII; J. H. Breasted, "The Foundation and Expansion of the Egyptian Empire," in *Cambridge Ancient History*, Vol. II; A. Erman, *Egypten und Egyptische Leben im Altertum* (Tübingen, 1923); R. Pöhlmann, *Geschichte der sozialen Frage und Sozialismus in der antiken Welt* (München, 1912), 2d ed.; J. P. Waltzing, *Étude historique sur les corporations professionelles chez les Romains* (Louvain, 1896), Vol. II, pp. 480 ff.; P. Vinogradoff, "Social and Economic Conditions of the Roman Empire in the Fourth Century," in *Cambridge Mediaeval History* (1911), Vol. I; L. Brentano, "Die Byzantinische Volkswirtschaft," in *Schmollers Jahrbuch*, Vol. XLI (1917); J. Brissand, *Le régime de la terre dans la société étatiste de Bas-Empire* (Paris, 1927); C. Diehl, *Byzance, grandeur et décadence* (Paris, 1928); A. A. Vasilieff, *Histoire de l'Empire byzantin* (Paris, 1932); P. A. Means, *Ancient Civilizations of the Andes* (New York, 1931); L. Baudin's paper on Agrarian Communities in pre-Columbian Peru, in *Revue d'histoire économique et sociale* (1927), No. 3. (Important fragments of this and Waltzing's, and Rostovtzeff's works are translated and published in Sorokin, Zimmerman, and Galpin's *Systematic Source Book in Rural Sociology* (Minneapolis, 1930), Vol. I, pp. 599–609); M. P. Lee, *Economic History of China* (New York, 1921); Ivanoff, *Wang-an-Shi* (St. Petersburg, 1909); R. Grousset, *Histoire de l'Asie* (Paris, 1922), Vol. II, pp. 325 ff.; M. Granet, *Chinese Civilization* (London, 1930); Chen Huan Chang, *The Economic Principles of Confucius* (New York, 1911), Vol. II, pp. 497 ff.; De la Mazallière, *Le Japon* (Paris, 1907), Vol. II, pp. 389 ff.; T. Ono, *Peasant Movements in the Period of Tokugawa* (1927); E. Denis, *Huss et la guerre des Hussites* (Paris, 1878); K. Kautsky, *Vorläufer des neueren Socialismus* (Stuttgart, 1909), 2 vols.; Sir John Malcolm, *History of Persia* (London, 1815), 2 vols.; T. Arnold, *The Caliphate* (Oxford, 1924); M. Hartmann, *Die islamische Verfassung und Verwaltung* (Leipzig, 1911); V. Pareto, *Les systèmes socialistes* (Paris, 1902–1903); H. Spencer, *Principles of Sociology* (New York, 1910), Vol. II, §§ 547–582. In these works further bibliographies are to be found.

[5] See the summarized cases in Spencer, *op. cit.*, Vol. II, §§ 547–582. See also R. Thurnwald, *Die Menschliche Gesellschaft* (Berlin and Leipzig, 1935), Vol. IV, quoted; R. H. Lowie, *Primitive Society* (New York, 1920).

In the above totalitarian state systems the government control and regimentation was exceedingly large; it embraced the greater part of the lives of the subjects. The government managed almost the whole economic life: production, distribution, consumption; it controlled the family and the marriage relationships; the religious, educational, recreational, military, and other activities and relationships. The situation was factually not very different in all the essentials (except the phraseology) from that in the contemporary totalitarian state systems of Soviet Russia, Fascist Italy, or Nazi Germany. All the patterns in all the essential fields of their behavior and relationship were prescribed for the citizens or the subjects. What kind of occupation an individual may enter; what, where, and when to work; where to live; what to eat, to wear, to use; what to believe; what rank or position to hold; what to think and to say; what to approve or disapprove; what to learn; whether to marry or not, and if to marry, whom, where, and at what age; how many children to have; which of these children to allow to live and which to expose to death. Briefly, the network of the state system was so closely woven that an individual could hardly take any step without touching it and bringing it into action. From an *external* standpoint his liberty was almost nonexistent; he was a kind of puppet pulled by the government; and the government was a kind of central "power station" from which came all the "motor power" that moved the subjects. Viewed in this light, these systems were the realization of the ideal of contemporary socialists, communists, and other "totalitarians" of our times. For this reason any claim that the contemporary totalitarianism is something quite new in human history is utterly wrong: if anything, the past was more totalitarian than the Western state systems of the nineteenth century.

Thus the state systems of different but synchronously existing state groups differ from one another in this respect.

If we compare the state system of the *same state* at various periods of its existence, we can easily see that it fluctuates between totalitarianism and *laissez faire* in the course of time. In these fluctuations two kinds of "swings" are noticeable: long-time and short-time spasmodic fluctuations. The first proceed slowly and gradually and extend over a long period of time; the second come suddenly and quickly go. Let us take, in the first place, the long-time swings in the history of the Roman and the Western states, and note, at least, the most conspicuous moments of the comparative "totalitarianism" and *laissez faire* in their existence. Then we can briefly take the short-time fluctuations.

In the history of the Roman state system, at least one period of an enormous long-time swing toward "totalitarianism" stands out, namely, the period beginning with the end of the third century A.D., and especially with the time of Diocletian. Besides the short-time squalls there were probably other long-time waves of expansion and contraction of government regulation, of "condensation" and "rarefaction," but possibly none of them reached the degree of totalitarianism of the period mentioned. The marks of this extraordinarily developed totalitarianism are (1) The Government becomes absolute: *Princeps legibus solutus est. Quod principi placuit — legis habet vigorem.* The emperor becomes a deity above the law; (2) complete centralization and all-embracing control by the state government of the population, in all its activities and relationships; (3) the centralized all-embracing planned economy of the State, which is now the exclusive and the main business corporation; (4) almost complete annihilation of private business and commerce; (5) complete loss of external freedom and self-government by the population; (6) degeneration of the money economy and replacement of money by "the natural" commodities and services: introduction of the "natural economy," ration system, with usual "ration cards" (*tesserae*); different rations given to different groups and strata of the population; (7) enormously increased army of the state officials and bureaucrats. Here we have on a large scale a well-developed state-socialist or totalitarian system. For those who know indeed the real character of the Soviet system in the period 1918–1922, its striking similarity — nay, identity — with the totalitarian system of Diocletian and the later Roman Empire needs no further evidence. Here is an abbreviated picture of the Roman state system of the period discussed.

All are regimented and controlled. For this purpose an enormous army of state officials is created. It robs and steals and aggravates the situation still more. The State needs gigantic financial means [to maintain the court, to feed the mob, army, officials, and to carry on wars]. . . . The work of the population and labor unions which before was free [unregimented by the State] now becomes regimented and hereditary. The *corporati* and *Collegiati* [the members of the governmentalized labor and occupational unions] now belong to the government, with all their possessions. The State that took upon itself the satisfaction of all needs — public and private — finally comes to the necessity of a complete regimentation of even private labor. . . . The empire is transformed into a huge factory where, under the supervision of the state officials, the population works for the emperor, the State, and private persons. Almost all industry is managed by the State. The State also distributes —

very unequally — the produce. The members of the trade and labor unions are not free persons any more, that work freely for maintenance of their families; they are now the slaves of the State, that are supported, like the officials, by the State, but very poorly and inadequately. . . . Never was an administration as cruel and quarrelsome with the population, and as inefficient and unproductive for the country. The regime was based upon compulsion: everywhere the hand of the State; its tyranny. Everywhere coercion recruits and holds the workers. Nowhere do private initiative and free labor exist.[6]

These lines give a most vivid idea of the situation. In this totalitarian form the Western Roman Empire dragged out its existence during the fourth and the fifth centuries until its fall. Likewise, in the Byzantine Empire the governmental regimentation was conspicuously high throughout its existence, rising still higher at some periods.

When the Merovingian and the Carolingian empires emerge, they start with a very considerable amount of governmental regulation and with a considerably "condensed" state system of social relationships. Nevertheless, it was far less totalitarian than the described Roman Empire. Then, with the development of feudalism, the medieval feudal State experiences an enormous "rarefaction" of its network and, respectively, an enormous decline of the regulatory, regimental, and controlling functions of its government. It is a clear case of dropping an enormous number of relationships from the state network and of the shrinking of state government interference. These dropped functions were taken over by other organizations.

Then, with the decline of feudalism and with the emergence of the so-called national state, the state system began again to "swell" and include an increasing number of social relationships. The process reached its culmination in the period of so-called "*Polizei-Staat*" or the absolutistic State of the seventeenth and eighteenth centuries. The state system of Louis XIV or Frederick the Great, or Maria Teresa and Joseph is the same system, with an enormous number of relationships included and quite compact with "relationship wires"; its government is absolutistic; its controlling and regimental functions are enormously expanded and concern almost all the important fields of the behavior of its subjects and their relationships: economic, religious, moral, educational, recreational, and so on. The swing toward totalitarianism was another long-time wave that in its rise and decline lasted about four centuries.

By the end of the eighteenth century it had spent itself, and its place was taken by the opposite swing toward *laissez faire* and liberalism and

---

[6] Waltzing, *op. cit.*, Vol. II, pp. 482-484. See the mentioned works of Rostovtzeff.

"individualism" and "contractualism." They reached high tide in the nineteenth century. Many relationships, such as liberty of speech, religion, the press, meetings, unionization, education, marriage (to a considerable degree); most of the economic activities, generally many relationships in "the pursuit of happiness and liberty" were dropped from the state network and left either to the free choice and contract of the individuals or were shifted to the networks of other social groups. The net result was, especially up to the last quarter of the nineteenth century, a conspicuous "rarefaction" of the state system of relationships, limitation of the government's power, control, and interference. The period was marked by the growth respectively of "democracy," "self-government," "liberty," "liberalism," "constitutional government," "contractual relationships," "rugged individualism," "private property," "private business," "private initiative," "equality of opportunity," "free associations," and other marks of the rarefied state system of relationships and of the limited amount of its regimental and regulatory functions. In the political and economic ideologies its reflections were the physiocratic, the free-trade, the liberal theories and philosophies.

With the end of the nineteenth century the signs of reaction against this comparatively *laissez-faire* state appeared and manifested themselves in the growing state regulation of labor, industry, business, and then of several other fields (a great number of measures aimed at the protection of child labor, the minimum wage, social insurance against sickness, old age, and the like; the regulation of commerce; interference into the relationship of the employer and employees; development of the state education system and compulsory laws concerning it; universal and obligatory military duty; interference in the family relationships; obligatory registration and regulation of marriages, births, divorces; an enormous number of measures concerning the public health and sanitation; and so on and so forth). Respectively governmental control and regulation started to expand again; at the beginning very slowly and gradually.[7] With the World War, they made at once a tremendous jump; they soared into the stratosphere — due to the war factor (see further in this chapter). After its termination, in some countries in some fields, they slightly declined, but for a short time only. Soon they resumed their upward movement. At the present moment we are living in an age of an enormous swing toward state totalitarianism. The trend is common to practically all the Western (and also to some of the Eastern) countries. In some

---

[7] Even in the United States, before the depression of 1929 and the New Deal, the trend was manifest. See *Recent Social Trends* (New York, 1933), chaps. xxv and xxix.

states, like Soviet Russia, Fascist Italy, Nazi Germany, the state totalitarianism has soared to "unbelievable" heights; in the United States of
America, England, and a few other countries, it has grown also, though
not to the same high level.

Its concrete forms and degrees vary from country to country; the
trend itself is under way in all the Western countries. Here it takes the
Soviet-Communist form; there, the Fascist; elsewhere the Hitlerite or
New Deal form; in other countries the Pilsudsky-Horty-MacDonald-
Baldwin-Blum forms. Whether we like it or not, we are living in an age
of a sharp rise of "totalitarianism," of an enormous condensation of the
Western state systems; of absolutization of the state power; and of an
increasing interference of the state government in all affairs and matters
which should and should not be its business.[8]

This brief outline gives an idea of at least the most conspicuous "highs
and lows" of the totalitarian and the *laissez-faire* swings, the condensation and rarefaction, expansion and contraction, of the Western state
system and its government, from the Merovingian-Carolingian times to
A.D. 1937.

There is hardly any doubt that other state systems that existed for
centuries experienced somewhat similar swings in their life history, as, for
instance, the Chinese, Japanese, many Arabian caliphates, Ancient Egypt,
several Hindu states, and some others.

The practical conclusion of this is that there is hardly any perpetual
tendency in state history either toward bigger and better "totalitarianism" or toward the *laissez faire*. Neither the partisans of the totalitarian
State — Socialist, Communist, Hitlerite, Fascist (the ideologists' absolutistic state, with its all-perfect bureaucratic guardian angels) nor the
partisans of the absolute *laissez faire* or its diluted forms — anarchists,
complete individualists (of the Stirner and Nietzsche type), liberal human

[8] The trend depends little upon the personality of the head of the government. In Russia
it was started by the Czarist Government in 1915, continued by the Kerensky liberal regime,
and pushed to its limit by the Communist Government, which now shows signs of some
recession from its previous extreme position. In the United States, the trend made a
jump under the regime of such a great partisan of individualism and self-government as
President Hoover (after 1929); and has been continued by the regime of President Roosevelt.
These cases are similar to that of Turgot, who in 1774 abolished many forms of state regulation
of trade and business; in 1775 he had to reinstrte most of them and add a few other regi-
mentations. The basic trends of sociohistorical processes depend little upon persons; only
the concrete forms and the degrees which the trend assumes seem to depend upon individuals
and leaders. In one country the trend assumes the Communist, in another, the Hitlerite
form; in one case it is pushed beyond any common sense; in another, within inevitable and
reasonable limits.

itarians, liberal democrats, with their "government of the people, by the people, and for the people," but not too much of it — none of these are supported by the sociohistorical reality in their contention that history steadily leads toward their favorite ideal.   Here, as in most other fields, history fluctuates, now giving the upper hand to the totalitarian, now to the antitotalitarian swing.   Partisans of the contemporary totalitarianism may cheer up : they are living in its rising tide ; partisans of the antitotalitarian state system may also console themselves : today belongs to their opponents, tomorrow will belong to their proponents.   This tomorrow may not come within their span of life ; but it will come, sooner or later.

What has been said of the long-time waves in this field of the state system can be said, with proper modifications, about any long-existing, organized, social system of relationship : the family, the Church, the guild, the trade union, the political party, and other organized groups.   All of them experienced the pulsation of "rarefaction" and "condensation" of their networks ; of the expansion and contraction of control of their governments.   This "rhythm" is an immanent trait of all the long-living organized systems of social interaction.

Now for the short-time fluctuations in this field.

B. *Short-time Squalls and Ripples.*   Their existence is evident. Each time a state declares either martial law or a state of siege ; each time it introduces dictatorship, in the Roman sense of this term ; each time, as we shall see, when its government suddenly expands its interference and begins to regulate and regiment relationships hitherto free from state control — in all these and many other cases (to be spoken of further) when the government's regulation and control expands, many social relationships at once are included in the state system of relationships.   As a result, the network of the state system becomes suddenly closer and the number of "wires" in it increases.

Similar short-time fluctuations occur practically in all organized groups or social systems, whether of the family, the religious group, or any other organized association.   As we shall see, such sudden short-time "convulsions" are, as a rule, the result of some sudden "emergency."

III. REASONS AND FACTORS OF THE LONG-TIME FLUCTUATIONS

As far as Ideational and Sensate cultures are concerned, logically no direct or very close relationship between these and the expansion or contraction of the state government interference is evident, with the following exceptions.

A. The ascetically Ideational culture (and its respective society) cares little for the State and its government; therefore, unless such a society becomes a prey to foreign invaders (as it does usually), no particularly "condensed" state system and totalitarian government should be expected in such a culture, society, or period.

B. The actively Ideational culture and society is likely to create a strong social body and a strong government. The body, however, is likely to be a religious organization, rather than the State, and the government accordingly would be that of the religious order rather than of the State. If the body in such a society happens to be the State, such a state and its government can be only the extreme theocracy discussed above in Chapter Five.

C. Therefore, the totalitarian (and secular) state with an omnimanaging government logically belongs mainly to the Sensate culture and society. Only in the Sensate societies and periods should it be expected to flourish; to rise with the rise of the Sensate culture and decline with its decline. Here, however, two main variants may be expected, according to the phase and variety of the Sensate culture: one, of the vigorous, compulsory type of the absolutistic state and government; the other, in the periods of overripe Sensate culture, of the soft, contractual type, with a considerable prestige and interference, but limited by Constitutions and "Declarations of the Rights of Man and Citizen."

Such seem to be the possibilities that logically should be expected. Are the expectations sustained by the data of history? Not perfectly (for the reasons indicated further), but to a tangible extent Here are a few broad classes of facts that seem to corroborate that.

(1) The predominantly Ideational Hindu culture rarely created for itself a powerful state, and the State has played in its life history a comparatively secondary role. The main role belonged to the Brahman caste, the caste of priests without church organization; teachers without state educational institutions; moral and social leaders without wealth, army, and support of state organization. India has known, of course, many states, and some of them, like the Maurya Empire, were very powerful. But these states were either theocratic or mostly organized by foreign invaders, or, in a few cases, by the Sensate groups and in comparatively Sensate periods. As such they remained social organizations foreign to the population, like the present British rule; they did not penetrate the heart and soul of India, and have always been something existing on the surface of its culture rather than as its organic and inner element. C. Bouglé well sums up the situation, stating:

In India there is no embryo of the State. The very idea of the state public power is entirely foreign to India. . . . All the state governments whatsoever seem to remain only on the surface of the Hindu world. . . . Because the Hindus live in isolated castes they appear to be created to be subjugated by anybody [externally] not permitting, at the same time, to be assimilated with anybody and to be united [into one real state organization].

Il manque à l'Inde la Cité. Une organisation proprement politique n'a pas été donnée la société hindoue, et la tradition religieuse a pu la dominer tout entiére.[9]

Perhaps this strong statement somewhat exaggerates the situation;[10] nevertheless, in essentials it stresses a real characteristic of the Hindu culture and societies. So far this case supports the proposition. In other cases of predominantly Ideational societies, like Tibet, we have the sacral state, with theocracy as its government. The proposition is again corroborated.

(2) If we turn to the verification of the propositions in time, in the life history of the Graeco-Roman and the Western cultures, they are not repudiated by the factual data. Indeed, if the early Greek and the Roman state were somewhat totalitarian in the period of domination of their Ideational culture, their totalitarianism was sacral and theocratic. (See above, Chapter Five.) With the progress of the sensatization of the Greek culture, the totalitarianism of the Greek States did not decrease but rather increased, and became secular (after the fifth century B.C.). The role of the State became in all matters more and more important, and the State replaced and took upon itself many a function which hitherto had belonged to the nonstate groups (the family, the *phile*, the religious, and other social bodies). Likewise in Rome, with the progress of Sensatism, after the second century B.C., the totalitarianism of the state began to increase and become secular. Due to specific factors, the increase continued almost up to the "end" of the Western Roman Empire (in the fifth century A.D.). But in the fifth century and after — and please note that only in the fifth century and after did the Ideational culture of Christianity become dominant — the state system of the empire quickly began to fall to pieces and weakened to such an extent that the historians style it the "fall and the end of the Roman Empire." When we enter the Ideational Middle Ages, we are confronted with a very weak state, far indeed from any totalitarianism. Even when the Merovingian and Caro-

[9] C. Bouglé, "*Note sur le droit et la caste en Inde,*" in *L'année sociologique* (1906), Vol. X, pp. 156.

[10] See some correction to that in Mazzarella, "*Le forme di aggregazione sociale nell India,*" in *Rivista italiana di sociologia* (1911), pp. 216–219.

lingian empires were created, they were still far from being "totalitarian." The place of the secular state was taken by the Christian Church and its organized system. The religious body became the most important and even the most powerful body social in the Ideational period, but not a secular totalitarian state. After the Carolingian Empire, the feudal state became something still less important; a rarefied, impotent, and insignificant social system of relationships, that played a very modest part and in no way remind one of the Hobbesian Leviathan. Thus, here again we see a nonexistence of totalitarianism and the all-controlling State in the period of domination of Ideational culture.

(3) Further history is no less instructive. With the rise of the Sensate culture, the secular state, in the form of the newly formed national monarchies, began to rise also. Step by step it grew; absorbed into its system a greater and greater number of social relationships that were outside its reach in the Middle Ages. Parallel to that, the state government, the monarchs, began to expand their interference, control, regulation, and regimentation. Soon they challenged the Church theocracy in the form of the Papal See. Subsequently this trend continued with the progress of the Sensate culture and in the seventeenth and eighteenth centuries resulted in the creation of the absolute monarchies and the *Polizei-Staat* — the real Leviathans, with the monarchs *legibus solutus*, with enormously expanded government control and regimentation, and all the other signs of totalitarianism. Finally, the settled and prosperous Sensate culture of the nineteenth century produced a secular state, as the most important and powerful among other social systems, but "normalized" and "constitutionalized" within certain limits. This "limitation" was due, on the one hand, to the overripeness of that culture. Its bearers, these "men and citizens of the Declarations," had sowed their wild oats and now wanted to enjoy their liberty without any undue annoyance from the State or its government. On the other hand, as we shall see, it was due to the comparative security, prosperity, and peace of the European society of the nineteenth century, as a specific factor (see further in this chapter and Chapter Eight). With the World War the factor of militarism appeared on the stage and led, as it regularly does (see the next part of this chapter), to a sudden flare-up of the swing toward totalitarianism. Under its influence, and then that of its aftermaths (economic crises, insecurity, depression, and so on) the overripe Sensate man "went to pieces," lost his balance, went wild. Hence, the most violent and extremely totalitarian trend of the postwar period in which we live.

This sketch shows that the propositions offered have a serious basis and are borne out by the main swings of history rather well. It gives an additional proof of the dependence of this quantitative aspect of social systems upon the type of culture. But, as mentioned, the connection is not exceedingly close; all the time it is influenced by the interference of other, special factors that are responsible for "short-time and intermittent" swings in this field. Most of the deviations from the line of the propositions are due to the play and interference of these special factors. When their influence is combined with the role of our culture variables and their fluctuations, in providing the main reasons for the long-time swings in the field, the essentials of the actual movement of the curve of the state totalitarianism and *laissez faire* become comprehensible and accountable.

Let us turn now to the special factors of the short-time and convulsive swings between totalitarianism and the *laissez-faire* poles of the state system and its government.

IV. FACTORS OF SHORT-TIME FLUCTUATIONS

These factors are numerous. The most important are three: (1) *war or peace;* (2) *economic impoverishment or prosperity;* (3) *social emergency of any kind. Other conditions being equal, governmental control in a given social system tends to increase in periods of great social emergency; and of these emergency conditions, particularly in the times of strenuous war and in severe economic crises where there is a scarcity of the most important means of subsistence for a large part of the population.*

All emergency conditions call forth an extraordinary effort on the part of the state government, which leads naturally to expansion of its activity, control, and regulation.

The role of the military factor was well analyzed by Spencer.[11] It goes without saying that as soon as a society enters war, the curve of government interference at once jumps and the state network of social relationships becomes more complicated. Instead of normal laws, martial law and a state of siege are introduced, which means an enormous expansion of government control. Many economic relationships heretofore uncontrolled by the State now become regimented by it: production, distribution, and consumption. Many other social relationships undergo a

---

[11] See Spencer, *op. cit.*, Vol. I, pp. 258–263; Vol. II, pp. 547–582; Vol. III, pp. 840–853. Spencer foresaw even the growth of the state totalitarianism, indicating, however, it would be only a passing stage in the life of mankind.

similar shift. The liberties and rights of the subjects or citizens are enormously curtailed. Military rule is absolute; it may concern anything that is urgent from a military standpoint; it imposes upon the population anything that is deemed necessary for military purposes. It may impose not only the draft into the army, but even mass execution of groups in the population. In a word, the fact of a sudden expansion of government control in time of war is unquestionable.

The main reasons for it are also axiomatic. Such a "totalitarian swing" is necessary for victory: of two nations equal in other respects, the nation that imposes a centralized and rigid discipline upon its population has more chances of being victorious than the nation whose efforts are not organized; which does not have a centralized system and strong discipline. It would be like a group of soldiers fighting the battle each on its own account, without the co-ordinated efforts by the commander in chief, and with soldiers who allow themselves, according to their fancy, now to fight, now to rest. Such a group will certainly be beaten by a similar group with a central staff co ordinating their efforts and a strong discipline, even the right to discipline some of them by death, if need be. The second reason is that the military regime of life in the barracks is in a sense "totalitarian" in its very nature. A soldier, especially during war, does not belong to himself. At any moment he can be sent to fight, to do whatever he is ordered, even to die. The commands are absolute and do not admit of any protest or discussion. The commanding officer, and especially the commander in chief, has the right of life and death over the army and even over the civilians. He is an absolute ruler. The regime of life in the military institutions is also "state communistic." The soldiers live in buildings not chosen by them; they eat whatever they are given, dress and do as they are ordered. Their time and activity, with the exception of a few hours, is most rigidly regimented. Their behavior also. In this sense, the army and the military regime have always been "totalitarian" par excellence. The best creators of totalitarianism, including the state socialism and state communism, have been not Marx or Engels or Lassalle or Lenin, but the greatest organizers of military forces and military empires: Jenghiz Khan, Tamerlane, Caesar, Napoleon, and the like.

If a country has long and frequent wars, such a regime becomes habitual for it. It extends beyond its army, over the whole country; as a result, the whole nation becomes "conditioned" to be totalitarian in the behavior and relationship of its members. There are other reasons, but these two are sufficient to explain why the factor of war and militarism facilitates the swing of the state system toward totalitarianism, while peace tends to work in the opposite way.

The whole matter is so clear and unquestionable, and is so well supported by the actual facts of history, that there is no need to go into its detailed corroboration.   Every war exhibits the above regularities.   The World War as well as the Italian-Abyssinian War displayed them magnificently, even in the Anglo-Saxon countries of traditional liberalism.   In Part Two of this volume, devoted to the study of the movement of war, we shall see that the medieval centuries were comparatively peaceful; and these centuries had a State either very far from any totalitarianism, or of only a moderate degree of "condensation" and government interference.   Then after the thirteenth century, the curve of war began to rise; and the state system and its government began to rise also.   In the seventeenth and partly in the eighteenth centuries war reached its climax; and the state totalitarianism reached its climax also.   The Revolutionary and Napoleonic periods were belligerent; and they were totalitarian in reality.   The nineteenth century (after the Napoleonic Wars) was comparatively peaceful; and the state system and its government became moderate, contractual, and limited.   The twentieth century, beginning with the World War, happened to be the most belligerent century so far; and the totalitarianism of the State and of its government soared into the "stratosphere."   In brief, we find in the essentials the tangible parallel movement of the curve of totalitarianism and that of war.[12]

Less known and evident is the "totalitarian" role of famine, impoverishment, and of severe economic crises of a given society.   Therefore, a little greater space needs to be devoted to the establishment of this logical and factual association.   Let us take the matter as concisely as possible.[13] In a society where there exists a differentiation into poor and rich an extraordinary impoverishment facilitates an expansion of government interference in economic relations, and, through that, an increase of governmental control in other fields of social life.   If the economic level of the masses remains the same, but the economic difference between the

---

[12] In much greater details these considerations were developed in my two Russian articles: "The Influence of War," in the *Ekonomist*, no. 1 (in Russian) (Petrograd, 1922); and in "War and Militarization of Society," in *Artelnoje Delo*, no. 1 (Petrograd, 1922).

[13] Again space does not permit me to go into the matter with the available details.   These can be partly found in my two articles: "Influence of Famine upon the Social-economic Organization of Society," in *Ekonomist*, no. 2 (in Russian) (1922) and "Famine and Ideology of Society," in *Ekonomist* (1922), nos. 4-5.   In still greater detail the problem was studied in my large monograph: *Influence of Famine and Impoverishment upon Social Life and Organization*, destroyed by the Soviet Government in the process of printing.

wealthy and the poor increases in such a way that the rich become still richer, the effect is similar because a relative enrichment of the wealthy is a relative impoverishment of other groups of the population, and vice versa. An increase of economic prosperity or a decrease of economic contrasts between the rich and the poor tends to decrease the economic control of the government. Such seems to be the second important factor of fluctuation of the amount of governmental interference. From the standpoint of the proposition it does not matter whether an increase of the interference is made in a peaceful or revolutionary way, by a conservative or revolutionary government, under the name of socialism or absolutism. What matters is that in some way it takes place, regardless of these details.

The reason for this is at hand : abundance of a necessity makes unnecessary any governmental regulation. Since we have plenty of air to breathe, our need is satisfied without any compulsory regulation. If there were a scarcity of this necessity the regulation would have become unavoidable. The same may be said of other necessities. Owing to a lack of space I cannot enter here into a more detailed discussion of the reasons for an increase of governmental control under the influence of the factor of impoverishment. Instead of such an analysis it would be better to show factually that the foregoing correlation really exists and has been regularly repeated in history. Such a regularity, exhibited in different societies and at different periods, is one of the best witnesses that the two phenomena are correlated.

Whether we take the records concerning great famines in the history of ancient Egypt, or ancient Greece and Rome, or China and Persia, or Russia and many medieval societies, we can but notice an expansion of the economic control of the government at such a period. On the other hand, except in the cases of "a militant state socialism" called forth by the factor of militarism, the greatest expansion of governmental control, amounting to a universal state socialism in the history of different societies and at different periods, has invariably happened in the periods of economic disorganization of the country and of impoverishment of its masses. Such are two series of facts which corroborate the proposed hypothesis.

An increase of governmental economic control in the periods of famine and impoverishment has been regularly manifest in the following phenomena : [14] (1) in an establishment or reinforcement of governmental

[14] All these functions are invariably found in the records of Egypt, Greece, Rome, China, Persia, India, Russia, and Europe, past and present. As a matter of fact, in the whole "unemployment relief" of the New Deal I do not find any single measure that is new and was not practiced in the past economic crises, beginning with the "relief measures" of the Pharaohs of Egypt.

control of exports and imports, which often amounted to governmental monopoly of foreign trade; (2) in an establishment of fixed prices on food and other necessities; (3) in governmental registration and tabulation of the entire amount of necessities in the country owned by its citizens; (4) in a complete control of purchase and sale of commodities, including amounts to be bought and conditions governing sales; (5) in governmental compulsion of private citizens' sending their commodities to market; (6) in requisition, to an extraordinarily large degree, of private necessities by the government; (7) in an establishment of numerous governmental agencies for the purpose of buying, producing, and distributing necessities among the population; (8) in the introduction of a ration system; (9) in an organization of public works on an extraordinarily large scale; (10) in a substitution of governmental control of production, distribution, and even consumption, of necessities for that by private individuals or corporations. All these and many similar phenomena have been regularly repeated in most dissimilar countries at most dissimilar times, as soon as famine and impoverishment have broken out. All this signifies great expansion of governmental interference in the economic relationships of the population and, through that, often in other fields of social interrelations. Here are a series of facts, a few out of many similar, which show this.

A. *Ancient Egypt.* The Bible gives us one of the oldest records which clearly shows the foregoing correlation. As a result of the great famine in the time of Joseph, the money, cattle, and land of the population of Ancient Egypt "became Pharaoh's." The people became the slaves of the government. The entire economic life began to be controlled by the government. In the modern terminology this means that everything was nationalized, and that the economic control of Pharaoh's government was expanded enormously at the expense of that of private individuals.[15] Other Egyptian records show that this was repeated several times in the history of Ancient Egypt. Its pharaohs and officials often stress in their records that "in years of famine they plowed all the fields of the nome, preserving its people alive and furnishing its food."[16] As war and famine, or danger of famine, were very frequent phenomena in Ancient Egypt, this accounts for a high level of governmental control throughout the history of Egypt. And yet, in the famine years and in periods of impoverishment, as the before-mentioned facts show, the control seems to

---

[15] See Genesis xlvii. 12–20.
[16] See J. H. Breasted, *Ancient Records of Egypt* (Chicago, 1906), Vol. I, §§ 523, 281, 189, 459, and others.

have jumped still higher.   The economic life of Egypt under the Ptolemy dynasty gives an additional example of this.   Economic disorganization of this period was accompanied by an extraordinary growth of governmental control which led to a transformation of society into a universal state-socialist organization.[17]

B. *China.*   More abundant and conspicuous confirmation of the hypothesis is given by the history of China.   It is the history of a society with very frequent famines and with a permanent danger of starvation. This accounts for an exclusively high level of governmental control in China throughout its history.   The organization of Chinese society has been in essence an "economic state socialism," with "many governmental regulations to control consumption, production, and distribution." [18] And yet, in the periods of great famine or impoverishment, governmental control expanded still more.   This, according to the records, has invariably happened in the time of Yao, in the years of famine during the Yin, the Chow, the Hans, the T'ang, the Sung, and other dynasties.   On the other hand, the attempts to introduce a real state-socialist organization, like the attempts of Wang Mang or Wang-an-Shih, regularly happened in the period of a great impoverishment of the country.[19]

C. *Ancient Greece.*   Aside from the factor of militarism, economic insecurity was responsible for a large degree of governmental control in Sparta, Athens, Lipara, and other Greek states.   R. Pöhlmann says: "The products of the Spartan agriculture were not sufficient to satisfy the necessities of the population.   The entire economic life was based on a very narrow and uncertain basis.   Every economic crisis, every delay or interruption of imports of necessities was very dangerous.   Shall we wonder that the strongest governmental control of economic life became inevitable?" [20]   In similar straits was Athens.[21]   In the periods of impoverishment and famine the governmental control intensified.

[17] See M. Rostovtzeff, *State and Personality in Economic Life of the Ptolemaic Egypt* (in Russian), in *Sovremennya Zapiski* (Paris, 1922), No. 10, and " Ptolemaic Egypt " in *Cambridge Ancient History* (Cambridge, 1924), Vol. VII.

[18] Chen Huan Chang, "The Economic Principles of Confucius," *University of Columbia Studies*, Vol. XLIV (New York, 1911), I, 168 ff.; II, 497 ff.

[19] See the detailed factual data in Mabel P. H. Lee, *The Economic History of China* (New York, 1921), pp. 40, 46, 58–60, 63, 77–80, 83, 92, 99, 101–104, 110, 122, 140, 155, *et passim.*

[20] R. Pöhlmann, *op. cit.,* pp. 32 ff. and 430 ff.   I quote its Russian translation (St. Petersburg, 1912).

[21] See A. Böckh, *Die Staatshaushaltung der Athenes* (Berlin, 1851), Vol. I, 125 ff.; Novosadsky, " The Struggle against Dearth in Ancient Greece," in *The Journal of the Ministry of Public Education* (in Russian) (St. Petersburg, 1917), pp. 78–80.

"As soon as the prices on the necessities began to go up, the state interference took extraordinary forms. For the struggle with the coming famine the State organized an extraordinary commission of Sitons with unlimited control of economic life." All mentioned effects of famine took place in an extraordinary degree. Often private control of economic relations was almost completely superseded by that of the government, in the production and distribution of the necessities and in the field of economic life of society generally.[22]

In the period of extreme impoverishment governmental control assumed the forms of the present-day totalitarianism. The government confiscated private lands and wealth, distributed them in such a way as it found necessary, nationalized what it wanted; in brief, pushed its control up to possible limits. Such were, for example, the periods of impoverishment after the Messina War and in the times of Agis IV, Cleomenes III, and Nabis in Sparta; after the Peloponnesian War in Athens (the periods of the Thirty and the Ten Tyrants), and in some other periods. Either in a legal way or in the form of revolution, under conservative as well as revolutionary dictators, state interference in such periods grew to its limits and assumed the form of state totalitarianism.[23]

D. *Ancient Rome.* Similar parallelism is given in the history of Rome. Here the years of famine, like the years A.D. 5, 8, 18, 52, were usually accompanied by a corresponding increase of the governmental control. Side by side with these small fluctuations we see that the periods of impoverishment of the masses were followed by an expansion of state interference which amounted sometimes to state socialism. It is well known that in the period from the second half of the second century B.C. to the beginning of the first century A.D. there were many acute economic crises in Rome. The same period is marked by the Corn Laws of the Gracchi (123 B.C.); by the establishment of a special institution for prevention of famine and for control of the public supply (104 B.C.); by the introduction of a ration system and public supply free of charge; by many nationalizations and confiscations and restriction of private economic enterprise; by a great increase of economic functions of the government.[24] Still more conspicuous was the discussed correlation in the period

[22] Novosadsky, *op. cit.*, pp. 80–82; Pöhlmann, *op. cit.*, pp. 235–236; Böckh, *op. cit.*, pp. 116–125; Francotte, "*Le pain à bon marché et le pain gratuit dans les cités grecques,*" in *Mélanges du droit publique grecque* (Paris, 1910), pp. 291 ff.

[23] See besides quoted books, P. Guiraud, *Études économiques sur l'antiquité* (Paris, 1905), pp. 68 ff.; G. Busold, *Griechische Geschichte* (Gotha, 1902–1903), pt. iii, pp. 1456, 1614, and 1628; B. Niese, *Geschichte der griechischen und makedonischen Staaten* (Gotha, 1893–1903), pt. ii, pp. 296 ff., and pt. iii, pp. 42 ff.

[24] See O. Hirschfeld, *Die kaiserlichen Verwaltungsbeamten* (Berlin, 1905), pp. 231 ff.; Waltzing, *op. cit.*, pp. 26–103; M. Rostovtzeff, *The Roman Leaden Tessera* (in Russian)

from the third century A.D. to the "end" of the Western Roman Empire. This was the time of economic decay of Rome. It was also the time of an establishment of a totalitarian economic organization in the Western Roman Empire. "The Empire was transformed into a big factory where, under the control of the officials, the population had to work. It was a real state-socialist organization of industry and labor. Almost all production and distribution of wealth was concentrated in the hands of the government." [25]   One who has observed the Soviet Communist system in the period from 1917 to 1922 can but notice the essential similarity of the Roman and the Soviet regimes.

E. *The Middle Ages.*   Here the same correlation is repeated many times. In 792–793 the famine broke out. As a result, "Charles the Great introduced the first fixed prices under its influence."   In 805 famine burst out again, and a decree was issued that *"ne foris imperium nostrum vendatur aliquid alimoniae"*; free trade was forbidden; fixed prices were reintroduced; the freedom of contracts was restricted; agriculture and industry began to be controlled more severely, and so forth.[26]   As in the Middle Ages famine was very frequent, this, besides the factor of war, seems to have been responsible for a relatively high State or Church government control of economic relations throughout the Middle Ages. It, however, jumped up in the years of famine. In the history of England such years were 1201–1202, 1315–1316, 1321, 1483, 1512, 1521, 1586, 1648–1649, and others. In the history of France such years were 1391, 1504–1505, 1565, 1567, 1577, 1591, 1635, 1662, 1684, 1693, 1709, to mention but a few cases. The same years were marked by an increase of government interference in economic relations. A historian of the food trade in France sums up his exhaustive study as follows: "As soon as famine was bursting out, governmental control became stronger; as soon as famine was weakening, the control weakened also." [27]

(St. Petersburg, 1903), pp. 111–113; G. Salvioli, *Capitalism in the Ancient World* (Russian trans.) (St. Petersburg, 1906), pp. 24 and 165–170.

[25] Waltzing, *op. cit.*, Vol. II, pp. 383–384; Duruy, *Histoire des Romains*, Vol. VIII (Paris, 1885), 550 ff.; see also S. Dill, *Roman Society* (New York, 1904).

[26] F. Curschmann, *Hungersnöte in Mittelalter* (Leipzig, 1900), pp. 71–75 *et passim*.

[27] Afanassieff, *The Conditions of Food Trade* (in Russian) (Odessa, 1892), pp. 1–3, 8, 17, 144–148, 155, and 158. A. Araskranianz, *"Die französische Getreidehandelspolitik bis zum Jahre 1789,"* in *Schmollers Staats und Sozialwiss. Forschungen* (Leipzig, 1882), Vol. IV, pp. 3, and 10–14. It is curious to note that this regularly happened even when the heads of the French Government were persons who were inimical to an expansion of governmental control of economic affairs. An example is given by Turgot. In 1774 he decreed a complete freedom of trade. In 1775, under the influence of the famine of 1774–1775, he was forced to annul his decree. The same happened with Nekker, Dupont de Nemure, and the National Assembly (see Afranassieff,

The discussed correlation is still more conspicuously exhibited in the history of Russian famines. Each of the periods of famine or of great impoverishment has been invariably followed by an increase of governmental control.[28]

In the light of this hypothesis it is comprehensible why governmental control in the form of the revolutionary or counterrevolutionary dictatorship usually increases in the periods of great revolutions. Such periods are marked by an extraordinary impoverishment and disorganization of economic life. Hence its result — an extraordinary increase of governmental control of the entire economic life of a revolutionary society. Sometimes it leads to an establishment of a "communist" or "state-socialist organization" in a revolutionary country, like the communist societies in Tabor (in revolutionary Bohemia), in Mühlhausen, in New Jerusalem, or in Paris in 1871, to mention but a few cases of that kind.[29] In other cases it assumes other forms of totalitarianism: absolutism, dictatorship, fascism, Nazism, etc.

Finally, a striking confirmation of the hypothesis has been given by the expansion of governmental control during the years of the war and after. During this period, not only in the belligerent, but in the neutral, countries, too, the control of economic life by the government increased enormously. In the belligerent countries it was due primarily to the factor of war, and secondarily to that of scarcity of food and other necessities. In the neutral countries the expansion of the interference was called forth principally by an increased scarcity of food and other necessities. The same two factors seem to have been responsible for the Communist experiments in Russia, Bavaria, and Hungary, not to mention milder socialist measures as well as varieties of fascism, Nazism, and other totalitarianisms of different color and degree in several other countries. From this standpoint the so-called "Communist regime" in all the countries mentioned has represented the expansion of governmental control up to its limits. An annihilation of private property; a universal nationalization, beginning with factories and land and ending with the last silver teaspoon; a complete annihilation of private commerce and trade; a regulation of the entire production, distribution, and even consumption

---

op. cit., pp. 299 ff., and 370–371). A similar thing occurred with President Hoover, after the crash of 1929.

[28] See the data in my paper, "Influence of Famine," in *Russian Economist* (Petrograd, 1922), no. 2.

[29] See the facts in Sorokin's *Sociology of Revolution* (Philadelphia, 1924), chaps. v and xiv.

of all products of the country by the government; a complete substitution of governmental control for that of private individuals — such have been the characteristics of the Communist regime in Russia in the period from 1917 to 1922.

This means an extreme expansion of governmental control. What were its causes? The answer in brief is as follows: Owing to the war the lack of necessities began to be felt in Russia already in 1915. After the same period there appeared the tendency of the expansion of governmental control in the economic field. The decrees of August 15, 1915, and October 25, 1915, which gave the right to officials to search, to tabulate, to confiscate, to requisition all private food and necessities could be regarded as a beginning of what later on developed into "Communism." Owing to the growth of impoverishment, due to the war, this process necessarily grew also. As the revolution only aggravated the economic situation, governmental control continued to grow during the Provisional Government, whose policy in this respect only pushed further that of the Czarist Government. At the time of the overthrow of the Kerensky regime private trade and commerce were almost annihilated; private industry and agriculture were greatly restricted, state control was expanded enormously. Owing to the factors of the civil war and the growth of impoverishment the Bolsheviki pushed this process up to its possible limits. In this way appeared the so-called "Communist regime," which, in the present terminology of the Communists themselves, was nothing but "Military and Starving Communism." The continuation of this process is no less instructive.

In 1920 the civil war was finished. In this way one of the factors of "Communism" ceased to work. At the same time everyone, except a small group of Communists and swindlers, was ruined. Economic differentiation disappeared. An equality in poverty was established. If my hypothesis is true, under such conditions we should expect an opposite trend, toward a decrease of government control. This is what actually happened. In 1921 the Bolsheviki were forced to introduce the New Economic Policy. It meant a step toward the so-called "capitalist regime"; it represented a reduction of the governmental control of economic life and an increase of private control, initiative, and autonomy. This trend was continued up to 1929, when several factors temporarily stopped it. But after 1934, when some improvement of economic conditions took place, the trend again reappeared and has lasted up to the present time.

Still more familiar is the expansion of government regimentation in the United States as well as in practically all the European countries during the years of the present depression. After the crash of 1929, no less a person than President Hoover, this great exponent of "rugged individualism," began, like Turgot in 1775, or the Czarist Government in 1915, the process of expansion. The depression continued, and President Roosevelt pushed expansion farther. A similar process has occurred in practically all European and non-European countries hit by the depression.

The foregoing series of facts, from ancient Egypt to A.D. 1937, a series which might be continued *ad libitum*,[30] if there were need and space, seem to show clearly the logical and factual validity of the hypothesis discussed.

If the hypothesis is true, it gives a sufficient basis for the following tentative inferences.

(1) Since a considerable expansion of government control of economic relations has been a result of impoverishment or of a disproportionate economic contrast between the wealthy and the poor classes, it follows that the very fact of great expansion itself is a symptom of economic disorganization of society.

(2) From this standpoint, the Soviet Communism and other forms of contemporary totalitarianism have been but a form of an extraordinary expansion of governmental control due to an extreme impoverishment of the population caused by the war. In this sense the totalitarianisms have been a manifestation of a great social sickness, but not of a social improvement.

(3) Other conditions being equal, if in the near future an aggravation of the economic situation of a Western society takes place, or economic inequality within it grows, an increase of governmental control is to be expected.

(4) If the future shows an improvement of the economic situation within such a society, or a diminution of economic inequality, a decrease of governmental control is likely to happen. It will probably manifest itself in the form of a decrease of popularity of totalitarianist demands for substitution of governmental control for that of private persons and corporations.

So much for this factor.

What has been said of war and impoverishment can be said of any social emergency that involves a considerable part of the population. Any such emergency tends to expand the regulative and controlling functions of the state (and other group) government, whether the emergency is an earthquake, a devastating tornado, a widespread epi-

---

[30] See other facts in L. Kawan, *Gli esodi e le carestie in Europa attraverso il tempo*. Publicazione della commissione italiana per studio delle grandi calamita (Roma, 1932), Vol. III.

demic, flood and inundation of a large area, or an extraordinary development of banditry and crime, or an explosion of ammunition warehouses, or a serious drought, or dust storms covering large areas, or something else. All these emergencies lead to an expansion of governmental activity; if the emergency is local, of the local agents of the government; if it is national, of the national agencies.

The proposition again is so self-evident and the facts of this association of emergency with the expansion of governmental functions are so numerous and have been recurring so regularly, from the remotest past up to this year's floods, droughts, earthquakes, tornadoes, and other — local and national — emergencies, that there is no reason to go into its detailed corroboration. From the oldest records of various emergencies up to this year's latest calamity,[31] with the invariable indication of the increased activities of the government, of extraordinary measures taken, of the introduction even of martial law, the association has regularly recurred and is almost axiomatic.

If there were not a permanent — normal — emergency in any society, in the form of the maintenance of law and order, no government would be necessary in it. For the group of ideally perfect creatures — wise, moral, exceedingly social and altruistic; creatures of angelic nature — hardly any government with its compulsory nature and its regimentation would be necessary. They themselves, of their own will, would do all that was needed. Unfortunately such a society of human beings does not exist. In any society of imperfect human beings, frequently unwise and egotistic, and sometimes even antisocial, no minimum of law and order seems to be able to exist without a policeman and all the compulsory apparatus of the government, from a fine up to prison and the electric chair. Under such conditions, some so to speak permanent emergency of a normal degree exists all the time in any state. Therefore some forms of government exist and must exist in any organized society.[32] If there were

---

[31] Floods and drought of 1936–1937. One can read a detailed analysis of the social effects of such an emergency in the record of the enormous explosion of ammunition in Halifax, in 1915, in S. H. Prince's *Catastrophe and Social Change* (New York, 1920). In it one can see how the emergency situation led at once to a tremendous flare-up of government activity. A similar development occurs in other emergencies.

[32] In this sense, the age-old story of the Fall and of the establishment of government as the least evil, after the Fall — the theory given in the Hindu, the Chinese, the Jewish, the Persian, the Greek, the Roman, and the medieval thought (shared and subscribed to particularly by the Church Fathers and the medieval Christian thinkers) — this theory, in so far as it considers the institution of government as an immanent satellite of imperfect human nature and society, is neither so silly nor so fallacious as many a superficial pseudo thinker styles it.

no such imperfections, society without compulsory government would have been possible and the ideal of anarchists would be realizable. As such ideal society does not exist, and all the time some emergency is present, a government is necessary. When an emergency grows, the government interference, compulsion, and regimentation grow. When the emergency declines, the latter decline also. Such is the factual and logical connection of these variables. And such are the main special factors of the short-time and sudden fluctuations of the social systems between totalitarianism and the *laissez-faire* anarchy. The above shows what in these swings is due to our main variables and what to the special factors. Combining them, we can account for the actual curve of these fluctuations in the life history of any social system.

V. LIBERTY IN ITS RELATIONSHIP TO TOTALITARIANISM AND THE LAISSEZ FAIRE IN THE STATE SYSTEM

Since liberty's formula is $\frac{SW}{SM}$, an expansion of the government inter-ference does not mean necessarily the limitation of liberty within either the state system or any other group. *If the expansion corresponds to the wishes of the members of the State* or other organized group, a totalitarian character of government is neither felt as a limitation of the liberty of the members, nor is it regarded as tyranny. It is estimated as a real social service, rather than an encroachment on the freedom and the rights of the members. In many religious sects, in many family groups, and generally in a group with a predominant familistic relationship, such a totalitarianism is welcomed and viewed as a positive value. Even in periods of war and emergency, dictatorship in a state and a swing to totalitarianism have often been willingly accepted.

On the other hand, if such an expansion of government regimentation is contrary to the wishes of the members, any step toward totalitarianism would mean a limitation of the liberty of the members, would be felt as such, and would be valued as tyranny, despotism, and the like. Such is the clear-cut, logical answer to the problem. It points out, first the one-sidedness of the contractual-liberal formula of liberty dominant in the nineteenth century. According to this, any expansion of government activity was viewed suspiciously as a potential limitation of the liberty of the citizens or members. Similar is the standpoint of anarchists. The above statement means that, contrary to these views, there are expansions of the government's activities which are not a limitation of the liberty of the members of the group. When in a group, especially in periods of calamity, the members wish the most vigorous action from the government, and the government fails to give it, such an abstention from expansion would be qualified by the members as a mere impotence and inefficiency of the government, and as a failure to render the social service expected.   On the other hand, the policy of the government *laissez faire* in many cases is not a service to the liberty of the members of the group, but serves often the opposite purpose; it is like the noninterference on the part of an onlooker into the relationship where a cruel gangster tortures a child, or a physically powerful person coerces, without any just reason, the weaker party into an activity or conduct harmful to that party. I stated in the preceding chapters that when the contractual relationships degenerate, they cease to guarantee the minimum of liberty to the weaker party and turn factually into a compulsory relationship, in which the stronger party coerces the weaker.   As the stronger party is almost always a minority in a group, the perfect noninterference of the government in such cases leads not to an increase of freedom for the subjects, but to its decrease.

These considerations show why totalitarianism per se is not necessarily a limitation of the liberty of the members; and the *laissez faire* per se is not necessarily identical with the regime of freedom of the members. Everything depends upon the kind of totalitarianism and the kind of *laissez faire*.   If the former is familistic, it is the best realization of the liberty of the group members.   If it is compulsory, it is undoubtedly a limitation of their liberty.   The same is true of the *laissez faire*.   If it is in accordance with the wish of the members of the group and if the members are highly social and properly behave themselves in regard to one another, as "brothers," the *laissez faire* is a free regime.   If the wish of the majority of the members suffering from the pseudo-contractual relationship is for a just and strong government that can help them and bridle the coercive section of the group, then the *laissez-faire* government is a shrine for a compulsory regime.

One can but agree with many historians who, for instance, estimated the growth of the national monarchy in Europe in its first stages after the thirteenth century, and the expansion of the monarchical control, as a phenomenon of protection of the masses against the feudal exploiters, and as their liberation.   Likewise, the first phase of development of the con- tractual relationships, beginning with the end of the eighteenth century, was also a liberating movement against the *unwelcomed* oppression of the degenerated monarchical absolutism, and the parasitical groups of the super-Epicurean aristocracy.   But the last phase of the contractual regime, at the end of the nineteenth and at the beginning of the twentieth century, seems to have degenerated into a pseudo contractualism in many respects; into a pseudo-contractual scheme, in which various unscrupulous politicians, financial powers, journalists, and many varieties of the high-brow, parasitical intelligentsia have been coercing and exploiting the large masses of the population of the most different social strata and occupations. That pseudo contractualism developed to the point where it led to the emergence of millions of people who wanted to work and could not find any work; who often wanted to earn their living for wages prohibited by the politicians' "protective laws." This phenomenon of the unemployment of millions in itself is a sign of the degeneration of real contractualism into pseudo contractualism. Therefore, a thoughtful person is hardly surprised that these masses have so easily given up the contractual (or, rather, pseudo-contractual) values; that they have conceded so willingly what the theorizers of liberal pseudo contractualism style "liberty and freedom"; and that some of the groups have followed most enthusiastically the banner of the totalitarian dictators of the present time. In other words, contractualism, liberalism, democracy, parliamentarism, the "rights of man and citizen," and other synonyms have become, at the beginning of this century, merely pseudo contractualism, pseudo liberalism, pseudo democracy, etc., to a considerable degree. Therefore they have ceased to be the equivalent and the guarantee of liberty and other related values and for this reason have been easily given up by the many groups in favor of totalitarianism in our day.

Does this mean that the contemporary totalitarianism is that of liberty? If it were familistic in its main nature, it would have been such. But, as we have seen, in its essentials it is not an incarnation of the familistic, but mainly of the compulsory society. The very presence of its harsh and severe coercive means used overliberally, without any restraint; its martial (juridically or factually) laws; the immense number of its victims and of its opponents; its reliance upon an unrestrained physical coercion — these and other symptoms are a fairly reliable barometer that it is not the totalitarianism desired by all, or, in some cases, by even the majority, or a large portion of the populations of the contemporary totalitarian countries. For these sections of the population it is certainly not any enlargement of their liberty, but a radical limitation of it, even in comparison with the shadow of liberty they enjoyed under the pseudo-contractual regime at the beginning of this century.

Being such, present-day totalitarianism is a child of the transitory conditions. As such, it cannot exist in its present form for any length of time; it must turn either into familistic totalitarianism and in this form give a liberty greater than the pseudo-contractual liberty, or into a regime of open and rude coercion which will result in mobilizing against itself the population, and sooner or later will either be overthrown or curbed by other than state groups, or will succumb with the decay of the population, that cannot resist the tyranny, cannot overthrow it, and cannot live under it for long as a vigorous, strong, and creative society. The decay of such a "broken reed" of population would drag down with itself also its totalitarian executioners.

VI. TRANSFER AND MIGRATION OF SOCIAL RELATIONSHIPS FROM ONE SOCIAL SYSTEM TO OTHERS

Up to the present time, we have been studying the rarefaction and condensation of social relationships within one, the state social, system. Now let us glance at what is happening to the social relationships that drop from the state social system and cease to be regulated by its government. If the social systems were limited by the State, and if each individual belonged to one social system only, then any social relationship dropped from the state system would mean its transfer into the sphere of the free choice of an individual. We know, however, that the real situation is different. Within the same population there exists an organization of this population not only in the state system, but in several other nonstate social systems that do not coincide with the state system and are different from it, such as the religious organizations (the citizens of the same state often belong to different religious organizations; some are Catholics, some Protestants, some Hebrews, some Mohammedans, etc.; and, vice versa, members of the same religious organization — for instance, the Catholic — are citizens of different states), the occupational group, the "nationality" group, the political party, etc. Likewise, the individual is a willing or nonwilling "partner" not only of the state group, but of many others outside it. Each of us is a citizen of a certain state, belongs to some religious organization (including the atheist societies); is a member of some occupational group; of some family; of a nationality; of a political party; of many associations and societies, each different from the state and from one another.

Under these conditions, inclusion of new relationships in the state system (expansion of its government control) or the exclusion from this system of some relationships that hitherto were a part of it, does not necessarily mean (respectively) a limitation of free choice or an increase of it for the individual, but in most cases it is a *transfer of the respective relationships from one social system to another.* If the feudal State lost some social relationships from its system, they were taken over by other social systems (particularly by the Church, by the feudal orders or estates, and the like) and began to be controlled and regulated by these nonstate organizations, instead of being left to the "free choice of the individual."

If the registration of marriages, births, deaths, and divorces was dropped in many cases from the network of the religious organizations (especially after the French Revolution), these relationships were not left uncontrolled by the social bodies, but were registered, regulated, and controlled by the State (in most of the Western countries). In other words, they were shifted from the regulative system of the religious group to the state group. In almost all cases of exclusion or inclusion, decrease or increase of the number of social relationships in a given network of social groups, the decrease or exclusion means a mere transfer of this dropped relationship to another social system, which begins its regulation ; the inclusion of a new social relationship into the state, or into the network of any other social group, means that it dropped from the social system of which it has been a part and is shifted into the given social system.

Such shifts, or "migrations," of social relationships from one social system to another are fairly frequent and normal phenomena. In moderate form, this movement goes on in any population, almost all the time. Now a certain relationship, say the prohibition of alcoholic beverages, which hitherto was regulated by the nonstate social groups, is included and begins to be regulated by the State; after some time, it is excluded, in its greater part, from the state system of relationships and begins to be regulated by other social groups (the family, the Church, the professional union, various prohibition societies, etc.). So it happens with a large number of social relationships. In some periods, such a "migration" assumes the mass character of a geologic earthquake; a large set of relationships is suddenly and en masse shifted from one social system to another — for instance, in the periods of the so-called "social revolutions." During the French, the Spanish, the Russian, or many other revolutions, most of the relationships that had been controlled by the Church before the revolution were suddenly shifted to the control of the Revolutionary state government. With the beginning of the Middle Ages, many relationships that were "fibers" of the Roman state system were dropped and taken over into the Christian Church social system. Social relationships in the field of marriage and divorce, and birth and death ; of education, recreation, religion — in fact, practically all fields of social life — have frequently been shifted from one social system to another. Education in most European countries, say a century ago, was mainly the business of the family and the religious group; then it migrated largely to the state system and began to be controlled by it, through its government and the ministry of education and instruction, with their numerous agents. Religion, in a certain period of the Middle Ages, and after the Augsburg Agreement, was included in the state system (*cuius regio, eius religio*) ; after the introduction of "freedom of religion," it was excluded from that control and migrated into the networks of other social systems. The relationship between a criminal and his victim was often not a part of the state system in the so-called tribal period. It was a matter of "self-redress" on the part of the victim, and of his family or clan. Then this relationship was transferred to the state system; self-redress was prohibited and the state government took upon itself the control and regulation of this relationship. In a so-called "capitalist society," most of the economic relationships between employers and employees in the field of production, distribution, and consumption are not a part of the state system; they are controlled by business corporations, associations, unions, including the family and the Church. The most essential traits of the socialist and communist and other totalitarian state systems at the present time is "nationalization" or "socialization" or "étatization" of most of the economic relationships. They are shifted into the state system and controlled by the state government either in all fields, as in the Soviet regime, or in most of the essential ones, as in other totalitarian systems of the present time. All the totalitarian governments control and regulate the main relationships in the field of production, distribution, consumption; in the field of interrelationships of employers and employees; in the field of prices, export, import, money, banking, and so on.[33]

[33] Romantic and naïvely enthusiastic socialists and communists, as well as other totalitarians, are not aware that, stripped of the beautiful dress of "derivations," the main difference between the capitalist and the socialist or communist system in this respect is that in the capitalist system most of the economic relationships are controlled by other than state social systems; in socialist, communist, and other totalitarian systems, they are controlled by the state officials. In the capitalist system the concrete individuals involved are businessmen, as the representatives of the nonstate system; in the socialist, communist, and totalitarian systems the controllers are state bureaucrats. It is not necessary to have a great enthusiasm for a businessman and his omniscience, omnipotence, wisdom, and sociality. But one is still less obliged to expect miracles from the state bureaucrat and politician, even if he does profess Karl Marx's creed. If anything, the latter is less omniscient and omnipotent and wise and altruistic than the plain Mr. Babbitt.

These examples give a sufficiently clear idea of the migration or transfer or shift or "mobility" of social relationships from social system to social system. It is one of the important and ever-present social processes.[34]

(1) Assuming that the totality of social interrelationships between the units of a given population is constant, the greater is the part of the relationships that compose the fibers of the network of a given social system — for instance, of the State — the smaller is the part that makes up the fibers of the network of other social systems. If the State is totalitarian and the government tries to control most of the social relationships between its citizens, there remains little to be regulated by the other nonstate groups in the population. Their network will be thin and rarefied; they will have few matters to control and regulate. If the State involves in its system all the relationships (a purely theoretical case hardly ever found in the social reality) there is no room for the existence and functioning of other than state social systems. The same can be said of any other group.

(2) The network of the relationships of any organized social system does not remain constant, quantitatively or qualitatively, in the course of time. Quantitatively, as we have seen, it now "swells," now shrinks and becomes rarefied. At a given period, some of the relationships are excluded; at another period some new relationships are included. Qualitatively also, the relationships that compose it do not remain the same. The relationship A — for instance, religion — now is a part of a given social system — for instance, of the State. Now it drops from this network and becomes a fiber in another social system. Thus the texture of the social relationships of a given group changes not only quantitatively but qualitatively.

(3) In regard to small social groups, sometimes their networks become so thin that there remain few, if any, social relationships in their system. Such a situation means the end of their existence as an organized social system.

[34] It is regrettable that in spite of its importance, the process is hardly mentioned in social-science literature; most social scientists are unaware of it; and the problem is practically untouched by social investigators. I hope that after it is brought to their attention, some talented young scholars will venture to study it monographically, instead of wasting their talents in a study of the hackneyed problems, with their respective hackneyed and outworn "techniques." My study of social mobility (*Social Mobility*, New York, 1927), somewhat stimulated a series of studies along the lines elaborated in that book; perhaps it is reasonable to expect that this paragraph will do the same in regard to the problem of the "Mobility, Migration, and Shift of Social Relationships from Group to Group."

(4) In the predominantly Ideational culture, the Ideational social systems, like the Church, "swell" quantitatively and include most of the qualitatively important relationships. In the predominantly Sensate culture, the Sensate social systems, like the state, the economic, and other organizations of a highly utilitarian nature, swell and involve in their systems most of the qualitatively important relationships.

(5) The above means that in the social life there is always present the process of migration of social relationships from one system to another.

(6) The intensity of this migration is not constant. There are periods when only a few social relationships shift; therefore the structure and configuration of the social systems remain in a universe of a given population almost unchanged. They exist, for all such periods, in the form they had at its beginning. Respectively, no social earthquakes occur in the organized or institutional life of the society. And there are periods when the migration of social relationships becomes rapid and on a large scale. Such sudden and mass migrations lead to: (a) a crumbling of many social systems, whose beams, timbers, and bricks are taken from them — many of these systems disappear; (b) a deep transformation of other social systems, due to the migration from their network of a series of relationships and to the inclusion of a series of new ones. This means that such periods are marked by a substantial modification of the institutional and structural aspects of society. It experiences an earthquake which creates havoc with its previous order. The periods of so-called revolutions (social, political, economic, religious, and others) are examples of the periods of such mass migrations of the social relationships from social system to social system. We shall meet this phenomenon in a subsequent part of this work devoted to the movement of internal disturbances.

(7) In these fluctuations, so far as the large and fundamental social systems are concerned, like the big state, the world religious, the national, the occupational, the family formation (not the single family, but the totality of the families of the same type), and others, there are limits; none of the groups can become absolutely totalitarian and drive all the other groups out of existence. In the process of the expansion of a given system there will always be a point of saturation beyond which the system cannot go, and if it tries, it soon fails. As a result the process of expansion gives place to the opposite process of contraction and rarefaction of the system, and the decline of its totalitarianism.

This means that in the totality of the most powerful social systems (the Church, the State, the family, the occupational, the national, even the racial unions, the political parties, etc.) *the comparative power and totalitarianism of each group* has not been constant in the course of time, in the same society, and in different societies. It fluctuates. Now, as in the Middle Ages, the Church may be the most powerful group; then, as in modern times, its power and totalitarianism may decline, while that of the State rises. So it is with the occupational systems, whose role at the present time is especially important. In like manner has been changing the influence of the family formation, of kinship, of nationality organizations, and of other social systems. Thus in this field we see the existence of highly important migrations of social relationships; the quantitative-qualitative fluctuation of the network of social relationships of a given social system; and orderly and disturbing periods in the life of a given society. So much for this point.

The foregoing gives an idea of the qualitative and quantitative fluctuation of the systems of social relationships; of how much, in these fluctuations, they depend upon our main variables, and to what extent they are independent of them. The next chapter will add a little more to the picture.

Chapter Eight

FLUCTUATION OF ECONOMIC CONDITIONS [1]

I. PRELIMINARIES

Economic conditions do not remain constant in any social system but are subject to unceasing fluctuation. Some of the changes are slight, others great. Some are of short duration; others, especially the great fluctuations, manifest themselves completely only with the passage of decades or even centuries. Some come gradually, others with unexpected suddenness.

The economists have studied intensively short-time fluctuations, those mainly of recent times; [2] but the long-time changes and the sudden and calamitous movements of economic conditions have been virtually neglected, except for such purely descriptive characterizations as appear in the works of historians. That these fluctuations occur, there is no doubt. Every long-existing social and economic system experiences them. For examples of such fluctuations in the relatively small economic organization, let us look at enterprises of smaller or greater size. Any organization of this sort, if it exists for some time, is subject to many economic ups and downs, and among these some movements are sharp, sometimes even mortal, leading to dissolution of the firm, corporation, business enterprise. One has no reason to assume that such catastrophic "turns" are infrequent, especially as regards recent years. The average

[1] In co-operation with G. Mickwitz, P. A. Ostrouchov, S. G. Pushkareff, P. Savitzky, E. F. Maximovitch.

[2] Most business cycles studied by contemporary economics belong to comparatively slight and short-time fluctuations. Previous to the last two decades investigation dealt mainly with fluctuations of three, five, seven, eleven years. At the present time the students of business changes talk of cycles of twenty-five or forty-eight years. There is hardly any doubt that eventually they will pass to the study of fluctuations of still longer duration. See A. C. Pigou, *Industrial Fluctuations* (London, 1927); W. C. Mitchell, *Business Cycles* (New York, 1930); S. S. Kuznets, *Secular Movements in Production and Prices* (Boston and New York, 1930); N. D. Kondratieff's paper in the *Archiv für Sozialwissenschaften*, Vol. LX; E. Wagemann, *Economic Rhythm* (New York, 1930). In these representative works will be found bibliographies and indications of the character of the economic investigations of business cycles.

duration, for instance, of such small enterprises as grocery, drug, hardware, and shoe stores in Buffalo during the decade 1918–1929 was from three to six years.[3]   Of larger corporations, like the automobile companies in the United States, 64 per cent of 181 concerns subjected to examination (1903–1926) continued in existence for less than ten years.[4]   An examination of the age composition and duration of life of 7338 Swiss joint stock companies for the period 1902–1920, discloses that the median life expectation at the moment of founding is about 28.67[5] years for all the companies. A similar study of the Italian joint stock companies (1902–1922) shows the average expectation of life to be 24 years, 10 months.[6]   Nor does a survey of the English limited companies for the period 1856–1928 give a different result.[7]   This means that even in the life history of the extensive business system the incidence of catastrophic change in economic and financial conditions is not so rare as many think.   Still less rare are the "bad turns" that do not put an end to the companies, but make the continuance of their existence exceedingly difficult.

The same can be said, *mutatis mutandis*, of still larger socioeconomic systems like cities, states, nations, or extensive religious or other organizations.   Many such entities existed and are no more.   Their disappearance as an integrated and separate individuality often indicates, among other things, a catastrophic impoverishment and the impossibility of their maintaining their economic existence.[8]   The incidence is considerable, likewise, of catastrophic (and sometimes of an exceedingly great positive) change in the economic well-being of various societies and of populations inhabiting vast or narrowly limited areas — change that does not put an end to their existence, but leads to famine, starvation, lack of the elementary necessities and all the other concomitants of such a situation. Any investigator of famines, epidemics, and sudden extreme forms of impoverishment meets them frequently.[9]   Every economic and general

[3] See E. D. McGarry, *Mortality in Retail Trade* (Buffalo, 1930), pp. 52–61.

[4] R. C. Epstein, "Producers' Growth Curves in Expanding Industry," in *Harvard Business Review* (1927–1928), Vol. VI, pp. 270–277.

[5] See the data and the sources in P. Sorokin, "Life-span, Age-composition and Mortality of Social Organizations," in *Mensch en Maatschappij*, 9e *Jaargang* (1933), nos. 1 and 2, pp. 69–85.

[6] *Ibid.*   [7] *Ibid.*

[8] See the data on the life duration of these and other social organizations in P. Sorokin, *op. cit.*

[9] Such an investigation was described in my *Influence of Famine on Social Life and Organization*, destroyed by the Soviet Government.   See, for instance, F. Curschmann, *Hungersnöte in Mittelalter* (Leipzig, 1900); L. Kawan, *Gli esodi e le carestie in Europa attraverso il tempo* (Accademia Nazionale dei Lincei, Roma, 1932).   See also P. Sorokin, *Social Mobility* (New York, 1927), chap. iii.

historian knows the incidence of the long-time ascending and declining trends of economic well-being that occur, from time to time, in the history of nations or countries.

The purpose of this necessarily concise chapter is not a study of long-time trends, nor, contrariwise, of sudden catastrophic changes, in the economic history of the Graeco-Roman and Western cultures, but an elucidation of the relationship between the fluctuation of the Ideational and Sensate types of culture and that of economic conditions. Is there indeed any genuine relationship between them? If there is, what is it? Do the countries and periods of dominant Ideational culture tend to be associated with economic poverty or prosperity? What is the association during Sensate periods and in Sensate countries? These are the problems to be discussed in this chapter.

The predominant opinion in the literature of the social sciences seems to answer these questions — even the larger problem of the relationship between the mentality, ideology, and economic processes — in positive fashion. Most of the investigators do not hesitate to assert that the mentality of culture — aesthetic, religious, scientific, philosophical, ethical — on the one hand, and the forms of economic organization and economic processes, on the other, are closely interrelated. Karl Marx and the partisans of the so-called economic interpretation of history base the existence of this relationship upon the determining role of the economic factor. In their opinion, economic conditions, beginning with the means and instruments of production, control the forms of social and economic organization and the whole "superstructure" of the mentality or ideology of culture.[10] Others reverse this relationship and base their contentions upon the determining influence of mentality and ideology, beginning with religion, upon economic phenomena and processes, or simply claim a two-sided mutual functional connection between them. The theories of Fustel de Coulanges, Max Weber, Le Bon, J. G. Frazer, C. Bouglé, R. H. Tawney, and others [11] represent different varieties of this point of view. However sharply opposed are the economic and the ideological or functional interpretation, both currents agree as to the existence of a close correlation between the economic conditions and culture mentality. But the careful investigator cannot accept this agreement as conclusive evidence of the actual existence of the correlation in fact. He must test its validity directly, at least within the special

[10] See the literature and the essential elements of the economic interpretation of history in P. Sorokin, *Contemporary Sociological Theories* (New York, 1928), chap. x.

[11] *Ibid.*, chap. xii.

field of his study. The subsequent pages give a summary of such a test and its results.

II. Relationship between the Main Types of Culture and Economic Conditions

If we mean by economic values the totality of the Sensate values concerned with the satisfaction mainly of bodily needs, and prized as the means of securing Sensate — that is, utilitarian, hedonistic, and eudaemonistic happiness and pleasure — it seems reasonable to expect that the predominantly Ideational cultures and periods must be less prosperous economically than are predominantly Sensate. In the completely Ideational mentality and culture the economic values logically occupy a much less important and less highly esteemed place than in the Sensate. Christ's statement that it is easier for a camel to pass through a needle's eye than for a rich man to enter into the Kingdom of God is a typical formulation of an attitude common to the Hindu, the Taoist, and other Ideational mentalities. Even, as in the Middle Ages,[12] when economic values and the institutions associated with them are of necessity admitted into the system, they are regarded merely as the lesser evil, unavoidable since the Fall of Man. Similar is the attitude of the Hindu lawbooks and other Ideational sources, where the theory of the Fall also figures and is used to explain the toleration of this lesser evil.[13]

Since the mentality of the members of the Ideational culture is "other-worldly"; since they supposedly take little heed of this world, and especially of its economic comfort, of money-making, the accumulation of wealth, and the like, they should give little attention to, and discharge little energy on, the economic aspect of this empirical illusory reality. Still less is such a society to be expected to make economic comfort its main goal and its main value. If anything, it should ignore, disdain, or be indifferent wholly to activities and efforts in this direction. Hence, like the ascetics, it should, viewed from the Sensate standpoint, be poorer in its economic plane of living, and generally in its economic achievements, than the Sensate society.

We are all aware, on the other hand, of the positively exalted, sometimes the most exalted, position which the economic values have in a Sensate

[12] For the theories of the Stoics and the Church Fathers about economic values, private property, wealth, and so on, see R. W. Carlyle and A. J. Carlyle, *A History of Mediaeval Political Theory in the West* (New York, 1930), Vol. I, chaps. i–iv, ix, *et passim* throughout the other volumes. See Chapter Thirteen, Volume Two, of this work, and the literature cited there.

[13] See, for instance, Narada, I, 1–3; Brihaspati, I, 1, in *Sacred Books of the East*, Vol. XXXIII (Oxford, 1889).

culture.   The Sensate society is turned toward this world and, in this world, particularly toward the improvement of its economic condition as the main determinant of Sensate happiness.   To this purpose it devotes its chief thought, attention, energy, and efforts.   Therefore, it should be expected to be richer, more "prosperous," and more "comfortable" than the Ideational society.

Moreover, besides the difference in the *quantitative* economic achievements of the two opposed types of society, we must also expect a *qualitative* difference : a difference in the forms of economic organization — the character of the social relationships involved in production, distribution, and consumption — and in the theory of economic value, price, interest, profit, wage, and so on.   And this qualitative difference must be at least as profound as that which exists in such other respects as personal liberty, political regimes, social leadership, art, systems of truth and ethics.   For instance, it is probable that the surplus profit of an Ideational society would be spent in the building of a magnificent — and "unprofitable" — cathedral or monastery; while that of the Sensate society would be invested in a business skyscraper, like the Empire State Building, or a stadium, or a town hall.   A capitalist in an Ideational society might finance religious crusades without any expectation of material compensation and profit; but in a Sensate society he would do no such thing, if it did not promise a generous financial return.   These are but casual illustrations of the millions of qualitative differences which are to be found in the economic organization and processes of the two societies.

However, *such relationships are to be expected only if in a culture the mentality and the actual behavior of its members are closely integrated.*   Offhand, we are not to assume that the *whole* of a culture of a given society — including the economic compartment — is in fact integrated.   Likewise, as will be shown in Chapter Fifteen, we must not postulate, without a test, that mentality and actual behavior of human beings are always closely integrated and logically consistent.   Who is not acquainted with persons whose words (or thoughts) and deeds are sorely contradictory?   Since we cannot assume that any culture is logically and causally integrated in all its compartments, or that all human beings are always consistent in their mentality and their behavior, we cannot stop at a merely theoretical statement of what we may logically expect to be the correlation of economics and culture mentalities, but must try the validity of the theories in the light of empirical facts.

Besides the existence within a system of fundamental discrepancies, *we must reckon with the possible interference of "accidental" and external conditions.* Suppose, for instance, a highly prosperous Sensate society is suddenly swept over by the black plague, or by some other "accident of history," like an earthquake, inundation, or drought on a large scale. Suppose, further, that it becomes involved in a disastrous war or a still more disastrous revolution. These external forces might easily ruin its prosperity, at least for a period. If, however, the data should show that, such disastrous impoverishments notwithstanding, the general economic level of a Sensate society still remains high even in these periods, or that it recovers quickly when the accidental forces cease to operate, then, as regards this culture, we should have support from history for our theory of association.

Finally, the expected correlation of economic conditions with culture type may be upset by *the "immanent consequences" of the high development or even overdevelopment of the Sensate or Ideational culture itself.* As is true of virtually any logical deduction or causal generalization, what we postulate concerning quantitative and qualitative differences of economic phenomena in Ideational and Sensate societies may be valid only within certain limits, beyond which their validity ceases.[14] Like any other variable or process, Ideational and Sensate cultures generate in the course of their existence a series of characteristic consequences that follow inevitably from their individual natures. Some of these consequences may operate in the direction of weakening and destroying the culture that generates them. Thus in the field of economic conditions, some of the consequences of Ideational culture may, in spite of its negativistic attitude to "prosperity," work toward an accumulation of wealth, careful and successful organization of economic activity, and therefore toward "prosperity." And, vice versa, some of the immanent consequences of Sensate culture may operate, in spite of the avowed positive attitude of the Sensate mentality toward economic values, in the direction of undermining its prosperity and eventually lead the Sensate society to impoverishment and a plane of living below that of the Ideational society.

For instance, an overdeveloped Sensate mentality, through making economic well-being the main value, breeds greediness, rapacity, the desire to get rich quick, jealousy, and the like. Everybody in such a society begins to fight for his "share" of happiness and prosperity. This leads often to conflicts between sects, classes, states, provinces, labor-employer unions, two or more different Sensate nations and states, and often results in riots, revolts, wars, class struggles, overtaxation, which ruin security

[14] See P. Sorokin, "The Principle of Limits," in *Publication of the Sociological Society of America* (1932), Vol. XXVI. In addition see Volume Four of this work.

and in the long run make economic prosperity impossible. As a consequence, the high level of economic conditions in such a society often declines. Such situations have not infrequently developed in the later stages of a Sensate culture. So it was in Greece especially after the fifth and fourth centuries B.C. So it was in Rome at the end of the Republic and especially in the second and subsequent centuries A.D. This is only one of many ways in which the Sensate culture may generate forces that begin to work against one of its main objectives — an improvement of economic well-being.

Similarly, Ideational culture also generates forces that work against its negativistic or indifferent attitude toward the accumulation of wealth and the establishment of economic well-being. For example, the increasing prestige of saints, ascetics, and spiritual leaders who in the most disinterested way devote themselves either to God or to alleviation of the pain and sorrow of this world, to the salvation of human souls, to the organization and spiritualization of their earthly life — such prestige not infrequently has led the masses of the people, rich and poor, to flock to the abode of the saint, the hermit, the great bishop administrator ; to flock and to bring their contributions ; to intrust, to give, to bequeath their wealth to them, as the servants of God and disinterested servants of mankind. Such bearers of Ideationalism often find themselves eventually amidst wealth which they did not seek. A colony of the followers grows up near the place of the hermit ; it soon expands into a monastery ; the monastery becomes richer and richer. This makes necessary a proper management of the wealth. The disinterested and rational management leads to a further increase of wealth, involves the Ideationalists deeper and deeper in organizational economic activities. These, successfully discharged, tend to expand more and more ; the expansion leads to a still greater devotion of time and energy to the management of the economic affairs of a larger and larger community. In this way, in spite of its negative position with respect to economic well-being and wealth, Ideationalism generates forces which often work toward an improvement of the economic situation, not only of Ideationalists themselves, but of a much larger community, to embrace which the economic and organizational functions of the Ideational managers expand. Such in fact was the history of the accumulation of wealth and the growth of economic functions in many a center of Ideational Christian, Buddhist, Taoist, Hindu religion. In this way, among several others, the otherworldly Christian Church became the richest property owner in the Middle Ages, deeply and inextricably involved in economic affairs, as organizer and manager of the economic and social life of medieval Europe. For the same reason other Ideational currents, like Taoism in China, have given rise to a large number of the cleverest statesmen and the greatest organizers of social and economic life. What Max Weber ascribes specifically to ascetic Protestantism is, in fact, an immanent consequence of the active Ideational mentality in general, at a certain phase of its development when the appropriate circumstances arise. The very fact of existence of theocratic political and economic regimes (see Chapter Five) is another evidence of this.

To sum up : *At a certain phase of its growth, the Sensate culture may generate the forces which tend to undermine and destroy the economic welfare demanded and stimulated by the Sensate mentality. Likewise, the Ideational culture, generally disdainful of, or indifferent to, an improvement of economic well-being, may generate forces that involve it in vast economic affairs and often lead to a noteworthy improvement of the economic situation of the group or society.*

Thus, one or more of the three sets of conditions that we have just considered — (1) the lack of a causal integration corresponding to the logical; (2) the influence of various external and "accidental" factors; and (3) the immanent consequences of each culture type operating against the very culture that generates them — may easily obliterate the relationships which should theoretically exist.

With these conditioning factors clearly understood, we can now turn to testing, by Graeco-Roman and general Western history, our logical deduction as to the correlation of economic circumstances with culture types. Have these theoretical relationships been empirically realized here? And if they have, to what extent?

One method of making the test seems straightforward enough : limiting ourselves to Graeco-Roman and Western societies from the sixth to the twentieth century, we begin by finding out the periods of unquestionable prosperity and unquestionable depression and drawing the curve of the main waves of economic change. Then, having plotted the movement of Ideational and Sensate culture in the history of these societies, we bring the two curves together in comparison, and, using either a statistical or some other technique, reckon the exact nature of the relationship between the rise and decline of each type of culture and the curve of the rise and fall of economic prosperity. If the curves run clearly parallel, if there is an obvious correlation (no matter whether positive or negative), we have here *one* important piece of evidence of the empirical existence of the association which we have postulated. Later, in order to get corroboration in social space, we can apply the same procedure to other cultures and societies and compare the results with those obtained for Greece, Rome, and the West.

Now this procedure, though logical and clear, is not easily carried through.   Contrary to fairly common opinion, the movement of economic conditions cannot be studied more easily, accurately, and objectively than ideological and other fluctuations.   Through many circumstances an objective estimation of the economic ups and downs in the history of any country is exceedingly difficult to make, even for recent times. It is still more difficult for the older periods.   First of all, the data on which appraisal must be based are often, and for the past centuries regularly, either quite unsatisfactory in nature or completely or partially lacking.   For this reason only the construction of an accurate curve is well-nigh impossible.   Second, a number of epistemological and logical difficulties enter the problem.   What is to be regarded as economic well-being?   What a good, what a poor, standard of living?   What prosperity, what depression?   Is our standard to be the amounts of money in the income and expense columns of a figurative account book?   Is it to be the quantity of meat, bread, ice cream, cocktails consumed?   The size of movie audiences?   The number and quality of clothes or automobiles bought? or other necessities and luxuries enjoyed?   Or the amount of coal, iron, and other basic commodities produced?   Or the rate of interest on various bonds and shares, and the stock market quotations? Or the velocity of circulation of capital, the amount of bank deposits, and the purchasing power of money?   Or employment and unemployment?   Or what?

When we talk of "standard of living," "prosperity and depression," and the like, all this appears to us clear and definite.   But we have only to go a little deeper into the matter to see that the seemingly clear things are in fact very complex, very puzzling, and dependent upon subjective judgments to an enormous degree.[15]   In current belief, if one's expenses show a comparatively large amount spent for "recreation and amuse-ment" (say for a *New Yorker* magazine, for ten visits to Coney Island, for ten attendances at the movies, five attendances at baseball games, and five at horse races) and also a considerable amount for "eats" in cafeterias, one's plane of living is supposed to be higher than the plane of living of a peasant who breathes the fresh air of his countryside free of charge; who plays and watches the village games, paying nothing; who without any

[15] For some of the complications and the various, widely different standards of judgment, see C. C. Zimmerman, *Consumption and Standards of Living* (New York, 1936).

rush eats more wholesome food that costs him less than the mediocre food
of "modern" eating places.   The standard of living is, like "freedom,"
as we have seen previously, not a purely "objective" phenomenon but
depends always upon individual tastes and the pattern of living regarded
as desirable by a given group.   Diogenes the Cynic regarded his spiritual,
as well as his economic, plane of existence (the Stoic-Cynic "self-sufficiency") as far higher and better than that of a Croesus living in the utmost material luxury and ostentation.   For a teetotaler the indulgence of
an Epicurean in wine, even if he be the most refined connoisseur, is a manifestation not of a higher plane of living, but of perversity, degeneration,
and animalism.   Hence, when somebody claims that he is giving the
indices and curves of a *purely* economic well-being — quite "objective"
and free from any personal bias — such an investigator must be forgiven
for his astonishing naïveté.   There is no such thing as *perfectly* objective
and *purely* economic well-being, no absolute standard of prosperity,
depression, a high or low plane of living.   After analysis, all these matters
are found to be dependent upon a subjective-objective judgment, in
which the so-called economic category is inextricably interwoven with
many noneconomic values and intangibles.   Any economic well-being is
in a great degree a state of mind, depending not only, and perhaps not so
much, upon the number of calories and vitamins consumed, the number
and make of automobiles in one's possession, the amount of clothing
purchased, and the like; but also upon the social and cultural circumstances (especially with regard to one's neighbors, the Joneses and the
Smiths), the mind, the mood in which, and the purpose for which, all this
is possessed and consumed.   A prisoner or a slave may have (hypothetically) the best food, the best clothing, a Rolls Royce, and all the luxuries;
and yet, a plain peasant or laborer would hardly envy his standard of
living.   A "playboy" of high society may have five of the best cars (in
order not to be outdone by others of high society), and yet a farmer may
get more enjoyment from his secondhand Ford.   Yet these different
points of view are all contained within a Sensate context.   Still deeper is
the "subjective element" from the standpoint of Sensate and Ideational
mentality.   Here the formulas of Sensate and Ideational liberty, given
above (Chapter Six), express accurately the difference between Sensate
and Ideational economic well-being.

Having pointed out this profound difference, I intentionally assume,
in the subsequent study of the quantitative economic fluctuations, the
Sensate standpoint, liberalized and diluted with some eudaemonistic
values.   *Economic well-being will thus refer to not merely a plane of living*

measured by dollars and cents or by the quantity and quality of the commodities consumed per capita, but also, and to no less an extent, the total sum of more complex values — material and immaterial — which — like power, prestige, control, freedom, contentedness, satisfaction of the desires (which depend upon the character of the mentality) and the like — have a utilitarian, hedonistic, and eudaemonistic significance. Among these values special weight is given to such items as freedom, health, mortality, morbidity; the comparative prestige and dignity of a given class among the other classes of a society; the comparative power of control and the organizational functions (directive and creative activity) a given class or country has; the comparative place of a given class on the social ladder; and such intangibles as the "feeling of contentment with one's position"; and the like. All this makes the eudaemonistic-Sensate concept of economic well-being more indefinite and complex than the "dollar-measured" or "consumption-measured" planes of economic living. But since the phenomenon of economic values is complex and embraces all these elements, the conception of it which considers them all is more accurate and more valid than the artificially simplified conception that disfigures it fundamentally and therefore entirely misleads.[16]

But the problems and difficulties here indicated, epistemological and otherwise, are only of one kind among many. For example, even if we can agree upon a clear definition of economic well-being, we have yet to decide what measuring stick, what business barometer, what index, we shall use to measure the magnitude and nature of changes in the economic condition of society. Even for the study of recent business fluctuations, barometers and indices are at best only very approximate and highly subjective in character. For an examination of the past most of the elements on which they are based (whether they involve the production of coal or of iron, bank deposits, the circulation of money, prices, the value of shares and bonds, unemployment, and the like) are simply

---

[16] In passing I call attention to a practice frequently indulged in by contemporary social science and fundamentally fallacious, namely, the attempt to give a "clear-cut" definition to everything, including phenomena that by their nature are neither clear-cut nor definite. If a nebula is "nebulous," the description of it must emphasize this property and must not make the nebula "clear-cut." In the sociocultural world there are numerous series of phenomena that are in many respects nebulous. "Well-being," "economic well-being," is one of these. In such phenomena there may be a central core, say a trait A (sensory, hedonistic, utilitarian, eudaemonistic value), which is surrounded by a multitude of parts and constituents that are neither definite, nor clear, nor perfectly distinguishable. Defining this sort of reality with mathematical precision simply disfigures the reality. Most of the clear-cut, "objective," and measurable items of income-expense type of definitions of economic well-being are faulty in this respect.

inapplicable.   For a few centuries ago all these items either did not play any important role in determining the economic conditions and the business situation generally, or played a role different from, even opposite to, that which they now have.

All this indicates only briefly why it is more difficult to deal with economic conditions than with such variables as styles in painting, materialism and idealism, and others treated in Volumes One and Two.   It explains very largely why economic historians have thus far preferred giving fragmentary or vague descriptions, which are sometimes hardly more than a guess, to attempting a systematic and measured appraisal of the conditions in different periods and countries.

If, however, the definition of economic well-being which has been assumed by the present writer be used as a base, if the data of the historians may be relied on and their conclusions admitted at least as to the periods of unquestionable prosperity and decline, if the appraisal of the comparative economic status of the periods studied be considered as no more than very approximate, if the main body of the best historical works in the field be carefully and competently studied and summarized — if all these conditions be observed and admitted, then it will be possible to construct indicators and draw curves which should show approximately, and without serious distortion, the relative economic status of the countries and periods in question and the chief movements toward prosperity and impoverishment.

This is exactly what has been done by a group of historians at my request.   For specified countries they have attempted to construct such rough indicators and to draw such curves.   Let the reader note, the indicators and curves are not my work but that of these historians, all of whom are specialists each in the field he is here chosen to treat.   The summaries, analyses, tables, bibliographies, submitted by each would make an extensive monograph for each of the countries dealt with.   All these copious materials have been considered fully for the present chapter, but for the reason of economy of space only the indicators and diagrams are recorded here.[17]

A few explanatory remarks are necessary at the outset.

First, for most countries the comparative status of economic well-being at each specified period (of one hundred or of fifty years) is expressed on a scale from 1 to 10.   The 10 here means an "excellent" economic situation, or the highest prosperity; 9, "very good"; 8, "good"; 7, "very satis-

<hr />

[17] The complete material at my disposal will be deposited in the Sociology Library of Harvard University.

factory"; 6, "satisfactory"; 5, "fair"; 4, "almost fair"; 3, "rather bad"; 2, "bad"; 1, "very bad."

Second, the criteria for the diagnosis of the economic situation on this scale are naturally different from the contemporary business barometers. As we have mentioned, the constituent elements of the contemporary business barometer are inapplicable for the past. Not coal, nor iron, nor other elements that play a major part in the contemporary business barometer were as important in the economic systems of the past as they are at present. Hence the criteria for diagnosing the economic status for the past centuries must vary from those ordinarily used today. All in all the diagnosis, in accordance with the definition of economic well-being, given above, is based upon the totality of the relevant symptoms but not upon one or two elements. And these symptoms are combined not mechanically through assigning a certain, and the same, weight to each element throughout all the periods, but rather thoughtfully, considering the total sociocultural and economic configuration of each period. Of the elements that entered into the diagnosis the following may be specially enumerated: (1) the very fact of the mention of the existence and increase of economic enterprises in a given period by contemporary chroniclers; (2) the testimony of these writers about impoverishment or prosperity; (3) the appearance and growth of comparatively large individual fortunes; (4) evidences of growth or decline in agriculture and agricultural enterprises, as well as in agricultural populations; (5) evidences of the foundation, growth, and multiplication of cities and city buildings (or evidences of their decline, and especially of those cities of an economic character in contradistinction to the purely military urban centers which are less important for our purpose as symptoms); (6) the opening and development of new trade routes by land, water, and air; (7) evidences of rise of labor movements; (8) expansion or shrinkage of the colonizing activity of a given country; (9) the movement of population: growth or decline in size and density, and the increase or decrease of mortality; (10) morbidity and epidemics; (11) direct evidences concerning the "standard of living": prices, wages, employment, unemployment, accumulation of wealth, and the like; (12) war and peace; (13) the flourishing or decay of the arts, philosophy, science (for these are frequently a manifestation of prosperity or decline), as they are seen in the creation or importation of art objects, the rise of artists, thinkers, or their importation from abroad; (14) the multiplication or disappearance of monasteries, cathedrals, and other religious centers, together with the accumulation or decline of wealth in them; (15) the growth or decay of schools and other institutions of religious and secular learning; (16) political unification or disintegration; (17) internal peace or disturbance (revolutions, riots, etc.); (18) political expansion or decline. And there are several others. All these symptoms are well known to the historian, and it is from the result of their combination often that he characterizes a period as prosperous or unhappy and impoverished and indicates the extent of its prosperity or poverty. For the present chapter these symptoms have been investigated systematically and their totality weighted upon the scale that we have already described.[18]

Third, the appraisal of the movement of economic well-being in each country for the specified periods is given, to begin with, for the country as a whole, and then for its chief classes of people, especially those who are the main bearers of the culture in its integrated state, whether Sensate, Idealistic, or Ideational. A general appraisal of the economic situation of the whole country does not mean to indicate that all its regions and provinces were equally prosperous or impoverished. It happens fairly frequently that while the greater part of a country is in good economic condition, some of its separate regions are suffering from want. The general characterization aims to show the prevalent condition of the majority of its regions and population.

Now in addition to this an appraisal of the situation of the main classes of people in the society is introduced, because, even though the country as a whole is on the upward trend, this does not mean, necessarily, that the economic situation of all its classes follows the same trend. On the contrary, it is thinkable that an upward trend for the whole country or for most of its people may be followed by a downward economic trend for this or that special class, and vice versa. This is particularly important in regard to those classes, like the aristocracy, the clergy, the intelligentsia, governmental officials, and — especially in the Sensate culture — the bourgeoisie, which are the main bearers of the given culture.

With these preliminary words of explanation, let us turn directly to the figures. We begin with Greece and Rome.

A. *Greece and Rome:* (1) *Comments.*[19] The data of the tables and Figure 3 bear chiefly upon the changes in general prosperity which can be

---

[18] The investigators experimented a great deal with these symptoms before using them systematically. One of the results of the experimentation is that, of the eighteen items listed, in each period of prosperity from nine to fourteen "symptoms of prosperity" appeared. Similarly, the periods of depression are marked by the presence of from eight to fifteen symptoms.

[19] Figure 3 has been drawn by Dr. G. Mickwitz.

supposed to have taken place in some of the most important realms of
the ancient world. Where it seems probable that the culture-creating
upper classes have not undergone the same development as the lower
strata of the population, additional information is given. Everyone
familiar with the researches in ancient history knows that the data
must be considered with the utmost caution. In order to obtain exact
scientific results they must be based on some kind of statistical accounts.

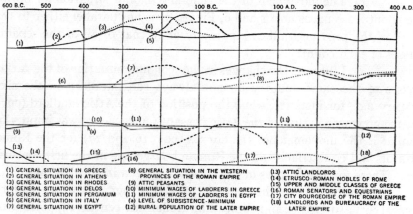

(1) GENERAL SITUATION IN GREECE
(2) GENERAL SITUATION IN ATHENS
(3) GENERAL SITUATION IN RHODES
(4) GENERAL SITUATION IN DELOS
(5) GENERAL SITUATION IN PERGAMUM
(6) GENERAL SITUATION IN ITALY
(7) GENERAL SITUATION IN EGYPT

(8) GENERAL SITUATION IN THE WESTERN
PROVINCES OF THE ROMAN EMPIRE
(9) ATTIC PEASANTS
(10) MINIMUM WAGES OF LABORERS IN GREECE
(11) MINIMUM WAGES OF LABORERS IN EGYPT
(a) LEVEL OF SUBSISTENCE-MINIMUM
(12) RURAL POPULATION OF THE LATER EMPIRE

(13) ATTIC LANDLORDS
(14) ETRUSCO-ROMAN NOBLES OF ROME
(15) UPPER AND MIDDLE CLASSES OF GREECE
(16) ROMAN SENATORS AND EQUESTRIANS
(17) CITY BOURGEOISIE OF THE ROMAN EMPIRE
(18) LANDLORDS AND BUREAUCRACY OF THE
LATER EMPIRE

FIG. 3. GENERAL ECONOMIC SITUATION IN THE ANCIENT WORLD,
600 B.C. TO A.D. 400

Now only the data about the position of laborers in Greece and Egypt
are founded on figures regarding salaries and expenses of living directly
recorded in inscriptions, chiefly of Delos, and in the Egyptian papyri.
In all other cases, while we are able to draw from literary sources, and
above all from the archeological material, some general conclusions as
to the improvement or aggravation of the economic situation during a
certain period, we cannot state anything specific about the extent of this
phenomenon. We do not gain anything like certainty by comparing two
"downs" in the line of fluctuations any more than we can judge which
period of improvement has reached the highest point. Several factors
quite inaccessible to us contribute to this condition, i.e., the density
of the population, the local extension of prosperity, the distribution of
incomes among rich and poor.[20]

[20] The following works sum up the results of the modern researches and form a suitable
introduction to the study of ancient economics. A general survey of the field is given by
the pages of the Cambridge Ancient History dealing with this subject. For archaic Greece:
J. Hasebroek, Griechische Wirtschafts- und Gesellschaftsgeschichte bis zur Perserzeit (Tübingen,
1931). For classical Greece: G. Glotz, Le travail dans la Grèce ancienne (Histoire universelle

If these curves depict the changes in the economic situation of Greece and Rome, and for the main classes of people in these countries, even with rough accuracy, the following conclusions are warranted.

(*a*) The economic well-being of both countries and of the main classes of its population fluctuated widely in the course of time.

(*b*) In these fluctuations there is no permanent trend in the advance from the earlier to the later stages of the cultures.

(*c*) The movement of the general economic situation for both of the countries (curves nos. 1 and 6, Figure 3) is not parallel either to that of all of the provinces taken separately or to that of all of the separate classes of each country.

(*d*) Likewise, the changes in the economic situation of the various classes of the same country do not always run parallel: in the sixth century B.C., for instance, while the position of the Attic landlord (curve no. 13) grew worse, that of the Attic peasant (curve no. 9) was improving. Similar is the movement of the curves (nos. 16 and 17) for the Roman senators and equestrians and the Roman bourgeoisie in the first centuries B.C. There are other cases of this kind to be seen in the diagram.

(*e*) Passing to the central concern of our study, we find the general curve of Greece and the leading Hellenistic centers supporting the logical theoretical position in regard to the negative association of eudae-monistically Sensate economic prosperity with the Ideational, and to its positive association with the Sensate, at the period of ascendance and before the decline of the culture. We see, for example, in the sixth century B.C. when Greek culture was still considerably Ideational, that the economic level was not very high. With the rise of the Sensate culture in the fifth and fourth centuries B.C. the curve of economic prosper-

---

du travail, Paris, 1920). With regard to trade: J. Hasebroek, *Staat und Handel im alten Griechenland* (Tübingen, 1928) and E. Ziebarth, *Beiträge zur Geschichte des Seeraubs und Seehandels im alten Griechenland* (*Hamburgische Universität, Abhandlungen aus dem Gebiet der Auslandskunde*, no. 30, Hamburg, 1929). Endeavors at calculating national income: E. Cavaignac, *Population et capital dans le monde méditerranéen antique* (*Publications de la Faculté des Lettres de l'Université de Strasbourg*, no. 18, Strasbourg, 1923). The Hellenistic Age: F. Heichelheim, *Wirtschaftliche Schwankungen der Zeit von Alexander bis Augustus* (Spiethoff, *Beiträge zur Erforschung der wirtschaftlichen Wechsellagen Aufschwung, Krise, Stockung*, no. 3, Jena, 1930); M. Rostovtzeff's articles in *Cambridge Ancient History;* The Roman Republic: T. Frank, *An Economic History of Rome* (Baltimore, 1927). The Roman Empire: M. Rostovtzeff, *Social and Economic History of the Roman Empire* (Oxford, 1926; revised German edition, 1930). Salaries and prices: A. Segré, *Circolazione monetaria e prezzi nel mondo antico ed in particolare in Egitto* (Roma, 1922). Later Empire: E. Stein, *Geschichte des spätrömischen Reiches* (Wien, 1928) and G. Mickwitz, *Geld und Wirtschaft im römischen Reich des vierten Jahrhunderts n. Chr.* (*Societas scientiarum Fennica, Commentationes humanarum litterarum*, Helsingfors, 1932), Vol. IV, no. 2.

ity rises also; and in some centers, like Athens (which led in this Sensate movement), its rise was very great even before the end of the fifth century. The greatest development of the Sensate culture occurred in such Hellenistic centers as Rhodes, Pergamum, and Alexandria. We see that in these centers the curve continued to rise after it had declined in Athens and in Greece as a whole; and rose until it reached levels considerably higher than had ever been approached elsewhere in Greece. As we pass to the subsequent centuries, especially to the second and the third centuries A.D. — when, as we have seen, the new Ideational culture began to rise and the previous Sensate culture was definitely on the decline — the curve of economic well-being tended to decline also. Thus far, then, the association that we have indicated as logically predictable seems to be supported in fact.

It is supported also by the movement of the economic situation of the Greek upper and middle classes in the centuries from the fifth to the first B.C. (curve 15). Roughly these classes were the chief bearers during these five hundred years of the integrated Sensate culture. With its rise in the fifth and the fourth centuries B.C. their economic welfare rose also, stayed high throughout the third century, and began to decline with the decline of the now overripe Hellenistic Sensate culture in the second and, probably, in the first century B.C.

Less notable, in fact barely distinguishable, is the association of the economic situation of either the Attic peasants or the laborers in Greece generally, with Sensate or Ideational culture movements. The economic position of these classes fluctuated within much narrower limits than did that of the upper and middle classes. If it rose with the rise of the Sensate culture, it began to decline earlier than for other classes and at a period when the Sensate culture was still strong and the Hellenistic centers (Rhodes, Pergamum, Egypt) were still developing to their climax. The meaning of such a loose relationship may possibly be that since these classes are rarely in any pronounced fashion the bearers of either type of integrated culture, and since their culture mentality is mainly Mixed, containing many "subcultural" or pseudo-Ideational elements, their economic position is influenced much less by the transformation of the integrated culture of upper and middle classes of their country than by various "accidental" forces and by the immanent consequences of culture. Hence, if this is true, the lack of a clear-cut relationship in the case of the lower classes does not necessarily invalidate the theory of associations for the Sensate and Ideational cultures, but indicates that in those sections of society where integration is not conspicuous we may have to look for various disturbing factors as furnishing the key to the truth. Thus in the period of the domination of the Ideational culture in Greece (before the sixth century and to a less degree in the sixth century itself), when the general economic level was comparatively low, the position of the laboring classes was necessarily low on this account, but not excessively as compared with the position of the upper classes, because of a considerable growth of the familistic relationship between the classes which, as was shown in Chapters Two, Three, and Four of this volume, is more highly developed in an Ideational society than in a Sensate. The rise of the general economic level with the development of the Sensate culture, at the time when the synthesis with the declining Ideational culture resulted in the Idealistic complex of the fifth and fourth century B.C., to some extent brought benefits to the agricultural and laboring classes. When, however, the Sensate culture reached a high level, it seems to have generated the forces which began to hinder a further increase of this sharing of the benefit by the laboring classes. Through the unbridled egotism and greed of the dominant Sensate class, which had now become too much "economically minded" and too little "socially minded"; through the weakening of familism, compassion, moral and religious checks against the exploitation of the weaker classes by the stronger; through development of contractual and compulsory relationships; and finally, through revolts, riots, excessive taxation of the rich by the masses and their leaders, the improvement of their condition was stopped and replaced, already at the climax of the Sensate culture and increasingly during its decline, by a turn for the worse. We shall meet a somewhat similar course of events in the history of France and Germany.

So much for Greece.

The general Roman economic situation (curve no. 6, Figure 3) is also in agreement with our hypothesis. We know that the movement of Rome to the Sensate culture, especially under influence of the Hellenistic culture, began to be manifest already in the third century B.C., became particularly strong in the second and first centuries B.C., and reached its climax in the first century A.D. Correspondingly, the economic curve shows a steady rise during these centuries with its height in the first part of the first century A.D. We have also seen that already in the second century A.D. the Ideational currents had become noticeable and then continued to rise. Similarly, beginning with the later first century A.D., the general curve of the economic situation turns downward and in the third and fourth centuries A.D. reaches levels notably lower than in the centuries of the climax of the Sensate mentality and culture.

Turning to the main bearers of the integrated culture — the Roman senatorial and equestrian classes, and for a later period the urban bourgeoisie — we observe that the curves of the economic situation of all these classes, in spite of some differences in time among them, rise and fall with the rise and fall of the Sensate wave.   For the senatorial class, as being less Sensate, the decline comes earlier; for the bourgeoisie later.   But all three classes (including the equestrians) "describe their parabola" within the general limits of the rise and decline of the Sensate culture.

The economic welfare of the laboring classes shows here again a very limited amplitude of fluctuation and a far looser connection, if any, with the changes in the culture.   Judged by the minimum wages in Egypt, this class had its best situation in the first, second, and third centuries A.D. — that is, in the centuries of a Mixed culture, with a declining Sensate and a rising Ideational type.   Though this Mixed period was not strictly Idealistic, it approached this state.   With the transition to the Ideational culture, before its full development, their position grew worse in the general downward movement of the economic conditions of the country.

Finally, the curves for the Attic landlords (13), Etrusco-Roman nobles (14), and the landlords and bureaucracy of the later Empire (18), are interesting.   We see that the first two landlord classes suffered an economic decline with the beginning of the decline of the Ideational culture and the rise of the Sensate in the sixth and fifth centuries B.C., while the landlords and bureaucracy of the later Empire experienced an improvement with the beginning of the rise of the Ideational culture in the third and fourth centuries A.D.   Here we are confronted with a situation to be met later on in the Middle Ages.   Such an economic fate may be due to the totality of the "accidental" forces, but it may also be the result of the association of these classes with the rise and fall of the Ideational culture and with some of the immanent consequences of that culture. This class, together with the priestly class, was the main organizer of the social, moral, and economic order in the Ideational society (before the sixth century); and for this reason, as is true of any class in any society that organizes its system of values, including the organization of the economic functions, it could not help improving its own situation.   What we know of the Attic landlord class (before the fifth century), of the early Etrusco-Roman landlord class, and — after the state adoption of Christianity — of the class of state officials and landowners suggests that these classes were indeed bearers of Ideational culture, working hand in hand with the sacerdotal Ideational class, supported and partly controlled by it (as after the legalization of Christianity) or themselves discharging

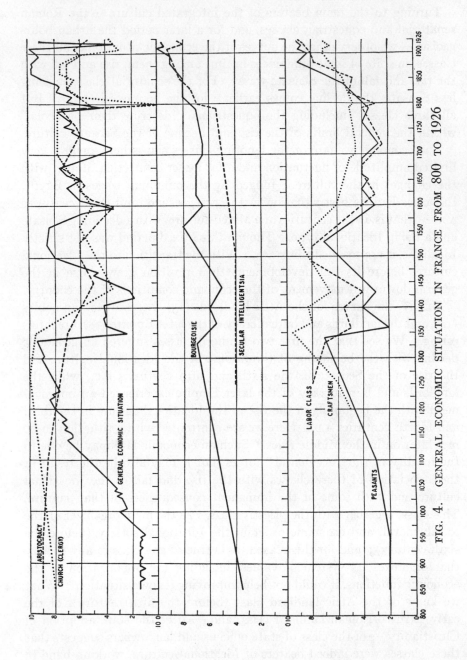

FIG. 4. GENERAL ECONOMIC SITUATION IN FRANCE FROM 800 TO 1926

to a considerable extent the religious functions of priest and of the organizers of the moral order of society (as in Greece and Rome before the fifth century B.C.). As the mouthpiece and integrators of Ideationalism, they were destined, as one of the immanent consequences of the development of their culture type, to improve their social and economic condition with its rise, and to suffer social and economic decline with its decay. Further, in so far as the system of social relationship in which they lived was mainly familistic and compulsory, and not contractual in any great degree, the decline and rise of familistic and, in part, compulsory relationships with the decline and rise of Ideational culture bound these classes to that culture by an additional tie.

Such seems to be the connection of the economic destiny of these various classes with our main variables. Besides this connection many other sporadic and incidental factors, independent of the types of culture, explain some of the fluctuations we meet with; but these factors do not concern us in this work and therefore can be passed by.

B. *France.* From Greece and Rome let us pass now to France as shown by Figure 4, which shows the main fluctuations in the field for France as a whole, as well as for its chief classes.[21]

(1) *Comments.* If the general curve representing the economic fluctuations in France reflects the reality approximately accurately, then it reinforces in essentials the major points previously made concerning Greece and Rome (see pages 230 to 237, points (a), (b), (c), (d), (e). By means of it we perceive at once that, judged from the Sensate standpoint, the general economic situation throughout the Ideational Middle Ages remains on the levels "very bad," "bad," "rather bad," and, at best, "almost fair." Up to the end of the eleventh century the curve does not pass beyond the stage "almost fair." To this extent our hypothesis of correlation is given positive support. We see also that, beginning with

[21] The appraisal is by Dr. E. F. Maximovitch. The diagram, and a volume of comments and evidences not given in this work, are based upon the work of the following authors (for the sake of economy of space the titles of the works are omitted here): G. d'Avenel, M. Augé-Laribé, P. M. Bondois, M. Block, A. Coville, G. Martin, C. E. Labrousse, K. Lamprecht, C. V. Langlois, R. Latouche, E. Lavisse, H. Lemonnier, E. Levasseur, A. Luchaire, M. Mariéjol, H. Marion, G. Monod, C. Petit-Dutaillis, P. Raveau, A. E. Sayous, H. Sée, K. von Tyszka, R. Vivier, G. Wiebe, L. Verriest, H. Pirenne, P. A. Scheffel, G. Lefebvre, M. Lair, Du Bourg, C. Seignobos, F. Simiand, E. Pariset, L. Godart, E. Tarlé, P. H. Ardasheff, F. Volters, N. P. Graziansky, V. Dalin, M. Kovalevsky, J. Kulisher, V. F. Levitski, E. V. Olovianishnikova, I. Loutchisky, N. Kareef, D. M. Petrushevski, M. N. Pokrovski, F. Potemkin, A. A. Suchov, N. P. Freiberg, A. Schulgin, N. Nikiforoff, P. Boissonade, F. Lot, and others, together with many collective works like the *Cambridge History*, statistical publications, chronicles, and other primary and secondary sources.

the end of the eleventh century, the curve starts to rise very rapidly and continues upward until the second quarter of the fourteenth century, reaching the level "very good" and even "excellent" at the climax of the Idealistic culture of these centuries.

We know that the end of the eleventh century marks the reappearance of the Sensate forms in most of the compartments of the Western culture, and the subsequent centuries bring further growth of the Sensate at the cost of a declining Ideational culture. The thirteenth century and a part of the fourteenth were Idealistic in most of the sections of Western culture generally. Thus again the rise of the Sensate culture and of economic well-being go hand in hand (minor and incidental fluctuations excluded).[22] Here we have a recurrence of what we met with in Greece and to some extent in Rome.

[22] Incidentally, confronting the curve of economic situation in Greece, Rome, and France, with the curves of the movement of war and internal disturbances (cf. Parts Two and Three of this volume), we see that in Greece in the centuries of the maximum of war and internal disturbances (fifth and fourth B.C.) these did not hinder the rise of economic prosperity, and the third and second centuries B.C., which were comparatively very peaceful both internally and externally, were, at the same time, centuries of economic decline. In Rome, likewise, economic improvement proceeded successfully from the fourth century B.C. to the first A.D., which centuries were the most belligerent. After the first century war declined and never reached the level of the third and the first century B.C. In spite of that the economic curve turned down in the first century A.D. The curve of the internal disturbances rose from the third to the first century B.C., and yet it did not stop economic improvement from the third century B.C. to the first century A.D.; and, vice versa, economic improvement during these centuries did not stop or impede the ascending trend toward internal disturbances. This means that the usual opinion that internal disturbances or wars occur mainly in the periods of impoverishment, or vice versa, is fallacious. This does not mean that the opposite statement, that war and revolutions occur mainly in the periods of prosperity, is a universal rule. It means, as explained in Parts Two and Three of this volume, that war, internal disturbances, and economic fluctuations all move fairly independently of one another and that the causes of war and revolutions are not mainly economic.

This statement is borne out also by the curve of economic fluctuations in France. We see that beginning with the end of the tenth century up to the middle of the fourteenth the economic curve was rapidly rising. In spite of that, the indicators of disturbances rose from 34 for the tenth century to 142 for the eleventh, 291 for the twelfth, 245 for the thirteenth. The fourteenth century is marked by a great impoverishment and the first part of the fifteenth century was also bad. And yet, the indicators for the disturbances fell to 117 for the fourteenth and 94 for the fifteenth. The sixteenth century shows a notable improvement in the economic situation; the disturbances again rise. Likewise, the absolute figures for the casualties of war as well as the strength of the army show a regular increase in both from the tenth to the fourteenth and subsequent centuries. Absolute figures are of course misleading, but they warrant the conclusion that war did not decline during these centuries. These correlations show the fallacy of the popular opinion that we have mentioned, give substantiation to the statement developed in Parts Two and Three of this volume that wars and disturbances have occurred in periods both of poverty and prosperity, and that there is no evidence that war or revolution is more associated with poverty than with prosperity. The

When, however, we pass to the fourteenth century we are confronted with a sudden decline of economic well-being. The decline was due partly to the immanent consequences of the rising Sensatism, which manifested itself to some extent in the Hundred Years' War. This war in its turn led to impoverishment. But in a considerable degree impoverishment was due also to an accidental cause in the form of the sudden epidemics of the Black Plague that carried off a large part of the population of Europe. But in spite of these powerful disturbing elements, the economic level still remains, all in all, above that of the centuries of the Ideational period. And when these elements have disappeared, the Sensate culture and society recover rapidly, and already in the fifteenth century show notable improvement which continues in the sixteenth century until the curve reaches the "very good" level — a level never reached in the Ideational period. At the end of the sixteenth century we have again a sudden short-time decline. This was the result, among other things, of the religious wars. Now the religious wars themselves were in a sense, just as the Reformation itself was, one of the immanent consequences of the developing Sensate culture and mentality. However, the decline was temporary, and even at its lowest level the economic situation remained considerably above that of the Ideational centuries. The seventeenth century brought with it a notable improvement once again, and from that time on, except for minor and temporary fluctuations, the curve rose steadily, continuing throughout the eighteenth and the nineteenth and in the prewar twentieth century. In the nineteenth and the first decades of the present century it reached the unprecedented height of the category "excellent." A war of unprecedented magnitude — again an immanent consequence of an overripe and rapacious Sensatism (as we shall see in Part Two) — led to a sharp decline in the plane of living. After the war the curve shows a rise again, but it does not at its high point in 1926 reach the prewar level; and at the present time, it is again on the decline. Whether this decline is the beginning of a long-time downward trend, the inner result of an overripe Sensate culture, or whether it is just a short-time fluctuation, like some of the preceding "accidental" declines, remains to be seen.

What is important in the curve for the centuries after the fourteenth is that it shows, in spite of the temporary declines due partly to the

---

curves and data given in this chapter substantiate this statement for other periods in the three countries mentioned, and there is further corroborating evidence for Germany, Austria, Russia, and England. The reader interested in the problem can easily make for himself further tests when reading Parts Two and Three of this volume.

"accidents of history" (just as a healthy man may be killed or temporarily incapacitated by an automobile or other accident), the successful economic orientation of the society and culture in the periods of rising and developed (but not overdeveloped) Sensatism. Even in the periods of the lowest economic level during these centuries, the Sensate society was (judged from the Sensate standpoint) better off than the Ideational at any time during its domination. The great economic vitality of the Sensate culture in this period is demonstrated also by the comparatively rapid recovery of the Sensate social organism from the shocks due to the terrific accidents or to the immanent consequences of Sensatism itself.

(2) *Reasons*. Taken as a whole the curve lends support to what we have on the basis of logic expected. Sensate culture tends to be associated, save for the limitations we have considered, with greater economic (hedonistic, utilitarian, or eudaemonistic) well-being, while the Ideational culture tends to be poorer and less prosperous in this respect. Such a statement does not mean that the Sensate man is cleverer and thus can solve the economic problems better than the Ideational man. It means that the Ideational man is less attentive to, less appreciative of, and less interested in, economic well-being; therefore he does not devote his mind and energy to this purpose to the extent that this is done by the Sensate man, for whom economic well-being is the alpha and omega of all effort. All the intellect of the Sensate man (see Chapters Three and Four, Volume Two), all his volition, and his activities (see Chapters Five and Thirteen, Volume Two; and the first four chapters of this volume) are centered on the achievement of wealth, which means for him to be happy, independent, free, powerful, respected, admired; to be a leader, a member of society; to have influence, prestige, and "everything in the world that money can buy" — because in a Sensate society money can buy almost anything. Ideational and Sensate mentalities are quite differently oriented in this and in many other matters. Therefore, the behavior of persons bearing them is different. Hence, the difference in the economic achievements of both. One man does not care for wealth much and therefore remains (often quite contentedly) poor; the other cares for it very much, devotes his efforts to its achievements, therefore multiplies his economic comforts far beyond the accomplishment of the Ideational man.

(3) *Classes*. Let us glance now at the movement of the curves for the leading classes of French society, those classes which have been the main bearers of the integrated culture, whether Ideational or Sensate. Figure 4 shows the main changes in the economic situation of the specified

classes. For our purposes short comments on the curves for the clergy and the Church, the aristocracy, the bourgeoisie, and the intelligentsia are sufficient.   The main bearers of the medieval Ideational culture were the clergy and the aristocracy as the landowning class.   From the curves we see that their position was the best in the Middle Ages.   With the decline of the Ideational culture the economic well-being and economic power of the Church and clergy decline also (after the thirteenth century).   In spite of several sharp rises during the subsequent centuries, the curve does not reach the medieval level, and continues to show a general declining trend.   The position of the aristocracy also was best during the early medieval centuries.   Because of the Crusades, the communal movements, and other factors — most of which were the first manifestations of the coming Sensate culture — the economic power and level of the aristocracy begin to decline even earlier than that of the Church and the clergy.   In a way the aristocracy experiences here what happened to the Attic and Etrusco-Roman landed aristocracy.   The French Revolution put an end to aristocracy as a social class.   Its place was taken by the great landowners.   But even this class, predominantly Sensate now, suffers a steady economic decline during the nineteenth and in the twentieth century.

In the Sensate culture the main bearers are the bourgeoisie and the secular, in a considerable degree free-thinking, intelligentsia.   A mere glance at the curves for these classes shows a steady rise with the growth of Sensate culture : for the bourgeoisie already beginning with the eleventh, and especially with the fifteenth century ; for the secular intelligentsia after the fifteenth century.   Both classes reached their comparative climax in the prewar period.

Thus again the data suggest that in each integrated culture, the classes that are its main bearers flourish (comparatively) when the culture blossoms, and decline when it declines.   This does not exclude temporary and "accidental" changes in the economic position of these classes, due to many extrinsic and other factors.   But the main trends of their rise and fall are bound up with the destiny of the culture itself of which they are the mouthpieces and integrators.

As to the peasant, labor, and craftsmen classes, their economic situation, as in Greece and Rome, is low in the period of Ideational culture (a consequence of the generally low economic conditions).   With the rise of the Sensate culture in the eleventh century it begins to rise, and reaches one of its highest points in the period of the Idealistic culture of the thirteenth and part of the fourteenth century, when the social and moral

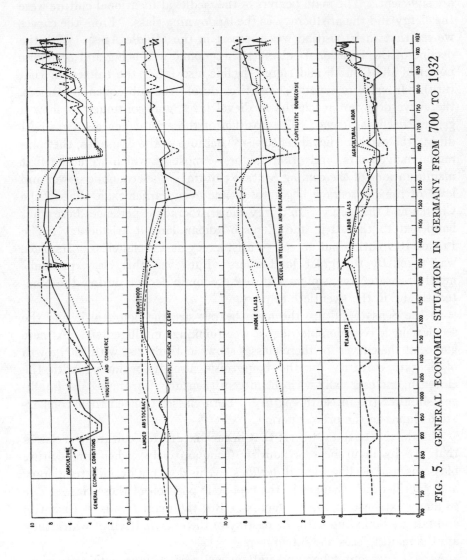

FIG. 5. GENERAL ECONOMIC SITUATION IN GERMANY FROM 700 TO 1932

precepts of the Idealistic periods were still operating to give them an increased share in an increased national wealth and income, and when the disastrous immanent consequences of the overdeveloped Sensatism were not as yet playing an especially important role. After that period, only in the nineteenth century does their economic well-being reach a level higher than that of the Idealistic period. This is the result of the exceptionally great economic achievements of an exceptionally powerful Sensate mentality and culture, with their unique scientific and technological progress. But the twentieth century here also, as in practically all the compartments of Western culture, gives the first strong warnings: the curve of economic improvement of these (and other) classes that rose rapidly and almost uninterruptedly throughout the nineteenth century now not only shows a decrease in rate of rise, but even goes downward. Whether this is going to be a short-time dip or is the beginning of a long-time downward trend remains to be seen. If the Western culture is in fact entering the declining stage of its Sensate form, and if the waves of the economic fluctuations of these classes are indeed, in part at least, bound up with the fluctuation of the main types of culture, then this warning symptom may be the beginning of a long-time economic decline. Otherwise, if the Sensate culture of our days is still vital and is going to emerge from the contemporary crises revitalized, then the economic decline of the twentieth century will be just an "accidental" short-time dip, to be replaced by a continuation of the previous rising trend.

C. *Germany.* Let us pass now to Germany as shown in Figure 5 on the opposite page.[23]

[23] Figure 5 and the analysis (which would make a volume by itself), not given here, were made by Dr. S. G. Pushkareff. The main works upon which the curves are based are by the following authors: L. Achner, A. Arndt, W. J. Ashley, G. von Below, L. N. Berkut, L. Beutin, A. Bilimowitsch, J. Borchardt, F. Bothe, T. Brauer, H. Brück, K. Bücher, A. Cohen, H. Cunow, F. Curschmann, E. Daenell, A. Dopsch, O. von Dungern, R. Ehrenberg, H. V. Festenberg-Packish, F. X. Funk, T. Geiger, T. von der Goltz, V. Grinevitch, A. Günther, K. Hanefeld, A. Hauck, H. Herkner, O. Hötsch, O. Hue, K. T. von Inama-Sternegg, J. Janssen, J. Jastrow, K. Kaser, G. F. Knapp, R. Kötzschke, M. Kovalevsky, G. Krüger (ed.), R. Kuczynski, J. M. Kulischer, F. X. Künstle, B. Kuske, K. Lamprecht, J. Lippert, A. Luschin von Ebengreuth, R. Meerwarth, N. Molschanowski, J. Müller, L. Oberascher, E. Otto, E. von Philippovich, A. Pöschl, P. Sander, A. Sartorius von Waltershousen, D. Schäfer, A. Scharnagl, P. Schumpeter, G. Schmoller, G. Schnapper-Arndt, G. Schnürer, H. von Schubert, P. Schutiakow, M. Sering, H. Sieveking, W. Sombart, T. Sommerlad, L. A. Veit, Ad. Wagner, A. Weber, M. Weber, J. Wernicke, G. Wiebe, K. Woblyi, W. Woytinski, F. Zahn, W. Zimmermann, F. Zoepfl. Dr. Pushkareff also used the *Kirchliches Handbuch* (A. Krose, ed.), *Kapital und Kapitalismus* (B. Harms, ed.), *Die deutsche Landwirtschaft*, and many collective works statistical and other publications, important *Schriften* and periodicals.

(1) *Comments*. Once more the occurrence of fluctuation in the general economic situation, the lack of any perpetual trend, and other traits mentioned above in regard to Greece and Rome, are present in the curve for Germany. As to the association of prosperity with the Sensate and of a comparatively modest economic situation with the Ideational culture, this is shown also by the curve, though not so conspicuously as in the case of France. We see that the Ideational period from 850 to the end of the eleventh century is marked by a rather low economic level. Beginning with the twelfth century the curve begins to rise and reaches the "good" stage in the thirteenth and the fourteenth centuries, and remains on this high level throughout the fifteenth and sixteenth centuries (minor fluctuations excluded, the chief of which was due to the Black Plague) up to the time of the Thirty Years' War, when it drops enormously and reaches one of the lowest levels thus far. But this "accident," and at the same time consequence, of the developing Sensate culture being over, it begins to rise again after 1650, and then it climbs steadily to an unprecedented height in the nineteenth and twentieth centuries, up to the World War, when it drops again greatly, as is the case in practically all the other countries of Europe.

A similar picture is given by the two general curves, one for the development of agriculture, the other for that of industry, with the difference that the development of industry and urban economics, when compared with agriculture, seems to be more highly favored by the growth of the Sensate culture (until the seventeenth century, after which agriculture began to become more and more "industrialized" and "urbanized" and therefore its fluctuations became more and more closely parallel to those of industry).

(2) *Classes*. The curves of the social classes, that are the chief bearers of the integrated cultures, whether Ideational or Sensate, show again a more direct connection with the main types of integration than the curves for the classes of the peasantry, agricultural laborers, and industrial workingmen. The latter fluctuate within narrower limits and manifest a much looser connection with the change of the dominant culture than those for its main bearers. In this respect they are similar to those of the lower classes in Greece, Rome, and France. The reason for the looser connection is that the mentality and mode of adaptation of the lower classes are less completely integrated than those of the bearers of the integrated culture.

(3) *Clergy*. The curve of the Roman Catholic Church reaches its highest point in the period up to about 1250, after which it begins to

decline, takes a great drop in the period of the Reformation, then subsequently rises again but never reaches the levels of the Ideational and Idealistic ages.   The comparatively "good" situation in the second half of the eighteenth and during the nineteenth century is the result of the generally very good economic conditions during these years, rather than of the specially favorable and influential position of the Catholic Church and clergy, as was true in the Middle Ages.   In the Middle Ages with their predominantly "fair" and "almost fair" and "bad" general economic situation, the position of the Catholic Church and its clergy was "fair," "good," and "very good" — that is, far above the general level of the country as a whole; in the nineteenth century especially, when the general economic situation of the country was "good," "very good," and even "excellent," the position of the Church and of the clergy was only "good," "satisfactory," and sometimes even only "fair."   If this difference is taken into consideration, the decline of the economic situation and power of the Catholic Church with the rise and triumph of the Sensate culture becomes particularly clear.

Similar is the situation of the knighthood and aristocracy, the privileged landed aristocracy.   Again their position was far above the general level of the country in the Ideational Middle Ages, reaching a climax in the eleventh and twelfth centuries.   After that there comes a decline, leading soon to the disappearance of the knighthood as a special class and to an especially great decline in the position of the landed aristocracy relative to the general situation of the country.   Even in the nineteenth century the landed aristocracy did not again reach the level of the eleventh and twelfth centuries; at best it enjoyed a "good" level while the country as a whole attained the "very good" and even the "excellent" economic status.

Thus here again we see that the main bearers of the Ideational culture, the Church (clergy) and the landed aristocracy, which was its ally in secular matters, had their best situation in the period of the domination of the Ideational, and that their position declined with the rise of the Sensate culture.   This parallels the history of Greece, Rome, and France.

If now we turn to the curves of the main bearers of the mentality of the Sensate culture, to the curves of the industrial bourgeoisie and secular intelligentsia and, in part, the secular bureaucracy, we see that the position of the intelligentsia and the bureaucracy (classes that hardly existed before the thirteenth century) was rising steadily with the growth of the Sensate culture up to the time of the World War.   Similarly, the capitalistic bourgeoisie appeared and climbed rapidly up the economic ladder with the rise of Sensatism, suffered a great setback with the economic decline of the second half of the sixteenth century and in the period of the Thirty Years' War.   But after this catastrophe it quickly recovered and resumed a steady climb during the rest of the seventeenth century, and in the eighteenth and nineteenth centuries, and in the twentieth up to the World War, after which it began rapidly to go down.   Thus, here also we find uniformities similar to those which we found in the curves of Greece, Rome, and France.

(4) *Workers*.   The peasants, the agricultural laborers, and the industrial workers existed at a low economic level in the Ideational centuries. This level improved with the beginning of the rise of the Sensate culture, reached a relatively high position in the Idealistic centuries, the thirteenth and the fourteenth.   After that these classes had to wait until the nineteenth century in order to reach a still higher status than that of the Idealistic period.   In the postwar twentieth century the curve of their economic situation, like that for France, dropped considerably.   In all these respects here again we find agreement with the economic norms of the lower classes in Greece, Rome, and France.   The reasons for it, so far as these fluctuations are connected with the rise and decline of the main types of culture, are the same as those which have been outlined above for the three countries already dealt with.

The curves for France and Germany (which up to the year 1500 includes Austria and central Europe) are, in their essentials, fairly representative of Europe generally.   Of course, due to local and "accidental" conditions, the curves of economic fluctuations in England, Russia, Spain, Italy, and other countries manifest several peculiarities and differences from those of France and Germany.   But with regard to the main points — namely, the comparatively poor situation in the period of the domination of the Ideational culture and the notable improvement with the rise of the Sensate culture — and with regard to the situation of the classes which are the main bearers of both forms of the integrated culture — these countries, at least Austria, England, and Russia, do not deviate from the norms we have just observed.   The curves for England, Austria, and Russia, together with the sources, the full data, and the analyses, are at my disposal.   These curves support this claim.   But for the sake of economy of space they are not given here.

D. *Corroboration in Social Space*.   The cultures of India, of Tibet, and, in part, of China have been and still are predominantly Ideational or Mixed.   Hence we are not surprised to discover that the economic conditions of these countries throughout their history have rarely risen above the satisfactory level. Only in some separate regions and provinces, or during some exceptional periods — and these periods seem to have been marked by the rise of the Sensate form — have "very good" and "prosperous" conditions prevailed. Thus, so far as relevant data have survived,[24] we have what seems to be a corroboration of our hypothesis in social space.

III. Main Conclusions

A. Viewed from the Sensate standpoint, the economic situation (as this term is defined in the present work) of a country or nation, or of any other large or small social system, does not remain constant, nor does it show any perpetual trend toward improvement, but fluctuates, now rising, now declining.

B. There are short-time and long-time fluctuations.

C. So far as the long-time trends are concerned, they may be partly due to the interference of "accidental" factors external to the social system, but also they show a perceptible association with the rise and decline of the main kinds of integrated culture and with the immanent consequences generated by the development of each culture type.

D. All in all, and for the reasons mentioned above, the dominantly Ideational societies tend to exist in economic conditions which are on a lower level (judged from the Sensate standpoint) than those of primarily Sensate cultures. The periods when the Ideational culture begins to decline and the Sensate to rise are marked by the beginning of the improvement of the economic situation of the social system as a whole (though not necessarily of all its parts). The rise continues and reaches one of its high peaks in the period of the Idealistic or Mixed culture. The highest levels are attained, however, at the time of the fullest development of the Sensate culture, just before its subsequent decline. When the culture reaches this summit of ripeness, it begins to generate strongly certain conditions ("immanent consequences") which operate against the Sensate culture as a whole, as well as against the economic welfare as one of its main values. The operation of these forces, manifest even in the periods preceding the climax of development, works in the direction of Sensate cultural and economic decline. Such are the general trends in the field of the relationships between the fluctuations of the economic conditions and that of the main types of culture. These relationships

[24] The available materials for India and China are scanty. But such as they are, we have tried to piece them together. For lack of space none of the details are given here.

do not appear where there is no integration of a culture as a whole, or where the culture is not integrated with its economic compartment. They may be temporarily, at least, obliterated by the intrusion of accidental external forces like plagues, famines, wars. They may be disturbed also by the operation of the immanent consequences of each culture. But in spite of all the influences of all these conditions, the associations postulated appear indeed to have existed, though not always fully or perfectly, in the history of Greece, Rome, and the West.

The associations are to be explained by the basic difference in mentality and even behavior of Sensate and Ideational man, a difference which is conditioned by the profound variance between the total system of Ideational and Sensate values, and especially of Ideational and Sensate economic values. In the Ideational culture the economic is viewed either negatively, or indifferently, or, at best, is admitted as the lesser evil within the limited range of necessity. In the Sensate system, it is either the main value by itself, or is included among the few main values. Therefore, the Ideational society devotes much less attention and energy to improving its economic well-being than does the Sensate society. The result is that the former does not attain such good results as the latter.

The reason for a comparatively high level of economic prosperity in a period of Idealistic culture seems to be comprehensible also. This is the period which to a notable extent enjoys the benefits of the increased economic efficiency of the Sensate mentality and efforts, and at the same time does not have, or has only in slight degree, the destructive immanent forces generated by the strongly developed and dominant Sensate culture. These forces are present only at their beginning stage and, in addition, are checked by the "inhibitions" (religious, moral, juridical, and others) of the Ideational culture which is still operative and still vital and as strong as the Sensate element.

E. As to the fluctuation of the economic condition of various classes of people in the same system, their economic curves do not all run parallel. While some classes are moving upward economically, others move downward. Even in the periods of rapid and great economic rise or decline, though most of the chief social classes move in one direction — hence the rapid increase or decrease of the prosperity of the social system as a whole — there always are one or more classes which are the losers or gainers.

F. Each of the main types of culture has one class or several classes which are its main bearers, agencies, and integrators. In the Ideational culture such classes seem to be mainly of two kinds: sacerdotal (the clergy, the priestly class, the Brahmans, the lamas, and so on), and the class of the religious landed aristocracy, which itself often discharges religious and sacerdotal functions and is always in close alliance with the sacerdotal class, as an allied companion, or as its secular instrumentality. In the Sensate culture, the main bearers are the capitalist-commercial bourgeoisie, the secular bureaucracy, and the secular — independent, free-thinking, "scientific," artistic, political — intelligentsia and the professional classes. The laboring classes, including the peasant and farmer, are rarely the main bearers and integrators of either type of culture. Their mentality, as a whole class, rarely reaches a high degree of integration.

G. All such integrating classes are immanently destined to elevate themselves socially and economically with the rise of their culture, and to decline with its decline. The sacerdotal class and the religiously minded groups of the landed aristocracy tend to become the organizing bodies and those most influential and economically most prosperous in the Ideational culture, while the classes of the moneyed bourgeoisie, of the secular intelligentsia, and of the secular officialdom thrive in the dominantly Sensate culture.

The reasons for this are readily comprehensible as far as the Sensate integrating classes are concerned. They are eager to become rich and powerful by their Sensate nature and, when the opportunity comes, they seize it and elevate themselves, no matter by what means and at what cost. Less comprehensible is the economic elevation of the bearers of the Ideational culture, the sacerdotal group, and the religious landed aristocracy; less comprehensible because, by definition, they should be disdainful of, or at least indifferent to, wealth and economic values. And yet, directly or indirectly, they elevate themselves greatly, as was true, for instance, of the Christian clergy in the Middle Ages, or moderately, as with the lamas of Tibet or the Brahmans of India. Such a "paradox" is the result of the immanent consequences of certain sociocultural conditions: in these cases of the leading organizational position these classes assume in Ideational periods. As soon as they are placed in that position, often imposed upon them by circumstances; as soon as they become the builders of the Ideational culture and of its social, moral, mental, and economic order, they cannot help elevating themselves, no matter whether they wish it or not. Here we have a prime example of the working of the general principle of immanent consequences running counter to the nature of their parental culture.

H. The fact that the clergy and the religious landed aristocracy tend to become the leading and organizing classes in the Ideational, and the capitalistic bourgeoisie, intelligentsia, professionals, and secular officials in the Sensate culture, offers us unexpected corroboration of the theory of the theocratic and secular political regimes developed in Chapter Five. Quite independently of the considerations and evidences brought together in that chapter, our present study of the fluctuations of the economic conditions of the main classes indicates that in the periods of the domination of Ideational culture the theocratic groups become in fact the leading classes even economically, with the secular classes occupying this position in the Sensate culture.

I. The alliance of the sacerdotal groups with the religious landed aristocracy, on the one hand, and of the capitalist bourgeoisie with the secular, free-thinking intelligentsia and professionals and secular officialdom, on the other, suggests, among other things, *that the moneyed bourgeoisie and secular intelligentsia are twin children of the same parent culture, born from it, and reared by it, and bound together in their destiny, in their rise and decline.* This means that the not infrequent quarrels between these brothers, and especially the frequent revolts of the free-minded intelligentsia against the "moneylenders," its denunciation of the "capitalist regime," its attempts to discredit and overthrow the "oppressor," are, when seen objectively, nothing but an effort to undermine and to overthrow the secular intelligentsia itself, a kind of suicide or self-destruction. If their destiny is bound together, if they both rise and fall with the rise and fall of the Sensate culture, then the decline of the moneyed economy, the so-called capitalist regime, or (more accurately) the contractual system of social relationships between economically minded human beings, must drag down also the secular intelligentsia itself. As a matter of fact, such revolts of the secular intelligentsia against its "elder brother," the capitalist, occur usually and with increasing frequency, not when the Sensate culture rises, and with its rise elevates the classes of the capitalist bourgeoisie and of the secular intelligentsia, but after the climax of the Sensate culture is over and when it has begun to decline. The growth of the revolts of the intelligentsia contributes in this way to the decline of the Sensate culture itself. Regardless of, and contrary to, what the revolting intelligentsia thinks of its actions and its ends, the immanent logic of history makes it a mere instrument — and even a blind instrument — for the achievement of objectives fundamentally different from its "subjective purposes." *Volentem fata ducunt nolentem trahunt.* The objective logic of cultural processes appears to be very different from the "derivations" and imagery which the persons involved — in this case the secular intelligentsia — believe in and fool themselves with. With proper modification the same may be said of the "elder brother" as well. At the declining stage of the Sensate culture, the capitalist class does its best to dynamite the ground upon which it stands. Its activities and policies also become more and more suicidal. It loses more and more energy, acumen, virility, determination, self-confidence, and especially self-respect, and the conviction of the sacredness and justice of its activity, of its position. The social utility of its functions decreases. It becomes mentally and morally and volitionally disarmed, weakened, and effeminate. Its actions lead to more and more results quite opposite from those expected, and harmful to the class. As a result, its social prestige and its power wane. In the postwar period we have witnessed a decline of both classes, the capitalists and the intelligentsia, in the revolt of the first against the second. The condition of the capitalist class and the intelligentsia of the declining Sensate is a sight as sore as that of the sacerdotal class and the landed aristocracy of the declining Ideational culture. To both the old statement that Jupiter makes devoid of reason him whom he is going to ruin is applicable. The immanent logic of cultural and social processes makes all these classes a kind of plaything of history : elevates when the proper culture rises, and puts down when it declines, regardless of the ideologies and motives and "derivations" with which these classes amuse themselves.

J. The social and economic conditions of the "integrating classes" fluctuate within far wider limits than those of the laboring and agricultural (peasant) classes. As to the changes which we have noticed in the economic condition of the laboring classes — their rather low position in the dominantly Ideational periods, its improvement in the periods of Idealistic culture (as in Greece in the fifth and fourth century, in Europe in the thirteenth century), and in the West during the nineteenth century — the reasons for them have been indicated above. To recapitulate : their economic position is low in the Ideational culture because the economic level in such a culture is generally low. Their position is relatively high in the periods of Idealistic culture, because in such periods the restraining and controlling forces of Ideational culture are still operating, while the forces of the economic efficiency of the Sensate culture are already at work toward an improvement of the economic situation generally and of these classes especially. The destructive immanent consequences of the Sensate culture are, as yet, not released in any great degree. With the increase of the general wealth, these classes get, in such periods, a comparatively larger share of the total national income. Subsequently, as after the thirteenth century A.D., further improvement is hindered and even regress takes place partly through the "accidental factors," partly through the destructive consequences of the developing Sensate culture — these consequences being of divers sorts, such as the increase of greed, the decrease of familistic feeling and justice among the leading classes with regard to the share of the total income of society to be given to the laboring classes, the growth of class conflicts, wars, and the like. A better organization of the integrating classes of the Sensate culture permits them to keep the laboring classes down, and to resist all their efforts to increase their share in the national income. When, however, as in the nineteenth century, the upward movement of general economic conditions becomes unprecedentedly rapid and great, it becomes possible for these classes to benefit themselves and to improve their situation, to some extent, through that general enrichment of all society. In addition, the fully developed Sensate culture and mentality lead these submerged classes to a better Sensate organization in the fight for their share in the national income against the leading classes ; and this likewise procures for them a somewhat larger share in the total income than before.

Thus, due to the general increase of wealth and to the increase of the share of the laboring classes in this increased wealth, their economic position improved enormously in the nineteenth century and the prewar period. War, revolts, revolutions, the increase of the class struggle, various political measures that not only take the eggs from the capitalist hen but often kill the hen itself — these and similar destructive consequences of the fully developed Sensate culture have overwhelmed us in the twentieth century. As a result, the general economic level has declined, and with this the position of the laboring classes has begun to decline.

Such, depicted in a very concise way, appears to be the connection of the economic conditions of the various classes of society with the change of the types of culture, and such is the explanation, expressed in simplified fashion, of the main fluctuations in the economic position of these classes, so far as these fluctuations are even loosely connected with our variables. For the rest, fluctuations are strongly influenced by accidental factors.

K. Turning to the twentieth century, we observe that the curve, which was steadily and rapidly rising throughout the nineteenth century, first undergoes a decrease in its rate of rise, and then with the beginning of the war and during the postwar period takes a downward direction. Here, then, we have a change quite similar to those of almost all the other curves of the Western culture in the twentieth century : the movement of scientific discoveries, systems of truth, Visual and Ideational styles in art, ethical theories, law codes, and so on. This economic fluctuation is additional evidence that a "turn" has indeed been experienced by Western culture; that none of these curves is misleading; that in their totality they give strong evidence of the deep crisis which the Sensate culture of our day is going through. Whether it is one of the short-time and minor crises, or, what seems to be more probable, the beginning of a long-time decline of the Sensate culture itself, cannot be stated certainly. But the fact of the deep and general crisis is beyond serious doubt.

L. The data given in this chapter corroborate the conclusions stated elsewhere in this work. They give evidence that wars and revolutions happen in periods of impoverishment as well as enrichment (see Parts Two and Three); that, therefore, the economic factors per se are not the primary or main causes of these phenomena. Likewise, the data unexpectedly bear out our theory of the fluctuation of the theocratic and secular political regimes and social leadership. Directly or indirectly they give support to practically all the previous statements where the economic factors are involved.

M. What we have just said gives an answer to the problem: Is the economic class of the sociocultural phenomena integrated causally with the rest of the culture? So far as the Graeco-Roman and the Western cultures are concerned, we discover the *existence of a definite association between the rise and fall of economic well being and the type of the dominant culture.* This means that our expectations on logical grounds are indeed realized by the actual causal and functional associations. Thus the answer to the problem is positive. And this seems to be applicable not only to the cultures studied but also to other cultures like the Hindu, the Tibetan, and, in part, the Chinese.

The association is, however, not close. It is definite, but it is frequently disturbed or partly dissolved by the intrusion of "accidental" forces of divers kinds, as well as by the complex set of the immanent consequences of the development of each type of culture. Economic processes and activities deal more closely with "nature," with the forces of the inorganic and organic world, than do many other cultural processes and activities. Therefore, the former depend upon, and are influenced by, the natural forces possibly more than the latter. Or, to put it in other terms, the margin of immunity of the economic system from the intrusion of the accidental forces heterogeneous to the economic system may be narrower than, for instance, that of the scientific, philosophical, artistic, and ethical systems. For this reason these "external" forces may change, disrupt,

modify, and disfigure the immanent development of the economic processes much more than they can upset the other cultural processes.
Hence, the perceptible but much looser association of the economic
fluctuations with our main variables, the chief types of integrated culture
and their major compartments. This means that our conclusions agree
with those of the economic interpreters of history, as well as of the opposite
type, who claim that the economic section is integrated with the rest of
the culture, including the ideological compartments. But in contradistinction to those theories, all of which assert equally that economic
processes are particularly closely related to the other compartments of
culture; in contradistinction especially to the "economic interpretation"
of history, which claims that they are associated so closely that any
change in these economic conditions is immediately reflected in the rest of
the compartments — in contradistinction to these, our conclusion is that
the economic connection is rather loose as compared with the correlation
of the other culture processes with one another. *Art and science, science
and religion, ethical systems and law, law and religion and art — these and
other especially "ideological" compartments of culture are interrelated and
change in much closer unison than do, for instance, economic conditions and
art, economic conditions and science, economic conditions and criminal codes,
economic conditions and any other compartment of culture.*

Such are the main inferences from the study of the *quantitative aspect*
of the fluctuation of economic conditions in the systems of integrated
cultures.

N. Translated into terms of human behavior these conclusions mean
that *there is a definite, though not close, association between the culture
mentality and the actual behavior of individuals and groups.* The domination of the Ideational mentality manifests itself — even in the field of
economic behavior — in a series of effects quite different from those upon
the corresponding groups in the Sensate culture. The contemptuous or
indifferent attitude toward all economic values dictated by the Ideational
mentality results in the *nonperformance* of many activities aimed at an
accumulation of wealth and the improvement of the economic conditions,
on the one hand, and, on the other, in the *toleration* and *performance* of
many acts which are not carried on by the Sensate man as being merely
a waste of time and energy; as being senseless, "uneconomic," and
"unprofitable." Among such acts may be, for instance, the investment
of the economic resources in an "unprofitable," though magnificent,
cathedral, or in a "useless" religious relic; or the bequeathing of all one's
property to an "idle" monastery, or to a missionary enterprise to spread

the Gospel; or the paying of a tenth or other portion of one's income to the priestly class; and the like. The Sensate mentality that makes economic value one of the greatest manifests itself behavioristically in the performance of many "economic" actions which Ideational man does not care to perform, and in the *nontoleration* and *nonperformance* of many acts which Ideational man does perform. Other conditions being equal, the Ideational culture mentality tends to make a society less prosperous economically than the Sensate mentality does. Thus, we find here fairly general evidence of the existence of some degree of association between the type of mentality and the type of behavior. Mentality and behavior in the economic field do not remain isolated and independent of each other, but are bound together to a considerable degree. The causal association is not everywhere close and leaves a considerable margin for the independent movement of the two variables, especially when various external and "accidental" forces interfere; nevertheless, it is quite clear and permits us to adhere to the above conclusion. In Chapter Fifteen the problem of the relationship between mentality and behavior will be taken up systematically, and we shall see that the conclusion reached here is sustained by other evidence.

O. This conclusion becomes still stronger if one examines not only the *quantitative fluctuations* of economic conditions in conjunction with the fluctuation of the types of culture, but the *qualitative forms* of economic organization and activities in each type of culture. Viewed from this qualitative standpoint, economic forms show thousands of differences in the Ideational and Sensate atmospheres. Beginning with the general attitude toward economic values or with the theories of capital; the place of wealth in the total system of values; the institutions of property and ownership, profit, interest, usury, price, alms, and bequests; theories of production and distribution and consumption, and ending with the forms of social relationships (familistic, or compulsory, or contractual) in the economic systems between their members and outsiders; and with the forms of use of the capital — in all these respects the economic forms and activities differ profoundly in Ideational, Idealistic, and Sensate cultures. This has been shown to some extent in the preceding parts of this work, especially in this part. Other investigators like Max Weber, F. de Coulanges, W. Sombart, A. Espinas, P. Huvelin, E. Durkheim, B. Malinowski, Hubert, Mauss, G. von Below, and many others, have also demonstrated it in many ways.[25] We still lack a work which offers a

[25] See Max Weber, *Gesammelte Aufsätze zur Religionssoziologie* (Tübingen, 1922–1923), 3 vols.; F. de Coulanges, *The Ancient City* (Boston, 1900); W. Sombart, "*Technik und Kul-*

systematic theory in this field; but the works that we have make it reasonably certain that the economic phenomena in their *qualitative* forms show a quite definite association with the corresponding forms of religion, ethical mentality, science, law, art, and other aspects of culture mentality. The economics of an Ideational society are fundamentally different from those of the Sensate society. The economic theory applicable to one type of society would be inapplicable in many respects to the other.[26]

As I do not in this work intend to develop systematically the theory of the *qualitative* forms of economic phenomena in each type of culture (a sorely needed investigation which still awaits a competent investigator), the above remarks must suffice for my purposes. For the present it is important only to note that the association of the quantitative fluctuations of economic phenomena with the types of culture becomes still more definite when the qualitative forms are also considered. Both the quantitative and qualitative aspects being taken together, the existence of an association between mentality and behavior in the economic sphere becomes indubitable.

---

tur," in *Archiv für Sozialwissenschaft* (1911); A. Espinas, *Les origines de la technologie* (Paris, 1897); B. Laum, *Die geschlossene Wirtschaft* (Tübingen, 1933). See other works referred to in P. Sorokin, *Contemporary Sociological Theories*, pp. 530 ff. and chaps. x and xii.

[26] Contemporary classical or "institutional" or other varieties of economics, as systematic theories of economic phenomena, are all in fact theories of the Sensate economic phenomena. If one attempts to apply them to the economic phenomena of an Ideational society, they will be found not to fit at any point, whether they be theories of production, distribution, and consumption, value, price, demand and supply, wages, interest, profit, capital, or any other. Even to a purely familistic society they are inapplicable; they are still less applicable to the Ideational-familistic society. This is often not understood. We must not be surprised that the results of such misapplication are mostly monstrous.

PART TWO

Fluctuation of War in Intergroup Relationships

FLUCTUATION OF WAR IN THE HISTORY OF GREECE, ROME, AND EUROPE: I. METHODOLOGICAL[1]

I. INTRODUCTION

In Chapter One I pointed out that the concepts of the organized group and the solidary group mean different things. A group may be solidary but not organized, and vice versa. All the organized groups with predominant compulsory relationships in them are examples of the organized but nonsolidary social systems of interaction. So far as the distribution of the rights and duties, functions and social positions, among the members of the group; social differentiation and stratification within it; and other characteristics mentioned are crystallized and enforced, the group and the social relationships between its members are organized. No matter whether the crystallized system of social relationships is maintained within the group by compulsion or contract or familistic forces, it is an organized system. As such, it has an order and constituted system of relationships between its members and parts. Its network of relationships is definite and functions in an orderly manner. The group has an internal order and peace, and is in a state of equilibrium, to use a fashionable and meaningless term,[2] no matter by what means this order, peace, or equilibrium is maintained: by solidarity and love of familism; by contractual utility and advantages; or by rude coercion (as in prisons).

Similarly, the *relationships between different groups interacting with one another can either be organized or not.* When two states have a crystallized system of relationships between them, with all the characteristics involved in that term (see Chapter One), the social relation or interaction between them is organized, no matter whether it is just or unjust, whether it is maintained by mutual solidarity of the states, or by their contractual

[1] In co-operation with Lieutenant General N. N. Golovine, formerly Professor in the Russian Imperial General Staff College and Chief of the Staff of the Russian Armies on the Rumanian Front during the World War, and Professor-General A. A. Saitzoff.

[2] Why it is meaningless, see P. Sorokin, "*Le concept d'equilibre est-il nécessaire aux sciences sociales?*" in *Revue internationale de sociologie* (September–October, 1936).

advantages, or by the coercion of one state by another. The relationships between them are respectively orderly and peaceful (or are in a state of equilibrium) without regard to what this order, peace, or equilibrium is due.

Any organized intragroup or intergroup system of social relationships experiences change in the process of its existence. These changes may be gradual or sudden, orderly or disorderly, slight or great, but any such network experiences them. Its change is one of the recurrent processes in the life history of any organized social group or intergroup relationship.

The change may be orderly, brought about by the constituted authorities of the group, according to its written or unwritten laws and constitution, or according to the desires and mores of its members. Such a change represents an orderly modification or reconstruction of the system of social relationships of a given group or intergroup, and by it the network of social relationships at no moment is broken or smashed or ceases to function. Like a house which is being renovated gradually, the system, in such a reconstruction, continues to preserve its identity, its continuity, and its functions. It, and the group, or the intergroup, remain completely organized in all such reconstructions.

In other cases, the change proceeds along different paths. The organized network of relationships of a given group, or the system of intergroup relationships, breaks down, contrary to, and regardless of, the laws, constitution, mores, and authorities. The house of social relationships, to use a simile, crumbles instead of being renovated and reconstructed. The existing crystallized system of social relationships goes to pieces before the new one is built and replaces it.

When this crystallized system is broken, the organized group becomes disorganized, the organized relationships between the groups cease to be such. By definition this means that the previously existing distribution of the rights, duties, functions, and social positions of the members of the group (within the group), or of the interacting groups in the intergroup relationship, ceases to exist as it was and becomes indefinite and confused. So become also the social differentiation and stratification within the group and between the groups. Order and peace (or equilibrium) disappear either in the life of the group, or in the relationship between the interacting groups. Instead, we have confusion; the interacting parties do not know what are their rights, duties, and functions, or generally the line of conduct, of each toward the others. The lines of social differentiation and stratification clearly delineated before now disappear. Instead of a definite structure of the body social, we have a confused mass of its elements.

Such a confusion leads generally to a growth of conflicts between the members (in the group) and between the interacting groups. Since "nobody knows" what is the proper relationship to one another, for this very reason the conflicts are likely to grow; what one party now regards as right, the other may feel as wrong. Increase of conflict means coercive antagonism in its open form, in the form of sheer violence applied by one party to another.

The outlined series of events follows: (1) breakdown of the crystallized system of relationships; (2) ensuing confusion; (3) increase of conflicts and antagonisms; (4) outburst of overt compulsion and violence in the relationship of the members of the group, or between the interacting groups. The outburst may assume in some cases mild forms, in others, the sharpest and rudest; in some cases the duration of disorder may be short — when the new crystallization takes place quickly — in others comparatively lasting. These variations occur, but an outburst of *confusion, conflict, overt violence* invariably follows any breakdown of the crystallized system of relationships.

When this process occurs within a group, we have the phenomenon of internal, or *intragroup, disturbance*, ranging from a little local confusion, disorder, riot, up to the greatest and bloodiest revolution possible, so far as the structure and functioning of its system of relationships is concerned.

When the process takes place in intergroup relationships, we have the phenomenon of the external or *intergroup disturbance*, ranging from a mild dispute, a straining and rupture of diplomatic relationships, army and navy preventive maneuvers, a few fights between a few members of the groups, and ending with the *ultima ratio* of solution of any conflict, external or intergroup: war, the sharpest outburst of violence in the breakdown of the system of intergroup relationships.

Thus internal and external disturbances — revolution and war — are but logical and factual consequences of the state of disintegration of the crystallized system of relationships. Their nature cannot be comprehended and a definition of them cannot be adequate, without the preliminary definition of the organized system of social relationships and its breakdown. When this is done, the concepts of internal and external disturbances of revolution and war follow by themselves.

Since that is so, a series of problems directly concerned with the study of sociocultural fluctuations arises, such as how often the breakdown of the crystallized system of relationships occurs in intragroup and intergroup relationships in the course of time; how great becomes the outburst of violence, quantitatively and qualitatively, in such breakdowns; how long these disturbances last; whether there is any trend in the course of time as to a decrease or increase of these external and internal disturbances; and a legion of other problems.

This explains why, in a study of the quantitative-qualitative fluctuations of the system of social relationships, the problem either of orderly reconstruction or of the *breakdown of the crystallized system of relationships cannot* be avoided. For the present, we shall omit the orderly way of the modification of the social system of interaction. If the space permits, we shall analyze it in a subsequent part of this work, together with many ever-recurrent processes in the life history of social systems of interaction, such as: origin or emergence of the system; its crystallization; the recruitment of its members; the placing of each in his social position; the horizontal and vertical shift of the members; and several other processes up to the termination of the existence of the organized system of interaction, or its death. At the present moment, we shall concentrate on the study of the breakdowns, with their external and internal disturbances.

This part is devoted to the study of the fluctuations of war, as the vastest and sharpest form of external or intergroup disturbances. The next part deals with the fluctuation of the internal disturbances or revolutions in the field of the system of social relationships.

Such a study — of war and revolution — is at the same time an examination of the outbursts of the sharpest forms of violence which occur in the life process of a group, or in a universe of interacting groups, from the standpoint of frequency, bloodiness, quantitative and qualitative magnitude, and other trends.

In such outbursts the compulsory relationships become not only dominant and monopolistic, between the conflicting parties, but they become overt, and, as a rule, unlimited and unrestrained by any law or constitution or other inhibitions of the organized system of relationships. As a rule, sheer force toward the opposite party tends to become the supreme arbiter, and "everything is permitted in regard to the enemy" tends to become the main principle.

The phenomenon of the breakdown of the system, with ensuing war and internal disturbances, happens in the process of existence of the most diverse organized social groups; within and between families; within and between business organizations, criminal gangs, religious associations, trade unions, villages, educational institutions, political parties, and other social groups. Most of them, if they exist long enough, experience these processes of external feuds and internal disturbances, if not always in the form of a bloody war, then at least in the milder phases of social struggle and conflict. For obvious reasons, all the internal and external disturbances in all the social groups cannot be studied here. For the sake of economy, we shall limit our study to the most important and historically registered disturbances that occur, on a large scale, in the vastest and most powerful systems of social interaction. The *interstate wars and intrastate disturbances satisfy this requirement.* They are not only the greatest and most influential, but they are to a considerable degree the resultant and the sum total of the most important internal and external disturbances within or between groups that live under the control of the state, or under that of the states involved in the war. If a disturbance inside a religious group, say, or between two religious sects, or two political parties, or two occupational unions, becomes considerable, it invariably involves the state where these groups live, and becomes also an internal or external disturbance to it.

When large masses of employees start a "national strike," as a weapon against their employers, the state machinery, the state government, the state laws are immediately involved, and either the State settles the matter, or, if it cannot, the strike becomes a state disturbance and sometimes develops into a riot, uprising, revolt, and revolution against the state system of social relationships and the state government. When the feud between, say, the Catholics and Protestants of two different states develops and assumes a large magnitude, the disturbance of the inter religious groups invariably involves the respective states and becomes an internal and external disturbance.

All such large and important disturbances that start within or between social groups other than the state involve, as a rule, the respective states and turn into internal or external state disturbances. For these reasons, the important internal and external state disturbances sum up and are the resultant of the most important disturbances that originate in other than state groups.

Only the small disturbances that do not exert a notable influence upon the lives and activities of the large groups may come and go without developing into state disturbances, though even there the State and its machinery are usually involved, as the police, the judge, the mediator, the jailer, and executioner. Partly as a matter of economy of effort, partly as a matter of necessity, and mainly as a matter of scientific knowledge, we can afford to ignore these ripples of small disturbances and concentrate on the external and internal disturbances that formally result in the interstate wars and intrastate disorders, riots, revolts, and revolutions.

Now let us turn to the study of the movement of war between states, as the vastest and bloodiest form of external or intergroup disturbance.

II. Methodological Explanations and Reservations

What has been the movement of war magnitude, measured either by strength of army or amount of casualties, in the life history of the Graeco-Roman and Western civilizations? Has it been decreasing, increasing, or fluctuating trendlessly? Has its movement been associated in some tangible way with the waves of the Ideational and Sensate cultures? To all these questions contemporary social science gives no adequate answer. No doubt there are hundreds of different, seemingly cocksure theories which give very definite answers in a firm and unhesitating way, but among them there is hardly any which is based upon the necessary minimum of evidence.

In the immense literature on the evolution of war and of peace, on their past, present, and future, exceedingly few authors [3] have tried to consult the sources of historical facts. Of these authors, so far as we know, only one or two attempt to study the problems systematically and quantitatively, for several countries and several centuries. The greater part of this literature is merely "inspirational," substituting for the actual history of the warfare the history which the authors consider desirable.

[3] Excellent, but purely historical, studies of a single war or of a few wars are, of course, very numerous. But the studies which deal with the problem of the course of war, its increase or decrease during a long period of time, for several centuries in several countries, have indeed been surprisingly few. Only two studies treating the problem from the comparative-quantitative point of view are known to us, namely, *Is War Diminishing?* by F. A. Woods and A. Baltzly (Boston, 1915); the other, *The Causes of War and the Conditions of Peace* by Q. Wright (London, 1935), came out after this work had been written and unfortunately gives only summary conclusions without any figures and actual data.

Of other factual studies of the above general type the following can be mentioned: L. Hobhouse, G. Wheeler, and M. Ginsberg, *The Material Culture and Social Institutions of the Simpler Peoples* (London, 1915), pp. 228 ff.; G. Bodart, *Losses of Life in Modern Wars* (Oxford, 1916) and *Militärhistorisches Kriegs-Lexikon* (Wien and Leipzig, 1907–1908); Hans Delbruck, *Geschichte der Kriegskunst im Rahmen der politischen Geschichte*, 6 vols. (Berlin, 1900–1929); O. Berndt, *Die Zahl im Kriege. Statistische Daten aus der neueren Kriegsgeschichte* (Wien, 1897); S. R. Steinmetz, *Soziologie des Krieges* (Leipzig, 1929); S. Dumas and K. Vedel-Petersen, *Losses of Life Caused by War* (Oxford, 1923); and a few others. The enormous "propaganda" literature in the field is practically worthless. The immense semiscientific literature, like the works of J. Novicow, M. Vaccaro, and others (on these see chap. vi in P. Sorokin, *Contemporary Sociological Theories*, New York, 1928) either has no systematic factual data or has mostly fragmentary, "illustrative" cases which do not and cannot prove anything.

The reason for such a situation is at hand, namely, the impossibility of a perfect or even satisfactory study of the problem. The difficulties which meet an investigator are so obvious and so insuperable that the problem cannot be studied and answered satisfactorily, no matter who studies it. A very brief survey of some of the difficulties shows this fact convincingly.

A. *Factual Difficulties.* (1) In many cases the *necessary data are lacking* concerning the size of the fighting forces, the number of human lives lost on each side, the proportion of the number of combatants to the total population of the countries involved in the war, the economic cost, the increase of morbidity and mortality in the civilian population, sometimes even the length of the war — in brief, all the essential elements important to determining the increase or decrease of the magnitude of war in the course of time. Up to the second half of the seventeenth century, and especially in the chronicles of Ancient Greece, Rome, and medieval times, a lack of even roughly accurate data is the rule; the presence of such data is exceptional. For this reason no one, no matter how competent he be or how capable and how numerous his assistants, could make an entirely satisfactory study of the problem. Estimates can be used, but any estimate introduces an element of uncertainty and inaccuracy. This, then, is the first source of error in the study.

(2) The next factual difficulty is the *unreliability and inaccuracy of much of the existing data.* Even in regard to the World War, 1914–1918, we do not have quite accurate figures for any of the belligerent countries. Even the official figures for that war show discrepancies, sometimes amounting to hundreds of thousands! (See the Appendix to this part.) How much more imperfect must be the data for the wars of the previous centuries! Each belligerent country tends to underestimate its own losses and to overestimate the losses of its enemy. In addition, the chroniclers and ancient historians often give purely fantastic figures, like Herodotus's estimate that there were a million men in the Persian army and the statements that armies of several hundred thousand took part in various medieval wars. Even when one uses the figures given by later, more critical, historians, for some of the wars, these figures are mainly estimates, not actual data, and therefore they are to some extent inaccurate.

(3) The third factual difficulty is with the *wars that lasted for a number of years.* The intervals between the many battles in such wars varied from days to weeks, months, or even years. Undoubtedly the size of the armies was not the same, nor the proportion of losses constant, in the various battles of even the same campaign. If we had exact data for

each battle we could, of course, have measured the individual battles. Unfortunately, however, we do not know how many small battles and skirmishes occurred, and seldom do we know how many men were engaged in such minor conflicts or how many were killed or wounded. This is especially important for wars before the sixteenth century when a "fighting army" represented something very indefinite and changing, now swollen by a large mass of the people of a given territory, and mercenaries, now reduced to a small group of professional fighters.

(4) There is another great difficulty in these wars of *long duration*. Compare the World War of the present century with any long war of past centuries. The period from 1914 to 1918 was possibly the first period of relentless, almost incessant, warfare lasting for four years. There was hardly a day without more or less conflict between the lines of the opposing armies, face to face in the trenches. The fighting was interrupted from time to time not so much by periods of peace as by still greater offensives. Consider, on the other hand, the Hundred Years' War, the Wars of the Roses, the Thirty Years' War, or, in fact, any campaign lasting for more than a few days. No such war continued without cessation for a hundred years, thirty years, ten years, or even for a full year. Such wars were really a series of battles often separated by long intervals of time. During these intervals the fighting forces were out of contact, or in only passive contact, with each other, as in the case of sieges.

The duration of wars being one of the variables of the magnitude of war, evidently two wars may be identical in their apparent duration (from the beginning to the peace) but quite different in actual length, and therefore quite different in magnitude. In one case a duration of four years may mean uninterrupted fighting, as in the World War, and in another the same period from the declaration of war to the conclusion of peace may include only five or six battles, each lasting for a day or two, with perhaps a dozen still shorter skirmishes. Arithmetically the length of the two wars is the same; in reality they are of quite different lengths. Translated into the language of actual fighting, the duration of the World War was much greater than the duration of the Hundred Years' War, or even than of several centuries of wars when each war means a series of battles occurring at long intervals of time. One can see how great this difficulty is and how easily it may lead to blunders.

(5) *Coalitional wars* cause further difficulty. Even if we know the size of the total army, we often do not know how large a share each of the allied countries had in it. Again we are forced to make estimates, which may or may not be accurate.

(6) Similarly, how can we make comparable the study of *naval* and *territorial* wars? What can we take as a unit for the essentially different types of warfare carried on by sea and by land?

(7) The next difficulty, an appalling one, is presented by the fact that no country whose wars are studied has been quite uniform throughout the centuries in population, size, and extent of territory, but has varied considerably from period to period in these respects. Moreover, on a territory at one time occupied by one state several states has existed at other times, and vice versa. During the centuries studied, certain states disappeared and others made their appearance. For instance, what we now style Italy did not exist at all before the second part of the nineteenth century. What really existed were several states on the territory of the present Italian kingdom. One of these states, Savoy, later on increased by Sardinia, was a kernel around which, through its dynasty, united Italy was gradually built. Somewhat similar was the case of Spain, while the variability of what we call Austria was very great. To a certain degree this difficulty is encountered with regard to all the other states studied.

Suppose we have certain data concerning the army's strength or casualties of war for Savoy in the latter part of the sixteenth century, when the duchy embraced only a small part of Italy. Suppose, further, that the respective figures for the Italy of the nineteenth or the twentieth century are much higher. Can we conclude from this that the magnitude of war activities increased proportionately from the sixteenth to the nineteenth or the twentieth century? Evidently not. For the sixteenth century the data refer to only a small fraction of the population of Italy. For the later centuries a much larger population and much greater area are in question. To make the data comparable it is evidently necessary to correct or "equalize" them in conformity with the changes in the countries studied. And obviously this cannot be done "accurately and exactly" for every war and every year or quarter century.

(8) Finally, data are similarly lacking on *the exact size of the population of each country studied*, during each of its wars. Before the seventeenth century not only data for each war but data in general are non-existent. We find only estimates, or fragmentary data for this or that locality, for this or that period, which in no way fill in the enormous gaps in the field. Again we must make estimates and run all the risk of being inaccurate.

Not to continue this list of difficulties and obstacles, although there are many others besides the ones mentioned, the above gives an idea of how utterly impossible it is to study the problem "perfectly" and how great the danger is of making gross blunders in such a study, cautious as the investigator may be.

B. *Methodological Difficulty*. The main *methodological* difficulty, added to all these factual difficulties, is the impossibility of making a "perfect translation" into purely quantitative language of any phenomenon that is *qualitative-quantitative*. Most sociocultural phenomena, including the phenomena of war and revolutions, are of this nature. Anyone who attempts to "measure" or to construct "indices" of the movement of crime, of business conditions, of the standard of living, of scientific progress, of religiosity, of divorce, of artistic activities, and so on, is confronted with the same methodological difficulty. He finds it impossible to translate the changes in any one of these processes into the purely quantitative language of the indices; for these processes are qualitative-quantitative in nature.

An illustration of this point was just given in the factual difference between the *real* duration of wars and their "arithmetical," or actual, time duration. A vast difference between two or more values which seem arithmetically equal is normal in the field of sociocultural phenomena. The most conscientiously made "translations" into indices — business indices not excepted — can be only very imperfect and based on several arbitrary assumptions which may or may not be sound. Here is an additional source of possible errors.

This brief survey of some of the difficulties involved explains why the social sciences do not give even remotely valid answers to the questions with which the chapter is opened, why a perfectly valid answer cannot be given, and why overcautious scholars prefer to pass the problem by as not lending itself to be studied satisfactorily. It also explains why, in the place of scientific theories, we have endless "weeds," intuitional, inspirational, and propaganda derivations, manufactured every day by journalists, politicians, statesmen, ministers, professors, and others equally careless of the factual verification of their contentions, but similarly cocksure in their preconceived beliefs.

In these conditions an investigator finds himself before an alternative. *Either he must pass the problem by, however important it be, in order not to take chances of making too many, or too great, blunders, or he must go ahead and take these chances. In this latter case the study would be of value only if he would try to be as careful and unbiased as possible in the study of the facts. The relevant facts he collects must be at least as complete as or more complete than in any other study hitherto made. He should not claim the privilege of infallibility or validity of his results, but should simply say, "Let us study the relevant facts as well as possible and then see what the results will be, without certainty as to whether they are accurate but with confidence that they are more reliable than purely inspirational theories or theories based upon only fragments of the existing data." He must put "all his cards on the table," in the sense of stating his assumptions explicitly and making the nature of his procedure perfectly clear to the reader. Finally, he must be ready to bear the most vicious, and for the most part, incompetent, criticism of a crowd of waiting critics, from ignorant journalistic "snipers" and politicians, pacifists and militarists, up to the finicky and meticulous scholar accustomed only to a study of little narrow topics and to the art of "straining at the gnats."*

Of these alternatives I chose the second, with all its conditions, especially the last. Some of the motives of this choice are obvious. The problem is too important to ignore it or to leave it to be handled "inspirationally." For my own curiosity I am interested in it; not finding any reliable answer to the personal quest in the field, I was forced to try to find the answer as well as I could. The tentative results based upon the available body of the data are better than results based upon mere wishes or upon fragments of these data. No exactness in detail can be claimed for such a venture; but I can at least urge in its favor that it has a more complete and more solid factual basis than either the offhand revelations of the inspirationalists, or even the studies hitherto made that cope with the problem set forth at the beginning of this part. Being possibly inexact in many details, it may nevertheless not be misleading in its essential conclusions when an appropriate criterion of validity is applied to it. The point is that there are different criteria of adequacy for a general map of a whole continent and for an inch map of a given county. Judged by the inch map any general map is fallacious; it shows straight lines where the inch map shows fancifully curved lines; it fails to show many roads, streams, and lakes, and a thousand other things, shown on the county map. And vice versa, by the scale of reference of the general map the inch map is incorrect, too. Those critics, however, who can apply the proper criterion in each case will find each map correct in its own way and each as necessary for its own purpose as the other — one for planning a journey from the Pacific to the Atlantic, the other for detailed orientation on reaching a given street and house.

In the general field of human knowledge both maps are necessary. For many purposes we need to familiarize ourselves with the meticulous map drawn by the historian of a given single event, single group, single war, or of even a detail of these limited areas; for other purposes we need a map of several eras or a survey of a whole continent, which may be little known.   We must use a broader perspective and longer vistas.   For such purposes even a very imperfect, grossly representative map may be of value, sometimes of great value.   It is clear, then, that any study of the facts of war for many centuries belongs to the same class as a general map of a vast and almost unexplored continent.

Comparing the chances that the inch map and the rough sketch map of the little-known continent also may be faulty, the inch map has not always nor necessarily the advantage.   Many of the "most exact" and minute studies made, supposedly, with "perfect scientific technique" have proven in due course of time to be utterly wrong, even tested by the "inch-map" criteria of validity.   And here we are concerned with many of the "most careful" and "controlled" of experimental, statistical, and historical investigations.   For a detailed historical study and its con-clusions to be utterly destroyed by the finding of a new "inscription" or "pot" is not a rare phenomenon.   Almost every day brings the down-fall of "minute quantitative" studies; and even of the exactness of routine problems not much need be said.   During the last five or ten years it has happened that many a research made with all "tests of reliability" and many volumes published by reputed authorities have been either wholly or partially wrong.

The same is true of general maps.   They have been hardly less liable to fallibility.   Since "*humanum errare est*" in making the inch map or the general map, in exploring either an unknown or a known region, one may be excused for adventuring into an unexplored region, preferring to err in this venture rather than be safe — and bored — in the home town, walk-ing no farther than from the drugstore to the grocery store day after day.

Trying to "know more and more about less and less," social sciences in recent times have perhaps walked too much between the drug and grocery stores not to become finicky.   We have been choosing the problems of study not so much by their importance as by a possibility of making a "fine and accurate study of the topic."   As a result we are overwhelmed with fine studies of the correlation between the number of windows in farmhouses and toilet rooms with and without running water; with many monographs on the armor of the Black Prince in a certain battle; with the large quantity of studies painfully elaborating the obvious, like "after the spring comes summer, then fall, and winter"; and so on.   Pushed too far in that direction, these investigations become a worthless parody on science.   To avoid this situation, once in a while, somebody has to take upon himself the doubtful privilege of selecting an important topic for his study, though it does not lend itself to an exact investigation. In this part (as well as in this whole work) I am volunteering to take such a subject for sake of my adventurous spirit (not to say for the sake of the welfare of science). Granting all the possible shortcomings, I bring no apology for the chapter. However great its defects be, they are possibly less than in most, if not in all, the studies of the problem on a general map basis. Let others who can do better do better; unfortunately they have not done so, as yet!

Stressing the difficulties of the study in the above, on the other hand I must say that, in spite of their enormity, they do not make quite hopeless the possibility of arriving at some conclusions at least roughly approximating accuracy in their main parts.

Many estimates were used in the place of actual data. But the use of estimates does not necessarily signify error. Everything depends upon the nature and upon the basis of the estimates, and upon the degree of accuracy desirable in a given investigation. All sciences dealing with an empirical world use estimates extensively in one form or another. In the "exact" sciences, when an astrophysicist, on the basis of a certain number of actual facts or relationships observed, "extrapolates" the observed actuality and builds a theory of the whole cosmos, he is professing to use estimates, and is erecting an immense theory on a definitely limited foundation. *Mutatis mutandis*, the process is the same when a physicist or chemist formulates a generalization or "unlimited law" on a limited basis of experimentation or observation. Almost any scientific law or generalization is in a sense "extrapolation" or "estimate."

This is still more certain in the biological and the social sciences. When a biologist like Cuvier reconstructs the whole anatomy of a prehistoric animal on the basis of a few bones; when, like Darwin and Lamarck, he frames an all-embracing theory of evolution on the basis of a number of "given factual points," he is estimating, and his theories are mainly "estimates." When, from a limited number of inscriptions or excavated pots or vases or from such contemporary testimony as has been preserved, a historian constructs a well-rounded description of the culture of a past period, he is giving an example of the wide use of the method of estimates in writing history. He draws the lines and coherent designs on the basis of the few scattered points on his canvas. He hardly ever has so "complete a set of facts" about the past as to make "filling in of the holes" unnecessary. Unavoidably, the "holes," as a rule, are very large.

Direct estimates and guesses in the narrow sense of the term are present in almost any historical work dealing with a relatively important topic. A mere description of a very narrow topic, such as this or that document, this or that pot, is perhaps possible without any estimate or speculative element. But as soon as an attempt is made to interpret an object or give it a meaning, a guess comes in by a back door, if not by the front.

All this, however, does not mean that in essentials astrophysics, chemistry, biology, and history are necessarily misleading. So far as we know and can judge, they contain a great deal of truth. Economics, political science, psychology, anthropology, and sociology are all full of estimates. And in spite of all that, all these disciplines do not consist only of errors, and perhaps do not contain so much of error as of something that can be styled relatively valid "truth."

This aside suggests that the use of estimates per se must not prejudice us against the validity of the results. If the estimates, like a line, have several actual data as their basis; if, further, the "line of estimates" is drawn in conformity with other circumstances which show the extreme limits beyond which the line cannot go; if one does not claim for the estimates the accuracy of a perfect "inch map" but claims only that in an uncharted country the lines are roughly accurate within a large margin of error granted in advance; and if in spite of allowances for as wide a margin of error as possible the conclusions remain essentially the same — given all these conditions, estimates are one of the most useful of instruments for making a first approximation to reality.

This is the case with the present study. As the reader can see from the detailed list of the wars (see the Appendix to this part) most of the Greek or the Roman war figures involve estimates concerning the strength of the army and the casualties. As such they are inaccurate from the standpoint of the inch map. However, from the standpoint of the continental map they are roughly representative. We are reasonably certain that the size of the Greek armies in any of the wars never exceeded 50,000 fighters. Only in two or three wars a figure approaching this size is found. This means that our estimates have a definite upper limit beyond which they cannot go. The totality of other data on various wars permit us grossly to guess the probable lower limit of these variables for each of these wars. If, therefore, the estimates err to some extent, they do not err so much as to be purely fantastic or to deviate from the reality to such an extent as to give entirely misleading results. Likewise, as the reader can see, most of the data of the medieval wars are estimates, and these estimates intentionally are made "uniform" for many wars of the same decades, and for the same country, say 20,000 for the strength of the army and 4 per cent for the losses. No doubt the real sizes of the fighting force and losses in these wars fluctuated considerably from war to war, even from one period of the same war to another. And yet, we can be reasonably certain that the figures used are within the limits of the possible maximum of the forces and the losses for the respective periods, because none of the critically analyzed records give a figure higher than the maximum assumed. As to the minimum, here again, in conformity with the conditions of the war, we used a guess, but a guess either based upon an actual figure preserved about another war adjacent to it in time and similar in conditions, or upon some other relevant circumstance.

For some of the wars we have a factual datum concerning the strength of the army and the losses in a certain battle. Therefore we are entitled to use these data, in many cases, as typical. For the wars of the seventeenth century and later, the situation is incomparably better because for these wars, in the majority of cases, we have roughly accurate data.

Such a procedure certainly introduces many inaccuracies. But considering that we are dealing with the continental map of many countries and many centuries, from the standpoint of the "scale" of such a map these inaccuracies and the probability of blunders are hardly much greater than many similar statements of the "inch-map" historians of a certain unique event or battle, from the standpoint of their respective "scale." Take, for instance, the following statements of the "inch-map" historians: "On April 25 (1813) Napoleon had at his disposal 145,000 men, including 10,000 cavalry and 400 guns. . . . The Allies at the most could only muster 80,000 men." "The French lost 18,000 men, the Allies only 10,000." [4] "At the head of 3000 men, this intrepid leader . . . had seized Tergoes." [5] "In the beginning of October, 1575, the eastern provinces of the Republic were ravaged by a predatory Tartar horde, said to be 120,000 strong." [6] "Over 6000 French were killed or wounded." [7]

Some of these statements are definitely approximate, like the "Over 6000 French" (how much over?), the others draw a straight line where, on the inch-map and in reality, there was a curved line; all the figures give round thousands or hundreds, which is not necessarily true. Likewise when we are told that in such and such battle the army was, say, 3000 men, the statement is not perfectly accurate. Even granting that

[4] *The Cambridge Modern History* (popular ed., New York, 1933), Vol. IX, pp. 517–518.
[5] *Ibid.*, Vol. III, p. 234.   [6] *Ibid.*, Vol. III, p. 92.   [7] *Ibid.*, Vol. IX, p. 467.

it really were 3000 before the battle (which is doubtful; more probably it was somewhat more or less than 3000), during the battle the exact number of the fighting men varies — at one moment some of them are kept in reserve, at another some are killed and wounded; in other words, if we take the real number of the fighting army it varies even during the duration of one battle, now more now less, and in no battle does it remain exactly constant. Insofar, on the scale of an inch map, the historians draw a straight line where in fact it should be curved, and give us also a kind of estimate instead of the exact figures. So far as the figure given approximates the actual, though varying, figure, the historian is perfectly right in his procedure. Dealing with a continental map, an investigator is in a somewhat similar position, with the difference that his continental map permits him to have a much larger amplitude of approximation. If it does not go beyond this many times larger range of the "legitimate error," his approximations can be as accurate as the approximations of an "inch-map" historian. From this standpoint, if in many wars instead of an estimated army of, say, 10,000, the real size of the armies were indeed 7500, 13,455, even 20,000, or 3000, the results when summed up for a series of wars of a given quarter century or century are not misleading. They are rough approximations to the reality and would show the difference between such a period and a period where the typical size of the army in many wars is estimated as 100,000. In the first case the sizes tended to gravitate around 10,000 and in the second around 100,000. The difference in the results roughly reflects the real change in the real war magnitude, though the real sizes were different from the assumed estimates of 10,000 and 100,000. In other words, though the data for most of the wars of the period before the seventeenth century are estimates, and therefore inaccurate, they are estimates based not upon mere fancy, but typical for the wars of the period, and based upon a certain amount of actual data. When, in addition to this, a large range of error for these estimates is granted in advance, sometimes up to 300 per cent, and in spite of this the conclusions reached hold, such a situation speaks well in favor of the rough reliability of these estimates and conclusions.

Now let us take the unreliability or the biased character of the actual existing data. There is no great danger of falling victim to really fantastic data from the past; their nature is too evident and has been too clearly exposed by prominent historians of the period of the war. As for the biases within reasonable limits, in a mass study of wars like this study, such biases would be present for all the centuries and all the parties, and so may cancel one another to a considerable degree. Besides, I do not claim perfect accuracy for the indicators, and admit a very wide margin of probable error. Such inaccuracies within reasonable limits (so narrow as to make it impossible to detect them) would not and cannot essentially change the results. As the reader can see below, the official and authoritative sources give figures for the World War differing sometimes by 1,000,000 to 1,500,000 soldiers. And yet, for the purposes of this study even such an enormous discrepancy does not make much difference; whichever figure we take, the maximum or the minimum, in both cases the magnitude of the World War comes out as unique and unprecedented.

As for the third factual difficulty presented by *wars of long duration*, with their many battles, the varying numbers engaged in these battles, and the varying numbers killed or wounded, this certainly may lead to errors. Again, however, the danger should not be exaggerated. It was greatly reduced, if not eliminated, by securing factual data for each important battle, whenever possible, and thus breaking up a long war into the series of separate campaigns of which it consisted. When a war could not be divided into campaigns, it was broken up into several separate periods, and each of these periods, again, was estimated on the basis of actual data concerning its battles, or the total size of the fighting forces on all the fronts of the war. This means a closer approximation to reality than if the whole war had been taken as a unit and estimated by the same values throughout its existence. In subsequent detailed descriptions of the wars, in the Appendix to this part, the reader will see that the averages of many long wars are based upon the data of the army's strength and the losses in several of its battles. If the war were conducted upon one front only, these actual figures give some basis for the average assumed. If it were conducted upon two or more fronts, respective correction is made, sometimes upon the basis of the actual data, sometimes hypothetically, but hardly exceeding the wide margin of error granted in advance.

Considering, further, that the same method is uniformly applied in all such cases and for all the centuries studied, the wide probability of error is eliminated to a considerable degree. And, however strange it may sound to persons who do not work on investigations of social phenomena en masse, this uniformity of method perhaps insures against erratic and violent fluctuation of the data even better than the use of a few, widely different actual data. A uniform "measuring stick" applied to all the centuries on the same principle makes the results, in a sense, more probable and comparable than results based merely upon a few fragmentary and quite widely divergent data about a few battles of the same long war.

What on an inch map of a given single war investigated in detail would have been an "unforgivable error" is our "salvation" in the case of the general map, and means "drawing a straight line" on sound principles, instead of showing the turns and curves seen on the inch map.

A more difficult problem, in view of the differences in the amount of actual fighting within the same length of time in different wars, is the problem of measuring the duration of long-continued conflicts. Fortunately the phenomenon of a lasting war with continuous and uninterrupted fighting appears for practically the first time with the War of 1914–1918, and to hardly any important degree previously. In all the centuries preceding the twentieth, the long wars consisted of a number of battles and skirmishes separated from one another by considerable intervals of time during which no important fighting occurred. In the Greek, the Roman, and the medieval wars these intervals were perhaps longer than in the wars of the seventeenth and subsequent centuries; but the difference was not fundamental.[8]

For these reasons, to measure the duration of the wars uniformly by the period between the opening of each war and the conclusion of peace does not necessarily lead to gross error. If anything, since the intervals of inactivity between engagements in long wars in the past seem to have been somewhat longer than in wars in more recent centuries, this method may minimize the real magnitude of the more recent wars and slightly exaggerate the magnitude of the wars of Greece, Rome, and the Middle Ages. But, in view of the results, I am ready to grant any reasonable "inflation" of the wars of the earlier periods.

As to the difficulty presented by the coalitional wars, in the cases where data about the share of each allied country in the total coalitional army were lacking, I had to use estimates based on the relative population of the allied countries and on other relevant circumstances. Such estimates are probably inaccurate to a considerable degree, but, in most cases, to a smaller degree than the maximum of probable error granted. Besides, at worst, such errors concern only the data for each allied country, not the data for the whole coalitional army. As only the latter count in the final computation of the magnitude of the war for all the countries studied from century to century, the errors that, we grant, may occur do not influence the totals for all the countries. If the share of one of the allies were overestimated, the share of the others must have been underestimated, while the total for the whole coalitional army remained uninfluenced by these partial overestimations and underestimations.

[8] Compare Q. Wright, *op. cit.*, pp. 30–35.

For comparison of *the territorial and the naval wars* no perfect measuring stick is available. As the best available basis for the appraisal of the magnitude of the naval wars we have taken the number of fighting men on the ships engaged in the battles, rather than the number of naval vessels. The size of the ships has varied too often and too widely to serve as an adequate basis for quantitative comparison. We grant that the size of the forces on the ships is far from being satisfactory as a basis, but it seems the best choice among the possibilities. Since naval battles are but a small part of all battles, and since the same stick — the size of the human forces of the navy — is applied uniformly to all such wars for all the centuries, the possible error can hardly be of particular significance and cannot greatly change the essentials of the conclusions reached.

Of the other factual difficulties mentioned, there remain two most formidable ones, the varying size of the countries studied and the lack of exact statistics, for the centuries before the eighteenth, as to the populations of these countries. Again there is no perfect way to combat the first of these difficulties. However, there are several circumstances which, in all probability, eliminate the greater part of the error and reduce it to limits within which it ceases to be misleading, so far as the essentials of the conclusions are concerned.

In the first place, for several of the countries studied, the variation in their size and population in the course of time is neither excessively great nor of such a nature as to be fundamentally harmful to the results achieved. Indeed, since we study ancient Greece as a unit, including all its states, the territorial as well as the populational unit for Greece remains practically the same throughout the centuries studied. The changes which occurred are relatively insignificant and therefore unimportant.

The situation with Rome or, rather, Roman Italy, is similar. Since Italy, primarily, is studied through the centuries from the fourth B.C. to the fifth A.D., the unit here again remains essentially constant. The Roman Empire, certainly, varied greatly in size from century to century within the above period. This I fully realize, and in the final computation of the indicators of war per 1,000,000 of the population I take these variations into consideration and reduce them to the same unit.

There is a similar situation in the cases of Great Britain, France, Russia, and, in part, the Netherlands. The main body of the territory of each of these countries and its population, when taken together with one or two other countries, is essentially unbroken and not radically different. What differences and variations there be are merely additions to, or subtractions from, one of the other countries studied, for these nine

European countries cover the greater part of the "European universe." When, finally, the movement of the war magnitude for all these countries taken together is computed, these changes correct one another and represent "variations" from one part of the "basket" to another, but within the same "basket universe." This means that if this variability factor is likely to lead to several errors in the indicators for individual countries, in the final computation of indicators for the "whole universe" of these countries, which is the main point of this study, this source of error becomes incomparably less dangerous, especially when necessary allowances are made.

Somewhat different is the situation in regard to Austria-Hungary, Germany, Italy, and Spain. The territory occupied by these countries at the beginning of the World War had certainly undergone enormous variations. For instance, we begin the study of the movement of the wars of Italy with the wars of the duchy of Savoy and Sardinia, which at the time occupies only a small part of Italian territory and is only one of eleven or more states.

With regard to Spain there is a somewhat similar situation. We begin our investigation with the moment when Castile and Aragon, which did not cover the whole Spanish peninsula, were unified. Evidently, our indicators of the wars of Italy and Spain will be misleading if they begin with the wars of the kernel states around which the modern states have grown, for each of these units at first embraced only a part of the population of its peninsula. Just because, when the other states united and were joined to the growing states of Italy and Spain, these units grew, therefore the indicators must grow. Any conclusion as to the increase of war in the course of history that might be drawn from the growth in the war indicators for these particular countries would obviously be misleading.

Mutatis mutandis, the same can be said of the empire of the Hapsburgs and, in part, of Germany. Our study of the wars of Germany begins with the wars in Prussia in the seventeenth century. Again, Prussia at that time did not contain several other states which were later united around it to form the German Empire. Prussia was a smaller unit than later Germany. A study of its wars does not embrace the wars carried on by the other German states, whereas the wars of Germany do. With Austria-Hungary the situation is still more complex and, if not corrected in some way, is likely to lead to enormous errors.

Clearly realizing these conditions in regard to these four countries in particular, I have tried to combat them by several procedures. So far as

Austria-Hungary is concerned, I study not so much the wars of Austria-Hungary as the wars of Central Europe as it was united in the Holy Roman Empire of the German nation.   This means that the unit studied throughout the centuries from the twelfth to the seventeenth is relatively constant, Central Europe in the form of the Holy Roman Empire.   When, beginning with the seventeenth century, the wars of Prussia-Germany are taken separately from the wars of Austria-Hungary, these two countries again embrace almost the whole of Central Europe; therefore the unit, Central Europe, remains essentially constant throughout the whole period studied.

In regard to Italy and Spain, though during the first few centuries studied the united state Castile-Aragon did not embrace all the population of the Spanish Peninsula, nor did Savoy and Sardinia embrace all of the Italian population, most of the other states of the Italian and Spanish peninsulas through all these centuries composed a part of either Austria, France, Spain, or Italy.   For this reason they enter into the study of the wars of these countries and are not left out.   For any single country this factor of the variability of its size, and the noninclusion of the wars of other states of Italy or Spain in the wars of the kernel state around which they have since united, may lead to the error of fictitious increase of its war indicators when the other states are incorporated in the kernel state. For the whole "European universe," however, so far as represented by the nine countries studied, this error is decreased to a considerable degree. In one way or another, the wars of these "other states" entered into the wars of either Austria, France, the Spanish Empire, or Italy.

Probably, however, not all the wars of those other states, nor all parts of Italy and Spain enter into the total war indicators for the whole universe of the nine countries studied.   Many a war of the Italian city states, the activities of the condottieri, the armed conflicts of various factions and groups, like the long conflicts of the Knights of St. John of Compostella and many others, either did not enter into the results or entered only in part, and often in a small part, leading thus to an underestimation of the war activities for the earlier centuries of European history.

This is still more true of the "private wars" in the Middle Ages.   The extent of these "private wars" was probably exaggerated by the early historians of the Middle Ages.   But, no doubt, these "wars" were numerous, and often disastrous and destructive, for the locality in which they occurred and for the small groups involved in these conflicts.   Most of such "wars" did not enter into our list of wars at all for two convincing reasons. First, strictly speaking they were not wars. They were something similar to what we style now "the gangsters' war," or "collective crimes," or "group redress." Since these are not considered for recent times, they were omitted for the earlier centuries also. In the second place, there is no possibility of computing and of "measuring" them on account of a lack of even the most approximate data. Formally these reasons are quite sufficient to justify their omission from any investigation of war. Factually, these private wars were probably a kind of substitute for the real wars during the earlier centuries. However, the omission of these "private wars" may lead to an undue underestimation of the war activities during the Middle Ages and to overestimation for the recent centuries.

For all these reasons, other allowances have to be made and have to be made liberally, within even the exaggerated margins of minimum and maximum. Since we seek only a rough approximation to reality, we make quite a liberal allowance, *doubling* and even trebling the magnitude of war activities for all the countries studied up to the sixteenth or seventeenth century, after which these factors of variability and of other conditions mentioned cease to play a notable role. It is probable that doubling more than amply compensates the possible underestimating of the wars of these countries for the centuries from the twelfth to the seventeenth, and that trebling makes these wars seem far greater than they really are. Such an allowance certainly must satisfy even the most ardent critic.

We are ready to grant the same allowance for early centuries for all the other countries studied, though there are hardly any serious reasons for doubling their war activities. But we are willing to be unduly liberal in our admission of the margin of possible error. Instead of being "stingy," we thus open wide the doors of this margin, so that no critic need break violently into the building of our results. And yet, with all these allowances, as we shall see, the essentials of the results will hold under the minimum and maximum points of the overliberal margin of error. So much for this difficulty ; with these corrections, considerations, and allowances it seems to be rendered harmless to a great degree.

The next complicating factor is presented by the fact that, especially in the wars for the centuries before the eighteenth, the *fighting force of a given country consisted not only of the soldiers of this country but also of foreign mercenaries or men enlisted in various ways into the army.* Sometimes the proportion of such "foreign fighters" was very considerable. Strictly speaking they had to be excluded, or at least separated, from the army of the citizens or subjects of a given country. This, however, is impossible in most of the wars of the centuries before the eighteenth. Insofar, the figures used contain another possibility of error. However, in the final computation of the relative indicators of war for the whole of Europe the error is again greatly mitigated. If in the Prussian or the French armies there were many foreigners, these foreign elements were usually from one of the nine European countries, and only rarely and in a small proportion from a population outside. In other words, they were from the same European "basket universe," and were included in computing the total.

The next point to be mentioned is the *exceedingly variable size of the fighting forces throughout the Middle Ages.* In some of its wars the fighting forces consisted only of "professional" fighters, and therefore were small; in other cases around that kernel was gathered together a large mass of additional fighters, various mercenaries, and an able-bodied local population which enlarged the army's strength considerably. Such a variability makes any estimate made for the wars of these centuries particularly uncertain. But again, the variability should not be exaggerated. One-time creditable "histories" about the enormous size of the Crusades, and of some other armies of the Middle Ages, now can be definitely discounted as fantastic. The maximum limits of almost all the medieval wars rarely, if ever, exceeded 20,000 (up to the wars of the fifteenth century). The main force of the fighters almost always consisted of the professionals, the nobility, the mercenaries, and soldiers by occupation. The temporary enlargement of this central force by the nonprofessional fighters was a somewhat episodic event and probably happened during all the centuries of the Middle Ages, without being a specific trait of a specific century. For these reasons, the estimates aim to give the strength and the losses of the central fighting force throughout these centuries. Though they deviate from the fanciful variability of the medieval reality, nevertheless the "straight lines" of the estimates do not necessarily disfigure the comparative picture of the war activities from century to century. These straight lines are uniformly applied to all these centuries, and are aimed at the central force of the military machinery, disregarding the unknown factor of the episodic enlargement of this central core by various nonprofessional fighters or professional mercenaries.

Finally, the difficulty presented by the lack of population statistics for the centuries before the seventeenth or eighteenth is not absolutely unconquerable. In the first place, there are many estimates by historians and specialists on population which permit us to arrive at some roughly correct figures, within a reasonable margin of error. Again we wish to be most liberal. As the reader will see later on, we are ready to grant the widest possible margin of error there, amounting to 300 per cent. Within these very wide limits, certainly, are included the actual populations for the centuries studied. If the essential conclusions still hold under the minimum and maximum points of this margin, there must be something valid in the results.

The factual difficulties, then, are real and serious, but are not absolutely unconquerable.

Let us turn now to the *methodological difficulties*. These difficulties, as aforesaid, consist mainly in the impossibility of perfectly "translating" qualitative-quantitative phenomena into the language of purely quantitative indicators. If, however, an investigator does not attempt to turn qualities into quantities but limits his task to *translating some of the purely quantitative aspects of the phenomena of war into quantitative language, no logical or epistemological obstacles to the enterprise exist*. If the investigator limits his task still more by considering only the most essential elements of the quantitative aspects of his subject, the task is a reasonable, not an impossible, one.

Are there quantitative aspects of the phenomena of war that can be counted? Evidently! The first such quantitative element is the size of the army, which is "countable" and "measurable." As to the casualties, here again units — individuals killed and wounded — exist, need not be invented, and can be counted. Such another quantitative element is the duration of the war, which has units of time in which it can be counted and compared with other time units.

This means that within the above limitations, and providing the investigator does not claim that these quantitative elements exhaust all the quantitative and qualitative components of war, a quantitative study of war in these respects is possible.

This study deals precisely with these three quantitative elements of war: *the strength of the army, the number of casualties (killed and wounded), and the duration of each of the wars studied*. No other aspect of the war phenomena is studied, not the economic losses, nor the morbidity and mortality of the civilian population, nor anything else. The conclusions reached are based upon the data of these three variables only, and concern these three aspects only, no more and no less. Therefore, all the claims, as well as the criticism, which involve other aspects of war movement not studied here should not be addressed to this study and its conclusions; they belong somewhere else.

Now turn more specifically to the material of the study, and its procedure, so far as it is not outlined above.

III. The Materials of the Study

We have taken almost all the known wars of Greece, Rome, Austria, Germany, England, France, the Netherlands, Spain, Italy, Russia, and Poland and Lithuania from the periods indicated in the subsequent tables (Chapters Ten and Eleven) to the present time, or, in the case of Greece and Rome, to the loss of Greek independence and to the so-called "end of the Western Roman Empire," respectively. The existence at least of some relatively and very roughly reliable data or estimates on war determines for each country the earliest period with which the study may start. The earlier periods, for which no data exist, have, of course, to be excluded.

In the way outlined above we have studied about [9] 967 important wars (not battles) divided about as follows among the different countries: in Greek history, 24; in Roman, 81; in Austrian, 131; in German, 24; in English, 176; in French, 185; in Dutch, 23; in Spanish, 75; in Italian, 32; in Russian, 151; in Polish and Lithuanian, 65.[10] Having obtained the data for the three variables for each of these wars, we then grouped these data by twenty-five-year periods for each of the variables, obtaining in this way three time series for each of these countries by twenty-five-year periods.

In regard to each of these wars it is attempted to give its duration, the strength of the army, and the number of the casualties. The duration is known in almost all cases and therefore presents no real difficulty. In many cases where two or more wars were waging concurrently, two wars

[9] We write "about" because there are certain wars which some historians count as single wars while others count each of these as two or more separate wars. The number, therefore, varies somewhat according to the procedure adopted. Then several small wars in adjacent years are united into one group. However, the number of wars as such in no way influences the absolute or the relative indicators.

[10] Here the reader may be puzzled by the fact that the number of the wars for some of the countries — like England, France, Russia, and Austria — is great while for some other countries — like Germany, Spain, Holland, and Italy — it is comparatively small. Such a contrast may appear unbelievable. The real reason for it is that the study of the wars for the countries of the second group starts only with the sixteenth or the seventeenth centuries, while the countries with the larger number of wars are studied beginning with the tenth or the eleventh centuries. As the countries with a small number of wars began their independent history only later, the wars which were carried on in their present territory before that entered into the history of the countries with the larger number of wars, and hence the contrast. It does not mean that one group of the countries has been more peaceful or military than another. See further Chapter Ten, where the real meaning of this contrast is explained.

each lasting one year counted, according to one method, as two years. As a result, the number of years of war for any one country may rise as high as 45 or 50 years within a quarter-century period. According to the other method each single year, no matter if one or more wars occurred during it, was counted as one year only. Subsequently the two methods are mentioned.

As to the strength of the army, in each war, and the amount of the casualties the following procedure is adopted and used uniformly throughout. For each war the total strength of the army means the typical size of the army multiplied by the number of years of a given war. In a very few cases when the total strength of the army is known (for instance the total mobilized forces or the like) this figure is considered also. Likewise, the total number of the casualties in a given war means the typical per cent of the casualty in regard to the strength of the army multiplied by the number of years during which the war lasted. The typical size of the army and the casualty in a given war is obtained by considering the actual strength of the army and of the casualty in its various battles, when the war had only one front. When the war had not one but two or more different fronts, a phenomenon almost entirely lacking in the wars before the seventeenth century, the typical size of the army in such a war is established either on the basis of the data concerning the total force on all the fronts or on the basis of an increase of the size of the army through its proportional increase according to the number of the different fronts and their respective importance. In such cases, the figure typical for one front of the war is doubled or trebled if the number of the fronts were two or three respectively, and if they were more or less equally important. If the second front were less important, the increase is proportionately less. In the wars of the seventeenth and of the subsequent centuries there exist, for many wars, roughly accurate factual data concerning the total size of the army on all fronts of a given war. Such data are naturally considered and used as part of the basis of the figure given.

When the total strength of the army in a given war, on its one or several fronts, is established, and when the typical per cent of the casualties in regard to the total army in the war is determined, the total number of the casualties for each given war is obtained, either by multiplication of the typical per cent of the casualties by the number of years, or by putting down the actual data which exist in regard to this item for a given war as a whole. For civil wars, where both sides belong to the same country, the strength of the army and of the casualty represents both parties; when the data exist only in regard to one party, the respective figures are doubled. *This means that the figures given for each period are aimed not so much to lay down the actual number of the mobilized or killed and wounded as to obtain a rough measuring device to see the comparative increase or decrease of war from period to period.* It is very important to keep this in mind.

The actual data are taken from authoritative historical sources, often ably summarized and elaborated by various special historical works like the often-quoted works of Delbruck, Bodart, and various encyclopedias of war and military science. For the sake of economy I reduce my references intentionally to comparatively few works, where the results of many monographic studies are given and well summarized. Such a fact does not mean, however, that either my or my collaborators' reading is limited by these comparatively few works (as one of the readers of the draft of this study assumed). When such data are lacking, and they are lacking for the majority of the wars of the past, my own estimates are introduced, as has been explained above. In which wars estimates, and in which wars the actual data, are used the reader can see from the detailed characterization and itemization of the wars of each country, in the next chapter of this work.

This procedure, for the computation of the total strength of the army and for the total number of casualties in each war studied, may tempt some too pretentious critics to think that I presume that for every additional year of the war duration the total typical size of the army is renewed, because the total size of the army in the accepted procedure is obtained through multiplication of the typical strength of the army by the number of years of the war duration. It is hardly necessary to say that no such presumption is made on my part. It is obvious that, in lasting wars, every year only a part of the army is renewed by new men called to the colors. If, however, such a procedure is accepted, it is a mere device for the estimation of the *comparative* strength of the army and of the losses by a uniform means in all the wars studied. In so far as the means is the same, and uniformly applied to all the wars studied, it serves the purpose of giving a rough idea of the *comparative* magnitude of the army and of the casualty of all the wars. When these figures are obtained they are summed up by quarter-century and century periods.

This mechanical division of the periods into twenty-five and one hundred years often leads to dividing one single war between two periods, and other similar inconveniences. But since we compare the fluctuation of the war activities in the course of time, such a division of time into equal units seems unavoidable for purposes of comparison. Whether the unit of time will be one minute, hour, day, year, or twenty-five years, any such unit is in a sense mechanical, and cuts across the social processes, but is absolutely unavoidable in such a comparative study. And there is no real difference whether the unit will be a minute, day, year, or one hundred years. As explained above, when we try to estimate the average strength of the war activity (or of any other sociocultural process) per minute, day, year, or one hundred years, we always draw a straight line from point to point, where in fact there exists a fluctuating, crooked, curved line, because the real strength of the process often does not remain constant within even every minute, hour, or day. Averages drawn for the change of the process from minute to minute on their scale may differ from the crookedly fluctuating strength of the processes within a minute no less than the averages for the change of the strength of the process from twenty-five to twenty-five years, or from one hundred to one hundred years, upon their respective scales. In other words, the continental map with its straight lines, where in fact are very crooked roads, deviates from the real direction of the roads to some extent but so does any inch map, and the deviation of the latter upon its scale is ordinarily no less than the deviation of the continental map upon its scale. So much for this point.

Such, in brief, is the material and procedure used for making the three time series. Providing that the initial data and the estimates do not err fundamentally, it will probably be agreed that each of these time series is one of the important indicators of an increase or decrease of war activities. It is understood that the figures, whether for separate wars or for periods of a quarter century and century, are *absolute figures not corrected by the size of the population*. Taken as such without correction per unit of population, they are misleading. Whether the "burden of war" is decreasing or increasing, the figures can roughly answer only when they are turned into *relative indicators computed per unit of population*.

After giving the absolute figures of the time series in the next chapter, I attempt to give relative indicators of the magnitude of war, or "burden of war," for Greece, for Rome, and for nine other European countries. The last part of the study deals with this problem and gives *"relative indicators"* of the army and casualty per unit of population in the history of Greece, Rome, and the whole of Europe from the twelfth to the twentieth century.

Concluding this "introductory-explanatory" part of the study, I can say that however great and numerous the shortcomings, the errors, the inadequacies, which I have frankly stressed and overstressed in the preceding remarks, may be, one thing seems very probable : such a study more nearly approaches the reality than mere guesses, than incidental and fragmentary statements, than theories made *ad hoc*, no matter by whom or with what intentions. We at least have now at our disposal as accurate an appraisal as possible of some one thousand wars "measured" uniformly by the same stick, and in as objective a way as I could design.

How misleading guesses, or even unsystematic "appraisals," can be, I can testify by my own experience. Like many others somewhat acquainted with history, I held certain preconceived ideas of the kind generally accepted, that such and such periods would give exceptionally high or exceptionally low indicators of war activities. When, however, the wars of the period in question were studied, the results sometimes quite contradicted my preconceived ideas.

In such cases I naturally felt that I must find out whether the figures were not playing me a trick and giving quite misleading results. So I proceeded to check and recheck the results. After sufficient study I had to recognize that in most cases the figures were right ; while the ideas that I had drawn from textbooks, journalistic articles, historical novels, prevalent opinions, and propaganda in various forms were wrong.

The point is that a given society at a given time, in its press, its textbooks of history, its "best sellers," and so on, particularly emphasizes this or that war or battle — for instance, the Napoleonic wars, the battle of Bunker Hill — and does not mention, or mentions only in passing, many larger wars. What does the average American high-school student, or college student for that matter, know of the wars of Ancient Egypt or even of the wars of the Middle Ages? The wars and the periods of which they know nothing do not exist for them. On the other hand, they have learned a great deal about Bunker Hill or the battles of any similar war that for various reasons were particularly emphasized by texts, addresses, and the press. The same is true of peace periods. The periods charged with "peace movements" and pacifistic speechmaking appear peaceful indeed, in spite of the fact of an intensive war activity.

The result is a kind of mental aberration and false perspective as to the comparative magnitude of wars and the periods in which they occur, quite similar to the illusion as to the comparative size of the moon and Jupiter; the former seems much larger than the latter and the naïve observer supposes it actually to be so. In a primitive or in a refined way most of us have this false perspective on various wars. Until one really "measures" the wars, and "measures" them systematically by the same rod, one cannot have a correct perspective as to their relative magnitude, and often one's mental vision will play tricks with judgment. The chances of this false perspective in the psychosocial atmosphere are perhaps more numerous than the chances of a false perspective in physical space.

In conclusion, I hope that this study will stimulate more competent persons to take the problem into their hands, and to make a better investigation than this. It is, in a way, no more than a pioneer survey of an unknown country, made without perfect instruments and without perfect training for the task. As such it is taken by me humorously as an adventurous enterprise, but this humorous attitude is not followed by any apology for it, on my part. In comparison with the other existing studies of the same problem, it does not need any apology.

Chapter Ten

FLUCTUATION OF THE MAGNITUDE OF WAR IN THE HISTORY
OF GREECE, ROME, AND EUROPE: II. ABSOLUTE FIGURES

In this chapter the absolute figures for each of the wars studied, as well
as the absolute figures for the three time series in the field of war, are given
for each of the countries mentioned, by quarter-century and century
periods. A glance at the table for each country gives an idea how the
war burden fluctuated in the history of each country in the course of time,
so far as this burden or war magnitude is "measured" by any of these
three series. Each of the variables being symptomatic in this respect,
the variables of the casualties and of the size of the army are particularly
important as indicators of the magnitude of war burden and of war
activities. As the reader can easily notice, these two variables have an
essentially parallel movement. Such parallelism is due mainly to a close
association which exists between the size of the fighting force and the
amount of human life lost, and partly to the necessity of using, in many
cases, estimates. The estimates of casualties for the wars for which the
actual data of the losses do not exist are based mainly upon the size of
the army in a given war and are computed in the form of varying percentages of the army's strength — two, five, or more per cent as the
totality of the evidence warrants in each case. It is probable that this
factor increased somewhat the parallelism of the movement of the two
variables; but it hardly disfigured their real relationship.

As mentioned above, the absolute figures for each of the time series,
when they are not computed per unit of population, are somewhat misleading. They must be given, however, because without them neither
the relative indicators of war burden per unit of population can be computed nor several other problems studied. After the absolute figures of
the movement of each variable are given, the relative indicators of the
size of the army and of the casualties per unit of population are computed
for all the nine European countries, in the next chapter. For Greece
and Rome the relative indicators are given in this chapter.

One additional remark is necessary. There is no serious reason to think, so far as our knowledge goes, that for the earlier centuries, for Europe from the eleventh to the sixteenth inclusive, many wars are omitted, or that the indicators are lower than they should be. However, we must consider the long time that has elapsed and the "obliterating function of time," the variation of the states studied in the course of time, tending to increase their size through incorporating states previously independent of them, and the "private wars," and similar circumstances mentioned. Due to these and similar factors it is not improbable that our indicators for the wars of these centuries are too low and should be raised considerably. In the subsequent absolute figures this is not done. But when we pass to a summary of the absolute figures for all these countries taken as a whole, the indicators for the early centuries are increased by *doubling*, an allowance which is probably more liberal than is necessary. Nevertheless, in a study like this where so many uncertainties exist, it is better to be more than less liberal, especially when in spite of even such "over-liberalism" the essential results remain still unchanged.

A. *Ancient Greece.* The main authorities for the construction of the lists of indicators are J. Beloch,[1] Hans Delbrück,[2] and W. S. Ferguson.[3] The use of these authorities means that we reject all fantastic figures about the size of the armies, the number of victims, and other items given by many uncritical sources, and believe that however questionable are some of the data given by Beloch, Delbrück, or Ferguson they probably approximate reality as nearly as other figures given by other specialists in the field. If instead of the estimates of these scholars we had taken estimates given by E. Meyer, or R. Pöhlmann, or a few other specialists, the final results would not have been essentially different from the results reached here, on the basis of the above main sources. In the footnotes and the Appendix to this part the references to these sources are abbreviated in the following way: B I, B II, and B III refer to the first, second, and third volumes of Beloch's *Griechische Geschichte;* B without any figure refers to his *Die Bevölkerung;* D I and D II, etc., refer to the first, second, and following volumes of the cited work of H. Delbrück; and F refers to Ferguson's work mentioned.

Using these and several other works for a basis, one must bear in mind that the absolute size of the Greek armies (and also of their adversaries), as well as their relative size in proportion to the population, was com-

---

[1] *Die Bevölkerung der griechisch-römischen Welt* (Leipzig, 1886) and *Griechische Geschichte,* 3 vols. (Strassburg, 1893, 1897, and 1904).

[2] *Geschichte der Kriegskunst im Rahmen der politischen Geschichte,* 1st ed. (Berlin, 1900) and 2d ed. (Berlin, 1908).

[3] *Hellenistic Athens* (London, 1911).

paratively small. In the fourth century B.C. Athens had in very few cases more than 6000 combatants, a figure only about 3 per cent of the approximately 200,000 population of Attica. Sparta with its Peloponnesian allies in the war of Boeotia, fourth century B.C., set forth only about 18,000 fighters, some 2 per cent of the population of the Peloponnesus, without Argos (the above population being near to 750,000).[4] The general size of the Greek armies, as well as of the armies of their adversaries, very rarely exceeded in any war 25,000 to 30,000 combatants.[5] Since the total population of Greece in the time of the Graeco-Persian and Peloponnesian wars was scarcely less than 3,000,000 (according to Beloch 3,051,000), this means that no more than 2 per cent of its population were involved actively in the war, or 4 per cent even in the most strenuous civil war, where the belligerent parties made their maximum military effort. As we shall see, this per cent is considerably lower than the per cent of population actively involved in a war in modern times.

This modest size (absolute and relative) of the armies is paralleled by the relatively low rate of loss of human life (in the form of killed and wounded) in the Greek wars. An idea of the size of the losses is given in two of the greatest battles of Alexander the Great: on the Macedonian side in the battle at Granicus (334 B.C.) 120 were killed, in the battle at Issus (333 B.C.) 450 were killed. In taking Tyre (July 332) about 400 were lost, and in the battle at Arbela (331 B.C.) about 500.[6] Likewise 500 were killed in the battle at Crannow,[7] and so on. In the last battles the casualties of the defeated side were probably higher, but there is no possibility of carrying out such a differentiation for all the wars studied. According to the generally accepted method of estimation of loss of human life in a war[8] — 1 killed per 3 or 4 wounded — this gives only from 1 to 2 per cent of the army for the Granicus battle, and from 4 to 8 per cent for the battles at Issus, Tyre, and Arbela, accepting 30,000 to 47,000 as the size of the Macedonian Army.[9] Only in the battle at Marathon (490 B.C.) were the losses of the Greeks about 25 per cent of their army (D I, 41, 50). As will be seen further, even this exceptionally high rate of loss would not be particularly high for many wars of the seventeenth, eighteenth, nineteenth, and twentieth centuries. In the wars after 431 B.C., when out of

---

[4] B, p. 23.

[5] D I, pp. 88, 171, and 184; B II, p. 337.

[6] B II, pp. 627, 643, and 648.

[7] F, p. 18.

[8] On the basis of the wars of the eighteenth and nineteenth centuries plus the World War, the norm is 1 killed per 3 to 4 wounded. See O. Berndt, *Die Zahl im Kriege, Statistische Daten aus der neueren Kriegsgeschichte* (Wien, 1897), pp. 91–92, table 67; Lt. General N. N. Golovine, *The Russian Army in the World War* (New Haven, 1931), p. 86.

[9] B II, p. 625.

85 years 55 were war years, the losses were not especially high, amounting to some 2 to 3 per cent on the average in single battles.[10] These and other data seem to show that the absolute magnitude of wars in Greece was not particularly high, with the exception of one century.

The scarcity of relevant data for Greek wars, plus data like the above, forces us to accept as a maximum size of the Greek armies, 30,000, and as a maximum rate of losses, 5 per cent, for big wars for which more exact data do not exist. Such an assumption is a rough approximation; in no single case do we meet a figure above 50,000. Even this figure is met only once. For smaller wars the estimate has to be respectively less.[11] For civil wars, which as a rule are more devastating and call forth greater military effort from the parties (of the same country), these norms should be raised. In the subsequent computation of the indicators (Tables 1 and 2) these values are doubled for the civil or inter-Greek wars.

Subsequently, in the Appendix to this part are given detailed figures enumerating all the wars studied, with values for each of the variables: the war's duration, the size of the army, and the extent of the losses. Anyone who is anxious to see them in detail and to check their accuracy and their sources is given thus a full opportunity.[12] So much for preliminary explanations.

In Table 1 these detailed figures are summed up for each quarter-century and century period. As mentioned, they are absolute figures not corrected by the size of the population — therefore, somewhat misleading.

---

[10] B II, pp. 336–337.

[11] Besides the figures given in the detailed list of the Greek wars, here are a few additional examples. In the war of 323 B.C. the Athenians had, all in all, about 10 regiments, of which 7, or about 5000 men, plus 2000 mercenaries with 500 horses, actively participated in the war. In the same year Antipater, the regent of Macedonia, started to suppress the revolt of Greece with 13,000 men, 600 cavalry, and 110 ships. (F., pp. 14–15.) Leonnatus, satrap of Phrygia, entered Thessaly with 20,000 plus 2500 cavalry. (Ibid., p. 15.) The united army of the Greeks had 20,000 plus 3500 cavalry against Leonnatus. (Ibid., p. 15.) The subsequent army of Craterus, who hurried to help Leonnatus after his defeat, was about 6000 Macedonians, 4000 new recruits, 1500 cavalry, and a few hundred archers, all in all about 12,000. (Ibid., p. 17.) And so on. "Fifty thousands, victorious Macedonians — more, perhaps, than any ruler of that country led into action either before or after," says Ferguson, stressing thus the exceptional size of an army of such a number. (Ibid., p. 19.) See in this work many other figures for the end of the fourth, the third, and the second century B.C., the period especially dark and little known. See other figures in the detailed list of the wars appended.

[12] It is understood that it is quite impossible to enumerate and measure all the small skirmishes between various Greek states and between the Greek and the non-Greek groups. Such "skirmishes" had naturally to be omitted or united in one prolonged warfare, with few troops, losses, and respectively low figures. Main campaigns, however, are tabulated as carefully as was possible for us. As this concerns all the centuries studied, such a shortcoming hardly disfigures the comparative war indicators for various centuries and quarter centuries.

The corrected indicators follow in Table 2. The inter-Greek wars are regarded as internal and, as for all internal (civil) wars, their figures are doubled, because in such cases both adversaries are of the same country.

TABLE 1. TOTAL MEASURES OF WAR FOR ANCIENT GREECE FROM 500 TO 126 B.C. BY QUARTER CENTURIES AND CENTURIES

Century and Quarter Century	Duration (Years)	Army's Strength (Number)	Casualties (Number)
500–401 B.C.	**91**	**1,694,000**	**88,660**
500–476	25	500,000	25,000
475–451	34	752,000	42,600
450–426	8	64,000	3,200
425–401	24	378,000	17,860
400–301	**85**	**2,413,000**	**144,050**
400–376	19	489,000	47,850
375–351	18	720,000	36,000
350–326	25	698,000	34,900
325–301	23	506,000	25,300
300–201	**48**	**1,225,000**	**54,400**
300–276	18	360,000	14,400
275–251	15	250,000	10,000
250–226	2	120,000	6,000
225–201	13	495,000	24,000
200–126	**11**	**205,000**	**9,100**
200–176	5	115,000	5,600
175–151	4	60,000	3,000
150–126	2	30,000	1,500

These data suggest the following conclusions.

(1) The curves do not show any continuous trend toward either the increasing or the decreasing of war during the period studied, measured by the movement of any of the three variables.

(2) According to the variables, Army's Strength and Casualties, the maximum falls on the fourth century, the fifth century being next.

(3) Toward the end of independent Greece the curves tend to go down.

(4) There is no strict periodicity in the ups and downs of war, and no uniform rhythm.

(5) The data on the duration show that in the accepted system of computation of the duration (see above, page 284), of 375 years studied, 235 years (or about 63 per cent) had an occurrence of war. Many of these wars did not last through a whole year.[13] If we just inquire how

[13] Any calendar year in which any war or its part occurred, no matter how long or short, is counted as a year with war occurrence. This is one of the reasons why our numbers of years with and without the occurrence of war is somewhat different for European countries from those given by F. A. Woods and A. Baltzly. They counted in a sense the real duration

many years of 375 studied had any occurrence of war and how many
years did not (and were therefore peaceful), the answer is about 213
years were war years; that is, the per cent of the years with war (or
wars) in that case is about 57 of the total number of Greek history studied.
Both figures show that in the history of Greece frequency of war was
much higher than many of us are wont to think.

(6) Although the data on the number of years with war in each twenty-
five-year period, compared with the data of the other variables, are in
some degree correlated, the association is remote and there is considerable
discrepancy. The variables, Army's Strength and especially Casualties,
seem to measure more adequately the magnitude or burden of war
than mere duration of war and peace periods.

(7) The fifth and fourth centuries B.C. are generally accepted as the
centuries of climax of Greek splendor, creativeness, and power. Scientific
discoveries and technological inventions, used as criteria of scientific
progress, numbered 26 in Greece in the sixth century, 39 in the fifth,
52 in the fourth, 42 in the third, and 14 in the second.[14] The indicators of
philosophical creativeness in Greece are: 38 for the sixth century; 99 for
the fifth; 152 for the fourth; 98 for the third; and 47 for the second
century.[15] Thus the movement of the magnitude of war, as shown by our
second and third variables, and that of the curve of scientific and philosophical creativeness run parallel in Greek history, giving the maximum
in the fourth century, next in the fifth, and falling lowest in the second
century. The third and second centuries are generally regarded as those
of the decline of Greek culture, of Greek genius, and of an enormous decline
of Greek political power, ending with a loss of the last simulacrum of
Greek sovereignty and political independence. The same centuries show
a decisive decline in war activities, which dwindled to a very low level.

---

of the war within an approximation of six months. We, as mentioned, proceeded differently.
(See their *Is War Diminishing?*, Boston, 1915, p.2.) The other reason why in this item
there is a discrepancy between their data, the data of G. Bodart, and ours, is that for some
of the periods the list of the wars studied is not equally complete in all three studies. For
instance, Bodart's computation of the years with and without wars for Austria, and especially for France in the seventeenth, eighteenth, and nineteenth centuries, does not include
the colonial wars at all. (See Bodart, *Losses of Life in Modern Wars*, Oxford, 1916, p. 78.)
Our study, and in part that of Woods and Baltzly, does include them. For most of the
periods our list of wars is somewhat more complete than that of Woods and Baltzly. Hence
the difference in the number of years with and without war in these three studies. However, for most periods the figures given in all three studies are close to one another.

[14] Computed from L. Darmstaedter, *Handbuch zur Geschichte der Naturwissenschaften und
der Technik* (Berlin, 1908). See Chapter Three of Volume Two of this work.

[15] The data will be given in Volume Four of this work. If we take a mere number of the
philosophers known, the relative position of the centuries will be the same.

We shall meet similar phenomena several times in the study of the other countries.

Such are the results shown by the *absolute figures*. They are in a sense misleading. Therefore it is advisable to inquire what the results will be if we try to compute the war burden or war magnitude "per unit of population," say per 1,000,000. It goes without saying that exact statistics of the population of Greece for the various centuries studied do not exist. What do exist are the estimates given by the best historians on the basis of the totality of available data. As a basis for our computation we take, as mentioned above, Beloch's estimates.[16] The estimates given by other specialists, like E. Meyer, R. Pöhlmann [17] and others, deviate somewhat from the figures given by Beloch, but not so much as to make any essential difference in our results.

For the simplest form of relative indicators we can take the army's strength and casualty figures for each of the specified centuries, divide them by the estimated population of the corresponding century, and multiply by 1,000,000. The result will be the relative indicator of the losses of human life — or of the main form of war burden or war magnitude per 1,000,000 of population. Under these conditions the relative indicators of war-burden magnitude for specified centuries,[18] per 1,000,000 of estimated population of Greece, will be as shown in Table 2.

TABLE 2. RELATIVE INDICATORS OF WAR MAGNITUDE FOR ANCIENT GREECE

Century	Measured by the Casualties	Measured by the Army's Strength
V B.C.	29,000 [1]	560,000
IV	from 48,016 to 36,012 [2]	804,333 to 603,250
III	from 18,170 to 13,600	408,333 to 306,250
II	from 3,033 to 3,640 [3]	82,000 to 68,333

[1] Assuming the population was 3,000,000, the estimate given by Beloch (3,051,000) for the period c. 432 B.C. B, p. 506; B II, p. 405.

[2] Assuming the population was from about 3,000,000 to 4,000,000. B, p. 497.

[3] Assuming the population remained around 3,000,000 or even decreased to 2,500,000. See B III, pt. 1, pp. 331–333, B, pp. 498–499.

From these rough and approximate figures one can see that the movement of the relative indicators is essentially the same as that of the absolute

[16] See B, p. 506 *et passim*. See also D I, pp. 13 ff. of the 2d ed.

[17] See E. Meyer, "*Die Bevölkerung des Altertums*," in *Handwörterbuch der Staatswissenschaften*, 3d ed. (Jena, 1909), Vol. II; R. Pöhlmann, *Die Ueberbevölkerung der antiken Grossstädte* (Leipzig, 1884).

[18] It is not possible to have any remotely reliable figures for the population of Greece for each of the twenty-five-year periods studied.

ones. The fourth century B.C. occupies the first place; next comes the fifth; and the least belligerent is the second century B.C. These results will remain if, instead of Beloch's estimates, any estimate of any of the greatest historians of Ancient Greece is taken. They will remain also if, instead of the assumptions made here, the figures for the population of these centuries are increased or decreased by 1,000,000 in either direction.

The detailed table for each war is given in the Appendix to this part.[19] Figures 6 and 7 give an idea of the relative magnitude of war by casualties and by army's strength for the centuries mentioned.

B. *Ancient Rome.* In regard to Rome all the above statements concerning the scarcity and unreliability of data are applicable in an even greater degree than to Greece. Here again, rejecting many fantastic figures and accepting data corrected by the severe criticism of many historians, we take as our foundation the data given in Delbrück's work. For the size of the population we take the data of Beloch, though we are not unaware that other authoritative historians (E. Meyer, R. Pöhlmann, J. Marquardt, and others) have given for some periods and items data considerably deviating from those given by Beloch or Delbrück. But these deviations are not so large as to change the results essentially.

In spite of all the painstaking work of historians, our difficulties here are even greater than in the case of Greece. Besides the scarcity or lack of data, the existing data given by various historians vary considerably even in regard to the best-studied wars of Rome. For instance, for the battle at Cannae in 216 B.C. the figures of the size of the Roman Army fluctuate from 86,000 (Delbrück and others) to 44,000 (P. Cantalupi).[20] Likewise the losses in this battle fluctuate, according to various historians, from about two-thirds of the army to one-third. Similar is the situation in regard to other wars, as the wars with Pyrrhus,[21] the battles at Heraclea, and others. There is still further complication from additional circumstances, the size and losses of the auxiliary armies of the allies, and the real portion of the total armies of the Empire which participated in a given war. If, in the time of the Republic, the greater part of the Roman armies fought actively in the important wars, in the time of the Empire most of the troops seem to have been stationed at the boundaries and often did not take active part in wars far from the area where they were stationed. Other complications might be mentioned also.

---

[19] See again p. 290 for meaning of abbreviated references in the footnotes and the Appendix.

[20] See D I, pp. 321 ff. of the 2d ed.; P. Cantalupi, "*Le legione Romane nella guerra d'Annibale,*" in the *Studi di Storia Antica* (Rome, 1891), Vol. I.

[21] See D I, pp. 301 ff. of the 2d ed.

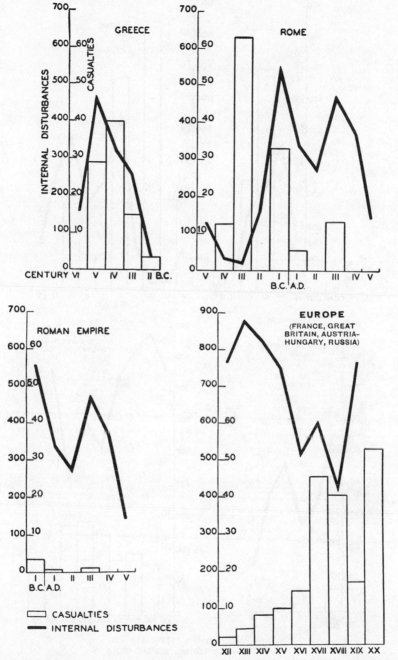

FIG. 6. RELATIVE WAR MAGNITUDE BY CASUALTIES AND INTERNAL
DISTURBANCES

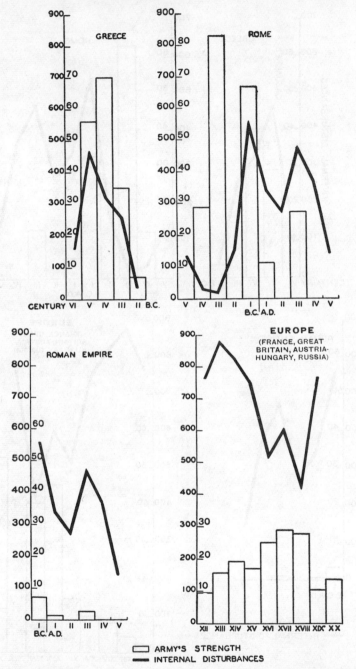

FIG. 7.   RELATIVE WAR MAGNITUDE BY ARMY'S STRENGTH AND IN-
TERNAL DISTURBANCES

Not to continue this "whining" about the lack and uncertainty of the data, the practical conclusion to be made is this: in view of this lack of data and the uncertainty of those which exist, it is safer (for the wars for which there are practically no data) not to base the estimates and indicators upon this or that fragmentary existing figure. It is better, instead, to use "the average coefficients," so to speak, suggested by the total data, as well as by the whole character and historical conditions of each war, and by general norms based upon facts given by many battles and wars. Such a solution is, of course, guesswork to a considerable degree; but it is a guess as good as any other and there are some reasons for regarding it as approximately trustworthy.

From the standpoint of this principle it becomes rather certain that the data of such wars as the Second Punic, and in part even that of the wars with Pyrrhus, are in no way typical of most of the Roman wars. Indeed, if Rome at the beginning of the second Punic War called to the colors 34,000 and up to 216 B.C. increased this army to 86,000, this gives from 3.4 to 8.6 per cent of the total free population of Rome enlisted in its army.[22] Eight per cent is an exceedingly high proportion: it is hardly found in the history of wars before the World War, where some of the countries called to the colors 10 and even a greater per cent of their populations. For the wars previous to the twentieth century even 5 per cent was exceptionally high. Likewise the losses in the battle at Cannae, whether we take them as one-third or two-thirds of the army, are exceptionally high. Since we have every reason to think that these figures for the second Punic War are, within the minimum and maximum mentioned, reliable, we do not believe it follows that these "norms" are typical for most of the Roman wars. For these wars the figures must be much lower, as is indicated by the few actual data. That assumption is warranted also by other evidences. For instance, the total size of the army of the Roman Empire hardly exceeded 250,000 at any time in its history. Augustus's army seems to have been somewhere around 225,000; the Empire's armies of the later period probably never exceeded 250,000, which is about ⅓ of 1 per cent of the total population of the Empire.[23]

Not giving here all our considerations, estimates are made, for the wars for which no actual data exist, with the following assumptions.

(1) The average rate of losses in the war is taken as about 5 per cent, which is most typical for the wars of the Ancient World, with the exception

---

[22] Assuming the free population to be about 1,000,000 at that time, as is given by H. Delbrück and some other historians. See D I, p. 309, of the 1st, and p. 349 of the 2d ed.

[23] See D II, pp. 170 and 228, 1st ed.

of such unique wars as the battle of Marathon or that of Cannae.   Since this rate is taken for all the wars for which actual and reliable data do not exist, the very constancy of this coefficient neutralizes its disfiguring effects upon the war movement from century to century.

(2) The duration of the wars is not guesswork, but it is known to a large extent for the majority of wars.[24]

(3) There is a greater element of speculation in the assumptions concerning the size of the armies fighting in a given war.   Their sizes are made up of three types.   For the wars before the Punic Wars, that is for the wars of the fourth century, the size of the armies is taken as about 20,000 (about four legions of Caesar).   This figure seems slightly high for the armies of the first half of the fourth century; but it is possibly somewhat low for the armies of the end of the fourth century and the beginning of the third.   In this way its inadequacies are neutralized and all in all it seems most nearly to approximate reality.   For the period beginning with the Punic Wars, the size of the armies in a war is taken as about 40,000 (8 legions), except for the wars for which data exist.   This seems to be the closest approach to truth.[25]   Finally, for the secondary wars and for the suppression of revolts (except that of Spartacus) the size of the armies in active operation is taken as near 20,000.

Such are the main assumptions made in our construction of the movement of war magnitude.   All the reservations and qualifications made in regard to the Greek detailed data and summarized time series, by twenty-five- and one-hundred-year periods, are to be applied to the Roman wars shown in Table 3.

The table suggests the following conclusions.

(1) According to the number of casualties the most belligerent centuries in the history of Rome were: the third B.C., and the first, and then the second B.C.; then the third A.D. and the fifth A.D.; the most peaceful centuries were: the first A.D. and then the fourth B.C.

(2) Here also we do not find any continuous trend toward an increase or decrease of war; it just fluctuates up and down.

[24] The words "to a large extent" are used because the character of war at that time was different from that of modern times, and the time duration between various battles of the same war was then much longer than in modern times. The factor permits some "subjectivity" — but within narrow limits — in the computation of duration of the wars.

[25] Note, we are talking of the size of the army actively engaged in a war, but not of the total army of the Roman Empire. This, as mentioned, was larger. According to the computation of D I, p. 310, 1st ed.; p. 349 of the 2d ed., even during the second Punic War, out of 18 legions of Rome, only 8 actively operated against Hannibal, while the remaining 10 were sent to Spain, Sicily, Sardinia, or composed the garrison of Rome and the human force of the navy.

TABLE 3. TOTAL MEASURES OF WAR FOR ANCIENT ROME FROM 400
B.C. TO A.D. 476 BY QUARTER CENTURIES AND CENTURIES

Century and Quarter Century	Duration (Years)	Army's Strength (Number)	Casualties (Number)
400–301 B.C.	**43**	**860,000**	**43,000**
400–376	2	40,000	2,000
375–351	11	220,000	11,000
350–326	7	140,000	7,000
325–301	23	460,000	23,000
300–201	**83**	**3,317,000**	**252,500**
300–276	21	581,000	44,100
275–251	18	732,000	45,200
250–226	12	440,000	22,000
225–201	32	1,564,000	141,200
200–101	**57**	**1,660,000**	**83,000**
200–176	8	240,000	12,000
175–151	4	80,000	4,000
150–126	24	560,000	28,000
125–101	21	780,000	39,000
100–1	**66**	**3,674,000**	**182,200**
100–76	20	1,200,000	60,000
75–51	30	1,734,000	86,700
50–26	10	620,000	29,500
25–1	6	120,000	6,000
1–100 A.D.	**29**	**784,000**	**38,800**
1–25	12	324,000	16,200
26–50	2	20,000	600
51–75	7	280,000	14,000
76–100	8	160,000	8,000
101–200	**28**	**1,120,000**	**56,000**
101–125	9	360,000	10,000
126–150	7	200,000	10,000
151–175	8	320,000	16,000
176–200	6	240,000	12,000
201–300	**42**	**1,620,000**	**80,600**
201–225	2	20,000	600
226–250	11	440,000	22,000
251–275	26	1,040,000	52,000
276–300	3	120,000	6,000
301–400	**26**	**1,235,000**	**61,450**
301–325	6	320,000	16,000
326–350	3	30,000	1,200
351–375	10	680,000	34,000
376–400	7	205,000	10,250
401–476	**37**	**1,400,000**	**70,000**
401–425	10	400,000	20,000
426–450	3	120,000	6,000
451–476	23	880,000	44,000

(3) According to the accepted system of computation of war duration, out of some 876 years studied, about 411 years or 47 per cent of the years had wars. If we count just the years with and without wars, regardless of how many wars occurred in the same year, then respectively 362 years, or a little more than 41 per cent, were years with war. Out of 35 quarter centuries studied, only 3 were free from serious wars.

The third century B.C. was in a sense the climax of Republican Rome (before its decline and passage into the Caesarist Empire) and also of its great expansion. This was the century to which the Romans later referred as the ideal and the virtuous. Likewise, the first century B.C. was that in which the Empire reached practically the limits of its expansion, except for small parts added later. It was also the century of bloody civil wars, and of the blooming and effervescence of Roman culture hardly excelled by any century of Roman history. It was the century of the greatest Roman statesmen and conquerors; of the greatest Roman philosophers, poets, artists, and scientists; of Cicero and Lucretius, of Horace and Virgil, of Varro and others. If by the mere number of scientific discoveries the first century A.D. is superior to that century (20 for the first century B.C. and 35 for the first century A.D.; 3 is the number of discoveries in the second century B.C.; 13 in the second century A.D., 6 in the third, 15 in the fourth, 4 in the fifth, and 1 in the sixth),[26] we must keep in mind that the jump from the second century B.C. to the first B.C. was the greatest, almost 700 per cent, while from the first century B.C. to the first A.D. it was only 75 per cent. During the subsequent centuries the curve of discoveries began to decline, never reaching the level of the first century B.C.; the situation is similar in the field of philosophical creativeness, where the record of the first century B.C. — so far as purely Roman philosophers and thinkers are concerned — was unbroken by any other century in Roman history.[27] All this means that here also the periods of greatest military effort coincide to a considerable degree with those of greatest growth of the Empire, of its cultural, political, and social effervescence. Second comes the first century A.D. — the most peaceful century. During it the impetus of creativeness of the preceding century continued and the Empire "rested" upon the achievements of the preceding centuries. All enemies conquered, the limits of expansion reached, it could afford to do so. There were wars, but mainly for defense, and as the enemies were not yet strong, and the "inner vigor" of the Empire was still great, the defensive wars were relatively easy. But as time went

[26] The figures are taken from Chapter Three of Volume Two of this work.
[27] See Volume Four of this work.

on, the vigor began to wane, and for this reason only, if for no other, the pressure of the enemies became stronger; therefore the defensive wars tended to grow, never reaching, however, the levels of the third and first centuries before our era. Along somewhat similar lines moves the curve of scientific discoveries and inventions, as well as that of philosophical and artistic creativeness.

(4) Table 3 shows further that though there is an association between the movement of the magnitude of war and that of the number of years with war and peace in the periods studied, the association is rather loose, and the amplitude of the swings of the three sets of figures is quite different. This means again that the mere number of years with war and peace is an inadequate indicator of the war and peace movement.

(5) No definite periodicity and no uniform rhythm are noticeable in the "ups and downs" of war movement, whether by twenty-five- or one-hundred-year periods. It is a varying and shifting rhythm.

Turning to the *relative indicators*, we remind the reader of all the reservations and warnings given above applying to Greece. The relative indicator of the burden or magnitude of war here also means the number of casualties divided by population and multiplied by 1,000,000. Here again, as the basis for the size of the population of Italian Rome and of the Roman Empire, we take the estimates of J. Beloch. However, it would not make an essential difference in the relative indicators given if we had taken other existing estimates, or if we should change the assumed figures of population of Italy 1,000,000 in either direction, and those for the population of the Roman Empire as a whole as much as 1,000,000 to 10,000,000. In such cases the contrasts between the indicators for various centuries would be slightly different, but the configuration of the curve from century to century would remain about the same as given in Table 4.

TABLE 4. RELATIVE INDICATORS OF WAR MAGNITUDE FOR ANCIENT
ROME MEASURED BY CASUALTIES

Century	Per 1,000,000 Population of Italy	Per 1,000,000 Population of the Empire
IV B.C.	12,666 [1]	
III	63,125 [2]	
I	33,127 [3]	3644 [6]
I A.D.	5,543 [4]	712 [7]
III	13,433 [5]	1343 [8]

[1] Assuming the population of Italy *c.* 3,000,000. See B, pp. 500–507; D I, p. 522, 2d ed.
[2] Assuming the population of Italy *c.* 4,000,000.
[3] Assuming the population of Italy *c.* 5,500,000.   [6] Assuming the population of the Empire *c.* 50,000,000.
[4] Assuming the population of Italy *c.* 7,000,000.   [7] Assuming the population of the Empire *c.* 54,000,000.
[5] Assuming the population of Italy *c.* 6,000,000.   [8] Assuming the population of the Empire *c.* 60,000,000.

If with the same assumptions concerning the size of the population we compute the relative indicators of the size of burden of the army "per 1,000,000," the results will be as shown in Table 5.

TABLE 5.　RELATIVE INDICATORS OF WAR MAGNITUDE FOR ANCIENT ROME MEASURED BY ARMY'S STRENGTH

Century	Per 1,000,000 Population of Italy	Per 1,000,000 Population of the Empire
IV B.C.	286,666	
III	829,250	
I	668,000	73,480
I A.D.	112,000	14,519
III	270,000	27,000

Thus the movement of the relative indicators from century to century is similar to that of the absolute figures, with the exception of the relative positions of the fourth century B.C. and the third century A.D. Here the burden of war in the fourth century B.C. is greater than in the third century A.D. We see further that the relative indicators for Greece and Roman Italy are not greatly different from each other nor from those for the European countries which we see later. Their minima are near to the minima for the European countries; their maxima are near to European maxima.

Indicators for the whole Roman Empire are lower than they should be, because the losses of the "natives" of various conquered provinces are not computed. But if we increase them greatly, they still will remain probably comparatively low. One must marvel at the ability of the Romans to maintain the *pax romana* with slight military activities. The *pax romana* was indeed an exceptionally good organization of peace in the vast Roman Empire.

For detailed indicators see the Appendix to this part.

C. *France.* The war movement can be studied considerably more easily in the history of France than in that of many other countries. This is due to the continuous territorial unity of France, to the comparative richness of the data, and to the relative lack of many of the complicating conditions found in the history of the wars of other countries.

Our study opens with 987, when the Carlovingian dynasty was succeeded by the Capets. The first century of the new dynasty was fairly peaceful — seemingly a military lethargy of France.[28] Then after Philip I and Louis VI (the second half of the eleventh century) the military

[28] *Encyclopaedia Britannica*, Vol. IX, p. 614.

activities increased. In the Crusades (except the sixth) France played a leading role. This explains why its share in these wars is proportionately greater than the shares of other countries. Until the Hundred Years' War the army and the military activity of France were, however, moderate. Even in the most important wars the size of the army did not exceed 8000 to 10,000.[29] The French Army of the Crusades likewise rarely exceeded 5000. The Anglo-French wars of the eleventh and twelfth centuries were also carried on with rather small armies. For instance, in one of the most important battles of the war of 1106–1125 (Brémule in 1119) there were only several hundred fighters on each side, and the losses did not exceed 1 per cent.[30] For these and other reasons, in the wars of France for which there are no definite data, and which occurred before the middle of the fourteenth century, the size of the army is accepted as about 5000, and the losses as about 2 per cent.[31]

The battles and truces of the Hundred Years' War are difficult to separate definitely in time, and different historians give different classifications in this field, except for definite dates like the truce of Brétigny, 1360, or of Troyes, 1420. We follow the classification in the chronological tables of Dujarric and Green.[32] The size of the armies is known for several battles of this war. For those for which data are lacking, the size is taken as about 13,000 — the average size of the armies in the two main battles of this war (Crécy and Agincourt). The rate of losses is taken as 5 per cent of the army. For the numerous inner strifes, the coefficients are assumed to be respectively 5000 and 2 per cent. For the Burgundian wars, the size of the army is taken as 17,000, and the losses as 5 per cent, as shown by the data in the special monograph of H. Delbrück.[33]

For the wars of the sixteenth century, the size of the army is accepted as about 25,000 — the average size of the armies in the Italian wars of Francis I and Henry II with Charles V. The losses are about 5 per cent. For the inner strifes (the wars with the Huguenots), the coefficient of the army is lowered to 20,000 and the losses to 2 per cent, as shown by the data concerning the main battles (Monconcourt and Coutras) of these wars.

[29] D III, pp. 427, 444, and 445.

[30] D III, pp. 417–421 and 412.

[31] As mentioned above, this concerns mainly the "regular" fighting forces; the incidental mass of fighters that once in a while gathered around these forces is not included for the reasons indicated above.

[32] G. Dujarric, *Manuel de chronologie de l'histoire de France* (Paris, 1920), pp. 54 ff.; J. R. Green, *A Short History of the English People* (London and Toronto, 1923), p. xx.

[33] H. Delbrück, *Perser und Burgunderkriegen* (Berlin, 1887).

The period from 1598 to 1635 is unique, being the only period of 37 years during which France did not have any important war.

Beginning with the seventeenth century, most of the wars have roughly reliable statistical data which permit us, with a reasonable degree of certainty, to assume the probable size of the army and the losses, even for those wars for which data are either scarce or lacking. It is to be noted that in the wars of the seventeenth and eighteenth centuries, the military effort of France was greater than the extent of the sacrifices of her population. The reason for this is a considerable proportion of foreigners in her armies. For instance, in the Thirty Years' War (1638) about 41 per cent of the total military regiments of France were made up of foreign soldiers. In the wars of Louis XIV about one third of the combatants were hired foreigners; even in 1789, on the eve of the Revolution, 29 per cent of the regiments were composed of foreigners.[34]

There is some uncertainty in the data concerning the colonial wars of France. We follow the data given in the work of G. Bodart.[35] For wars of this type the coefficients are computed nearest to the most similar and "adjacent" colonial wars for which data exist. As a rule, the size of the colonial armies is estimated as between 10,000 and 20,000, and the losses as approximately 1 per cent. For internal or civil wars the figures are doubled. Likewise the figures are increased for the wars that had more than one front, though such wars were very few before the seventeenth century.

Table 6 shows the movement of war magnitude for France by quarter-century and century periods.

TABLE 6. TOTAL MEASURES OF WAR FOR FRANCE FROM 976 TO 1925 BY QUARTER CENTURIES AND CENTURIES

Century and Quarter Century	Duration (Years)	Army's Strength (Number)	Casualties (Number)
976–1000	1	10,000	200
1001–1100	**7**	**40,000**	**800**
1001–1025	—	—	—
1026–1050	1	10,000	200
1051–1075	1	5,000	100
1076–1100	5	25,000	500

[34] D IV, p. 261.

[35] *Losses of Life*, cited. See also S. Dumas and K. Vedel-Petersen, *Losses of Life Caused by War* (ed. by H. Westergaard). Losses due to sickness are not included. They are indicated, however, in detailed data in the Appendix to this part.

TABLE 6. TOTAL MEASURES OF WAR FOR FRANCE FROM 976 TO 1925
BY QUARTER CENTURIES AND CENTURIES — *continued*

Century and Quarter Century	Duration (Years)	Army's Strength (Number)	Casualties (Number)
1101–1200	**42**	**175,000**	**3,500**
1101–1125	21	65,000	1,300
1126–1150	7	40,000	800
1151–1175	2	10,000	200
1176–1200	12	60,000	1,200
1201–1300	**78**	**554,000**	**11,080**
1201–1225	33	259,000	5,180
1226–1250	20	165,000	3,300
1251–1275	11	60,000	1,200
1276–1300	14	70,000	1,400
1301–1400	**62**	**1,264,000**	**59,240**
1301–1325	10	76,000	1,520
1326–1350	12	330,000	16,050
1351–1375	23	483,000	23,250
1376–1400	17	375,500	18,475
1401–1500	**75**	**1,320,000**	**61,620**
1401–1425	26	331,000	14,390
1426–1450	21	525,000	26,250
1451–1475	12	212,000	9,580
1476–1500	16	252,000	11,400
1501–1600	**90**	**2,831,000**	**107,650**
1501–1525	17	681,000	34,050
1526–1550	19	590,000	28,900
1551–1575	27	845,000	29,650
1576–1600	27	715,000	15,050
1601–1700	**85**	**5,054,000**	**658,280**
1601–1625	3	105,000	2,850
1626–1650	40	1,724,000	163,800
1651–1675	26	1,205,000	159,550
1675–1700	16	2,020,000	312,080
1701–1800	**83**	**8,355,000**	**1,055,200**
1701–1725	21	2,470,000	250,100
1726–1750	14	1,800,000	208,800
1751–1775	7	1,050,000	168,000
1776–1800	41	3,085,000	428,300
1801–1900	**121**	**7,826,000**	**1,769,183**
1801–1825	36	4,512,000	1,273,450 [1]
1826–1850	31	386,600	12,229 [2]
1851–1875	30	2,620,400	472,404 [3]
1876–1900	24	307,000	11,100 [4]
1901–1925	13	9,030,000	3,682,000

[1] With losses of the non-French contingents in French armies the figure for the army's strength should be raised by 100,000 to 200,000; for losses, by 40,000 to 80,000.

[2] With losses from sickness in colonial wars, 49,450.

[3] With losses from sickness in colonial wars, 490,000.

[4] With losses from sickness in colonial wars, 20,000.

According to the size of the army, as well as the number of casualties, a steady trend toward an increase of war from the eleventh to the twentieth century is shown. Only the nineteenth century drops to a slightly lower figure of the army's strength from the eighteenth century. With this exception, the trend of growth of the absolute figures is quite steady. Especially great is the jump — both absolute and relative — in the army's strength and even more in the casualties of the seventeenth century and the beginning of the eighteenth, the period of Louis XIV which was one of unquestionable cultural and political hegemony of France in Europe. The next great jump is made at the end of the eighteenth century and in the first quarter of the nineteenth — again the period when France undoubtedly led Europe in many respects. Toward the end of the nineteenth century the war activities sharply fall far down, as happens in almost all other countries of Europe. This explains, as will be shown later on, the appearance and rapid diffusion of beliefs and theories about the disappearance of war and peaceful progress in internal and external relations. In a study of internal disturbances (see Part Three) it is shown that the same period was marked by comparatively great order, or a low level of internal disturbances. Such an atmosphere was naturally conducive to the spread of beliefs in the disappearance of war and in "orderly progress." The twentieth century, however, gave a mortal blow to such beliefs : the figures of the army's strength as well as of casualties flared up to "unbelievable" heights, unprecedented in all the previous wars ; alone they exceed the respective figures for any of the previous centuries and of the six centuries, from the eleventh to the seventeenth, taken together so far as the army's strength is concerned.

In regard to casualties the losses of 1901–1925 are little less than all the losses for all the previous centuries taken together. At least they exceed all the losses for the centuries from the eleventh to the eighteenth, even if these latter are doubled. We shall see that the same result is given by the absolute figures of all the other European countries which participated actively in the war of 1914–1918. Therefore, however staggering and unbelievable the result, there seems to be no possibility but to accept it. Perhaps when the absolute figures are "translated" into the relative per unit of population the result will change somewhat (see pages 340 to 348), but for the absolute indicators the result stands, and are and will be the same in any similar study of the magnitude of war, measured from the standpoint of the same variables with which we deal in this investigation. Later we shall discuss the question more fully and shall see fairly convincing reasons for thinking that the above indicators for the first quarter of the twentieth century incline to underestimate rather than overestimate the World War.

Of 950 years of French history studied, war occurred in 657 years, or some 80 per cent, according to the accepted systems of measurement of war duration. In the simpler system of computation of years with one or more wars, about 482, or 50 per cent, of the 950 years had an occurrence of war. Of 34 quarter centuries, only one was free from important war. No periodicity and no uniform rhythm are noticeable.

It is almost impossible to give the relative indicators of the magnitude of war in various centuries in the history of France on account of lack of data on the French population during the earlier centuries studied. For this reason, for France, as well as for other European countries taken separately, such indicators are not given. Instead, the relative indicators for all the nine European countries taken together are presented later. Such relative indicators not only are more important and can be computed more easily, but approximate reality somewhat better than the indicators for each separate country.

See the detailed indicators in the Appendix to this part.

D. *Russia.* Our study of the war-peace movement in Russia before the eighteenth century meets the usual difficulties in the form of lack of reliable data. Here, however, this difficulty is particularly great, because the military history of Russia has not been much nor critically developed. It is true that at the end of the nineteenth century a large effort was made in this direction when seven volumes of *The Encyclopedia of Military and Naval Sciences* were published under the general editorship of such an authority as General Leer; and in the years from 1910 to 1913 there appeared sixteen volumes of the *Military Encyclopedia*. But in spite of the participation of prominent specialists in these publications, the data concerning our topic are highly unsatisfactory for the earlier centuries. The authors seem often to have accepted figures without any serious critical anaylsis. Such figures as 100,000 in the Russian Army in the battle at Kalka in the thirteenth century; 150,000 in the army of John the Terrible in his siege of Kazan (1552); 150,000 in the Lithuanian War of 1534; 280,000 in the Lithuanian War of 1563; 100,000 in the War of 1590–93; 100,000 in the Crimean War of 1686; the same figures for the army at Tula (1607), and so on,[36] are quite unbelievable and impossible. Likewise such losses as 40,000 [37] at the Kulikovo battle with the Tartars

---

[36] See Leer's *Encyclopedia of the Military and Naval Sciences*, Vol. II, p. 46; Vol. III, pp. 98 and 576; Vol. IV, pp. 584–585.

[37] Sytin's *Military Encyclopedia*, Vol. XII, p. 382.

in 1380 are incredible; for if we accept even such a high loss in this battle as 10 per cent of the army, the loss of 40,000 makes the size of the Russian Army about 400,000 — a figure absolutely fantastic.

These and similar data cannot be taken seriously. The chronology of Russian military history is also little studied, especially in the works of European and foreign historians. So far as the chronology of the wars of Russia is concerned, we follow the data of Leer's and Sytin's encyclopedias mentioned above, which in spite of their defects seem to give more adequate data than any foreign source.

Accepting certain data as near reality, plus the size of the armies of various European countries at corresponding periods, plus general considerations dictated by the whole history of wars, on these bases we take the following average figures for the armies and losses for the centuries enumerated.

(1) The tenth to thirteenth centuries, about 10,000 and about 2 per cent; for the wars with the Mongols, which were more strenuous, the figures are doubled. For the fourteenth and fifteenth centuries, the above values are doubled (20,000 and 4 per cent). For the sixteenth century, the fragmentary data indicate 30,000 as the typical size of the army and 4 per cent for the losses. For the seventeenth century, the typical size is about 40,000 and 5 per cent the typical rate of losses. For the wars of the subsequent centuries, there exists a body of data sufficiently reliable to make any estimate unnecessary, with the exception of a few — mostly secondary — wars.

(2) The conquests of Caucasus and of Central Asia, which lasted about half a century (with small interruptions), are considered each as one continued war. The beginning of the Caucasian War is taken as 1816, instead of the usual 1795, because up to 1816 the war was actually with Turkey and Persia and only after 1816 was the war with the native population of Caucasus really started.

(3) By the War in Central Asia is meant all the military operations in the territory of Turkestan from 1842 to 1884.

(4) Finally, all civil wars are estimated by doubled coefficients.

Table 7 shows the movement of war magnitude for Russia by quarter-century and century periods.

In Table 7 the movement of both main variables by one-hundred-year periods shows the familiar growing trend with but few exceptions. Again the figures for the twentieth century are staggeringly high, almost equaling in army's strength and exceeding especially in casualties the total figures for all the previous centuries taken together. However unbelievable this

TABLE 7. TOTAL MEASURES OF WAR FOR RUSSIA FROM 901 TO 1925
BY QUARTER CENTURIES AND CENTURIES

Century and Quarter Century	Duration (Years)	Army's Strength (Number)	Casualties (Number)
901–1000	**20**	**200,000**	**4,000**
901–925	1	10,000	200
926–950	1	10,000	200
951–975	16	160,000	3,200
976–1000	2	20,000	400
1001–1100	**20**	**203,000**	**4,600**
1001–1025	—	—	—
1026–1050	9	86,000	1,720
1051–1075	3	30,000	600
1076–1100	8	87,000	2,280
1101–1200	**45**	**480,000**	**12,000**
1101–1125	22	220,000	4,400
1126–1150	9	100,000	3,200
1151–1175	8	100,000	3,200
1176–1200	6	60,000	1,200
1201–1300	**71**	**875,000**	**29,200**
1201–1225	39	495,000	16,000
1226–1250	18	220,000	8,400
1251–1275	4	40,000	1,200
1276–1300	10	120,000	3,600
1301–1400	**40**	**870,000**	**36,900**
1301–1325	7	140,000	5,600
1326–1350	6	120,000	4,800
1351–1375	17	340,000	13,600
1376–1400	10	270,000	12,900
1401–1500	**43**	**915,000**	**37,900**
1401–1425	9	180,000	7,600
1426–1450	4	80,000	3,200
1451–1475	4	135,000	6,300
1476–1500	26	520,000	20,800
1501–1600	**84**	**2,473,000**	**117,770**
1501–1525	29	870,000	34,800
1526–1550	6	180,000	7,200
1551–1575	37	1,028,000	57,520
1576–1600	12	395,000	18,250
1601–1700	**63**	**2,296,000**	**118,750**
1601–1625	15	780,000	39,000
1626–1650	14	281,000	14,030
1651–1675	25	880,000	44,000
1676–1700	9	347,000	21,750
1701–1800	**66**	**4,908,000**	**751,630**
1701–1725	26	2,260,000	323,000
1726–1750	10	498,000	29,460
1751–1775	15	1,260,000	171,000
1756–1800	15	890,000	228,170
1801–1900	**138**	**6,343,320**	**777,340**
1801–1825	37	2,130,000	360,800
1826–1850	44	1,576,320	138,320
1851–1875	45	1,905,000	206,620
1876–1900	12	732,000	71,600
1901–1925	11	17,620,000	6,371,000

may appear, there seems to be no basis for claiming that the result is misleading as far as "regular" army and casualties in a narrow sense are concerned.

If one takes all the armies of Russia in all the wars of the preceding centuries (about 19,563,000), even doubles and triples the size for the tenth to the sixteenth centuries inclusive, and adds these figures together, one will obtain a figure not far above the size of the Russian Army in the wars of the twentieth century. The same can be said even more of the casualties in the wars of the twentieth century (some 6,371,000) compared with all the wars of the preceding centuries (about 1,900,000). Here, too, the last quarter of the nineteenth century was relatively peaceful.

Of 1025 years studied, 592 years, or some 57 per cent, according to one system of computation, and 471 years, or about 46 per cent, according to the other system had an occurrence of war. Of 41 quarter centuries only one was free from important war.

See the detailed indicators in the Appendix to this part.

E. *England.* The investigation of the wars and military efforts of England along the lines of our study meets several peculiar difficulties. First of these is the dual character of the wars: before the seventeenth century England's wars were mainly on land, while after that they became, to a great extent, naval. The territorial wars and the naval campaigns are so different in character that they cannot be measured accurately by the same criteria, on the same basis. For this reason the variables studied cannot be quite comparable in their continuity for the periods before and after the seventeenth century. The contrast between the two kinds of war is compensated to some extent by the fact that for the land wars a large-sized army and a low per cent of losses are typical, while for the naval wars a small-sized navy-army and a high per cent of losses are typical. Nevertheless there remains some incomparability in the wars of these two periods and the comparable continuity of the variables becomes guesswork to a large degree, in spite of every effort to make it accurate.

The second difficulty consists in the lack of data for many wars of England, especially for the period before the fourteenth century. This is true of the wars on English soil as well as of those in France, where the English Crown had large possessions. The same may be said of many local wars (with Ireland, Scotland, and several civil wars in England) of the period from the fifteenth to the seventeenth century.

The third difficulty — even for the period of the seventeenth to the nineteenth centuries — is the coalitional character of many wars in which

England participated. If the data for the whole coalition exist, they are essentially lacking as to how large was the share of the English Army in number and in losses in these wars.

The fourth difficulty is the scarcity of data concerning numerous colonial wars of Great Britain carried on in the eighteenth and the nineteenth centuries.

All these obstacles mean that a series of assumptions is quite inevitable in "measuring" the war fluctuations in England and, in spite of great care in making these assumptions, several errors may result should they be wrong.

Having stressed the dangers and uncertainties, the assumptions made in this work are as follows.

(1) The average size of the army for the wars before the Hundred Years' War is accepted as about 5000 to 6000. The few existing data show such figures and make the assumption justifiable. Only for the Welsh wars in the last quarter of the thirteenth century is the size raised from 9000 to 15,000. The size of the English armies in the coalitional wars for that period (the Crusades, the Bovines, etc.) is accepted, where specific data are lacking, as around 5000, and the losses as about 2 per cent of the army. Before the beginning of the Hundred Years' War (around the middle of the fourteenth century) the population of England was about 2,500,000, less than half that of France or of the Holy Roman Empire.[38] Therefore the share of England in the coalitional armies of that period (with France and the Holy Roman Empire) could hardly exceed one-fourth or one-third of the whole. Such a share would give the figure near to 5000. As these wars were not strenuous for England, the losses could hardly exceed 2 per cent of the army.

(2) For the Hundred Years' War with its varied periods of fighting and factual truces, we accept the classification of these periods in the chronological tables of G. Dujarric and J. R. Green.[39]

(3) The size of the English Army, for the periods of this long war for which data are lacking, is assumed to be near the average of the sizes given by Delbrück, Fortescue, and the *Encyclopaedia Britannica;* namely, around 15,000.[40] The rate of losses is accepted as 5 per cent of the army, which is typical for wars of normal intensity. For the small and the internal wars of this period the size of the army is assumed to be about

---

[38] *Handwörterbuch der Staatswissenschaften*, Vol. II, pp. 890–892.

[39] G. Dujarric, *op. cit.*, pp. 54 ff.; J. R. Green, *op. cit.*, p. xx.

[40] See H. Delbrück, *op. cit.*, Vol. III, pp. 466 and 480; J. W. Fortescue, *History of the British Army* (London, 1899), pp. 32–33 and 44; *Encyclopaedia Britannica*, 14th ed., Vol. VIII, p. 501.

5000, or for both sides about 10,000; the losses, about 2 per cent of the army. For the important wars of the fourteenth to the sixteenth centuries the assumed indicators are 15,000 for the army and 5 per cent for the losses; for the small civil wars, 5000 and 2 per cent respectively. During that period the population of England remained almost the same in size as before, and there is no evident reason to think that the size of the armies and losses tangibly increased. We accept for the coalitional wars of the seventeenth and eighteenth centuries, in which as a rule England fought against France in alliance with Holland and the Holy Roman Empire, the proportional relationship of the armies of the coalition of $1 : 1.5 : 2$, respectively, for the Netherlands, England, and Austria. In other words, in the coalitional English-Dutch army the share of the English Army is assumed to be 60 per cent, in the coalitional Austrian-English Army, 45 per cent. For the secondary wars of this period coefficients are taken which are given by the nearest wars for which data exist.

(4) The size of the army for the colonial — mainly Indian and African — wars, which England carried on after the middle of the eighteenth century, and for most of the ordinary wars in India (where data are lacking) is accepted as about 15,000 and the losses as about the normal 5 per cent of the army (losses from sickness excluded). The existing data show that the size of the army in these wars fluctuated from 2000 or 3000 to 100,000 (e.g., the army of Lord Hastings in the war of 1817 [41]). This last figure is exceptional. Most of the armies were nearer to 10,000 than to 100,000.

(5) For the African colonial wars the average size of the army is taken as near to 10,000 and the typical rate of losses as about 2 to 3 per cent. With the exception of the war with the Boers, for which data exist, most of the other wars were carried on with armies of about 10,000, rarely reaching 20,000. Likewise in the wars with the African natives the English losses were relatively low, due to the enormous disparity in war weapons and technique of the English and the natives.

(6) The participation of England in several ordinary interventional wars of the nineteenth century is estimated by the same coefficients of 10,000 for the size of the army, and 2 to 3 per cent for the rate of losses.

(7) For important civil and internal wars the average figures are doubled for size of the army as well as for losses.

Table 8 shows the movement of war magnitude for England by quarter-century and century periods.

[41] See the *Encyclopaedia Britannica*, Vol. XII, p. 194.

TABLE 8. TOTAL MEASURES OF WAR FOR ENGLAND FROM 1051 TO 1925
BY QUARTER CENTURIES AND CENTURIES

Century and Quarter Century	Duration (Years)	Army's Strength (Number)	Casualties (Number)
1051–1075	1	6,000	550
1076–1100	—	—	—
1101–1200	**62**	**356,000**	**6,940**
1101–1125	20	10,000	100
1126–1150	19	175,000	3,500
1151–1175	11	117,000	2,340
1176–1200	12	54,000	1,000
1201–1300	**61**	**725,000**	**17,260**
1201–1225	17	110,000	2,550
1225–1250	10	79,000	1,580
1251–1275	13	156,000	5,130
1276–1300	21	380,000	8,000
1301–1400	**78**	**1,630,000**	**64,010**
1301–1325	24	443,000	8,860
1326–1350	16	297,000	13,050
1351–1375	19	420,000	21,000
1376–1400	19	470,000	21,000
1401–1500	**76**	**1,770,000**	**86,100**
1401–1425	29	555,000	25,350
1426–1450	21	525,000	26,250
1451–1475	17	480,000	24,000
1476–1500	9	210,000	10,500
1501–1600	**93**	**1,824,000**	**90,600**
1501–1525	13	390,000	19,500
1526–1550	26	695,000	34,750
1551–1575	23	269,000	13,650
1576–1600	31	170,000	22,700
1601–1700	**55**	**1,519,000**	**160,140**
1601–1625	6	160,000	8,000
1626–1650	21	680,000	58,600
1651–1675	18	379,000	39,540
1676–1700	10	300,000	54,000
1701–1800	**76**	**2,518,000**	**310,580**
1701–1725	25	1,320,000	226,000
1726–1750	8	290,000	28,900
1751–1775	13	462,000	24,100
1776–1800	30	446,000	32,580
1801–1900	**115**	**1,670,800**	**140,528**
1801–1825	36	720,000	78,590
1826–1850	24	174,000	6,720
1851–1875	28	437,400	37,428
1876–1900	27	339,400	17,790
1901–1925	13	7,815,000	3,094,550

Except for the smaller size of the army in the seventeenth century compared with that in the sixteenth, and that of the nineteenth compared with
that of the eighteenth century, and for the lower number of casualties
in the nineteenth century compared with the eighteenth, the essential
direction of these main variables for England is similar: toward an
increase from the earlier to the later centuries.

Here again, the figures for the first quarter of the twentieth century
exceed, in number of casualties, those of all the preceding centuries taken
together.   Even if we double and treble the total figure of casualties for
the centuries from the eleventh to the sixteenth, the figure for the first
quarter of the twentieth century will still be greater than for all the preceding centuries taken together.   The relative indicators (per unit of
population) may give somewhat different results, but, as we shall see, not
fundamentally so.   The magnitude of the wars of the twentieth century
— in the aspects in which war is "measured" in this study — will still
remain quite extraordinary in its extent.

Using the accepted system of computation of duration of wars, of
875 years studied, 630 years, or some 72 per cent, were war years.   Using
the simpler system mentioned above, of 875 years studied, 493 years, or
about 56 per cent, had an occurrence of war.   Of 35 quarter centuries
studied, only one was free from important war.   This means that England
was busy with war activities as frequently, at least, as most of the other
countries.   Until the second quarter of the nineteenth century, England's
curve of war, judged by the movement of both variables by century
periods, fairly systematically rises, doing so especially abruptly in the
fourteenth and eighteenth centuries.   But in the nineteenth century,
as in most of the other countries, it tends to go down.   In the twentieth
century, the curve reaches an unparalleled high level.   The centuries of
the strong rise of war were, all in all, centuries of an extraordinary growth
of political power and of cultural creativeness of England.

If one compares the number of years with and without war in each half
century as it is given here and in the work of F. A. Woods and A. Baltzly,[42]
one sees that for several half centuries the figures in both works are practically identical; for several others they diverge, our figures for the
years with wars being generally higher.   The reason for that divergence
has been given above.   The same is to be said of the similarity and divergence of this point in the data for the seventeenth, eighteenth, and
nineteenth centuries given in G. Bodart's *Losses*, cited.   This is true of
all the European countries studied.

[42] See p. 34.

No periodicity nor uniformity of rhythm in the ups and downs of war movement is noticeable. For the reasons mentioned above, the relative indicators for England are not given. They will be given, as said earlier, for all nine European countries taken together.

See the detailed indicators in the Appendix to this part.

F. *Austria-Hungary*. All the previous reservations are to be applied here. Before the nineteenth century the data for Austria-Hungary which are needed for our purposes are neither complete nor exact. Neither the exact statistics for population, nor for size of armies, nor for rate of loss of human life, nor for other relevant variables, exist in complete and satisfactory form. Only with the Thirty Years' War does the situation begin to be somewhat better. This means that for the wars before the seventeenth century the factual basis is uncertain. Our tentative approximation for most of the wars must be based not so much on fragmentary data, as on estimates warranted by the data, as well as on the total conditions of the period and the country, plus some norms discovered in the study of wars generally.

As has been mentioned, until the seventeenth century "Austria-Hungary" means practically the territory of the "Holy Roman Empire of the German Nation," whose main part [43] was Austria. After Prussia was formed, and became the kernel of the German Empire in the seventeenth century, "Austria-Hungary" means the more limited empire as it was formed under Charles V (1526) and as it existed until 1918. Up to the Thirty Years' War the data are scarce and very fragmentary, especially for the tenth to the thirteenth centuries. However, these data justify us in making some approximations. The average size of the Empire's army for these (the tenth to the thirteenth) centuries seems to have been between 2000 and 10,000, the latter figure being the exception rather than the rule; only in such big battles as that at Bovines (1214) and in the campaigns of Frederic II (1237) and in the battle at Lechfelde (955) was an army of 7000 to 10,000 used. In most of the other battles it was somewhere around 2000 or 3000.[44] Even in the campaigns of Frederic Barbarossa, or in the Crusades (especially the Second, Third, and Fifth), the army of the Empire did not exceed some 2000 or 3000. These and several other facts warrant the assumption that the typical size of the army of the Holy Roman Empire for these centuries (the tenth to the

[43] Because from 1438 the rulers of the Empire (with the one exception of Charles Albert of Bavaria) were the Hapsburgs of Austria. Even before that time three emperors were from the same dynasty.

[44] See D III, pp. 427–428, 362–363, 113, 357, 228–229, in the 2d ed., chap. ix, *et passim*.

thirteenth, inclusive) was from 3000 to 10,000 combatants when war had one front and was not internal. The typical rate of losses for most of the wars of that period is assumed to be 5 per cent of the army.

From the fourteenth to the sixteenth centuries inclusive, the size of the army somewhat increased, averaging 12,000. For the wars of Charles V at the beginning of the sixteenth century it reached 20,000 to 25,000 and more when war had more than one front. On the other hand, in the wars with the Swiss, the Austrian Army hardly ever exceeded 3000.[45] The typical rate of losses for these centuries is assumed to be about 10 per cent of the army, because some data give such an approximation, because the wars of these centuries became more intensive and devastating, and finally because the wars of the seventeenth century, especially the Thirty Years' War, for which fairly reliable data exist, gave still higher rates of losses.

Beginning with the seventeenth century, the situation in regard to data improves considerably : they become more reliable and more numerous. Starting with the Thirty Years' War (1618–1648), figures increase for the size of the army (which in that war reached the unprecedented size of about 100,000) as well as for losses. After that time the wars became bigger and more strenuous. For the Thirty Years' War the figures are based not only upon the size of the armies in separate battles, but also upon the general size of the participating armies. As there were a number of German contingents among the armies which were adversaries of the Empire, this fact also warrants taking the indicator of the army in this war as not lower than 100,000. The exceptionally high figure for this war, which indeed largely ruined the territory and population of the Empire, is explained thus. The data for the eighteenth century are still more complete, while for the nineteenth century, especially for its second part, they are roughly satisfactory with actual figures existing for almost all the wars. The data for the World War are obtained from the Austrian *Reichsarchive*.

For all the civil and internal wars — that is, for the wars between the nations of the Holy Roman Empire up to the seventeenth century, and between the peoples of Austria-Hungary after the seventeenth century — the coefficients are doubled, as has been done for other countries. The reason for this is that in such wars both adversaries belong to the same state; therefore the State as a whole supports double the army and double the losses.

Table 9 shows the movement of war magnitude for Austria-Hungary by quarter-century and century periods.

[45] See more details in D III, pp. 572 and 591.

TABLE 9. TOTAL MEASURES OF WAR FOR AUSTRIA-HUNGARY FROM
1101 TO 1925 BY QUARTER CENTURIES AND CENTURIES

Century and Quarter Century	Duration (Years)	Army's Strength (Number)	Casualties (Number)
1101–1200	**36**	**150,000**	**7,500**
1101–1125	2	9,000	450
1126–1150	8	39,000	1,950
1151–1175	12	36,000	1,800
1176–1200	14	66,000	3,300
1201–1300	**29**	**218,000**	**10,900**
1201–1225	2	12,000	600
1226–1250	18	123,000	6,150
1251–1275	5	17,000	850
1276–1300	4	66,000	3,300
1301–1400	**27**	**103,000**	**6,575**
1301–1325	11	26,000	2,600
1326–1350	1	2,000	200
1351–1375	—	—	—
1376–1400	15	75,000	3,775
1401–1500	**69**	**995,000**	**99,000**
1401–1425	8	25,000	2,500
1426–1450	13	240,000	24,000
1451–1475	21	300,000	30,000
1476–1500	27	430,000	43,000
1501–1600	**115**	**2,630,000**	**257,000**
1501–1525	37	470,000	45,000
1526–1550	40	1,200,000	116,000
1551–1575	21	620,000	62,000
1576–1600	17	340,000	34,000
1601–1700	**100**	**6,996,000**	**1,560,000**
1601–1625	20	1,240,000	274,000
1626–1650	26	2,810,000	830,000
1651–1675	15	526,000	64,000
1676–1700	39	2,420,000	392,600
1701–1800	**80**	**9,068,000**	**1,504,730**
1701–1725	31	3,826,000	688,210
1726–1750	22	1,790,000	202,500
1751–1775	7	1,190,000	400,000
1776–1800	20	2,262,000	214,020
1801–1900	**32**	**2,030,000**	**226,000**
1801–1825	9	950,000	156,000
1826–1850	18	380,000	7,800
1851–1875	3	500,000	56,000
1876–1900	2	200,000	7,000
1901–1925	5	7,000,000	3,000,000

Here both variables grow from the twelfth to the fourteenth century;
in the fourteenth they fall considerably, to make a big jump in the fifteenth century, after which they continue to grow fast until the seventeenth, flaring up from century to century. In the eighteenth they

remain high, the army's strength grows, but the casualties slightly decline. After the first quarter of the nineteenth they fall greatly, rising in the third quarter of this century but again falling to the medieval level, thus giving a comparatively low figure for the nineteenth century. In the twentieth century, as in all the other countries which participated in the World War, both curves for Austria-Hungary go into the "stratosphere."

According to the system of computation used for Table 9, 501 years, or 55 per cent, were war years. By the simple method the data show further that of some 900 years studied, about 361, or some 40 per cent, had an occurrence of war. Out of some 34 quarter centuries studied, we find only two free from important war. Here again we do not find any definite periodicity or rhythm in the ups and downs of the war movement from period to period. The century as well as quarter-century figures do not show any continuous trend toward increase, decrease, or constancy. Again the figures reach their climax, or rise with particular strength, in the period of the greatest political power and cultural influence of the country, the fifteenth to nineteenth centuries. Then comes, as in all European countries, a decline of war in the nineteenth century, which is ended by the flaring up of war activities in the twentieth century in which the great Empire was practically "exploded," and, at least for the time being, turned into a small political monstrosity — a big city with a small section of country to keep it alive. Such a monstrosity can hardly live for long without a radical change, either in the form of dissolution as an independent body politic, or of re-establishment in some normal shape, where a large head is not placed upon a "baby's neck, body, and feet."

So much for the absolute figures of war for this country. For the reason mentioned above, the relative indicators are not given here — it is easier to give such indicators for the nine European countries studied taken together.

For the detailed indicators see the Appendix to this part.

G. *Germany.* As mentioned earlier, our investigation of the wars of Germany begins with the middle of the seventeenth century. Up to that time its wars were studied under Austria-Hungary (the Holy Roman Empire). In the second half of the seventeenth century Prussia, which later became the uniting center of Germany, got its independence in the Brandenburg Duchy and Eastern Prussia, which freed herself from Polish domination in 1657.[46] In 1700 Prussia became a kingdom and sub-

---

[46] Eastern Prussia became the personal dominion of the Hohenzollerns in 1525 (Albrecht of Brandenburg), but only in 1657 was it freed from feudal dependence on Poland, to which belonged the rights of a suzerain.

sequently united — first in the Zollverein ; then in the North German Confederation ; then, since 1871, in the German Empire — all the states within the territory of the present Germany.

The necessary data are more complete and satisfactory here because they deal with only the last four centuries, when data generally are more adequate. The main difficulties are due, for the second half of the seventeenth and the first half of the eighteenth centuries, to the lack of accurate data concerning the degree of the participation of Prussia in the coalitional wars on the side of the Holy Roman Empire. However, the existing data permit us to make a fairly sound approximation in these respects.

Considering several relevant circumstances, the population of Prussia in the second half of the seventeenth century seems to have been somewhere between 1,900,000 and 1,500,000. In 1740 it was about 2,240,000. The army of Prussia around 1688 was 29,000. In the middle of the eighteenth century it was about 100,000, about 4.4 per cent of the population of 2,240,000 of that time — an unusually high per cent, especially for peacetime. It has been typical, however, for Prussia and serves as an indication of that country's strenuous militarization.[47]

The degree of intensity with which Prussia participated in the Wars of the Coalition (against Louis XIV) was not exceedingly great, because the burden was put mainly upon its more powerful allies — Austria, Spain, England, and the Netherlands. In comparison with them, Prussia of that period was a small power.[48] For this reason its interests were not very great in these wars and therefore its military efforts could not have been very strenuous. This is also shown indirectly by the fact that the territorial changes of Prussia for that period — the annexations and losses being the most important result of the wars of that time — were almost negligible : from 1688 to 1740 only a small part of Pomerania and a few other insignificant territories were added.[49] These and similar considerations justify us in accepting the size of the Prussian Army in these coalitional wars of the seventeenth and the first part of the eighteenth centuries as about 20,000 (except for the wars for which actual data exist and those that had more than one front) ; and the rate of losses as around 3 to 4 per cent, instead of 5 per cent, of the army.

[47] For the population and the size of the army see in D IV, pp. 304 and 280 of 1st ed. It is to be noted, however, that Prussia at that time used a large number of foreigners in its armies.

[48] While its population was about 2,000,000, the population of France was about 19,000,000, of Spain 7,620,000, of Austria probably near to that of France. See *Handwörterbuch der Staatswissenschaften*, Vol. II, pp. 891–895, 3d ed.

[49] See Vidal de la Blache, *Atlas général. Cartes historiques* (Paris, 1929), p. 38.

Since we are studying the wars not only of Prussia but of all the territory which since 1871 has become the German Empire, we consider not only the Prussian Army, in the Napoleonic and the Austro-Prussian War of 1866, but all the German armies fighting in these wars, both for and against Prussia (like the armies of the Rhenish Confederation and Saxony, in 1806–1813, and the South-German armies, in the War of 1866). The only exception is made for Hanover, which remained a part of England.

Table 10 shows the movement of war magnitude for Germany by quarter-century and century periods.

TABLE 10. TOTAL MEASURES OF WAR FOR GERMANY FROM 1651 TO 1925 BY QUARTER CENTURIES AND CENTURIES

Century and Quarter Century	Duration (Years)	Army's Strength (Number)	Casualties (Number)
1651–1675	9	158,000	5,540
1676–1700	13	260,000	10,400
1701–1800	**29**	**1,891,000**	**360,120**
1701–1725	18	360,000	63,600
1726–1750	8	295,000	24,900
1751–1775	7	1,050,000	262,500
1776–1800	6	186,000	9,120
1801–1900	**12**	**3,028,000**	**458,862**
1801–1825	5	595,000	159,900
1826–1850	2	28,000	2,800
1851–1875	4	2,385,000	295,962
1876–1900	1	20,000	200
1901–1925	6	13,010,000	6,060,100

By one-hundred-year periods the magnitude of war increased systematically from the seventeenth to the twentieth century, reaching in the twentieth an unprecedented value, greater in both variables than for all the preceding centuries taken together. Of 275 years studied, about 79 years, or some 29 per cent, were war years, by the system used in Table 10; by the simpler system about 76 years, or some 28 per cent, had war. The per cent is much lower than in the countries discussed previously. Of the 13 quarter centuries studied, there was none free from war. In the curve of German casualties a periodicity of some 25 years' duration appears: since 1676 each quarter century with a low war indicator is followed by one with a high indicator, and so the rhythm has gone, up to the present time. In the curve of army's strength a similar rhythm appears from 1800 on.

Though the degree of militarization of Prussia-Germany has been, as noted above, rather high, the actual war activities of the Hohenzollern Empire were, up to the twentieth century, hardly higher than those of some other great European countries. This suggests that potential militarization — the keeping even in peacetime of a relatively large army in proportion to the population — and active militarism in the sense of actual warfare are not identical and not necessarily quite parallel.

For the detailed indicators see the Appendix to this part.

H. *Italy.* Before 1870, by "Italy" we mean the kingdom of Savoy (Sardinia). Until the second half of the nineteenth century Italy was, as Metternich put it at the Vienna Congress, a geographic concept rather than a united body politic. We take Savoy (Sardinia) because mainly through and around it various political bodies on the territory of Italy were united in one Italian state, and we take 1559 as a starting point in our study, for after that date Savoy became an Italian state, instead of being one of the states of the Burgundian group.

This substitution of one state for the whole population of Italy, on the one hand, undoubtedly leads to an underestimation of the military activities of the Italian peoples up to the second half of the nineteenth century. On the other hand, since after the nineteenth century, especially beginning with its second part, the data are computed for practically all Italy, which would lead naturally to an overestimation, even if the war activities of the whole Italian population did not increase in the nineteenth century. The units whose wars are studied have changed. This makes the absolute and the relative figures, if computed, of war movement in Italy unreliable and, so far as Italy as such is concerned, very inaccurate or, at the best, only roughly representative. Nevertheless, we have computed the indicators, for they can satisfactorily serve another purpose : they can and must enter as an element into the computation of the absolute and relative figures for the whole of the nine European countries studied.

Most of the other parts of Italy, besides Savoy (Sardinia), during the period studied were either parts of other European countries or were ruled by members of their royal houses, like the Hapsburgs, the Bourbons, etc. Their military activities therefore enter into our figures as a part of the war figures of other European countries — Austria, Spain, and France. If to these parts of Italy we now add Savoy-Sardinia, we get almost the whole of Italy as a unit for war activities — a unit which remains essentially the same for the whole period studied. This eliminates to a considerable degree omission or undue variability of the war activities of some parts of Italy. Under this procedure almost all its parts in one way or another enter as elements in the total war indicators of the nine countries studied, making the whole, so to speak, constant [50] throughout the centuries covered. Such is the reason for introducing the Italian figures, however faulty they may be when taken for Italy only.

In the seventeenth and eighteenth centuries Sardinia was among the most important of the independent Italian states.[51] Its population was about 2,500,000 in the second half of the eighteenth century.[52]

In regard to this state we find the usual difficulties: lack of statistical data for many of its wars, uncertainty as to the size of the army and the losses in the coalitional or quasi-coalitional wars in which it participated. Most of the indicators up to the nineteenth century are therefore estimates based on total existing data — both direct and indirect — and the known circumstances. These estimates may or may not be accurate, but in their essentials they should not grossly err. Some of them follow: since the population of Sardinia was about 1,670,000 c. 1700,[53] in the sixteenth and seventeenth centuries it was probably less, hardly far from 1,000,000; since Prussia of that period — although small it was larger than Sardinia and maintained a particularly strenuous military organization — had an army of 29,000 in the second half of the seventeenth century, the Sardinian Army must have been much less: even according to the Prussian high norms it could not be more than 14,000 to 19,000. In the sixteenth century it was probably still less, hardly larger than 10,000; as to the losses, they seem not to have been high, and were probably around 3 to 4 per cent, since Sardinia could scarcely have had an exceedingly vital interest in these wars, and the "barometer of interest in war" — the addition and loss, or the mobility, of the territory — was for that period practically stationary (with only the acquisition of Saluces).[54] For the coalitional wars of the eighteenth century the proportion of the Sardinian Army was not far from one-third of the combined armies (with Austria and France), which gives a figure not deviating notably from the above.

For the Napoleonic period (1805–1814), when Sardinia was included in the French Empire, the data are as follows.

(1) According to the computations of Bodart, the number of Italian combatants in the French Army was, in the wars of 1809 and 1812, 20,000

---

[50] See Chapter Eleven where various allowances are made to increase this "constancy."

[51] Because Parma with Piacenza, the kingdom of the two Sicilies, Toscana, Milan, and so on, were headed by the Bourbons, or the Hapsburgs.

[52] For the sake of uniformity, up to 1870 — the date of unification of Italy by the kings of the Savoy dynasty — we use the term Sardinia, though the title of that kingdom was established only in 1720.

[53] *Handwörterbuch*, Vol. II, p. 894.   [54] See Vidal de la Blache, *op. cit.*, pp. 28–29.

and 32,000 respectively. According to Berndt, in 1812 it even reached 45,000.

(2) According to Bodart, the losses of the Italian contingents in the Wars of 1813–1814 were respectively 12,000 and 5000, which, compared with the average losses of the French armies in the Napoleonic wars — about 20 per cent — would make the size of the Italian contingents for these years 60,000 and 25,000 respectively.[55] Thus the average size of the Italian contingents in the Napoleonic armies was about 36,000. Of these, about one-third were probably Sardinians (its population at that time being about one-third of the population of all Italy). This gives some 12,000 for the size of the Sardinian Army and 20 per cent for its losses in the Napoleonic wars.

Table 11 shows the movement of war magnitude for Italy by quarter-century and century periods.

TABLE 11. TOTAL MEASURES OF WAR FOR ITALY FROM 1551 TO 1925 BY QUARTER CENTURIES AND CENTURIES

Century and Quarter Century	Duration (Year)	Army's Strength (Number)	Casualties (Number)
1551–1575	4	40,000	1,200
1576–1600	23	230,000	7,100
1601–1700	**49**	**510,000**	**17,100**
1601–1625	9	90,000	3,300
1626–1650	19	190,000	6,000
1651–1675	12	140,000	4,200
1676–1700	9	90,000	3,600
1701–1800	**61**	**556,500**	**41,190**
1701–1725	16	375,000	18,450
1726–1750	13	146,500	15,040
1751–1775	—	—	
1776–1800	5	35,000	7,700
1801–1900	**22**	**692,000**	**53,860**
1801–1825	10	118,000	21,900
1826–1850	2	150,000	7,000
1851–1875	8	382,000	22,860
1876–1900	2	42,000	2,100
1901–1925	5.5	5,060,000	1,783,000

Table 11 shows a continuous trend in both variables for the last three centuries. Here the last three-quarters of the nineteenth century were also comparatively very peaceful. Again the gigantic caliber of the World War comes out clearly; the figures for both main variables for the first quarter of the twentieth century greatly exceed all the figures for all

[55] See G. Bodart, *Losses*, pp. 44–47 and 126; O. Berndt, *op. cit.*, p. 29.

the previous wars taken together. Of 366 years studied, 133 years, or some 36 per cent, by the simpler system of computation, and 137 years or some 37 per cent by the other system, had an occurrence of war. Of the 15 quarter centuries, only one is free from war. Here again the number of years of war and peace in each period deviates considerably from the total movement of the other variables of war magnitude.

For the detailed indicators see the Appendix to this part.

I. *Spain.* Our study of Spanish wars begins with the period of the union of Aragon and Castile, after the death of Henry IV of Castile in 1474 and of John II of Aragon in 1479. From this union in 1479 and from the downfall of Granada — the last Moorish state in Spain — in 1492 Spain emerged as an independent state whose history is continuous up to the present time.[56] This explains the second half of the fifteenth century as the starting point in our study.

There are several factors which greatly complicate the study of the Spanish wars for our purposes. One of them is that since the middle of the fifteenth century the possessions of the Spanish dynasty in Italy (the Aragon dynasty of Naples from 1443) led to several wars carried on mainly by the Spanish forces. Another is the unification of Spain, the Holy Roman Empire, the Italian possessions of the Aragon dynasty, of Milan, and of the Burgundian heritage, under Charles V as ruler. This led, for the period from 1519 to 1556 especially, to an inextricable mixture of the history and the wars of Spain with those of Austria, or the Holy Roman Empire, and of some other countries. In these wars headed by Charles V it is impossible to divide accurately the share of the Spanish armies from the other countries which were parts of the forces of Charles V. However, the role of the Spanish forces seems to have been unquestionably dominant and decisive in all these wars (the role of the celebrated Spanish infantry of the sixteenth century, etc.). Therefore, in this maze of interrelations, one is entitled to view the military activities of Spain as near to those of the whole monarchy of Charles V.

After the abdication of Charles V in 1558, practically until the peace of Utrecht in 1713, a part of the Netherlands (except the seven northern provinces), Sicily, Milan, and for some time (from 1581 to 1668) Portugal, continued to be parts of Spain. Only since 1713 has the territory of Spain nearly coincided with its present territory. These complications make our variables liable to considerable error for several periods, however great the care and effort exerted to obtain accurate figures.

---

[56] See the details in Don Rafael Altamira y Crevea, *Histoire d'Espagne* (Paris, 1931), pp. 45, 50, 53–55, 62, 68, 103–113, *et passim.*

Besides these complications there are several other difficulties in a quantitative investigation of war fluctuation in Spanish history. First of these is the proportional share of Spanish military effort (her army and losses) in the numerous coalition wars carried on by Spain in alliance with Austria, England, France, etc.   What this share was is not known exactly. One guide is the size of the Spanish population compared with that of her allies for a definite period.   This size was approximately 6,750,000 around 1570; 7,620,000 around 1723; 10,260,000 around 1787; and 11,500,000 around 1800.[57]   The size of one of her allies, France, was about 19,000,000 around 1696–1699, and about 23,000,000 around 1785–1787.   The size of the United Kingdom (Great Britain and Ireland) at the time of Napoleon was around 16,300,000.   In other words, in the period of coalition with these countries the size of the population of Spain was smaller than that of France or England.   The population of Austria for the sixteenth and seventeenth centuries is unknown, though it was hardly below that of France.   But in the Austrian coalitions the Spanish Army was fully exploited by the Hapsburgs (especially the Spanish infantry, as the experience of the Thirty Years' War shows). For these and several other reasons, liable however to considerable error for the wars of the coalitions, we assume the following proportions of Spanish contingents in the whole coalitional armies: with Austria (the Holy Roman Empire), 60 per cent of the total army; with France, 30 per cent; with England, 40 per cent of the total army.

The next difficulty in our study is the widely different character of the Spanish wars.   Side by side with "usual" war, Spain carried on a considerable number of so-called colonial wars and expeditions, for the majority of which no data exist as to size of the armies or losses.   Such were the wars with the Moors and the Turks in Africa in the sixteenth and seventeenth centuries.   Only approximate estimates can be made for such wars, based on several facts.   It is known that the size of the normal Spanish Army at the beginning of the sixteenth century as established by Cardinal Cisneros (the *charte* of 1516 concerning the establishment of the *gente de la Ordenanza*) was about 30,000.[58]   On the other hand, the maximum size of the Spanish Army in the sixteenth and seventeenth centuries in its major engagements hardly ever exceeded 50,000. The typical size was possibly near to 30,000 for these centuries.   For the African colonial wars the probable size was somewhere between 10,000 and 30,000 combatants.

[57] See the *Handwörterbuch der Staatswissenschaften*, Vol. II, pp. 891–895 and 992–993 (the tables).   [58] Altamira y Crevea, *op. cit.*, p. 140.

Finally, a considerable number of the Spanish wars were practically civil wars, like the little-studied Carlist Wars of the nineteenth century, and the still less known but similar wars of the preceding centuries. The size of the armies in such wars can only be guessed, as somewhere between 10,000 and 20,000. The rate of losses for the wars for which there are no data is assumed to be near the average rate in wars neither too easy nor too strenuous, that is, 5 per cent of the army.

Table 12 shows the movement of war magnitude for Spain by quarter-century and century periods.

TABLE 12. TOTAL MEASURES OF WAR FOR SPAIN FROM 1476 TO 1925
BY QUARTER CENTURIES AND CENTURIES

Century and Quarter Century	Duration (Year)	Army's Strength (Number)	Casualties (Number)
1476–1500	17	270,000	13,500
1501–1600	**128**	**3,239,300**	**160,365**
1501–1525	25	396,000	18,300
1526–1550	23	485,500	24,275
1551–1575	35	1,075,800	53,790
1576–1600	45	1,282,000	64,000
1601–1700	**124**	**3,371,000**	**558,740**
1601–1625	30	637,000	46,250
1626–1650	37	1,150,000	277,500
1651–1675	37	874,000	107,240
1676–1700	20	710,000	127,750
1701–1800	**40**	**1,178,000**	**94,250**
1701–1725	16	542,000	49,850
1726–1750	12	186,000	21,900
1751–1775	4	180,000	9,000
1776–1800	8	270,000	13,500
1801–1900	**71**	**2,216,000**	**166,290**
1801–1825	32	794,000	75,190
1826–1850	16	510,000	25,500
1851–1875	10	362,000	18,100
1876–1900	13	550,000	47,500
1901–1925	7	890,000	44,500

Since Spain virtually did not participate in the World War, her figures for the first quarter of the twentieth century do not show the extraordinarily high values found in those of the countries which did. Here the climax of war activity falls at the period of greatest splendor, power, and economic-cultural influence of Spain, the sixteenth and seventeenth centuries. With their decline the war curves decline also. Here once more we meet what we have met several times: war activities become particularly strong and extensive in periods of expansion, power, and splendor of the culture of a given country. Of 450 years studied, some 300 years, or about 67 per cent (in the other system of computation 387 years or 85 per cent), had an occurrence of war. Of 18 quarter centuries none was free from war. No steady trend, no periodicity, no uniform rhythm are noticeable. As in other countries, the movement of years with war and peace and the movement of the other war curves are somewhat associated, but very loosely so.

For the detailed indicators see the Appendix to this part.

J. *Holland*. Study of the wars of Holland begins with the revolt of the "Beggars" in 1566–1567, which opened the long fight of the Netherlands with Spain and led in 1579 to the independence of the seven northern provinces [59] which composed the territory of contemporary Holland. Up to that time the Netherlands was not an independent state, having belonged in part to France, Burgundy, and Spain.

During the seventeenth and eighteenth centuries the territory of Holland remained little changed. From 1795 to 1813 it was incorporated by France (the Republic of Batavia and later the kingdom of Louis Bonaparte and Napoleon); in 1815 it was made independent with the inclusion of Belgium; since 1830 it has existed in the limits of contemporary Holland. In spite of these vicissitudes it functioned in fact as an independent state and could be taken as a unit for our investigation.

The main difficulties in our study of war movement in Holland are due to uncertainty as to how great was its share in the coalitional armies in the wars of the seventeenth and eighteenth centuries. Notwithstanding the existence of data concerning the size of the army and the losses of the whole coalition, data are very scarce so far as the share of the Netherlands is concerned. For an estimate of the military effort of this country in these wars we must rely upon several general considerations of the military possibilities of Holland in these campaigns. When all the important facts are considered, perhaps it is not greatly misleading if we take the proportional role of the Netherlands in these wars of coalition as 1, compared with 1.5 for England and 2 for Austria. In other words, in the Anglo-Dutch coalitions Holland's share is given 40 per cent of the total military effort; in the Austro-Dutch coalitions, 30 to 35 per cent of the whole effort; in the Austro-English-Dutch coalitions the share of Holland is estimated as about 25 per cent of the whole army.

[59] Though Spain recognized the independence of the "United Provinces" *de facto* only in 1609 and *de jure* in 1648, factually since 1579 they functioned as an independent state.

Another difficulty is the exact size of Holland's armies and their losses in the French campaigns of 1795–1812, when these armies fought on the side of France and were a part of the French armies. Considering the small size of the French Batavian armies for the period when Holland was the Batavian Republic — between 10,000 and 20,000 — it is reasonable to assume that the size of Holland's army in these wars hardly exceeded 10,000. At the end of the Napoleonic regime, when Holland fought against France, its army, for instance in the battle of Waterloo, was about 18,000. Considering these and additional data for the beginning and the end of these French-Dutch campaigns, it is hardly misleading to assume that the typical size of the Dutch armies for that period was about 15,000.

A similar difficulty exists for the exact size of the Dutch Army in its war with Belgium supported by France and England in 1830–1833. For this war the size of the Dutch armies is assumed to be about 50,000 — near to the size of the French — the main army of intervention.

For many wars there exist factual data for the extent of the losses sustained by the Dutch armies. For those for which they do not exist, the coefficient of the losses typical for the moderately strenuous wars, namely 5 per cent of the army, is accepted. Only for those wars where the Dutch armies were within the French armies is the figure raised to 10 per cent (for the French armies it was about 20 per cent).

Table 13 shows the movement of war magnitude for Holland by quarter-century and century periods.

One peculiarity immediately strikes the eye: since 1833 Holland has been free from war — a privilege not shared by any other country for such a long period. If the curve of war in other countries, especially in the larger ones, had been going in that way, believers in eternal peace would have had a fairly substantial foundation for their hope. Unfortunately the truth is very different from this *desiderium*. In other respects the data do not deviate radically from those of other countries. As in several others, the maximum of war activities falls here at the period of the climax of power and commercial and cultural activity of the country, the seventeenth century. The decline of the power and influence of the country (compared with other countries) is followed here by a decline of war activities. This phenomenon has been met before several times. Of 375 years studied, about 165 years or 44 per cent (181 years or 49 per cent in the other system of computation) had an occurrence of war. Otherwise, no periodicity and no uniform rhythm are noticeable.

For the detailed indicators see the Appendix to this part.

TABLE 13. TOTAL MEASURES OF WAR FOR HOLLAND FROM 1551 TO 1925 BY QUARTER CENTURIES AND CENTURIES

Century and Quarter Century	Duration (Year)	Army's Strength (Number)	Casualties (Number)
1551–1600 [1]	**35** [1]	**1,280,000** [1]	**64,000** [1]
1551–1575	10	30,000	1,500
1576–1600	25	1,250,000	62,500
1601–1700	**89**	**2,823,000**	**289,700**
1601–1625	14	545,000	41,000
1626–1650	26	210,000	118,000
1651–1675	35	688,000	59,600
1676–1700	14	380,000	71,100
1701–1800	**38**	**1,123,000**	**169,730**
1701–1725	16	680,000	134,100
1726–1750	7	133,000	14,630
1751–1775	—	—	—
1776–1800	15	310,000	21,000
1801–1900	**19**	**428,000**	**33,844**
1801–1825	15	228,000	23,844
1826–1850	4	200,000	10,000
1851–1875			
1876–1900	Peace	—	—
1901–1925			

[1] Half century only.

K. *Poland and Lithuania.* Our study of the wars of Poland begins with 1386, the year of personal unification of Poland and Lithuania under Jagello, Grand Duke of Lithuania, and the foundation of the dynasty of Jagellons.[60] There are practically no data concerning the wars before that date, and they are incomplete after that date. Even for the wars of the fourteenth and fifteenth centuries, in which fall the most important wars of Poland, there are exceedingly few and fragmentary reliable sources. The same difficulty is met for the subsequent centuries up to 1795, the third partition of Poland, after which it ceased to exist as a really independent state up to its resurrection in the twentieth century. This explains why for most of the wars of Poland estimates are used instead of the actual data. Some of the data are given, but in several cases they were very questionable in their accuracy and therefore had to be rejected.

In conformity with the norms taken for Russia for the Polish wars of the fourteenth and fifteenth centuries the typical size of the army is taken as 20,000, and the proportion of the losses as 4 per cent. The main conflicts of Poland of that period were largely with Russia, and these

[60] See O. Halecki, *La Pologne de 963 à 1914* (Paris, 1933).

norms appear for both countries as most probable. A series of wars of
Poland-Lithuania with the Teutonic order investigated by Delbrück
supports this assumption : for instance at the battle of Tannenberg,
1410, the Polish Army's strength did not exceed this figure.[61]

For the wars of the sixteenth century the norms similar to those for
Russian wars of this period — and again the principal wars of Poland
were with Russia — are accepted, namely, the average size of the army
as about 30,000 and the proportion of losses as 4 per cent. Some of the
concrete data of various sources are given in the subsequent descriptions
of the wars, but many of them are rejected as hardly probable. For
instance, such a figure as an army of 100,000 which besieged Pskov in
1581-1582 is evidently incredible : none of the European armies had
such strength, even half of it, during that century.

For the smaller wars, like those with Crimea and with Cossacks, the
figures are naturally smaller, around 15,000.

For the wars of the seventeenth and eighteenth centuries we are here,
as in other countries, upon somewhat firmer ground. For many wars
approximate actual data exist and therefore can be used as comparatively
reliable. For the wars of these centuries for which the data do not exist
they can be estimated roughly upon the basis of the actual data of other
Polish wars of that period. Only in the wars with "Cossacks" — many
of which were simultaneously revolts — is there great difficulty. Being
a kind of sporadic, unorganized outburst they were very different in their
magnitudes. Accepting the figures given by various investigators for the
revolt under the leadership of Bogdan Khmelnitzki (1647-1649) as
maximal, for other smaller Cossacks' wars (led by Nalivaiko, Sagaidat-
schny, Pavluk, Ostranitza) the figures are taken respectively smaller.

The Polish Army in the Great Northern War (1701-1706, 1709-1721)
was composed of the Polish as well as Saxon soldiers. There is no possibility of separating the comparative proportions of these elements, therefore
the estimates given include both. For the War for Polish Succession —
the war carried on mainly in Italy and Germany and in which the fate of
Poland was decided by other than Polish powers — the size of the Polish
army is taken similar to that of the Russian Army which occupied Poland.
These figures are considerably lower than those given, for instance, by
A. Podhorsky,[62] who estimates 40,000 as the size of the army in this war.

---

[61] Delbrück, op. cit., Vol. III, pp. 539 ff. The 80,000 army of Jahn-Albrecht in his war,
1497-1498, mentioned by Lewinski-Corwin, can hardly be taken seriously. E. Lewinski-
Corwin, The Political History of Poland (New York, 1917), p. 123.

[62] A. Podhorsky, La Pologne. Les Guerres (Paris, 1929), Vol. I, p. 63.

The reason for that is the contradiction of this estimate with many other conditions and with the comparatively insignificant role which Poland played in this war.

In application to Poland, the factor of several fronts of the same war — the factor which makes it necessary to increase the size of the army in comparison with that given in this or that battle — is almost nonexistent : the coalitions of the adversaries of Poland were almost always so little organized and unified in their efforts that the wars of the coalitions were often a series of separate wars to be singled out from one another and respectively estimated as such.

Table 14 shows the movement of war magnitude for Poland and Lithuania by quarter-century and century periods.

TABLE 14. TOTAL MEASURES OF WAR FOR POLAND AND LITHUANIA FROM 1386 TO 1800 BY QUARTER CENTURIES AND CENTURIES

Century and Quarter Century	Duration (Year)	Army's Strength (Number)	Casualties (Number)
1386–1400	4	80,000	3,200
1401–1500	**80**	**1,640,000**	**65,600**
1401–1425	20	340,000	13,600
1426–1450	11	320,000	12,800
1451 1475	18	360,000	14,400
1476–1500	31	620,000	24,800
1501–1600	**73**	**2,170,000**	**90,500**
1501–1525	29	795,000	31,800
1526 1550	10	240,000	9,600
1551–1575	17	460,000	17,700
1576–1600	17	675,000	31,400
1601–1700	**74**	**3,227,000**	**348,380**
1601–1625	16	1,065,000	59,250
1626–1650	16	630,000	77,550
1651–1675	25	1,124,000	154,480
1676–1700	17	408,000	57,120
1701–1800	**33**	**1,458,000**	**218,560**
1701–1725	21	394,000	60,540
1726–1750	3	60,000	1,200
1751–1775	6	914,000	130,820
1776–1800	3	90,000	27,000

Here the army as well as casualties grow up to the seventeenth century inclusive, and then in the last century of the existence of Poland — the eighteenth — before its regeneration in the twentieth century, they decline considerably. Here the climax falls also upon the sixteenth and seventeenth centuries when Poland reached perhaps the peak of its power and glory. Of 414 years of Polish history considered, some 265 years or some 64 per cent had an occurrence of war. In another system of computations the per cent is about 58. In other respects the results corroborate the conclusions reached before.

For the detailed indicators see the Appendix to this part.

Chapter Eleven

SUMMARY AND MAIN RESULTS

I. ABSOLUTE FIGURES

Still on the plane of absolute figures, for the armies' strength and the casualties, we can attempt to make a summary of their movement for four of the countries studied from the twelfth century [1] to 1925. There are four countries which it is possible to study in this way, France, England, Austria-Hungary, and Russia. The remaining five countries, at least formally, enter the scene later, and therefore a summary for all nine countries would make comparison unfair, or even impossible, in regard to the later centuries. However considerable were the variations of the above four countries, they preserved essentially their continuity as well as the constancy of their territory and population. It is true that the total for these four countries is somewhat unfair in regard to the later centuries, because Germany before the sixteenth century figured in Austria-Hungary; and a considerable part of Italy, Holland, and Poland also entered the data for earlier centuries. For this reason, totals for the four countries from century to century tend to overestimate some what the figures for earlier centuries, before the seventeenth, and to underestimate somewhat the figures for the seventeenth and later centuries.

TABLE 15. SUMMARY FIGURES BY CENTURY PERIODS FOR FRANCE, ENGLAND, AUSTRIA-HUNGARY, AND RUSSIA FROM 1101 TO 1925

Century	Army's Strength (Number)	Casualties (Number)
1101–1200	1,161,000	29,940
1201–1300	2,372,000	68,440
1301–1400	3,867,000	166,729
1401–1500	5,000,000	285,000
1501–1600	9,758,000	573,020
1601–1700	15,865,000	2,497,170
1701–1800	24,849,000	3,622,140
1801–1900	17,869,800	2,912,771
1901–1925	41,465,000	16,147,550

[1] Not all of these four countries have complete data for the tenth and eleventh centuries; therefore the summary results can be given only beginning with the twelfth century.

Table 15 shows the summarized results by century periods of the movement of the army's strength and of casualties for France, England, Russia, Austria-Hungary, from the twelfth to the twentieth century.

Since the summary deals with the same four countries for the centuries compared, the figures, as absolute figures, are roughly comparable, though recognizing the slight overestimation for earlier centuries, explained above.

Before proceeding with the analysis of these figures, let us sum up the figures for all the nine countries,[2] keeping in mind, however, that such a summary tends to inflate unduly the figures for the later centuries, for the reason just opposite to the one indicated in the preceding paragraph (see Table 16).

TABLE 16.   SUMMARY FIGURES BY CENTURY PERIODS FOR NINE EUROPEAN COUNTRIES FROM 1101 TO 1925

Century	Army's Strength (Number)	Casualties (Number)
1101–1200	1,161,000	29,940 [1]
1201–1300	2,372,000	68,440 [2]
1301–1400	3,947,000	169,929 [3]
1401–1500	6,910,000	364,220 [4]
1501–1600	16,707,300	896,185 [5]
1601–1700	25,796,000	3,711,090 [6]
1701–1800	31,055,500	4,505,990 [7]
1801–1900	24,233,800	3,625,627 [8]
1901–1925	60,425,000	22,035,150 [9]

[1] Only Austria, England, France, Russia.
[2] Only Austria, England, France, Russia.
[3] Plus Poland for one quarter.
[4] Plus Spain.
[5] Plus Italy and the Netherlands.
[6] Plus Germany (all nine).
[7] All nine countries.
[8] All nine countries.
[9] All nine countries.

In Table 16 the data are comparable beginning with the second part of the seventeenth century, after which time all nine of the countries are present.

So far as the absolute figures are concerned, whether in Table 15 or in the comparable study (Table 16), they show a steady but uneven growth of the size of the army and the number of the casualties, from the twelfth to the eighteenth centuries inclusive, a notable decrease in the nineteenth century, and an unprecedented flare-up in the first quarter of the twentieth century. The casualty figure for that quarter exceeds the total casualty for all the preceding centuries taken together (in Tables 15 and 16). The figure for the army's strength is also exceptionally high

[2] Though Poland formally is not existent in the nineteenth century, factually its population, soldiers, and casualties are present in the form of the part of the army and the casualty of the countries which divided Poland.

(in both tables). Though it does not exceed, it is lower than the total for the previous centuries taken together, its stunning-size, especially when it is remembered that it is only for one quarter century, is evident. The above means then, first, that *within the centuries studied there is no continuous trend, according to the tables; after an increase from the twelfth to the eighteenth centuries both figures are less in the nineteenth.* Second, as far as the absolute figures stand, *they do not warrant any claim for the existence of some continuous trend toward a disappearance or decrease of war.* Third, the figures for both variables show at the same time that the rate of increase of the size of the army and of the casualty has not been the same; all in all *the casualty rates increased faster than the strength of the army.* According to Table 15 (of the four countries), while the army's strength increased from the twelfth to the twentieth century by about 36 times, the rate of casualty increased by about 539 times; according to Table 16, the army increased by 52 times, the casualty by 748 times. In both cases the increase of the casualty is from 14 to 15 times greater than the increase of the army's strength.

This means that regardless of the size of the army, recent and modern wars have tended to become more devastating in their killing and wounding power, so far as such killing power is measured by the per cent of casualties in reference to the size of the "regular" fighting forces. This is shown more clearly by Table 17, which roughly estimates the casualties in each century as a per cent of the size of the army, for the four countries in Table 15.

TABLE 17.   PERCENTAGE OF CASUALTIES IN FOUR COUNTRIES
FROM THE TWELFTH TO THE TWENTIETH CENTURY

Century	Casualties as Per Cent of Army's Strength
XII	2.5
XIII	2.9
XIV	4.6
XV	5.7
XVI	5.9
XVII	15.7
XVIII	14.6
XIX	16.3
XX	38.9

With but slight differences the same results are given by Table 16. The invention and introduction of gunpowder in the fourteenth century,[3]

[3] "The first well-authenticated case of its use in war was in Edward III's Crécy campaign in 1346." C. L. Spaulding, H. Nickerson, and J. W. Wright, *Warfare, A Study of Military Methods from the Earliest Times* (New York, 1925), p. 406.

and the subsequent development of technology, physics, and chemistry, gave, by the progress of the technique of war, more destructive means of warfare. Especially great "progress" was shown in this respect by the wars of the seventeenth and then of the twentieth centuries when many new weapons were introduced, such as military airplanes, perfected machine guns, tanks, more powerful cannons, explosives, poisonous gas, and the like. The above percentages reflect in absolute figures the progressive perfecting of the means of exterminating human life in the wars of the last four centuries, especially the twentieth. One machine gun (not to mention poison gas, big Berthas, tanks, explosives) is more efficiently deadly than picks, spears, bows, arbalests, and swords of dozens of knights, the weapons of the twelfth century.[4]

It is true in war, as in many other phenomena, that poison calls for counterpoison, new danger for new protection, action for reaction. Just as the weapons of the twelfth century led to the use of armor, high walls for the cities, and other means of protection, the deadly weapons of modern warfare called forth many means of protection against them. There is, however, one notable difference in the protective devices then and now. Formerly they aimed to protect human life by minimizing the deadliness of the danger; armor protected the body of the knight from many dangers and minimized the losses. Now the means of protection aim to protect both sides, not so much through various devices which minimize the total losses, as through infliction of the maximum losses upon the adversary. This modern protection in warfare is a mad race in the invention and use of ever stronger destructive means against the adversary. Explosives, guns, machine guns, airplanes, poison gas, probably germs of epidemics and of devastating maladies, in future wars, are not protection, like armor or the unassailable city wall, which reduced losses of both sides, but are hellish means of mutual destruction. As both adversaries use them the result is maximization of the losses of both sides.[5]

When this factor alone is properly considered, it is comprehensible why

---

[4] It should be pointed out that this efficiency is discussed only with reference to the fighters, and to the killing and wounding form of casualty; losses from diseases and epidemics among the soldiers, and still more losses in the civilian population and among incidental fighters, do not concern us here.

[5] This conclusion stands even when we consider an uprooting of the vanquished army in the wars of the past. Even under such conditions the losses of the vanquished party rarely exceeded some 25 or, as in the battle of Cannae, 50 per cent. But such losses were very exceptional, as has been shown above. I refer to the typical losses of the armies involved in the wars of a given period. Small parts of an army have often been exterminated almost completely in the past as well as in the present wars.

the losses in the World War amounted to 30 and 40 per cent of the army, instead of 1, 2, and 5 per cent as in the wars of the past.

Another condition should be mentioned in connection with losses. As the armies of the medieval centuries were mainly armies of knights and nobility, with their code of chivalry and honor, a code which was enforced to a considerable extent, the losses were minimized. As soon as the adversary was wounded, taken, or overpowered, he was not necessarily killed; more often his life was spared for ransom, or by reason of the code. At the present time, poison gas, shell bullet, bomb, explosive, do not and cannot have any "code" of chivalry or honor; they strike anything and anybody that happens to be in their way. Besides, the "international laws of war" proved themselves during the World War to be fairly noneffective. Instead, the principle "all is fair in war" was the main "code." Recent wars in Asia and Africa have shown that still more clearly. This is another factor leading to greater losses now than in the wars of earlier centuries.

A still more important factor contributing to the high per cent of casualties in the twentieth century is the *real* duration of war. Here the World War was unique. Our figure for its duration is computed on the usual basis, from the beginning of the war to the date of peace. This gives about four years. The duration of any war in the past is computed upon the same purely "arithmetic" basis. However, as was explained above, four years' duration of the World War and four years' duration of the earlier, especially the medieval wars, are quite different quantities. The World War was filled with incessant warfare; every day, even every hour, the enemies faced and exterminated each other. These were, indeed, four years of continuous fighting, practically without interruption. A war four years long in past centuries was in fact mostly inaction, lacking much real fighting, interrupted only once in a while by this or that battle, skirmish, or engagement. The duration of real fighting in the Hundred Years' War was in fact many times shorter than in the World War. When this condition is considered in all its enormous importance it is understood why the number and the per cent of casualties in the twentieth century is so exceptionally high,[6] and why the real magnitude of the World War was gigantic, actually greater

---

[6] A similar conclusion is reached by other investigators. "If all the losses of the hundred years which lie between the Napoleonic wars and the World War of 1914–1918 are counted, the result will prove a fraction only of the number of deaths during the World War." H. Westergaard in Editor's Preface to S. Dumas and K. Vedel-Petersen, *Losses of Life*, quoted. See also Q. Wright, *op. cit.*, pp. 32–43.

than the figures show. In the light of these considerations Table 17 of the growing percentages of casualties with reference to strength of the army, as well as the exceptionally big figure of casualties for the twentieth century, appear to reflect the real changes in this field adequately, if not in details, then in essentials. So much for the absolute figures.

II. Relative Indicators of the Movement of War from the Twelfth to Twentieth Century

As has been said, the absolute figures are given, regardless of the changes in the size of population for the centuries studied. As such they are, in a sense, misleading, if they are interpreted "atomistically." Let us now see what the results will be if the absolute figures, for casualties, as the main burden of war, or for army's strength are corrected per unit of population; for instance, if they are computed per 1,000,000 population at the middle of the century under investigation. Such figures will be relative indicators. First of all let us compute the relative indicators for all the nine countries studied for the centuries from the seventeenth to the twentieth. In order to obtain them we shall take the absolute figures for the army's strength and casualties for the countries for each century, divide them by 90 per cent [7] of the population of Europe during the middle of that century, and multiply the result by 1,000,000. The same is to be computed for the four countries in Table 15. The reason for this is that beginning with the seventeenth century we have roughly reliable estimates of the population of Europe. Before the seventeenth century considerable guesswork is present in any of the existing estimates. If, however, we make widely different assumptions as to the rate of growth and the size of population in each century, and if under these widest minimums and maximums the results remain essentially the same, such a procedure is strong evidence that, if not in the details, then at least in the essentials, the relative indicators are valid.

Multiplying the absolute figures for casualties and for army's strength for each century by 1,000,000 and dividing them by 90 per cent of the population for the middle of the respective century, or, in the case of the twentieth century, by the population of 1910 as the nearest date, we

[7] As a round approximation the population of the nine countries is taken as near 90 per cent of the population of all Europe. During the latter part of the eighteenth century and all the nineteenth, the population of these countries composed from 80 to 90 per cent of the population of Europe. See C. Gini, M. Boldrini, L. Berardinis, and G. Zingali, *Demografia* (Torino, 1930), table on pp. 548–549.

obtain the following relative indicators of the burden of the army and of the casualties for the seventeenth to the twentieth centuries, inclusive.[8]

TABLE 18. RELATIVE INDICATORS OF WAR ACTIVITIES BY CENTURY PERIODS FOR NINE EUROPEAN COUNTRIES

Century	Army's Absolute Strength	Casualties	90 Per Cent of Population	Relative Army	Magnitude of Casualty
XX	60,425,000 [1]	22,035,150 [1]	401,000,000 [2]	150,685 [1]	54,955 [1]
XIX	24,333,800	3,645,627	238,000,000 [3]	101,823	15,234
XVIII	31,055,500	4,505,990	135,000,000 [3]	230,041	33,377
XVII	25,796,000	3,711,090	100,000,000 [3]	257,960	37,111

[1] For the first quarter only. As mentioned, the figure underestimates the indicator for the twentieth century. If there are going to be wars in the remaining part of the twentieth century, and after 1925 there have already been a few, though small, wars, the indicators for the twentieth century are likely to rise.
[2] In 1910.
[3] About 1850, 1750, 1650. See the figures in C. Gini and others, *op. cit.*, table on p. 548.

As we shall see in Table 19, the relative indicators computed in the same way for the above four countries for these centuries give figures which, though slightly different, are identical to the above so far as the comparative position of the centuries is concerned, both in regard to the strength of the army and the casualties. From the seventeenth to the twentieth centuries, so far as the army's strength per population is concerned, the greatest burden of war was in the seventeenth century, then the eighteenth, and the lightest was in the nineteenth century. The twentieth century, in its one quarter, did not exceed the burden of the seventeenth and the eighteenth centuries, but exceeded the nineteenth century. Considering, however, that in one quarter it exceeded more than half of the indicators of the seventeenth and of the eighteenth century, the twentieth century is to be given, so far, first place in relative burden of the army per population. On the other hand it is also shown

[8] Of course such a procedure is very elementary and rough, but there is no need to use the most delicate laboratory weight, sensitive to one-thousandth of a milligram, in a butcher shop. Under the conditions of the present problem with its rough estimates, the use of more complicated and refined methods for estimating population is superfluous. Furthermore, the figure for the twentieth century is not quite comparable in this case with the figures for the other centuries. As the absolute figures for the twentieth century are only for its first quarter, while for the other centuries the army's strength as well as the casualties are the totals of four quarters, the figure for the twentieth century would tend to decrease the magnitude of the army and of the casualties for that century. If during the remaining three quarters of the twentieth century there are new wars, and if the population does not grow rapidly up to 1950, which is very improbable, the figure for the twentieth century will have to be higher; the greater the wars up to A.D. 2000 the higher the indicator. Keeping this in mind, the relative indicators for the first quarter of the twentieth century, in spite of their incomparability, have some value; though they underestimate the real magnitude of its wars, they still show how big these wars were in comparison with the wars of the previous centuries.

that war magnitude, measured by this criterion, has not been systematically increasing from the seventeenth century on but, on the contrary, was decreasing in the eighteenth and nineteenth centuries in comparison with the seventeenth century. The relative indicator shows also that though the army's strength per population in the twentieth century was exceptionally great, nevertheless it was not so bewilderingly great as is shown by the absolute figures. While the absolute figures of the army's strength for the first quarter of the twentieth century greatly exceed any two of the preceding centuries, the seventeenth, the eighteenth, and the nineteenth, taken together, the relative indicator shows quite a different picture. It only exceeds the indicator of the nineteenth century, but is almost twice as small as the indicators of the seventeenth and eighteenth centuries.

Thus the relative indicator gréatly corrects the impression given by the absolute figures. To sum up, according to the relative indicator of the army's strength, the first place is to be given to the seventeenth, the second to the eighteenth, and the third to the nineteenth century. If the twentieth century have no wars in its remaining three quarters, it will occupy the third place and the nineteenth century the fourth. If it have them, then it will depend upon their number and magnitude which place will belong to it. Judged by the relative indicators of one quarter century only, it occupies the most belligerent place of all the quarter centuries from the seventeenth century to 1925.

If now we take the relative indicators of the casualties, probably the most important criterion of war, they tell definitely and unequivocally that *the curse or privilege to be the most devastating or most bloody war century belongs to the twentieth; in one quarter century it imposed upon the population a "blood tribute" far greater than that imposed by any of the whole centuries compared. The next place belongs to the seventeenth, and then comes the eighteenth century; the nineteenth century appears to be the least bloody of all these centuries concerned.* But it is again necessary to stress the fact that the relative indicators of casualty of the twentieth century are much less bewildering than the absolute figures. Though it remains the highest even in this respect, yet its relative difference is not so astounding. Thus the conclusion given by the relative indicators of the army's size, as well as of casualties per population in the centuries compared, is that the *twentieth century, so far, was the most belligerent, then the seventeenth, eighteenth, and nineteenth respectively. The war burden imposed by the twentieth century is particularly great in the casualties or blood tribute, while in the size of the army it does not occupy a unique position.* We shall see that the same results are given by the relative indicators of the four countries mentioned for these centuries.

Such is the comparative position of these centuries in regard to the magnitude of war. However rough are the figures used, as most of the figures for these centuries are actual data, not guesses, the above conclusions are probably roughly accurate.

Much more doubtful becomes the situation when we try to compute the relative indicators for the centuries from the twelfth to the sixteenth, inclusive — not only because the absolute figures for the army's strength and the casualties for these centuries are mainly estimates, but also because the population of the countries studied for these centuries is unknown. Since, however, this whole part is in a sense a venture in systematic guesswork, it may be advanced into this field also, trying, however, to be as careful as possible. For the reason indicated above, no relative indicators for all the nine countries can be computed for the centuries from the twelfth to the sixteenth inclusive. *Only in regard to the above four countries may such a venture be attempted.* Considering that they embrace at least one-half of the European population, the results, if they be not misleading, may be typical for the whole of Europe, at least in their essentials.

Since we have the absolute figures for the army's strength and for the casualties of these countries from the twelfth to the twentieth centuries, we need now a computation of the relative indicators by population of these countries for each of these centuries. Under the necessity of estimate for the earlier centuries I shall resort to various hypothetical assumptions, with maximum and minimum limits which probably embrace in their range the actual size of the population of these countries in each century. The first is this: the increase of the population of Europe from 1600 (95,000,000) to 1700 (139,000,000) was, according to the data, about 46 per cent; from 1700 to 1800 (187,700,000) about 35 per cent; from 1800 to 1900 (398,007,431) more than 200 per cent.[9] A few studies of the movement of medieval population, for instance the estimates of K. Lamprecht, R. Kötzschke, K. T. von Inama Sternegg, G. Schmoller, W. Sombart, K. Bücher, E. Lévasseur, G. von Mayr, and others, give widely fluctuating rates of increase from century to century, from a decrease to an increase of 25 to 300 per cent, according to the place and the period.[10]

[9] *The rate of increase of the population of Europe in the nineteenth century is rightly and unanimously regarded as exceptional and can in no way be applied to the Middle Ages.*

[10] For instance, R. Kötzschke gives the following figures for the German population: about 2,500,000 to 3,000,000 in the ninth century; about 3,000,000 to 3,500,000 in the tenth

If we assume an average increase of about 40 per cent from century to century in the Middle Ages, from the twelfth to the sixteenth century inclusive, with the exception of the fourteenth century when the population decreased from one-fifth to one-third, such an allowance will probably be about the best rough approximation to the reality.[11] However, we should cover all possibilities. In addition to the 40 per cent rate of increase, let us assume smaller (20 per cent) and larger (60 per cent) rates of increase, a range which in all probability embraces the possible fluctuations in population growth of these countries [12] during the twelfth to the sixteenth centuries inclusive. As a matter of fact, the three sets of figures given in Table 19, for the population of these four countries in the centuries from the twelfth to the sixteenth inclusive, include practically all the estimates of competent historians. The computation of the relative indicators remains the same, and all the other qualifications mentioned above are applied here also. Now the table follows. (Figures 6 and 7, pages 297 and 298, give a pictorial idea of the movement,

---

century; about 5,000,000 to 6,000,000 c. 1039–1056; about 7,000,000 to 8,000,000 c. 1152–1190; about 15,000,000 at the beginning of the fourteenth century; and about 20,000,000 c. 1500. See R. Kötzschke, *Grundzüge der deutschen Wirtschaftsgeschichte, bis zum 17. Jahrhundert* (Jena, 1921), pp. 73 ff. and 116. G. Schmoller gives about 2,000,000 to 3,000,000 at the time of Caesar; about 12,000,000 c. 1250–1340; regress in the fourteenth century, after the Black Death; and about 15,000,000 c. 1600–1620. G. Schmoller, *Grundriss der allgemeinen Volkswirtschaftslehre* (München, 1923), pt. 1, p. 173. K. Lamprecht's rates of the increase of the population (*Vermehrungskoefficient der Bevölkerung*) are more liberal for the centuries from ninth to thirteenth; then the rate fell in the fourteenth century. K. Lamprecht, *Deutsches Wirtschaftsleben im Mittelalter*, Vol. I, pt. i, p. 163; see the statistical data in the appendix to the work (Leipzig, 1885), Vol. I, pt. ii. W. Sombart gives more conservative figures and rates for the growth of the population. See his *Der moderne Kapitalismus* (München and Leipzig, 1922), Vol. I, p. 253.

Not quoting others, especially the French estimates of E. Lévasseur, the above shows a considerable divergency of estimates, but the divergency is, after all, not radical; and what is still more important, in none of these estimates is the average rate of the increase from the eleventh to the seventeenth century, when all these centuries are taken, higher than 100 per cent per century; all in all, when all the centuries are taken, the rate is considerably below that of doubling of the population per century. The same is to be said of most of the French, English, and other estimates, beginning with the data given by the political arithmeticians: John Graunt, William Petty, Gregory King, I. P. Süssmilch, Deparcieux, and ending with the estimates given by the modern historians and populationists.

[11] It is to be noted that a more rapid increase of the population given by the above and other historians concerns mainly the centuries before the thirteenth. Beginning with the twelfth and the thirteenth centuries most of them give a lower rate of increase than for the centuries from the eighth or the ninth to the twelfth.

[12] The rate of growth for small and modest territories or areas fluctuated, of course, much more strongly, as, for instance, Lamprecht's study of the growth of population in the valley of the Moselle from 800 to the thirteenth century shows. But the rate for the whole European universe fluctuated naturally within much narrower limits.

under the assumption of 40 per cent increase of the population from the twelfth to the seventeenth century, except the fourteenth with its decrease of the population.)

TABLE 19.   RELATIVE INDICATORS OF WAR ACTIVITIES BY CENTURY PERIODS FOR FRANCE, GREAT BRITAIN, AUSTRIA-HUNGARY, AND RUSSIA

Century	Total Population [1]	Relative Magnitude of Army's Strength	Relative Magnitude of Casualties
XX[2]	305,000,000 [2]	136,278	52,943
XIX	171,530,000	104,179	17,034
XVIII	90,000,000	276,100	40,246
XVII	55,000,000	288,455	45,403

Three Assumed Sizes.   Relative Magnitude under the Specified Assumptions

	A	B	C	A	B	C	A	B	C
XVI	45 m.[3]	39 m.	35 m.	216,844	250,205	278,800	12,734	14,693	16,372
XV	35 m.	28 m.	25 m.	142,857	171,428	200,000	8,143	10,179	11,400
XIV	25 m.	20 m.	18 m.	154,680	193,350	214,833	6,669	8,336	9,263
XIII	18 m.	15 m.	13 m.	131,777	158,133	182,462	3,802	4,563	5,265
XII	13 m.	12 m.	10 m.	89,308	96,750	116,100	2,303	2,495	2,994

[1] In 1910, 1850, 1750, 1650, 1550, 1450, 1350, 1250, 1150.   [2] One quarter century only.   [3] m means million.

The relative indicators for the seventeenth to the twentieth centuries for these four countries are slightly different from the relative indicators for all nine countries, but they are reasonably similar and give the same order of belligerency to the centuries, measured by the army's size as well as casualties per population. The conclusions given above are well sustained by these indicators and therefore need not be repeated. Turning to the relative indicators for the twelfth to the sixteenth centuries inclusive, we are led to the following conclusions.

So far as the relative strength of the army is concerned, there is no clear-cut trend from the twelfth to the seventeenth century, or from the twelfth to the twentieth century. The indicators are the lowest for the twelfth century; then, under all three assumptions, they grow from the twelfth to the fourteenth century, inclusive; drop somewhat in the fifteenth century; then rise during the sixteenth and seventeenth centuries; drop in the nineteenth century; and rise again in the twentieth century. The maximum falls within the seventeenth century (with the exception of the twentieth, if it should have a considerable number of wars during its remaining three quarters). Thus there is no continuous trend toward either an ever-increasing or decreasing size of the army per population. The burden of the army in the nineteenth century is lower than all the other centuries with the exception of the twelfth. The false impression given by the absolute figures of the army's strength for the twentieth century is again corrected; in the system of the relative indicators the twentieth century does not stand out, in this respect, as something quite extraordinary.

Considerably different are the results given by the relative indicators of casualties per population. Under all three assumptions in regard to the size of the population, there is found a continuous trend toward an increase in this "blood tribute" for the wars from the twelfth to the seventeenth century, inclusive; after that they decline in the eighteenth and especially in the nineteenth centuries to reach a climax in the twentieth century. The minimum falls within the twelfth and the maximum within the twentieth century, in spite of the fact that the indicator for the twentieth century is only for one quarter. These indicators show a particularly sharp increase from the sixteenth to the seventeenth century. Such a sharp rise (paralleled by a sharp decline in the nineteenth century) probably reflects the reality, for we know that the wars of the seventeenth century, beginning with the Thirty Years' War, became more strenuous and bloody than before. But it may also be a result of an inadvertent underestimation of the casualties in the wars of the twelfth to the sixteenth centuries; however small the probability, the possibility should be granted. We may grant hypothetically that the losses of these centuries were twice as great as they are given. Such an assumption would make the typical per cents of the casualties for these centuries from 4 and 5 to 10 and 12, instead of the estimated typical per cents from 2 and 3 to 5 and 8. Such a double percentage in all probability greatly exaggerates the casualties of these centuries; nevertheless let us be liberal and grant it. The relative indicators will be twice as large as given in Table 19, but even so, the trend, increases, and decreases remain respectively the same. Since the nineteenth century gives a decrease in spite of the fact that, in the main, the actual data for the seventeenth to the twentieth centuries are used, such sharp fluctuations seem really to exist in this field, and to reflect the great increase in the killing and wounding power of war in the seventeenth century in both efficiency and scale.

However this may be, such is the result given, and it stands under all three sizes of the population assumed, and under doubling the casualties of the wars of the twelfth to the sixteenth centuries. The main results given by the relative indicators can now be summed up in a few statements.

(1) All in all, especially in regard to the casualties, the twelfth to the sixteenth centuries were much less bloody, and therefore much less

belligerent than the seventeenth, eighteenth, and the twentieth centuries. In regard to the size of the army (per population) there is no such consistent difference.

(2) Of the later centuries, the nineteenth appears to have been, comparatively, very peaceful, especially in its last quarter. The burden of war that it imposed upon the population by the relative size of the army, as well as of the casualties, was comparatively very low, much lower than in the seventeenth and the eighteenth centuries, and rather similar to the burden of the sixteenth century.

(3) The twentieth century, so far, appears to be the most bloody within the period of European history studied, with respect to the relative casualties; the same century occupies an exceedingly high position with respect to the relative burden of the army.

(4) The study discloses a lack of any continuous trend (in relative indicators) during the centuries investigated. We have not been moving to ever bigger and more bloody, nor to ever smaller and less bloody war. If from the twelfth to the seventeenth centuries war, measured by the relative indicators of casualties, and also by the relative indicators of the army's strength, was growing, during the eighteenth and especially the nineteenth century it was decreasing. After that it greatly increased again, in the first quarter of the twentieth century. Thus we have longtime fluctuations without any continuous trend either to the so longed for and so necessary Paradise of peace, or to the so dreaded and so tragic Inferno of bigger and bloodier war.

(5) It is interesting to note that the relative indicators obtained for the European countries do not differ greatly from the relative indicators obtained for Greece and Rome. The maximums and minimums in casualties are very similar in both cases; in the strength of the army the difference in maximum is greater, but not incomparably so.[13] (See figures 6 and 7, pages 297 and 298.)

Such an outcome in this "guessy" adventure is one of the evidences that the results are not entirely misleading. In this connection it is to be noted that the record indicator of the relative magnitude of casualty is held by third-century Rome, with an indicator of 63,125, while the twentieth-

---

[13] The relative indicators of the army's strength for Rome and Greece are computed in the case of Rome only for the population of Italy, which makes the indicators for the third and first centuries B.C. considerably higher than the maximum figure given for European countries. Meanwhile in the Greek Army a considerable part was played by "foreigners." The Roman Army, especially in the centuries after the third B.C., was recruited not only from the population of Italy but from all parts of the Roman Empire. This is the evident and the main reason for the difference.

century indicator is 54,955 (for nine countries). However, the Roman indicator is for the entire third century while the twentieth-century indicator is only for its first quarter. A few wars of considerable magnitude occurring in the remaining three quarters of that century will mean that the Roman record will be beaten. Whether this happen or not, nobody can predict.

III. The Absolute and Relative Magnitude of War Activities of the Various Countries Studied

If we inquire which of the countries studied in their respective centuries has had the largest army and casualties (absolute figures), the answer is given by the following order of countries for each specified century.

In regard to the *army's strength* the order, beginning with the country with the largest army and ending with the smallest army, is as follows in each of the centuries studied (see Tables 6, 7, 8, 9, 10, 11, 12, 13, 14).

XII. Russia, England, France, Austria
XIII. Russia, England, France, Austria
XIV. England, France, Russia, Austria
XV. England, Poland, France, Russia, Austria, Spain
XVI. Spain, France, Austria, Poland, England, Russia, Holland, Italy
XVII. Austria, France, Spain, Poland, Holland, Russia, England, Italy
XVIII. Austria, France, Russia, England, Germany, Poland, Spain, Holland, Italy
XIX. France, Russia, Germany, Spain, Austria, England, Italy, Holland
XX. Russia, Germany, France, England, Austria, Italy, Spain, Holland

This list shows that so far as absolute figures of the size of the army are concerned, the comparative position of the countries is changing in the course of time, now one country occupying the first position, now some other one. Of course the small countries are not expected to hold a first position for obvious reasons. Nevertheless, we see that even their positions change greatly; Holland occupied fifth place in the seventeenth century, among the eight countries, while in the nineteenth and the twentieth it occupied last place.

A similar picture is given in regard to the *absolute* figures of the casualties in the centuries studied. In this respect the order of the countries is as follows, according to the century.

XII. Russia, Austria, England, France
XIII. Russia, England, France, Austria
XIV. England, France, Russia, Austria
XV. Austria, England, Poland, France, Russia
XVI. Austria, Spain, Russia, France, England, Poland, Holland, Italy
XVII. Austria, France, Spain, Poland, Holland, England, Russia, Italy

XVIII. Austria, France, Russia, Germany, England, Poland, Holland, Spain, Italy
XIX. France, Russia, Germany, Austria, Spain, England, Italy, Holland
XX. Russia, Germany, France, England, Austria, Italy, Spain, Holland

Thus in absolute figures Austria, Russia, and France have had the tragic privilege of bearing the greatest number of casualties in the centuries studied. Here again we see that, all in all, the place of various nations is shifting from century to century.

It goes without saying that the absolute figures do not give an idea as to the relative or real size of the army or of the casualties in relation to the size of the population. Such figures can be given only when the absolute figures are divided by the size of the population of the countries studied. Taking a rough estimate of the size of the population about the middle of the respective century and dividing by it the absolute figure of the casualties of that century, we obtain the rough relative indicators [14] of the comparative burden of casualties borne by each specified country in the specified centuries. These are shown in Table 20.[15]

TABLE 20. RELATIVE INDICATORS OF THE CASUALTY BURDEN OF THE SPECIFIED COUNTRY (PER UNIT OF POPULATION)

Country	XX	XIX	XVIII	XVII
Russia	41.1	11.1	21.5	7.9
Austria	48	5.8	94.0 [1]	130.0 [1]
England	66.5	5.0	30.1	20.0
France	92.0	51.0	45.8	36.6
Germany	94.7	13.1		
Italy	53.1			
Spain	2.2	11.0	11.8	
Holland	—	5.7	84.8 [1]	161.0 [1]

[1] This exceptionally high figure is due not only to the high casualty of the population of Austria and the Netherlands in the wars, but also to a large quota of foreign soldiers employed in the Austrian and the Netherlands' armies as well as participating in the battles. For this reason the figure notably exaggerates the real burden of the casualties borne by the population of Austria and the Netherlands. With this reservation, the figure is nevertheless symptomatic, showing the excessive burden of the wars of that century in the Netherlands and Austria. The figure for England in the twentieth century exaggerates the burden because a considerable part of her army and casualties were those of the Dominions. If the populations of the Dominions were included in the denominator, the figure would be notably lower.

[14] These relative indicators are very approximate; neither the exact data exist for the size of the population for the centuries before the eighteenth, nor those for the proportion of foreigners in the army of the given country, nor dozens of other relevant data, can be computed.

[15] The relative indicators are obtained through the division of absolute figures for the casualties of each country by its population for the specified centuries (in 1910, 1850, 1750) and cutting from the result the last three figures. The figures for the population of each country for each century are taken from the *Demografia*, quoted. *Handwörterbuch der Staatswissenshaften* (Jena, 1909), Vol. II, table on pp. 548–549; for Russia from the *Statistical Yearbook of Russia* for 1913, and for 1916 (in Russian).

These figures need correcting in the sense that in many countries these casualties were borne not only by their population, but also by soldiers who fought for the country but were "foreigners" to it. Even in the World War, and therefore in the twentieth century, in the armies of England, France, and to a much less extent in some others, there was a notable part of such foreign participation. As mentioned above, in the past, in the English, Dutch, French, Austrian, Spanish, and other armies there was always a considerable portion of such strangers. In addition, in the armies like the Austrian in the seventeenth century were fighting soldiers taken from other countries which were either a part of the Holy Roman Empire, or related to the country in various ways. When this factor is considered, it leads to several corrections, sometimes of considerable importance.

Assuming that the populations of these countries for the seventeenth and the eighteenth centuries were near, or between, the two widely different estimates given for several countries, the data lead to the following conclusions. In the twentieth century the largest military burden per capita is carried by Germany, then by France, England, Italy, Austria, and Russia;[16] the smallest is carried by Holland and Spain. In the nineteenth century, the first place is occupied by France; then come Germany, Russia, Spain, Austria, Holland, and England. For each and all the countries, with the exception of Holland and Spain, the burden in the nineteenth century is many times lighter than in the twentieth century. In the eighteenth century the first places are occupied by Austria-Hungary, Holland, and France; then come England and Russia. In the seventeenth century the greatest burden is carried by Holland and Austria-Hungary, the smallest by Russia.

It is quite impossible to compute, even very roughly, the relative indicators for each country before the seventeenth century. Even the indicators given for the later centuries can be but very approximate. Granting that they correctly give the burden of casualties per unit of population, one must not conclude that they take every relevant condition into consideration and that the burden is quite adequately represented by the above figures. Besides the point indicated above, there are other conditions which are important. For instance, the indicator for

---

[16] However, France and England had a very considerable part of "natives" and men from the colonies and dominions in their armies. Therefore, figures for these should be notably lowered. See the size of these "native" and colonial forces in the English Army in T. J. Mitchell and G. M. Smith, *Medical Services. Casualties and Medical Statistics of the Great War* (London, 1931), pp. 2-5. It is a volume in the English official *History of the Great War*. For France see H. Corda, *La guerre mondiale* (Paris, 1922), p. 413 (Table 7).

Russia stands relatively low, due to her large population. But the burden of war in such a large country cannot really be distributed evenly among all the people of its vast area, some of whom were exempted from, or not admitted into, the army; the real burden has been much heavier for some parts of the population than is shown by the figure. Similar considerations should be applied to the indicators in general. Their only function is, at best, to show very roughly some comparative situations in the field, with all the limitations and reservations necessary for their proper interpretation.

All in all, a table made in this way confirms the conclusions reached above concerning the relative and absolute fluctuation of the magnitude of war from the seventeenth to the twentieth century. It confirms also the contention that the magnitude of "militarism" or "war effort" or "war burden" shifts from country to country in the course of time. Furthermore, Table 20 shows that there are no consistently peaceful and consistently militant countries. Although Holland has been peaceful during the last hundred years, it was particularly belligerent during the seventeenth and eighteenth centuries. *Mutatis mutandis*, the same can be said of all other countries. The popular opinion that democracies are much less belligerent than autocracies seems to be unwarranted by our data. In the twentieth century the relative magnitude of the war activities of democratic England (measured by casualties) was higher than of Spain; of France, higher than of Austria or Russia. In the nineteenth century democratic France was not more pacific than "autocratic" Germany, Russia, or Spain. During the seventeenth century, England did not occupy a lower position than Russia.

IV. THE PERCENTAGES OF YEARS WITH AND WITHOUT WAR

What is the comparative position of the countries in regard to the per cent of the total number of years studied, with war and with peace? Do they all have the same position in this respect, and enjoy an equal portion of years with war and years with peace? Such is the first question to be answered.

The data for the question have been given above. All we have to do here is to present the data in the form of a summary table which gives them in an easily comparable and understandable way. When put in this form the data look as shown in Table 21.[17]

[17] Here the simpler way is taken: each year with an occurrence of war or wars, no matter how long or how many, is counted as one year with war.

TABLE 21.   PERCENTAGE OF YEARS WITH WAR

Country	Per Cent of Years with War of the Total Number of Years Studied	Country	Per Cent of Years with War of the Total Number of Years Studied
Greece	57	Italy	36
Rome	41	France	50
Austria	40	England	56
Germany	28	Russia	46
Holland	44	Poland and Lithuania	58
Spain	67		

Table 21 shows that Germany has had the smallest (28) and Spain the largest (67) per cent of years with war, the other countries occupying various positions between the two. All in all, about 50 per cent of the years in these countries had an occurrence of war, and the difference between the maximal and the minimal figures is not excessively great. This does not mean that during 50 per cent of the time these countries have had war and during the remaining 50 per cent, peace. Many wars lasted much less than a whole year; therefore, the period of peace in the history of these countries is certainly larger than the per cent of years with peace according to the table. Even so, the per cent of years with war seems to have been much greater than is usually thought. So far, war phenomena seem to have been almost as common and " normal " as peace phenomena. The percentages given do not mean, of course, that the years of war and peace in the history of any one country have been evenly distributed; some periods have had uninterrupted war during two, five, ten, or thirty, and so on, years; other periods have had several years of undisturbed peace. But, as has been shown above, periods of peace as long as one quarter of a century have been exceedingly rare in the history of the countries, and a period up to 100 years or more of peace is almost unique, given in the history of Holland; in some of these countries such periods did not occur at all. Almost every generation (25 to 30 years) in the past, with very few exceptions, has been a witness of, or an actor in, war phenomena.

V. The Problem of Periodicity in the Fluctuation of War Magnitude

There have been several theories claiming that there exists a certain and definite periodicity in the rhythm of war and peace, in the comparative increase and decrease of war phenomena. As examples of such theories, two can be mentioned here. The first is the astrophysical, almost astrological, theory of R. Mewes. The essence of his theory is:

The periods of war and peaceful culture blossoming are influenced mainly by the position of the three great planets: Jupiter, Saturn, and Uranus, in regard to the Sun. Upon this position depend the great periods of dryness and bareness and moisture and fertility of the Earth.[18]

These periods in their turn determine — through climatic and similar influences, where the sun and the sunspots play a decisive part — human behavior and social events.[19]

According to Mewes the above three planets recur in the same position in regard to the sun every 675.5 years. This period breaks up into six shorter periods of 111 to 112 years.

During this period of 111 or 112 years there are usually two periods of war and two periods of blossoming of arts and sciences, each period being about 27.8 years [on the average].[20]

After this, the author gives a long table of the periods of war and peace with the blossoming of the arts and sciences, beginning with 2400 B.C., and ending with A.D. 2100. This enormous span of time he divides into forty periods of 111 to 112 years, and each period into smaller ones of 27 years, on the average, attempting to show that these periodicities have really existed in human history and are supported by it. It would take too much time and energy to reproduce here his tables in full. Instead, a part will give sufficient idea of the author's periodicities.

111-year	(a)	290–318 A.D.	Wars of Diocletian, Maximilian, Constantine, etc.
period	(b)	318–346	Introduction of Christianity; Nicean conclave and organization of the Christian Church.
	(c)	346–380	Migration of the peoples and wars of that period.
	(d)	380–401	Theodosius the Great, San Paolo, Vulgata, St. Augustine, Ulfilas.
111-year	(a)	401–429	Germanic wars, Alaric, Athaulf, Radagais, Walja, Genserich.
period	(b)	429–450	Organization of the German States, Leo I.
	(c)	450–486	Wars against Huns, under Attila.
	(d)	486–512	Conversion of the Franks into Christianity, and so on.

---

[18] K. Mewes, *Kriegs und Geistesperioden im Völkerleben und Verkundigung des nachsten Weltkrieges* (Leipzig, 1922), pp. 7 and 17.

[19] The sun, in conjunction with the above planets, is the final source of the periodicity of war and peace, of mental stagnation and progress, and of other important social events.

[20] Mewes, *op. cit.*, p. 8.

Interrupting his series, let us take more recent times and their periods.

111-year	(a) 1737–1765	Friedrich II. Silesian wars, etc.
period	(b) 1765–1793	The second blooming period of German literature, etc.
	(c) 1793–1821	Napoleonic wars.
	(d) 1821–1848	Arts and Sciences : Schopenhauer, R. Mayer, etc.
111-year	(a) 1848–1876	The Prussian and the German wars, etc.
period	(b) 1876–1904	Blooming period of the arts and sciences.
	(c) 1904–1932	World War [21]
	(d) 1932–1960	Peace, inner development, and progress.
111-year	(a) 1960–1988	Wars.
period	(b) 1988–2016	Peace.
	(c) 2016–2044	Wars.
	(d) 2044–2072	Peace.

And so on, *ad infinitum*, so long as the Earth goes around the Sun and mankind lives and acts on this planet. . . .   The great wars come usually in the periods of the great drought [*Durre*], that is in the times of the low level of the ground water [*Grundwasser*] while the periods of the great blooming of the arts and sciences, industry and commerce and culture generally happen at times of the maximal level of ground water.[22]

Such maximal and minimal periods were :

Maximum period, 1487 to 1518, the period of Michelangelo, Raphael, Leonardo da Vinci, Albrecht Dürer, Columbus, Vasco da Gama, B. Diaz, Martin Luther, the discovery of America, the Renaissance, and the Reformation.

Minimum period, 1518–1544, war era — the peasants' wars, the wars of Charles V, François I, religious wars, etc.

Maximum period, 1544–1576 : the deepening and expansion of the religious movement, while in the next

Minimum period, 1576 to 1598, we had the Dutch wars and revolts. The next

Maximum period, 1598 to 1625, was again the time of Galileo, Kepler, Descartes, Bacon, Shakespeare, Tycho de Brahe, etc.   The next

Minimum period, 1625 to 1654, was marked by the great Thirty Years' War.   The subsequent

Maximum period, 1654 to 1682, was a time of progress and elevation of Brandenburg, the time of Leibnitz, Sir Isaac Newton, Huygens, R. Boyle, Stahl, and the brilliant period of the arts, literature, sciences, etc., of the first part of the reign of Louis XIV.   The subsequent

[21] It is interesting to note that this war period was predicted in the first edition, published in 1896.

[22] Mewes, *op. cit.*, pp. 8–12.

Minimum period, 1682 to 1710, was the period of the great wars for the Spanish inheritance, the Northern wars (of Russia, Sweden, Poland, etc.) ; the Turkish wars, etc.   The next

Maximum period, 1710 to 1737, was again a time of blooming, of Voltaire, D. Hume, Wolff, Friedrich Wilhelm I, etc.   The period of 1737 to 1765 was the period of the three Silesian wars of Friedrich the Great. The next

Maximum period, 1765 to 1793, was marked by Goethe, Schiller, Herder, Wieland, Kant, Lavoisier, Black, Priestley, Cavendish, C. L. Berthollet, Dayton, Richter, Euler, Lagrange, Laplace, inventions of the steam engine, and other great inventions of the period.   Then comes again the

Minimum period, 1793 to 1821 ; then again the

Maximum period, 1821 to 1848 ; then the

Minimum period, 1848 to 1876 ; the

Maximum period, 1876 to 1904 ; the

Minimum period, 1904 to 1932 ; to be followed by the

Maximum period, 1932 to 1960, and so on.[23]

Such is the essence of this curious, half naïve, "numerological" theory of the periodicity of war and peace.   On the preceding pages not only is it outlined in essence, but also the essence of the evidences used is given ; the above periodization is not based upon any additional historical data or anything else given by the author, but just upon the above statements, almost fully reproduced here.   It is evident that Mewes's arrangement of the historical periods is just "intuitional," where a few facts are picked up to suit the preconceived scheme.   Not mentioning evident blunders and purely fantastic "history" in many parts of this long list of periods, the slightest test is sufficient to show that the periods of war and cultural blossoming (peace) are cut according to the wishes of the author, but contrary to the evident facts.   Let us confront, for instance, a few of his periods of warfare and peace with our figures of casualties for these periods.   Though the years of his periods do not coincide with ours, nevertheless they admit a confrontation.   The comparison is given in Table 22.[24]

Table 22 shows that several of the periods qualified by Mewes as peaceful were in fact belligerent, and several of his periods of war were in fact more peaceful.   Similar would be the results if instead of casualties

---

[23] *Ibid.*, pp. 14–17.

[24] Since Mewes's "evidences" concern mainly central Europe and France, the figures of these countries only are given.

we should take the size of the army. This confrontation shows the purely "inspirational" character of Mewes's qualifications and of his whole periodization.

TABLE 22.   COMPARISON OF MEWES'S AND SOROKIN'S STUDIES

Mewes's Periods of War and Peace			Our Absolute Casualty Figures for	
			Austria	*France*
Peace	1487–1518	1500–1525	45,000	34,050
War	1518–1544	1526–1550	116,000	28,900
Peace	1544–1576	1551–1575	62,000	29,650
War	1576–1598	1576–1600	34,000	15,050
Peace	1598–1625	1601–1625	274,000	2,850
War	1625–1654	1626–1650	830,000	163,800
Peace	1765–1793	1776–1800	214,000	428,300

Discussing the question of periodicity in the figures of each country, we have seen that only in the history of Germany, Russia, and Italy for a few centuries are there noticeable periodicities of 25 or 50 years. That is all. In the other countries nothing like this or any other periodicity is noticeable.[25]   More than that, if one should take the chronology of wars in the history of any country studied, one would hardly find any kind of periodicity. As an example let us take the detailed chronology of the periods of peace and war in the history of France, year by year, the length of a given war followed by the length of the subsequent period of peace, and so on. The war periods are given in Roman, the peace periods in Arabic figures, expressing the duration of war or peace in units of one year. (In these symbols the actual duration of war-peace periods in the history of France is as follows. The year ending war and starting peace, or vice versa, is included in both periods.)

I–40, I–40, I–25, IV–7, XXIII–14, I–4, III–20, I–4, I–3, I–13, IV–3, VII–2, III–3, XXIV–2, II–8, IV–3, VIII–4, I–9, I–2, I–14, VIII–3, IV–2, IV–9, IV–11, and so on.

No regular periodicity is noticeable here, whether of 25, 27, 33, 50, or 56 years' duration. Instead, we find an enormous variety of rhythms. After prolonged wars several times there occur long periods of peace, but not always. In the earlier history the alternation of war-peace periods is slower and the peace periods longer than in later history. But again there are many exceptions to this rule.

[25] Q. Wright claims also the existence of the periodicity of fifty years during the last three centuries. Unfortunately he gives only fragmentary data for its support. These data are insufficient to warrant the claim. *Op. cit.*, pp. 32–36.

R. Mewes, like many others,[26] ascribed to the process of history a periodicity which it does not have, or at least which has not been discovered.

To sum up, none of the periods claimed, whether the 27-year periods of Mewes, or the 10- to 12-year periods of Sasse, or the 30- to 33-year periods of several other "numerologists," or the 50-year period of Q. Wright, so far have been proven, and they can hardly be proven. The same is true of the much longer periods of 111, 300, 500, 600, 675 years, and so on, claimed by various authors. All that we can say is that the war-peace curve fluctuates, but in its fluctuations, with the exceptions mentioned, no regular periodicity or uniform rhythm is noticeable.

Considerably more interesting, and more factual, is the theory set forth by J. S. Lee concerning the periodicity of the internecine wars in the history of China (Figure 8).[27] For the discovery of any long-time periodicity there is hardly any better country than China with its long history. Dr. Lee took the Chinese chronicles and computed almost all the occurrences of the internecine wars in the history of China from 221 B.C., the period with which the data become relatively complete and reliable, to the present time. He plotted the curve of their number by five-year periods for the 2150 years studied. The results of the computation and plotting have disclosed the existence of three long-time periods of about 810 to 780 years: the first from 221 B.C. to A.D. 589; the second from 589 to 1368; the third from 1368 up to the present time. Each of these long-time periods begins with a flaring up of civil war which is quickly ended, and the country enters a prolonged period of peace, marked by enormous technical and cultural achievements. After about the second half of the period of the curve, it begins to rise, showing shorter periods of peace, and a greater and greater number of wars. One period ends and a new period begins with a general internecine war and anarchy with their satellites. Then again the same phenomena are repeated. In each of these 800-year periods the curve of war has seven main waves; the smallest of these seven jumps is the fifth in each of the three periods. Such is the essence of this very laconic study.

[26] R. Mewes's theory is just a sample of numerous similar theories set forth by astrologers, numerologists, astrophysicists, climatologists, geographers, and so on. Astrological literature is filled, since the most ancient times and until the present, with varieties of this kind of theory, some flat, some ingenious, all more or less naïve. The literature of "numerologists," of astrophysicists, of the partisans of the decisive role of sunspots, climate, or geographic conditions in human affairs is also rich with theories of this kind. They were outlined in Chapter Ten of Volume Two of this work.

[27] See J. S. Lee, "The Periodic Recurrence of Internecine Wars in China," in the *China Journal*, March-April, 1931.

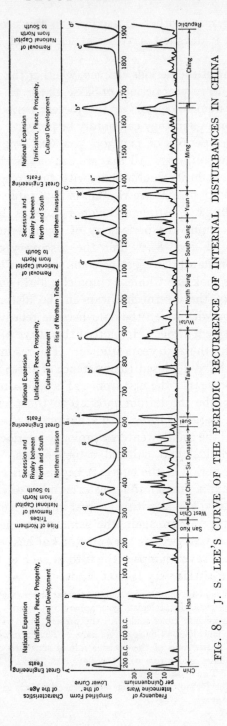

FIG. 8. J. S. LEE'S CURVE OF THE PERIODIC RECURRENCE OF INTERNAL DISTURBANCES IN CHINA.

It should be noted that the author plots, not the fluctuation of the magnitude of war in our sense, but merely the number of wars in each five-year period in the span of 2150 years. Putting aside many points which are not clear in the study, points concerning the sources, method, etc., and taking the study at its face value, one can say, however, that the conclusions of the author somewhat overshoot the data and the diagram which he gives. Studying them as they are given, especially the real, unsmoothed curve, one finds that the curve's configurations in each of the three long periods are far from being identical, similar, or, indeed, periodic. In the first period one finds from 10 to 12 main rises; in the second, 9; in the third, which seems to be incomplete, only from 4 to 5 as yet. And the length of time which separates the jumps in each of the three periods, as well as the height of the waves, is neither uniform nor equal, nor similar in general. In other words, the data of the author hardly give any real periodicity or uniform rhythm. What they give is a "trendless" shifting in the rhythm and in the number of recurring internecine wars. And that possibly is all that they entitle us to deduce.

In such an interpretation the results are similar to results obtained in our study of the movement of the magnitude of war in the history of Greece, Rome, and the other European countries. As has been mentioned, they do not show any real periodicity, with a few exceptions. Of course, in our study we do not have such a long continuous history of one country as did Lee. And yet, even in the shorter history of Greece and Rome we find a rise and fall, but no regular periodicity. Again, in the history of the four, and of the nine, countries taken together we find a rise of casualties from the twelfth to the seventeenth century, a downward movement in the eighteenth and the nineteenth, and a flaring up in the twentieth century. If each of these European countries be taken separately, in some of them the absolute indicators steadily increase from the twelfth to the twentieth century; in some others, like Holland, they rise and fall to the zero line; in still others they move erratically. The same result is given by the relative indicators from the seventeenth to the twentieth century. No universal uniformity, no definite periodicity is present.

These considerations are sufficient, until real evidence to the contrary is given, to cause us to conclude that, so far, no regular periodicity, no uniform rhythm, no universal uniformity of the curve of war movement in all of the countries studied are identifiable.[28] History seems to be neither as monotonous and uninventive as the partisans of the strict periodicities

[28] Similar are the results in all the movements studied in the present work.

and "iron laws" and "universal uniformities" think; nor so dull and mechanical as an engine, making the same number of revolutions in a unit of time. It repeats its "themes" but almost always with new variations. In this sense it is ever new, and ever old, so far as the ups and downs are repeated. So much for periodicity, rhythms, and uniformity.

VI. The "Evolution and Progress" of War Movements

A. *What Has Been in the Past?*   If we could not accept the periodic and "cyclical" theories in the field studied, still more definitely must we reject all the "linear" theories here, which have been dominant since the end of the eighteenth century and throughout the nineteenth. As we have seen in Chapter Ten of Volume Two, one of the most important characteristics of the mentality of the nineteenth century was a belief in "bigger and better" progress and providential *de facto* evolution. The gods were dismissed, and their place taken by a real *deus ex machina*, blind, mechanical, or "emergent," which steers the course of the world and of mankind steadily to an ever "higher and better" level. This dogma was naturally applied also to war and to internal disorders. In the relatively peaceful international and internal conditions of the Victorian nineteenth century, it was quite natural to believe that a linear eternal trend must be found in the field of war, and that it could only be the trend of ever-decreasing war until its final disappearance; there would also be ever-decreasing violence in the sphere of the inner progress of societies. Hence the inevitability of the disappearance of war and of an orderly progress as one of the firmest beliefs of the nineteenth century. It was handed down to the twentieth century, and it is still believed in to a strong extent as the last word of science, in the countries which have escaped a real catastrophe. Hence all this large crop of flat and ingenious, philistine and philosophical, superficial and ponderous, theories which have claimed that war is disappearing from human history, that the time is around the corner when a lamb will be co-operating with a lion, "mutual understanding" and "world-wide co-operation" will be realities, and when all weapons will be turned into electric toasters, golf clubs, and radio receivers. Hence come all these commendable "outlawing wars" and tragicomical "magic" operations to oust the last traces of war through "rubbing shoulders around the same table," through carrying long paper beautified with millions of endorsed names, from the Pacific to the Atlantic, and from the Atlantic to Lake Geneva, and so on and so forth. Hence come also an enormous number of supposedly scientific theories trying to prove convincingly that war is indeed disappearing, as we move along the linear trend from the cave to Main Street and from the paleolithic or neolithic man to Mr. Babbitt of the twentieth century. Some have not been satisfied even with this rather long stretch of time, and have tried to prove that war has certainly been disappearing (and most assuredly does not dare to stay!) as we move from the amoeba or protozoan to the nineteenth- and twentieth-century civilization of *homo sapiens*.

It would be tedious and useless to reproduce these theories, or even the best among them. I have dealt with them rather extensively in one of my previous works, and those readers who wish may study them there.[29]

What shall we say of all these theories, conceptions, and beliefs? Taken as a manifestation of wishes, they are very noble and commendable, and deserve every kind of success. Taken as a scientific description of reality and the real direction of social processes, they are nothing but beautiful beliefs, contradicted at almost every step by the "ugly facts." The above data do not support them at all. A sudden disappearance of war, when after thousands of years of human (and animal) history mankind has reached the twentieth century with the magnitude of war unprecedented, not in its smallness, but in its greatness! One must have strange logic to see disappearance in these and other data given![30] Further, the data, as has been mentioned, do not show any eternal steady trend, either toward constant increase or constant decrease of war. Neither in the European countries taken together, nor in Greece, nor Rome, nor even in the quoted studies of the movement of the Chinese internecine wars for 2150 years, is there a linear tendency noticeable.

As in the data presented there is nothing to support the claim of disappearance of war in the past, so is there nothing to support the claim, in

---

[29] See P. Sorokin, *Contemporary Sociological Theories* (New York, 1928), chap. vi.

[30] It is to be noted that all four investigations of the movement of war in the history of Europe — Woods and Baltzley, Q. Wright, Dumas, and Petersen, and my own — are in essential agreement in this point. All four find that there is no trend of war disappearance or decrease as we pass from the earlier to the present century. And these four studies are, so far, the only existing studies that deal with the problem systematically and not "intuitionally" or "fragmentarily." For the future, it is enough to take the postwar movement of the military budgets of all the countries, the size of the standing and reserve army, the accomplished facts like the Italian-Ethiopian or Japanese-Chinese wars, in order to have almost no basis for a belief that war is over. The present work has possibly shown that the crisis in our whole present culture is infinitely deeper and more serious and tragic than most people think. The possibility of a gigantic catastrophe, including war, is also much greater than many think. This should be understood by all who want to avoid it and to give their mind, and will, and effort to the noblest and most urgent task of its prevention or minimization. The proverbial ostrich policy of minimization of the danger does not help in that task. One has to have courage to look at the grim reality squarely. And such a courage is the first condition for a success of the preventive or minimizing efforts.

spite of the exceptionally high figures for the twentieth century, that there has been (or will be) any steady trend toward increase of war. No, the curve just fluctuates, and that is all. Such a solution is psychologically disquieting; we seem to crave some clear and certain trend; we do not like "erratic, irregular, and aimless" fluctuations. We prefer a certainty, even be it a certainty of inferno. And yet, such a predilection is insufficient to force history to give a steady trend where it does not exist, or to postulate its existence where the facts deny it. These erratic fluctuations mean that in any society at any moment two sets of forces are incessantly working and struggling with each other. One set tends to create, magnify, and sharpen the antagonisms of a given state with other states; the other set works for solidarity and peace. At one period the first set becomes dominant and leads to wars, or to their increase. At another period, the second set becomes overwhelming and results in the ending, or in the decrease, of wars. Hence come the erratic ups and downs of war and of peace.

Such is the answer to this problem, however unpleasant it may be to many, including myself.[31] If one be not entitled to claim the existence of an "eternal trend of evolution" toward a steady increase of war, one is still less entitled to claim the opposite. Any trend so far has been only a part of a curve, changing its direction, sooner or later. So much for what has been.

B. *What Is Going to Be in the Future?* Is the tragedy of war going to have a happy ending or is it going to continue in human history? Is war going to increase, decrease, or what will it do? My answer to that is, "I do not know." All that can be said is that, since no linear trend toward either a continued increase or decrease has been shown up to the present time, it is little probable that a trend would appear and go "forever" in the future. More probable is it that the curve of the magnitude of war will continue its "erratic" ups and downs in the future as it has done in the past. Though in the twentieth century, so far, it has flared up to an exceedingly high level, it is hardly probable that it will continue to rise forever; sooner or later it must reach its "saturation point," whatever it be, and then it must begin to fall. So at least it has behaved in the past, and in a like manner most of the fundamental social processes. On the other hand, since war has been almost as "habitual" a phe-

[31] It is hardly necessary to mention that, as for me, like most of mankind for all the centuries of its existence, and no less than most ardent but nonmilitant pacifists (militant pacifists are the most virulent creators of war), I wish most sincerely "Glory to God in the highest and, on earth, peace and good will." But here I am busy not with what I wish, but with what really has been, regardless of my wish.

nomenon in human history as peace, it is not to be expected that it can suddenly disappear forever with its curve falling to the zero line and staying there always. Such a dream is a beautiful one, but to believe in its possibility amounts almost to a belief in a great miracle. "Blessed are those who believe." But there seems to be little chance for transformation of such a dream into reality. At least at present there are almost no serious symptoms of such a miracle. Popular faith in the League of Nations, the "International Conferences," the peaceful "Foreign Policy Associations," in the mile-long petitions, in the pacifist movement, and so on and so forth, with all the verbosity associated with them, is one of the fashions which, like many fashions, come and go quickly without serving the real purpose intended for them. With all due respect for these institutions and movements in the work of eliminating war, they factually have been much more impotent than the institution of *pax romana*, in the Roman Empire, of the Holy Roman Empire, and especially the Roman Catholic Church in the Middle Ages, or even than the "Holy Alliance" of the emperors and kings after the Napoleonic Wars.

After somber reflection one can scarcely look forward to seeing a dove bringing the olive sprig of eternal peace. This does not mean that in the future a relative peace for some length of time cannot occur (relative peace in the sense of lack of a great war, for moderate wars have been, and are, going on all the time in spite of the League of Nations and other panaceas of peace). Perhaps, as has happened several times before, a relatively long peace will bless our generation after the extraordinary bloodshed of the World War. Perhaps a new conflagration will occur soon. We do not know, but whichever happens, neither war nor peace is likely to be eternal. The great tragedy, with its piano and forte, will probably be continued.

VII. THE CURVE OF WAR IN THE LIFE HISTORY OF A NATION

Since neither the cyclically periodical nor the linear theories of war evolution are valid, either in application to the history of mankind or to the history of any particular country, the question arises, Is there any other uniformity of war evolution, in the sense of its increase or decrease, in the life history of a nation? Can we say that wars are more frequent and greater at the earlier stages of such a history? Or does the magnitude of war tend to grow as we proceed from the earlier to the later stages of the existence of a nation? Are neither of these suppositions valid, and does something different really take place?

It is hardly possible to answer these questions fully, because the vast realm of history of many nations, both past and present, has been studied too little from this standpoint. It is possible, however, to advance four propositions.

The first has already been outlined above, namely, that there is almost no uniform curve of the evolution of war magnitude applicable to all countries and nations. The preceding material shows that it is considerably different for various countries. The curve of the war magnitude of Greece has little resemblance to the curve of Rome, in terms of the absolute or of the relative figures for our two variables. Both are considerably dissimilar to the curve of the nine European countries taken together. The curves of the separate European countries are again essentially unlike. And all these curves are different from the curve of the internecine wars in China as shown in Dr. Lee's study. The pet assumption of the nineteenth century, that all peoples and societies pass through the same stages and exhibit similar curves of development of their culture and of any of its parts, being wrong in general, proves itself quite unwarranted in the field of war also.

The second proposition has also been shown above. There is no continuous linear trend in the evolution of the magnitude of war in the course of time, either toward increase or decrease of war, in the life history of all the nations studied. Instead, we have erratic curves varying from country to country in their shape.

The third proposition is that the remotely parabolic curve of war evolution, in the sense of its magnitude, which we met in the case of Greece and, so far, in the case of Holland, is again not universal; most of the other countries studied do not show it.

The fourth proposition, the positive one, is as follows : *In the life history of nations, the magnitude of war, absolute and relative, tends to grow in the periods of expansion — political, social, cultural, and territorial — of the nation at least as frequently as in the periods of decline. In such periods of blossoming the war activities tend to reach the highest points, probably more frequently than in the periods of decay, and vice versa. War tends to fall in the periods of "sinking" or decay of a given nation, when its political, military, economic, and cultural influence, among and upon other nations, is on a decline, at least as frequently, probably even more frequently, than in the period of growth and blossoming.* Such seems to be one of the relatively valid, but limited, generalizations. Before giving its limitations and reservations, let us briefly remind ourselves of the facts which support it. In the preceding chapter, this fact has been pointed out in regard to many countries. The fourth and fifth centuries B.C. give the highest figures, both absolute and relative, of war for Greece. And the same centuries were the climax of its expansion, growth, culture, and influence. The third and first centuries B.C. were similar periods in the history of Rome. Of the European countries, putting aside the twentieth century, Holland had its climax of war magnitude in the seventeenth and eighteenth centuries, Spain in the seventeenth and sixteenth centuries. These centuries in the history of these countries were again the period when the power, influence, and splendor of their cultures were at the peak. The role and influence of Holland and Spain during the nineteenth and twentieth centuries have been steadily declining : from great powers they slid down to be second- and third-class powers; and from being main cultural centers of Europe, the position they occupied during the previous "military" centuries, they have shifted to a much less important role, now transcended greatly by other countries. The Austria of the Hapsburgs has its highest indicators, absolute and relative, in the seventeenth, eighteenth, and sixteenth centuries, when it occupied the first place in the military scale. The same centuries were the climax of the international and cultural power of Austria. In the nineteenth century, in both military and cultural influence, its role was already more modest. Contrast with this the history of Germany. Its growth — cultural, economic, political, and international — was steadily progressing from the seventeenth to the twentieth century. Especially important were its power and influence in the eighteenth and nineteenth centuries. Correspondingly we see that its absolute indicators of war were steadily growing from the seventeenth to the twentieth century. France possibly had its greatest power and influence, military as well as cultural, in the seventeenth and eighteenth and nineteenth centuries. The same centuries give the highest indicators of war in its history. Russia has become an international power, and then a great power, since the time of Peter the Great (the end of the seventeenth and the beginning of the eighteenth century). The same centuries — the seventeenth, eighteenth, and nineteenth — give the highest absolute figures of its war magnitude. England shows the highest relative indicator of war in the sixteenth, seventeenth, eighteenth centuries; and in these centuries England emerged as a great empire and cultural center. Poland had its climax of warfare in the seventeenth century, and decline in the eighteenth.

These facts seem to support our proposition, to an extent. Logically it is easy to understand why it must be so. The expansion of any empire, if it does not take place in a sparsely populated area, like the American continent where the United States developed, can be made only at the cost of the territory of other nations. In order that this may be possible, these other nations must be conquered, because none is willing to present itself, its population, its territory, and its resources as a free gift to any other nations. Since the victim of the expansion must be subjugated and conquered, this means war, the only real instrument of subjugation. Hence war's increase in the period of expansion. Hence, for its increase to be possible, the conquering nation must be strong and resourceful. In order to be strong and resourceful in war, it must be strong in its population, in its economic resources, in its inner order, and its mental and moral qualities. These last are as important a factor of military victory as any other. Otherwise no military strength can be possible. This explains why the periods of expansion and growth of a given nation coincide frequently with the periods of the increase of war and of biosocial and cultural blooming of the country; why, on the other hand, a nation which is weak and secondary becomes often more peaceful. This latter may be true either because the nation is so small and weak that it dares not take the chance of assaulting any other nation, or even of resisting the claims of the others, however unjust they may be, or because such a nation is put into factual dependence upon a stronger nation and is relatively protected by its stronger boss and captor, or, finally, because such countries, by mutual agreement of the "strong dogs," are put in a "golden cage of neutrality" for some time unbroken by the stronger "dogs." The reasons for this coincidence are so clear and almost axiomatic that it is no wonder the facts support the proposition. It means a tragedy of human culture and history, but they have been tragic indeed.

What one must wonder at is that so many sweet and "vegetarian" theories, quite contradictory to the facts as well as to the obvious reasons, have been set forth and have been sold successfully to the public. By these noble, though "vegetarian," theories are meant all theories which claim that cultural effervescence is always incompatible with war; that any war happens at the periods of, and lead always to, cultural decay; that no military nation has been great in its culture and cultural contributions; that peace always leads to and stimulates cultural progress; that the most peaceful countries have always been the greatest creators of culture; that the growth of war in the history of any nation is a sure sign of its decline; and so on and so forth.[32] However commendable are the moral and other motives which are behind these "sweet" theories,

[32] See about these theories in P. Sorokin, *op. cit.*, chap. vi, and especially pp. 328 ff. and 349 ff.

from the standpoint of facts and logic they are wrong. They are possibly all right from the standpoint of what ought to be, but they are without foundation from the standpoint of what has been and is. The situation is more adequately depicted by Joseph de Maistre. Following Machiavelli, he says:

The best fruits of human nature, arts, sciences, great enterprises, great conceptions, and virile virtues, prosper especially in time of war. It is said that nations reach the peak of their grandeur only after long and bloody wars. The climax of Greek civilization was reached in the terrible epoch of the Peloponnesian War; the most brilliant period of Augustus followed immediately after the Roman civil wars and proscriptions. The French genius was bred by the wars of the League, and was polished by the war of the Fronde. All great men of the time of Queen Anne (1665-1714) were born amidst a great political commotion. In brief, they say that blood is a fertilizer of the plant called Genius. . . . I do not see anything less pacifistic than the periods of Alexander the Great and Pericles; the periods of Augustus, Leo X, François I, Louis XIV, and Queen Anne.[33]

De Maistre, as we shall see, certainly overshoots the mark; nevertheless, in the light of the data given he is as much right as is necessary to disprove the opposite "soothsaying" theories mentioned. There is a considerable portion of truth contained in his statements, as well as in our above proposition, well warranted by a detailed study of the curve of war magnitude in the centuries investigated, and in the curves of the movement of scientific inventions, philosophical and musical creativeness (not to mention the movement of the social sciences and of the other arts) We have seen that the absolute and the relative curves of war magnitude in Europe, measured by casualty, have steadily been growing, from the twelfth to the seventeenth century, after which the relative indicators fall in the eighteenth and the nineteenth centuries while the absolute indicators continue to rise. The curve of inventions and discoveries in the natural sciences (see Chapter Three of Volume Two) also goes up (in the absolute number of discoveries and technological inventions) from the thirteenth to the twentieth century, a growth which evidently could not have occurred if war were as destructive to science and art as is claimed by the above "sweet" theories.

In Chapter Three of Volume Two we have seen that the rate of increase of discoveries and inventions began to slow down beginning with the second half of the nineteenth century, the period when war magnitude absolutely and relatively went down. A still more important fact is

[33] J. de Maistre, *Œuvres* (Lyon, 1891-1892), Vol. I, pp. 36-37.

shown by the detailed study of the discoveries and inventions by separate countries. In most of the countries, the greatest, and possibly the most important, discoveries were made in the centuries having a particularly great war activity. Here are typical data for most of the countries studied. In Holland the number of discoveries in mathematics were as follows, by century periods : in the fourteenth century, 1 ; in the fifteenth, 1 ; in the sixteenth, 8 ; in the seventeenth, 11 ; in the eighteenth, 9 ; in the nineteenth, 4. Now let the reader glance back at the war figures of Holland, and he will see that both curves are quite parallel in their rise and fall. If, instead of Holland, we take Germany in the same field, mathematics, we get a different picture from that of Holland, but again one in agreement with its war curve (absolute figures) : in the seventeenth century the number of the discoveries and inventions here is 14 ; in the eighteenth, 18 ; in the nineteenth, 33. Again in France, and in other countries, in many (but not in all) quarter-century periods which were particularly belligerent, there occurred very high numbers, much higher than in many peaceful quarter centuries.

I could give many cases, from all the countries studied, of the same "parallelism" of the war movement and the movement of scientific discoveries and inventions. But the above cases suffice for our present purposes. It is enough to add that the seventeenth century gives the highest indicator of war magnitude for all Europe up to the twentieth century ; and the same century was possibly the greatest period of scientific progress. The fundamentals of contemporary natural science are still essentially those of the seventeenth and the very beginning of the eighteenth centuries.[34]

All this does not mean that war is the main or general cause of scientific progress. That is wrong, and here is the weak point of De Maistre's statement. It means, decidedly, that the claims of the above "vegetarian" theories of the negative association of war and science and art are naïve and fantastic. It means, further, an additional evidence of my proposition that the periods of high war activities and great political, military, and cultural blossoming in the history of the countries studied coincide often (with exceptions to be mentioned further). This coincidence does not indicate that a great war is the cause of a great scientific blossoming or, vice versa, that a great scientific and cultural blossoming is the cause of a great war. But it means that both are manifestations

---

[34] What is said of science and inventions can be said of the movement of the curves of philosophical creativeness and of musical creativeness, and other art forms. These movements will be given in Volume Four.

of numerous still deeper forces which create, simultaneously with great military power and political influence, great scientific and cultural blooming. Just as healthy youth manifests itself simultaneously in several anatomical, physiological, psychological traits and in several forms of behavior characteristics of a healthy and young organism, so the general blooming state of the social body manifests itself in both forms of exuberance.

Such is the meaning and reason for the first limitation of the proposition discussed. Its second limitation is more serious. *Not all wars and not all great wars are necessarily a manifestation of exuberance, or the biosocial and cultural effervescence of a given society.* Some, though seemingly the minority, may be the manifestation either of the decline and "old age" of a given society, or of the end of an epoch, in its sociocultural life history, and the transition to another epoch, one not necessarily better or more brilliant, but quite different from the preceding epoch of the society's culture. For instance, for Austria the war of 1914–1918 was hardly an effervescence of the superabundance of its energy and creative vitality. It was rather the final explosion of a brilliant torch which had burned magnificently during at least a thousand years. For all Europe the World War may also be a sign of the beginning of the end of the brilliant "Epicurean culture," which blossomed magnificently for some six hundred years from the period of the so-called Renaissance and the Reformation, and which possibly is coming to an end now, to be replaced by a new culture as different from the last as it was different from the medieval culture. Whether this allusion is valid or not, just now is unimportant. What is important is that such wars are shown to be manifestations of "old age," of the coming end of either the political or sociocultural body, or an end of an epoch in its life history. On the other hand, *there are peaceful periods marked by a notable blooming of arts and sciences and culture.*

For this reason the above proposition is not given as an absolute rule; it must have serious limitations and exceptions. But with those amendments it stands as a more valid generalization than most of the linear, cyclical, periodic, and other theories discussed. In the life history of a nation, in its occupied areas, most of the periods of its political, social, economic, moral, and mental effervescence, the most brilliant periods in its history, the period of the climax of its grandeur, power, magnificence, and genius are usually also the periods of its high militarism and warfare. The reverse, however, is less valid. *We cannot say that every period of warfare and great belligerency is necessarily a period of grandeur and blooming.*

These reservations make the proposition more accurate. And the data given warrant the belief that the proposition is not without foundation.

It is outside the scope of this study to discuss hundreds of other aspects of the sociology of war.[35] This study has only one problem to answer, how the magnitude of war has behaved in the course of time, and this question is answered within the limited span of time and the limited number of countries studied. A few other problems have been, and will be, touched briefly because they are related to the main problem of this work and because our material throws some light upon them.

VIII. War Movement and Fluctuation of the Ideational and Sensate Types of Culture

What are the reasons (causes and factors and independent variables) of the fluctuation of war? And is the fluctuation connected in some way with the rise and decline of the Ideational and Sensate types of culture?

As to the first question, it is enough to say that the prevalent theories that try to see the causes (factors and variables) either in climate and geographic conditions; or in instinct of pugnacity of the herd; or in human nature generally, and the struggle for existence particularly; or in race and heredity; or in this or that economic factor; or in this or that political regime; or in the size and the density of the population; or in a lack (or overabundance) of education; or in many other (biological or sociocultural) specific factors — all such theories can, at the best, account for only certain details of the curves of war fluctuation for this or that special war or some aspects of such a war; [36] but they do not and cannot account for the greater part of the fluctuation curves of war in the countries studied, whether they are taken separately or together. In order to see that, it is enough to take the curves or the data of the tables and try to account for their movements through any particular factor, like poverty and prosperity, means and instruments of production, increase and decrease of the size and the density of the population, monarchy and republic, autocracy and democracy, good and bad government, conservatism and progressivism, religiosity and irreligiosity, collectivism and individualism, literacy and illiteracy, ignorance and education, high or low morality, spirit of nationalism or internationalism, simplicity and

---

[35] See many of them discussed in P. Sorokin, *op. cit.*, chap. vi, and in S. R. Steinmetz, *Soziologie des Krieges* (Leipzig, 1929). Sociology of war battles is especially carefully studied in the forthcoming *Sociology of War* by General N. N. Golovine.

[36] See the shortcomings of such explanations in P. Sorokin, *op. cit.*, chap. vi.

complexity of the international world of nations, or any other factor out of many offered in the field.[37] A conscientious and competent scholar would find it utterly impossible to get a satisfactory explanation in such a way. None of these factors can account for a greater part of the fluctuation of war magnitude. The above data on the movement of war show that wars happen in the periods of prosperity and depression; under both autocratic and democratic regimes; in the countries with prevalent illiteracy and literacy; in agricultural and industrial societies; in the "liberal" and "conservative" nations; among the peoples of different nationalities and races; in an international milieu comparatively simple and complex; in the societies with diverse religions, diverse density of the population; and so on and so forth. None of these and other factors taken separately can account for either the frequency and distribution of war in social space or for its increase and decrease in time. If I were involved in a systematic analysis of "war causation" (which analysis is outside of this work) I would start my search with an investigation of the conditions that follow from the very definition of war as *a breakdown of the organized relationship between the states* (see Chapter Nine). *Such a breakdown or, if one prefers, disruption of the existing interstate equilibrium, is the absolute condition of possibility of any war.* By definition, and by fact, any war presupposes such a breakdown of the organized *status quo* relationship and comes as its resultant. Respectively *all the "factors" which facilitate this breakdown are the factors of war; all the factors that reinforce the organized relationships between the states are factors of peace, no matter whether these organized relationships between the states A and B are just or unjust, fair or unfair, or what not.*

Most of the investigators of war causation are in agreement with this proposition and have expressed it in various forms.[38]

The disagreement begins when the next step is taken, and the question is raised as to what are exactly the factors that facilitate the breakdown or reinforce the organized *status quo* relationships? Answering it, many investigators choose some one "variable" — for instance, the change in the size and the density of the population, or the modification of the means and technique of production, or prosperity or depression, or the political regime and the like — and try to prove that this one chosen variable is the real and the main cause of war (or peace). As mentioned, here is the point where they make their blunder. Not denying that the

---

[37] See several other factors in Q. Wright's and Steinmetz's works quoted.

[38] See the literature and theories in my *Contemporary Sociological Theories*, chap. vi. See also Q. Wright, *op. cit.*

chosen factor may account for this or that detail, this or that ripple in the curve of the war movement, it cannot, as such, account for the greater part of the war curve. For the sake of brevity, an analogy will explain the point. The breakdown in health of an individual, or his death, can be, and mostly is, the result of many and diverse factors, combined in diverse configurations. It may be now the result of age; now of accident; now of overwork; now of wrong or insufficient diet; now of general unhealthy conditions of living; now of an inherited weak constitution; now of an infectious disease caught; or of several other factors of a diverse nature. This comparatively simple, and in many essential respects similar, phenomenon called breakdown in health (or death) is not due to one factor alone, and not even to one kind of combination of the same factors, but to most diverse factors and in most varied combinations. It is true, the diversity of factors would reflect upon the secondary traits of the breakdown or death, making breakdown A different in these traits from that of B and C and D. Nevertheless, the net result, the fact of the breakdown or death A and B and C and D, remains the resultant of many and diverse factors, combined in several different configurations. Still more valid is this conclusion in regard to war. The breakdown of the organized intergroup relationship may be due now to the factors A C M; now to A N G; now to B C J M; now to other factors in different combination. Now the famine or impoverishment, or great density of the population or a great destructive invention, given in a certain sociocultural configuration, can lead to a breakdown of the relationships between the famished state A and opulent state B; now prosperity and imperialistic tendencies to maintain it, and the low density of the population, in collaboration with other factors, can lead to war. Now the "decline" configuration, now the "blossoming" configuration, discussed may be the factors. In some cases the militant pacifists or the great development of technique and physicochemical sciences are one of its factors; in others, the militant militarists and scientific ignorance, and so on. Whatever are the factors and their combination, one thing seems to be certain: none of the *single* biosocial variables is the main or the sufficient factor of *all* the wars, and none can account for war's fluctuation. Almost always, war is the result of the concurrence of many factors. According to the character of the concurrence, the same factor A can play different, even opposite, roles; in configuration with the conditions B N M D it may be a factor of war; in combination with the factors C K L E it may be a factor of peace. Taken per se, such a single factor is neither the direct reason for war nor for peace.

This explains why the numerous attempts to see the cause of war in this or that *single* factor — and such is the enormous majority of the theories of war causation — are faulty at their very source. This means also that a further step along the study of the war causes should consist of an analysis and delineation of the few main and typical combinations of the factors that most frequently lead to the breakdown of organized relationships and then to war. If the investigator (or investigators) succeed in singling out, say, the factorial complexes A N D, N C K, A M C K L, B J V, and a few others, as the most frequent configurations that facilitate a breakdown and lead to war, the problem of war-peace causation would progress a great deal. Without that, the attempts to explain war through any of the single factors do not promise much and in all probability will continue to be a failure, as all such attempts have hitherto been. At the best, only some local and secondary traits of war can be accounted for in that way. Hardly more.

This means that on this point I am not going to explain the war-peace movement through our main factors: Ideational and Sensate culture. However large are these variables, even they, in my opinion, are insufficient to account directly for all the essential movements of the war-peace curve. What they seem to be able to account for are some of the specific traits of war and some of the movements of the above curves. In other words, I am not going to apply these "keys" directly to all the doors of war-peace. But some of these doors they seem to unlock satisfactorily. The main doors are as follows.

A. *Wars of the dominant Ideational culture (or period) tend to assume the form of religious or Ideational wars more frequently than the wars of the dominant Sensate culture (and period). These rarely have religious or Ideational color.* They are wars of economic, imperialistic, utilitarian, and other Sensate colors mainly: wars for "a place in the sun," for "white man's domination," for maintenance of high standards of living, for exploitation of the rich natural resources unexploited by the native savages, for political independence, and so on and so forth. (Of course, these reasons are usually set forth in much more high-sounding terms and mottoes. The recent Italo-Abyssinian and Japanese-Chinese-Mongolian wars, plus the mottoes of the World War, give typical examples of this "beautification" of the Sensate values through high-sounding speech reactions.) The proposition is self-explanatory logically, and is well supported by the actual facts of history. With the rise of Ideational Christian culture in the Roman Empire, the wars of Rome, already in the fourth century, as the wars of Constantine the Great, Julian the

Apostate, and other wars show, began to be colored more and more by religion. Most of the medieval wars are religiously colored. I mean not only the Crusades, or wars for spreading or protecting Christianity;[39] or wars and campaigns against heretics; or wars connected with the struggle between spiritual and secular powers for supremacy; or, as in Byzantium, wars connected with the iconoclastic controversy; but few of the important wars of the Middle Ages were waged without involving the Roman Catholic See and religious reasons. Even in the period of transition from the Ideational to the rising Sensate culture, the religious element continued to play a conspicuous role in the wars of the Reformation, the League, and others. Only beginning with the eighteenth century did religious colors of war fade so much as to become almost unnoticeable, and subsequent wars assumed explicitly the secular-Sensate color.[40]

When tested in social space, the proposition seems to be tangibly corroborated also. It means that in such a culture or society the Ideational motives, reasons, forces, factors, play a more important part in the breakdown of the interstate relationships or in a military invasion of the pagans and heretics, and all the groups that are not the members of a given Ideational culture, than those of the Sensate culture. In a study of the war-peace reasons in Ideational cultures and societies, these Ideational factors have to receive much greater attention than in a study of these reasons in a Sensate milieu.

[39] Charles the Great's statement is typical in this respect. "Nostrum est secundum auxilium divine pietatis sanctam ubique Christi Ecclesiam ab incursu paganorum et ab infidelium devastatione armis defendere et indices catholice fidei agnitione munire." E. Chénon, *Histoire générale du droit française* (Paris, 1925), Vol. I, p. 343.

[40] This means not only a change of the color; but it is one of the examples of the rule: *the same factor, for instance, religious or economic, is not an equally efficient causal factor in profoundly different cultures.* The religious reasons are more efficient (even causally) in the dominant Ideational culture than they are in the dominant Sensate culture. Economic factors are less "efficient" in the dominant Ideational culture than in the Sensate. For many habituated to "mechanistic-naturalistic" thinking, this proposition is a revolutionary paradox. They axiomatically assume that the role of any given factor, for instance economic, remains the same in all societies and cultures. The same "constant efficiency" they ascribe to any other factor. Respectively the partisans of the "economic interpretation of history" view the economic factor as equally efficient in Ideational and Sensate societies and cultures, however different they are. The same in regard to any other variable. Such an assumption is unwarranted. The "efficiency" of any factor is not constant. "Economic interpretation" of Sensate man, society, culture, has a real basis in application to such man, society, culture; while in application to Ideational man, society, culture, it is mainly fallacious. For the present, these lines explain *the principle of varying efficiency of the same factor in profoundly different cultures and societies.* Later on, in Volume Four, I shall return to it. It is one of the most important methodological principles of the sociocultural sciences. Replacement of the opposite principle by it must profoundly change the character of the social sciences.

B. *Per se, possibly neither Ideational nor Sensate culture is more belligerent or peaceful than the other.* If Ideational society may not be anxious to start a war to obtain Sensate advantages, it may start a war to exterminate the infidels, the heretics, or to convert them to the true religion or to make it triumphal, *ad majorem gloriam Dei.* If Sensate society is not interested to fight for these values, it is highly interested to improve its Sensate welfare and standard of living, or to maintain them against encroachment through preventive and repressive wars; or in exuberance of vitality to defend and expand its prestige, glory, and integrity, to carry its banner *urbi et orbi,* and the like. On the other hand, both societies have their own inhibitory forces: Ideational in the religious and other absolute commandments (prohibition of war by God, etc.); Sensate in utilitarian considerations of danger, discomfort, death, bloodshed, poverty, destruction of wealth, and the like.

In a word, it is not evident logically that one type of society has a greater amount of war or peace factors or a greater amount of inhibitions. Their militant and inhibitory forces are different; but there is no clear evidence that one has to be more militant than the other. A well-ordered and crystallized Ideational society may be as peaceful or militant as the well-ordered Sensate.

Our data (see the relative indicators and diagrams) show that both predominantly Ideational Europe of the twelfth century and predominantly Sensate Europe of the nineteenth century had a comparatively low level of war magnitude; that predominantly Ideational Rome of the fourth century B.C., and predominantly Sensate Rome of the first century A.D., or Greece of the third and second century B.C. all had a low magnitude of war. It is true that in Europe the low level of war in the Ideational twelfth century is much lower than in the Sensate nineteenth century. On the other hand, the war level of the Sensate first century A.D. in Rome is lower than that of the more Ideational fourth century B.C. So these data in a sense neutralize each other and do not permit us to draw any other conclusions except the above proposition.

C. *The periods of transition from the Ideational to the Sensate, or from the Sensate to the Ideational, phase of culture are the periods of notable increase of war activities and war magnitude.* If crystallized and settled cultures of both types, Ideational and Sensate, tend to be comparatively peaceful (unless a strong external factor intervenes) when their system of values and their network of social relationship are firm and strong, *the periods of transition from one type of culture to another* must be logically the periods of comparative conflagration of war. Why must such transitional

periods be expected to be comparatively militant? Because transition
from one type of culture to another means: (1) disintegration of the
cultural system of values: scientific, religious, philosophical, artistic,
juridical, and moral; (2) so far as the main types of social relationship — familistic, contractual, and compulsory, with all their derivatives
— have been found to be tangibly associated with the main types of
culture (see Part One of this volume), the transition from one type of
culture to another means also disintegration of the existing form of the
system of social relationships: the previous system begins to crumble;
the new system is not crystallized as yet; (3) so far as many other relationships have been found to be associated with these types of culture
— such as the form of government, of freedom, of governmental regulation, and others — the transition means again the upsetting of the
previously existing system of values and relationships without replacing
it by a new one. All this means that in intragroup as well as in intergroup relationships, the previously existing distribution of the rights,
duties, functions, social positions, and generally the previously existing
"conditioned" forms of the social relationships and conduct of the
members of the group or of the interacting groups are decidedly upset;
no new map of conduct and relationship is established as yet. As a result,
the force and compulsion explode, not inhibited by any generally recognized and rooted system of social values and system of social relationships;
force tends to become the supreme arbiter and the *ultima ratio* in intergroup and in intragroup relationships. Hence, a rise of war in such
periods. Such, in brief, is the logical reason for the expectation discussed.
In Part Three of this volume, in slightly modified form, we shall meet
it, developed more than here.

Is this logical expectation corroborated by the actual data? It seems
it is. Here, however, one should keep in mind several circumstances.
Since war is an interstate phenomenon, there may be several possibilities
as to the transitional phase of the states involved. Only one of the states
may be in transition; both or all states involved; a part of the states
involved, while the other part may be in a crystallized and firm Ideational
or Sensate culture. Then, of the states involved, both or all may be moving from Ideational to Sensate or from Sensate to Ideational culture;
one — or part — may be moving from Ideational to Sensate, while the
other part may be in transition from Sensate to Ideational. The next,
and a very important condition to be kept in mind, is that *the transitional
period within a given group must come, and factually does come, somewhat
earlier than it manifests itself outside of the group, in its intergroup relation-*

ships, and in the international world as such. If the groups involved are not in transition, no transitional period can occur in their interrelationships. Only after the groups involved enter the transition, and the disintegration of the previous culture progresses to some extent in the group (or groups) — only after that may its manifestation be expected to come in the intergroup relationships. In other words, *some lag of the manifestation of the transition in international relationships from that within the groups involved has to be expected. This lag may be short or long.* Its form and length depend upon many circumstances, such as whether only one or part of the groups (states) involved are in transition, or all of them; what kind of transition it is for each state; whether the states are small and homogeneous in their culture or are large; and the like. Due to these circumstances, not to mention the interference of many other external factors, the rise of war in the periods of transition can hardly be expected to be too regular or to be quite synchronous with the rise of internal disturbances as the manifestation of transition within the state or group. When the groups are relatively small and homogeneous, the external wars and internal disturbances may rise almost synchronously. When the groups are large and heterogeneous, there may be a lag in the rise of the curve of war from that of the internal disturbances in the groups involved.

After these considerations, let us glance at our relative indicators for Greece, Rome, and Europe.

A study of all the compartments of culture of Greece has shown that the fifth and the fourth centuries B.C. were the periods of transition from Ideational to Sensate culture, in the history of Greece, while, beginning with the third century, Sensate culture became more or less crystallized and dominant there. Looking at the relative indicators of war and their curves in Figures 6 and 7 we see that the fourth and the fifth centuries were most belligerent centuries in Greek history. In the third and then in the second centuries, the curve of war falls sharply. In other words, the factual movement-of-war curve is in conspicuous agreement with the logical expectation discussed. Turn now to the curve of Rome. Here, the fourth century B.C. gives a low indicator of war. If it is unknown how great was the Ideationality of the Roman culture in the fourth century B.C., it is certain it was greater than in the subsequent centuries. The culture of Rome — Ideational, to a considerable extent — was not disintegrated as yet in the fourth century B.C.; it was firm, strong, and crystallized. So was its system of social relationships. So far the low indicator for that century agrees with the expectation. The third century gives a sudden and an enormous rise of war. It is the most militant century in Roman history. Though the Roman culture began possibly to disintegrate somewhat in that century, the disintegration was not so great as to warrant such a rise of war magnitude. In other words, the rise of the war curve in that century may be explained by the interference of other factors than the transition discussed. Considering that war depends not only upon the given society but upon the other society that attacks and forces the war upon a given society, this rise of the war curve in the third century, due mainly to the Punic Wars, can be accounted for through the Carthaginian invasion rather than by the factor of transition. (What was the status of the Carthaginian culture at that time, I am not in a position to state. If it were in the state of transition discussed, then even the third century would be corroboration of the hypothesis discussed.) Passing to the second and the first centuries B.C., we know that they were the centuries of transition from the Mixed or Ideational culture to one somewhat Sensate. The first century B.C. was in a sense the most transitory century in Roman history. We see the respective indicators (absolute and relative) for the second century B.C. much higher than for the fourth (the third century omitted), and for the first century B.C. still higher, occupying the second position in all the centuries of Roman history studied. So far, the war curve of these centuries agrees with the hypothesis offered. The first century A.D. is the century of a comparatively crystallized Sensate culture. Respectively, the war indicator for it is very low. This is again in agreement with the expectation. Low remains also the indicator for the second century, though it is higher than for the first (in absolute figures). In that century the Sensate culture began to be undermined, but not very much, as yet. The third century A.D. is definitely the century of transition from the Sensate to the coming Ideational culture. Exactly in accordance with the hypothesis, the curve of war rises notably. Unfortunately, there are no data to compute the relative indicators for the subsequent centuries. The absolute figures show, however, a beginning of the decline of the curve of war for the fourth and the fifth centuries A.D. If the absolute data are indicative, this decline is also in agreement with the hypothesis. The beginning of the fourth century A.D. had already witnessed the legalization of Christianity, then its elevation into the dominant cult of the Empire, and, with it, the definite triumph of its Ideational culture. In other words, in these centuries Ideational culture was already crystallized to a considerable degree; the transitional status was weakened; hence, a decline of the war curve.

Thus, with the exception of the third century B.C., for Rome the factual movement of the curve of war goes in essential agreement with the logical deduction.

Perhaps still greater is the accord of the movement of the relative indicators of war for Europe with the logical expectation. Unfortunately, it was impossible to compute the relative indicators for the centuries before the twelfth. But the absolute figures for a few countries for one or two centuries before the twelfth warrant the conclusion that the war magnitude during those centuries was possibly still lower than in the twelfth. This means that the medieval centuries of domination of strongly crystallized Ideational culture were the centuries of comparatively very low belligerency. We know that after the twelfth century European culture entered the transitional period. Some of its compartments had entered it already at the end of the twelfth, others in the thirteenth, still others in the fourteenth, fifteenth, sixteenth, and the seventeenth centuries. Likewise, some of the European countries, like Italy, entered it earlier than some others. All in all, the centuries from the thirteenth up to the seventeenth were transitional centuries. In perfect agreement with this, Figures 6 and 7 show a systematically rising trend of war from the thirteenth to the seventeenth century inclusive. Partly (in some compartments and countries) in the fifteenth, partly in the sixteenth, and for all the compartments and all the main European countries toward the end of the seventeenth, the Sensate culture became dominant and crystallized. After the seventeenth century, according to the hypothesis, we shall expect a downward movement of war curve. It indeed goes down in the eighteenth and — especially — in the nineteenth centuries. The crystallized Sensate culture, like the crystallized Ideational, gave a comparative peace during these centuries. Finally, we have seen in practically all the compartments of the Western culture a sharp turn — a revolt against the overripe Sensate forms at the end of the nineteenth and in the twentieth century. The revolt means a sudden entrance into an intensive transitional stage. In accord with that, the curve of war movement for the twentieth century also soars.

Thus the war curve for Europe goes on, practically in perfect agreement with the logical expectation. All in all, the movement of war by century periods agrees well with the hypothesis, with a possible exception of the third century B.C. in Rome. As the relative indicators for separate European countries could not be computed, I cannot test the hypothesis by the factual war movement for each of these countries. It is probable, however, that if and when such data are obtainable, and all the minor

swings between Ideational and Sensate poles of the culture of these
countries are established, they will show a tangible correlation.   This is,
however, a conjecture.   What is important is that the factual data, so far
as they are at hand, tangibly warrant the hypothesis.   In a modified
form it is also warranted, as we shall see in the next part, by the movement in the internal disturbances.   Since the hypothesis is logically
comprehensible; and since it accounts for almost all the major movements of war curves at hand, it seems to be entitled to claim validity, and
a validity perhaps greater than any other hypothesis in the field.   As
mentioned, these do not and cannot account for even a considerable part
of the actual movements of the war curves; therefore, however fashionable and concrete and congenial to the Sensate mind their factors are
(economics, population, sunspots, etc.), they do not stand the test and
therefore should be relegated to the class of local and subsidiary factors.
This means that most of the popular theories of war causation are fallacious.   This means also that when various political groups try to
prevent war and organize peace either through preaching birth control
(to reduce the density of the population as an alleged cause of war);
or by advocating a certain political regime — communism, fascism,
democracy — as the panacea against war; or clamor for limitless prosperity, as the surest means to eliminate war; or stage big demon-
strations with energetic red-flag waving as an organization of peace; or
transfer the manufacture of munitions from the private firms to the
state bureaucrats — these and hundreds of similar "medicines" against
war are mostly "pseudo medicines" of the contemporary shamans,
magicians, and "medicine men."   They do not touch the main cause
and therefore have remained, and will remain, essentially impotent.
Their impotency has been demonstrated with especial clearness in the
twentieth century and still more clearly in the postwar years.   All the
endless efforts to promote these "panaceas" have not prevented wars;
and have resulted in the development of intensive war psychology
and sinister preparation for future wars on an appalling scale in all
countries.   *One of the main — and I am inclined to say even the main —
weapons against war is the crystallization of the system of cultural values
and of social relationships.*   Until this is achieved, the efforts to prevent
war are likely to be fruitless.   The hypothesis possibly sounds abstract;
but so sounds the Newtonian law in comparison with baseball rules,
and a treatise in chemistry in comparison with a popular "cookbook."

   Let us turn now to the next part, which deals with the fluctuation
of the internal disturbances and their *ratio sive causa.*

PART THREE

Fluctuation of Internal Disturbances in Intragroup Relationships

FLUCTUATION OF INTERNAL DISTURBANCES IN THE HISTORY OF GREECE, ROME, AND EUROPE: METHODOLOGICAL[1]

Tension and relaxation, sickness and health, crisis and repose, incessantly alternate in the life process of an individual. They usually coexist with one another, but now one alternative, now another, becomes dominant and colors the corresponding part of the life process. A similar pulsation seems to occur in the life process of a society. It also has its periods of tension and relaxation, stormy crisis and quiet order, or, to use Saint Simon's terms, its "organic and critical periods." The existence of this pulsation is well known and does not need to be discussed further. But its many aspects, and among them some important ones, are much less known.

In this study I am going to take several of these aspects and investigate them somewhat more systematically than has hitherto been done. Here are some of the problems. What is the general relationship between the "critical" and the "organic" periods in the life history of various societies when they are taken in a long-time perspective? Compared with the organic periods, are the periods of social storms something extraordinary and abnormal, as many seem to think? Are these conditions recurrent, and if so, is their recurrence periodical? Do all the recurring storms have the same pattern as to the suddenness of their explosion, their length, their intensity, etc., or do they vary widely from case to case? Do the curves of tranquillity and storms run parallel in the countries which belong to the same "cultural continent," and do the "ups" and "downs" of the curves occur simultaneously in these countries? Are there among the various countries some which are orderly and some which are stormy par excellence? Is there in the course of time a steady trend toward a progressive decrease of critical periods — decrease in their length, violence, frequency of occurrence, etc. — followed by a corresponding increase of periods of internal social peace, as we are assured by prevalent opinion? Are social disturbances indeed becoming more human, less

---

[1] In co-operation with N. S. Timasheff and S. Oldenburg.

bloody, less spasmodic?   And are we drifting toward a social life where
no inner storms will occur and where an incessant orderly progress will
replace the bumpy shifts from stagnation to revolution and from revolution to reaction, as Auguste Comte believed, and as, after him, almost all
the social and biological scientists of the Victorian and post-Victorian age
believed?   If such a trend is lacking, is there any generally steady trend
in this field at all?   Is the occurrence of social storms more frequent at the
early periods of the life history of a given society or do they tend mainly
to concentrate and mature at the later periods of this life history?   Do
these internal disturbances run parallel with the movement of the external
wars of a given group, or does each of these two curves have its own
course unrelated to the other in any uniform way?   Do the internal disturbances tend to occur mainly at the period of healthy growth and
cultural blossoming in the existence of a certain group, or do they tend
to concentrate dominantly at the stages of decline?   Finally, are they in
some way associated with the pulsation of Ideational and Sensate cultures?

In regard to these and several other aspects of the pulsation discussed,
our knowledge is limited indeed.   A considerable number of theories in
the field represent a farrago of beliefs and wishes rather than a carefully
checked scientific theory.   For this reason they do not fill the hiatus entirely.   The subsequent pages attempt, if not to fill the gap, then at least
to contribute something which will make it smaller and less "swampy"
than it is at the present time.

Before passing to the study, let it be said here that *in an investigation
of these problems the uncertainties, the possibilities of error, and all the other
dangers, are probably even greater than in the study of war movement.   For
the sake of economy of time and space I shall not enumerate them as was done
in regard to wars, but the reader should be warned of them, and the critic should
not think that I am unaware of them.*   Anybody who attempts to tackle
these problems meets difficulties at every step, and realizes the dangers
possibly more fully and clearly than any critic.   For this reason the
results are neither given as being perfectly accurate, nor are they claimed
to be infallible.   On the other hand, careful and laborious study has given
the investigator an ever-increasing feeling of confidence that the most
essential results are not misleading, and that at any rate they are possibly
more reliable than any unsystematic *dicta* in the field, or any generalization derived, however carefully, from a very limited number of cases of
disturbances.   Besides, this study has an advantage possessed by neither
the purely speculative studies nor the thorough historical studies based

upon a limited number of cases: here all the data and the procedure are laid "naked" before the reader; he can go through them, check each and all of them, and in this way test their accuracy or error.   In the purely "philosophizing" studies, as well as in those based upon few cases, such a possibility is lacking.   There is no evidence by which to verify whether or not the conclusions are accurate, or whether the generalization derived from the few cases is or is not valid.

Let these remarks be noted, and let them suffice here without further details concerning the lack of data, their uncertainty, the difficulty of finding an adequate measuring stick.

Let us dispense with the technical preliminaries as briefly as possible.

The material of this study includes most of *the recorded internal disturbances of importance*, from the relatively small disorders to the biggest revolutions, which have taken place in the life history of Greece, Rome, France, Germany (Central Europe), England, Italy, Spain, the Netherlands, Byzantium, Poland, Lithuania, and Russia.   The very fact of its mention in the annals of history is considered a sign of the importance of an internal disturbance.   Quite insignificant disorders which do not affect the life of the country in any appreciable way usually pass by without leaving any traces in the records of history.   Even if they are mentioned by some of the contemporaries who happen to witness such disturbances, as for instance a local strike or small riot reported by the newspapers, they are soon forgotten and have little chance of being passed on to subsequent generations.   Some exceptions to this rule possibly exist, but they hardly vitiate it

The analysis of the disorders and tensions in Ancient Greece embraces not only the Greece of the Balkan peninsula, but also the independent Greek states outside, which, like Syracuse and other Sicilian Greek city states, actively participated in the life of Greece proper.   The disturbances in the Greek settlements in Asia Minor, which since the sixth century B.C. were under Persia, and in other Greek colonies which did not participate actively and closely in the life of Greece proper, are not included.

The analysis of the phenomena studied in the Roman Empire takes for each specified period the territory and the population which at that period constituted the Roman Empire.

For the centuries which preceded the crystallization and emergence of France, Germany, and Italy, the territories and the populations included are those which later composed these nations and countries.   After the establishment of these nations the varying territories and populations which belonged to each of them at any given period (with the exception of Holland, mentioned further) are considered as the territory (and the population) of each country. By Germany, from the ninth to the eighteenth century, is meant the varying territory and population of Central Europe which belonged to, or was under the power of, the German kings and German archchancellors. Roughly it embraces the territory of the Holy Roman Empire (up to 1804), then, from 1815 to 1866, that of the *Deutscher Bund;* after that the German Empire and Austro-Hungarian Empire, without Hungary, Galicia, Bosnia, and Dalmatia. Burgundy and Italy are excluded from Germany. Bohemia and other western Slavic countries are put under Germany only after the period of their subjugation to, or entrance into, the German kingdom.

Before the establishment of the united British kingdom, England is considered within the limits of England proper, without Wales, Scotland, and Ireland. For the subsequent periods it is taken within the limits of the territory and population which composed Great Britain at each period. The colonies and overseas dominions are excluded.

The Netherlands are considered to be within the limits of contemporary Holland and Belgium. The disturbances in these territories are excluded from those of France and of Germany in our investigation and are kept as a unit within the territories indicated.

Spain is taken within the limits of the Iberian peninsula, exclusive of Portugal; Byzantium, within its proper limits and omitting the possessions in Western Europe; Russia, within the territory subject to the Grand Dukes of Kiev, then to the Grand Dukes of Vladimir and of Moscow, then to the Moscovy Czars and to the Emperors of Russia. This means that Galicia and Western Russia, which since the thirteenth and fourteenth centuries respectively became subjected to Lithuania and Poland, are excluded from the Russia under consideration. Poland and Lithuania are taken within the territory that belonged to them, at the beginning separately, then together. Temporary dynastic liaisons of Poland with Hungary and Bohemia are disregarded. After the division of Poland in 1795, the disturbances on the territories previously Polish are considered within the territories of the countries that divided it.

From these remarks one can see that under the same name at different periods, different territories and different populations are considered. These are incessantly varying for each country. If we had been studying the movement of the magnitude of the disturbances "atomistically," per 1000 or 1,000,000 people, or per square mile, such a changing territory and population would have made the study absolutely impossible.

However desirable and important such an atomistic study, per 1000 people, or per square mile of inhabited territory, would be, it would be impossible to make, because for internal disturbances we do not have even the scanty quantitative material — the number of persons involved in the disturbances, the number of persons killed or wounded in them, the number of square miles in the area of a given disturbance — which we have for the external wars studied. Even if we had such material, it would not be the only way of studying the movement of the magnitude of internal disturbances, nor even the best or most adequate. The point is that the importance of the internal disturbances for a given country depends not only upon the *number* of persons involved, or the *number* of persons killed, or the *number* of square miles over which a disturbance is spread, but upon many other circumstances, such as whether the disturbances happen only in the capital city of the country with its limited area (in units of miles) or whether they involve vast stretches of the little-inhabited country with its few hamlets and villages, and so on. Many disturbances with a large number of persons involved and a large number of killed, and those with large areas in the rural districts, often have failed to affect the regime of the country or its government in any appreciable way, while others, much more modest in these aspects, have affected the life of the country in a very noticeable way.

In view of the impossibility of an atomistic study on account of the lack of data, and in view of its inadequacy if made just mechanically and arithmetically, an investigator of the problem is forced to devise here some other procedure, however rough, in its turn, it may be. The only procedure possible seems to be an *organico-proportional method* of study of the magnitude of inner disturbances in the course of time.

Its essence can easily be grasped from the following comparison. Suppose we want to study the frequency of occurrence and the gravity of sickness in the life process of an individual. In the course of time the number of cells, the number of pounds of weight, the number of inches of stature, and the enormous number of other aspects of the organism incessantly vary. In spite of this there is the possibility of a study of the frequency and the gravity of the occurrence of sickness in the life process of the organism as such, regardless of the number of cells and units of mass in its body. More than that; there is the possibility of studying specific classes of sickness according to the main parts of the body, such as heart disease, lung disease, diseases of the digestive organs, or the nervous system, of the organs of hearing or of sight. In spite of the fact that each of these organs and systems incessantly varies in the life process of the organism, each of them is present from birth to the moment of death. Such a study is not atomistic, not per 1000 cells or per pound of weight of the body. It is organico-proportional in the sense that the final unit is the varying organism as a whole and that proportionality consists in taking as a specific unit a certain organ or system of the body and in studying the occurrence of the disease per such organ or system — for instance, the frequency and the gravity of occurrence of heart disease or of "nervous disturbances" in the course of the life process of the organism from its earlier stages to the later. As a matter of fact such studies have been made since the remotest times, and we know the typical curves in regard to a specific kind of diseases, e.g., heart diseases in this life process of the organism increase toward old age; other diseases are typical of childhood; and so on.

The same procedure can be applied to the real (in contradistinction to the nominal) "social systems" or social groups. Each of them may vary as to the size of its population and its territory; nevertheless, it is not impossible to study the frequency and the gravity of the occurrence of internal disturbances at various periods of its existence, providing the criteria for the measurement of magnitude and frequency of the disturbances are not purely atomistic and arithmetical, but proportional to the whole group at any period of its existence studied. If we take, for instance, the number of persons involved in the disturbances as a criterion of their magnitude, such a mere number would evidently be misleading in the greatly varying population of the groups under investigation. Two disturbances in which the same number, say 10,000 persons, are involved would be quite unequal if one happens in a group of 100,000,000 and the other in a group of 10,000,000. But if we can ascertain that in these two groups two disturbances involved about the same *proportion* of their population and of their *social* area (not the purely physical one), and were of the same duration, and resulted *proportionately* in the same amount of violence, and were followed by about the same consequences proportionately (for instance, an overthrow of the government), though the disturbances are arithmetically quite different, *proportionately* they are the same. Therefore, if they happen in the life process of the same group at various phases of its existence, although the group is different arithmetically in all these respects, the magnitude of the two disturbances — also arithmetically unequal — is equal from this proportional standpoint so far as a given group is concerned. (For other groups their effectiveness is, of course, different.)

Such is the essence of this organico-proportional criterion for the rough estimate of the comparative magnitude of disturbances in the course of the existence of a varying group.   In such a procedure the variability of the population and of the other quantitative traits of the group becomes inessential to the study.   If the estimating procedure is devised so as to incorporate in itself the above principle of proportionality, the results may be comparable and indicative.

This general principle explains the subsequent method of constructing the indicators for the measurement of the comparative magnitude and the frequency of occurrence of internal disturbances in the history of the above countries, as well as for a study of their "ups" and "downs" in the course of their existence.

It needs no argument to show that the comparative magnitude of internal disturbances is not the same.   Some are colossal and some quite insignificant.   What has been said in regard to war magnitude can be said about internal disturbances.

What has been said concerning the impossibility of a perfect "translation" of a qualitative-quantitative phenomenon like war into language which is purely quantitative holds for internal disturbances also.   Only a few of their quantitative aspects permit an approximate translation into such language.

In regard to war it has been shown that it has several purely quantitative aspects which, as such, permit computation and measurement. Internal disturbances also have several such aspects.   If the exact numerical data were obtainable in regard to the duration of a disturbance, the absolute and the relative proportion of the population involved in it, the number of killed and wounded, the number of buildings demolished, the extent of the *social* area of a given disturbance, the number and class of the cities, villages, and other settlements in which the disturbances occurred, it would be possible to compute all these items and then to make corresponding indicators.

Such indicators would not translate and measure all the quantitative, and more especially the qualitative, aspects of the internal disturbances; but they would roughly appraise the quantitative aspects for which the data exist.   Of these quantitative aspects four seem to be particularly important: (1) the proportional extent of the *social* (not merely geographical) area of the disturbance (social space); (2) the proportion of the population involved actively in the disturbance (for and against it); (3) the duration of the disturbance; (4) the proportional intensity (the amount and sharpness of violence and the importance of effects) of the disturbance.

In addition to these, several qualitative aspects like, for instance, the predominant nature of the disturbance — political, economic, religious, nationalistic — may be studied separately from the above four quantitative variables of the magnitude of the disturbance. Our concept of magnitude is composed as nearly as possible of the combination of these four variables. They do not embrace all the aspects of the disturbance, but they seem to embrace its most significant quantitative aspects. *Other conditions being equal, the greater the proportional extent of the social area of the disturbance, the greater the proportion of the population involved in it, the greater its intensity and the longer its duration, then the greater is the comparative magnitude of the disturbance.* As such, this magnitude aims to estimate, and does estimate, only those aspects which enter into it as an element or a variable; it does not aim to estimate other aspects of it, especially the qualitative one. However, if these variables are indeed the most important ones, the total indicator of the magnitude of the disturbance may also indirectly be one of the best barometers for the magnitude and the importance of many other effects of the disturbance.

Such are the essential variables of which the proportional magnitude of an internal disturbance is made. The reader has undoubtedly noticed that in the above all these variables are put in proportional (but not in absolute) terms. This is but a realization of the *organico-proportional* principle discussed above. As will be shown, the principle of proportionality is carried throughout all the details of the four variables with their subdivisions from which the concept of the total magnitude of the disturbance is composed. Here we do not give the number of people, or the number of killed, or the number of square miles, but we give the *proportional* values or indicators for each disturbance in regard to each of these variables and their subdivisions on certain arbitrarily assumed scales of values.

The evaluation of each disturbance on such assumed scales involves an element of subjectivity; and here lies a source of probable error. But there seems to be no way to avoid either such arbitrary scales or the assignment of certain values to each disturbance studied on such a scale. In order to limit the element of subjectivity and to obtain the scale which can reflect the fluctuation of the magnitude of the disturbances from period to period as nearly as possible like the reality, we have tried, in an experimental way, *several different scales and procedures for the appraisal of the magnitude of the disturbance.* After several experiments which led us to think that the scales and procedures were unsatisfactory, we carried through *three different scales or procedures*, each of which involved a large amount of computation and other work.   *Having carried them through all our data and received the results through each of these three different scale procedures, we observed one important fact: in spite of the considerable differences in the scales and procedures used in these three different computations, the essential results or the main "ups" and "downs" of the three curves of the movement of the magnitude of the disturbances happened to be fairly consistent.*   As the reader can see from Figure 9, the configurations of the

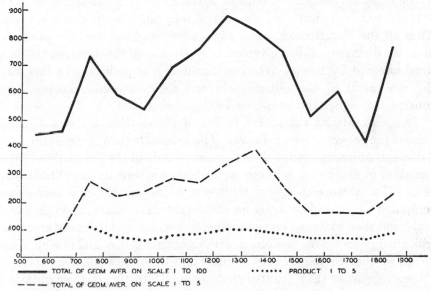

FIG. 9.   FLUCTUATION OF INTERNAL DISTURBANCES IN EUROPE FROM
500 B.C. TO A.D. 1900 SHOWN BY THREE CURVES

fluctuation of the magnitude of the disturbances are similar — or parallel — to one another in all three curves.   The differences concern mainly the minor fluctuations and their amplitude.   Such a consistency of results in all three different scale procedures used is a sign that the scales, as well as the procedures, possess some validity.   It also gives us additional reason to believe that, however numerous may be the mistakes and blunders of the study — due not to any fault of mine, but to the lack of data and to other circumstances beyond the control of any investigator — the subsequent tables and figures in their essentials may reflect the sociohistorical reality without serious distortion.   These three different scales and procedures are in brief as follows.   In two curves of Figure 9 the scale is the same: from 1 to 5 for the social area; from 1 to 10 for the duration; from 1 to 5 for the intensity; and from

1 to 4 for the proportion of the masses involved in the disturbance. Using the same scale, the magnitude of the disturbance in one curve was measured by the *product* of these four variables; that is, the values given to each disturbance in regard to its social area, duration, intensity, and masses on the above scale were *multiplied* and the product of these four values was taken as the value of the magnitude of the disturbance. As the variables on the scale were limited, and the enormous fluctuations of the variables eliminated, both in advance, the product appeared to be a fairly sound indicator of the magnitude under such circumstances. Thus all the disturbances, some 1622, were weighted, and the products of all the disturbances in a given country, then in all the countries studied, were summed by twenty-five- and hundred-year periods. In this way the movement of the disturbances and their respective curves were constructed. (See the lowest curve, Figure 9.)

Then, considering the strong feeling of the statisticians who demand a use of the *geometric average instead of the product* in such circumstances — a demand quite reasonable where the amplitude of the fluctuation of the variables is enormous, but not so necessary where the amplitude was reduced in advance to a very limited scale, as was the case here — we computed the *geometric average* for each of the disturbances upon the same scale, and then summing up the geometric averages of all the disturbances which happened in the respective periods of twenty-five and one hundred years, we constructed for each country and for all of them the curves of the movement of their internal disturbances. In this way we obtained a second and variant form, shown in Figure 9 (second curve), indicating the fluctuations of the disturbances.

Finally, we took a third variant, which stands at the foundation of the subsequent study. In this third variant the *scale employed was larger than in the preceding one, namely, from 1 to 100* (with the modifications which will be explained later) for each variable, instead of the scale 1 to 5, 1 to 4, and 1 to 10, as in the preceding two variants. The magnitude of each disturbance was measured here by the *geometric average* of its variables on that scale. Finally, in the computation of the movement of the disturbances for all the countries studied, *each of the countries was weighted separately on the scale from 1 to 5*, a method that was not followed in the preceding two variants. Such a weighting is necessary because — though a given revolution may be the greatest in a given country (for instance, in Holland) and therefore has to be accorded the highest values on the scale in comparison with another great revolution in a much bigger and powerful country (for instance, in France or Russia) — it would be small in its absolute magnitude, since Holland is much smaller than France or Russia.   In view of this obvious fact, the geometric average of each disturbance in each country was multiplied by the value given to the country on the scale 1 to 5, in constructing the movement of the disturbances for the whole of Europe (upper curve of Figure 9).

Such were the three different scale procedures carried on throughout the study.   The reader can see now that they were considerably different. And yet, if not the minor fluctuations and the amplitude of the fluctuations, the essential long-time tides of the "ups" and "downs" of the three curves happen to be notably similar in all three variants.   This fact may have more than a casual significance.

It would be exceedingly cumbersome to give in this study the full and detailed results of all the three variants.   Even with one variant the study is cumbersome and complex enough.   Therefore, the essential results of the movement of disturbances in all three variants are given in Figure 9 which depicts the curves of all the variants together.   By glancing at it the reader can see how far they are similar, how far dissimilar.   This is enough to indicate generally the nature of the results of each variant. For the rest, the subsequent part of the study is based upon the third variant primarily, since, after many trials, it appeared to be better than the others.

We can now turn to a more detailed description of the technical details of the third variant used in the study, beginning with the scale and its divisions.

I. As to the Social Area of the Disturbance

It goes without saying that the greater the social area involved in the disturbance, the greater is the disturbance, other conditions being equal. But social area is not the number of square miles over which the disturbance spreads : it may spread over thousands of miles of a little-inhabited subarctic region, and yet its weight and social effects may be much less than those of a disturbance in one big city occupying a few square miles. Generally, disturbances in the main cities of a given country, which are the centers of interaction and influence, are much more weighty than in small cities or in villages that lie upon the periphery of the nation's life and whose system of interaction is very small and limited.[2]   Through this central position and the vast system of interaction and the concentration

---

[2] See the discussion of urban and rural systems of interaction and contact and influence in P. Sorokin and C. Zimmermann, *Principles of Rural and Urban Sociology* (New York, 1929). pp. 48 ff.

of the means of communication, contact, control, and coercion, such main foci of population affect the rest of the country much more than the places which are on the periphery of the system of interaction and control. From this standpoint there is a great deal of truth in the familiar saying that Paris rules France, *i.e.*, that the metropolis governs the rest of the country.   Without developing in detail this line of thought, it is sufficient to note that this principle explains the subsequent grading of the disturbances from the standpoint of the social area where they happen and over which they are spread.

On the scale 1 to 100 the following values are given to the following disturbances so far as their social area is concerned :

 1 to a disturbance of a local character in a rural county or similar limited area.

 3 to a similar disturbance in several rural counties or in a small town.

 5 to a disturbance in a larger town.

 10 to a disturbance in several towns of medium size or in one important city or in a small feudal region or a small province.

 20 to a disturbance in a larger feudal region or larger province or in a part of a capital city.

 40 to a disturbance in several large provinces or in the whole capital city.

 60 to a disturbance in the capital city and spread over several provinces.

 80 to a disturbance where almost the whole country is involved.

 100 to a disturbance in the entire country.

Such are the values given to different disturbances from the standpoint of the social area involved.   The *proportional* nature of these gradations is clear from their scale evaluations.   Arithmetically the one provincial city or rural district may be enormously different at two periods in the history of a given country, but proportionally they may be about the same.

II. As to the Duration of the Disturbance

Other conditions being equal, the longer the duration of a disturbance, the larger is its magnitude.   Here, as with all other variables, several considerations have to be kept in mind.   Usually a notable "explosion" is preceded and followed by several smaller disorders.   In a single and short explosion such tremors possibly count for more than in a long-lasting disturbance.   Other complicating circumstances are also to be considered in grading disturbances from the present aspect.   Without enumerating them in detail, we have tried to give as much weight as possible to these complicating circumstances in the following value scale of disturbances considered from the standpoint of duration :

1 to a disturbance of momentary duration, where only one short-time shock is noticeable.

3 to a longer disturbance.

5 to a disturbance that lasted several months.

10 to a disturbance of the duration of about one year.

Then for every additional year up to five years' duration, the value 5 is added to 10; thus a disturbance of about five years gets a value of 30. If the disturbance lasted from six to fifteen years, 4 is added to every year of duration above the five years with their value of 30. Thus the disturbance of fifteen years gets a value of 70. If the disturbance lasted more than fifteen years, then 3 is added for every additional year above fifteen. In this way a disturbance of twenty-five years' duration gets a value of 100. The same value of 3 is added for every year above twenty-five.

III–IV. As to the Intensity of the Disturbance and the Masses Actively Involved in It

The greater the amount of violence displayed and the larger the social classes involved actively in a disturbance, the greater the magnitude of the disturbance, other conditions being equal.

From the standpoint of the classes involved, the disturbances are arranged in the following five divisions : (1) disturbances actively engaging a few individuals (plots, murders, etc.) ; (2) those involving a small group ; (3) those involving a large social class (extensive occupational, economic, racial, national groups, or a large political party, or a religious denomination, etc.) ; (4) those involving larger masses of the population (several extensive classes) ; (5) those involving practically all the active and adult population.

From the standpoint of the *amount of violence and the number of sociopolitical changes*, the disturbances are divided into five classes also : (1) those without violence ; (2) those with slight violence ; (3) those accompanied by destruction of life and property : murders, fights, arson, lootings, sackings, and other forms of violence on a considerable scale ; (4) those accompanied by an even larger amount of violence and by the overthrow of the government in various centers, but without serious and lasting sociopolitical effects ; (5) those involving violence on a still larger scale, followed by the irrevocable overthrow of the central government and by deep and lasting sociopolitical consequences.

Now disturbances of these five classes are given the values 1, 3, 5, 7, and 10 respectively, for each of the two variables, *i.e.*, for the masses involved and for the amount of violence. But in final grading both variables are combined and the values given to the disturbances from this combined standpoint are shown in Table 23.

TABLE 23.   VALUES GIVEN TO INTERNAL DISTURBANCES

		By the Amount of Violence and Effects				
		I	II	III	IV	V
	I	1	3	5	7	10
By the	II	3	10	15	20	30
Masses	III	5	15	25	35	50
Involved	IV	7	20	35	50	70
	V	10	30	50	70	100

In this combined table, if a disturbance belongs according to one variable in the third class but according to the other in the fourth, it is given a value of 35; if it belongs both to the fifth and second classes it is given a value of 30; and so on.

Such are the four components of the magnitude of the disturbance, the scales for each component and the values of each scale given to specified classes of disturbances. *The magnitude of each disturbance is made up of the geometric average of the four values given to it with regard to its social area, duration, social masses involved, and the amount of violence and sociopolitical effects* — the values of the masses and of the violence being combined as explained above. By summing up the geometric averages of all the disturbances that occurred in a given twenty-five- and then a one-hundred-year period, we obtain the indicator of the magnitude of disturbances for such periods.[3] By taking the figures for all such periods we obtain comparative indicators of the movement of the disturbances in the history of the given country from period to period.

Finally, so far as the movement of the disturbances for all these countries taken together is concerned, for almost the whole of Europe, the indicator of the movement of the magnitude of disturbances for each twenty-five-year period is made up of the indicators of the disturbances for this period of time in each country, multiplied by the weight of the country on a scale 1 to 5. The figures for all the countries studied are then summed up and the sum divided by the number of the countries for the given period. The result is made the indicator of the disturbance for all the countries during the time under investigation. A series of such indicators gives an idea of the increase and decrease of the disturbances from period to period.

[3] Besides this total sum of the geometric averages for twenty-five- and one-hundred-year periods, the geometric average for each such period was computed; but for several obvious reasons it was found less adequate than the total of the geometric averages and therefore discarded.

As to the weight values given to each country on the scale 1 to 5, they are as follows:

Spain, up to the end of the fifteenth century (the time of political unification), 3; for the sixteenth and seventeenth centuries (the period of great power), 5; after the seventeenth century, 3.

France, throughout the whole period studied, 5.

England, up to the middle of the eleventh century (the Norman Conquest), 3; after that to the present, 5.

The Netherlands, to the end of the sixteenth century, 1; for the seventeenth century, 3; after that to the present, 1.

Germany, up to the end of the eighth century, 3; up to the present, 5.

Italy, throughout the whole period studied (especially in view of the location of the Roman Catholic See there), 5.

Byzantium, up to the middle of the seventh century (the period of the loss of most of its Asiatic possessions and of Egypt), 5; up to the end of the twelfth century (the conquest by the Crusaders in 1204), 3; after that, 1.

Poland and Lithuania, up to the end of the fourteenth century (the time of unification), 3; up to the middle of the seventeenth century (the period of great power), 5; after that up to the time of the division of Poland, 3.

Russia, up to the middle of the thirteenth century (when it falls into parts and is subjugated by the Tartars), 5; up to the end of the fifteenth century (when it is again united into a great power), 3; after that, 5.[4]

Thus we have outlined all the necessary details for the construction of indicators of the magnitude of disturbances as well as for the estimation of the movement — increase and decrease — of the magnitude in the course of time for all the countries studied.

It is granted in advance that the method has many an important shortcoming. Not all the significant disturbances of the past are recorded. Many of those that are recorded furnish hardly any definite data for the the estimation of their magnitude. Moreover, it is probable that several of the disturbances which are recorded have been overlooked by our study. Further on, the whole attempt to estimate the magnitude of the disturbances introduces several assumptions which are arbitrary but unavoidable, no matter who the investigator, assumptions involving such matters as the scale, the assignment of the values on such a scale for each disturbance, the recourse to a geometric or any other average, and so on. All this is granted without question. From the standpoint of the Platonic absolute truth, the entire attempt is unsatisfactory. But Platonic absolute truth does not exist in this imperfect empirical world with its imperfect knowledge and truth, especially in the field of the social sciences; therefore, we have to apply relative criteria for the appraisal of the pro-

[4] Again the scale is somewhat arbitrary and conservative, but sound in its essentials.

cedure. The whole problem can be put in the following way : Are the defects in this study so great as to vitiate hopelessly the result ; are they greater than in other studies in the field ; and is there any other way, free from these shortcomings, which can promise better and more reliable results? When the questions are so put — and only in such a way can they be asked by any intelligent critic or scholar — then the answer to them all can, in our opinion, only be in the negative.

Yes, the records of the disturbances, especially for the remote past, are incomplete ; but they are incomplete for any study and for every scholar who takes the problem over. This cannot be helped. In view of the scarcity of concrete data about many disturbances, it is true that an element of guess is inevitable. But this again is an obstacle for any investigator. I grant even that it is probable that of the recorded disturbances some — though a very small minority — have escaped my investigation. But, so far as my knowledge goes — and it is reasonably certain at this point — my study has collected, analyzed, and systematically estimated a far greater number and a far more nearly complete list of disturbances than any other study made up to the present time. Its conclusions are based upon an examination of some seventeen hundred disturbances — a number never approached by any other investigation. I do not even know any treatment of the movement of disturbances for a long period of time which is based upon an analysis of so many as a few hundred cases. In fact, most of the theories — and there are many — about the historical trends and tendencies and the line of evolution and progress in this field have been either pure guesses, based upon almost nothing, or generalizations derived from a study of a few disturbances in a given period or taken haphazard from different periods. Under such circumstances no apology is needed for the possible shortcomings of the present work. Of course, in a forest one cannot at once build a perfect city with fine, smooth sidewalks and perfect gardens. But the plan and essential structures of such a city are given in this study. Others can polish and improve it, if they will labor, filling a few holes here and there and in other cases replacing our data by more accurate ones, if they can. But all this can hardly change the results essentially, if any such study — even by a large committee of scholars endowed with hundreds of thousands of dollars — be founded upon the bases similar to these established here.[5]

[5] A kind of law of diminishing returns operates also in the field of the scientific investigation of several problems. Numerous cases may be cited in which, after a study of the movement of prices or other phenomena by one scholar, single-handed, investigations of the same problem by large national and international groups gave results which differed very little practically.

As to the element of arbitrariness, it is per se neither a vice nor a virtue. There is no science, no theory, which is not based upon some arbitrary principles, from arithmetic, geometry, mechanics, and physics to economics and ethics. The point is whether the assumptions made are reasonable and sound, or, at last, as reasonable and sound as is possible within the field of the problem. The assumptions made in this study do not contain anything illogical or unsound per se. They are not perfect; but no perfect "translation" of the qualitative-quantitative sociocultural phenomena is generally possible, as mentioned before. Of the possible imperfect translations our attempt is probably as good as any made hitherto. Therefore, for a severe critic — and such critics exist — there is only one ground upon which to assail soundly the assumptions of this study, namely, to deny radically the entire possibility of applying quantitative estimates to the study of the sociocultural phenomena in the field. "Any quantification, however approximate, is out of place in such a study." Such critics — and most of them are probably historians — would be right if these phenomena had not had quantitative among other aspects, and if correspondingly it were possible to escape the necessity of making — in verbal or numerical form — some sort of quantitative statements in the field. But such is not the case. "Increase and decrease" of disturbance, of anarchy, of social order and internal peace; "a great and a small disturbance"; "a period of long and profound order"; "great and small revolution"; "disturbances on a large scale" — what are these aspects but quantitative? They are put in a verbal, not a numerical form, but this does not change their quantitative nature. These quantitative aspects and the quantitative direction of this form of social process (order-disorder) is as certainly present in the disturbances as in the processes of the increase and decrease of birth and death rates, of coal and iron production, of murder and suicide, and what not. Perhaps to measure adequately these aspects in our field is more difficult than in some others, but the existence of the quantitative aspects in it is unquestionable. To deny this is to make a falacious assumption, infinitely worse than the assumptions criticized by the critic. Since the phenomena studied have the quantitative aspect, it is comprehensible why all who have studied them carefully, beginning with the historians, have not escaped the necessity of making in some form quantitative judgments and statements. If for a shallow reader they are unnoticeable, the reason is, besides the shallowness, the verbal but not numerical character of such statements. Who of the serious historians does not speak of "great revolutions," "small disorders," "considerable riots," "large sackings and lootings," "very violent," "comparatively bloodless," "long," "short living"; or of a "comparatively orderly (or disorderly) period," a "time of crisis," an "increase of disturbances," a "transition from a period of profound internal order to that of disorder and instability"? Here are a few examples: "We have traversed a period of ninety years — forty years of profound peace, fifty of an almost constant revolution." [6] "This was bad; but matters soon became worse." [7] The revolution shook "social and political order to its very foundations." [8] "For a whole generation the Roman State enjoyed a profound calm, scarcely varied by a ripple here and there on the surface." [9] "Great conflict. . . ." [10] "Fearful commotion. . . ." [11] "Never has an ancient civilised people in so short a space of time made such wholesale havoc of its old institutions." [12] "The French Revolution is the most important event in the life of Modern Europe." [13]

In thousands of forms such quantitative statements are met with in almost any historical work.[14] The above explains why they are unavoidable.

If such is the real situation, then the whole problem is narrowed to the question: Which is better scientifically, the indefinite and vague quantitativism of the above type, or a more definite numerical quantitativism of the kind used in this work? All in all, with some exceptions for specific conditions and problems, I prefer the quantitativism of the kind used here. It is more economical: in a few tables it permits one to cover enormous periods and to cover them more pointedly, accurately, and systematically than is possible in hundreds of pages of vague verbal quantitative descriptions. Such an economy is something by itself. In our study the basis, the assumptions, the measuring stick are placed clearly before the reader; nothing is left in the dark. The reader knows

[6] T. Mommsen, *The History of Rome* (Everyman's Library ed.), Vol. IV, p. 369.

[7] *Ibid.*, Vol. IV, p. 138.

[8] *Ibid.*, Vol. IV, p. 326.

[9] *Ibid.*, Vol. IV, p. 67.

[10] *Ibid.*, Vol. IV, p. 73.

[11] *Ibid.*, Vol. IV, p. 132.

[12] *The Cambridge Modern History* (New York and Cambridge, 1934), Vol. VIII, p. 177.

[13] *Ibid.*, Vol. VIII, p. 754.

[14] On the basis of my special test of this proposition, I suggest that the reader take at random any historical work in the field as well as almost any history of social and political movements, and with a pencil in his hand read them carefully, noting all such verbal quantitative statements. I can assure him in advance that he will find them in abundance. The humorous side of the situation is that some of the authors who are vigorously opposed to quantitativism in history are particularly prone to use verbal quantitative statements in their work, thus calling to mind once more Molière's hero who talked prose but was not aware of it.

at once what he is dealing with, how the figures are obtained, what they mean.   In most of the indefinite verbal quantitative judgments all this remains unknown : the judgments are a kind of mystical pronouncements of the scholar, whose bases, reasons, measuring stick, even exact meaning, remain hidden.   They can be neither checked nor verified, rejected nor accepted.   They are just a kind of *dicta* to be believed in and not questioned.   In our case, if the reader does not want to accept the results or the assumptions, he at least knows what he is rejecting.   But the most important advantage of the method used is that it has a definite and uniform measuring stick, systematically applied to all the recorded disturbances ; and the universe of the disturbances studied embraces almost all the recorded cases during the long stretches of the history of each of the countries under examination.   This advantage is generally absent from the verbal quantitative statements and theories.   In most cases no clearly thought-out means of measuring is used ; when it is used, uniformity is not ascertained.   Therefore, such judgments are always stamped more or less by the mark of intuition, guess, incidentalism.   The very nature of the verbal statement does not permit dealing with a large number of disturbances.   Most languages have only six words for comparison : small, smaller, smallest ; and great, greater, greatest.   Therefore verbal quantitative specifications like great and small, more or less, increase and decrease, rise and decline, growth and decay, are limited in meaning and cannot be applied to even a series of a few dozens of disturbances with any exact power of expressing the magnitude of their movement and fluctuation.   In such phrases a few cases, two to ten, perhaps, can be described approximately in their quantitative aspects. Larger numbers of them make the terms meaningless and therefore inapplicable.   For the same reason a verbal quantitativist cannot uniformly apply his measuring stick, if he has any, to all the disturbances compared and cannot therefore even properly compare them.   The numerical indicators, having no peculiar weakness in comparison with the verbal quantitative statements, do not have their limitations.   This explains why generalizations and judgments made by many verbal quantitativists have, almost without exception, been based upon very few cases and have, therefore, had a very narrow and unstable factual basis.   These considerations are sufficient to show why, not being an ardent quantitativist at all, I find that only some sort of system of numerical indicators can describe, more or less accurately, the movement of the phenomena studied, and why I use them and prefer them to the other verbalist procedure, so far as the quantitative aspect of the processes is concerned, and

why I am not disturbed by the numerous criticisms of the verbal quantitativists of all degrees of serious and superficial knowledge, criticisms
which I expect (being so far a psychologist as well as a sociologist).
Whatever and however great are the weaknesses of this study, it is more
systematic, more complete than, and as logical as any study of the subject
hitherto made.   It needs no specific apology.[15]

So much for the concept of the magnitude of the disturbances and the
procedure for the estimation of their movement in the course of time.
Now one more classification, involving an additional aspect of the disturbances, an aspect which is qualitative and does not enter into the
concept of magnitude.

[15] How little, indeed, is known in the field and how erratic are the supposedly scientific
and competent judgments was, in a sense, experimentally tested in connection with the present
study.   A preliminary draft was submitted for criticism to several eminent scholars, who
kindly read it and made several helpful constructive suggestions.   Then, in order to see what
weaknesses might be found in it by the severest critic, who might manifest all the force of
his criticism without any apprehension, it was arranged that the preliminary draft of this, as
well as the work devoted to the movement of war, be given by a prominent scholar to two
critics whose names would remain unknown to me.   These two anonymous critics wrote,
one a very lengthy criticism in which the writer tried to tear the whole work to pieces, using
abundantly on every page strong words, like "nonsense," "absurdity," and so on, but giving
very little of the factual and logical bases for his highly emotional utterances.   The important
and somewhat humorous aspect of the entire criticism by two supposedly competent critics
(they are historians) is that each of them found as the main defect of my work entirely opposite
and mutually contradictory sins.   One, the particularly antagonistic critic, found that my
curves and tables run contrary to all historical knowledge of the real movement of the disturbances.   The other, fair-minded and, in my opinion, a much more competent scholar
than the first, accused me of using a very complex and cumbersome procedure for proving
what "every qualitative historian knows and agrees on."   So here we are : one critic finds
that almost all the movements of the curves of this study are contrary to what competent
historians accept as true ; the other, that they are in conformity with such knowledge and
that there seems to exist among historians in that field information so well known and generally accepted that all my scales, tables, and other procedures are unnecessary.   Enjoying
the delightful role of the *tertius gaudens* I had great pleasure in reading these two anonymous
criticisms, and what I have said above partly explains the enjoyment.   It is sufficient to say,
that if before reading these criticisms I had had some hesitation as to the comparative value
and adequacy of this study, my hesitation almost entirely disappeared afterwards.   Having
gone once more over the primary data, introducing further improvements and modifications
in which some of the real shortcomings indicated by the critics were diminished or eliminated,
I decided definitely to publish it, and I am now prepared to face whatever criticism of this
sort may arise.   With the present lack of any real knowledge in this field, the fair and competent criticism will improve the rough building constructed here ; the unfair and unen-
lightened criticism will only show, if not immediately then in the long run, its own shallowness
and incompetence.   If there were space enough, I should like to reproduce the suggestions
of my two anonymous critics *verbatim*, supplemented by a few remarks of my own.   In a
sense it would be an instructive performance.   Unfortunately a lack of space and a possible
unwillingness on the part of the critics that their criticism be published *verbatim*, do not
permit my following any such plans.

V. As to the Predominant Qualitative Nature and the Main Objective [16] of the Disturbances

These are divided into five classes :

A, predominantly political disturbances, the main objective of which is a change of the existing political regime.

B, predominantly socioeconomic disturbances, directed toward a modification of the existing social and economic order.

C, national and separatistic disturbances, the main objective of which is national independence, or autonomy, or the elimination of disfranchisements, or the achievement of some other privileges and advantages.

D, religious disturbances.

F, disturbances with specific objectives — like some personal change in the government; resistance to a specific law, or tax, or other concrete measure — and disturbances without any single dominant objective but with two or more equally strong objectives.

It is to be noted that from this standpoint the disturbances are not graded quantitatively (for obvious reasons) but are just marked according to their class. These qualitative pigeonholings are to be regarded as very approximate. It can hardly be questioned that any social disturbance has several reasons and several objectives. On the other hand some movements are marked by the fact that they show one of these characteristics more conspicuously than the others. In many disturbances such "predominant color" is lacking; therefore they are lumped together into a group called "mixed." In some others one can perceive readily the prominence of either the political, or the religious, or any other "nature." In the tables in the Appendix to this part, all the disturbances are divided into five groups: A, B, C, D, F (F = mixed).

Such is the system of classification and differentiation of disturbances. It is not exhaustive, but it gives a sufficiently detailed passport to each of them; it embraces most of the important characteristics — quantitative and partly qualitative — of the disturbances; takes into consideration most of their substantial traits; therefore, it grasps something of the real diversity of the processes studied. The organico-proportional nature of the variables, as well as of the total measure of the magnitude of a disturbance, is now clear. Such proportional units permit us to make rough comparisons between the magnitudes of the disturbances in a varying social body.

[16] The term "main objective" is not necessarily to be interpreted in the sense of nominalistic, conscious, and well-reasoned objectives for all the participants in the disturbance. It means the realistic objectives of the movement itself usually manifest in its mottoes, slogans, and shibboleths and in the essential nature of the movement as shown in the process of its realization, regardless of whether this objective effect was planned intentionally or not.

It is to be noted that though the amplitude of the scale 1 to 100 is broad enough, its neutralization of values by the geometric average may somewhat diminish the difference between the *numerical values* of the magnitude for the greatest and the smallest of the important disturbances studied. (Note: we study only "important" disturbances.) The real magnitude of the greatest revolutions and of the smallest of the important disturbances may possibly differ much more than the relationship between, say, the values 1 to 100. Therefore it is not improbable that the amplitude of the fluctuation of the curve of the disturbances in this work is narrower than in the reality and, also, that the magnitude of the greatest revolutions in our data is smaller than in reality. Admitting this possibility, on the other hand, one is in a sense safer being rather conservative than being too liberal in the assigning of widely different values to different disturbances. Since we do not go so far as to contend that the subsequent indicators are perfectly accurate and that they show not only the gross contrasts but also exactly how much greater or smaller were the disturbances compared, such conservatism is justifiable. If it tones down somewhat the real amplitude of the fluctuation of the disturbances from period to period; and if it in some cases diminishes the magnitude of the particularly spectacular, much talked of, and much magnified revolutions, like the present Russian Revolution, or the great French Revolution, or the great Revolution in the Netherlands, then it compensates for this possible shortcoming by avoiding many of the inaccuracies which may appear when a too liberal and wide scale of values is taken for the ranking of the disturbances. Admitting thus the possibility of an underestimation of the magnitude of the great revolutions in the system of measurement accepted, one should, on the other hand, keep in mind the possibility of a false perspective of the real size of the disturbances, a distortion similar to that discussed in the previous part in regard to war magnitude. The point is that here also, for various reasons, some of the disturbances like the great French Revolution or the American Revolution are mentioned and talked of, and as a result they are particularly "popular." Thus they appear especially great in their dimensions when compared with some other little-known and seldom-mentioned disturbances. (Such events as the taking of the Bastille or the Battle of Bunker Hill appear to be enormous and become the occasions for national holidays, though both were in fact events of very modest dimensions, especially the affair of the Bastille.) In this not always fortunate perspective, the magnitude of such spectacular and popular disturbances tends to become enlarged, while that of some others, less known, though in fact no less great, becomes in popular estimation comparatively quite small.   Considering this bias, perhaps it will not appear so strange when on subsequent pages the reader sees that the periods of some such popular and spectacular disturbances in our indicators do not always appear as the most extraordinarily turbulent, while other periods of which most of the intelligent nonspecialists have no knowledge, appear more disorderly than their reputation makes them.   Such a result may be due partly to the accepted system of measurement of the magnitude of disturbances, a measurement which perhaps underestimates the periods of some of the great revolutions : but it may be due also to the reflection of a reality which is more accurate in the system of indicators than in popular opinion with its false perspective.

Considering that our total indicator of the movement of disturbances agrees all in all with the movement of the number of disturbances from period to period, we have an additional reason to believe that the accepted system of measurement of disturbances is not misleading in its essential results.   If, however, the scale accepted underestimates, indeed, the great revolution and overestimates the small ones, the future and better studies can easily remedy the defect by using a larger scale than ours.

A few additional remarks are sufficient to dispense with the technical details of the construction of the indicators.   As has been mentioned, all the disturbances of these countries which are recorded in substantial and competent standard texts are studied and "ranked."   This means that no selection and no sampling is made by us, but all the recorded disturbances are taken.   In regard to each of the disturbances, the historical work upon which the ranking is based is indicated with its relevant pages in the detailed list of the disturbances for each country given in the Appendix to this part.   This means that the subjective bias of the investigator is practically eliminated from the study, except perhaps in cases where the historical description of the disturbance is so indefinite and incomplete that it permits the giving to its several variables somewhat different marks for each on our scale.   If such subjectivity is present, it can hardly vitiate the essential results, because in the majority of cases the description of the disturbance is sufficiently definite to give it an exact grading on our scale, or at the worst one of two adjacent grades, and this cannot change the fundamental nature of the disturbance.

Although all the disturbances considered in the best standard historical works are taken for each country studied, this does not mean that these histories record all the small disturbances.   Most of the small "social ripplings" are not set down ; but most of the important ones are.

As the position of all the countries studied is identical in this respect, and also the position of various periods in the history of a given country — with perhaps a slight inflation of the disturbances for the more recent period, compared with those of the earlier ones — the lack of records for "teapot" social storms does not vitiate the results concerning the movement of the important — that is, the recorded, and they are recorded because they are important — internal disturbances. In regard to them our study includes almost 100 per cent or the whole "statistical universe" of these disturbances.

The periods with which study of the disturbances begins and ends for each country are indicated in detail in the tables. For this reason they need not be specified here. Altogether there are 84 disturbances in the history of Greece; 170 in that of Rome; 49 for Byzantium; 173 for France; 150 for Germany; 162 for England; 251 for Italy; 235 or 242 (if seven disturbances which were wars rather than disturbances be included) for Spain; 103 for the Netherlands; 167 for Russia; 78 for Poland and Lithuania.[17] A total of 1622 to 1629 disturbances is listed for all these countries.

Before passing to the study of the results, two other methodological details should be mentioned here. The first concerns the nature of the affairs which should be classed as internal disturbances: disorder, riots, revolutions, and other such manifestations of social tension and social crisis. The point is that two or more occurrences which in their external appearance are similar may be quite dissimilar in their meaning, if they happen to occur under quite different social and political regimes. For instance, a public meeting of the opposition for a criticism of the policy of the ruling party in a democratic regime, or a public demonstration of protest under such a regime, in most cases is not to be classed as an internal disturbance at all. It is permitted by law, by sociopolitical mores, and by the everyday practice of such a society. The same meeting or public demonstration for criticism of the government, in a society where such meetings are prohibited, becomes a manifestation of social tension and disturbance. This explains why in the list of social disturbances are included only happenings which violated the existing social order and laws of the period and of the society in which they occurred. The reasons for such a procedure are so evident and self-explanatory that no further comment is needed.

This rule has particular weight for the early centuries of European

---

[17] As in the case of war the difference in the number of the disturbances for various countries is due mainly to the length of time for which the history of each country is studied in this work.

history. The private revenge and self-redress of offenses by the injured party, so widely practiced during these centuries, and the private wars among feudal lords of the same rank in the feudal hierarchy were not a violation of the existing laws and mores. On the contrary, they were permitted, sometimes even demanded, by these laws. Such cases evidently cannot be classed as internal disturbances. Therefore they are excluded from this class in our study. Quite different is the situation in the case, for instance, of a revolt of a vassal against his suzerain, or a duke against his king, or a baron against his duke-suzerain, where the fealty oath is broken; or the case of any other disturbance which was a violation of the existing laws. These should be, and are here, considered as internal disturbances, in spite of the fact that often externally they look quite like the other phenomena of physically violent motions permitted by the existing laws and mores.

For a similar reason social disturbances of purely or mainly international character (wars between various countries, the revolt of a conquered country against its victorious foreign invaders — as, for instance, the riots of the French communes against the English invaders during the Hundred Years' War, the wars of Louis XI with the dukes of Burgundy after the evaporation of the fealty, etc.), — were also excluded from the class of internal social disturbances. The reason is again evident: they are not symptoms of the inner tension and inner disturbance of one part of the same social system against another, but phenomena of international tension and disturbance, which are the objects of study in the previous treatment of war movement.[18]

We have now outlined fully the material, sources, territories and groups, and the time span within which the phenomena of inner social tensions and disturbances are studied. Several rather routine qualifications and reservations, all of which are well known to the investigator and are mentioned in the part on war movement, need not be repeated here for the reason of the economy of time and space. So much for the technicalities. Now we can turn to a consideration of the results themselves.

[18] There were several instances of an intermediate nature, which were simultaneously internal disturbance and international war. Such cases are entered in both lists: that of wars and that of internal disturbances.

Chapter Thirteen

MOVEMENT OF INTERNAL DISTURBANCES BY COUNTRIES

The essential results of the study of the fluctuation of the magnitude of disturbances in the life history of the countries studied are given in the subsequent tables and figures by quarter-century and century periods. They follow with the minimum of comments.

I. INTERNAL DISTURBANCES OF ANCIENT GREECE

TABLE 24. TOTAL OF THE GEOMETRIC AVERAGE OF INTERNAL DISTURBANCES OF ANCIENT GREECE FROM 600 TO 126 B.C. BY QUARTER CENTURIES

Quarter Century	Number of Disturbances	Measure of Disturbances	Total for the Quarter
600–576 B.C.	4	8.07 10.63 20.80 7.05	46.55
575–551	2	15.13 10.63	26.06
550–526	3	10.63 10.63 17.54	38.80
525–501	3	4.93 20.80 12.16	37.89
500–476	5	9.66 13.39 9.09 11.45 9.66	53.25
475–451	8	9.09 7.66 7.11 27.14 14.42 41.21 23.42 12.16	142.21

TABLE 24. TOTAL OF THE GEOMETRIC AVERAGE OF INTERNAL DISTURB-
ANCES OF ANCIENT GREECE FROM 600 TO 126 B.C. BY QUARTER
CENTURIES — *continued*

Quarter Century	Number of Disturbances	Measure of Disturbances	Total for the Quarter
450–426 B.C.	5	25.77 9.66 15.18 17.38 16.07	84.06
425–401	13	8.03 19.13 14.42 10.10 10.13 21.54 17.54 10.16 4.64 15.43 15.43 27.14 9.66	189.25
400–376	5	6.69 19.13 7.37 7.37 9.66	50.22
375–351	8	18.17 18.47 15.18 16.13 20.80 13.57 7.06 12.16	124.54
350–326	6	11.45 9.66 15.43 18.17 12.81 19.13	86.65
325–301	4	17.10 12.16 15.43 14.42	59.11
300–276	4	21.54 14.42 21.54 14.42	71.92
275–251	4	14.42 8.88 33.02 10.63	66.95

TABLE 24.   TOTAL OF THE GEOMETRIC AVERAGE OF INTERNAL DISTURB-
ANCES OF ANCIENT GREECE FROM 600 TO 126 B.C. BY QUARTER
CENTURIES — *continued*

Quarter Century	Number of Disturbances	Measure of Disturbances	Total for the Quarter
250–226 B.C.	2	16.13 11.12	27.25
225–201	7	14.42 8.43 16.13 10.63 12.60 21.54 9.66	93.41
200–176	2	9.66 9.66	19.32
175–151	—	—	—
150–126	1	17.10	17.10

TABLE 25.   TOTAL OF THE GEOMETRIC AVERAGE OF INTERNAL DISTURB-
ANCES OF ANCIENT GREECE BY CENTURIES

Century	Number of Disturbances	Number of Years with Disturbance	Total of the Geometric Averages for the Century
VI B.C.	12	13	149.30
V	30 [1]	51	468.77
IV	23	23	320.52
III	17	22	259.53
II (first 3 quarters)	3	4	36.42

[1] In a few cases the number of the disturbances by century periods is slightly smaller than the sum of the disturbances of the four quarters of that century in Table 24.   The slight discrepancy is due to the fact that the disturbances which occurred between two quarters are counted as two disturbances in the tables by quarter centuries. If, however, there were one disturbance, in this table by century periods such a disturbance is counted as one, since it falls within the century period.   For the same reason the total number of disturbances by century periods, in some cases by one to four, is higher than the total number of disturbances given in the Appendix.   If a disturbance continued from, say, 898 to 902, it falls in both centuries and so gives, in the century table, two disturbances and thus increases slightly the number of the disturbances in the table.   Such an increase is, however, insignificant and does not change the magnitude of the disturbance, because in such cases it is divided between respective centuries.   In the study of the frequency of disturbances their real number is considered.

Ancient Greece. If we take century periods, whether we judge on the basis of the totals of the geometric averages, of the number of years with a disturbance, or of the frequency of disturbances, the most peaceful was the first half of the second century, then the sixth century, and near to it the third century B.C.   The most disorderly were the fifth and the fourth centuries.   Of the quarter centuries the periods 425–401 B.C. (with the magnitude 189.25);   475–451 (142.21);   375–351 (124.54);   225–201

(93.41) ; 450–426 (84.06) ; and 350–326 (86.65) were the most turbulent, while the periods 200–126, 575–551, and 250–226 were the most orderly. (See Figure 10.)

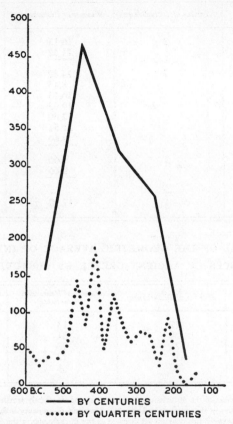

FIG. 10.   MOVEMENT OF INTERNAL DISTURBANCES IN ANCIENT GREECE

If we inquire in which of these periods the greatest single revolutions happened, the answer is in the periods 460–440 (with the magnitude 49.19) ; 464–455 (41.21) ; 467 (37.14) ; 403 (27.14) ; 265–261 (33.02). (The detailed tables in the Appendix to this part show exactly what these disturbances were.)

On the basis of these data one is entitled to conclude that in the history of Greece the most turbulent centuries and periods were, like those periods of the maximum of war activities, not the periods of decline but of resplendence, when Greek culture reached its peak — the fifth and fourth centuries.[1] In general, the curve of disturbances, judged by century periods, goes parallel with the curve of war. Here, then, we have a refutation of the claims that disturbances occur always in the period of decline. We shall see that some of them do occur in such periods, but not always, nor even as a general rule. What the situation is exactly we shall discuss more substantially in Chapter Fourteen of this volume. For the present it is enough to note the fact.

No continuous trend, no regular periodicity, and no uniformity in the amplitude of the ups and downs by quarter centuries, nor by century periods, are noticeable.

As to the characteristic nature of the disturbances, the data show (see the detailed list of disturbances in the Appendix to this part) that predominantly political disturbances were most common and frequent; then came the nationalistic and socioeconomic disturbances. Greece did not have religious disturbances in any tangible degree. The data show also that socioeconomic disturbances happened most often in the fifth century, while nationalistic disturbances were predominant in the fourth and partly in the third centuries, appearing at a later stage of the development of the Greek bodies politic. This does not mean that these reasons — the socioeconomic and the nationalistic — did not play any role in other periods; the socioeconomic played a very conspicuous role in the disturbances of the third and partly in the disturbances of the second century. But they were screened or cloaked in the exterior forms of disturbances of a political or a mixed nature.

Other comments will be given in Chapter Fourteen.

---

[1] This confirms, and is confirmed by, the following statement of a prominent historian. "There had been sedition *within* the Greek cities from time immemorial, and when the factional wars ceased entirely, as in the later Hellenistic days, internal peace followed, but it was the peace of a graveyard. . . . The march of progress in Greece was accompanied by revolutions. . . . Class struggles had not prevented extraordinary progress in the past; why should they do so in the future? . . . Struggles of this sort were destructive of property, undoubtedly, but the material prosperity of Athens had not been ruined by them, and Greece, as a whole, maintained a higher standard of living in the fourth century B.C. than ever before." W. S. Ferguson, *Hellenistic Athens* (London, 1911), pp. 3-5.

II. Internal Disturbances of Ancient Rome

TABLE 26.   TOTAL OF THE GEOMETRIC AVERAGE OF INTERNAL DISTURB-
ANCES OF ANCIENT ROME FROM 525 B.C. TO A.D. 500 BY QUARTER
CENTURIES

Quarter Century	Number of Disturbances	Measure of Disturbances	Total for the Quarter
525–501 B.C.	1	24.66	24.66
500–476	3	16.67 7.37 28.84	53.08
475–451	1	10.63	10.63
450–426	4	24.66 12.16 12.16 9.66	58.64
425–401	1	8.43	8.43
400–376	1	12.16	12.16
375–351	—	—	—
350–326	1	16.87	16.87
325–301	—	—	—
300–276	1	18.17	18.17
275–251	—	—	—
250–226	—	—	—
225–201	—	—	—
200–176	4	14.45 9.09 9.09 12.16	41.79
175–151	2	12.16 19.57	31.73
150–126	2	24.10 17.10	41.20
125–101	3	7.66 10.00 25.96	43.62
100–76	10	12.16 43.09 12.16 30.37 7.66 30.37 35.37 8.43 9.66 19.91	209.38

TABLE 26.   TOTAL OF THE GEOMETRIC AVERAGE OF INTERNAL DISTURB-
ANCES OF ANCIENT ROME FROM 525 B.C. TO A.D. 500 BY QUARTER
CENTURIES — *continued*

Quarter Century	Number of Disturbances	Measure of Disturbances	Total for the Quarter
75 51 D.C.	5	15.92 34.76 10.63 19.57 12.16	93.04
50–26	9	50.00 19.13 16.13 14.42 24.66 24.66 14.42 28.23 8.11	199.78
25–1	6	4.05 14.42 12.16 9.66 9.66 4.64	54.59
1–25 A.D.	7	9.66 12.16 9.66 14.42 5.85 17.10 9.66	78.51
26–50	6	9.09 8.43 6.69 10.00 7.37 8.43	50.01
51–75	10	3.68 13.87 13.39 3.91 21.54 20.80 36.84 17.10 21.90 11.45	164.48
76–100	4	9.66 4.93 20.80 14.42	49.81

TABLE 26.   TOTAL OF THE GEOMETRIC AVERAGE OF INTERNAL DISTURB-
ANCES OF ANCIENT ROME FROM 525 B.C. TO A.D. 500 BY QUARTER
CENTURIES — *continued*

Quarter Century	Number of Disturbances	Measure of Disturbances	Total for the Quarter
101–125 A.D.	2	27.14 8.43	35.57
126–150	3	27.59 7.37 16.51	51.47
151–175	5	11.45 9.66 19.57 12.16 14.42	67.26
176–200	7	10.63 14.42 8.43 24.66 22.89 18.17 14.42	113.62
201–225	5	12.16 14.42 24.66 8.43 20.80	80.47
226–250	7	12.16 4.64 14.42 18.17 7.66 17.54 22.89	97.48
251–275	10	18.17 22.89 35.93 28.84 26.21 7.66 20.80 9.66 7.94 20.80	198.90
276–300	8	14.42 14.42 12.16 14.42 10.63 9.66 9.66 13.57	98.94

TABLE 26.   TOTAL OF THE GEOMETRIC AVERAGE OF INTERNAL DISTURB-
ANCES OF ANCIENT ROME FROM 525 B.C. TO A.D. 500 BY QUARTER
CENTURIES — *continued*

Quarter Century	Number of Disturbances	Measure of Disturbances	Total for the Quarter
301–325 A.D.	7	3.68 12.16 16.87 25.20 16.87 15.36 19.31	109.45
326–350	5	7.66 6.69 15.36 6.08 13.39	49.18
351–375	11	13.39 7.66 4.64 16.51 20.80 12.16 4.64 6.08 16.51 9.66 7.37	119.42
376–400	8	9.66 7.94 13.92 4.22 7.21 15.36 18.17 14.42	90.90
401–425	6	9.66 15.87 12.16 9.66 14.42 14.42	76.19
426–450	3	16.51 9.09 3.91	29.51
451–475	3	9.28 9.28 9.28	27.84
476–500	1	9.28	9.28

TABLE 27.   TOTAL OF THE GEOMETRIC AVERAGE OF INTERNAL DISTURB-
ANCES OF ANCIENT ROME BY CENTURIES

Century	Number of Disturbances	Number of Years with Disturbance	Total of the Geometric Averages
V B.C.	8	11	130.78
IV	2	2	29.03
III	1	1	18.17
II	11	16	158.34
I	28	44	556.79
I A.D.	27	28	342.81
II	17	24	267.92
III	30	46	475.79
IV	31	34	368.95
V (first three quarters)	13	13	142.82

Rome. Considering the century periods, whether on the basis of the total of the geometric averages or on the basis of the number of years with disturbances, the most disorderly centuries were as follows: the first century B.C., the third century A.D., and then the fourth, the first, and the second centuries A.D. The most orderly centuries were the third, fourth, fifth B.C., and the fifth A.D. Of the single disturbances, the greatest occurred in the years 49–46 B.C. (with the magnitude 50.0); 91–89 B.C. (43.09); 80–79 B.C. (35.57); 87 B.C. (30.37); 83–82 B.C. (30.37); 80–72

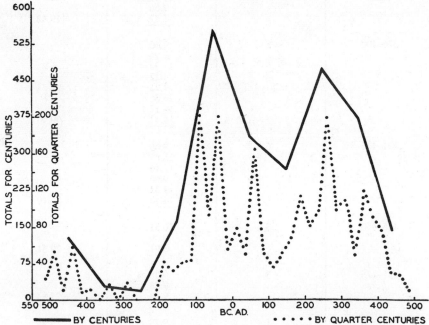

FIG. 11.   MOVEMENT OF INTERNAL DISTURBANCES IN ANCIENT ROME

B.C. (35.83); 73–71 B.C. (34.76); and A.D. 69 (36.84). The most disorderly quarter centuries were 100–76 B.C. (209.38); 50–26 B.C. (199.78); A.D. 51–75 (164.48); A.D. 351–375 (119.42); and A.D. 176–200 (113.62). (See Figure 11.)

Here the curve of disturbances has a different course from the curve of war; while the third century B.C. shows the highest indicator of war, its indicator for disturbances is the lowest. The struggle for life and death with Carthage, not to mention the other international conflicts of Rome in that century, seems to have been followed by a maximum of inner order and the elimination of inner strife. Likewise, the first century A.D., the lowest in war activities, has a relatively high figure of internal disturbances. On the other hand, the first century B.C. has here the highest figure of disorderliness and also a very high figure of war. In other words, in the history of Rome we do not meet any uniformity as to the movement of the curves of disturbances and of war.

Again, confronted with the periods of blossoming and decline of the Roman culture, the curve of the disturbances does not exhibit any uniformity. The first century B.C. was one of the highest peaks of Roman power and culture and the same century was the most turbulent. The same can be said of the first century A.D. On the other hand, the third century A.D. was already the beginning of the decline; and yet it occupies the second place from the top in internal disturbances.

Here then, in contradistinction to Greece, we meet a diversity of relationships between disturbances and sociocultural and political blossoming. This means a refutation of the theory that an increase or an abundance of internal disturbances is always or as a rule a symptom of the growth and healthy blossoming of a country. In some cases that seems to be so; in others it is not so at all. The matter seems to suggest that there are various kinds of disturbances. Some of them are the "birth pains of a healthy child"; others are the agony of senility and disintegration. Sweeping uniform generalizations, so commonly set forth, here, as well as in many other cases, either fall short of the mark or overshoot it.

No continuous trend and no clear periodicity are noticeable, except that in seven centuries out of ten the second quarter is marked by a drop in the indicator of disturbances.

Finally, the predominant "color" of the disturbances indicates that the earliest forms were mainly political and socioeconomic. After the second century B.C., when Rome had already become an empire, the usual disease of empires quickly built up of diverse peoples and countries, the separatistic, nationalistic, and regional movements, appeared and persisted up to the fourth century A.D., when their place was taken by religious strifes and disturbances. Finally, as we move from the earlier to the later centuries of Roman history, the proportion of "mixed" disturbances tended, with minor fluctuation, to grow. Their growth seems to suggest an increasing complexity of internal antagonisms, a growing interweaving of diverse interests, motives, objectives, and a complication of the social structure in its lines of differentiation and stratification.

III. Internal Disturbances of Byzantium

TABLE 28. TOTAL OF THE GEOMETRIC AVERAGE OF INTERNAL DISTURB-ANCES OF BYZANTIUM FROM A.D. 526 TO 1400 BY QUARTER CENTURIES

Quarter Century	Number of Disturbances	Measure of Disturbances	Total for the Quarter
526–550 A.D.	1	16.14	16.14
551–575	—	—	
576–600	1	17.97	17.32
601–625	2	17.37	
		44.16	61.53
626–650	1	20.00	20.00
651–675	1	9.66	9.66
676–700	2	7.36	
		12.59	19.95
701–725	2	7.36	
		42.36	49.72
726–750	2	11.45	
		30.34	41.79
751–775	—	—	—
776–800	4	15.17	
		5.84	
		24.66	
		7.36	53.03
801–825	5	7.36	
		10.06	
		10.06	
		10.06	
		22.91	60.45
826–850	—	—	—
851–875	1	7.36	7.36
876–900	—	—	
901–925	—	—	
926–950	1	27.61	27.61
951–975	2	5.18	
		18.46	23.64
976–1000	2	39.81	
		34.74	74.55

TABLE 28.   TOTAL OF THE GEOMETRIC AVERAGE OF INTERNAL DISTURB-
ANCES OF BYZANTIUM FROM A.D. 526 TO 1400 BY QUARTER CENTURIES
— *continued*

Quarter Century	Number of Disturbances	Measure of Disturbances	Total for the Quarter
1001–1025 A.D.	1	12.16	12.16
1026–1050	4	3.91 11.29 11.45 12.79	39.44
1051–1075	1	10.06	10.06
1076–1100	2	10.06 10.06	20.12
1101–1125	1	3.91	3.91
1126–1150	—	—	—
1151–1175	—	—	—
1176–1200	5	16.14 13.40 17.10 12.79 14.66	74.09
1201–1225	2	16.14 21.53	37.67
1226–1250	—	—	—
1251–1275	1	5.18	5.18
1276–1300	—	—	—
1301–1325	—	—	—
1326–1350	2	16.14 43.05	59.19
1351–1375	1	10.06	10.06
1376–1400	3	7.48 13.40 13.40	34.28

TABLE 29.   TOTAL OF THE GEOMETRIC AVERAGE OF INTERNAL DISTURB-
ANCES OF BYZANTIUM BY CENTURIES

Century	Number of Disturbances	Number of Years with Disturbance	Total of the Geometric Averages
VI [1]	2	3	33.51
VII	5	14	111.14
VIII	8	19	144.54
IX	6	8	67.81
X	5	12	125.80
XI	8	8	81.78
XII	6	6	78.00
XIII	3	4	42.85
XIV	6	15	103.53

[1] Three quarters of the century only.

Byzantium. Measured either by the totals of the geometric averages or by the number of disturbances, or even by the totals of the years with disturbance, the curve of disturbances here is very different from the curve of Greece and Rome. Taken by century periods, it rises steadily from the sixth through the seventh, and reaches its climax in the eighth century; it falls in the ninth and rises again in the tenth century; it declines steadily from the eleventh to the thirteenth inclusive;

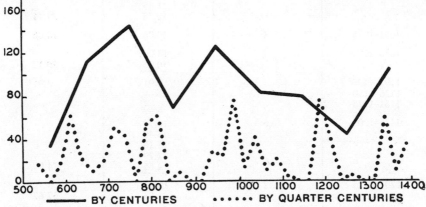

FIG. 12. MOVEMENT OF INTERNAL DISTURBANCES IN BYZANTIUM

and then flares up in the fourteenth century again. Of the quarter-century periods, the most turbulent were 1176–1200 (74.09); 976–1000 (74.55); 801–825 (60.45); 601–625 (61.53); 1326–1350 (59.19). The curve resembles the Greek and Roman curves in that its first century, the sixth, was peaceful; the climax of disturbances also falls at early maturity; and then the curve fluctuates without any definite trend. That the climax here is farther from the middle line of existence, and falls within the first third of the life process, is perhaps due to the fact that the Byzantine culture was, in a way, transplanted as a mature culture from Rome and Greece, instead of being a spontaneously and gradually grown culture. Therefore, it may be that the virulence of the disturbance forces would naturally show itself earlier under these conditions than would be the case if this culture had grown gradually by itself, from simple conditions.

Of the single disturbances, the largest occurred in the years 1341–1347 (43.05); 711–717 (42.36); 603–610 (44.66); 741–743 (30.34); 976–980 (39.81); 987–989 (34.74). It is to be noted further that the brilliant period of Justinian (emperor from A.D. 527 to 565) — and in general the brilliant sixth century — is marked by a very low rate of disturbance (only two disturbances, one in 532 and the other in 599–602); the seventh and the eighth centuries, a period of decline, had a rate of disorder which was high; while the twelfth and thirteenth centuries, again a period of decline, had a low rate. The blooming and prosperous ninth, tenth, and eleventh centuries were marked again by a low as well as high disturbance occurrence. Most of the disturbances here are of the "mixed" type. In the eighth, ninth, twelfth, and thirteenth centuries religious disturbances played a considerable part. (See Figure 12.)

Again we do not find any linear trend or definite periodicity in the movement of the disturbances over the course of time. While in Greece the last century of the Greek independence is marked by a low rate of turmoil, the last century of the existence of Byzantium displays a comparatively high explosion of disturbances.

IV. Internal Disturbances of France

TABLE 30. TOTAL OF THE GEOMETRIC AVERAGE OF INTERNAL DISTURBANCES OF FRANCE FROM 526 TO 1925 BY QUARTER CENTURIES

Quarter Century	Number of Disturbances	Measure of Disturbances	Total for the Quarter
526–550 A.D.	2	17.38 5.64	23.02
551–575	2	9.08 15.85	25.93
576–600	3	5.18 24.66 6.70	36.54
601–625	3	10.00 11.45 9.08	30.53
626–650	—	—	—
651–675	1	17.10	17.10
676–700	1	38.28	38.28
701–725	4	21.88 21.88 21.88 15.17	80.81
726–750	—	—	—
751–775	2	34.74 17.10	51.84
776–800	—	—	—
801–825	—	—	—

TABLE 30.   TOTAL OF THE GEOMETRIC AVERAGE OF INTERNAL DISTURB-
ANCES OF FRANCE FROM 526 TO 1925 BY QUARTER CENTURIES — *continued*

Quarter Century	Number of Disturbances	Measure of Disturbances	Total for the Quarter
826–850 A.D.	5	26.18	
		26.18	
		15.17	
		31.05	
		18.63	117.21
851–875	1	12.42	12.42
876–900	1	5.18	5.18
901–925	1	15.85	15.85
926–950	1	4.64	4.64
951–975	1	8.07	8.07
976–1000	1	6.08	6.08
1001–1025	—	—	—
1026–1050	4	12.59	
		30.02	
		6.08	
		10.54	59.23
1051–1075	4	10.54	
		24.66	
		20.80	
		9.08	65.08
1076–1100	2	9.08	
		9.08	18.16
1101–1125	7	17.10	
		12.59	
		6.08	
		14.66	
		14.42	
		19.59	
		11.45	95.89
1126–1150	6	9.08	
		12.16	
		8.07	
		10.02	
		9.52	
		8.07	56.92
1151–1175	3	8.07	
		8.07	
		18.15	34.29
1176–1200	9	7.21	
		8.07	
		24.66	
		8.07	
		8.07	
		9.52	
		7.65	
		8.07	
		20.80	102.12

TABLE 30.   TOTAL OF THE GEOMETRIC AVERAGE OF INTERNAL DISTURB-
ANCES OF FRANCE FROM 526 TO 1925 BY QUARTER CENTURIES — *continued*

Quarter Century	Number of Disturbances	Measure of Disturbances	Total for the Quarter
1201–1225 A.D.	14	6.26	
		15.17	
		17.06	
		8.07	
		8.07	
		6.76	
		7.65	
		17.38	
		7.21	
		9.52	
		14.42	
		6.08	
		9.08	
		9.08	142.41
1226–1250	5	15.85	
		18.15	
		15.85	
		8.07	
		15.85	73.77
1251–1275	1	11.45	11.45
1276–1300	1	17.38	17.38
1301–1325	2	8.07	
		10.06	18.13
1326–1350	1	6.76	6.76
1351–1375	3	4.64	
		7.92	
		16.52	29.08
1376–1400	5	11.45	
		8.43	
		16.52	
		7.21	
		19.59	63.20
1401–1425	2	11.45	
		19.59	31.04
1426–1450	4	7.12	
		12.59	
		4.21	
		4.64	28.56
1451–1475	3	8.43	
		8.43	
		10.06	26.92
1476–1500	1	8.43	8.43
1501–1525	—	—	—
1526–1550	3	7.65	
		12.16	
		10.76	30.57

TABLE 30. TOTAL OF THE GEOMETRIC AVERAGE OF INTERNAL DISTURB-
ANCES OF FRANCE FROM 526 TO 1925 BY QUARTER CENTURIES — *continued*

Quarter Century	Number of Disturbances	Measure of Disturbances	Total for the Quarter
1551–1575 A.D.	5	2.08 10.00 11.45 27.61 13.27	64.41
1576–1600	6	26.54 44.46 9.08 8.55 4.86 8.55	102.04
1601–1625	4	5.13 11.45 12.16 4.78	33.52
1626–1650	8	14.36 4.86 10.00 7.92 4.86 28.25 10.00 12.59	91.84
1651–1675	5	10.06 24.66 3.68 4.21 17.10	59.71
1676–1700	2	3.15 9.66	12.81
1701–1725	5	23.28 9.44 24.66 4.70 5.84	67.92
1726–1750	2	3.15 9.66	12.81
1751–1775	3	7.36 6.08 3.04	16.48
1776–1800	5	3.04 6.08 6.70 10.47 79.43	105.72

TABLE 30. TOTAL OF THE GEOMETRIC AVERAGE OF INTERNAL DISTURB-
ANCES OF FRANCE FROM 526 TO 1925 BY QUARTER CENTURIES — *continued*

Quarter Century	Number of Disturbances	Measure of Disturbances	Total for the Quarter
1801–1825 A.D.	8	3.91	
		6.70	
		3.91	
		23.28	
		19.59	
		3.68	
		4.64	
		5.64	71.35
1826–1850	10	20.32	
		8.07	
		8.87	
		18.46	
		2.48	
		5.84	
		2.46	
		20.32	
		11.45	
		8.07	106.32
1851–1875	4	12.16	
		3.68	
		10.00	
		21.53	47.37
1876–1900	1	9.68	9.68
1901–1925	2	14.66	
		14.66	29.32

TABLE 31. TOTAL OF THE GEOMETRIC AVERAGE OF INTERNAL DISTURB-
ANCES OF FRANCE BY CENTURIES

Century	Number of Disturbances	Number of Years with Disturbance	Total of the Geometric Average
VI [1]	7	9	85.43
VII	5	13	85.91
VIII	6	13	142.65
IX	6	14	134.81
X	4	5	34.64
XI	9	27	142.47
XII	25	37	289.22
XIII	21	39	245.01
XIV	11	10	117.17
XV	10	11	94.95
XVI	13	30	197.02
XVII	18	24	197.28
XVIII	13	32	202.93
XIX	23	21	234.72
XX [2]	2	2	29.32

[1] Only last three quarters.　　　　[2] One quarter only.

France. Measured either by the totals of the geometric averages or by the number of disturbances, the most turbulent centuries in the history of France have been the twelfth, thirteenth, nineteenth, sixteenth, seventeenth, and eighteenth. The most orderly have been the tenth, seventh, and fifteenth centuries, the rest occupying an intermediary position. The last quarter of the nineteenth century was also very quiet. Looking at the quarter-century figure, one can see diversity in the amplitude of fluctuation from order to disorder. In some cases,

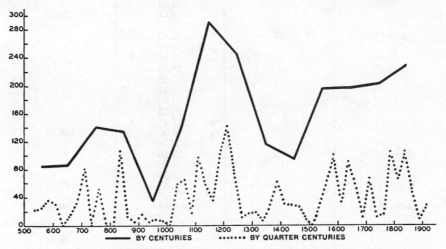

FIG. 13. MOVEMENT OF INTERNAL DISTURBANCES IN FRANCE

for instance in the eighth and ninth centuries, we have a sharp passage from one quarter with no disorder to one with a figure of 117.21, or from a disorderly quarter with an indicator of 80.81 to the next, perfectly orderly, with a zero indicator. In other words, a very brisk and sharp transition from quiet order to great turbulence, within the span of some twenty-five years or less, may take place. In other cases, the ups and downs of the curve of disturbances from one quarter century to another are gradual, rising or falling within a narrow limit. No particular uniformity is shown in this point. Sometimes the grade of the curve is gradual, and sometimes it turns sharply, with sudden jerks. The point is worth noting because there have been many theories set forth of "universal gradualness" in any social trend. These theories have contended that "*natura non facit saltum*," that nature does not make any jumps, always proceeding gradually, "evolutionally," and imperceptibly. Like many other quietistic generalizations, such a claim unduly interpolates a specific case into a universal rule.

The curve of the total of geometric averages by century periods moves essentially parallel with the curve of the frequency of disturbances, but deviates from the curve of the number of years with disturbance. None of these curves shows any noticeable periodicity, nor any continuous trend over the course of time.   The curves just fluctuate erratically.

Of the single disturbances, the greatest occurred in the years 1788–1799 (79.43);   678–686 (38.28);   760–767 (34.74);   844–845 (31.05);   1572–1577 (39.81);   1585–1593 (44.46).

The most turbulent quarter centuries were 1201–1225 (142.41); 1826–1850 (106.32);   826–850 (117.21);   1176–1200 (102.12);   1576–1600 (102.04);   1826–1850 (106.32);   1776–1800 (105.72).   (See Figure 13.)

It is impossible directly to compare the movement of disturbances with the movement of war in the history of France, because for war we have only absolute figures while here the indicators are relative.   Such a confrontation will be made for the whole of Europe.   For the present it is enough to say that the courses of these two curves are probably somewhat independent.   Here we do not find either a steadily increasing trend of disturbances from the earlier centuries to the seventeenth, or an unprecedented jump in the twentieth century, or several of the other characteristics of the curve of war.   What the relationship between them is will be discussed more fully in Chapter Fourteen.

The figures show, further, that it is impossible to contend that a great increase and explosion of disturbances occurs invariably, either in periods of "progress" and resplendence of the country, from the sociocultural, political, and economic standpoints, or in periods of decline.   On the one hand, such exceptionally brilliant periods as the period of Charlemagne (the last quarter of the eighth and the first quarter of the ninth centuries) and the period of Louis XIV were orderly; while on the other hand such prosperous and progressive periods as the second and third quarters of the nineteenth century were turbulent.   The same is true of several other periods.   Again, the tenth century can hardly be considered as a particularly brilliant period, and yet it was orderly and quiet.   In brief, here we meet the same lack of uniformity which has been met in the history of Rome and Byzantium and which will be encountered several times more.

Besides the "mixed" disturbances, the political and socioeconomic are predominant in the history of France.   In the centuries of consolidation of the Carlovingian Empire, the nationalistic, regional-separatistic disturbances played a considerable part.   Finally, the thirteenth century and, more especially, the sixteenth and seventeenth centuries are marked by the conspicuous role of religious disturbances.

V. Internal Disturbances of Germany and Austria

TABLE 32. TOTAL OF THE GEOMETRIC AVERAGE OF INTERNAL DISTURBANCES OF GERMANY AND AUSTRIA FROM 701 TO 1925 BY QUARTER CENTURIES

Quarter Century	Number of Disturbances	Measure of Disturbances	Total for the Quarter
701–725 A.D.	2	7.65 13.58	21.23
726–750	6	20.80 11.45 11.45 16.52 9.08 13.58	82.88
751–775	1	17.10	17.10
776–800	6	17.10 17.10 17.10 24.66 7.92 27.16	111.04
801–825	—	—	—
826–850	3	20.00 10.00 25.12	55.12
851–875	4	7.92 7.92 5.64 14.66	36.14
876–900	4	10.76 11.29 3.91 7.65	33.61
901–925	3	13.58 10.06 15.85	39.49
926–950	5	12.05 12.05 13.58 14.66 5.64	57.98
951–975	4	8.43 10.02 8.43 13.87	40.75
976–1000	4	6.93 11.45 13.58 6.54	38.50

TABLE 32. TOTAL OF THE GEOMETRIC AVERAGE OF INTERNAL DISTURB-
ANCES OF GERMANY AND AUSTRIA FROM 701 TO 1925 BY QUARTER
CENTURIES — *continued*

Quarter Century	Number of Disturbances	Measure of Disturbances	Total for the Quarter
1001–1025 A.D.	8	11.45 3.91 6.70 8.43 7.21 11.45 12.16 10.06	71.37
1026–1050	3	10.06 12.59 14.66	37.31
1051–1075	10	11.45 6.76 5.31 5.18 11.45 4.64 9.66 19.14 12.05 17.10	102.77
1076–1100	1	31.05	31.05
1101–1125	4	10.06 7.21 11.45 10.02	38.74
1126–1150	1	13.90 20.80 14.66 11.45	60.81
1151–1175	4	5.84 15.52 16.52 3.39	41.27
1176–1200	5	10.19 22.91 16.52 27.16 15.31	92.09
1201–1225	1	10.00	10.00
1226–1250	2	11.45 21.30	32.75
1251–1275	2	49.01 15.17	64.18

TABLE 32. TOTAL OF THE GEOMETRIC AVERAGE OF INTERNAL DISTURB-
ANCES OF GERMANY AND AUSTRIA FROM 701 TO 1925 BY QUARTER
CENTURIES — *continued*

Quarter Century	Number of Disturbances	Measure of Disturbances	Total for the Quarter
1276–1300 A.D.	9	7.65 9.66 12.59 4.21 14.66 11.45 12.05 5.18 6.05	83.58
1301–1325	2	12.10 6.70	18.80
1326–1350	7	10.02 10.02 10.02 24.66 10.02 17.10 14.66	96.50
1351–1375	4	10.02 10.02 11.45 12.79	44.28
1376–1400	3	21.53 15.85 5.18	42.56
1401–1425	1	21.88	21.88
1426–1450	4	21.88 21.88 19.14 15.85	78.75
1451–1475	1	10.02	10.02
1476–1500	3	10.02 15.17 21.53	46.72
1501–1525	4	4.21 4.21 13.58 27.61	49.61
1526–1550	2	13.58 15.85	29.43
1551–1575	3	7.12 4.21 4.21	15.54

TABLE 32.   TOTAL OF THE GEOMETRIC AVERAGE OF INTERNAL DISTURB-
ANCES OF GERMANY AND AUSTRIA FROM 701 TO 1925 BY QUARTER
CENTURIES — *continued*

Quarter Century	Number of Disturbances	Measure of Disturbances	Total for the Quarter
1576–1600 A.D.	—	—	—
1601–1625	1	11.45	11.45
1626–1650	1	6.70	6.70
1651–1675	—	—	—
1676–1700	—	—	—
1701–1725	1	5.31	5.31
1726–1750	—	—	—
1751–1775	—	—	—
1776–1800	3	12.05	
		10.76	
		10.00	32.81
1801–1825	2	10.76	
		12.16	22.92
1826–1850	4	17.10	
		6.70	
		7.36	
		22.91	54.07
1851–1875	1	4.64	4.64
1876–1900	2	7.66	
		9.66	17.32
1901–1925	9	4.64	
		7.66	
		9.09	
		36.73	
		12.79	
		15.17	
		10.76	
		4.21	
		6.70	107.75

TABLE 33.   TOTAL OF THE GEOMETRIC AVERAGE OF INTERNAL DISTURB-
ANCES OF GERMANY AND AUSTRIA BY CENTURIES

Century	Number of Disturbances	Number of Years with Disturbance	Total of Geometric Averages
VIII	15	18	232.25
IX	11	13	124.87
X	16	15	176.72
XI	22	27	242.50
XII	16	38	232.91
XIII	13	45	190.51
XIV	16	20	202.14
XV	9	12	157.37
XVI	9	12	94.58
XVII	2	2	18.15
XVIII	4	4	38.12
XIX	9	11	98.95
XX	9	8	107.75

Germany and Austria. Practically all the previous remarks made in regard to France and Rome are applicable to Germany, or rather to the German bodies politic of central Europe.   There is no continuous trend, and no periodicity. (See Figure 14.) Using our main criterion, as well as the actual number of disturbances, the most turbulent centuries —

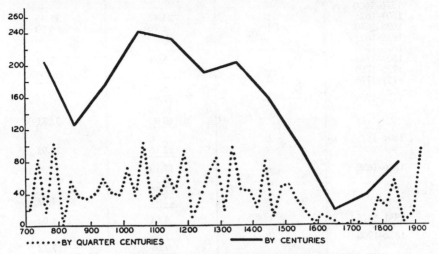

FIG. 14. MOVEMENT OF INTERNAL DISTURBANCES IN
GERMANY AND AUSTRIA

twentieth, eleventh, twelfth, eighth, and fourteenth — were rather in the earlier stages of German history than in the later centuries. The sixteenth, seventeenth, and eighteenth centuries, especially the seventeenth, were much more orderly than in many other countries. But the nineteenth century and more especially the twentieth, broke the orderly record and turned the declining curve of disturbance upward. However, the second part of the nineteenth century was notably free from turmoil in Germany.

Here again the passage from orderly to disorderly, or from less orderly to more orderly, quarter-century periods is, in some cases, sharp and abrupt, in other cases gradual and "evolutionary." No uniformity is given on that point.

The largest disturbances occurred in the years 1241–1273 (70.31); 1847–1849 (22.91); 1918–1919 (36.73); 1077–1080 (31.05); 1190–1109 (27.16); 792–794 (27.16); 784–785 (24.66); 1524–1525 (27.61); and other big disturbances are scattered throughout several centuries. The most turbulent quarter centuries were 1051–1075 (102.77); 776–800 (111.04); 1176–1200 (92.09); 1276–1300 (83.58); 1326–1350 (96.50); 1901–1925 (107.75); 726–750 (82.88).

In approximation one can say that no uniform relationship with the war curve is present. Both curves seem to move fairly independently.

A similar lack of uniformity is present in the relationship of the disturbances and the sociocultural, economic, and political blooming or decay.

Finally, most of the disturbances seem to belong to the "mixed" class. The fifteenth, sixteenth, and seventeenth centuries are marked by the domination of religious disturbances; nationalistic-separatistic disturbances played some role in the tenth, eleventh, and for a short time at the end of the eighteenth and the beginning of the nineteenth centuries.

VI. Internal Disturbances of England

TABLE 34. TOTAL OF THE GEOMETRIC AVERAGE OF INTERNAL DISTURB-
ANCES OF ENGLAND FROM 651 TO 1925 BY QUARTER CENTURIES

Quarter Century	Number of Disturbances	Measure of Disturbances	Total for the Quarter
651–675 A.D.	3	5.13 14.66 17.38	37.17
676–700	4	15.17 14.66 27.16 5.18	62.17
701–725	6	11.45 12.79 12.79 10.06 16.52 9.66	73.27
726–750	3	21.53 5.13 8.03	34.69
751–775	8	16.07 19.59 5.13 10.06 4.35 21.88 7.37 10.06	94.50
776–800	8	8.87 5.18 5.18 5.18 6.70 8.87 24.10 21.70	85.78

TABLE 34.   TOTAL OF THE GEOMETRIC AVERAGE OF INTERNAL DISTURB-
ANCES OF ENGLAND FROM 651 TO 1925 BY QUARTER CENTURIES —
continued

Quarter Century	Number of Disturbances	Measure of Disturbances	Total for the Quarter
801–825 A.D.	5	13.04 11.45 21.53 24.66 12.79	83.47
826–850	3	17.10 5.18 5.18	27.56
851–875	2	6.70 24.66	31.36
876–900	3	21.53 8.43 9.66	39.62
901–925	—	—	—
926–950	6	12.05 14.42 19.59 10.02 5.18 11.45	72.71
951–975	6	10.06 12.79 15.17 7.65 7.21 12.16	65.04
976–1000	—	—	—
1001–1025	2	14.66 16.52	31.18
1026–1050	2	14.66 7.21	21.87
1051–1075	6	9.66 9.66 11.45 11.45 55.22 12.59	110.03
1076–1100	2	10.06 8.43	18.49
1101–1125	2	3.15 5.31	8.46

TABLE 34.   TOTAL OF THE GEOMETRIC AVERAGE OF INTERNAL DISTURB-
ANCES OF ENGLAND FROM 651 TO 1925 BY QUARTER CENTURIES —
continued

Quarter Century	Number of Disturbances	Measure of Disturbances	Total for the Quarter
1126–1150 A.D.	3	5.31 10.00 39.96	55.27
1151–1175	3	9.24 4.47 23.82	37.53
1176–1200	—	—	—
1201–1225	3	41.21 13.58 10.06	64.85
1226–1250	2	5.13 15.17	20.30
1251–1275	2	15.17 22.91	38.08
1276–1300	4	13.58 12.05 12.05 25.94	63.62
1301–1325	5	17.10 17.06 14.42 12.05 16.52	77.15
1326–1350	2	12.59 5.18	17.77
1351–1375	—	—	—
1376–1400	5	24.10 14.66 5.13 19.14 3.16	66.19
1401–1425	6	25.28 9.08 7.65 9.66 8.43 4.64	64.74
1426–1450	1	17.10	17.10
1451–1475	3	34.74 43.75 43.75	122.24

TABLE 34. TOTAL OF THE GEOMETRIC AVERAGE OF INTERNAL DISTURB-
ANCES OF ENGLAND FROM 651 TO 1925 BY QUARTER CENTURIES —
continued

Quarter Century	Number of Disturbances	Measure of Disturbances	Total for the Quarter
1476–1500 A.D.	6	38.28	
		10.02	
		7.65	
		13.58	
		7.65	
		4.64	97.81
1501–1525	1	6.70	6.70
1526–1550	5	7.92	
		17.10	
		11.45	
		5.64	
		18.15	60.26
1551–1575	4	7.36	
		8.43	
		3.55	
		8.43	27.77
1576–1600	2	17.10	
		17.38	34.48
1601–1625	3	3.91	
		5.64	
		5.64	15.19
1626–1650	5	2.92	
		5.64	
		10.00	
		77.27	
		9.05	104.88
1651–1675	4	18.11	
		4.43	
		8.43	
		7.65	38.62
1676–1700	5	9.08	
		4.47	
		6.70	
		25.59	
		4.47	50.31
1701–1725	2	4.47	
		17.10	21.57
1726–1750	2	6.70	
		19.14	25.84
1751–1775	2	4.64	
		7.92	12.56

TABLE 34.   TOTAL OF THE GEOMETRIC AVERAGE OF INTERNAL DISTURB-
ANCES OF ENGLAND FROM 651 TO 1925 BY QUARTER CENTURIES —
continued

Quarter Century	Number of Disturbances	Measure of Disturbances	Total for the Quarter
1776–1800 A.D.	4	11.45 9.66 7.65 12.79	41.55
1801–1825	4	5.84 6.29 3.55 3.91	19.59
1826–1850	4	10.06 16.52 9.66 4.64	40.88
1851–1875	1	6.70	6.70
1876–1900	1	9.08	9.08
1901–1925	2	12.79 16.52	29.31

TABLE 35.   TOTAL OF THE GEOMETRIC AVERAGE OF INTERNAL DISTURB-
ANCES OF ENGLAND BY CENTURIES

Century	Number of Disturbances	Number of Years with Disturbance	Total of Geometric Average
VII	7 [1]	10 [1]	99.34
VIII	28	31	288.24
IX	12	18	182.01
X	12	14	137.75
XI	12	16	181.57
XII	7	22	101.26
XIII	11	21	186.85
XIV	12	14	161.11
XV	15	28	301.89
XVI	12	15	129.21
XVII	17	27	209.00
XVIII	10	11	101.52
XIX	10	12	76.25
XX	1	3	29.31

[1] For two quarters of the century only.

England. There is no continuous trend and no periodicity. The most disorderly centuries were the fifteenth, eighth, seventeenth, thirteenth, ninth, and eleventh. The most orderly were the nineteenth, twelfth, and eighteenth. The twentieth century has shown a rising tide of disturbances compared with the preceding half century. But the rise up to 1925 has been moderate.

Of the single disturbances the largest occurred in the years 1641–1649 (77.27); 1066–1070 (55.22); 1688 (25.59); 1650–1652 (27.16); 1455–1483 (34.74, 43.75, 43.75, 38.28); 1138–1153 (49.20); 692–694 (27.16); 1215–1217 (41.21); 1265–1267 (22.91); 1297–1300 (25.94); 1381 (24.10);

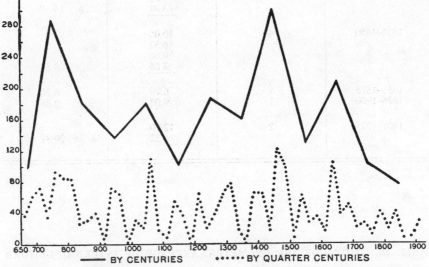

——— BY CENTURIES   •••••• BY QUARTER CENTURIES

FIG. 15. MOVEMENT OF INTERNAL DISTURBANCES IN ENGLAND

1400–1408 (28.44). The most turbulent quarter centuries were 751–775 (94.50); 776–800 (85.78); 801–825 (83.47); 1451–1475 (122.24); 1476–1500 (97.81); 1626–1650 (104.88); 1051–1075 (110.03). Again there is no tangible periodicity or trend, and there are both sharp and gradual turns of the curve from period to period. (See Figure 15.)

One can hardly discover any uniform relationship between the movement of the curve of disturbances and the movement of the curve of war, or between the former and the periods of progress or decay in the history of the country.

From the fifteenth to the eighteenth centuries the disturbances have a marked religious color. Throughout almost the whole period studied the nationalistic-separatistic disturbances have also played a tangible role. Most of the other disturbances were of a "mixed" nature.

VII. Internal Disturbances of Italy

TABLE 36.   TOTAL OF THE GEOMETRIC AVERAGE OF INTERNAL DISTURB-
ANCES OF ITALY FROM 526 TO 1925 BY QUARTER CENTURIES

Quarter Century	Number of Disturbances	Measure of Disturbances	Total for the Quarter
526–550 A.D.	3	13.90	
		9.29	
		7.36	30.55
551–575	2	31.05	38.41
		7.36	
576–600	1	31.55	31.55
601–625	1	9.08	9.08
626–650	2	7.36	
		11.45	18.81
651–675	3	7.36	
		24.10	
		7.36	38.82
676–700	3	10.76	
		7.65	
		9.66	28.07
701–725	7	24.70	
		17.10	
		13.58	
		10.06	
		11.45	
		11.45	
		14.16	102.50
726–750	7	16.53	
		7.65	
		5.13	
		18.15	
		11.06	
		7.36	
		7.36	73.24
751–775	5	9.50	
		10.06	
		9.66	
		9.66	
		7.58	46.46
776–800	5	7.57	
		17.10	
		13.58	
		12.79	
		0.59	51.63
801–825	4	14.88	
		3.91	
		15.85	
		8.43	43.07

TABLE 36. TOTAL OF THE GEOMETRIC AVERAGE OF INTERNAL DISTURB-
ANCES OF ITALY FROM 526 TO 1925 BY QUARTER CENTURIES—*continued*

Quarter Century	Number of Disturbances	Measure of Disturbances	Total for the Quarter
826–850 A.D.	9	9.50	
		15.17	
		14.09	
		16.14	
		7.36	
		4.12	
		17.10	
		8.43	
		7.65	99.56
851–875	2	4.12	
		10.02	14.14
876–900	10	14.66	
		5.84	
		5.84	
		9.08	
		11.45	
		6.54	
		4.12	
		7.65	
		4.12	
		20.32	69.62
901–925	5	7.36	
		18.15	
		4.12	
		15.17	
		9.29	54.09
926–950	7	14.66	
		19.59	
		5.84	
		5.18	
		7.36	
		10.02	
		12.05	74.70
951–975	6	11.45	
		6.08	
		7.36	
		7.92	
		6.70	
		12.59	52.10
976–1000	8	14.66	
		11.45	
		10.02	
		17.10	
		4.12	
		5.84	
		12.79	
		10.02	86.00

TABLE 36. TOTAL OF THE GEOMETRIC AVERAGE OF INTERNAL DISTURB-
ANCES OF ITALY FROM 526 TO 1925 BY QUARTER CENTURIES — *continued*

Quarter Century	Number of Disturbances	Measure of Disturbances	Total for the Quarter
1001–1025 A.D.	6	8.87	
		12.79	
		12.39	
		33.57	
		12.05	
		3.91	83.58
1026–1050	7	7.92	
		6.70	
		9.08	
		19.59	
		10.00	
		10.76	
		7.04	71.09
1051–1075	4	4.12	
		12.05	
		12.05	
		9.08	37.30
1076–1100	3	12.79	
		10.76	
		15.17	38.72
1101–1125	2	15.85	
		17.38	33.23
1126–1150	1	10.00	10.00
1151–1175	6	6.70	
		6.70	
		10.76	
		28.84	
		11.94	
		11.54	72.48
1176–1200	2	17.30	
		23.23	40.53
1201–1225	2	7.92	
		11.45	19.37
1226–1250	5	33.65	
		6.08	
		7.21	
		4.47	
		7.04	58.45

TABLE 36. TOTAL OF THE GEOMETRIC AVERAGE OF INTERNAL DISTURB-
ANCES OF ITALY FROM 526 TO 1925 BY QUARTER CENTURIES—*continued*

Quarter Century	Number of Disturbances	Measure of Disturbances	Total for the Quarter
1251–1275 A.D.	16	9.66	
		8.07	
		9.08	
		8.07	
		10.02	
		5.18	
		18.15	
		5.60	
		7.04	
		5.60	
		11.45	
		25.12	
		5.60	
		4.86	146.14
1276–1300	9	11.45	
		12.79	
		13.58	
		5.60	
		5.60	
		5.60	
		5.60	
		5.60	
		3.68	71.50
1301–1325	16	14.73	
		5 60	
		9.08	
		5.60	
		3.91	
		5.60	
		10.76	
		12.05	
		5.60	
		6.29	
		11.45	
		10.76	
		10.76	
		5.60	
		5.60	
		10.26	134.15
1326–1350	8	7.92	
		4.86	
		5.84	
		10.76	
		11.45	
		12.79	
		16.14	
		10.76	80.52

TABLE 36.   TOTAL OF THE GEOMETRIC AVERAGE OF INTERNAL DISTURB-
ANCES OF ITALY FROM 526 TO 1925 BY QUARTER CENTURIES—*continued*

Quarter Century	Number of Disturbances	Measure of Disturbances	Total for the Quarter
1351–1375 A.D.	9	6.70 4.47 10.02 7.04 5.84 10.00 8.55 15.17 6.02	73.81
1376–1400	11	18.08 13.58 5.84 12.59 12.59 8.43 10.02 18.41 15.52 9.08 19.59	143.73
1401–1425	8	10.00 5.60 9.66 10.02 15.52 17.10 15.17 11.45	94.52
1426–1450	4	9.52 5.31 17.10 11.45	43.38
1451–1475	4	11.45 9.66 3.15 8.07	32.33
1476–1500	8	15.52 4.12 6.70 14.66 4.54 14.66 8.07 5.84	74.11
1501–1525	3	9.08 10.02 9.66	28.76

TABLE 36.   TOTAL OF THE GEOMETRIC AVERAGE OF INTERNAL DISTURB-
ANCES OF ITALY FROM 526 TO 1925 BY QUARTER CENTURIES—*continued*

Quarter Century	Number of Disturbances	Measure of Disturbances	Total for the Quarter
1526–1550 A.D.	4	7.92 6.29 4.12 3.91	22.25
1551–1575	2	19.14 7.58	26.72
1576–1600	3	7.57 3.15 4.47	15.19
1601–1625	2	2.46 3.15	5.61
1626–1650	2	2.15 21.88	24.03
1651–1675	1	3.15	3.15
1676–1700	2	4.64 6.70	11.34
1701–1725	2	3.15 15.17	18.32
1726–1750	1	13.58	13.58
1751–1775	1	15.17	15.17
1776–1800	1	15.17	15.17
1801–1825	3	9.08 6.29 19.14	34.51
1826–1850	3	15.17 6.70 34.74	56.61
1851–1875	1	14.66	14.66
1876–1900	3	7.21 8.43 5.18	20.82
1901–1925	5	10.06 5.31 4.21 23.82 20.80	64.20

TABLE 37. TOTAL OF THE GEOMETRIC AVERAGE OF INTERNAL DISTURB-
ANCES OF ITALY BY CENTURIES

Century	Number of Disturbances	Number of Years with Disturbance	Total of Geometric Averages
VI	6[1]	8[1]	100.51
VII	9	10	94.78
VIII	19	36	273.83
IX	24	54	226.39
X	26	36	266.89
XI	20	34	230.69
XII	11	32	156.24
XIII	32	38	295.46
XIV	42	43	352.21
XV	24	23	244.34
XVI	12	14	92.92
XVII	7	8	44.13
XVIII	5	9	62.24
XIX	10	13	126.60
XX	5	6	64.20

[1] For three quarters of the century only.

Italy. All in all, the Italian peninsula seems to have been one of
the most turbulent regions in Europe (see Figure 16); especially from
the eighth to the sixteenth centuries the total indicators for Italy (taken
as a geographical region) seem to be noticeably higher than in most
European countries. Considering that Italy, in connection with the
Roman Catholic See, was the focal point where all the antagonistic

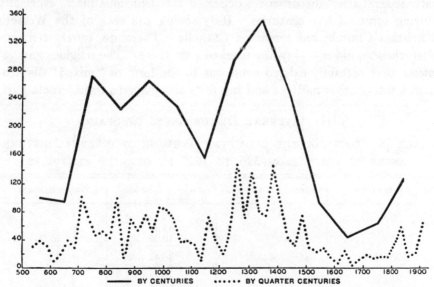

FIG. 16. MOVEMENT OF INTERNAL DISTURBANCES IN ITALY

III — 3ᵉ

interests of most of the European countries converged and clashed, such a conclusion is not surprising. According to the indicators, the fourteenth, thirteenth, eighth, tenth, fifteenth, eleventh, and ninth centuries were especially disorderly. The sixteenth, seventeenth, and part of the eighteenth centuries were comparatively quiet. But the nineteenth and the twentieth centuries have shown themselves more turbulent than the preceding three centuries. This means again that no continuous trend toward the increase or decrease of disturbance is shown during the centuries studied.

The biggest single disturbances occurred in the years 1848–1849 (34.74); 1158–1162 (28.84); 1174–1178 (28.84); 1234–1241 (33.65); 566–567 (31.05); 590–591 (31.55); 720–732 (30.69). The most turbulent quarter centuries were 701–725 (102.50); 826–850 (99.56); 1251–1275 (146.14); 1301–1325 (134.15); 1376–1400 (143.73); 1401–1425 (94.52).

As Italy is here considered as a territorial unit, no comparison of the curve of disturbances with the curve of war is possible. The confrontation of the century indicators of disturbances with the centuries of socio-cultural and economic blooming of most of the states in Italy seems to support the previous conclusion that there is hardly any positive or negative uniform relationship between these two "variables."

Again, most of the disturbances were "mixed" in their nature. The existence of city states for several centuries explains why the "national-istic-separatistic" disturbances occupied a conspicuous place, especially during some of the centuries. Italy, being the seat of the Western Christian Church, has remained Catholic. Therefore, purely religious disturbances did not play any marked part there. The religious antago-nisms that certainly existed come out in the form of "mixed" disturb-ances, where other motives and interests also played a considerable part.

VIII. Internal Disturbances of Spain

TABLE 38. TOTAL OF THE GEOMETRIC AVERAGE OF INTERNAL DISTURB-ANCES OF SPAIN FROM 526 TO 1925 BY QUARTER CENTURIES

Quarter Century	Number of Disturbances	Measure of Disturbances	Total for the Quarter
526–550 A.D.	3	13.39 13.39 10.00	36.78
551–575	4	46.42 22.89 19.13 18.17	106.61

TABLE 38.   TOTAL OF THE GEOMETRIC AVERAGE OF INTERNAL DISTURB-
ANCES OF SPAIN FROM 526 TO 1925 BY QUARTER CENTURIES — *continued*

Quarter Century	Number of Disturbances	Measure of Disturbances	Total for the Quarter
576–600 A.D.	4	18.17 19.57 31.58 16.51	85.83
601–625	3	11.45 11.45 16.51	39.41
626–650	3	21.90 12.60 14.12	48.62
651–675	2	14.12 19.57	33.69
676–700	2	5.65 12.16	17.81
701–725	1	31.07	31.07
726–750	6	17.10 21.90 31.58 19.13 17.10	125.94
751–775	8	27.59 22.89 9.09 17.38 11.45 9.09 11.45 39.60	148.54
776–800	4	8.80 11.45 9.44 7.49	37.18
801–825	4	6.69 7.94 7.94 4.64	27.21
826–850	5	13.57 25.96 13.92 24.77 9.66	87.88

TABLE 38. TOTAL OF THE GEOMETRIC AVERAGE OF INTERNAL DISTURB-
ANCES OF SPAIN FROM 526 TO 1925 BY QUARTER CENTURIES — *continued*

Quarter Century	Number of Disturbances	Measure of Disturbances	Total for the Quarter
851–875 A.D.	6	27.59	
		11.45	
		9.44	
		9.66	
		11.45	
		9.66	79.25
876–900	9	7.66	
		3.98	
		12.60	
		7.66	
		13.04	
		9.09	
		9.09	
		17.10	
		9.09	89.31
901–925	7	0.82	
		5.59	
		22.89	
		13.10	
		12.44	
		6.08	
		7.66	68.58
926–950	6	4.66	
		22.89	
		7.66	
		10.00	
		18.17	
		7.66	71.04
951–975	7	20.80	
		9.66	
		11.45	
		13.39	
		13.39	
		9.66	
		7.21	85.56
976–1000	4	18.12	
		14.42	
		8.93	
		18.17	59.19
1001–1025	10	4.64	
		6.69	
		26.21	
		21.90	
		9.66	
		16.13	
		10.63	
		26.21	
		10.63	
		10.63	143.33

TABLE 38.   TOTAL OF THE GEOMETRIC AVERAGE OF INTERNAL DISTURB-
ANCES OF SPAIN FROM 526 TO 1925 BY QUARTER CENTURIES — *continued*

Quarter Century	Number of Disturbances	Measure of Disturbances	Total for the Quarter
1026–1050 A.D.	8	11.45 10.63 10.63 11.45 18.17 6.69 5.31 7.66	81.99
1051–1075	7	15.87 5.31 5.31 14.42 8.43 9.44 7.94	66.72
1076–1100	3	5.31 10.00 14.42	29.73
1101–1125	6	26.21 20.80 4.64 4.64 10.77 19.73	86.79
1126–1150	5	4.93 9.66 18.17 10.16 27.14	70.00
1151–1175	6	18.17 14.42 9.09 14.42 11.45 12.16	79.71
1176–1200	1	12.60	12.60
1201–1225	5	13.58 10.63 12.16 18.10 16.51	70.98
1226–1250	2	5.17 4.22	9.39

TABLE 38.   TOTAL OF THE GEOMETRIC AVERAGE OF INTERNAL DISTURB-
ANCES OF SPAIN FROM 526 TO 1925 BY QUARTER CENTURIES — *continued*

Quarter Century	Number of Disturbances	Measure of Disturbances	Total for the Quarter
1251–1275 A.D.	4	10.00 23.21 20.80 19.57	73.58
1276–1300	8	11.45 11.45 22.89 8.43 13.57 24.66 6.69 17.60	116.74
1301–1325	6	8.80 10.00 13.39 29.32 9.44 26.21	97.16
1326–1350	6	8.43 27.32 5.15 19.57 24.66 5.31	91.14
1351–1375	4	10.40 24.66 22.89 16.51	74.46
1376–1400	5	10.00 20.80 9.66 8.43 8.43	57.32
1401–1425	4	18.17 7.94 8.43 12.16	46.70
1426–1450	6	8.43 20.80 18.17 14.42 14.42 16.51	92.75

TABLE 38. TOTAL OF THE GEOMETRIC AVERAGE OF INTERNAL DISTURB-
ANCES OF SPAIN FROM 526 TO 1925 BY QUARTER CENTURIES—*continued*

Quarter Century	Number of Disturbances	Measure of Disturbances	Total for the Quarter
1451–1475 A.D.	5	11.45 13.92 30.72 27.14 13.57	96.80
1476–1500	6	13.57 6.08 11.45 6.54 7.94 18.09	63.67
1501–1525	5	9.05 11.45 23.80 34.20 17.10	95.61
1526–1550	1	9.66	9.66
1551–1575	1	25.96	25.96
1576–1600	2	6.08 9.66	15.74
1601–1625	2	3.91 6.08	9.99
1626–1650	2	10.00 22.43	32.43
1651–1675	4	4.07 13.10 3.11	29.16
1676–1700	—	—	—
1701–1725	1	25.91	25.91
1726–1750	—	—	—
1751–1775	1	9.66	9.66
1776–1800	—	—	—
1801–1825	6	4.64 14.42 3.91 3.91 50.00 7.66	84.54

TABLE 38.   TOTAL OF THE GEOMETRIC AVERAGE OF INTERNAL DISTURB-
ANCES OF SPAIN FROM 526 TO 1925 BY QUARTER CENTURIES — *continued*

Quarter Century	Number of Disturbances	Measure of Disturbances	Total for the Quarter
1826–1850 A.D.	8	8.43 10.00 66.49 7.66 5.31 5.31 6.69 22.89	132.78
1851–1875	7	10.00 10.00 8.43 7.66 7.66 39.15 53.30	136.20
1876–1900	6	13.64 6.69 6.69 3.51 4.22 8.43	44.98
1901–1925	6	6.69 4.64 8.68 21.54 5.31 10.00	56.86

TABLE 39.   TOTAL OF THE GEOMETRIC AVERAGE OF INTERNAL DISTURB-
ANCES OF SPAIN BY CENTURIES

Century	Number of Disturbances	Number of Years with Disturbance	Total of Geometric Averages
VI	12 [1]	21 [1]	239.22
VII	10	10	139.53
VIII	20	32	342.73
IX	23	48	283.55
X	22	34	284.46
XI	28	38	314.77
XII	18	27	256.46
XIII	19	39	270.69
XIV	19	31	320.08
XV	21	43	299.92
XVI	9	15	146.97
XVII	8	20	81.58
XVIII	2	13	35.57
XIX	27	43	398.50
XX	6	6	56.86

[1] For three quarters of the century only.

Spain. Here Spain, for the early centuries, means the territorial abode of several states rather than one state. The most turbulent centuries were the nineteenth, eighth, fourteenth, fifteenth, tenth, eleventh, ninth, and the thirteenth. (See Figure 17.) The most orderly centuries were the eighteenth, seventeenth, and seventh. The largest single

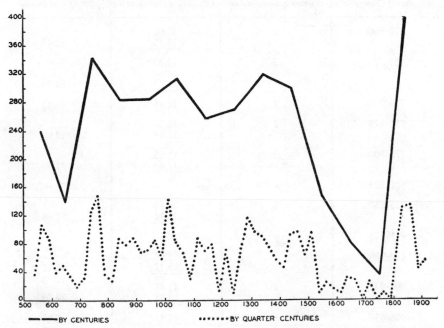

FIG. 17. MOVEMENT OF INTERNAL DISTURBANCES IN SPAIN

disturbances occurred in the years 766–777 (48.40); 1461–1472 (30.72); 1520–1522 (34.20); 1868–1870 (39.15); 1872–1876 (66.94); and the most turbulent quarter centuries were 551–575 (106.61); 726–750 (125.94); 751–775 (148.54); 1276–1300 (116.74); 1826–1850 (132.78); 1851–1875 (136.20); and 1001–1025 (143.33).

Again the turns of the curve from period to period are in some cases sharp and sudden, in others slow and gradual. No periodicity and no continuous trend are noticeable. Among the disturbances, those of nationalistic-separatistic nature played a prominent part in Spanish history. One can hardly see any uniformity in the relationship between the curve of disturbances, the curve of war, or the curve of sociocultural and political blossoming or decay.

IX. Internal Disturbances of The Netherlands

TABLE 40. TOTAL OF THE GEOMETRIC AVERAGE OF INTERNAL DISTURBANCES OF THE NETHERLANDS FROM 676 TO 1925 BY QUARTER CENTURIES

Quarter Century	Number of Disturbances	Measure of Disturbances	Total for the Quarter
676–700 A.D.	2	41.02 11.45	52.47
701–725	3	21.53 21.53 21.53	64.59
726–750	1	11.45	11.45
751–775	2	11.45 11.45	22.90
776–800	2	11.45 11.45	22.90
801–825	—	—	—
826–850	2	28.84 28.84	57.68
851–875	—	—	—
876–900	2	25.94 15.17	41.11
901–925	2	11.45 18.15	29.60
926–950	1	11.45	11.45
951–975	2	8.43 11.75	20.18
976–1000	2	7.84 9.08	16.92
1001–1025	2	13.58 21.53	35.11
1026–1050	1	13.58	13.58
1051–1075	3	11.45 13.58 21.53	46.56
1076–1100	1	15.17	15.17
1101–1125	2	18.15 13.58	31.73
1126–1150	5	21.53 11.45 27.12 8.43 6.76	75.29

TABLE 40. TOTAL OF THE GEOMETRIC AVERAGE OF INTERNAL DISTURB-
ANCES OF THE NETHERLANDS FROM 676 TO 1925 BY QUARTER CEN-
TURIES — *continued*

Quarter Century	Number of Disturbances	Measure of Disturbances	Total for the Quarter
1151–1175 A.D.	2	11.52 11.45	22.97
1176–1200	1	9.08	9.08
1201–1225	4	24.66 16.52 8.58 11.45	61.21
1226–1250	1	28.66	28.66
1251–1275	4	10.76 23.49 8.55 13.58	56.38
1276–1300	3	13.58 7.28 8.07	28.93
1301–1325	8	27.31 10.76 10.76 27.61 13.58 11.43 6.08 6.70	114.23
1326–1350	7	11.43 8.07 4.21 11.45 10.76 10.02 2.06	58.00
1351–1375	8	18.55 19.59 9.08 17.10 6.70 8.07 7.21 6.08	92.38
1376–1400	5	6.08 14.63 12.05 7.65 21.88	62.29

TABLE 40.　TOTAL OF THE GEOMETRIC AVERAGE OF INTERNAL DISTURB-
ANCES OF THE NETHERLANDS FROM 676 TO 1925 BY QUARTER CEN-
TURIES — *continued*

Quarter Century	Number of Disturbances	Measure of Disturbances	Total for the Quarter
1401–1425 A.D.	5	18.15	
		21.88	
		10.02	
		7.31	
		14.59	71.95
1426–1450	4	21.93	
		7.29	
		17.10	
		10.76	57.08
1451–1475	3	10.76	
		6.08	
		8.55	25.39
1476–1500	1	7.65	7.65
1501–1525	—	—	—
1526–1550	—	—	—
1551–1575	3	7.65	
		17.10	
		9.68	34.43
1576–1600	1	60.37	60.37
1601–1625	2	21.78	
		8.43	30.21
1626–1650	2	7.12	
		7.21	14.33
1651–1675	1	8.43	8.43
1676–1700	2	10.76	
		5.31	16.08
1701–1725	1	5.31	5.31
1726–1750	1	17.54	17.54
1751–1775	—	—	—
1776–1800	5	28.84	
		34.20	
		22.91	
		9.66	
		9.08	104.69
1801–1825	1	15.85	15.85
1826–1850	1	34.74	34.74
1851–1875	1	5.31	5.31
1876–1900	1	6.08	6.08
1901–1925	—	—	—

TABLE 41. TOTAL OF THE GEOMETRIC AVERAGE OF INTERNAL DISTURB-
ANCES OF THE NETHERLANDS BY CENTURIES

Century	Number of Disturbances	Number of Years with Disturbance	Total of Geometric Averages
VIII	8	8	121.84
IX	4	10	98.79
X	6	11	78.15
XI	7	11	110.42
XII	8	36	139.07
XIII	11	44	175.18
XIV	27	51	326.90
XV	12	18	162.07
XVI	3	31	94.80
XVII	7	16	69.05
XVIII	7	10	127.54
XIX	4	4	61.98
XX	—	—	—

The Netherlands. The fourteenth, thirteenth, fifteenth, twelfth, eighteenth, and eighth centuries were the most turbulent here. The nineteenth, seventeenth, tenth, sixteenth, and ninth centuries were the most virtuous in this respect.[2] The first quarter of the twentieth century was also most orderly. (See Figure 18.)

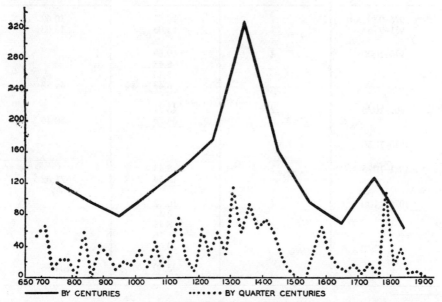

FIG. 18. MOVEMENT OF INTERNAL DISTURBANCES IN THE NETHERLANDS

[2] The fact that the century of the Great Revolution (1572–1609) gives a low figure of disturbances is, to some extent, surprising, in spite of the fact that the Great Revolution is the biggest of all the single disturbances of the Netherlands, with the geometric average 91.83, a

Of the single disturbances, the three largest occurred respectively in the years 1572–1609 (91.83); 1788–1790 (34.20); 1830 (34.74); 1220–1245 (37.24); 678–686 (41.02). Of the single quarter centuries, the most disorderly were 1301–1325 (114.23); 1351–1375 (92.38); 1776–1800 (104.69). Again one does not find any definite periodicity or any trace of a steady trend.

Most of the disturbances were of the "mixed" type; of the specific types, the religious appear in the sixteenth and seventeenth centuries; the nationalistic-separatistic in the eighth, tenth, twelfth, thirteenth, and especially in the nineteenth and eighteenth centuries.

No uniform relationship, positive or negative, with war movement or with the periods of progress and decay, is noticeable.

X. INTERNAL DISTURBANCES OF RUSSIA

TABLE 42. TOTAL OF THE GEOMETRIC AVERAGE OF INTERNAL DISTURBANCES OF RUSSIA FROM 926 TO 1925 BY QUARTER CENTURIES

Quarter Century	Number of Disturbances	Measure of Disturbances	Total for the Quarter
926–950 A.D.	1	10.62	10.62
951–975	1	13.03	13.03
976–1000	4	19.59	
		8.43	
		8.43	
		8.43	44.88
1001–1025	2	45.71	
		34.75	80.46
1026–1050	—	—	—
1051–1075	2	8.43	
		12.59	21.02
1076–1100	7	16.52	
		8.43	
		8.43	
		18.16	
		9.66	
		9.66	
		33.50	104.36

value not exceeded by any single disturbance in all the countries studied. Considering that the sixteenth century, however, had only two other disturbances and that particularly spectacular disturbances tend to appear to us as especially great, and that the Great Revolution was spread over thirty-seven years, falling into two different centuries, the result is perhaps not so strange as it may look at first glance.

TABLE 42. TOTAL OF THE GEOMETRIC AVERAGE OF INTERNAL DISTURB-
ANCES OF RUSSIA FROM 926 TO 1925 BY QUARTER CENTURIES — *continued*

Quarter Century	Number of Disturbances	Measure of Disturbances	Total for the Quarter
1101–1125 A.D.	3	11.46 18.16 9.66	39.28
1126–1150	4	9.66 12.16 38.64 18.46	78.92
1151–1175	7	28.97 8.67 11.45 10.62 9.66 34.76 34.76	138.89
1176–1200	5	9.66 13.58 7.36 28.23 7.36	66.19
1201–1225	8	16.71 10.62 13.49 18.03 24.66 5.39 10.62 10.62	110.14
1226–1250	7	10.62 9.66 10.62 17.10 19.59 11.45 16.14	95.18
1251–1275	5	8.67 10.62 19.14 7.36 21.88	67.67
1276–1300	7	16.98 16.98 10.62 31.84 5.47 10.62 9.66	102.17

TABLE 42.   TOTAL OF THE GEOMETRIC AVERAGE OF INTERNAL DISTURB-
ANCES OF RUSSIA FROM 926 TO 1925 BY QUARTER CENTURIES — *continued*

Quarter Century	Number of Disturbances	Measure of Disturbances	Total for the Quarter
1301–1325 A.D.	8	9.66 4.64 16.98 4.64 11.56 29.24 19.59 6.70	103.01
1326–1350	10	6.88 8.43 7.65 6.04 3.91 8.43 11.46 11.46 9.66 9.66	83.88
1351–1375	7	9.07 7.36 12.89 13.09 9.66 9.66 5.64	67.37
1376–1400	3	9.66 10.62 3.56	23.80
1401–1425	7	9.66 9.66 7.65 9.07 9.66 10.62 3.63	59.35
1426–1450	2	54.45 32.82	87.27
1451–1475	3	26.25 3.91 10.02	40.18
1476–1500	3	4.64 8.43 8.43	21.50
1501–1525	—	—	—

TABLE 42.   TOTAL OF THE GEOMETRIC AVERAGE OF INTERNAL DISTURB-
ANCES OF RUSSIA FROM 926 TO 1925 BY QUARTER CENTURIES — *continued*,

Quarter Century	Number of Disturbances	Measure of Disturbances	Total for the Quarter
1526–1550 A.D.	3	10.00 15.89 11.16	37.05
1551–1575	—	—	—
1576–1600	3	6.74 8.43 3.91	19.08
1601–1625	1	79.44	79.44
1626–1650	3	6.88 15.31 15.89	38.08
1651–1675	5	9.29 11.46 34.75 15.89 7.65	79.04
1676–1700	4	10.62 9.66 11.46 13.58	45.32
1701–1725	4	8.43 9.66 13.09 8.43	39.61
1726–1750	5	6.70 5.18 5.84 5.64 5.12	28.48
1751–1775	12	14.42 8.43 3.55 7.81 3.55 8.43 5.12 5.12 3.91 3.55 12.89 35.56	112.38

TABLE 42.   TOTAL OF THE GEOMETRIC AVERAGE OF INTERNAL DISTURB-
ANCES OF RUSSIA FROM 926 TO 1925 BY QUARTER CENTURIES — *continued*

Quarter Century	Number of Disturbances	Measure of Disturbances	Total for the Quarter
1776–1800 A.D.	1	3.55	3.55
1801–1825	3	5.84 5.84 7.94	19.62
1826–1850	7	6.71 27.51 5.84 5.12 7.21 17.95 6.71	76.15
1851–1875	3	7.65 10.62 21.53	39.80
1876–1900	4	2.46 22.91 5.84 3.56	34.77
1901–1925	6	28.25 5.12 39.17 7.21 6.73 63.08	149.56

TABLE 43.   TOTAL OF THE GEOMETRIC AVERAGE OF INTERNAL DISTURB-
ANCES OF RUSSIA BY CENTURIES

Century	Number of Distrubances	Number of Years with Disturbance	Total of Geometric Averages
X	6 [1]	6 [1]	68.53
XI	11	23	205.84
XII	19	46	323.28
XIII	26	35	375.16
XIV	28	28	277.76
XV	14	40	208.30
XVI	6	8	56.13
XVII	13	30	201.88
XVIII	22	24	184.02
XIX	17	29	160.34
XX	6	11	149.56

[1] For three quarters of the century only.

Russia. Of the century periods, the most disorderly were the thirteenth, twelfth, fourteenth, fifteenth, eleventh, and seventeenth, the twentieth century being so far also exceptionally disorderly. The most peaceful were the sixteenth, tenth, and nineteenth. Of the single disturbances, the largest occurred in the years 1014–1019 (45.71); 1169–1175 (34.76); 1425–1440 (58.08); 1446–1462 (59.07); 1604–1613 (79.44);

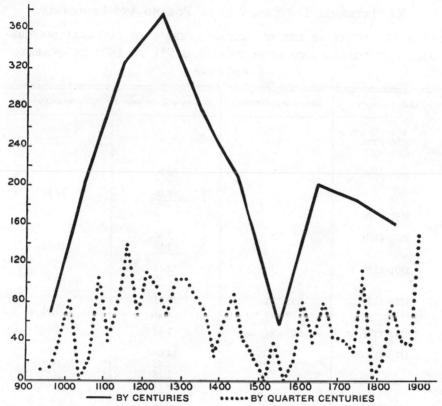

FIG. 19.   MOVEMENT OF INTERNAL DISTURBANCES IN RUSSIA

1667–1671 (34.75); 1773–1741 (35.56); 1905–1906 (39.17); 1917–1921 (63.08). Of the single periods by quarter centuries the most turbulent were 1076–1100 (104.36); 1151–1175 (138.89); 1201–1225 (110.14); 1276–1300 (102.17); 1301–1325 (103.01); 1751–1775 (112.38); 1901–1925 (149.56). (See Figure 19.)

Besides the political and socioeconomic disturbances, the national-separatistic ones played a considerable role in several of the centuries studied. The predominantly religious disturbances appeared in the seventeenth century. Most of the disturbances were, however, of a "mixed" nature.

Other remarks made previously as to the lack of any continuous trend, periodicity, or uniformity in the relationship between the curve of disturbances and the curve of war, or in the relationship of the periods of progress and decay, are also applicable here.

XI. Internal Disturbances of Poland and Lithuania

TABLE 44.   TOTAL OF THE GEOMETRIC AVERAGE OF INTERNAL DISTURB-
ANCES OF POLAND AND LITHUANIA FROM 951 TO 1800 BY QUARTER
CENTURIES

Quarter Century	Number of Disturbances	Measure of Disturbances	Total for the Quarter
951–975 A.D.	—	—	—
976–1000	—	—	—
1001–1025	—	—	—
1026–1050	3	12.16 5.18 58.48	75.82
1051–1075	—	—	—
1076–1100	2	7.36 12.16	18.52
1101–1125	2	32.43 17.38	49.81
1126–1150	2	28.25 7.36	35.61
1151–1175	1	7.92	7.92
1176–1200	4	14.66 7.48 7.48 33.81	63.43
1201–1225	2	29.00 14.66	43.66
1226–1250	3	26.18 20.80 16.18	63.16
1251–1275	8	4.62 13.58 10.76 13.58 10.76 13.58 9.08 9.08	85.04

TABLE 44.   TOTAL OF THE GEOMETRIC AVERAGE OF INTERNAL DISTURB-
ANCES OF POLAND AND LITHUANIA FROM 951 TO 1800 BY QUARTER
CENTURIES — *continued*

Quarter Century	Number of Disturbances	Measure of Disturbances	Total for the Quarter
1276–1300 A.D.	5	13.58 20.80 18.15 14.66 14.66	81.85
1301–1325	2	36.73 11.45	48.18
1326–1350	2	5.84 9.29	15.13
1351–1375	—	—	—
1376–1400	6	7.92 32.42 17.10 3.91 14.66 7.65	83.66
1401–1425	3	5.60 14.66 9.08	29.34
1426–1450	6	18.15 6.54 12.16 4.64 14.66 7.21	63.36
1451–1475	2	14.66 16.52	31.18
1476–1500	1	5.64	5.64
1501–1525	1	5.64	5.64
1526–1550	—	—	—
1551–1575	1	5.64	5.64
1576–1600	6	7.65 3.15 14.66 15.52 19.59 10.76	71.33
1601–1625	3	20.80 8.55 13.58	42.93
1626–1650	3	13.58 19.59 21.88	55.05

TABLE 44.   TOTAL OF THE GEOMETRIC AVERAGE OF INTERNAL DISTURB-
ANCES OF POLAND AND LITHUANIA FROM 951 TO 1800 BY QUARTER
CENTURIES — *continued*

Quarter Century	Number of Disturbances	Measure of Disturbances	Total for the Quarter
1651–1675 A.D.	4	23.26 21.53 10.76 14.66	70.21
1676–1700	2	14.66 13.58	28.24
1701–1725	2	7.36 7.12	14.48
1726–1750	1	11.45	11.45
1751–1775	2	11.45 7.36	19.81
1776–1800	1	11.45	11.45

TABLE 45.   TOTAL OF THE GEOMETRIC AVERAGE OF INTERNAL DISTURB-
ANCES OF POLAND AND LITHUANIA BY CENTURIES

Century	Number of Disturbances	Number of Years with Disturbance	Total of Geometric Averages
X [1]	— [1]	— [1]	— [1]
XI	5	14	94.34
XII	9	25	156.77
XIII	17	38	273.71
XIV	9	24	146.97
XV	12	18	129.52
XVI	8	10	82.60
XVII	12	21	196.43
XVIII	6	6	57.19

[1] Two quarters only.

Poland and Lithuania. Of the century periods the most turbulent
were the thirteenth, seventeenth, twelfth, fourteenth. (See Figure 20.)
The most peaceful were the tenth, eighteenth, sixteenth, and eleventh.
Of the quarter-century periods the most disorderly were 1026–1050
(75.82); 1251–1275 (85.04); 1376–1400 (83.66); 1576–1600 (71.33); and
1651–1675 (70.21). Of the single disturbances the largest were 1034–1043
(58.48); 1102–1108 (32.43); 1194–1206 (62.81); 1377–1382 (32.42).
A glance at the data of either century or quarter-century periods is
sufficient to indicate that no continuous trend, or periodicity, is given.
The indicator is very low in the earliest centuries, then rises and reaches
a climax in the thirteenth century, after which time it steadily declines

during the fourteenth, fifteenth, and sixteenth centuries, flares up in the seventeenth, and enormously declines in the eighteenth century, in the last century of the independence of Poland (before its regeneration in the twentieth century). This last point reminds one of a similar situation in Greece and other countries. Here we seem again to have the maximum of disturbance in the centuries of the greatest power and splendor of the Polish-Lithuanian Empire.

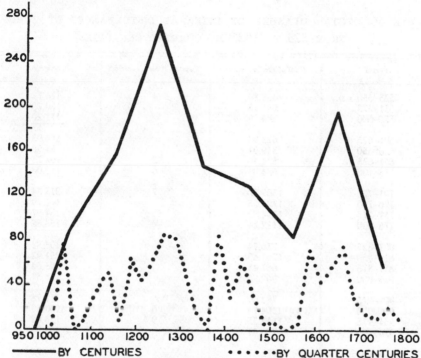

FIG. 20. MOVEMENT OF INTERNAL DISTURBANCES IN POLAND AND LITHUANIA

Having now in our possession the factual data on the movement of the internal disturbances in the countries studied, we can turn to a summary and more profound analysis of several problems only touched heretofore.

XII. INTERNAL DISTURBANCES OF EUROPE

Europe. When the above indicators for separate countries are summed up by the quarter-century and century periods, they give the following picture of the movement of internal disturbances. The summing up, as mentioned, is done in the following way: the indicators of all the countries in a given period are multiplied by the comparative weight of the country among other countries in a period on a scale of 1 to 5; then these indicators are summed up and for each period divided by the number of the countries which enter into the summary of the period. Table 46 shows for each period the number of the countries, and then the total indicator for all countries, and the average indicator (the total indicator divided by the number of the countries) in each specified quarter-century and century period.[3]   (See also Figure 21.)

TABLE 46.   TOTAL MEASURE OF INTERNAL DISTURBANCES OF EUROPE FROM 525 TO 1925 BY QUARTER CENTURIES

Period	Total of the Indicators	Number of the Countries	Average
525–550 A.D.	458.89	4	114.72
551–575	641.13		160.28
576–600	684.79		171.20
601–625	623.93		154.98
626–650	339.91		84.98
651–675	521.16	5	104.23
676–700	684.01	6	114.00
701–725	1507.40	7	215.34
726–750	1223.55		174.79
751–775	1294.82		184.97
776–800	1112.14		158.88
801–825	726.74		103.82
826–850	1763.45		251.92
851–875	667.41		95.34
876–900	969.95		138.57
901–925	782.69		111.78
926–950	1264.73	8	158.09
951–975	1112.55	9	123.62
976–1000	1295.44		143.94
1001–1025	1772.17		196.91
1026–1050	1478.97		164.33
1051–1075	1737.84		193.09
1076–1100	1256.18		139.57
1101–1125	1284.37		142.71
1126–1150	1734.30		192.70
1151–1175	1887.16		209.68
1176–1200	1963.97		218.22
1201–1225	2176.65		241.85
1226–1250	1648.26		183.14
1251–1275	2010.18		223.35
1276–1300	2111.01		234.56

[3] The number of the countries varies, but since the indicator is the sum of the indicators for all the countries in the period, divided by the number of the countries in such a period, the total indicator is roughly comparable, in spite of the varying number of the countries. After 950 the number of the countries remains practically the same up to 1925.

TABLE 46. TOTAL MEASURE OF INTERNAL DISTURBANCES OF EUROPE FROM 525 TO 1925 BY QUARTER CENTURIES — *continued*

Period	Total of the Indicators	Number of the Countries	Average
1301–1325 A.D.	2100.43		233.37
1326–1350	1812.87		201.43
1351–1375	1283.90		142.66
1376–1400	2245.87		249.54
1401–1425	1297.70	8	162.21
1426–1450	1752.89		219.11
1451–1475	1549.73		193.72
1476–1500	1386.70		173.34
1501–1525	918.60		114.83
1526–1550	947.05		118.38
1551–1575	864.78		108.10
1576–1600	1349.67		168.71
1601–1625	1081.28		135.16
1626–1650	1808.24		226.03
1651–1675	1226.00		153.23
1676–1700	728.66		91.08
1701–1725	890.13		111.27
1726–1750	430.44		53.81
1751–1775	871.36		108.92
1776–1800	1132.69		141.56
1801–1825	1085.92	7	155.13
1826–1850	2703.23		386.18
1851–1875	979.91		139.99
1876–1900	599.37		85.61
1901–1925	2071.28		295.89

TABLE 47. TOTAL MEASURE OF INTERNAL DISTURBANCES OF EUROPE BY CENTURIES

Century	Average	Century	Average
VI[1]	446.20	XIII	882.90
VII	458.19	XIV	827.00
VIII	733.98	XV	748.38
IX	589.65	XVI	509.56
X	537.43	XVII	605.50
XI	693.90	XVIII	415.56
XII	763.31	XIX	766.91

[1] Three quarters only.

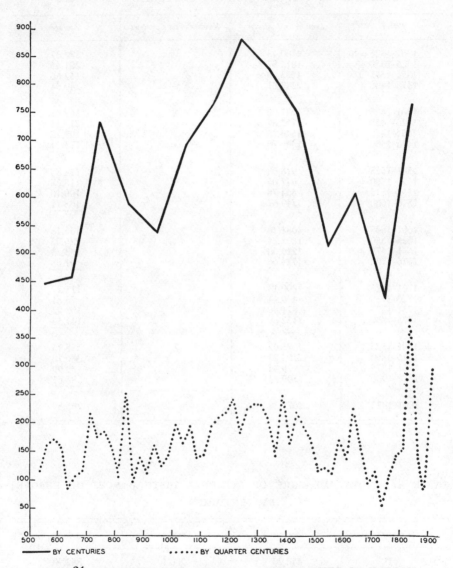

FIG. 21. MOVEMENT OF INTERNAL DISTURBANCES IN EUROPE

Chapter Fourteen

SUMMARY AND MAIN RESULTS

A. The first important conclusion concerns the *frequency of occurrence of important social disturbances in the life of social bodies.* Usually it is thought that they are fairly infrequent events. Meanwhile the data at hand show — and show consistently for all the countries studied — that on the average one notable social disturbance happens in about six years, for some countries in five years, for others in seventeen years. If, instead of taking the average time span per significant social disturbance, we ask ourselves what is the average number of years without a disturbance per years with a disturbance, then the results will be still more striking.[1] They indicate that the relationship between the years with disturbances and those without them fluctuates between one to two and one to eight, depending upon the country. On the average in most of the countries studied, to one year with a significant social disturbance there have been only about five peaceful years, free from inner social tensions and storms. Table 48 gives more exact data in the field.

Even with the relatively wide deviation of Byzantium from the record of other countries (which is due in all probability to a less careful recording of the disturbances in the history of that country) the averages for the occurrence of disturbances (in years) and for the ratio of years without disturbance to years with disturbance[2] are remarkably close. And this in spite of the enormous difference between countries and the times in which they have been making their history! The importance of these figures is that the occurrence of social disturbances is far from being so infrequent on the average as is usually thought. On the average, in about

---

[1] That the results in this case must be different from the preceding case follows from the fact that some of the disturbances have continued for more than one year, for perhaps as many as ten years, or longer.

[2] This means any year in which a disturbance occurred, regardless of actual duration, if this was less than one year. If it were possible to compute this relationship in terms of weeks or days — without and with disturbance — there is no doubt that the relationship would be noticeably greater; that is, the number of peaceful days per day with disturbance would be considerably greater than the above number of peaceful years per year of disturbance. The lack of data does not permit us to make such a computation.

every six to eight years one social disturbance may be expected. Internal disturbances, like tensions and sickness in the living organism, or storms in external nature, seem to have been occurring rather frequently in the life process of all the social bodies studied, regardless of whether they existed in the comparatively remote past, as in Greece and Rome, or have been in existence in recent times, as is true for most of the other countries, and regardless of what period of their history is taken, whether early or late. In this sense disturbances are "normal" occurrences in the life process of social groups.

TABLE 48.   FREQUENCY OF IMPORTANT SOCIAL DISTURBANCES

Country	Number of Years Studied	Number of Disturbances in Period	Average Occurrence of Disturbances (in Years)	Number of Years with Disturbance	Average Ratio of Years without to Years with Disturbances
Ancient Greece (600 B.C. to 146 B.C.)	454	84	5.4	122	(2.7)
Rome (509 B.C. to A.D. 476)	985	170	5.8	219	(3.5)
Byzantium (532–1390)	858	49	17.5	89	(8.6)
France (531–1933)	1402	173	8.1	246	(4.7)
Germany and Austria (709–1933)	1124	150	7.5	204	(4.5)
England (656–1933)	1277	162	7.9	247	(4.2)
Italy (526–1933)	1407	251	5.6	365	(2.9)
Spain (467–1933)	1466	242	6.1	424	(2.4)
The Netherlands (678–1933)	1255	103	12.1	263	(3.8)
Russia (946–1933)	987	167	5.9	280	(2.6)
Poland and Lithuania (1031–1794)	763	78	9.8	146	(4.3)

The preceding figures are, of course, averages. Such would be the average frequency of disturbances if they were distributed evenly in the course of time. But such evenness is lacking. Some periods have abundant disturbances, which sometimes continue for many years; other times are free from important social storms. Therefore, the actual distribution of disturbances in the course of time is somewhat different from those averages. A glance at the data in the Appendix to this part shows that once in a while, though rarely, periods have occurred when there was no disturbance during the whole of a quarter century. In a few such periods — in all countries and for all the time studied, there are hardly more than ten cases — internal peace existed for about half a century. More detailed tables show that Byzantium knew two peaceful periods, one lasting about seventy-eight years (from 867 to 945), the other sixty-four (from 1118 to 1182). The Netherlands knew one which lasted about ninety years (1476 to 1566). Germany had one of seventy-nine years' duration (1634 to 1713), another of eighty years (1713 to 1793). France had one of about sixty-one years' duration (769 to 830); Rome one of fifty-five years (342 to 287 B.C.) and another of eighty-nine years (287 to 198 B.C.). All the other countries knew only a few periods of about a quarter of a century free from important internal disturbances. This means that wide deviations from the above averages are very few, and that the wider the deviations, the fewer they are. All in all, each generation is likely to have one or more important social disturbances during its life span.

B. Another suggestion follows from Table 48. It is a fairly common opinion that *there are nations "inherently" disorderly and inclined to anarchy and disturbances, and nations which are, by God's will or for racial or some other reasons, destined to be orderly and free from social convulsions.* Most of the conservative proponents of this theory include their own nation in the "orderly" class; most of the radicals, who are Don Quixotes of revolution, in the "revolutionary." During the last few years there have been not infrequent occasions for hearing that, for instance, "these Slavs and Russians are anarchists by nature, while we (the British, the French, the Americans, etc.), thank heaven! are an orderly nation." Variations on this theme have been numerous and ingenious. *A glance at Table 48 is sufficient to dissipate these theories. All nations are orderly and disorderly, according to the times.* At the best, some of them show somewhat less inclination to social disturbances than others. But the difference is not serious, and even this small discrepancy is likely to decrease if we should deal with their completed history, as for example with that of Greece and Rome. This last point means, as we shall see further (pages 493 to 496), that there is an observable tendency for a few of the countries (but not all) to have their disturbances decrease at the later stages of their history, after their climax is over, and the glory and the fame are in the past. For instance, the Netherlands show a low disturbancy during the last two or three centuries, and a high one during the time that they were engaged in making a place for themselves under the sun. Something similar we see in Greece, Rome, and Poland and Lithuania. This will be discussed later in more detail. For the present, the above data and these hints are sufficient to dissipate the myth of orderly and disorderly nations "by nature." The difference between peoples in this respect is small and does not warrant any such theory.

The partisans of orderly and disorderly nations may, however, find refuge in the contention that though the incidence of disturbances is common to all nations, they nevertheless differ radically in that revolutions proceed in the orderly nations without any, or with little, violence, while in the disorderly nations they are always violent, bloody, and cruel. During these last few years such arguments have been heard many times. Is such a claim valid? The answer is given by Table 49, which lists the percentages of the disturbances among the nations studied, according to the degree of their intensity and violence. From the standpoint of intensity all the revolutions are divided into five classes, beginning with Class I, the "pure and bloodless" disturbances, and passing in order to Class V, the most violent among the disturbances in both the quantitative and the qualitative aspects. In other words, our indicators of the intensity of disturbances are very near to being in fact what might be called the indicators of the violence, cruelty, and bloodiness of the disturbances. This is particularly true of the first three classes.

TABLE 49.   INTENSITY OF REVOLUTIONS BY COUNTRIES — BY CLASS

COUNTRIES	I		II		III		IV		V		Total	
	No.	Per Cent	No.	Per Cent	No.	Per Cent	No.	Per Cent	No.	Per Cent	No.	Per Cent
Greece	1	1.2	11	3.1	30	35.7	24	28.5	18	21.4	84	100
Rome	2	1.2	49	28.8	79	46.5	19	11.2	21	12.5	170	100
Byzantium	2	4.0	1	2.0	10	20.4	36	73.6	0	0	49	100
France	17	9.9	43	24.5	74	43.0	33	19.2	6	3.4	173	100
Germany and Austria	12	8.0	24	16.0	73	48.7	39	26.0	2	1.3	150	100
England	15	9.2	41	25.3	51	31.5	52	32.2	3	1.8	162	100
Italy	13	5.1	35	13.9	88	35.1	112	44.7	3	1.2	251	100
Spain	4	1.7	46	19.5	132	56.2	43	18.3	10	4.2	235	100
The Netherlands	2	1.9	17	16.5	58	56.4	20	19.4	6	5.8	103	100
Russia	8	4.7	98	59.0	36	21.4	19	11.3	6	3.6	167	100
Poland and Lithuania	5	6.4	5	6.4	55	70.5	13	16.7	0	0	78	100
Total	81		370		686		410		75		1622	

What tale does Table 49 tell? Does it justify the above claims? Does it indicate that in the moments of social madness (or if one prefers, "social inspiration") some nations remain quite sane and angelic, while some others turn into madmen and beasts?

The table shows that there are some differences between the nations in this respect, but they are neither great nor consistent. This means that England and France, for instance, show the highest percentage of disturbances of those in Class I (the least violent) and in this point seem to be at the top of the list of the least violent countries. When, however, we find the predominant type of disturbances there, we see that their "mode" falls into Class IV and Class III, while the "mode" for all the other countries falls either into Class II, III, or IV. This means that all in all the English and French disturbances cannot be regarded in any way as less violent than, for instance, the Russian or German or Spanish or Dutch or the Roman. It can be said, in general, that for most of the countries there is hardly any possibility of drawing a real distinction between the degrees of intensity and violence of their internal disturbances. Practically all of them have shown a tendency to become "madly bestial" in many of their disturbances.[3] Only from a narrowly relative standpoint is it possible to indicate one or two nations whose disturbances seem to have been, all in all, slightly more violent than those of the other nations. On the basis of the data, the first place in this respect seems to belong to Greece, whose percentage of Class V disturbances is excessive. However strange it may appear in the light of the contemporary Russian Revolution with its endless cruelties, so far the Russian disturbances seem not to have been more violent than those of other countries: 64 per cent of all the Russian disturbances fall into classes I and II, and only 36 per cent into the remaining more violent classes. Such an indicator is not shown by any other country among those studied. Other countries, generally speaking, occupy about the same position in this respect. All this means that the contention discussed is also a myth based on a mere wish and imagination. Together with the preceding data these results are enough to dissipate the legend of "orderly" and "disorderly" peoples.

Another conclusion suggested by Table 49 is that only about 5 per cent of all 1622 disturbances studied occurred without violence and about 23 per cent with slight violence. More than 70 per cent were accomplished and followed by violence and bloodshed on a considerable scale. This means that *those who dream of a "bloodless revolution" have little chance (some five chances out of one hundred) to accomplish their*

---

[3] During these years I have heard many times the argument that "if Communism would come to our country it would certainly be free from its Russian excesses and terror and bloodshed and other barbarisms." It is hardly necessary to say that such arguments show only that their advocates are very naïve and optimistic persons who seem to have no knowledge of at least the few revolutions in their own country, and no eyes and ears for an adequate grasp of the disturbances which occurred before their very doors, as during the transitory Communist regime in Hungary, in various parts of Germany, or in China where cruelties were perpetrated to a degree hardly less, if not more, intense than in Russia.

dream. He who aspires for a disturbance must be ready to see violence and to be a witness or victim or perpetrator of it. This is true for all nations and groups.

C. The third item concerns the *duration* of the disturbances. From this standpoint there are ten different classes, beginning with the disturbances which lasted only a few days and ending with those which lasted for more than twenty-five years.[4] The questions arise: What is the proportion of short and long disturbances? What is the predominant type of their duration? Are there appreciable differences in this respect between the disturbances of various countries? Is there any observable trend showing that in the course of time they tend to become either shorter or longer?

These questions are answered by Table 50, which gives the actual and the per cent figures for the duration of the disturbances studied.

TABLE 50.   DURATION OF REVOLUTIONS BY COUNTRIES — BY CLASS

COUNTRIES	I		II		III		IV		V–VIII		IX–X		Total
	No.	Per Cent	No.	Per Cent	No.	Per Cent	No.	Per Cent	No.	Per Cent	No.	Per Cent	No.
Greece	22	26.2	36	**42.8**	12	14.3	3	3.6	10	11.9	1	1.2	84
Rome	42	24.7	88	**51.8**	21	12.3	9	5.3	10	5.9	0	0	170
Byzantium	8	16.3	22	**44.9**	7	14.3	1	2.0	11	22.5	0	0	49
France	28	16.3	69	**39.5**	34	19.8	10	5.9	32	18.6	0	0	173
Germany and Austria	20	13.4	40	26.6	53	35.4	10	6.6	26	17.4	1	0.6	150
England	28	17.3	67	**41.4**	33	20.4	8	4.9	25	15.4	1	0.6	162
Italy	85	33.7	67	26.5	44	17.7	17	6.9	37	14.8	1	0.4	251
Spain	45	19.1	108	**46.0**	23	9.8	22	9.3	36	15.3	1	0.4	235
The Netherlands	7	6.8	24	23.3	37	**35.9**	4	3.9	28	27.2	3	2.9	103
Russia	30	18.5	74	**44.0**	24	14.3	4	2.4	32	19.0	3	1.8	167
Total	315	20.4	595	**38.5**	288	18.6	88	5.6	247	15.2	11	0.7	1544

From these data it follows that for the majority of the countries taken separately *the predominant type of disturbance is of Class II, that is, of a few weeks' duration.* Only in Germany and Austria, and the Netherlands is the predominant type that with a duration of several months, while in Italy it is that of a few days. Next come the disturbances with durations of a few days and a few months (Classes I and II). Then the proportion of disturbances of longer duration decreases as the duration increases;

---

[4] A disturbance is considered as one and long-lasting when it is continuous, without any clear interruption by a long interval of time. Where such an interruption was present, and, on the basis of several other symptoms, two disturbances were distinct rather than a mere continuation of one another, the disturbances were counted separately.

disturbances with durations of above ten years are lacking altogether in the history of several countries, in others they are below 1 per cent of all the disturbances. Only in the Netherlands and in Russia are they above 1 per cent. In general, disturbances with a duration of less than one year compose about 80 per cent of all the disturbances. Disturbances with a duration of more than one year make about 15 per cent of the total. Thus *most of the internal crises in the life process of a social body* (like sicknesses in the life process of an individual) *come and pass their acute stage within a period of a few weeks*. Only a small proportion last for one year or more.

The same data show again that, although differences exist in regard to the duration of disturbances in various countries, they are not fundamental. On the contrary, the proportionate duration of the specified disturbances is closely similar in most of the countries studied, especially if disturbances with a duration of about one year or less are taken. The main deviations occur in the records of Byzantium and the Netherlands; but even they are not conspicuously great. This suggests again that there is no particularly strong basis for qualifying some nations as "bent to disorders," and some others as "bent to be orderly." This uniformity suggests also that the occurrence of the disturbances, their frequency, and their duration seem to be controlled by forces and conditions which lie very deep, far below the specific cultural and other circumstances, in which these countries differ markedly. If such surface factors were responsible for these phenomena, we should expect to find much more marked differences in the occurrence, frequency, and duration of disturbances, because the contrasts between the cultures of Greece, Rome, Byzantium, England, Russia, France, are great. If, in reality, the situation is different and the similarities in the disturbances far outweigh the differences, this means that these overt variables are not the main factor in the situation. I do not suggest that the deeper factors are biological or cosmic or climatic, and that we must turn to heredity, sunspots, climatic conditions, to explain them. Such an explanation would also be a surface explanation, only still more unsatisfactory than that of the different cultural variables. What I imply by the phrase "deep factors" is that as death is immanently connected with life, and inevitable for any human individual, irrespective of all external and cultural and climatic conditions, likewise a social disturbance is perhaps an immanent trait of sociocultural life itself, and in this sense is inescapable and in its essentials is manifested similarly in all the social bodies. The relatively slight differences may be conditioned by this or that specific cultural or biological or cosmic factor — just as the duration of individual life may be somewhat prolonged or shortened by such factors — but the very reason why such disturbances occur, and occur along much the same lines in these diverse countries, lies probably in this immanent connection of social life and internal tensions.   Here, probably, we meet again the same fact of the immanent self-regulation of social processes which any thoughtful investigator of such processes often comes across.   We met it in the dynamics of scientific discoveries and inventions, in the changes of philosophical currents, aesthetic styles, mentality, fashions.   The fact discussed seems to belong to the same category of the immanent self-regulation of social processes.   A clearer and more specific definition of what is understood here by these deep and immanent causes of disturbances will be given on pages 496 to 505.

Finally, it is enough to glance at Greece, Rome, and Byzantium — the countries which existed a long time ago — and at those existing now, in order to see that there is no important difference between the duration of their disturbances.   We cannot say that they were uniformly longer or shorter in the countries of the past compared with those of the present. Likewise, if the detailed data are examined for the duration of disturbances in the same country, beginning with the earliest and ending with the latest, they also show no uniform trend, in fact almost no trend at all. Here we strike, then, the first blow at the popular opinion that in the course of time disturbances tend to disappear, and to become shorter, less violent, and less inevitable.   We find nothing corresponding to this pleasant view in the data of their duration.   And nothing corresponding to it shall we find in the data concerning the other aspects of disturbances. This popular opinion is one of the pleasant wishes dressed in pseudo-scientific garb by the *chefs* of the social sciences of the Victorian and post-Victorian period, many of whom are still living amongst us.   Historical processes just go on erratically without any continuous trend in this respect as they have gone on before.

D.   In spite of all the vicissitudes and changing conditions within the system of the indicators accepted, the magnitude of the disturbances fluctuates from century to century much less than is usually expected. If we take all the European countries studied from the sixth to the twentieth century, the amplitude of fluctuation of the magnitude of the disturbances is between 414.65 and 882.90; that is, in the most turbulent century the disturbances are only a little more than twice greater than in the most orderly century.

If we take the indicators of the quarter centuries, the difference is naturally greater, the maximum figure being here 300.46 and the minimum figure 53.81, the maximum exceeding the minimum by five to six times. Such swings are not exceedingly wild. They indicate some permanently working forces, inherently connected with the essence of the social life itself, which do not permit either a complete elimination or the unlimited growth of disturbances. As soon as the curve of disturbances approaches either the minimum or the maximum level, a reaction sets in and sends its course in the opposite direction.

E. *In these "reactions" we observe several times, although not always, that when the curve approaches especially close to the minimum or maximum limits, the counteraction also becomes especially strong.*

We do not need a mystical or numerological interpretation when, as so often (though not always), we see that the further and the more sharply a curve swings in one direction the stronger is the reaction which sends it back again. It is simply that the swing from order to disorder, and the reverse, seems to have a limit, as do almost all sociocultural phenomena, and as physicochemical and biological processes apparently do. Besides indicating the comparatively narrow limits of the maximum and the minimum fluctuation of our indicators, the above suggests that deep within social life are forces, possibly two opposing sets, that manifest themselves in such pulsations. When one set of forces becomes too strong, other forces, in some way or for some reason, are set in motion in the opposite direction.

F. *The indicators for either quarter century or century periods show no continuous trend, either toward bigger and better "orderly progress" or toward ever-increasing disorderliness.* The curve fluctuates, that is all one can say. The popular theory that social change tends to become more and more orderly, more and more free from violence as "civilization progresses," is, then, nothing but a "pleasant myth."

This myth has sprung up often before, usually when the social life of a given century has been comparatively well organized. It reappeared in Europe in the second half of the nineteenth century, and during the last quarter of this same century spread among scholars and the public at large, becoming a "scientifically established fact." One reason why so utterly improbable a theory was accepted by so many scholars as well as by the public in general is shown by Table 46; the third quarter of the nineteenth century was more orderly than the three quarters preceding it; the fourth quarter (85.61) was more orderly than any of the preceding forty-three quarters from the sixth to the twentieth century, only two quarter centuries, 1726–1750 (53.81) and 626–650 (84.98), being

slightly more orderly. Social conditions like these naturally are conducive to the popularity of such theories.

Since the end of the eighteenth and the first half of the nineteenth
century had been a period of considerable storm and stress, the comparative orderliness of the succeeding fifty or sixty years encouraged the
belief that thenceforward orderly would replace disorderly change. The
fact that it was also a relatively peaceful period led to similar theories
that war would disappear. The condition of prolonged prosperity in the
United States before 1929 favored the seductive idea sponsored and
claimed by the leading scientific authorities that from then on economic
fluctuations would be less and less violent and more and more successfully
controlled. All such myths are likely to prosper in similar conditions and
to captivate most minds, especially since the authorities show no particular desire to learn from experience or from history, and since often,
while operating supposedly with "perfect scientific technique," they
forget to use longer spans of time and, sometimes, certain elementary
rules of logic in their studies.

In this field of disturbances as well as in the field of war, the data do not
give the slightest support for any such myth of bigger and better orderly
progress, or for the opposite myth of a steady movement toward greater
and more frightful disorder. Both the processes studied fluctuate, not
according to "linear" conceptions of historical processes, but erratically
or "variationally." They lead neither to the paradise of orderly progress
nor to the inferno of permanent anarchy or "permanent revolution," to
use the expression of Bolshevist theorizers. Neither has the fantastic
dream of linear movement the slightest support in facts. So much for
this point.

G. *According to Table 46, there is hardly any definite periodicity in the
ups and downs of internal disturbances.* Their tempo, as well as their
rhythm, is varied. From one period to the next *piano* or *pianissimo*
replaces *forte*, and the reverse.

Contrast, for instance, the quarter-century periods in the ninth,
eleventh, and seventeenth centuries. Sometimes for several successive
quarter centuries — two, three, four, or even ten — the level is low, or is
generally high. To see this, one need only glance at the figures of the
eighth, twelfth, eleventh, thirteenth, fourteenth, and fifteenth centuries.
During these periods the indicators remain generally high or generally
low and throughout the whole set of periods fluctuate gradually and
within relatively narrow limits. This means that Table 46 shows no
uniform rhythm, no recurrent change within a given span of time. So

all the fashionable theories which try to interpret sociocultural processes by a mechanistic principle and to ascribe a definite periodicity to these are wrong, in this field as well as in most others.[5]

One of the best and certainly one of the most original theories in the field is that of political periodicities, set forth by Giuseppe Ferrari, a thinker much less well known than he deserves to be.[6] So far as this theory of periodicity applies to revolutions or disturbances, we may summarize it as follows. There is periodicity in practically all political processes. The average length of such a political period is about that of the active life of a generation — thirty-one years. Ignoring unimportant exceptions and deviations, one may say that every thirty-one years the political generation is supplanted by a new one of very different character and aspirations. Is there any definite order in the sequence of generations and the characteristics of these generations? Yes, according to Ferrari; the generations, in their characteristics follow a definite order. Moreover, each four generations form a still longer period of some 115 to 120 years.

The series begins with a generation of "predecessors," the theorizers and ideologists of the new order. They are not involved in any practical overthrow of the existing order and often do not even strive to undermine it at all. This generation merely analyzes political phenomena, mildly criticizes many of the existing forms, tries to understand them, and sets forth various theories about them. A by-product of this purely theoretical and often wholly academic work is a critical attitude toward the existing order, and a tendency to replace or reconstruct this order according to the principles explicitly or implicitly stated by the "predecessors."

Next come "revolutionaries." Permeated by the ideologies of the "predecessors," this generation attempts to put these ideologies into practice; it puts down the existing order and replaces it by a new one nursed by the "predecessors." This is a generation of men of action rather than of thought. It has the will power, determination, energy, and one-sided fanaticism to try to realize in social life the prescriptions that the predecessors formulated, but would probably not have ventured

---

[5] Almost the only periodicity in *sociocultural processes* is found in those of purely sociocultural origin, like New Year's Day, Christmas Day, or annual holidays of a religious or civic nature, as the traditional Fourth of July. But even these live only as long as the tradition on which they are founded, and change or die out when this is replaced by a different one. Besides, strange as it may sound, those hunting for periodicity have looked for it in every other field but this.

[6] See his *Teoria dei periodi politici* (Milano-Napoli, 1874).

to carry out themselves. In other words, the generation of "revolution-aries" is a natural sequence of the generation of the "predecessors."

Again, a quite different generation succeeds the "revolutionaries" — the generation of "reactionaries." Through the extreme and fanatical activities of the "revolutionaries," social life as a whole hardly improves; rather, it becomes worse. Many social problems are unsolved. All the excesses and outrages of the "revolutionaries," together with their failure to establish the paradise to which they aspired and which they promised to bring about, naturally arouse and set in motion a strong reaction against their policies. Their successors disapprove of most of the things to which the revolutionaries aspired, and approve of the opposite measures, trying to put them into practice. However, this generation, like the generation preceding, goes to excess and does not succeed in solving the problems of its time. As this generation of reac-tionaries draws to an end, the unsoundness of its policies and the unsound-ness of the policies of the revolutionaries become equally apparent. Both parties prove failures. As the excesses of both lose their previous fasci-nation, the sound middle way appeals more and more strongly, and so a place is prepared for the fourth generation, the "accomplishers" (*le generazioni risolutive*).

This is the lucky generation. Free from fanaticism of either kind, and coming on the scene just when conditions are ripe for a sound solution of most of the "problems of the moment," it is easily successful with these problems. It puts the country in good order again, in a state of prosper-ity, and of political and social well-being. Thus the cycle of four gener-ations closes.

Then the sequence begins again. Under the prosperity and well-being of the generation of accomplishers, human thought and inquiry quietly germinate. In the next thirty years they flare up and again there is a generation of predecessors, followed by one of revolutionaries, then by one of reactionaries. And the cycles are closed again by a generation of accomplishers, to be replaced once more by the predeces-sors, and so on.

This is the essence of the theory. Ferrari tries to show that his theory of periodicity of generations, each generation covering some thirty years, his theory of a four-generation cycle of about 115 years, and his theory of a sequence of generations are indeed corroborated by historical data. He arranges the whole history of several European and of certain Asiatic countries to show that the facts really point to such periodicities.

It is not now our task to criticize the principles of Ferrari's work, or of many others based on generation periodicity.[7] For our present purposes it is enough to note that, according to Ferrari, there must be an outburst of disturbances and revolutions about every 115 or 120 years, each time that a new generation of the "revolutionaries" comes to the scene. Our data do not support this contention. The data that Ferrari gives to support it can hardly be said to be more accurate and more reliable than our list of disturbances and our indicators. His body of facts is rather thin, selected on a very arbitrary basis, and arranged according to subjective principles, and has many quite evident errors and shortcomings. Ferrari's data, therefore, hardly prove his contentions, interesting and intriguing as they are.

His theory is perhaps much better than dozens of other somewhat similar theories claiming that there is periodicity in the movement of internal disturbances. Without surveying and criticizing these claims, it is possible to say, in general, that no one has so far succeeded in showing the existence of periodic cycles in this field. Almost all such theories have been based either upon mere speculation and imagination or upon illustrations picked one-sidedly; none have been based upon a systematic study of all the important disturbances or of most of them. In view of these defects, and in the light of the facts given above, we must decline to regard these theories as valid. The duration of the "cycles" from one high or low point to another varies, as does the amplitude of the fluctuations.

Next it must be noted that in the light of the incessant changes in rhythm and tempo, and of the differences in the length of time between the turns and those succeeding them, most of the fashionable theories of foreseeing, forecasting, and of later "engineering," planning, and controlling the course of sociocultural processes can hardly be taken seriously. They are mainly a manifestation of the wishes of persons who mistake their own wishes for accomplished facts.[8]

These data mean also that no uniformly "gradual" or, on the other hand, no uniformly "abrupt mutations" are seen in the changes in direction and in degree of the order-disturbance processes. The popular

---

[7] Again, the literature is enormous and there are many varieties of the theory, the essence of which is very old. See an incomplete survey of these theories in F. Mentré, *Les générations sociales* (Paris, 1920); K. Mannheim. *"Das Problem der Generationen,"* in *Kölner Vierteljahrshefte für Soziologie*, Vol. VII, nos. 2 and 3. See the literature there. See additional literature in this work, Volume Two, pp. 381–382. The problem will be analyzed in Volume Four.

[8] See P. Sorokin, "Is Accurate Social Planning Possible?" in *American Sociological Review* (1936), Vol. I, no. 1.

theories that "nature makes no leaps," that everything moves step by step through a regular evolution, that the course of sociocultural processes has no "sharp turns," caesuras, or abrupt punctuations, all elevate a partial case into a universal rule without exceptions. Gradual changes do occur. But side by side with them are "sharp and sudden turns," unexpected shifts from *fortissimo* to *pianissimo*, from *largo* to *allegro vivace*, and so on. This is particularly clear when one takes each disturbance separately and plots it on a chart. The time span between them as well as their magnitude do show an incessant variation.

H. Tables 46 and 47 show which of the centuries and quarter centuries in the history of the greater part of the European continent have been particularly stormy and which particularly quiet. The turbulent centuries from the sixth to the twentieth were the thirteenth, fourteenth, twelfth, nineteenth, fifteenth, eighth, and eleventh. The maximum of disturbances fall within the thirteenth and then the fourteenth; the minimum fall within the eighteenth, seventh, sixth, and sixteenth centuries.

If quarter-century periods are taken, the most turbulent periods were: 1826–1850; 1901–1925; 826–850; 1201–1225; and 1301–1325. The most orderly periods were: 1726–1750; 1876–1900; 1676–1700; 851–875; 601–625. The most orderly and turbulent quarter-century periods for each of the seven countries separately studied were indicated above. Almost every country had one or more twenty-five-year periods with practically no important disturbances.

I. Table 46 shows, as mentioned, that the *last quarter of the nineteenth century was remarkably orderly;* of fifty-six quarter centuries from 525 to 1925 only two had a slightly lower figure of disturbances. Shall we wonder that in that orderly "capitalistic" milieu theories of assured "orderly progress" sprang up and were generally accepted? *At its height, therefore, the "capitalistic regime," which it is now the fashion to curse, was the most orderly of social systems and gave the greatest assurance of internal and external peace and of Sensate liberty and freedom for individuals.* In the light of this datum it is childish rather to ascribe to it all the vices of both anarchy and militarism and to strive to establish internal and external peace and the maximum of Sensate liberty by destroying capitalism and creating socialism, fascism, communism, Hitlerism, and other "isms" of today. It is very doubtful whether such regimes can give what capitalism gave at its height; as we have seen so far they seem to lead, if anywhere, precisely to the increase of war and of disturbances, and to a radical limitation and final elimination of Sensate individual liberty.

J. The data show, further, *where we now stand on the historical road.*
The indicators are not carried beyond 1925. If they were, the data for
the first third of the twentieth century would be still more conspicuous
and definite. Even as it stands, the figures show that *after the very
peaceful final quarter of the nineteenth century, Europe entered the stormy
period of the twentieth.* The indicator for the first quarter of the twentieth
century is exceptionally high. From 525 to 1925 only one quarter century
shows itself more turbulent than the 1901–1925 period. We are in a
rising tide of internal disturbances. Since 1925 there have been a large
number of disturbances, and of great magnitude, in Germany and Austria,
France, and Spain; and the number of smaller disturbances in England,
Italy, and Russia is also great. *On its face value, as the figure shows, the
first quarter of the twentieth century, 1901–1925, was not only the bloodiest
period in the entire history of the international conflicts of mankind but also,
when internal disturbances are considered, was one of the very turbulent
periods.* Such is the almost unavoidable conclusion from our data on
war and disturbances.

This, then, is the latest point of "social progress and evolution" to
which we have come. This conclusion will certainly startle all the
manufacturers and consumers of the "sweet applesauce" theories that
civilization is progressive through a process of orderly change toward
universal peace. They will undoubtedly ponder over it a little; and it
would be very useful for them, no matter who they are — for the partisans
of these theories are not, in the main, simple and ignorant people, but
rather "highbrows and authorities" — to consider whether they have
not been believing in their own wishes rather than heeding ugly facts,
and whether they have not been too confident and too light-hearted in
their theories and conclusions. *The twentieth century, so far, has been the
bloodiest period and one of the most turbulent periods — and therefore one of
the cruelest and least humanitarian — in the history of Western civilization
and perhaps in the chronicles of mankind in general.*

What its further course will be I am not in a position to predict. But
Table 46 shows where we are on the long historical turn and where we
have been. It is probable that sooner or later the curve will turn down;
but how soon no one can tell.

K. If we inquire as to whether the movement of internal disturbances for the eight European countries studied is connected directly and
synchronously with the movement of international war, the answer
must be in the negative. Comparing the curve of war movement
with the curve of the disturbances, both by century and quarter-century

periods, we see that *so far as century periods are concerned, each process has had a course independent of the other, without either positive or negative association.*   While war indicators increase by casualties and by army's strength from the twelfth to the seventeenth century inclusive (see Figures 6 and 7) the indicators of disturbances show no such tendency; they tend rather to decrease from the fourteenth to the nineteenth century. But while the indicator of war in the nineteenth century declines, the indicator of disturbances, on the contrary, rises greatly.   Thus, their movements for these centuries were rather opposite or "compensatory." But for the centuries from the twelfth to the fourteenth and from the seventeenth to the eighteenth their course was parallel rather than compensatory.

Finally, both increase in the first quarter of the twentieth century; but the war figure increased enormously while the disturbances increased much less.   Thus, there is no evident consistency in the relation between the two indicators for the century periods.   For the period from the fourteenth to the seventeenth century the relation, if any, is negative or compensatory; the increase in war is followed by a decrease in internal disturbances.   But the other centuries give a different picture and do not permit us to formulate any general rule from the single fact that there is a negative relation between the two variables for these centuries.

In a desire to elucidate the problem somewhat more, the annual and the quarter-century indicators of both processes in the history of Greece, Rome, and Russia were subjected to a detailed statistical analysis.   No definitely consistent relationship between the two variables was found. There did seem to be a slight indication that *disturbances tend to occur more frequently during and around years of war, being more frequent in war years, and in the years immediately preceding and following wars, and becoming rarer as we move further in either direction from the years of war.* For instance, of all the 207 years with disturbances in Rome studied, 96, or 45 per cent, occurred during years of war, 19 within one year before or after a war, 11 within two years before or after a war, 9 within three years, 11 within four years, 7 within five years, 5 within six years, 4 within seven years, 3 within eight years, then 4, 3, 4, and 4 within 9, 10, 11, and 12 years, respectively, after a war; 180 disturbances out of 207 are distributed in this way, while the remaining 27 cases of disturbances occurred at a still greater distance from a war.[9]

---

[9] Here are a few additional data.   Of 375 years of Greek history studied (500 to 126 B.C.), for disturbances as well as for wars, 127 years or 34 per cent of all the years studied were free from war as well as disturbance; 140 years or 37 per cent had war alone, without dis-

Considering, however, that war occurred in 41 per cent of the total number of years of Roman history, this result is less conclusive than may appear at first glance. In the history of Russia, 35 of the 70 disturbances from 1450 to 1925, or 50 per cent, occurred in years of war. War occurred, however, in about 46 per cent of all the years studied. The result is again very inconclusive, failing to show any definite and uniform association between the processes studied.

When the relation between war and disturbances in Greece is studied, the picture is somewhat similar. *There may be a very slight tendency for disturbances to occur more frequently in a period of war and in the years nearest war years; but the tendency is neither strong, consistent, nor quite tangible.* The above figures for Rome show that there were 9 disturbances within three years before a war and three years after, but 11 disturbances within four years from a war ; as we move farther from the war years and reach a period 8 years before or after a war the trend toward decreasing frequency of disturbances practically disappears. Also, in Rome there occurred 27 cases of disturbances in years at a considerable distance from years of war. On the other hand, several periods of war, and especially of very strenuous wars, like the Punic Wars, were, as mentioned, periods of deepest internal peace, discipline, and order. All this indicates that the relationship between war and internal disturbance is neither simple, uniform, nor close. It seems to depend on the kind of war as well as on the kind of disturbance, not to mention the total constellation of historical and sociocultural circumstances.

Such an ambiguous and indefinite result is perhaps due to the fact that in our analysis we did not divide the wars into victorious and unsuccessful. Mere common sense, together with slight historical observation, seems to suggest that victorious wars are much less likely than unsuccessful wars to be followed or preceded by internal disturbances. During and after the World War revolutions took place in Bulgaria, Turkey, Germany, Austria, and Russia — that is, in the defeated countries — while England, France, Italy, and Serbia, or the United States of America, did not have any revolution or disturbance that led to the overthrow of the

---

turbance : 35 years or 10 per cent had disturbance alone ; and 73 years or 19 per cent had both. The total number of the years with disturbance was 108, or 29 per cent; with war, 213, or 57 per cent.

Of 877 years of Roman history studied (400 B.C. to A.D. 476) 404 years or 46 per cent were free from war and disturbance ; 266 years or 30 per cent had war alone ; 111 years or 13 per cent had disturbance alone ; finally 96 years or 11 per cent had both. The total number of years with war was 362, or 41 per cent, with disturbance, 207, or 24 per cent. Such a result suggests a very slight association between war and disturbance.

existing regime or was as great as those disturbances in the defeated countries. Likewise, Russia, after her defeat in the Russo-Japanese War of 1904–1905, had a revolution, during 1905–1906, while Japan had no disturbance. After being defeated in war in 1912, Turkey had a revolution and deposed Abdul-Hamid, while nothing like this happened in the victorious countries. Likewise, France had a revolution after being defeated in the Franco-Prussian War; and one might give a long list of such cases from recent as well as from remote periods.

If this consideration has any importance, then it is clear why our analysis showed no more definite relationship between the variables. We put together all the wars, successful as well as unsuccessful, and so, of course, obscured any consistent relationship which may have existed between them. It was advisable, therefore, to try to discover the connection between the movement of disturbances and the movement of successful and unsuccessful wars.

Such a study, however, proved very difficult. Many disturbances have been of a purely local nature, small in magnitude and somewhat undefined as to the exact time and duration of their occurrence. Many disturbances by peasants and workers have been a kind of unrest or milling around spread over a number of years, with only occasional outbursts here and there. Then there were several "palace revolutions" involving only a small faction without any active participation by the masses.

On the other hand, many wars, especially of the colonial or half-colonial type, continued for ten, twenty, or more years, so giving a long uninterrupted period of war. Again, other wars of lasting nature consisted of several battles, some victorious and some not. Finally, wars are often indefinite in result, without victor or vanquished. All this makes a comparison of all wars listed with all disturbances impracticable and incapable of yielding definite results.

In view of this fact, another procedure seemed advisable, namely, to take only the biggest wars and biggest revolutions during recent centuries, for which data are comparatively accurate. However, even this method is not irreproachable; some of the biggest disturbances happened in time of war, and quite an insignificant war, while some of the biggest wars were synchronous with disturbances of a purely local character and insignificant magnitude. Even in the few cases when a defeat in war seemed to have been followed by a big disturbance, some specific circumstance, like the death of the king, occurred at the same time, making it impossible to decide whether the unsuccessful war or the death of the ruler was the really important factor in causing the disturbance. And there are dozens of such "obscuring" circumstances. All this material should be kept in mind.

There follow the approximate results of a study of several samples from several countries. In Russia since 1600 there have been 14 great disturbances.[10] Of these 14, 4 occurred during or immediately after big and unsuccessful wars, 6 in a period of peace, and 1 during a successful war. Three others occurred in somewhat indefinite circumstances; it is hard to say whether or not the war was successful, or whether the war resulted from the disturbance or was its "cause."

Thus the relationship is quite indefinite. If, on the other hand, we take the biggest wars for the same period, the results are about the same. Some of these big wars continued for a number of years, like the Napoleonic Wars, or the northern wars of Peter the Great. For a number of years they were unsuccessful, and for a number, successful; but in neither phase were they followed by any disturbance of importance. In the unsuccessful Crimean War of 1853–1856 there was only one, relatively very small, disturbance, in 1854–1855, among the soldiers. Another unsuccessful war, the Russo-Japanese, 1904–1905, was followed by a great revolution. The World War, 1914–1917, was followed by a great revolution. (Here again, however, it is hard to style the war unsuccessful, since up to the revolution of 1917 neither the Allies nor Russia was vanquished; Russia stepped out of the war and lost it as a result of the Revolution.) In brief, the results of the study are very indefinite.

The history of France from 1600 on gives similar results. From 1600 to 1925 we find 13 great disturbances.[11] Seven of these 13 occurred in peaceful times when, except for two quite insignificant colonial expeditions, no war was going on. Among the 7 great disturbances were those of 1830 and 1848; 3 big disturbances definitely happened during or immediately after unsuccessful wars. The remaining 3 occurred in somewhat indefinite circumstances, during wartime, but when success or defeat was somewhat uncertain. When, on the other hand, we take all the big wars from 1600 to 1925, we find at least 25 wars of comparatively large magnitude. During 17 of these, at least, not less than 5 being unsuccessful, none of the great internal conflicts above mentioned occurred, either while hostilities continued or immediately after the close of the campaign. During each of the remaining 8 wars a big disturbance occurred, 4 of

---

[10] 1604–1613; 1648; 1650; 1667–1671; 1668; 1689; 1698; 1707–1708; 1751–1753; 1773–1774; 1830–1831; 1863; 1905–1906; 1917–1921.

[11] 1620; 1625–1628; 1635–1637; 1662–1664; 1675; 1702–1710; 1706–1709; 1789–1799; 1815; 1830; 1834; 1848; 1870.

these disturbances being losing wars, 1 successful, and the remaining 3 only partially successful or of indefinite outcome.

These results seem to corroborate all the previous ones. Two other samples from two other countries lead to similar conclusions. On the basis of all these data, one must say that, *contrary to expectation, the data do not definitely show a positive association between unsuccessful wars and big disturbances nor between victorious wars and the absence of such. At best they yield only a very slight association between unsuccessful wars and disturbances.* As a study of the presence or absence of association between war in general and disturbances did not disclose any close uniform relationship between these, one has to conclude, at least until more refined analysis makes the question clear, *that the two processes proceed fairly independently of each other and that no direct nor quite tangible interdependence is shown.* There seem to be signs of slight dependence, but these signs are not strong enough for us to insist firmly that this dependence exists.

This means that the widely held opinion that there is a close dependence between these processes, and especially between unsuccessful wars and disturbances, needs some limitations, reservations, and toning down. The mere occurrence of an unsuccessful war as such is not sufficient to produce an important disturbance, if the country is not disorganized, mentally and morally, or otherwise. On the contrary, as has happened several times — to the Romans in the Punic Wars, the Russians in the "Fatherland War" with Napoleon, and to Belgium when invaded by the Germans — defeat, great danger, and privations, instead of demoralizing and disorganizing the invaded and defeated country, may make it strong as iron. Instead of an explosion of internal disturbances being caused by such conditions, these latter may decrease or entirely disappear. Only in a country with weak "nerves" and discipline and little solidarity may disturbances be started by successful or by unsuccessful wars or without any war whatsoever, by almost any incident or insignificant event.

Taking all this into consideration, it is clear that war, as such, no matter whether successful or not, is neither a necessary nor a sufficient condition for starting or reinforcing internal disturbances. Conversely, an important internal disturbance is neither necessary to start a war nor sufficient to start or greatly to increase one. It may at best be one of the factors. But whether a disturbance facilitates or inhibits a war or a war inhibits a disturbance depends also upon the totality of the other socio-cultural conditions — moral, mental, religious, economic, and political — of the given moment. This seems to be the meaning of the lack of close association or correlation between the two processes discussed. In the light of these data, the theory that internal disturbances breed wars, and wars breed internal disturbances, seems greatly to exaggerate the real relationship.

Data from various other countries studied corroborate this hypothesis. In Greece, for instance, the curves of war and disturbances are parallel for several periods, reach their maximum in the same centuries, the fourth and fifth, and then decline; but in Rome the direction of movement of one curve for several centuries is practically opposite to that of the other; the third century B.C. has the highest indicator of war and the lowest indicator of disturbances, while the first century A.D. has the lowest indicator of war and one of the highest of internal disturbances; a similar relationship is found in several other periods. Data for other countries also show the same contrast in the movement of the two curves, parallel during some periods, moving in opposite directions in others, and similarly with the total indicators of both processes, for all the European countries studied, as we have seen. So much for the direct relationship of the two processes to each other. *As we shall see, they are related to each other, but only in the identity of the main factor — the transition factor — that causes both processes.* But from the identity of their main cause, it does not follow that they must be either synchronous or must be the direct cause of each other.

L. We must touch upon the problem already discussed when we traced the movement of the curve of the magnitude of war in relation to the periods of blossoming and decay in the history of the countries studied. Do internal disturbances tend to increase regularly in periods of bloom and well-being or of decay, or do they occur erratically, regardless of these periods? Taking the indicators of disturbances by centuries, the results can be summed up as follows.

In Greece the disturbances reached their peak mainly in the fifth and fourth centuries B.C., when the power, culture, and social life of Greece were at their summit. In Rome the peak of the disturbances occurred in the first century B.C., the second highest point in the third century A.D., and the third and fourth highest in the fourth and first centuries A.D. If the two centuries just before and after the birth of Christ can be regarded as the summit of Roman power and culture, these had already begun to decline by the third and fourth centuries A.D. On the other hand, the curve of disturbances is low in the fifth century A.D. and the third and fourth B.C., the fourth and third centuries B.C. being the periods of most vigorous growth, the fifth A.D. decidedly one of decline.

The data on Byzantium are likewise inconsistent.   On the one hand resplendent periods of prosperity, when culture was at its height, have a low indicator of disturbances.   Such are the "Golden Age" of the sixth century, especially the time of Justinian (527–565), and the period extending, roughly, from the beginning of the Macedonian dynasty in 867 to the end of the tenth century.   On the other hand, centuries of decline like the thirteenth and, to some extent, the twelfth, have also low indicators, the thirteenth even much lower than the more flourishing tenth century. Then we find the highest indicators of disturbances in the seventh and eighth centuries, which were disastrous and agonizing, in spite of the activities and reforms of such rulers as Leo the Isaurian (717–741), and in the tenth, which all in all seems to have been a healthy and prosperous period.   This means that here again we find no uniform and consistent relation between periods of decline and a decrease in disturbance.   If the quarter-century periods are examined instead of the century periods, the results are similar.   The only significant thing, perhaps, is that the climax of disturbances here falls upon the difficult, disastrous, and declining centuries, the seventh and eighth, while just the opposite is true of Greece.

There is hardly any essential difference in the results of other countries studied, whether we use periods of centuries, quarter centuries, or even shorter times.   It is beyond the scope of this study to make such a detailed comparison.   A few cases will suffice.   Instances can easily be multiplied by any reader who uses the indicators of disturbances given here and his own knowledge of cultural, social, and economic conditions in any one of the countries and during any of the periods here studied.

In the preceding chapter in commenting briefly on the various tables for separate countries, we mentioned this same inconsistency between the curves of internal disturbances and general sociocultural conditions in other countries.   Not to go over the facts again or analyze the problem in further detail, we must conclude that *in periods either of blossoming or of decline, disturbances have sometimes increased in number and have sometimes decreased.*

If this conclusion is valid, there must be various kinds of disturbances. Some seem to be like the tensions of childbearing and of healthy growth, which are often associated with pain and with internal disturbances of the organism.   Others are disturbances of illness or of senility.   The former occur when the growth of the social group, the nation, is sound and rapid.   The growing vital forces cannot be contained in the old network of social relations, and therefore disturb or disrupt it here and there.[12]

Disturbances during social decline and disorganization result from the waning of the vital and creative forces of a given society or from some extraordinarily unfortunate combination of external circumstances, which makes an orderly life impossible for the group. Such disturbances are attempts, mostly blind and desperate, to "do something" to get rid of impossible conditions; and so occur during periods of decline and decay. A more detailed study of many great revolutions indicates that not all, nor perhaps even most, but at least many of them, occurred in just such periods of disorganization and decline.[13] These statements in modified form will presently be substantiated further; meanwhile let us mark the net result of this discussion.

Disturbances have occurred not only in the periods of the decay and decline of society, but in its periods of blossoming and healthy growth. For those whose minds are accustomed to run along the track of mechanical uniformity only, this conclusion will be somewhat disturbing and unsatisfactory. They crave by all means simple "uniformity." From their standpoint nothing would do but a positive or negative correlation of

---

[12] Several studies of relatively small disturbances, like industrial strikes, show that these usually tend to increase when economic and business conditions are on the upgrade and tend to decrease in periods of normal, not excessive, depression. Here, then, on a smaller scale, we have a phenomenon like the increase of disturbances in periods of blossoming and sound growth. See A. H. Hansen, "Cycles of Strikes," in *American Economic Review* (1921), Vol. XI, pp. 616–621. P. Sorokin, *Contemporary Sociological Theories* (New York, 1928), pp. 576 ff.

[13] Marxian theorists and several who hold diluted Marxian theories are right in saying that disturbances occur in periods of social growth — K. Marx's "pain of childbearing" — and in periods of "social maladjustment." But they are wrong in so far as they mean by "growth" only the change in means and instruments of production that, in their opinion, always disrupts other social relationships, and in so far as by "maladjustment" they mean a progressive change in economic conditions, particularly in the technique of production, not accompanied by changes in "nonmaterial culture" which lag behind changes in material culture. They are elevating a special case into a universal rule. A society may grow and its culture may blossom in many forms without the occurrence of any noticeable changes in economic technique, or in the network of economic relationships. Likewise decline and maladjustment may come about in many ways which the theory of the lagging behind of nonmaterial culture does not explain.

In fact, throughout the medieval centuries in all the countries studied there was little, if any, change in the technique of production and in economic productive forces — certainly no appreciable change — within periods of 25 or 50 years. The indicators, however, often rose and fell greatly within such short periods. This evidence, if there were no other, would be enough to disprove such an "economic interpretation" of the dynamics of internal disturbances. Other arguments against these theories will be found in my *Contemporary Sociological Theories*, chap. x and pp. 742–746.

disturbances with periods of either bloom or decline. Since the data do not bear out this explanation, we shall have to disregard the desires of various wishers.

M. Does the fact that disturbances occur in both periods really mean that no "uniformity" can be found in that "diversity"? Is it not possible to find in that diversity — almost opposition — of periods of bloom and decline something which belongs to both periods and in which both are similar? If so, might not this be the common factor "producing" disturbances in both periods? Is there anything which might serve as such a factor?

With this idea in mind let us glance more attentively at the indicators, by centuries, of disturbances — first at the indicators for all the European countries studied and then at the indicators for separate countries. We find the following interesting phenomena. For the sixth and seventh centuries indicators are low (446.20 and 458.19). For the eighth century the indicator is very high (733.98); in the ninth, tenth, and eleventh centuries there is a considerable drop (589.65, 537.43, and 693.90 respectively); and it rises considerably in the twelfth century and reaches the highest points in the thirteenth and fourteenth centuries (882.90 and 827.00), followed by a decline in the fifteenth (748.38), during which century the curve is still high but notably lower than before; then they greatly decline in the sixteenth (509.56) and stay low in the seventeenth (605.50) and the eighteenth, when up to the last quarter of the eighteenth they give the lowest point (415.56). The curve then begins to rise and jumps greatly in the nineteenth century (766.91). Notwithstanding a temporary sharp decline in the last quarter of the nineteenth century, it flares up in the first quarter of the twentieth. Thus *we have three main peaks; in the eighth, in the thirteenth and fourteenth centuries, and in the nineteenth and twentieth. After each peak the wave of disturbances subsides and remains low till the next peak.*

Have these facts a meaning, and can an interpretation be found to fit them that will be satisfactory from a logical standpoint also? The answer is given by the whole character of this work, namely, all three peak periods are the periods of transition, either in the whole culture of Europe and in its system of social relationships, or in the system of social relationships only. We know already that the thirteenth and fourteenth centuries were those of the greatest transition of European culture and society from the Ideational to the Sensate form and from the feudal to the modern system of social relationships (from predominantly familistic to coercive-contractual; from theocracy to the secular regime, from Ideational freedom to Sensate; from the feudal regime to the national monarchies, and so on).

In all these respects, these centuries were the greatest turning point in all European history; with the greatest breakdown of the system of social values and of social relationships. Therefore the curve of the disturbances reaches the highest point during these centuries. They would be expected logically to be centuries of disturbances, and they were such in fact. The hypothesis of transition, with its breakdown of the system of values and relationships, as set forth in the preceding part in regard to war movement, accounts for this peak.

Can it account for the peaks of the eighth and the nineteenth and twentieth centuries? As for the nineteenth and especially the twentieth century, it accounts for it easily; we have seen that the twentieth century is transitional in all the compartments of European culture. As for the end of the eighteenth and the first part of the nineteenth century (which is responsible for the comparatively high indicator for the nineteenth century), we know also that this was the period of the "liquidation of the postmedieval relationships" in the system of social organization, and especially the period of transition from the predominantly compulsory to the predominantly contractual relationships. This was demonstrated in Part One of this volume; there was also shown all the profound importance of such a shift from one main type of social relationship to another. This shift was accomplished roughly in the period opened by the French Revolution of 1789 and the first few decades of the nineteenth century (see Part One of this volume, particularly Chapters Three and Four). Such a transition from one fundamental type of social relationship to another had to call forth, according to the hypothesis, a rise of the curve of the disturbances; and this curve did indeed rise. Beginning roughly with the second part of the nineteenth century, Europe settled definitely into the comfortable new contractual house, and the fever of disturbances subsided. But toward the twentieth century, Sensate culture itself began to show signs of disintegration, and with it the contractual system of social relationships was disturbed. Both entered the sharp stage of transition. (See Chapters Three and Four of this volume, Chapter Fifteen of Volume Two, and the whole of this work.) Hence the rapid rise of the curve in the twentieth century.

Finally, as to the eighth-century peak, it also agrees with the hypothesis. It was the period of the so-called Carolingian Renaissance. If it did not mean a fundamental change in the culture, which remained Ideational before and after it, it accomplished nevertheless some important modifications in it. Its transitional character was, however, mainly in the system of social relationships; in the forms of social, economic, and political organization or reorganization; and in this field it was a genuinely transitional period. As such, it had to give rise to disturbances; and it certainly did.

Thus all the three main peaks seem to be well accounted for by the hypothesis of transition. The same hypothesis accounts for the comparatively low level of disturbances in the other centuries: from the ninth to the twelfth; from the fifteenth to the eighteenth inclusive (except its last decade); and from the second part of the nineteenth to the beginning of the twentieth century. These were the settled periods in the type of dominant culture, as well as in that of the system of social relationships. Even a slight rise of the curve in the seventeenth century is accountable from this standpoint; it was the last stand of the Ideational culture and its satellites to regain its dominance. The effort failed, and the question was definitely settled.

Thus the hypothesis of the transition accounts for these tidal waves of disturbances.[14] It means that, *other conditions being equal, during the*

[14] A careful reader may find a contradiction between the explanation by that hypothesis of the main movements of war in the preceding part, and the movement of the disturbances. He may notice that in these two cases my apportioning of the transitional periods is not identical. However, if such a reader studies the matter more carefully, he will see that there is no contradiction. In both cases the twentieth century was set forth as the period of transition; in both the thirteenth and fourteenth centuries are transitional periods; all the other centuries are qualified similarly. The only centuries that seem to be qualified somewhat differently in their roles are possibly the fifteenth and the sixteenth. Here they are regarded as the centuries of a sufficiently crystallized Sensate culture; in the preceding part their transitional aspect was stressed. That they were simultaneously both is emphasized throughout the whole work. Yes, in the fifteenth century, in many countries, the victory of the Sensate culture became fairly clear; therefore, culturally, the societies began to settle into the pattern of that culture. But it was only the beginning of the process of crystallization. Therefore, the curve of disturbances for that century is slightly lower than for the fourteenth, but it is still very high, which indicates its transitory nature. Only in the sixteenth century, when the crystallization had progressed, did the curve go down much. In the field of international relationships, especially in the vast international world of Europe, the transitory aspects of these centuries had to last longer and operate more vigorously than in the field of the purely internal relationships of the States of Europe. As I pointed out in Chapter Twelve, in a vast and heterogeneous international world the settling and crystallization of the interstate relationships must often lag from that within the groups involved. If the main European states only began to put their houses in Sensate order in the fifteenth and sixteenth centuries, in their interstate relationships during these centuries they still remained in the confusion of transition from the Ideational to the Sensate order. And the character of the religious wars of the sixteenth and seventeenth centuries testifies to this, besides other evidences given in this work, up to the sudden twist in the seventeenth century in many compartments of culture. When this and similar circumstances are kept in mind, no contradiction will be found, for the simple reason that all in all these centuries from the thirteenth to the seven-

periods when the existing culture, or the system of social relationships, or both, undergo a rapid transformation, the internal disturbances in the respective societies increase; when they are strong and crystallized, the internal disturbances tend to decrease and stay at a low level. This conclusion follows logically from all that is said in this work, and agrees with the facts about disturbances. We have seen that these occur in periods of bloom and of decline, in periods of prosperity and of poverty, and in periods when society moves upward with particular rapidity and during the phase of its rapid downward movement.

This "inconsistency" is quite consistent in the light of the above hypothesis. Indeed, the established social order and cultural system may be, and is, as easily unsettled in periods of rapid enrichment, vigorous blossoming, as in periods of catastrophe and decline. The well-knit network of social relationships may be, and is, as easily disrupted by a "boom" as by misfortune. As Cinderella, touched by the fairy's wand, forgot her regular bedtime, so when any individual or group is unexpectedly enriched, the regular habits of the man or the social order of the group may be disrupted, as easily perhaps as by tragedy.

Whatever factors lead to a rise and decline of each main form of culture and system of social relationship (and in passing I may say that the main factors calling forth change are "immanent" or "inherent" in cultural and social life itself, and that these factors in the course of time will bring any sociocultural order to confusion), *the main and the indispensable condition for an eruption of internal disturbances is that the social system or the cultural system or both shall be unsettled.* This datum seems to fit the facts much better than most of the popular theories. These theories, that ascribe internal disturbances either to growing poverty and "hard material conditions" or, on the contrary, to material progress, and that correlate them either with periods of decay or with periods of bloom, are sharply contradicted by relevant facts as well as by the bulk of the indi-

---

teenth were indeed transitional centuries; so far as the intragroup relationships and culture are concerned, for most of the European countries (except Russia), the transitional status decreased from the thirteenth to the sixteenth centuries; so far as the interstate relationships and culture are concerned, they proceeded rather *crescendo* from the thirteenth to the seventeenth centuries. If, in a vast urban area, many houses and their surroundings are modernized at a given moment, a time must elapse before the whole area in its entirety will be modernized. The debris of the reconstruction in the area will be seen a long time after a part or even the majority of the houses are reconstructed. The intragroup adjustment is one thing; the intergroup reconstruction is another, especially when the world of the intergroup relationships is vast and complex. When it is comparatively small, as in ancient Greece, then the intragroup and the intergroup reconstructions may be close and almost synchronous with each other.

cators.   However hard living conditions may be in a given society, if the framework of its relationships and values is unshattered, no disturbances will be forthcoming.   The members of such a society may be dying of starvation and yet not revolt ; or, anyhow, make fewer attempts to revolt than members of a perfectly comfortable society in which the sociocultural system of values is loose.   If one can imagine a society where everyone has the standard of living of a millionaire but sociocultural relationships and values are not crystallized, this society will be more turbulent and disorderly than one where even the main physiological needs are barely satisfied and half-starvation is the normal standard of living but where the sociocultural framework is strong and definite and the members of the society believe in the same values and live by them.

Here is a situation quite similar to that which one finds when studying suicide, and crime and punishment.   Many still believe the main factors in the increase of these phenomena to be poverty as such, or other material misfortunes and "uncomfortable conditions."   But even superficial study radically refutes these "theories of simplicists."

Suicide is no more frequent among the poor than among the rich — less frequent, if anything.   In previous centuries, when the standard of living was lower, suicides were less frequent than in the last two centuries and especially in the last few decades.   E. Durkheim conclusively showed that all these conditions have little to do with suicide and that the main condition is the destruction of the network of sociocultural relationships ("*anomie*"), resulting in the demoralization of the individual or an increase in his psychosocial isolation.[15]

The public and criminologists, by and large, do not yet realize that they are on the wrong track when they ascribe an increase in criminality to mental deficiency, to illiteracy, to poverty of a low standard of living, or to similar conditions.   They overlook such well-known facts as that the standard of living in this country has risen during the last forty or more years without decreasing criminality, that periods of business prosperity are not regularly followed by a decrease in crime, and that in many countries much poorer than the United States criminality is not higher than here, but much lower.   If sociocultural values are definitely crystallized, a given system of social relationships (with the distribution of the "rights and duties") is strong, a uniform standard of right and wrong is inculcated in each member of the society from his earliest childhood, and

---

[15] See E. Durkheim, *Le Suicide* (Paris, 1912).   See also P. Sorokin and C. Zimmerman, *Principles of Rural and Urban Sociology* (New York, 1929), chap. vii; M. Halbwachs, *Les causes du suicide* (Paris, 1930).

these standards invariably are enforced, the pressure of public opinion is uniform and undivided, and any act violating the rules and mores is felt to be really sacrilegious and appalling. In these circumstances the members of such a society would bear enormous hardships and privations before they would turn to crime.

If, on the contrary, the sociocultural framework is unsettled and broken, individuals lose a transsubjective guide, pressure, and control. Neither can uniform forms of conduct be inculcated in such conditions, nor can a unanimous public opinion exert its pressure, nor is there an attitude of "abhorrence" of crime. Such a society is a "house divided against itself." The result is increased demoralization, "revolt against the law and obligatory mores"; hence an increase in crime. This was shown more extensively in Chapter Fifteen of Volume Two.

The phenomena of social disturbances are fundamentally like the phenomena of criminality. The main difference is in scale. When a few individuals kill, steal, or rob others, the isolated cases are called "crimes." When the same actions are perpetrated on a large scale and by the masses, the phenomena are called "riots," "disturbances," "revolutions," and so on. Accordingly most of the disturbances [16] spring from, and develop in, exactly the same sort of situation as does criminal demoralization among individuals. The determining factor in each case is the condition of the sociocultural network of values and relationships.

This hypothesis not only explains the movement of the indicators for the countries taken together, but also explains many of the ups and downs of the indicators for separate countries. If in Greece the maximum number of disturbances fall within the fifth and fourth centuries B.C., it is because these centuries were, as we have seen, precisely the centuries of the meeting ground of the Ideational period which was nearing its end and the Sensate wave which was beginning in the life history of Hellenistic culture. These centuries were the height of Greek culture and political power. Their position was the same as the position of the eighth and thirteenth to the fifteenth, and the nineteenth to the twentieth centuries.

In the third and second centuries B.C. the new Hellenistic or Sensate order was already crystallized and firm. Hence the low indicators of disturbances, in spite of the fact that the centuries were those of the decline of Greek power and splendor.

---

[16] Except a few, started and factually carried through for the highest sociocultural values, without perpetration of bloody and violent actions. But, as we have seen, the per cent of such disturbances is very small.

No less instructive is the curve of disturbances in Rome. It is relatively high in the fifth century B.C., and no wonder. This was the century when the struggle between the patrician and the plebeian systems of social relationships was resolved, when the old order of social relationship ended and the new began — a century, therefore, with an unsettled social network of relationship at least, if not with a greatly disturbed system of cultural values. Toward its end, the new order had sufficiently crystallized so that the indicators of disturbances in the fourth and third centuries B.C. were exceptionally low. We know how "virtuous" these centuries were and how rigid was the network of their social relationships and cultural values. Roman writers are practically unanimous in stressing the opinion that they were the centuries of unspoiled virile mores and unity of firm convictions. Hence the orderliness of these centuries, though life in them was not particularly comfortable or easy.

Toward the second half of the second century B.C., not without the influence of the infiltrating Hellenistic Sensate culture, the sociocultural order began to be undermined and weakened. Hence an upward movement of disturbances began, and reached a climax in the first century B.C. As anyone acquainted with Roman history knows, that century again was the meeting ground for the dying, though still fruitful, order of Republican or traditional Rome, and the new Caesarean Rome that was just beginning. It was the century of rise of Sensate culture and decline of the Mixed or even Ideational culture of the preceding period. In this it is the replica of the other centuries of transition, the fifth to fourth B.C. in Greece, and those in Western culture.

Note the further development. Though during the first century A.D., and the subsequent centuries up to the fifth A.D., disturbances subsided from their level in the first century B.C., the level, nevertheless, remained very high. Why should this be so, in spite of the fact that all in all the first and second centuries of our era were peaceful, prosperous, and comfortable? Because these were all centuries of transition from the Hellenistic-Roman sociocultural order to the radically different sociocultural-Ideational system of Christianity. The contrast between the two opposite systems was so great and so deep that the struggle could not be settled in one or two centuries. We know it continued and increased rather than decreased from the first to the third century, which was marked by the maximum of disturbances during these centuries. In the fourth, which brought the victory and the legalization of the Christian sociocultural system, a falling trend in disturbances was already marked. In the fifth century the fall was enormous. Why? In that century the new Ideational sociocultural system was above question, recognized *urbi et orbi*, crystallized, and definite. According to the hypothesis under discussion, the curve of disturbances could but go down. And it did go down, in spite of the fact that so far as material conditions — safety, comfort, and general "economico-material" configuration — were concerned, the fifth century was one of the poorest of periods.

I regret that data for the Western world for the subsequent centuries, the sixth and seventh, could not be obtained. For Italy and Byzantium we have data. The indicators for these countries show that the falling curve of disturbances in the fifth century A. D. was not accidental; throughout the sixth and seventh centuries in Italy and the sixth in Byzantium the curve remained low. Low it is also for all the four countries, France and Spain added, for these centuries. The newly crystallized sociocultural order, then, continued to exist during these periods and in spite of all vicissitudes, especially in Italy, prevented disturbances from breaking out on a large scale. But in the eighth century in Italy and in Byzantium and in most of the other countries, disturbances increased enormously. This increase, for the reasons given, corroborates our hypothesis well.

The reader may test its validity by indicators of disturbances and by the historical data on the conditions of the network of sociocultural values and relationships. *It is not my contention that the factor stressed explains all the ups and downs in the curves of disturbances.* But I do claim that the factor of the status of the sociocultural network of relationships and values is enough in itself to "explain" the main "ups and downs" of the curves in all the societies studied. It is one of the most important reasons, perhaps even the most important reason, ever present and inherent in all the disturbances, their presence or absence, their increase or decrease. In this respect, then, the course of internal disturbances differs from the course of war, but both have an essentially similar set of "causative" factors.

N. In view of all this it is easier to understand the facts emphasized in the previous chapters. Let us recall them.

The first is that inner tensions and disturbances seem to be phenomena inseparably connected with the existence and functioning of social bodies. Indeed, they are no less, but rather more, inseparably connected than tensions, crises, and sickness with biological organisms. If few of these organisms, if any, are free from such crises during their whole existence, still fewer social bodies — practically none — are free from disturbances during their more or less prolonged and more or less complete history.

Among our samples we have not met any. And I can say with a reasonable degree of certainty that hardly any social body — be it political, religious, economic, tribal, or what not — or any sufficiently large aggregate of the population of a particular locality, would be free from such disturbances. These are no less "natural" and "common" than storms in ordinary weather conditions.

Second, disturbances occur much oftener than is usually realized. Only rarely does it happen that two or three decades in the life history of a vast social body pass without them. On the average of from four to seven years, as a rule, one considerable social disturbance may be expected. The fact that these phenomena occur so frequently confirms our conclusions that they are inseparable from the very existence and functioning of social bodies. If this be so, then it is evident that the usual method of accounting for these phenomena as the fault of a government, an aristocracy, or a mob, or of revolutionaries, or any other group, as due to this or that set of special conditions and factors — in brief, the habit of regarding disturbances as something quite abnormal and in need of being explained by special extraordinary factors and the faults or misdeeds of various agencies or individuals — is superficial and unscientific. Disturbances seem to be no less "normal" than periods of order, only less frequent, and seem no more to need a special explanation than order does. Their "causes" are as deep in social life itself as the "causes" of internal peace. A set of special conditions, like a poor government, a selfish aristocracy, stupid mob-mindedness, poverty and war, may play a secondary role in reinforcing or weakening, accelerating or retarding, disturbances, but these are only secondary factors. Even without them, disturbances, like storms, would frequently occur. So they have occurred under stupid and under wise governments, under conditions of war and of peace, in monarchies and republics, in democracies and aristocracies, in prosperity and poverty, in ages of "enlightenment" and of "ignorance," in urbanized and industrial as well as in rural and nonindustrialized countries ; and in other most diverse circumstances. To continue, therefore, to look upon them as something exceptional, abnormal, accidental, and incidental to social life itself is no more scientific than to look at indispositions, sicknesses, painful experiences, in the life of an individual as incidental. In some form, with some frequency, they occur to practically everyone before his life is over and, whether we like it or not, are a very essential part of life.

In stressing these facts before, I have indicated that they suggest that we must look far deeper for the "causes" of disturbances than is usually done. Now we have the deep, the inherent, causes before us. Since the main cause is perhaps the status of the sociocultural framework of relationships and of values, and since sooner or later, on account of immanent change inherent in any sociocultural system, such a system is bound to be unsettled, "withered," and broken, the sociocultural order of every society is bound to have periods of transition and with them rising tides of disturbances. On the other hand, any new system, if only it survives, will surely become crystallized and settled. This means that any society will also have periods when the wave of disturbances subsides, and hence the similarity of all societies in these respects, and the similarity of all the societies studied in the frequency and the magnitude of disturbances. All this "explains" the somewhat vague statement about deep and inherent causes that I made before. And these remarks may give further support to the validity of the hypothesis discussed. So much for this point.[17]

O. Another important problem in the field of internal disturbances, as of any other important social process, is to *what extent the direction, and particularly the quantitative direction, of the process is the same in various countries of the same "cultural continent" during the same period.* In other words, do disturbances, for instance, increase simultaneously in all the countries, or in several of these, or do they increase in some while decreasing in others? The answer, in the field studied, is given by the above figures.

Concentrating our attention on European countries (because the time for the others is relatively short and the countries few), we see that from the seventh century to the twentieth there was no century in which, for all the countries studied that then existed, including Byzantium, the curves of disturbances had the same direction, upward and downward, respectively. It should also be noted that there are no two countries among those studied in which the curves were parallel or had the same direction in all the centuries. From the dissimilarity one deduces that all the conditions bearing on the phenomena of disturbances may not be quite the same in all these countries. On the other hand, the fact that the direction of several curves is identical suggests that in any given century the basic conditions relevant to the phenomena of disturbances may be somewhat similar in several countries. Somewhat similar conclusions follow from the more detailed data for the quarter centuries. According to these data, in two quarter centuries the curves were parallel

---

[17] *Cf.* C. Cossio, *El concepto puro de revolución* (Barcelona, 1936); A. Poviña, *Sociologia de la revolución* (Cordova, 1933).

in six countries out of seven. Of the other quarter centuries the picture is less uniform, showing now four, now five, countries moving in one direction and the others in the opposite one. Again there are two countries in which the movement of the curves has been parallel in all the quarter-century periods.

All this means that the forces generating disturbances rarely, if ever, work in one country only. For good or bad, they seem to work in the areas of several countries simultaneously. So the Philistine's remark, so often heard regarding a revolution in some other country — "It doesn't concern us. Thank heaven, we are a different state and nation" — as well as the proverbial policy of noninterference in the disturbances of another country, means, at least half the time, that the attempt at self-consolation is based on a very fragile foundation. Perhaps the rulers and citizens who hold such opinions do wish not to interfere in the disturbances of a foreign country and hope that these will not spread over their own country. But, as the data show, the reality does not pay much attention to these wishes; disturbances started in one country usually spread over or are independently originated in several others. So it was in the past, and so it is in the present. Most statements like the above result from something like the proverbial ostrich policy, plus, often, a great deal of hypocrisy.

PART FOUR

Culture, Personality, and Conduct

Chapter Fifteen

RELATIONSHIP BETWEEN TYPES OF CULTURE AND TYPES OF PERSONALITY AND BEHAVIOR [1]

I. PRELIMINARIES

That the dominant type of culture molds the type of mentality of human beings who are born and live in it, we conclude at once from the evidence of the preceding chapters. The scientific, philosophical, religious, aesthetic, moral, juridical, and other opinions, theories, beliefs, tastes, and convictions — in brief, the whole *Weltanschauung* — of human beings in an Ideational society are shaped to the Ideational pattern, while those of the persons living under the dominance of a Sensate culture are formed by the Sensate mold. Only those who have their physical being in the realm of a given culture, but are neither a part of it, nor come in psychosocial contact with it — only such persons and groups can escape this conditioning of their mentality by the culture of the physical space in which they live.[2] With these exceptions, therefore, the mentality of every person is a microcosm that reflects the cultural microcosm of his social surroundings. This may be stated more specifically in the following fashion.

[1] In co-operation with J. V. Boldyreff.

[2] It is hardly necessary to remind the reader of the simple fact that mere adjacency in physical space and time does not necessarily mean adjacency in social space and time. Prisoners and strangers live physically in a culture that surrounds them, and yet are not a part of it. Hypothetically, a person born in the prison of a given city, and kept in it, may be touched very little by the culture of the city, if the "culture of the prison" is fundamentally different. Large social classes, like slaves and serfs, may be touched little by the dominant integrated type of culture of the free classes. In fact, there is always some contact with the dominant culture of all the people who live in it — even of prisoners, strangers, slaves, and serfs — and if not directly, then indirectly, the dominant culture stamps their mentality along the lines of this contact. But the contact is often slight, limited by few special elements, and therefore the dominant culture conditions their mentality only in these few respects. Moreover, theoretically, and often even in fact, two different cultures may coexist in the same physical space, in the same area of a city, or region. When these almost self-evident facts are taken into consideration, it will be comprehensible why in the same physical area there are persons with different types of mentality. Assuming that a certain type of culture is *dominant* in a given area or population, it follows that there will also be the dominant type of mentality molded by it.

Other conditions being equal, (1) the mentality of a person will be clearly Ideational if he has had a contact only with the pure Ideational culture.   The same is true with regard to the Sensate culture.   (2) The mentality of a person will be Mixed if he has been in contact with different types of culture.   The mixture will represent a combination of the elements of the various cultures involved.   (3) The mentality of a person will be unintegrated, for instance, pseudo-Ideational, if he has been associated with only an unintegrated culture, or with a multitude of different cultures of contradictory character.   An exception to the rule is provided by the comparatively rare case where a synthesis is achieved of various elements of different cultures in one integrated unity.   The Idealistic culture is an example of this.   Not only are these exceptions rare, but they hardly ever are absolute in the sense that the integration is perfect and embraces all the aspects of the sociocultural mentality. There are, in fact, always "odds and ends" in such mentalities that stand in contradiction to the central type of integration.

So much for this comparatively simple and clear point.

It is quite another matter with the problem of the *relationship between the dominant type of culture and the actual behavior or conduct* of the persons who are a part of it.   The difference between the two problems is clear. To repeat Ribot, a person may know perfectly well Kant's *Critique of Practical Reason*, and may enthusiastically write a most scholarly commentary on it, and yet in his actions and behavior be at great variance with it and with his own mentality in this field.   A man may agree with and extol the Christian principle of loving one's neighbor as oneself, and yet in his actual behavior be the most egotistic of individuals.   Who does not know the type of persons who preach sincerely the virtues of honesty, altruism, chastity, moderation in drinking and eating, and so on, and who in their behavior quite frequently transgress in these respects? Still better known is the type of hypocrites whose speech reactions and actions are normally in contradiction.   Similarly, we are quite familiar with our everyday practice of beautifying our often prosaic, selfish, even ugly actions by means of high-sounding, noble-appearing "motivations," "rationalizations," and "derivations."   When a lion devours a lamb, he does not tell us that he does it for the sake of God, humanity, the proletariat, the nation, communism, fascism, international welfare, and so on. Among human beings it is not an infrequent occurrence that the worst actions, whether wholesale murder, or rape, or torture, or robbery (by criminals, by revolutionaries, by the powerful rich, and others), regularly find noble and often quite sincere justification on the part of their perpetrators. I stress the fact that such "beautification" is often quite sincere.

All this means that in contradistinction to the close connection between the dominant type of culture and mentality, the relationship between the dominant type of culture and conduct or behavior is likely to be loose, even perhaps imperceptible. Hence the necessity of a special study of this problem.

II. Main Propositions

A. *First Proposition. The relationship between the two variables — the character of the dominant culture and the character of the conduct of the persons that live in it — either cannot be very close or cannot be as close as the correlation between the dominant culture and the mentality of these persons.*

However different from each other are the Ideational and Sensate cultures, the societies that are the bearers of such cultures have of necessity a general fund of similar activities. This fund is composed in the first place of all those *acts necessary for the satisfaction of the elementary biological needs*. The members of the Ideational and Sensate societies must eat, drink, have shelter, sleep, work, reproduce their kind, defend themselves against agencies and forces menacing their existence, and so on. Though the extent to which these biological needs are satisfied and the forms which satisfaction takes may widely differ in such societies, there is a common minimum for all societies, whether Sensate or Ideational. *The existence of such a minimum lessens the contrast in behavior between the members of an Ideational and those of a Sensate culture. And the decrease in contrast points to diminution of the closeness of the relationship between culture and mentality.* This is the central reason for the hypothesis stated in the first proposition.

If this proposition be developed fully (and it is not the purpose of the present chapter to do so), it will explain why even in the conspicuously Ideational societies (say, in ascetic monasteries) the activities of their members are far from being entirely otherworldly; why they take the Sensate reality much more seriously in their behavior than in their mentality; why they satisfy many of their biological needs — say hunger or sex — much more fully than they profess to do; why so often they "sin" and fall victim to the "flesh"; why hypocrisy or cynical adaptation is so frequently met with among even the most Ideational of societies; why the discrepancy between ideologies and acts is such a common phenomenon; why "rationalization" and ennoblement, through "derivations" and ideologies of cruel, sometimes bestial, acts are a perennial trait of all societies; why crime, revolution, egotism, avidity, lust, and so on, are present, to some extent, in the Ideational as well as the Sensate groups. In spite of inhibitory cultural forces, the pressure of elementary biological needs is never reduced to zero. It forces the members of even the most radical Ideational society to perform regular activities for their satisfaction. There are some exceptions, of course, among individuals who neglect these needs even to the point of death; but this cannot apply to the living society of which these exceptional individuals are members. Not infrequently even the inhibitory nature of the culture mentality is broken down by the pressure of the biological residues. In other cases they are responsible for the molding of the mentality itself, which thus assumes the form of a mere justification, a rationalization, an ennoblement, of the behavior that is the result of these residues, even though such behavior is fundamentally in contradiction with the main principles of the mentality. In such cases the principle "Don't kill" is twisted into "For the glory of God (or progress, or communism, etc.) kill the infidels, the enemy." The principle "Abstain from lust" assumes the form of encouraging religious prostitution, and other forms of sexual indulgence, all justified on religious, political, moral, or other grounds. Still more common is the confiscation of the property of others and the accumulation of riches, contrary to the maxims "Seek poverty," "Take no heed of the morrow," "It is easier for a camel to go through the eye of a needle than for a rich man to enter into the Kingdom of God."

All this explains why the relationship between the dominant culture and conduct cannot be very close; why in the field of conduct the difference between the members of the Ideational and Sensate societies is much less than in the field of culture mentality.

B. *Second Proposition.* If we should stop at this hypothesis, as many do, we should commit a great blunder. Having emphasized the fact that the relationship between culture and conduct is not always close, we are yet not entitled to conclude that there is no observable relationship whatever. The first proposition must, therefore, be supplemented by a second. It may be formulated thus: *Though the relationship between the dominant culture and the behavior of its bearers is not always close, nevertheless, it does exist. In application to the various types of culture, this means that the bearers of the Ideational and Sensate cultures differ from one another not only in their mentality (ideas, opinions, convictions, beliefs, tastes, moral and aesthetic standards, etc.) but also in their behavior and personality. All in all, the conduct of the Ideational man would be more Ideational than that of the Sensate man, and vice versa. Similarly the per-*

sonality — understood here to mean the total mentality plus conduct of an individual — of the Ideationalist is also more Ideational than the personality of the member of a Sensate culture. The difference between the bearers of the Ideational and Sensate cultures is less great with respect to conduct and personality than to mentality; nevertheless, the difference exists and is quite readily perceptible.

This second proposition follows, first of all, from the fact that there is hardly any clear-cut boundary line between mentality and behavior. They imperceptibly merge into each other, and many phenomena of mentality are at the same time phenomena of conduct and behavior, and vice versa. All the main compartments of culture mentality which have been analyzed previously in the present work — arts; systems of truth (science, philosophy, religion), moral systems, systems of law; forms of political, social, and economic organizations; and so on — are not only the phenomena of mentality, but also the phenomena of behavior in the most overt, "behavioristic" sense. Their creation and their existence and functioning in any culture presupposes an incessant stream of actions and reactions — that is, of behavior — on the part of the members of the culture. The creation of the Parthenon or the Chartres Cathedral involved the capital and labor (in the sense of the wealth and actions) of thousands of persons for a notable length of time. The creation and continuation of the activities of any institution, whether the Roman Catholic See, the Rockefeller Institute, Harvard, or the University of Paris; a research institute, theater, law court, moral sect; scientific, philosophical, religious, artistic, ethical, political, juridical, economic, or other social body, organization, or system — the creation, the existence, and the functioning of any of these are carried on through an incessant activity, *i.e.*, through the behavior, in the most overt sense of this term, of a few or of many human individuals. *Since, as we have seen, these activities assume one form in an Ideational and a quite different form in a Sensate society with respect to all the sociocultural compartments, this means that a very large part of the conduct and behavior of the members of an Ideational culture assumes Ideational forms, while those of the members of a Sensate society take on Sensate forms.* It is not a phenomenon of mentality only but of behavior also, that members of medieval society build a cathedral, whereas members of another society build Radio City; that A leaves his property to a monastery, B to a university, and C to a society of atheists; that Phidias creates the statue of Athena, an unknown artist the statue of Christ the Good, and Rodin or Canova molds a statue of Sensual Love. Likewise, it is not only mentality but also a long and complicated chain of overt actions that is embodied in preaching the New Testament or the gospel of communism.   And so with all other phenomena of culture mentality.   To the extent that this work has shown that Ideational, Idealistic, Mixed, and Sensate cultures have their own forms of mentality in all the main fields of sociocultural relationships ; to the extent that any phenomenon of this culture mentality is at the same time a phenomenon of overt behavior — to these limits *the conduct and behavior of the members of any such culture is conditioned by it, and stands in a consistent and clear association with it*.   These considerations are so self-evident that there is hardly any need to develop the argument further.

Placed on its inferences, this conclusion means (1) that the *forms* or *patterns* of almost all the overt actions and reactions (or conduct and behavior) of the members of each dominant type of culture are shaped and conditioned by it ; (2) that each culture, to some extent, stimulates many activities and inhibits many others in conformity with its nature ; (3) that only the actions and reactions that are most closely related to the elementary biological needs experience, in conformity with our first proposition, a comparatively mild conditioning by the dominant culture, *so far as the performance or nonperformance, the frequency, and the intensity of their satisfaction are concerned*.   The forms in which these activities are discharged are also conditioned by the dominant culture : for instance, the forms of marriage, the forms of property, the forms of securing elementary safety.   Only in this particular field, and in these particular respects, the conditioning role of the dominant culture seems to be less than in other fields of human conduct.

If the second proposition is valid, then it follows that (*a*) in Ideational societies and periods the desire to satisfy biological needs and the level — the frequency, intensity, and in part, extensity — of their satisfaction, necessarily tend to be less high than in a predominantly Sensate society, the Idealistic and Mixed societies occupying an intermediate position. Chapter Eight, on the fluctuation of economic conditions, supports this inference clearly.   Though the relationship between the type of culture and the level of economic conditions has been found to be not very close, nevertheless it is reasonably clear and perceptible ; (*b*) if the second proposition is valid, then in Ideational societies and periods we must expect to find a higher proportion of personalities of the Ideational type, and this type must be more pronounced qualitatively than in the predominantly Sensate periods.   And vice versa.   The proportion of the Sensate type of personality, with an unbridled desire for the satisfaction of the biological impulses, should be higher in the Sensate society than in the Ideational and Idealistic. But the relationship between the type of culture and type of conduct is not claimed everywhere to be complete or as close as between the type of culture and mentality; even the highest proportions should not be expected to reach beyond comparatively limited levels.

Thus our two major propositions mean that not only are the *forms and stimulation and inhibition* of certain actions and reactions conditioned by the type of culture, but also the activities closely related to the satisfaction of the elementary biological needs.

A complete verification of inference (2) is impossible for evident reasons: history does not record to what extent and how frequently and greedily all the members of a given society satisfied their biological needs, how strong were their lusts of the flesh, how sensual, ascetic, or balanced they were in eating, drinking, and the like. Even in the case of historical personalities whose life and conduct are comparatively well known (Caesar, or St. Augustine, or Henry VIII, or Savonarola, or any other), we never can be sure that the portrait given by a historian is accurate, exactly characterizes the subject's behavior with regard to the actions and reactions closely associated with the biological needs. The fact that different historians not infrequently give quite different pictures of the same personality (see, for instance, the recent "debunking" biographies of Washington, Lincoln, Queen Victoria, Napoleon, and compare them with the earlier idealized biographies; or the portraits of, say, Robespierre given by a "conservative" and by a "radical" historian) is evidence of the difficulty of achieving objective accuracy: the historian's picture is often a portrait of the historian himself rather than of the personality whom he thinks he depicts. These and many similar considerations explain why a satisfactory verification of inference (2) by means of actual historical material is impossible.

On the other hand, a rough approximation to such verification may be attempted. Suppose we take the *totality* of the historical personalities of a given period in a given society and compare them with the *totality* of historical personalities in the same society at other periods. This totality at each period is the integrator and the bearer of the dominant culture. The very fact that the individual became a person of historical significance means that he was deeply involved in the culture of his time and place. The fact that we take the totality of the historical individuals for each period, of all who have left traces in the annals of history, no matter in which compartment of culture their activity lay — in science, philosophy, religion, art, law, ethics; in social, political, economic, or other fields — makes the group "representative." It is more representative than the group chosen from only one profession or field of cultural activity because, as we have seen in the first part of Volume One, in the same society various groups — for instance, the Roman Catholic popes, the kings, the captains of finance, and the clergy — differ notably from one another as to the comparatively Ideational and Sensate nature of their conduct.

As to the uncertainty and unreliability of the portraits given by historians of such personalities, we should not go too far in our skepticism. If we do not know just how sensual many historical figures were and whether their behavior was nearer to the Ideational or the Sensate type, in regard to many others we can be reasonably certain of their type of conduct. Nobody would contend that Alexander Borgia, or Louis XIV, or Julius Caesar, or Napoleon, or Catherine the Great were ascetic, nonsensual, or Ideational in their conduct and personality. Likewise, nobody would place in the Sensate class St. Francis of Assisi, or Pachomius the Great, or Diogenes the Cynic, or such popes as Gregory I and St. Celestine. Similarly, no historian would place Plato, or Aristotle, or Dante, or Queen Victoria in any class but the Mixed. In spite of all the uncertainties, the profile of some figures is conspicuously Sensate, of others Ideational, and of others Mixed. If within these modest limits historical portraiture is unreliable, then there is no science of history, and the work of all historians must be dismissed as mere whim.

If, therefore, we put all such pronounced types into the Ideational or Sensate class, and place in the Mixed class all those whose behavior does not belong conspicuously with either of the extremes; if, next, we compute the percentage of each type in the totality of the historical personalities of each period, we shall then have some very rough data as to the frequency, increase, and decrease of each type in the various cultures under comparison. Since the number of persons involved in each of the periods is rather large, the few errors of classification that may be made by investigators are not very important: a few misplaced personalities do not change appreciably the total result for each period or for all the periods compared.

I shall now present three sets of data aimed at the verification of our hypothesis of the correlation of behavior personality with cultural types.

First, the indicators of the type of personality of *all the historical figures*, for each period compared, in all fields of culture in the societies of Greece, Rome, and Western Europe, as they are mentioned in the

Encyclopaedia Britannica. The group thus involves the totality of the personalities in the annals of each period so far as the *Encyclopaedia* represents them. This certainly embraces the overwhelming majority of the names known to history.

Second, the indicators of the type of personality of the Roman Catholic popes from the earliest to the present time; and of the English, French, Russian, Austrian, and German monarchs.[3] As we have already mentioned, if the personalities of different occupational groups of the same time were compared, the result would be misleading: the nature of the occupation determines the prevalence of a certain kind of personality — one type in one occupation and a different type in another. But when the leaders of the same great social organization, such as the Christian Church or one of the Western empires, are compared in various periods, the fluctuation of the frequency of the Ideational and Sensate types thus disclosed may have high symptomatic value.

Third, the apportionment of the historical figures of each period among the main compartments of culture (*i.e.*, religion, science, philosophy, art, business, politics, etc.). Suppose that for a certain century in Greece 80 per cent of all the known historical persons are engaged in religious activities, and none in business; suppose further that for the following century persons in the field of religious activities compose only 25 per cent of the total, and the percentage of those in business is 30. Such a change in the course of two centuries is fairly reasonable evidence of a change in the conduct and activity of the entire body of social and cultural leaders during these times, not merely of a few individual figures. In brief, the change is general in the field of social behavior for the totality of historical personalities.

Let us now turn to the first set of data, that is, to those which roughly show the fluctuation of the proportion of Ideational, Sensate, and Mixed (the unknown being put into the class of the Mixed) types among the totality of historical figures. I take these data from Mr. John V. Boldyreff's doctoral thesis. A few explanatory notes are necessary before Table 51 is given. First, Mr. Boldyreff recorded all the persons for each period that are mentioned in the ninth edition of the *Encyclopaedia*

---

[3] Why these groups were chosen is evident. The personalities of the popes and kings are comparatively much better known to history than those of many other historical figures. Moreover — unlike artists or scholars — being the heads of powerful social institutions, kings and popes follow one another in uninterrupted series as long as the institution lasts. Important also is the fact that this same headship of an organization means close dependence of pope or king upon it, so that, if the organization experiences a shift in type of culture, the shift is likely to be reflected in the personality of the leader.

Britannica. Next he computed the number of the lines devoted to each person, as a rough indicator of his influence. Each was then "diagnosed" on the basis of the characterization given in the *Encyclopaedia* itself and other historical sources, and put into the Sensate, Ideational, or Mixed class of personalities, according as his Sensate needs were maximal (Sensateness) and his efforts great to satisfy them by the transformation of the external *milieu* (energy), or his needs minimal and his chief energies devoted to non-Sensate and otherworldly values, or his needs and efforts intermediate to those of the other two both quantitatively and in their nature. Then the geometric averages for the total number of persons and lines of each type, for each period, were computed. The sum of the geometric averages for all three types of personalities for each period was then taken to be 100 per cent, and from this basis the percentage of each type for each period was computed. Table 51 gives the absolute figures for the geometric averages as well as the percentages.[4]

From these figures we may draw several important observations. First, within every fifty-year period (with five exceptions, which are undoubtedly to be explained as the result of lack of data) all the three types of personality and conduct are to be found coexisting side by side. There is only one period in the Graeco-Roman and Western societies when all the historical personalities were either Ideational, or Sensate, or Mixed. Second, all in all, when conduct and personality are considered, the Ideational type is less frequent than the Sensate or Mixed. This is comprehensible because, as has been mentioned several times in this work, the Ideational ways of behavior are more difficult to follow than the Sensate or Mixed. They require an inhibition of the natural physical needs and desires of an organism, while the other ways are the path of least resistance even of the stimulation of these needs and desires. Third, looking now at the fluctuation of the percentages of each type from period to period, we notice that, notwithstanding the erratic movements, there are definite long-time waves of the relative rise and decline of each type: (1) The period 950 to 851 B.C. appears as dominated by the Sensate type of personality. Considering that the last stage of the Creto-Mycenaean culture

---

[4] The table includes, besides the historical figures of Greece, Rome, and the Western World, a sprinkling from the other countries and regions. But these compose an insignificant part of the whole and do not change the results in any important degree. (For the period of A.D. 500 to 1400 inclusive, Arabia is excluded.) To repeat, it should be kept in mind that the entire computation and classification were done, not by me, but by Mr. Boldyreff, who at the time of his investigation did not know the results of my study as to which centuries and periods in the Graeco-Roman and the Western World appeared to be predominantly Ideational, Sensate, or Mixed.

TABLE 51. GEOMETRIC AVERAGES FOR TYPES OF HISTORICAL PERSONS FROM 950 B.C. TO A.D. 1849 INCLUDED IN ENCYCLOPAEDIA BRITANNICA

PERIOD	Ideational		Mixed		Sensate	
	Number	Per Cent	Number	Per Cent	Number	Per Cent
950–901 B.C.	0	0	0	0	17.9	100
900–851	13.7	12	0	0	102.7	88
850–801	0	.0	18.0	100	0	0
800–751	21.6	53	0	0	19.2	47
750–701	53.4	76	11.8	17	5.2	7
700–651	9.8	34	11.1	38	7.9	28
650–601	21.5	22	35.6	37	38.6	41
600–551	69.6	38	61.0	34	50.7	28
550–501	120.4	40	67.5	22	114.2	38
500–451	124.6	37	107.6	33	100.9	30
450–401	68.6	11	228.9	38	306.2	51
400–351	79.6	13	326.0	56	180.7	31
350–301	43.2	7	279.9	45	290.1	48
300–251	33.1	12	192.1	70	59.7	18
250–201	12.6	5	85.3	35	148.1	60
200–151	12.5	5	96.3	39	145.1	56
150–101	0	0	43.6	45	51.8	55
100–51	16.9	4	112.4	24	333.8	72
50–1	69.4	11	224.2	35	339.1	54
0–49 A.D.	179.9	31	119.3	21	272.9	48
50–99	46.0	9	219.2	43	240.7	48
100–149	100.0	26	208.4	55	72.0	19
150–199	23.7	7	238.4	76	54.7	17
200–249	121.5	43	133.5	47	29.8	10
250–299	102.7	56	32.8	18	46.9	26
300–349	78.0	23	126.2	37	139.0	40
350–399	204.7	40	190.2	38	111.7	32
400–449	80.4	22	165.2	45	123.7	33
450–499	22.8	11	113.4	52	80.4	37
500–549	77.9	28	84.6	30	115.9	42
550–599	45.6	30	58.6	39	48.0	31
600–649	58.5	40	45.2	31	42.2	29
650–699	29.6	15	19.0	29	17.2	26
700–749	43.1	44	15.3	16	38.7	40
750–799	33.8	48	12.6	18	23.6	34
800–849	57.0	36	74.1	47	26.3	17
850–899	91.0	37	76.6	31	76.8	32
900–949	16.8	14	51.7	42	54.5	44
950–999	18.1	10	75.6	42	87.2	48
1000–1049	38.2	15	75.0	29	148.5	56
1050–1099	24.4	6	145.6	37	218.7	57
1100–1149	72.5	17	176.6	41	177.3	42
1150–1199	74.8	15	210.9	41	228.0	44
1200–1249	66.1	15	166.9	36	231.3	49
1250–1299	172.0	33	185.9	35	167.0	32
1300–1349	91.4	26	181.7	51	81.2	23
1350–1399	144.6	23	152.5	24	330.4	53
1400–1449	141.4	18	322.7	42	302.1	40
1450–1499	240.9	15	602.1	38	730.9	47
1500–1549	543.4	17	1037.5	33	1543.1	50
1550–1599	485.9	14	1429.7	41	1528.1	45
1600–1649	537.0	12	1861.5	42	2023.5	46
1650–1699	949.4	19	1641.8	34	2179.0	47
1700–1749	724.0	17	2014.4	44	1534.0	39
1750–1799	901.6	10	3566.6	41	4329.9	49
1800–1849	1460.0	9	7301.1	50	5870.5	41

appears to us as the overripe Sensate, we find this dominance in such a period to be in accordance with our hypothesis. (2) The period 850 to 801 B.C. appears transitional with respect to types of personality. This again is in agreement with the nature of the culture of the period. (3) The period 800 to 501 B.C. is marked by a notable rise in the percentage of the Ideational types. We have seen that the Greek culture of that period in all its main compartments showed itself to be predominantly Ideational. Thus, here again our hypothesis is well supported. (4) The period 550 to 451 B.C. appears as well balanced, the Ideational, Sensate, and Mixed types being in an even proportion, with a slight domination of the Ideational. This tallies with the Idealistic character of the culture of the times. (5) The period 450 B.C. to the beginning of our era shows a decisive change from the preceding age. The percentage of the Ideational type falls greatly, while those of the Sensate and Mixed types grow. The period is marked by a decisive domination of Sensate and Mixed personalities. We know that the culture of this period was definitely Sensate. The agreement again is noteworthy. (6) Beginning with our era the data show a turn : during the first two centuries there is a sudden but unstable and intermittent spurt on the part of the Ideational type (31, 9, 26, 7, 43 per cent for the fifty-year periods from the year A.D. 1 to 249). This again seems to agree with the violently transitory character of this period which was turning away from the dominant Sensate to the coming Ideational culture. (7) Then, notwithstanding erratic fluctuations for a few fifty-year periods, the figures show a perceptible trend toward an increase of the percentage of the Ideational type of personalities, especially after A.D. 500 and throughout the subsequent centuries up to roughly A.D. 899. From 900 to 1199 there is a decline and then again a rise from 1200 to 1399, after which the curve assumes a steady downward trend in favor of either the Mixed or Sensate types. Even with the fall during the period from 900 to 1199, the percentage of the Ideational type is notably higher during these three centuries than during the periods of the domination of the Sensate culture, as, for example, 950 to 801 B.C. and 450 B.C. to the beginning of our era, and A.D. 1700 to 1849. This again is in agreement with our hypothesis. (8) The period from 1250 to 1849 is marked by an almost regular decline of the frequency of the Ideational type and a corresponding rise of that of the Sensate and Mixed types. The period 1750 to 1849 shows one of the lowest percentages for the Ideational type. This again is in agreement with the hypothesis. Even such a detail as a slight rise of the figure for the period 1650 to 1699 (from 12 to 19) for the Ideational type is perhaps not accidental. We know that this period was that of the Catholic Counter-Reformation and of a strong ascetic Protestantism, and we have noticed in many compartments of culture a sudden swing toward Ideationalism in these times.

Thus, the evidence is that historically there is an association between the type of dominant culture and the frequency of the type of conduct and personality. In the Ideational period the frequency of Ideational conduct and personality, among the figures of historical importance at least, is notably higher than in the period of the Sensate culture. To this extent our second proposition is supported by this empirical study made by another investigator, on the basis of such a source as the *Encyclopaedia Britannica*.

We have support in these data also for the first proposition of the present chapter, namely, that the relationship between the dominant type of culture and the behavior of its participants is far less close than that between the dominant type of culture and mentality. While in his mentality many a person of, say, an Ideational period appears to be an Ideationalist, in his conduct, so far as it concerns the biological needs and their satisfaction, he is far from Ideationalism, and belongs either to the Mixed or the Sensate type. Hence the figures in Table 51. Even in the dominantly Ideational periods, the Sensate type not only does not disappear but either composes the majority or is as widespread as the Ideational type. While in almost all the cultural curves that appear in Part Two of Volume One and Parts One and Two of Volume Two of the present work, the mentality of the Middle Ages and of other similar periods often shows a complete or very strong domination of the Ideational *mentality* in the arts, systems of truth, social relationships, law, and ethics, there is only a *relative* increase for the same periods of the percentage of persons with Ideational *behavior*, and this rarely reaches even 50 per cent of the whole. The difference between the 100 per cent of Ideationalism in mentality and the 30, 40, 48 per cent of Ideationalism in personality and conduct is a rough measure of the much looser connection of the type of culture with behavior, as compared with the closeness of the connection between the type of culture and mentality.

Let us now consider the more detailed data concerning the Roman Catholic popes.[5] Table 52 gives the comparative frequency of each type

[5] Here again I give only summary results. The sources, the literature, the detailed diagnosis of each pope, are all omitted. It is enough to say that each person, on the basis of the best historical sources, was analyzed from the standpoint of his sensate needs and desires (Sensateness), his efforts to satisfy those needs (Energy), the nature and extent of his adaptation to the *milieu* (Adaptation). As to the needs and the behavior, all the popes were divided into seven classes: Very Sensate (3), Notably Sensate (2), Sensate (1), Balanced (0); Idea-

by two-hundred-year periods. Before turning to Table 52 one must realize that the nature of the position of the pope as the head of a predominantly Ideational institution, the Christian Church, requires an Ideational type of personality and precludes, except in periods of the decline of the Church and its corruption, the occupation of such a position by a notably Sensate type of personality. Therefore we must expect that the entire body of popes [6] should exhibit the pre-eminence of the Ideational type over the Sensate. But the frequency and degree of Ideationalism (in respect to Sensate needs and adaptation-behavior) may possibly fluctuate from period to period. This is what is shown by Table 52: Roman popes, A.D. 42 to 1937 by two-hundred-year periods with cumulative value of the ratings of the popes whose pontificates were within the nearest two-hundred years, divided by the number of whole pontificates in this period.

TABLE 52.   TYPES OF ROMAN CATHOLIC POPES

		CUMULATIVE VALUE		
Year	Number of Popes	Sensateness	Energy	Adaptation
42–235	18	II.ii	0.0	I.iii
236–440	26	I.vi	0.iv	I.ii
441–642	28	0.vii	0.5	0.0
643–844	29	I.ii	0.2	0.vii
845–1044	44	0.iv	0.0	0.ii
1045–1241	31	0.viii	0.8	0.0
1242–1447	28	0.v	0.4	0.0
1448–1644	28	0.0	1.0	0.3
1645–1846	19	0.iv	0.i	0.ii
1847–1937	5	0.0	0.4	0.0

Looking at the table we see that though the whole series is dominated by the Ideational personality, nevertheless, the conspicuously Ideational type (marked by II and then by I) is centered in the first centuries of the

tional (I), Notably Ideational (II), Very Ideational-Ascetic (III). Small roman figures mean decimal fraction of the Ideational ranks I, II, III. Arabic decimal fractions, the same in regard to sensate ranks 1, 2, 3. In Tables 52 and 53 the data are given concerning only the sensate needs and adaptation-behavior. The full material is deposited in the Library of the Sociology Department of Harvard University. Many graphs that show the results pictorially are also deposited there.

[6] But the nature of the group as a whole does not preclude the appearance now and then of a Sensate type. As a matter of fact there were several such popes: Boniface II (530–532), Vigilius (538–555), Boniface VI (896, was pope for a few days), John XII (955–964), Benedict IX (1032–1044), Alexander VI (1492–1503), Sixtus IV (1471–1484), Julius II (1503–1513), and a few others.

existence of the Christian Church, before its legalization, or in any case, in the period before 942. After that, with the exception of the century between 1045 and 1144, the conspicuously Ideational type disappears. Its place is taken mainly by the "neutral" or Mixed (all the periods marked by o) or by the very slightly Ideational type (the periods marked by o.i, o.ii, and so on). Some periods, like 1342–1549 and 942–1044, are characterized by the domination of a slightly Sensate type.

Thus Ideationality is centered in the first ten centuries of our era (just as in Table 51 of all the historical persons). After that it somewhat declines quantitatively and qualitatively. The greatest decline falls upon the fourteenth, the fifteenth, and the sixteenth centuries, when the Sensate type appeared most frequently and in its most extreme form. We know that these were centuries of the greatest corruption of the Roman Catholic Church and of the greatest crisis experienced by it. When, with the Counter-Reformation, it was cleaned of this corruption, and at the same time became almost exclusively a spiritual power — the secular power becoming divorced from it *de jure* and to a considerable extent *de facto* — the Mixed and slightly Ideational type of personality again became the norm for the position of the pope, though the Ideationalism now became much more moderate and subdued in nature than during the first centuries of the existence of the Christian Church.

Hence, even in this series, we find some definite correlation between the type of the dominant culture and the frequency of the type of personality.[7]

[7] Any thoughtful person can easily understand why for the last four centuries one cannot expect a systematic rise of the Sensate type among the popes. Such a rise would be possible only if the Christian Church ceased to be what it is — that is, ceased to be an Ideational institution, the bearer of the Ideational mentality — and turned entirely into a worldly institution, perfectly Sensate in its mentality, culture, and nature. Such a transformation would mean the end of Christianity and the Christian Church — no less. In so far as it has continued to exist as Christian Church and religion, it remains still a predominantly Ideational institution, and as such can recruit its heads only from the Ideational, or, at the worst, the Mixed type, but not from the Sensate. Only if it should experience a corruption of its very nature, somewhat similar to what it suffered in the fifteenth and sixteenth centuries, would the Sensate type of popes be natural as it was natural in those centuries of corruption. Therefore, the prevalence of a slightly Ideational and, at least, of a non-Sensate type of popes from the sixteenth to the twentieth centuries in the Catholic Church is in its own way evidence of the existence of a relationship between the dominant type of culture — in this case of the culture of the Christian Church — and the dominant type of the personality of its leaders. On the other hand, the fact that among the popes of these centuries only a few were of a notably Ideational type (of the degrees II and I, and none of the degree III of Ideationalism) is a symptom that though the Roman Catholic Church has remained predominantly Ideational, it is a modified, subdued, less ascetic, form of Ideationalism than that of the early centuries of its existence. Behavior type and culture type are thus intertwined.

Let us now glance at a second group of similar data, that concerning the kings and their types of personalities. In contradistinction to the pope's office, the occupation of the king by its nature cannot as a rule be successfully carried on by a conspicuously Ideational personality. An ascetic entirely divorced from this Sensate world would not be a good king. If anything, he might ruin the kingdom more completely than could a shrewd and profligate Sensualist. Therefore, as I have mentioned in one of the earlier chapters of this work (see Volume One, page 106), the dominant type of royal personality can be expected to be Sensate or Mixed. We have seen that this was historically so (see Table 2 of Volume One). But again the frequency of the fluctuation of the more or less Sensate type, or of the Mixed type of personality in this position, may show what our hypothesis postulates, namely, some relationship with the fluctuation in the dominant type of culture.

Table 53 deals by two-hundred-year periods with the kings of France, Russia, Austria, and England. The results are arrived at by dividing the cumulative values of the ratings of the kings for each period by the number of reigns during that time.[8]

TABLE 53. TYPES OF MONARCHS

CUMULATIVE VALUE

	Year	Sensateness	Energy	Adaptation
French Kings	987–1180	0.6	0.5	0.5
	1180–1380	0.1	0.9	0.5
	1380–1589	1.4	0.8	1.4
	1589–1793	1.6	0.6	1.4
Russian Kings	1303–1506	0.1	0.7	0.4
	1506–1725	0.7	0.7	0.9
	1725–1917	1.0	0.7	0.8
Hapsburg Kings of Austria	1276–1458	0.ii	0.9	0.5
	1458–1657	0.i	0.3	0.1
	1657–1848	0.i	0.2	0.1
	1848–1922	1.5	1.0	1.0
English Kings	800–1016	0.1	0.3	0.4
	1016–1216	1.3	1.4	1.7
	1216–1413	0.0	0.2	0.1
	1413–1603	0.4	0.3	0.5
	1603–1820	0.0	0.0	0.0
	1820–1910	1.2	0.0	1.0

[8] Here again I give a summary, only based on the scale which I have indicated: III, II, I, 0, 1, 2, 3, from the standpoint of each king's Sensateness, energy, and adaptation. The detailed diagnosis of each king, the sources and references, and other materials are deposited in the Library of the Sociology Department, Harvard University.

A glance at the figures for the French, Russian, and Hapsburg monarchs shows us a clear trend, passing from the medieval to the present period, to Sensateness and the Sensate adaptation. In this respect the data agree with the results of Tables 51 and 52 and support our hypothesis. The rising tide of the Sensate Western culture has been followed even in this particular item by an increasing proportion of the more Sensate type of behavior and personality among the kings. Only the case of the English rulers deviates considerably from this. But the deviation does not contradict the trend fundamentally. It is in agreement with the larger tendencies traced out in Table 51 for all the historical persons taken together and to some extent for the special group of Roman Catholic popes. The evidence for all the historical persons shows a decrease of the Ideational type for the period A.D. 950–1249, and this is matched among the English kings by an increased indicator of Sensateness. For the period 1250–1399 the data for all historical persons indicates an increase in the proportion of the Ideational type, which is paralleled among the English kings by a decrease of the indicator of Sensateness for the nearest corresponding period, 1216–1413. Similarly, the next decrease of the indicator of Sensateness of the English monarchs, which occurs in the period 1603–1820, is in agreement with the temporary proportionate increase of Ideationalism for all historical persons during the years 1650 to 1749. Finally, the latest period, the nineteenth century, is marked in both Tables 51 and 53 by an increase of the Sensate type of personality.

To sum up : however erratic are the fluctuations of curves for the monarchs, especially when they are made for each king separately, all in all, when considered by periods of one or two centuries, they display, if not a close, at least a clearly perceptible, correlation with the fluctuation of the main type of culture. These data thus stand in support of our second proposition.

Finally, we turn to the fourth category of data : they concern the apportionment of historical figures among the various fields of activity at a given period. As we remarked earlier in the present chapter, it is neither accidental nor unimportant that at one time a large proportion of the historical persons becomes notable through, say, business activity, while at another time the leading group is engaged in the field of religion. If in a given society at a given period 75 per cent of the leading persons make their mark in business, while in another period 90 per cent become important through religion, these facts mean, among many other things, that in the first period the society was "business-minded," centered on economic concerns, oriented in a Sensate milieu, but that in the other period it was "religious-minded" and, if the religion was Ideational, oriented Ideationally both in the mentality and the behavior of its members. It means also that just because the society was Sensate and eco-nomical-minded, its leaders devoted their energy and brains — in other words their behavior — to an achievement of business or Sensate purposes; or that because the society was religious, the chief thought and efforts were directed along the channels of religious activity. These considerations explain why data of this fourth category bear closely upon our problem and compose an important body of evidence for its solution.

For these data I am indebted once again to Mr. Boldyreff. Mr. Boldyreff listed all the historical persons named in the *Encyclopaedia Britannica*, arranging them by fifty-year periods from the remotest times to the year 1849 and noting the number of lines of print devoted to each. This enumeration was done for the whole world as a unit, as well as for each country separately. To summarize the results for each period, the geometric average of the number of the persons involved and the number of lines of print for all of them together were computed. All the persons mentioned in the *Britannica*, taken by periods, were further divided into ten main occupational classes through which their historical importance was achieved : religion, statesmanship, literature, humanistic scholarship, science, philosophy, business, fine arts, music, miscellaneous. The geometric averages of the number of persons and lines of print in each of these ten fields of activity for each period were computed, for the whole world and for individual countries. Then the absolute figures for these geometric averages were turned into percentages, the total of the ten fields for each period being taken to represent 100 per cent. In this way Mr. Boldyreff obtained rough, but so far the vastest and possibly the best, numerical indicators of the fluctuation of the proportion of historical persons in each of these ten fields from period to period, for the whole world and for the separate countries. In Table 54 I give only the percentages for two fields, religion and business. Though the figures refer to the whole world for the periods given in the table, the figures deal mainly with the fluctuations in Greece, Rome, and the Western World. The other countries outside these enter into the table, but their share is comparatively quite insignificant ; therefore, it does not influence the main changes of the percentages in any appreciable way. I give only the percentages of the men that became important through religious and business activity, because these two fields are diametrically opposite, the one being nearest to the Ideational (religious activity), the other to the Sensate (business). Activity in the other fields — statesmanship, literature, scholarship, fine arts, and so on — may, by their nature, be either Ideational or Sensate. What they were in any specific case we cannot know without further details of the nature of the efforts of the individuals in those fields of endeavor. Therefore, they cannot serve our purpose here.

These explanations are sufficient for an understanding of what the figures in Table 54 mean.[9]

TABLE 54.   GEOMETRIC AVERAGES FOR HISTORICAL PERSONS ENGAGED IN RELIGIOUS AND BUSINESS ACTIVITY INCLUDED IN ENCYCLOPAEDIA BRITANNICA

EXPRESSED IN PERCENTAGES

Period	Per Cent Religion	Per Cent Business	Period	Per Cent Religion	Per Cent Business
900–851 B.C.	17.1		500–549 A.D.	20.2	
850–801			550–599	48.4	
800–751	26.0		600–649	65.0	
750–701	74.6		650–699	82.8	
700–651	33.7		700–749	48.1	
650–601	39.1		750–799	35.2	
600–551	38.3		800–849	46.0	
550–501	14.2		850–899	45.7	
500–451	9.1		900–949	44.3	
450–401	.6		950–999	26.2	
400–351	.5		1000–1049	33.0	
350–301		1.0	1050–1099	39.8	
300–251		5.5	1100–1149	34.1	.7
250–201			1150–1199	38.1	
200–151			1200–1249	28.7	
150–101	7.5	2.5	1250–1299	28.9	3.1
100–51	1.3		1300–1349	19.2	2.6
50–1	2.1		1350–1399	30.1	4.5
0–49 A.D.	46.2		1400–1449	20.7	5.1
50–99	7.5		1450–1499	14.8	6.4
100–149	38.1		1500–1549	26.0	2.6
150–199	30.2		1550–1599	18.7	2.1
200–249	54.6		1600–1649	12.0	1.7
250–299	74.5		1650–1699	18.9	1.4
300–349	58.3		1700–1749	15.0	1.8
350–399	61.6		1750–1799	5.2	3.1
400–449	54.0		1800–1849	6.5	4.8
450–499	18.1				

[9] As we have pointed out, the percentages for religion and business for each period are computed on the basis of a total of 100, which is made up of the averages of *all* the ten fields of activity.

The more detailed data for Greece, Rome, and all the European countries individually are in substantial agreement with the main fluctuations of religion and business in this summary table for the whole world.   Therefore, they are not given separately here.   Later on they will be published by Mr. Boldyreff.

A glance at the figures shows at once the comparatively high percentage for religion and zero for business for the period 800 to 501 B.C. This agrees with the Ideational character of this period in all the main compartments of the Greek culture, as well as with the data concerning behavior given in this chapter. After 500 B.C. the percentage for religion rapidly declines and soon, beginning with the year 350 B.C., becomes zero, and remains so up to the period 150 to 101 B.C., when it rises again, though it remains low up to the beginning of our era. On the other hand, in the period 350 to 101 B.C. business activity for the first time (on the basis of the *Britannica*) becomes an avenue through which historical importance may be achieved. The results confirm the Sensate character of the Hellenistic culture and lend weight to our hypothesis. Beginning with our era the percentage for religion rapidly rises, reaches an extraordinarily high level in the sixth and seventh centuries B.C. (up to even 82 per cent of all the historical persons), and stays very high until 950, after which it subsides somewhat (though it still remains high) up to the year 1200; then slowly a declining trend creeps in. Beginning with the sixteenth century the percentage for religion rapidly declines and reaches a very low level for the latest period, 1750 to 1849. The movement of the business percentage proceeds in opposite fashion. After the beginning of our era it falls to zero and stays at zero until the period 1100 to 1149. Then it reappears and begins to grow, especially after 1250 to 1299. Subsequently, with some fluctuations, it steadily maintains itself, and beginning with 1650 to 1699 it continues to grow to the latest date, 1800 to 1849.

These figures display a notable agreement with the rise and decline of the waves of Ideational and Sensate culture from 800 B.C. to our time. In other words, this set of evidence — and it is rather important — supports the two propositions before us very well. If the detailed data for separate countries were set forth here, they would show that support to be even stronger.

The evidence given in this chapter, together with the data presented by the preceding chapter on economic fluctuations, and with other relevant materials throughout this whole work, all shows that not only logically but causally the dominant character of a culture and that of behavior are definitely integrated; that in an integrated Ideational or Sensate society, not only the dominant mentality becomes correspondingly Ideational or Sensate, but the actual *behavior* also becomes Ideational or Sensate, in whatever field it acts and, what is more important, even in the *field of activities closely related to the satisfaction of the urgent biological needs.* Though the integration of this latter part of behavior with the dominant type of culture is not so close as is the mentality, nevertheless it is quite perceptible and beyond question.

These conclusions mean that, in an integrated culture, the type of overt behavior of its bearers is correlated with it and the culture mentality; that the type of culture and mentality do not stay isolated from, or ineffective with regard to, overt actions or to their "residues," "prepotent reflexes," "biological drives," or "proclivities." On the contrary, they not only determine the "forms" and "patterns" of behavior but also the frequency and intensity of doing or leaving undone acts dictated by the biological needs. In this respect the conclusions strongly deviate from the popular assumptions of Sensate times that "mentality," "ideology," "derivations," and "derivatives" are either mere playthings in the hands of biological or material needs, or something which merely "beautifies," "rationalizes," or serves them, or something which, as "impotent illusion," stays apart from them, neither being influenced by nor influencing them. Since we find that the overt behavior is definitely integrated with the dominant type of culture, such conclusions — especially as that the ideology (culture mentality) and action behavior are independent of one another — become fallacious. In integrated cultures both behavior and mentality become parts of one integrated system. The integration is not perfect, but it exists.

This means, to go a step further, that human behavior in the integrated culture is not completely — even not in its greater part — illogical, or nonlogical, or alogical, as again many have asserted. The fact of its association with the culture is evidence of its logicality and its consistency with the major premises of one particular culture mentality in which it exists.

Finally, the conclusions we have reached mean that there are indeed Ideational, Sensate, Idealistic, and Mixed (including the unintegrated) forms of behavior and types of personality, and that each type occurs most often in, respectively, the Ideational, Sensate, Idealistic, or Mixed society.

This chapter completes the major task which I set for myself at the beginning of this work. Having shown that the key principles of this study do indeed apply to the field of culture mentality, bringing order and meaning to a chaos of traits, events, objects, I then demonstrated that these same principles bring similar order and significance to the welter of fragments and details in the field of human action and reaction, that is, in the field of behavior.

The groundwork is done and the frame erected. From now on in the final, fourth, volume of this work I can employ my chief efforts and whatever materials are available, in completing, strengthening, and finishing the structure whose foundations are laid in these volumes.

Chapter Sixteen

POSTSCRIPT

We have traveled a long way. Having set our objective at the beginning of the journey, we have moved toward it step by step, never, through difficulty or distraction, losing it from our view.

It would be superfluous to attempt to summarize here the conclusions that we have reached in these volumes. In their preliminary form they have been given, piece by piece, in all the preceding pages. For their systematic unfolding, development, and consolidation, on the other hand, one chapter would be insufficient. To such tasks an entire book, Volume Four, of the present work will be devoted. There, on the basis of the main body of the factual material already presented, with the addition of supplementary data, we shall offer a systematic theory of social and cultural life processes, their types, directions, fluctuations, trends, rhythms, and tempos, together with a clear analysis of all the methodological problems involved in the present investigation and in the study of sociocultural phenomena generally.

For the moment, then, in this Postscript, it seems best to limit ourselves to a few words by way of interlude. These words concern the present status of Western culture and society. That both are in the midst of a crisis is nowadays a commonplace observation. But most people, even the "leaders" in thought and action, seem still to think the crisis is either purely economic, or perhaps political, or the result of some other partial maladjustment (!) — one of the many through which Western society passed many times, even during the last century. They still believe that it will soon be over, that prosperity seems indeed to be "around the corner." Accordingly their prescriptions for "the way out" are mainly of a kind of surface rubbing medicine. They seek to cure either a purely local economic maladjustment through the cancellation of debts, disarmament, regulation of banking, advertising technique, inflation, and nationalization of industry; or a purely political maladjustment through this or that modification of the national and international bodies politic, through the "rubbing of shoulders" around the same table, through the signing of gigantic rolls of paper and their transportation from the Pacific to the Lake of Geneva, and through other forms of contemporary magic.

I admire this optimism and I wish the optimists every success.   I am even prepared to see a temporary improvement of economic, and perhaps even political, conditions.   But if all the analysis of the preceding chapters is even roughly correct, I find the usual diagnosis of contemporary "maladjustments" utterly wrong.   The organism of the Western society and culture seems to have not merely a number of local or superficial ailments, but to be undergoing one of the deepest crises of its life.   The crisis is far greater than the ordinary; its depth is unfathomable, its end not yet in sight, and the whole of the Western society is involved in it.   It is the crisis of a Sensate culture, now in its overripe stage, the culture that has dominated the Western World during the last five centuries.   It is also the crisis of a contractual (capitalistic) society associated with it.   In this sense we are experiencing one of the sharpest turns in the historical road, a turn as great as any of the other few made by the Graeco-Roman and Western cultures in passing from Ideational to Sensate, and from Sensate to Ideational, phases.

We have seen during the course of the present work quite definite signs of such a turn.   Not a single compartment of our culture, or of the mind of contemporary man, shows itself to be free from the unmistakable symptoms.   We have observed, also, that these signs, this "handwriting on the wall," are particularly clear as we approach the end of the nineteenth and advance into the twentieth century.   The curves of painting, sculpture, music, and literature; of movement of discoveries and inventions; of the "First Principles" of science, philosophy, religion, ethics, and law; up to those of wars and revolutions — all make a violent turn as we approach our time.   Shall we wonder, therefore, that if many do not apprehend clearly what is happening, they have at least a vague feeling that the issue is not merely that of "prosperity," or "democracy," or the like, but that involving the whole of the contemporary (Sensate) culture, society, and man?   If they do not understand it by intellectual analysis, they feel sharply the painful claws of the events, whether they be kings or housewives.

Shall we wonder, also, at the endless multitude of incessant minor crises that have been rolling over us, like ocean waves, during the last two decades?   Today in one form, tomorrow in another.   Now here, now there.   Crises political, agricultural, commercial, and industrial!   Crises of production and distribution.   Crises moral, juridical, religious, scientific, and artistic.   Crises of property, of the State, of the family, of industrial enterprise, of the republic and monarchy, autocracy and democracy, dictatorship and self-government, capitalism and socialism, fascism and communism, nationalism and internationalism, pacifism and militarism, conservatism and radicalism.   Crises of truth, of beauty, of justice, of righteousness.   Crises of the whole system of values of our culture.   Each in a rich variety of forms and with varying degrees of power, but endlessly rolling, its roar reverberating in every daily newspaper.   Each of the crises has battered our nerves and minds, each has shaken the very foundations of our culture and society, and each has left behind a legion of derelicts and victims.   And alas! the end is not yet in view.   Each of these crises has been, as it were, a movement in a great terrifying symphony, and each has been remarkable for its magnitude and intensity.   Each movement has been played, during the last three decades, by enormous human orchestras, with millions of choruses, stage performers, and actors.   In 1911 the four-hundred-million-piece Chinese orchestra began one of its first festivals.   This still goes on, and the mountain of its contributor victims grows higher and higher from year to year.

In 1914 a new brass band of many nations with hundreds of participants started its deadening "*Marche Militaire:* 1914–1918."   The effects of this performance were appalling.   The stage — the soil of this planet — was soaked with blood.   Most of our values were poisoned by gas; others were blown to pieces by artillery.   The very foundations of our society and culture cracked. . . .

Before this festival had ended, the Russian orchestra of some 160,-000,000 virtuosi set forth its own variation entitled "Communist Revolution."   The first blow of its percussion instruments overthrew the social and cultural system of the old Russia.   Subsequent movements have shaken the whole human world.   The performance has been so brilliant that millions of onlookers have acquired a profound distaste for the old-fashioned music of the capitalist system and gone mad with the communist modernism.   In Russia millions of listeners and participants have died in the process.   Other millions have sunk to the bottom of human misery, and, weary and half dead, have been longing for the end of their hopeless and joyless existence.   Still other millions have been thrown into the social gutters, left moaning their desperate calls for help, and finding neither response nor assistance.   The festival still continues magnificently, with ever new tricks and surprises.   Having saturated the soil of Russia, the red fertilizing blood begins now to flow across its boundary, into the soil of the onlookers of this "marvelous experiment."

Dozens of other companies — Turkey and Hungary, Austria and Germany, Bulgaria and Rumania, Spain and Portugal, Italy and Poland, Abyssinia and Manchukuo, the Central and South American states, Japan and Arabia, Palestine and Egypt, Syria and Afghanistan — have also been giving their crisis festivals. Some of them, like the Central and South American orchestras, have turned it into a daily entertainment; others, like Abyssinia and Manchukuo, played it to their own death. Meanwhile, the vast continent of India, too, has taken definite steps to stage its gala concert. For several years the immense India orchestra has already been rehearsing. At the first rehearsals the symphony was played *pianissimo*. Then it was replaced by the *moderato* of nonviolent resistance, more and more often intercepted by a sharp *staccato* of machine guns and drums, bombs, and the blows of police sticks. There is hardly any doubt that soon we shall hear the *fortissimo* of this thundering festival.

If we turn our ears to Europe, we can hear, without the need of any short-wave radio, as many crisis festivals as we like. One day various fascists occupy the stage; another, communists; then the Hitlerites; then the Popular Front — red shirts and black shirts and brown shirts and silver shirts, and blue shirts and green shirts. At one moment the Spanish crisis is on the front page; at another, the French or Austrian; and all accompanied by news of the shakiness of the English pound, or the American dollar, or the French franc, or the German mark. Then come "cordial co-operation and mutual understanding" between Chinese and Japanese; or blessed salvation of Abyssinia from itself; or a Soviet demonstration of "pacifism" and a plea for the "sacredness of the contracts" on the part of a government that broke all contracts; or other forms of similar "international solidarity and good will." They give for a moment excellent publicity to that otherwise forgotten homeopathic family physician, the League of Nations, or call forth one of the endless international conferences of the "shepherds of the people" to "adjust the maladjustment," after which there usually spring up a dozen new maladjustments where before there was only one.

Up to 1929 the blessed Land of the Pilgrims was free from the crisis vogue. We preferred to listen to the crisis concerts of the other countries while at home we enjoyed mainly the *andante cantabile* of "sweet prosperity." Since the end of 1929 our taste seems to have changed. Prosperity has fallen at least temporarily into disfavor. The crisis music has also captured our fancy. From any radio we hear now almost exclusively either the "classical" or "crooning" versions of the crisis of industry and agriculture, of employment and unemployment, of education and morals, of stock-market crashes, of bank failures; the *adagio lamentoso* of dissipated luxury; the *marche funèbre* and *in memoriam* of faded hopes; the *requiem* to evaporated fortunes; the *allegro non troppo* of the murmurs of dissatisfaction; the *crescendo* of the criticism of the existing order; and occasional *scherzos* of hunger marchers, "sit-down strikers," and clashes between police and radicals. With a lag of a few years we also have acquired the taste for the new music.

These are but a few of the variations on the main theme of today's symphony of history. The total number of all the variations is immense. Not only the economic and political systems, but every important aspect of the life, organization, and culture of the Western society is included in the crisis. Its body and mind are sick and there is hardly a spot on its body which is not sore, nor any nervous fiber which functions soundly.

We are seemingly between two epochs: the dying Sensate culture of our magnificent yesterday and the coming Ideational culture of the creative tomorrow. We are living, thinking, and acting at the end of a brilliant six-hundred-year-long Sensate day. The oblique rays of the sun still illumine the glory of the passing epoch. But the light is fading, and in the deepening shadows it becomes more and more difficult to see clearly and to orient ourselves safely in the confusions of the twilight. The night of the transitory period begins to loom before us and the coming generations, perhaps with their nightmares, frightening shadows, and heart-rending horrors. Beyond it, however, the dawn of a new great Ideational culture is probably waiting to greet the men of the future.

Such, it seems to me, is the position we are at on the road of history. The evidence of all the preceding chapters points in this direction. And we find our conclusion in an irreconcilable contradiction with the other current diagnoses.

First of all, it stands in sharp contradiction to all the theories of a "moderate," "sensible," and "orderly" progress. Not realizing that their progress cult is already out of date, a throng of intellectuals, humanitarians, pacifistic and progressive parlor socialists, liberal ministers, professors, politicians, and a legion of intellectual Rotarians and Kiwanians of all kinds still profess this credo. They look at the historical process as at a good little boy who steadily advances from the first grade to graduation and progressively becomes bigger and better. They depict "the next stage" as a paradise where milk rivers flow between shores of ice cream, where all arms are remade into golf clubs, radio receivers, and electric toasters, and where "international co-operation," "mutual understanding," and "good will" reign supreme. No war, no crime, no insanity, no bloodshed, no foolishness, no trouble; there the happy existence of the contented and highly progressive ladies and gentlemen (both being blessed with birth control). All the labor is performed by mechanical appliances. Everybody's dinner consists of asparagus, fried chicken, ice cream, and pie à la mode, with cocktails before and liqueurs after the meal. Everybody will have plenty of leisure for shopping, golfing, driving, bridge playing, spooning, and especially for attending conferences on sex problems, the League of Nations, and the Love Your Neighbor Society. Everybody will have full opportunity to educate himself through reading every best seller and all the Book of the Month Club selections; through listening to the radio addresses of the latest "authorities"; through glancing over the "Literary" and "Readers'" and "Scientific" digests; and, finally, through movies, dance halls, and television.

Instead of this paradise, alas! my thesis offers a rather gloomy time of blood, cruelty, and misery, with "humanity uprooted," with the sweet humanitarian dreams thrown to the winds, and — what is more important — with the main and eternal values trodden down. Even the culture of tomorrow, as I see it, is in no way going to resemble this cloud-cuckoo land of the after-dinner imagination. Created in its present specific form in the second half of the nineteenth century, this utopia has been one of the fascinating soap bubbles with which contented Victorian Europe liked to amuse itself. This Europe being on the wane, its bubbles are bursting. Anybody who likes this utopia is welcome to its hearty enjoyment. On my part I hear distinctly the *requiem* that the symphony of history is playing in its memory.

My theory is no less contradictory to all the ideologies of a violent and revolutionary progress *à la sans-culotte, à la* Karl Marx-Lenin-Stalin, or *à l'anarchie*. After all, the difference between the theories of moderate and violent progress is small: it amounts to a mere difference in the temperament of the devotees and the technique of progress-promotion. Both parties are equally over-Sensate and both believe in a Sensate advance, but the moderates do not wish to rush its realization. They dislike bloodshed, loss of their savings, and having their parlors invaded by ruthless and crazy mobs. The extremists, on the contrary, want to hurry along progress by all means, at any cost, and regardless of whether or not others wish to enter their paradise. They have little or nothing to lose. Therefore, they are not afraid of being ruined, or of shedding blood, or of any other of the riotous occurrences of revolutionary progress making.

These revolutionary schemes are but utopias of a disintegrated mind, of demoralized man, and come as the by-product of the disintegrated culture of the transitionary period.   As we have seen in Part Three of this volume, the periods of the disintegration of social and cultural systems are regularly marked by the emergence of such schemes, and by revolts of the masses of humanity with *un*integrated minds led by groups of intellectuals with a *dis*integrated mentality.   The emergence and growth of the power of these unintegrated and disintegrated minds are two of the decisive characteristics of the fading day of the passing epoch.   These mobs and their leaders are the vultures that appear when the social and cultural body is decomposing.   Their eternal historical function is to pull it to pieces, and thus, though involuntarily, to clear the ground for a new life.   Creation is not given to them.   Both their "constructive" plans and they themselves are flesh of the flesh of the last phase of the disintegrating culture, with all the unpleasant traits of such a phase and without the virtues of the Sensate culture at its climax.

At the best, only a few of the traits of the coming integrated culture and society may possibly find, in distorted form, an echo in their schemes. With this exception, their utopian culture and society are as different from the society and culture to come as the familistic society differs from the compulsory, and the Ideational from a disintegrated Sensate culture.

Finally, *my thesis has little in common with the age-old theories of the life cycle of cultures and societies with its stages of childhood, maturity, senility, and decay.*   These conceptions have recently emerged once again in the works of Spengler and others.   We have seen that in their cyclical form such theories are untenable.   We can leave them to the ancient sages and their modern epigoni.   Neither the decay of the Western society and culture, nor their death, is predicted by my thesis.   What it does assert — let me repeat — is simply that one of the most important phases of their life history, the Sensate, is now ending and that we are turning toward its opposite through a period of transition.   Such a period is always disquieting, grim, cruel, bloody, and painful.   In its turbulence it is always marked by a revival of the regressive tendencies of the unintegrated and disintegrated mentality.   Many great values are usually thrown to the winds and trodden upon at such a time.   Hence its qualification now as the great crisis.

Crisis, however, is not equivalent to either decay or death, as the Spenglerites and cyclicists are prone to infer.   It merely means a sharp and painful turn in the life process of the society.   It does not signify the end of the traveled road or of the traveling itself.   Western culture did not end after the end of its Ideational phase. Likewise, now when its Sensate phase seems to be ending, its road stretches far beyond the "turn" into the infinity of the future.

These summary remarks show that our theory and diagnosis are not a variety of any of the above conceptions, of any moderately linear, revolutionarily progressive, or cyclical-decay-and-decline ideologies. The theory developed here stands by itself, unrelated to any of the dominant social philosophies of the present. It does not need their support nor approval, because its feet are stronger than theirs and stand upon a much firmer foundation.

For the champions of the overstuffed, after-dinner utopia the theory may appear pessimistic. In a sense it is. But from a deeper standpoint it is highly optimistic. It is optimistic because it shows sociocultural forces to be infinitely richer in creative power than does the inflexible ideal of these utopians. It is richer than any theory based on the Sensate, or Ideational, or Mixed form of culture taken alone, because it embraces all these, and gives *suum cuique*. And it is also optimistic, because it does not predict either the death or decay of the Western culture and society. If it points to the decline of the present Sensate phase and the probability of a grim transition, at the same time it indicates the possibility of the rise of a new magnificent Ideational culture, society, and man. Such a standpoint raises no fear of the temporary decline, nor even regrets it. Any value at the time of its decline deserves gratitude and compassion but not admiration. Still less does it deserve the efforts to keep it alive when a new value — as great and as good, perhaps — is coming.

Mankind should be grateful to the Sensate culture for its wonderful achievements. But now when it is in agony; when its product is poison gas rather than fresh air; when through its achievements it has given into man's hands terrific power over nature and the social and cultural world, without providing himself with self-control, with power over his emotions and passions, sensate appetites and lusts — now, in the hands of such a man, with all its achievements of science and technology, it is becoming increasingly dangerous to mankind itself and to all its values. And for the same reasons for which a bomb or gun in the hands of a child or an imbecile is dangerous for himself and for others.

The most urgent need of our time is the man who can control himself and his lusts, who is compassionate to all his fellow men, who can see and seek for the eternal values of culture and society, and who deeply feels his unique responsibility in this universe. If the conquest of the forces of nature is the main function of the Sensate culture, the taming of man, his "humanization," his ennoblement as the participant in the Divine Absolute, has always been the function mainly of the Ideational culture. The Sensate culture did its best in the way of degrading man to the level of a mere reflex mechanism, a mere organ motivated by sex, a mere semi-mechanical, semiphysiological organism, devoid of any divine spark, of any absolute value, of anything noble and sacred. Such a debasement now becomes increasingly dangerous for the Sensate man himself. Hence the urgency of the shift from Sensatism to Ideationalism, from the subjugation and control of nature by man to the control of man by himself.

This control is impossible without a system of absolute values. Absolute values are irreconcilable with the Sensate mentality and culture, which by their nature are relative, utilitarian, hedonistic, and expedient only. Hence the logical necessity and practical urgency of the shift to a new Ideational culture. Such a man can be trusted with the power created by the Sensate culture. Even with the present power and technique, such a man could build a society and culture with less poverty and misery, free from individual and group hatred, nobler, more just, more human, and more godly, than the present phase of our Sensate society.

Such shifts have happened before. They usually happened when a given Sensate or Ideational culture began to menace mankind and the whole system of supreme values. Sociocultural system, in making these shifts, has shown itself wiser than the contemporary actors who resisted such change. We may trust it in the beginning of the contemporary transition from the superannuated Sensate to a new Ideational culture.

In the light of these considerations, my theory and diagnosis are truly optimistic. *Le roi est mort, vive le roi!* "In my Father's house are many mansions. . . ." "Verily, verily, I say unto you . . . ye shall be sorrowful, but your sorrow shall be turned into joy. . . . A woman when she is in travail hath sorrow, because her hour is come : but as soon as she is delivered of the child, she remembereth no more the anguish, for joy that a man is born into the world."

APPENDIXES

Appendix to Part Two

DETAILED DESCRIPTION OF WARS STUDIED

GENERAL NOTE: For the sake of economy in the subsequent detailed data, the following abbreviations are kept throughout all the description of the wars: (1) the brief specification of the war and its dates; (2) its duration in years; (3) average strength of the army; and in parenthesis are given the actual figures in the specified battles of the war with reference to the source; (4) the total for the army in the whole war, obtained through the typical figure multiplied by the number of the years during which the war lasted; (5) the number of casualties, given in per cent of the army's strength and then turned into an absolute figure; (6) number of the main fronts upon which the war proceeded. Often there are given abbreviated references, like D I, 82, which means Delbrück, Vol. I, p. 82 of the work indicated on page 290. Once in a while additional explanatory remarks are added. Following this "key" the reader can easily grasp the meaning of the subsequent detailed data for each period. The dates like 11/V, 1813 mean day, month, and year. All the reservations and qualifications given in the text should be borne in mind in interpreting these data, and especially the figures for the size of the army and of the casualties. As explained on pp. 285 and 286, these figures represent, in a considerable degree, a measuring device for finding a comparative increase or decrease of war from period to period.

ANCIENT GREECE [1]

500–476 B.C.

——————— Graeco-Persian War, 500–476, 25 years. 20,000 (D I, 82) gives 500,000 for the whole period; 5% gives 25,000 as the total of the casualties for the whole period. It is true that in the battle of Marathon the losses reached at least 26% (D I, 50) but, as mentioned, this battle is unique and is in no way typical for the other battles in this war.

Total of the army for the period: 500,000; for the casualties: 25,000.

475–451 B.C.

——————— Graeco-Persian War, 475–451, 25 years. An average strength for the army of 20,000 gives 500,000 for the period; 6% gives 30,000 casualties for the period. 6% is taken because in the battle in 458 such were the losses of the Athenians (B I, 489).

Messenian-Spartan War, 463–455, 9 years. 14,000 Athenians (B I, 480) but a civil war, and therefore 28,000 for both sides. The total of the army's strength for the whole is 252,000; 5% gives 12,600 casualties.

Totals for the period, respectively: 752,000 and 42,600.

450–426 B.C.

——————— Graeco-Persian War, 450–449, 2 years. 20,000 (D I, 82) gives 40,000 and 5% gives 2000.

Peloponnesian War, 431–426, 6 years. 2000 (in the battle at Spartalos there were 2000 fighters,

D I, 95). Civil war and therefore 4000 for both armies. Duration of 6 years gives 24,000, and 5% gives 1200 for the losses.

Totals for the period: 64,000 and 3200.

425–401 B.C.

——————— Peloponnesian War, 425–404, 22 years. 8000, for both sides 16,000 (in the battle at Delion, 424, 8000 Boeotians, D I, 96; at Mantinea, 418, 7000 to 8000 Spartans, D I, 96). Total army was 352,000, and at 5% the losses were 17,600.

Retreat of 10,000 Greeks (*Anabasis* by Xenophon), 401–400, 2 years; 13,000 (B II, 138). Total 26,000 and 1% or 260 losses (B II, 138).

Totals for the period: 378,000 and 17,860.

400–376 B.C.

——————— With the Persians in Asia Minor, 399–393, 7 years. The strength of the army was 7000 (B II, 141–145), giving 49,000 for the period, and at 5% the losses were 2450.

Corinthian (internal), 394–387, 8 years. 20,000 (in the battle at Nemea, 394, 20,000, B II, 197); for both sides 40,000, and a total of 320,000 for the period. The Spartan losses were at 14% and the Allies' at 5.5% (B II, 197), giving a total of 44,800.

Spartan-Theban War, 379–376, 3 years. 40,000 for both sides or 120,000 for the period and 5% or 6000 losses.

Totals for the period: 489,000 and 47,850.

[1] For key see p. 290.

375–351 B.C.

———————— Spartan-Theban War, 375–362, 14 years. 40,000 for both sides (6000 Boeotians at Leuctras in 371; 33,000 Boeotians and 32,000 Spartans at Mantinea, 369, B 154 and D I, 132). Total 560,000 and 5% or 28,000.

The Holy War against the Phocians, 355–351, 4 years. 40,000 for both sides, 160,000 for the period of the war and 5% or 8000 losses.

Totals for the period: 720,000 and 36,000.

350–326 B.C.

———————— The Holy War, 350–341, 10 years. 40,000, total 400,000, and 5% or 20,000.

Macedonian-Athenian War, 341–338, 4 years. 30,000 (at Chaeronea, 338. 30,000 on each side, B II, 564–566). Total 120,000 and 5% or 6000 losses.

Expedition of Alexander against the Illyrians, 335, 1 year. 10,000 and 5% or 500.

War with the Persians of Darius, 334–333, 2 years. From 30,000 to 47,000 was the strength of the army (D I, 171–172), making an average strength of 35,000 and a total of 70,000; 5% or 3500 losses (at Granicus, 334, 2%; at Issus, 333, 7%, D I, 153, 162, 172).

Conquest of Syria, Phoenicea, Egypt, 332, 1 year. 35,000 (D I, 171–172) and 5% or 1750.

War with the Persians and the Conquest of Asia, 331–328, 3 years. 30,000 (D I, 184), total 90,000 and 5% or 4500.

Expedition to India, 327–326, 2 years. 30,000 (D 184), total 60,000, and 5% or 3000.

Totals for the period: 698,000 and 34,900.

325–301 B.C.

———————— End of Alexander's expeditions. War in Persia, 325, 1 year. 30,000 and 5% or 1500.

Wars of the Diadochi, 323–301, 23 years. Here are included all the numerous wars of the Diadochi which occurred upon Greek territory and in which various states were involved, such as the wars led by Polyperchon, Cassander, Antigonous, Demetrius, the Four Years' War, and so on. These wars went on almost uninterruptedly during this period. 22,000 (at Grannon, 28,500, F 18); Polyperchon's army 25,000; Cassander's army 4000 (F 18); at Gasa 23,000 with Demetrius, and 15,000 with Ptolemy (D I, 207). Total 506,000 and 5% or 25,300 (500 at Grannon, F 18). Many of the battles were naval (F 15–135).

Totals for the period: 536,000 and 26,800.

300–276 B.C.

———————— Numerous — but mainly small — wars between the Diadochi and the foreign rulers, upon Greek territory, with participation of Greeks, such as the campaigns of 296, 293, 290, 288, 283, 282, 278, 274; the First and Second Syrian wars; Chremonidean War; and several others. Duration about 18 years. 20,000, with a total of 360,000, and 4% or 14,400.

Totals for the period: 360,000 and 14,400.

275–251 B.C.

———————— Similar to the preceding period but possibly the battles were less numerous and smaller. The totals are probably lower also, about 250,000 and 10,000.

250–226 B.C.

———————— Spartan-Achaean War, 227–226, 2 years. 30,000 and for both sides 60,000. Total 120,000 and 5% or 6000 (including other small conflicts).

225–201 B.C.

———————— Spartan-Achaean War, 226–221, 5 years. 30,000 and for both sides 60,000 (29,000 on one side at Sellasia, B 210). Total 300,000 and 5% or 15,000.

Aetolian-Achaean Unions War, 222–217, 4 years. 15,000 and 30,000 for both sides (15,000 Aetolians, B 145). Total 120,000 and 5% or 6000.

Aetolian-Macedonian War, 212–207, 5 years. 15,000, total 75,000, and with 4% or 3000.

Totals for the period: 495,000 and 24,000.

200–176 B.C.

———————— First Macedonian-Roman War, 200–197, 4 years. 25,000 (8000 Macedonians at Athens, F 274; 25,000 at Cynocephala, B 210). Total 100,000 and 5% or 5000.

Roman-Aetolian League War, 189, 1 year. 15,000 and 4% or 600.

Totals for the period: 115,000 and 5600.

175–151 B.C.

———————— Second Macedonian-Roman War, 171–168, 4 years. Hardly more than 15,000 Greeks. Total 60,000 and 5% or 3000.

150–126 B.C.

———————— Achaean War, 147–146, 2 years. 15,000 (at Leukopetra 14,600, B 156). Total 30,000 and 5% or 1500 losses.

ANCIENT ROME [1]

400–376 B.C.

———————— Invasion of the Gauls, 390–389, 2 years. 20,000 gives a total strength of 40,000 for the war, and the losses at 5% gives 2000.

Totals for the period: 40,000 and 2000.

375–351 B.C.

———————— War with Etruscans, Rutilius, 355, 1 year. 20,000 and 5% or 1000.

Second war with the Gauls, 360–350, 10 years. 20,000 gives 200,000 and 5% or 10,000.

Totals for the period: 220,000 and 11,000.

[1] Note these additional abbreviations to those given on p. 290 of the text.

E — Leer, *Entziklopedia voiennykh i morskikh nauk* (Lieutenant General Leer, *Encyclopedia of the Military and Naval Sciences*), in Russian (St. Petersburg, 1895).

S — *Voiennaia Entziklopedia* (*Military Encyclopedia*), published by Sytin (St. Petersburg, 1913).

En — *Encyclopaedia Britannica*, 14th ed. (London, 1929).

The figures which are given after these abbreviations mean the pages.

350–326 B.C.
————— Second war with the Gauls, 350–348, 2 years. 20,000 gives 40,000 and 5% or 2000.
First war with the Samnites, 343–341, 2 years. 20,000 gives 40,000 and 5% or 2000.
Latin War, 340–339, 2 years. 20,000 gives 40,000 and 5% or 2000.
Second war with the Samnites 326, 1 year. 20,000 and 5% or 1000.
Totals for the period: 140,000 and 7000.

325–301 B.C.
————— Second war with the Samnites, 325–304, 22 years. 20,000 gives 440,000 and 5% or 22,000 losses.
Carthaginian War, 311, 1 year. 20,000 and 5% or 1000.
Totals for the period: 460,000 and 23,000.

300–276 B.C.
————— Third war with the Samnites, 298–290, 8 years. 20,000 gives 160,000 and 5% or 8000.
Wars with the Etruscans, Gauls, Lucanians, and the Tarent, 285–276, 6 years. 20,000 gives 120,000 and 5% or 6000.
War with the Tarent and Pyrrhus, 282–276, 7 years. 43,000 (Heraclea 36,000–50,000, D I, 262) gives 301,000. Losses 10% (Asculum up to 10%, D I, 265) gives 30,100.
Totals for the period: 581,000 and 44,100.

275–251 B.C.
————— War with the Tarent and Pyrrhus, 275–272, 4 years. 43,000 gives 172,000 and 10% or 17,200.
First Punic War, 264–251, 14 years. 40,000 (in 263 in Sicily 40,000, B 379) gives 560,000 and 5% losses or 28,000.
Totals for the period: 732,000 and 45,200.

250–226 B.C.
————— First Punic War, 250–241, 10 years. 40,000 gives 400,000 and 5% or 20,000 losses.
Illyrian War, 229–228, 2 years. 20,000 gives 40,000 and 5% or 2000.
Totals for the period: 440,000 and 22,000.

225–201 B.C.
————— Gaul (Cisalpine) Roman, 225–222, 4 years. 26,000 (S VII, 157) gives 104,000 and 5% or 5200.
Second Punic War, 218–201, 18 years. 70,000 (Cannae, 216, 70,000, D I, 281) gives 1,260,000. Losses 10% (up to 66% at Cannae, D I, 297) gives 126,000. (The battle at Cannae was exceptional for the whole war. The high rate of strain of this war, however, is indicated by the doubled index of losses.)
First Macedonian War, 215–206, 10 years. 20,000 gives 200,000 and 5% or 10,000.
Totals for the period: 1,564,000 and 141,200.

200–176 B.C.
————— Second Macedonian War, 200–197, 4 years. 20,000 gives 80,000 and 5% or 4000.

Syrian War with Antiochus the Great, 192–189, 4 years. 40,000 gives 160,000 and 5% losses or 8000.
Totals for the period: 240,000 and 12,000.

175–151 B.C.
————— Third Macedonian War, 171–168, 4 years. 20,000 gives 80,000 and 5% or 4000.
Totals for the period: 80,000 and 4000.

150–126 B.C.
————— Third Punic War, 149–146, 4 years. 40,000 gives 160,000 and 5% or 8000.
Achaean War, 147–146, 2 years. 20,000 gives 40,000 and 5% or 2000.
Lusitanian War with Viriathus, 146–140, 7 years. 20,000 gives 140,000 and 5% or 7000.
Numantian War, 141–133, 8 years. 20,000 gives 160,000 and 5% or 8000.
Slaves' insurrection in Sicily, 134–132, 3 years. 20,000 gives 60,000 and 5% or 3000.
Totals for the period: 560,000 and 28,000.

125–101 B.C.
————— War with Jugurtha, 111–106, 5 years. 40,000 gives 200,000 and 5% or 10,000.
Invasion of the Cimbri and Teutons, 113–101, 13 years. 40,000 gives 520,000 and 5% or 26,000 losses.
Uprising of slaves in Campania, 103–101, 3 years. 20,000 gives 60,000 and 5% or 3000 losses.
Totals for the period: 780,000 and 39,000.

100–76 B.C.
————— Allies' War, 91–88, 4 years. 40,000, doubled 80,000, gives 320,000 and 5% or 16,000.
Civil war between Marius and Sulla, 88–82, 7 years. 80,000 (the figure for the size of the armies is doubled because both adversaries are Romans) gives 560,000 and 5% losses, or 28,000.
First war with Mithridates the Great, 87–84, 4 years. 30,000 (D I, 402) gives 120,000 and 5% or 6000.
Insurrection of Sertorius in Spain 80–76, 5 years. 40,000 (doubled because internal) gives 200,000 and 5% or 10,000.
Totals for the period: 1,200,000 and 60,000.

75–51 B.C.
————— Insurrection of Sertorius in Spain, 4 years. 40,000 (doubled because both adversaries are Romans) gives 160,000 and 5% or 8000.
Second war with Mithridates, 74–64, 11 years. 40,000 gives 440,000 and 5% or 22,000.
Insurrection of the gladiators and of Spartacus, 73–71, 3 years. 60,000, doubled 120,000, gives 360,000 and 5% or 18,000.
Expeditions to Gallia of Julius Caesar, 58–51, 8 years. 55,000 (expedition against Helvetians 40,000, D I, 437; Alesia 70,000, D I, 466) gives 440,000 and 5% or 22,000.
Parthian-Roman of Crassus, 54–53, 2 years. 47,000 (47,000 Romans, D I, 405) gives 94,000 and 5% or 4700.

Conquest of Syria and Palestine by Pompeius, 64–63, 2 years. 40,000 gives 80,000 and 5% or 4000.

Totals for the period: 1,734,000 and 86,700.

50–26 B.C.

——————— Civil war between Julius Caesar and Pompeius, 49–48, 2 years. 75,000 (32,000 with Caesar, 43,000 Pompeius, D I, 499–500) gives 150,000 and 5% losses or 7500.

Pontine War with Pharnaces, 47, 1 year. 20,000 and 5% or 1000.

Egyptian War of Julius Caesar, 48–47, 2 years. 40,000 gives 80,000 and 5% or 4000.

Carthaginian War, 46, 1 year. 80,000 for both sides and 5% or 4000. Enormous losses of the natives at Tharsus are not included.

Hispanian War, 45, 1 year. 90,000 (Gnaeus 13 legions, Caesar 8 legions, S XI, 60–61) and 3% for both sides (Munda-Caesar 1500 or about 3% S XI, 60–61) gives for both sides 3000.

Civil war of Antonius and Octavius against Brutus and Cassius, 42, 1 year. 80,000 (doubled because internal) and 5% or 4000.

Parthian-Roman War of Antonius, 36, 1 year. 40,000 and 5% or 2000.

Civil war of Octavius with Antonius, 31, 1 year. 80,000 (doubled because internal) and 5% or 4000.

Totals for the period: 620,000 and 29,500.

25–1 B.C.

——————— German wars of Drusus and Tiberius, 12–9, 4 years. 20,000 gives 80,000 and 5% or 4000.

German wars of Drusus and Tiberius, 8–7, 2 years. 20,000 gives 40,000 and 5% or 2000.

Totals for the period: 120,000 and 6000.

1–25 A.D.

——————— German War of Drusus and Tiberius, 3–5, 3 years. 20,000 gives 60,000 and 5% or 3000 losses.

Insurrection of Pannonia and Dalmatia, 5–9, 4 years. 20,000 gives 80,000 and 5% or 4000.

Defeat of the legions of Varus, 9, 1 year. 24,000 (18,000–30,000, D II, 77) and 5% or 1200 losses.

Expedition of Germanicus into Germany, 14–17, 4 years. 40,000 (14, 20,000, D II, 104; 15, 60,000, D II, 3) gives 160,000 and 5% losses or 8000.

Totals for the period: 324,000 and 16,200.

26–50.

——————— No data, probably zero, with only a few expeditions, very small, about 2 years at 10,000 gives 20,000 and 3% losses or 600.

51–75.

——————— Batavian War 69–70, 2 years. 40,000 gives 80,000 and 5% or 4000.

Judean War, 66–70, 5 years. 40,000 gives 200,000 and 5% or 10,000 losses.

Totals for the period: 280,000 and 14,000.

76–100.

——————— British War, 78–85, 8 years. 20,000 gives 160,000 and 5% or 8000.

Totals for the period: 160,000 and 8000.

101–125.

——————— Dacian wars of Trajan, 101–106, 6 years. 40,000 gives 240,000 and losses 5% or 12,000.

War with Parthians, 114–116, 3 years. 40,000 gives 120,000 and 5% or 6000.

Totals for the period: 360,000 and 18,000.

126–150.

——————— Revolt of the Jews, 132–135, 4 years. 20,000 gives 80,000 and 5% or 4000.

Second Judean War, 135–137, 3 years. 40,000 gives 120,000 and 5% or 6000.

Totals for the period: 200,000 and 10,000.

151–175.

——————— Wars of Marcus Aurelius with Parthians, 162–165, 4 years. 40,000 gives 160,000 and 5% or 8000.

War with Marcomani, 169–173, 4 years. 40,000 gives 160,000 and 5% or 8000 losses.

Totals for the period: 320,000 and 16,000.

176–200.

——————— War of Marcus Aurelius with Marcomani, 177–180, 4 years. 40,000 gives 160,000 and 5% or 8000.

Parthian War of Septimius Severus, 198–199, 2 years. 40,000 gives 80,000 and 5% or 4000.

Totals for the period: 240,000 and 12,000.

201–225.

——————— Few small expeditions, 2 years. 10,000 gives 20,000 and 3% or 600.

226–250.

——————— War of Alexander Severus with Artaxerxes, 232, 1 year. 40,000 and 5% or 2000 losses.

Persian War, 241–250, 10 years. 40,000 gives 400,000 and 5% or 20,000.

Totals for the period: 440,000 and 22,000.

251–275.

——————— Persian War, 251–271, 21 years. 40,000 gives a total of 840,000 and 5% or 42,000 losses.

Expedition of Aurelianus against the Alemanni, 270–272, 3 years. 40,000 gives 120,000 and 5% or 6000 losses.

Expedition of Aurelianus into Gallia and with Zenovia of Palmyra, 273–274, 2 years. 40,000 gives 80,000 and 5% or 4000.

Totals for the period: 1,040,000 and 52,000.

276–300.

——————— Expedition of Probus into the region of Nekkar's River, 276–278, 3 years. 40,000 gives 120,000 and 5% or 6000.

Totals for the period: 120,000 and 6000.

301–325.

———— Civil wars of Constantine with Maxentius and of Licinius with Maximinus, 312–313, 2 years. 60,000 (doubled because both adversaries Roman) gives 120,000 and 5% or 6000.

First war of Constantine with Licinius, 314, 1 year. 50,000 (doubled because internal) (Constantine's army not more than 25,000, D II, 301) gives 50,000 and 5% or 2500.

Second war of Constantine with Licinius, 322–324, 3 years. 50,000 gives 150,000 and 5% or 7500 losses.

Totals for the period: 320,000 and 16,000.

326–350.

———— Few small expeditions, about 3 years at 10,000 strength gives 30,000 and losses about 4% gives 1200.

351–375.

———— German expeditions of Julianus, 356–359, 4 years. 70,000 (357, 13,000–15,000 Romans, D II, 273; later not more than 60,000–80,000, D II, 227) gives 280,000 and 5% losses or 14,000.

War of Julianus with Constantius, 360–363, 4 years. 80,000 (doubled because internal to the Roman Empire) (up to 40,000, E VI, 314–330) gives 320,000 and 5% gives 16,000.

Persian War of Julianus, 362–363, 2 years. 40,000 gives 80,000 and 5% or 4000 losses.

Totals for the period: 680,000 and 34,000.

376–400.

———— War of Valens with the West Goths, 376–378, 3 years. 15,000 (10,000–15,000, D II, 280–292) gives 45,000 and 5% or 2250.

Gothic Wars of Theodosius the Great, 379–382, 4 years. 40,000 gives 160,000 and 5% or 8000.

Totals for the period: 205,000 and 10,250.

401–425.

———— War of the Western Empire with the West Goths (Alaric), 401–410, 10 years. 40,000 gives 400,000 and 5% losses or 20,000.

Totals for the period: 400,000 and 20,000.

426–450.

———— Invasion of the Huns, 449 (Attila), 1 year. 40,000 and 5% or 2000.

The same in 451, 1 year. 40,000 and 5% or 2000 losses.

The same in 452, 1 year. 40,000 and 5% or 2000.

Totals for the period: 120,000 and 6000.

451–476.

———— Invasion of the Vandals under Genseric, 455–475, 21 years. 40,000 gives 840,000 and 5% or 42,000.

War with Odoacer and conquest of Rome, 476, 1 year. 40,000 strength and 5% losses 2000.

Totals for the period: 880,000 and 44,000.

FRANCE [1]

976–1000.

———— War with Charles of Lothringen, 991, 1 year. The strength of the army was 10,000 for both sides and the losses were 2% or 200.

Totals for the period: 10,000 and 200.

1001–1025.

———— No important wars are recorded for the first quarter century.

1026–1050.

———— War of Henry I for the Burgundian succession 1031, 1 year. The strength was 10,000 for both sides and the losses 2% or 200.

Totals for the period: 10,000 and 200.

1051–1075.

———— War of Philip I in Flanders, 1071, 1 year. 5000 strength and 2% gives 100 as the losses.

Totals for the period: 5000 and 100.

1076–1100.

———— War with England, 1098, 1 year. 5000 strength and 2% or 100.

First Crusade, 1096–1099, 4 years. 5000 (Antiochia 28/VI, 1098, 2000 crusaders, D III, 417; Ascalon 12/VIII, 1099, maximum 10,200 crusaders, D III, 418–419). Total 20,000 and 2% or 400 losses.

Totals for the period: 25,000 and 500.

1101–1125.

———— War with England, 1106–1125, 20 years. 3000 (Brémule 20/VIII, 1119, 400, D III, 412; the figure is enlarged in comparison with the battle at Brémule, because this single battle cannot be considered as typical for the whole war). Total 60,000. 2% losses (losses less than 1%, D III, 412; see above remark) gives 1200.

Expedition against Emperor Henry V, and into Champagne, 1124, 1 year. 5000 and 2% or 100.

Totals for the period: 65,000 and 1300.

---

[1] Meaning of the abbreviations in the detailed tables:
D — as before.
Du — Dujarric, op. cit.
S — as before.
L — G. Bodart, Losses, quoted.
B — G. Bodart, Militär-historisches Kriegslexikon (Wien und Leipzig, 1907–1908).
E — Leer's Encyclopedia
Z — O. Berndt, op. cit.
Ba — R. Ballester, Histoire de l'Espagne (Paris, 1928).
C — H. Corda, La guerre mondiale (Paris, 1922).
G — Médecin Inspecteur General J. Coubert, Étude statistique des pertes subies par les français pendant la guerre 1914–1918 (Paris, 1920).
En — as before.
Other works cited in this Appendix.
Roman figures like 28/VI, 1098, mean month: June 28, 1098.

1126–1150.
————————— War with England, 1126–1128, 3 years. 15,000 and 2% or 300, taking the average strength of the army at 5000.

Expedition of Louis VII against Champagne, 1142, 1 year. 10,000 (for both sides) and losses 2% or 200.

Second Crusade of Louis VII and of Emperor Conrad III, 1147–1149, 3 years. 5000 gives a total of 15,000 and 2% or 300.

Totals for the period: 40,000 and 800.

1151–1175.
————————— Armed conflicts with England, 1169 (Du 40), 1 year. 5000 and 2% or 100.

Armed conflicts with England, 1174, 1 year. 5000 and 2% or 100.

Totals for the period: 10,000 and 200.

1176–1200.
————————— War with England, 1188–1189, 2 years. 5000 gives a total strength of 10,000 and 2% or 200 losses.

Third Crusade (of Philip Augustus, Richard the Lion Hearted, and Frederic Barbarossa) for France, 1189–1191, 3 years. 5000 gives 15,000 and 2% or 300.

War with England, 1194–1200, 7 years. 5000 gives 35,000 and 2% or 700.

Totals for the period: 60,000 and 1200.

1201–1225.
————————— Fourth Crusade (without participation of the crown), 1202–1204, 3 years. 2000 (the figure of the army's strength is lowered because the expedition did not have the character of a war of the whole of France). Total 6000 and 2% or 120.

War with England, 1202–1204, 3 years. 5000 gives 15,000 and 2% losses gives 300.

War with England, 1213–1214, 2 years. 9000 (Bouvines 27/III, 1214, not more than 8000–10,000, D III, 427). Total 18,000 and 2% losses or 360.

War with England, 1215–1216, 2 years. 5000 gives a total of 10,000 for the war, and 2% gives 200 for the losses.

War with England, 1216–1217, 1 year. 5000 and 2% or 100.

War with England, 1223–1225, 3 years. 5000 gives 15,000 and 2% or 300.

First Albigensian War, 1207–1215, 9 years. 10,000 (for both sides). Total 90,000 and 2% or 1800.

Second Albigensian War, 1216–1222, 7 years. 10,000 (for both sides). Total 70,000 and 2% or 1400.

Third Albigensian War, 1223–1225, 3 years. 10,000 gives 30,000 and 2% or 600.

Totals for the period: 259,000 and 5180.

1226–1250.
————————— War with England, 1226, 1 year. 5000 and 2% or 100.

Third Albigensian War, 1226, 1 year. 10,000 (for both sides) and 2% or 200 losses.

Civil war, 1226–1231, 5 years. 10,000 gives 50,000 and 2% or 1000.

Civil war, 1233–1234, 2 years. 10,000 gives 20,000 and 2% or 400 losses.

War with England, 1242–1243, 2 years. 5000 gives a total of 10,000 for the war and 2% gives 200 as the losses.

Fourth Albigensian War, 1226–1229, 4 years. 10,000 (for both sides) gives 40,000 and 2% or 800.

Fifth Albigensian War, 1244, 1 year. 10,000 and 2% or 200.

War with England, 1245, 1 year. 5000 and 2% or 100.

Seventh Crusade, 1248–1250, 3 years. 5000 gives 15,000 for the total strength and 2% or 300.

Totals for the period: 165,000 and 3300.

1251–1275.
————————— Seventh Crusade, 1251–1254, 4 years. 5000 gives 20,000 and 2% or 400.

First insurrection, "Pastoureaux," 1251, 1 year. 10,000 (for both sides) and 2% or 200.

War with Flanders, 1253–1255, 3 years. 5000 gives 15,000 and 2% or 300.

War with England, 1259, 1 year. 5000 and 2% or 100.

Expedition of Charles of Anjou into Italy, 1268, 1 year. 5000 and 2% or 100.

Eighth Crusade, 1 year. 5000 and 2% or 100.

Totals for the period: 60,000 and 1200.

1276–1300.
————————— War with Castile, 1285, 1 year. 5000 and 2% or 100.

War with Aragon, 1284–1291, 8 years. 5000 gives 40,000 and 2% or 800.

War with England and Flanders, 1294–1298, 5 years. 5000 gives 25,000 and 2% or 500.

Totals for the period: 70,000 and 1400.

1301–1325.
————————— War with England, 1324–1325, 2 years. 5000 gives 10,000 and 2% or 200.

War with Flanders, 1301–1305, 5 years. 8000 (Coutray 11/VII, 1302, 8000, D III, 444–445). Total 40,000 and 2% or 800.

War with Flanders, 1314, 1 year. 8000 and 2% or 160.

War with Flanders, 1315, 1 year. 8000 and 2% or 160.

Insurrection of the Pastoureaux du Midi, 1326, 1 year. 10,000 (for both sides) and 2% or 200.

Totals for the period: 76,000 and 1520.

1326–1350.
————————— War with England, 1326–1327, 2 years. 5000 gives 10,000 and 2% or 200 losses.

War with Flanders, 1328, 1 year. 5000 and 2% or 100.

Hundred Years' War with England, 1339–1347, 9 years. 35,000 (Crecy 26/VIII, 1346, up to 20,000, D III, 466; there were two fronts, E VII, 301–304). Total 315,000 and 5% or 15,750 for the losses.

Totals for the period: 330,000 and 16,050.

1351–1375.

———————— Insurrection of Étienne Marcel, 1357–1358, 2 years. 15,000 (for both sides) gives 30,000 strength for the war, and 2% losses or 600.

War with England, 1354–1360, 7 years. 25,000 (two fronts) gives a total of 175,000 and 5% or 8750 losses.

War with England (in Bretagne), 1363–1364, 2 years. 13,000 gives 26,000 and 5% or 1300.

Intervention in Castile against England on the side of Henri de Trastamare, 1366–1369, 4 years. 13,000 gives 52,000 and 5% or 2600.

War with England, 1368–1375, 8 years. 25,000 (two fronts) gives 200,000 and 5% or 10,000 losses.

Totals for the period: 483,000 and 23,250.

1376–1400.

———————— War with England, 1376–1389, 14 years. 25,000 (two fronts) gives a total strength for the war of 350,000 and 5% losses or 17,500.

Insurrection in Paris of the "Maillotins" and "Tuchins," 1382, 1 year. 10,000 (for both sides) and 2% or 200.

War with Flanders, 1382, 1 year. 13,000 and 5% or 650.

Expedition against the Turks, into Hungary, 1396, 1 year. 2500 (Nikopole 25/IX, 1396, 2500, D III, 492) and 5% losses or 125.

Totals for the period: 375,500 and 18,475.

1401–1425.

———————— Burgundian civil war, 1405–1407, 3 years. 12,000 (for both sides) gives 36,000 and 4% or 1440.

Burgundian civil war, 1408–1410, 3 years. 10,000 (for both sides) gives 30,000 and 4% or 1200 losses.

Burgundian civil war, 1411–1415, 5 years. 10,000 gives a total of 50,000 and 4% losses or 2000.

War with England, 1411–1420, 10 years. 18,000 (Agincourt 25/X, 1415, 4000–6000, D III, 480, two fronts, E 301–304). Total 100,000 and 5% or 5000.

War with England, 1421–1422, 2 years. 20,000 (two fronts) gives a total of 40,000 and 5% or 2000 losses.

War with England, 1423–1425, 3 years. 25,000 (two fronts) gives 75,000 and 5% or 3750 losses.

Totals for the period: 331,000 and 14,390.

1426–1450.

———————— War with England, 1426–1439, 14 years. 25,000 (two fronts) gives 350,000 as the total strength for the war, and 5% gives 17,500 for the losses.

War with England, 1440–1444, 5 years. 25,000 (two fronts) gives 125,000 and 5% or 6250 losses.

War with England, 1449–1450, 2 years. 25,000 (two fronts) gives 50,000 and 5% or 2500.

Totals for the period: 525,000 and 26,250.

1451–1475.

———————— Hundred Years' War (the end), 1451–1453, 3 years. 25,000 (two fronts) gives 75,000 and 5% losses gives 3750.

War of the Civil League, "du bien publique," 1465–1466, 2 years. 12,000 (for both sides) makes 24,000 for the war, and 2% losses makes 480.

Burgundian War, 1468, 1 year. 10,000 (for both sides) and 2% or 200.

War of 1470–1474, 5 years. 18,000 (Hericourt 13/IX, 1474, 18,000, D III, 629). Total 90,000 and 5% or 4500.

War with England, 1475, 1 year. 13,000 and 5% or 650.

Totals for the period: 212,000 and 9580.

1476–1500.

———————— Burgundian War, 1478–1479, 2 years. 30,000 (for both sides; Granson 2/III, 1476, 14,000, D III, 633; Murten 22/VI, 1476, 18,000–20,000, D III, 633). Total 60,000 and 5% or 3000.

Insurrection in Bretagne ("La Guerre folle"), 1485–1488, 4 years. 10,000 (for both sides). Total 40,000 and 2% or 800.

War with England (in Bretagne), 1489–1492, 4 years. 13,000 gives a total of 52,000, and 5% losses gives 2600.

Italian War of Charles VIII, 1494–1497, 4 years. 15,000 (scattered fronts; Fornouc 6/VII, 1495, 9000, Du 78). Total 60,000 and 5% or 3000.

First war of Louis XII for Milan, 1499–1500, 2 years. 20,000 (19,500, S XI, 148). Total 40,000 and 5% or 2000.

Totals for the period: 252,000 and 11,400.

1501–1525.

———————— Second war of Louis XII for Naples, 1501–1504, 4 years. 40,000 (15,000–33,000, S XI, 148; two fronts: 23,000 in Spain and 20,000 in Naples, E III, 518). Total 320,000 and 5% or 16,000.

War with Venice ("Cambrian League"), 1508–1510, 3 years. 32,000 (S XI, 148). Total 96,000 and 5% or 4800.

War with the "Holy League," 1511–1514, 4 years. 35,000 (two fronts, E III, 550; Ravennes 11/IV, 1512, 23,000, D IV, 82–89). Total 140,000 and 5% or 7000 losses.

Second war of Francis I for Milan, 1515, 1 year. 30,000 (Marignano 13–14/IX, 1515, 30,000, D IV, 98). Total 30,000 and 5% or 1500.

First war with Charles V, 1521–1525, 5 years. 19,000 (Pavia 24/II, 1525, about 20,000, D IV, 110–111; Bicocca 27/IV, 1522, 18,000, D IV, 104). Total 95,000 and 5% or 4750.

Totals for the period: 681,000 and 34,050.

1526–1550.

———————— Second war with Charles V, 1527–1529, 3 years. 25,000 gives a total of 75,000 and 5% gives 3750.

Third war with Charles V, 1536–1538, 3 years. 40,000 (two fronts) gives 120,000 and 5% or 6000.

Fourth war with Charles V, 1542–1544, 3 years. 75,000 (three fronts: 40,000 in Spain; 40,000 in Luxembourg; 5000 in Italy, E III, 556). Total 225,000 and 5% or 11,250.

War with England, 1544–1546, 3 years. 25,000 gives 75,000 and 5% gives 3750 losses.

War with England, 1548–1550, 3 years. 25,000 gives 75,000 and 5% or 3750.

Insurrection in 1548, 1 year. 5000 and 2% or 100 losses.

Intervention in Scotland, 1546–1548, 3 years. 5000 gives a total of 15,000 and 2% losses gives 300.

Totals for the period: 590,000 and 28,900.

1551–1575.

————— War of Henry II with Charles V, 1552–1556, 5 years. 25,000 (two fronts, E III, 557–558). Total 125,000 and 5% or 6250 losses.

War with England, 1557–1559, 3 years. 25,000 gives 75,000 and 5% or 3750.

War with England, 1559–1560, 2 years. 25,000 gives 50,000 and 5% or 2500.

War with England, 1562–1564, 3 years. 25,000 gives 75,000 and 5% or 3750.

War with Spain, 1556–1559, 4 years. 30,000 (two fronts, 24,000, S XI, 156). Total 120,000 and 5% losses or 6000.

First war of the Huguenots, 1562–1563, 2 years. 40,000 (for both sides) gives 80,000 and 2% losses or 1600.

Second war of the Huguenots, 1567–1568, 2 years. 40,000 gives 80,000 and 2% or 1600.

Third war of the Huguenots, 1568–1570, 3 years. 40,000 (Moncontour 3/X, 1569, 19,000 Huguenots and 23,000 Catholics, D IV, 223). Total 120,000 and 1.5% (losses of Catholics 1.5%, D IV, 222) gives 1800.

Fourth war of the Huguenots, 1572–1573, 2 years. 40,000 gives 80,000 and 2% or 1600.

Fifth war of the Huguenots, 1575, 1 year. 40,000 and 2% or 800.

Totals for the period: 845,000 and 29,650.

1576–1600.

————— Sixth war of the Huguenots, 1577, 1 year. 40,000 and 2% or 800.

Seventh war of the Huguenots, 1580, 1 year. 40,000 and 2% or 800.

War of the "League," 1585–1594, 10 years. 40,000 or 400,000 for the war, and 2% losses or 8000.

War with Savoy, 1600, 1 year. 25,000 and 5% or 1250.

Eighth war of the Huguenots, 1585–1598, 14 years. 15,000 (for both sides; Coutras 20/X, 1587, 6000–7000 on each side, D IV, 223). Total 210,000 and 2% or 4200.

Totals for the period: 715,000 and 15,050.

1601–1625.

————— War with Savoy, 1601, 1 year. 25,000 and 5% or 1250.

Insurrection of the Huguenots, 1621–1622, 2 years. 40,000 (for both sides) gives 80,000 and 2% gives 1600 for the losses.

Totals for the period: 105,000 and 2850.

1626–1650.

————— Insurrection of the Huguenots, 1626, 1 year. 40,000 and 2% or 800.

Mantuan War, 1629–1631, 3 years. 10,000 (L 84) gives 30,000 and 5% gives 1500.

Thirty Years' War in Germany, 1635–1648, 14 years. 35,000 (4 fronts, E II, 22–24, and VII, 546–555; Rocroi 19/V, 1643, 23,000, B 70; average strength of the French armies in Germany 20,000, L 85). Total 490,000 and 25% losses (Rocroi 17.5%, B 70; Thionville, 1639, 33%, L 85; Allersheim, 1645, 33%, L 85) gives 122,500.

War with Spain, 1635–1650, 16 years. 60,000 (3 fronts: Barcelona naval, 1642, 12,000, B 68; Rocroi, 1643, 23,000, L 86–88). Total 960,000 and 30% losses (Barcelona, 1642, naval, 6.6%, B 68; Lens, 1648, 28%; Fontarabia, 1638, 33%) gives 28,800. (The principal burden of the struggle of France was exactly in her war with Spain, 1635–1650, which cost France about 300,000 losses, while her war with Germany cost only 80,000 killed and wounded, L 85–86, 88.)

War with England, 1627–1629, 3 years. 23,000 (La Rochelle 15/VIII, 1627, until 18/X, 1628, 23,000, B 53). Total 69,000 and losses at 5% or 3450.

The Fronde, 1648–1650, 3 years. 45,000 (for both sides) gives 135,000 and losses 5% or 6750.

Totals for the period: 1,724,000 and 163,800.

1651–1675.

————— War with Spain 1651–1659, 9 years. 50,000 (three fronts; Valenciennes, 1656, 25,000, L 86–88; Arras 24/VIII, 1654, 15,000, B 82). Total 450,000 and 10% losses (Dunkirchen, 1656, 13%, L 86–88; Arras 6, 6%, B 82) gives 45,000.

The Fronde, 1651–1652, 2 years. 45,000 gives 90,000 and 5% or 4500.

War with England, 1666–1667, 2 years. 20,000 gives 40,000 and 5% or 2000. (France took only slight part in this war, L 89.)

Devolution War, 1667–1668, 2 years. 20,000, gives 40,000 and 5% or 2000. (France took only slight part in this war, L 89.)

Second war of Louis XIV, 1672–1675, 4 years. 120,000 (three fronts: in the Netherlands, 100,000, E V, 364–365; Seneffe 11/VIII, 1674, 50,000, B 94; Turkheim 5/I, 1675, 33,000, B 96). Total 480,000 and 21% losses (Altenheim, 1675, 29%, L 90–91; Seneffe 12%, L 90–91) gives 100,800.

War with Turkey, 1664–1670, 7 years. 15,000 (two fronts, L 89: 6000 in Hungary, 1664, L 89; 10,000 to help Venice on the Island of Crete, 1669, L 89). Total 105,000 and losses 5% makes 5250.

Totals for the period: 1,205,000 and 159,550.

1676–1700.

————— Second war of Louis XIV, 1676–1679, 4 years. 120,000 (3 fronts, E V, 364–365; Mont-Cassel 11/IV, 1677, 30,000, B 101; St. Denis les Mons, 1678, 40,000, L 90–91). Total 480,000 and 14.6% losses (Agosta, naval, 1676, 19%, B 98; Mont-Cassel 15%, B 101; St. Denis les Mons 10%, L 90–91) gives 70,080.

"Reunion" war, 1683–1684, 2 years. 20,000 gives 40,000 and 5% or 2000.

Third war of Louis XIV, 1688–1697, 10 years. 150,000 (5 fronts, E V, 365, and VII, 292; Neerwinden 29/VII, 1693, 80,000, B 118; Steenkerke

3/VIII, 1692, 57,000 B 117; Fleurus 1/VIII, 1690, 50,000, B 112; La Hougue, Barfleur, naval, 1692, 20,000, B 116). Total 1,500,000 and 16% losses (Neerwinden 15%, B 118; Steenkerke 12.3%, B 117; Fleurus 12% B 112; La Hougue, Barfleur, naval, 25%, B 116) gives 240,000.

Totals for the period: 2,020,000 and 312,080.

1701-1725.

——————— War for Spanish Succession, 1701–1713, 13 years. 170,000 (5 fronts: Italian 77,000 in 1705; Dutch 100,000 in 1708; German 60,000 in 1703; Spanish 40,000 in 1708–1709, plus naval, E III, 402–404; Velez Malaga, naval, 1704, 24,000, B 138; Malplaquet 11/IX, 1709, 90,000, B 160). Total 2,210,000 and 11% losses (Velez-Malaga 9%, B 138; Malplaquet 12%, B 160) gives 243,100.

War of the "Quadruple Alliance," 1718–1720, 3 years. 20,000 gives 60,000 total strength, and 5% gives 3000 losses. (France took only slight part in this war, L 98.)

Insurrection of the "Camisards" in Languedoc, 1702–1706, 5 years. 40,000 (for both sides; 20,000–30,000, L 94) gives 200,000 and 2% or 4000.

Totals for the period: 2,470,000 and 250,100.

1726-1750.

——————— War for the Polish Succession, 1733–1738, 6 years. 66,000 (two fronts; Parma 29/VI, 1734, 53,000 French and Sardinians, B 180; Siege of Kehl 18–30/X, 1733, 33,000, B 160–179). Total 360,000 and 14% losses (Parma 8%, L 98; Guastalla, 1734, 15%) makes 50,400. (General losses during the whole war 50,000, L 99.)

War for the Austrian Succession, 1741–1748, 8 years. 180,000 (4 fronts, E I, 45–48; Lawfeldt 2/VII, 1747. 98,000, B 211; Fontency 11/V, 1745, 60,000, B 201; Rocoux, 1746, 110,000, L 99). Total 1,440,000 and losses 11% (Lawfeldt 10%, B 211; Fontency 9.3%, B 201; Piacenza, 1746, 16%, L 100) gives 158,400 (total losses 140,000, L 99).

Totals for the period: 1,800,000 and 208,800.

1751-1775.

——————— Seven Years' War, 1756–1763, 7 years. 150,000 (5 fronts: in Germany about 125,000–140,000 and in America 10,000, E VII, 142–167; Rossbach 5/XI, 1757, 41,000, B 220; Minden, 1759, 52,000, B 231; Quiberon, naval, 1759, 10,000, B 236). Total 1,050,000 and losses 16% (Kloster Kampen, 1760, 14%, L 101; Rossbach 8%, L 102; Quebec, 1759, 33%, L 103; Minden 9.5%, B 231; Quiberon, naval, 1759, 30%, B 236) gives 168,000 (total losses 170,000, L 100–101).

Totals for the period: 1,050,000 and 168,000.

1776-1800.

——————— War with England (North American), 1779–1783, 5 years. 30,000 (3 fronts, E VII, 382; Dominica, naval, 1782, 19,000, B 261; Yorktown 19/X, 1781, 19,000 Americans and French, B 260–263). Total 150,000 and losses 14% (Cap St. Vincent, 1780, 17%, L 104; Dominica 15.8%,

B 261; total losses 20,000) gives 21,000 as the total losses. (General losses during the whole war no less than 20,000, L 104.)

First Coalitional War, 1792–1797, 6 years. 250,000 (4 fronts, Netherlands 65,000–180,000, Reinish 90,000–100,000, Italian 25,000–40,000, Spanish 30,000–50,000, E VI, 270–281; Tourcoing 18/V, 1794, 70,000, B 292; Jemappes 6/XI, 1792, 45,000, B 270; Valmy 20/IX, 1792, 52,000, B 269; Wattignies 15–16/X, 1793, 45,000, B 283; Cateau Cambresis 26/IV, 1794, 90,000, B 299; Rivoli 14–15/I, 1797, 22,000, B 318). Total 1,500,000 and losses 12% (Rivoli, 1797, 10%, L 106; Wattignies, 1793, 11%, L 106; Tourcoing, 1794, 4.3%, L 106) makes 180,000. (The losses during this war on the average were between 8% and 15%, L 105.)

Second Coalitional War, 1789–1800, 3 years. 200,000 (6 fronts, in Switzerland 50,000, Germany 108,000, Italy 58,000–80,000, Netherlands 14,000, Naples 34,000, naval, E VI, 281–284; III, 536–544; I, 154–160; V, 58–60; Trebbia 17–20/VI, 1799, 33,000, B 337; Novi 15/VIII, 1799, 35,000, B 340; Zurich 25–26/IX, 1799, 33,500, B 339; Marengo 14/VI, 1800, 28,000, B 355; Bergen 19/X, 1799, 29,000 Franco-Hollanders, B 339; against Naples 15,000, L 111). Total 600,000 and losses 16% (Trebbia 29%, B 337; Novi 20%, B 340; Zurich 13%, B 339; Marengo 23.2%, B 355; Bergen 4.5%, B 339; Hohenlinden, 1800, 4.5%, L 114) gives 96,000.

War with England (revolutionary), 1793–1800, 8 years. 25,000 (3 fronts, Netherlands 14,000, Ireland 4000, naval, E VI, 270–289; Quessant, naval, 1794, 18,000, B 290). Total 200,000 and losses 23% (Quiberon Bay, naval, 1795, 8%, B 290; Aboukir, naval, 1798, 34%, B 290; Quessant, naval, 1794, 27.5%, B 290) gives 46,000.

War in Vendée, 1793–1796, 4 years. 50,000 (for both sides; Nantes 29/VI, 1793, 12,000 Republicans and 38,000 Vendeans, B 271–284; Lugon 14/VIII, 1793, 10,000 Republicans and 35,000 Vendeans, B 271–284). Total 200,000 and losses 29% (Dol 32% with the Republicans, L 107; Cholet 16% with Republicans and 20% with Vendeans, L 107; Le mans 10% with Republicans and 70% with Vendeans, L 107) gives 58,000.

Egyptian expedition of Bonaparte, 1795–1800, 6 years. 20,000 (Embaheh "Pyramids" 21/VII, 1798, 20,000, B 324). Total 120,000 and losses 7% (Embaheh "Pyramids" 1.5%, B 324; Mont-Thabor 16/IV, 1799, 12.5%, B 331) gives 8400.

Insurrection in San Domingo, 1791–1800, 9 years. 35,000 (L 115) gives a total of 315,000 and losses at 6% gives 18,900 (total losses 35,000, L 115).

Totals for the period: 3,085,000 and 428,300.

1801-1825.

——————— Second Coalitional War, 1801, 1 year. 200,000 (6 fronts) and losses 16% gives 32,000. (The figures are similar to the ones which are given for the first part of this war in the preceding quarter of a century.)

War with England (revolutionary), 1801–1802, 2 years. 25,000 (3 fronts) gives 50,000 and 23% or 11,500.

Third Coalitional War, 1805, 1 year. 200,000 (3 fronts, 200,000 in Germany, 40,000 in Italy, E I, 60–65; Austerlitz 2/XII, 1805, 65,000, B 369). Total 200,000 and losses 15% gives 30,000 (Austerlitz 15.3%, B 369. General losses for France 30,000, L 48).

War with Russia and Prussia, 1806–1807, 2 years. 150,000 (2 fronts, 160,000 in Germany, 3000 in Ionic Islands, E II, 277–284 and I, 78; Jena 14/X, 1806, 54,000, B 372; on the same day, Auerstadt 27,000, Z 50; Pr. Eylau 8/II, 1807, 75,000, B 380; Friedland 14/VI, 1807, 87,000, B 383). Total 300,000 and losses 18% (Jena 11%, B 372; Pr. Eylau 30.6%, B 380; Friedland 13.8%, B 383) gives 54,000.

War with Austria, 1809, 1 year. 180,000 (3 fronts 115,000–180,000 in Austria; 70,000 in Italy and Dalmatia, E I, 65–70; Aspern-Esling 21, 22/V, 1809, 85,000, B 405; Wagram 5, 6/VII, 1809, 160,000). Losses 20% (Aspern-Esling 21.7%, B 405; Wagram 18.8%, B 409) gives 36,000. The figure is considerably lowered in view of the presence of large Italian and non-French contingents in the army. If these are included, losses are much greater, up to 110,000, L 49).

War with Spain, 1808–1814, 7 years. 36,000 (Bailen 19/VII, 1808, 22,000, B 389; Siege of Saragossa 19/XII, 1808, 20/II, 1809, 50,000, B 394). Total 252,000 and losses 20% gives 50,400.

War with England, 1803–1814, 12 years. 150,000 (2 fronts, in Spain up to 161,000, E III, 393–402; Talavera de la Reina 27–28/VII, 1809, 47,000, B 410; Oporto 29/III, 1809, 16,000, B 395; Albuera 16/V, 1811, 18,000, B 425; Salamanca 22/VII, 1812, 42,000, B 432; Vittoria 21/VI, 1813, 60,000, Z 53; Trafalgar, naval, 21/X, 1805, 20,000 French and Spaniards, B 366). Total 1,800,000 and losses 27% (Talavera de la Reina 15.1%, B 410; Oporto 12.5%, B 395; Albuera 44%, B 425; Salamanca 24%, B 432; Trafalgar, naval, 40%, B 366) gives 486,000.

With Russia, 1812, 1 year. 300,000 (Borodino 7/IX, 1812, 124,000, B 438; general size of the armies 300,000 French and 312,000 allies, L 126). Losses 55.2% (Borodino 22.6%, B 438; general losses 280,000, L 127–128) gives 166,600. (The coefficient of losses is increased twice because of an extraordinarily great amount of losses, almost a complete extermination of the French Army at the end of the campaign, with the deduction of prisoners and dead from sickness, half of the entire contingent perished.)

War of 1813–1814, 2 years. 450,000 (2 fronts, 440,000 in Germany and France, 45,000 in Italy, E V, 405–417; Bautzen 20–21/V, 1813, 167,000, B 450; Leipzig 16, 18–19/X, 1813, 175,000, B 461; Laon 9–10/III, 1814, 52,000, Z 58). Total, 900,000 and losses 40% (total losses 310,000 French and 55,000 allies, L 46–47; Bautzen 15%, B 450; Leipzig 25.7%, B 461; Laon 23%, Z 58) gives 360,000.

100 Days' War, 1 year. 85,000 (Waterloo 18/VI, 1815, 72,000, B 487). Losses 42% (Waterloo 42%, Z 119) gives 35,700.

Egyptian expedition, 1801–1802, 2 years. 20,000 gives 40,000 and 7% gives 2800 losses.

Insurrection of San Domingo, 1801–1803, 3 years. 35,000 gives 105,000 and 5% losses gives 5250.

Spanish expedition, 1823, 1 year. 100,000 (Ba 273) and 3% losses (general losses of French 3100, i.e., about 3%, L 139) gives 3000.

Totals for the period: 4,512,000 and 1,273,450.

1826–1850.

——————— War with Turkey (Navarin), 1827, 1 year. 2600 (Navarin 20/X, 1827, 8000 English, French, and Russians, B 492). Losses 8.8% (Navarin 8.8%, B 492) gives 229.

War with Holland, 1832, 1 year. 50,000 (Siege of the Antverpen, 1832, 50,000 French, Du 83). Losses 1% (Antverpen; less than 1%, L 139) gives 500.

War with Portugal, 1834, 1 year. 20,000 and 1% or 200.

On the Madagascar, 1829, 1 year. 10,000 and 1% or 100.

The same, 1845, 1 year. 10,000 and 1% or 100.

War in Mexico, 1838–1839, 2 years. 10,000 gives 20,000 and 1% or 200.

War in Algeria, 1830–1847, 17 years. 12,000 (Isly 14/VIII, 1844, 10,000, B 501; siege of the Constantine, 1839, 13,000, Du 84). Total 204,000 and losses 5% (Isly 7000, i.e., 0.7%, B 501; general losses up to 47,000, L 141, but mainly from sickness; therefore not included) gives 10,200.

War in Argentine, 1838–1840, 2 years. 10,000 gives 20,000 and 1% or 200.

War in Cochin China, 1847, 1 year. 10,000 and 1% or 100.

Roman expedition, 1849, 1 year. 10,000 and 1% (general losses 1570, L 139) gives 100.

War with Morocco, 1843–1844, 2 years. 10,000 (10,000 French, Du 85) gives 20,000 and 1% or 200.

Expedition to Uruguay (Obligado), 1845, 1 year. 10,000 and 1% or 100.

Totals for the period: 386,600 and 12,229. (If losses from sickness in the war in Algeria and from all causes in Roman expedition are included, then the losses are 49,499.)

1851–1875.

——————— Crimean War, 1854–1856, 3 years. 100,000 (2 fronts, in Crimea 32,000 in 1854, 100,000 in 1855, Black Sea 31,000, Baltic Sea, E II, 300–332; Chernaja Rechka 16/VIII, 1855, 25,000, B 516; Inkerman 5/X, 1854, 38,000, B 515; average army's strength IX, 1854, 32,000; V, 1855, 100,000, Z 35). Total 300,000 and losses 17.4% (Inkerman 23%, L 141; Alma 20/IX, 1854, 8%, L 141; general losses 54,000, L 141 and general army's strength 310,000, L 142, or 17.4%) gives 52,200.

Austro-Italian War, 1859, 1 year. 140,000 (general army's strength 140,000, L 143; Solferino

24/VI, 1859, 106,500, Z 62) and losses 12% (general losses 12%, L 143; for the whole war; Solferino 8.9%, Z 62) gives 16,800.

War with China, 1862–1864, 3 years. 20,000 gives 60,000 and 1% or 600 losses.

War with Annam, 1857–1862, 6 years. 20,000 gives 120,000 and 1% or 1200.

Syrian War, 1860, 1 year. 10,000 and 1% or 100.

Cochin-Chinese War, 1861–1862, 2 years. 10,000 gives 20,000 and 1% or 200.

War in Mexico, 1861–1867, 7 years. 20,000 gives 140,000 and general losses up to 5000 (L 141).

War for defense of the Papal State, 1860–1861, 2 years. 10,000 gives 20,000 and 1% or 200.

Franco-Prussian War, 1870–1871, 2 years. 900,000 (general average of the French army's strength up to 900,000, L 147; Gravelotte Saint-Privat 18/VIII, 1870, 112,900, A 67; Orleans 3–4/XII, 1870, 60,700, Z 70). Total 1,800,000 and losses 22% (general losses up to 200,000, L 148; Worth 29.2%, L 146; Gravelotte Saint-Privat 6.5%, Z 67; Sedan 18.9%, Z 69; Orleans 3.3%, Z 70) gives 396,000.

In Tonkin, 1873–1874, 2 years. 200 gives 400 and 1% or 4.

In Rome (against Garibaldi), 1867, 1 year. 10,000 and 1% or 100.

Totals for the period: 2,620,400 and 472,404.

1876–1900.

———— War with Tonkin, 1883–1885, 3 years. 20,000 makes 60,000 and general losses 4200 (L 154).

War with China, 1884–1885, 2 years. 20,000 gives 40,000 and 2% or 800.

War with Tonkin, 1894, 1 year. 20,000 and 2% or 400.

War on Madagascar, 1883–1885, 3 years. 10,000 gives 30,000 total and 1% losses or 300.

War on Madagascar, 1895–1897, 3 years. 10,000 gives 30,000 and 2500 losses (general losses, for 1896, 5700, but almost all from sickness, L 155; from 1896 to the end 650).

Tunis, 1881–1882, 2 years. 20,000 gives 40,000 total and 2% losses or 800.

Morocco, 1893–1894, 2 years. 20,000 gives 40,000 and 2% or 800.

Dahomey, 1890–1892, 2 years. 10,000 gives 20,000; total losses 700 (for 1890, 130, for 1892, 540, L 154).

Sudan, 1890–1894, 4 years. 10,000 gives 40,000 and 1% gives 400.

Siam, 1893, 1 year. 10,000 and 1% or 100.

Boxers' insurrection, 1900, 1 year. 7000 (IX, 1900, 6700, S IV, 614–622) and losses 1% (losses less than 1%, S IV, 614–622) gives 100.

Totals for the period: 307,000 and 11,100.

1901–1925.

———— Morocco, 1907–1912, 6 years. 50,000 makes a total of 300,000 and 2% losses gives 6000.

World War, 1914–1918, 5 years. Total for the army, 8,410,000 (2 fronts, French 2,780,000 in July, 1917; Balkan 264,000 in July, 1918; army's strength: 15/VIII, 1914, 2,690,000; 1/VII, 1915, 2,660,000; 1/VII, 1916, 3,000,000; 1/VII, 1917, 3,050,000; 1/VII, 1918, 2,920,000; 1/XI, 1918, 2,850,000, C 408). Total losses 3,660,000 (total called to colors 8,410,000, C 407; total number of killed and wounded 3,660,000, G, figure used 43.5%). For many details see in *Les armées françaises dans la grande guerre* (official French history of the war), 8 vols. (Paris, 1927–1928). The official total data given by different sources and authors show, however, enormous discrepancies in France as well as in other countries.

Riffian War, in Morocco, 1925–1926, 2 years. 160,000 (En I, 28) gives 320,000 and 5% or 16,000 losses.

Totals for the period: 9,030,000 and 3,682,000.

RUSSIA [1]

900–950.

———— Expedition of Oleg to Byzantium, 906, 1 year. 10,000 was the strength of the army, and the losses 2% or 200.

Expedition of Igor to Byzantium, 941, 1 year. 10,000 and 2% or 200.

Totals for the period: 20,000 and 400.

951–975.

———— Expedition of Sviatoslav I to Bulgaria, 957–972, 16 years. 10,000 gives 160,000 total strength for the war, and 2% losses or 3200.

Totals for the period: 160,000 and 3200.

976–1000.

———— Expedition of Vladimir I against Khorvats (Galicia), 981, 1 year. 10,000 and 2% or 200.

Expedition to Chersonese, 988, 1 year. 10,000 and 2% or 200.

Totals for the period: 20,000 and 400.

1001–1025.

———— No trustworthy data exist.

1026–1050.

———— War of Yaroslav with Mechislav of Poland, 1031, 1 year. 10,000 and 2% or 200.

[1] Meaning of the abbreviations in the detailed tables:
E — Leer's *Encyclopedia*, quoted.
B — Bodart, *Militär-historisches Kriegslexikon*.
Z — as before.
G — N. Golovine, *The Russian Army in the World War* (New Haven, 1931).
S — as before.
Gr — *Grajdanskaia Voina 1918–1921*, ed. by A. Bubnov, C. Kameneff, M. Tukhachevsky, and P. Eideman. (*The Civil War 1918–1921*, 3 vols.) (Moscow and Leningrad, 1930.)
Other works cited in this Appendix.

Byzantine Expedition of Vladimir Yaroslavo-
vitch, 1043, 1 year. 6000 (expedition, 1043,
6000, E VIII, 463) and 2% or 120.
Russo-Lithuanian War, 1038–1044, 7 years.
10,000 gives 70,000 and 2% or 1400.
Totals for the period: 86,000 and 1720.

1051–1075.
——————— Against Polovcians, 1061, 1064, 1068,
3 years. 10,000 gives 30,000 and 2% or 600.
Totals for the period: 30,000 and 600.

1076–1100.
——————— Expedition of Vladimir Monomakh to
Silesia, 1076, 1 year. 10,000 and 2% or 200.
Into Polotsk province, 1078, 1 year. 12,000
(internal) and 4% or 480.
Into Chernigov province, 1078, 1 year. 15,000
(internal) and 4% or 600.
Against Polovcians, 1093–1096, 4 years. 10,000
gives 40,000 and 2% or 800.
Against Polovcians, 1100, 1 year. 10,000 and
2% or 200.
Totals for the period: 87,000 and 2280.

1101–1125.
——————— Against Polovcians, 1103–1116, 14
years. 10,000 gives 140,000 and 2% or 2800.
Against "black hats," torks, and berendei,
1116–1123, 8 years. 10,000 gives 80,000 and 2%
or 1600.
Totals for the period: 220,000 and 4400.

1126–1150.
——————— Against Polovcians, 1126, 1 year.
10,000 and 2% or 200.
Against Polovcians, 1149–1150, 2 years. 10,000
gives 20,000 and 2% or 400.
War of Urii Dolgorukii with Izzaslav Mistislavovitch, 1146–1150, 5 years. 12,000 (internal)
gives 60,000 and 4% or 2400.
Russo-Lithuanian War, 1132, 1 year. 10,000
and 2% or 200.
Totals for the period: 100,000 and 3200.

1151–1175.
——————— War of Urii Dolgorukii with Izzaslav
Mistislavovitch, 1151–1154, 4 years. 15,000 (in-
ternal) gives 60,000 and 4% or 2400 losses.
Against Polovcians, 1165, 1 year. 10,000 and
2% or 200.
Against Polovcians, 1168, 1 year. 10,000 and
2% or 200.
Against Polovcians, 1170, 1 year. 10,000 and
2% or 200.
Russo-Swedish War, 1164, 1 year. 10,000 and
2% or 200.
Totals for the period: 100,000 and 3200.

1176–1200.
——————— Against Polovcians, 1183–1185 ("Slovo
o Polku Igorevi"), 3 years. 10,000 gives 30,000
and 2% or 600.
Against Polovcians, 1191, 1 year. 10,000 and
2% or 200.
Against Polovcians, 1199, 1 year. 10,000 and
2% or 200.

Russo-Swedish War, 1188, 1 year. 10,000 and
2% or 200.
Totals for the period: 60,000 and 1200.

1201–1225.
——————— Against Polovcians, 1202–1215, 14
years. 10,000 gives 140,000 and 2% or 2800.
Expedition of Mistislav the Audacious against
Chudi and Templars, 1212–1213, 2 years. 10,000
gives 20,000 and 2% or 400.
Against Kiev, 1214, 1 year. 20,000 (internal)
and 4% or 800.
Against Urii II and Yaroslav Vsevolodovitch,
1215, 1 year. 15,000 (internal) total strength and
4% losses or 600.
Into Galicia province, 1219–1222, 4 years.
10,000 gives 40,000 and 2% or 800.
Russo-Lithuanian War, 1210–1225, 16 years.
15,000 gives 240,000 and 4% or 9600.
Mongol invasion, 1224, 1 year. 20,000 and 5%
or 1000.
Totals for the period: 495,000 and 16,000.

1226–1250.
——————— Mongol invasion into Russia (Batyi),
1237–1240, 4 years. 20,000 gives 80,000 and 5%
or 4000.
Expedition of Alexander Nevsky against Sweden and Livonian Knights, 1240, 1 year. 10,000
and 4% losses or 400.
The same, 1242, 1 year. 10,000 and 4% or 400.
Russo-Lithuanian War, 1226–1234, 9 years.
10,000 gives 90,000 and 3% or 2700.
Russo-Lithuanian War, 1245–1247, 3 years.
10,000 gives 30,000 and 3% losses or 900.
Totals for the period: 220,000 and 8400.

1251–1275.
——————— Russo-Lithuanian War, 1251–1252,
2 years. 10,000 gives 20,000 and 3% or 6000.
Russo-Lithuanian War, 1263, 1 year. 10,000
and 3% or 300.
Russo-Lithuanian War, 1274, 1 year. 10,000
and 3% or 300.
Totals for the period: 40,000 and 1200.

1276–1300.
——————— Russo-Lithuanian War, 1276–1277,
2 years. 15,000 gives 30,000 and 3% or 900 losses.
Russo-Lithuanian War, 1285–1286, 2 years.
15,000 or total 30,000 and 3% or 900.
Russo-Swedish War, 1295–1300, 6 years.
10,000 gives 60,000 and 3% or 1800.
Totals for the period: 120,000 and 3600.

1301–1325.
——————— Russo-Lithuanian War, 1320–1321,
2 years. 20,000 gives 40,000 and 4% or 1600.
Russo-Swedish War, 1301, 1 year. 20,000 and
4% or 800.
Russo-Swedish War, 1311–1313, 2 years.
20,000 gives 40,000 and 4% or 1600.
Russo-Swedish War, 1317–1318, 2 years.
20,000 gives a total strength of 40,000 and losses
at 4% or 1600.
Totals for the period: 140,000 and 5600.

1326–1350.

———————— Russo-Lithuanian War, 1346, 1 year. 20,000 and 4% or 800.

Russo-Swedish War, 1337–1338, 2 years. 20,000 gives 40,000 and 4% or 1600.

Russo-Swedish War, 1348–1350, 3 years. 20,000 gives 60,000 and 4% or 2400.

Totals for the period: 120,000 and 4800.

1351–1375.

———————— Russo-Lithuanian War, 1355–1359, 4 years. 20,000 gives 80,000 and 4% or 3200.

Expedition of Olguerd the Lithuanian against Russia, 1368–1372, 5 years. 20,000 gives 100,000 and 4% or 4000.

Tver War of Dmitri Donskoy, 1368–1375, 8 years. 20,000 gives 160,000 and 4% or 6400.

Totals for the period: 340,000 and 13,600.

1376–1400.

———————— War of Dmitri Donskoy against the Horde, Oleg of Riazan, and Yagailo the Lithuanian, 1376–1382, 7 years. 30,000 gives 210,000 and losses 5% or 10,500.

Russo-Lithuanian War, 1385, 1 year. 20,000 and 4% or 800.

Russo-Lithuanian War, 1395–1396, 2 years. 20,000 gives 40,000 and 4% or 1600.

Totals for the period: 270,000 and 12,900.

1401–1425.

———————— Russo-Lithuanian War with Vitoft, 1401–1408, 8 years. 20,000 gives 160,000 and 4% or 6400 losses.

Invasion of Edigey on Moscow, 1408, 1 year. 20,000 and 6% or 1200.

Totals for the period: 180,000 and 7600.

1426–1450.

———————— Russo-Lithuanian War, 1426–1428, 3 years. 20,000 gives 60,000 and 4% or 2400.

Russo-Lithuanian War, 1445, 1 year. 20,000 and 4% or 800.

Totals for the period: 80,000 and 3200.

1451–1475.

———————— Kazan Expedition of Ivan III, 1467–1469, 3 years. 30,000 gives 90,000 and 5% or 4500.

Novgorod War of Ivan III, 1471, 1 year, 45,000 (internal; Shelon battle, 1471, 40,000 Novgorodians, and 5000–8000 of Moscow armies, E III, 569) and 4% or 1800 losses.

(Several inner strifes and half-private suppressions made with quite insignificant forces are not included.)

Totals for the period: 135,000 and 6300.

1476–1500.

———————— Kazan Expedition of Ivan III, 1478, 1 year. 20,000 and 4% or 800.

Kazan Expedition of Ivan III, 1487, 1 year. 20,000 and 4% or 800.

Kazan Expedition of Ivan III, 1496, 1 year. 20,000 and 4% or 800.

Novgorod Expedition of Ivan III, 1477, 1 year. 20,000 and 4% or 800.

Overthrow of Mongolian yoke, 1480, 1 year. 20,000 and 4% or 800.

War of Ivan III with Lithuania and Livonian Order, 1482–1500, 19 years. 20,000 gives 380,000 and 4% or 15,200 losses.

Russo-Swedish War, 1496–1497, 2 years. 20,000 gives 40,000 and 4% or 1600.

Totals for the period: 520,000 and 20,800.

(See the note for 1451–1475.)

1501–1525.

———————— War of Ivan III with Lithuania and Livonian Order, 1501–1503, 3 years. 30,000 and 4% or 3600 from a total of 90,000 for the war.

War of Vassilii III with Kazan, 1506–1507, 2 years. 30,000 gives 60,000 and 4% or 2400 losses.

War of Vassilii III with Kazan, 1523–1524, 2 years. 30,000 gives 60,000 and 4% or 2400.

Lithuanian War of Vassilii III, 1507–1508, 2 years. 30,000 gives 60,000 and 4% or 2400.

Lithuanian War of Vassilii III, 1512–1522, 11 years. 30,000 gives 330,000 and 4% or 13,200 losses.

Crimean War of Vassilii III, 1515–1523, 9 years. 30,000 gives a total of 270,000 and losses at 4% gives 10,800.

Totals for the period: 870,000 and 34,800.

1526–1550.

———————— War of Vassilii III with Kazan, 1530, 1 year. 30,000 and 4% or 1200.

Russo-Lithuanian War, 1534–1537, 4 years (S IV, 584). 30,000 gives 120,000 and 4% or 4800.

War of Ivan IV with Kazan, 1550, 1 year. 30,000 and 4% or 1200.

Totals for the period: 180,000 and 7200.

(See the note for 1451–1475.)

1551–1575.

———————— War of Ivan IV with Kazan, 1551–1552, 2 years. 40,000 gives 80,000 and 5% or 4000.

War with Astrakhan, 1554, 1 year. 30,000 (E III, 577) and 4% or 1200.

War with Crimea, 1554–1559, 6 years. 13,000 (1555, 13,000, E III, 578) gives 78,000 and 4% or 3120.

Russo-Swedish War, 1554–1557, 4 years. 30,000 gives 120,000 and 4% or 4800.

Livonian War of Ivan IV, 1554–1564, 11 years. 30,000 gives 330,000 and 4% or 13,200.

War of Ivan IV with Poland and Sweden, 1563–1575, 13 years. 30,000 (E VI, 222) gives 390,000 and losses 8% (Assault of Pskov 7/VIII, 1581, 8%, E VI, 222) gives 31,200.

Totals for the period: 1,028,000 and 57,520.

(See the note for 1451–1475.)

1576–1600.

———————— War of Ivan IV with Poland and Sweden, 1576–1582, 7 years. 35,000 gives 245,000 and 5% or 12,250.

War with Sweden, 1590–1593, 4 years. 30,000 gives 120,000 and 4% or 4800.

Invasion of Crimean Tartars, 1591, 1 year. 30,000 and 4% or 1200.

Totals for the period: 395,000 and 18,250.

(See the note for 1451–1475.)

1601–1625.

———————— Internal Wars of the "Time of Troubles," 1604–1612, 9 years. 60,000 (three different fronts, internal and external in nature, E VII, 243–246; E II, 473) gives 540,000 and 5% or 27,000.

War with Sweden, 1614–1617, 4 years. 40,000 gives 160,000 and 5% or 8000.

War with Poland, 1617–1618, 2 years. 40,000 gives 80,000 and 5% or 4000.

Totals for the period: 780,000 and 39,000.

1626–1650.

———————— War with Poland, 1632–1634, 3 years. 67,000 (up to 67,000, E VI, 110–111) gives 201,000 and losses 5% or 10,050.

War with Crimea, 1632–1641, 10 years. 6000 (Asov, 1640, 6000, E I, 88) gives 60,000 and 5% or 3000.

First Northern War, 1650, 1 year. 20,000 and 5% or 1000. (The participation of Russia was slight.)

Totals for the period: 281,000 and 14,050.

1651–1675.

———————— First Northern War, 1651–1660, 10 years. 20,000 (Volkovysk 18/VI, 1657, 10,000, B 84; see the preceding remark) gives 200,000. Losses 5% (Volkovysk 33%, B 84; the per cent of losses at Volkovysk cannot be considered as typical for the whole war) gives 10,000.

First Polish-Russian War for "Little Russia," 1654–1655, 2 years. 40,000 gives 80,000 and 5% or 4000.

Second Polish-Russian War for "Little Russia," 1658–1677, 9 years. 40,000 gives 360,000 and 5% or 18,000.

Razin's Mutiny, 1667–1670, 4 years. 60,000 (internal) gives 240,000 and 5% or 12,000 losses.

Totals for the period: 880,000 and 44,000.

1676–1700.

———————— War with Doroshenko and Turkey, 1676–1678, 3 years. 40,000 gives 120,000 and 5% or 6000.

Crimean Expedition of Prince Golitzin, 1687, 1 year. 40,000 and 5% or 2000.

The same, 1689, 1 year. 40,000 and 5% or 2000.

Azoff Expedition of Peter I, 1695–1696, 2 years. 45,000 (1695, 35,000, 1696, up to 54,000, E I, 89) gives 90,000 and 5% or 4500.

War with China on the Amur River, 1689, 1 year. 10,000 and 2% or 200.

Second Northern War, 1700, 1 year. 47,000 (Narva 30/XI, 1700, 40,000, B 123; the figure is an average of the figures for the whole war, battles at Narva and Poltava) and losses 15% (Narva 20%, B 123) or 7050.

Totals for the period: 347,000 and 21,750.

1701–1725.

———————— Second Northern War (continued), 1701–1721, 21 years. 100,000 (four different fronts for the war; Poltava 9/VII, 1709, 54,000, B 159) gives 2,100,000 and losses 15% (Poltava 9.5%, B 159) or 315,000.

Expedition to Pruth River, 1711, 1 year. 40,000 (Falchi 27/VII, 1711, 40,000, B 165) and losses 5% (Falchi 5%, B 165) or 2000.

Persian War, 1722–1723, 2 years. 40,000 (86,000, E V, 605; an average figure for the wars of Peter the Great is accepted because the figure of 86,000 is evidently exaggerated) gives 80,000 and losses 5% or 4000.

Expedition of Prince Bekhovitch-Tcherkasky to Khiva, 1716–1717, 2 years. 20,000 gives 40,000 and 5% or 2000.

Totals for the period: 2,260,000 and 323,000.

1726–1750.

———————— War for the Polish Succession, 1733–1735, 3 years. 20,000 (the participation of Russia in this war was of secondary significance, and with France, Russia in reality did not fight at all) gives 60,000 total strength and losses at 5% or 3000.

Russo-Austro-Turkish War, 1736–1739, 4 years. 57,000 (Stavuchani 28/VIII, 1739, 60,000, B 187; Perekop 2/VI, 1736, 54,000, B 183; Ochakov 12/VII, 1737, 60,000, B 185) gives 228,000 and losses 7% (Ochakov 6.6%) or 15,960.

Russo-Swedish War, 1741–1743, 3 years. 70,000 (Helsingfors 4/IX, 1742, 60,000, B 193; total up to 114,000, E III, 334) gives 210,000 and 5% or 10,500 losses.

Totals for the period: 498,000 and 29,460.

1751–1775.

———————— Seven Years' War, 1756–1762, 6 years. 100,000 (two fronts, in East Prussia the army up to 100,000, E VII, 142–167; Gr. Jagersdorf, 1757, 55,000, B 220; Zorndorf 25/VIII, 1758, 52,000, B 227; Kunersdorf 12/VIII, 1759, 52,000, B 232) gives 600,000 and losses 23% (Gr. Jagersdorf 11%, B 220; Zorndorf 34.6%, B 227; Kunersdorf 22.9%, B 232) or 138,000.

Russo-Turkish War and War against Polish Confederates, 1768–1774, 7 years. 80,000 (four different fronts; Kagul 21/VII, 1770, 40,000, B 251; Perekop 15/VI, 1771, 32,000, B 252; Siege of Silistria 18–30/VI, 1773, 50,000, B 253; Larga 4/VII, 1770, 40,000, B 250; Chesma, naval, 1770, 7000, B 251) gives 560,000. Losses 5% (Kagul 2.5%, B 251; Chesma, naval, 7%, B 251) gives 28,000.

Pugatcheff's Mutiny, 1773–1774, 2 years. 50,000 (internal; Pugatcheff's army up to 15,000, 1773, E VI, 224) gives 100,000 and 5% or 5000. (The significance of this mutiny is near to a war of an average strain.)

Totals for the period: 1,260,000 and 171,000.

1776–1800.

———————— Russo-Austro-Turkish War, 1787–1791, 5 years. 110,000 (two different fronts; general strength of Russian armies up to 155,000, E VI, 603–606; Machin 10/VII, 1791, 36,000, B 268; Ochakov 17/XII, 1788, 90,000, B 264; Ismail 22/XII, 1790, 32,000, B 267) gives 550,000 and losses 33% (Ochakov 35%, B 264; Ismail 31.5%, B 267) or 181,500.

Russo-Swedish War, 1788–1790, 3 years. 22,000 (Viborg, 1790, naval, 26,000, B 266;

14,000–20,000, E VII, 55) gives 66,000 and losses 4% (Viborg, naval, 4%, B 266) or 2640.

Polish Insurrection, 1792–1794, 3 years. 17,000 (Maciejowice 10/X, 1794, 12,000, B 300; Assault of Prague 4/XI, 1794, 22,000, B 300) gives 51,000 and losses 8% (Assault of Prague 8%, B 300) or 4080.

Russo-Persian War, 1796, 1 year. 43,000 (E V, 605) and 5% or 2150.

Second Coalitional War, 1798–1800, 3 years. 60,000 (three different fronts, 17,000 in the Netherlands, 65,000 in Italy, 24,000 in Switzerland, not quite simultaneously, E I, 154–160; III, 536–544; VIII, 339–343; Trebbia 17–20/VI, 1799, 17,000, B 337; Novi 15/VIII, 1799, 15,500, B 340; Zurich 25–26/IX, 1799, 23,000, B 339; Bergen 19/IX, 1799, 23,000 English and Russians, B 340) gives 180,000 and losses 21% (Trebbia 13.5%, B 337; Novi 14%, B 340; Zurich 26.5%, B 339; Bergen 9.5%, B 340) or 37,800.

Totals for the period: 890,000 and 228,170.

1801–1825.

————— Second Coalitional War (continuation), 1801, 1 year. 30,000 and 21% or 6300.

Third Coalitional War, 1805, 1 year. 100,000 (two fronts, 116,000 in Bohemia, 13,000 in Naples, E I, 61–77; Austerlitz 2/XII, 1805, 67,000, B 369) and losses 19% (Austerlitz, 19.3%, B 396) or 19,000.

Against France, 1806–1807, 2 years. 110,000 (two fronts, 122,000 in East Prussia and 22,000 in Ionic Islands, E II, 280, and I, 77–79; Preussisch-Eylau 8/II, 1807, 74,500, B 380; Friedland 14/VI, 1807, 61,000, B 383) gives 220,000 and losses at 33% (Preussisch-Eylau 27.7%, B 380; Friedland 33%, B 383) or 68,200.

English-Russian War, 1807–1812. (There were no armed conflicts of any significance.)

Swedish-Russian War, 1808–1809, 2 years. 20,000 (Orowais 5/IX, 1808, 7700, B 390; the figure is increased in accordance with the Russian-Swedish War of 1788–1790, because the battle at Orowais is not typical) gives 40,000 and 14% losses (Orowais 14%, B 390) or 5600.

Russo-Turkish War, 1806–1812, 7 years. 80,000 (two fronts, 80,000 in Moldavia, 40,000 in Caucasus, E IV, 615–625; Bazardjik 3/VI, 1810, 23,000, B 417; Batin 7/IX, 1810, 22,000, B 419) or 560,000 and losses 8% (Bazardjik 7%, B 417; Batin 9%, B 419) or 44,800.

"Fatherland War," 1812, 1 year. 150,000 (Borodino 7/IX, 1812, 122,000, B 438) and losses 27% (Smolensk 17–18/VIII, 1812, 10% and Borodino 42.6%, B 438) or 40,500.

War of 1813–1814, 2 years. 300,000 (Bautzen 20–21/V, 1813, 66,000, B 450; Leipzig 16, 18–19/X, 1813, 122,000, B 461; Craonne 7/III, 1814, 100,000 Russians and Prussians, B 476; Laon 9–10/III, 1814, 46,000, Z 58) gives 600,000 total strength for the war. Losses totaled 145,000 (L 46–47; Bautzen 11.3%, B 450; Leipzig 22.8%, B 461; Craonne 22%, B 476; Laon 8.2%, Z 58).

"One Hundred Days' War," 1815. Russian army did not participate in the armed conflict.

Russo-Persian War, 1803–1813, 11 years. 30,000 (the general strength of the entire Caucasian Army, which acted principally against the Persians, reached, in 1809, 43,000, S XI, 224; for this reason, whereas the number of real fighters could not be more than half of the shown strength, the figure is taken as 30,000) gives 330,000. The losses at 8% (the assault of Lenkoran presents an exception, general percentage of losses was much lower, and for that reason a normal figure is taken near to the Turkish War of 1806–1812) gives 26,400 (Lenkoran 25/XII, 1812, 56%, S XIV, 587).

Caucasian War, 1816–1825, 10 years. 10,000 (average strength of the detachments was not more than 10,000, S XI, 226–228) gives 100,000 and losses 5% or 5000.

Totals for the period: 2,130,000 and 360,800.

1826–1850.

————— Russo-Persian War, 1826–1828, 3 years. 30,000 (the figures are taken near to the Russo-Persian War of 1803–1813) gives 90,000 and 8% or 7200.

Caucasian War, 1826–1850, 25 years. 41,000 (Chechnia, 1832, 11,000, S XI, 230; general strength, 1837, 85,000, S XI, 232; detachment of Grabbe's, 1842, up to 25,000, S XI, 234; 1844 expedition 44 batteries, S XI, 234) gives 1,025,000. Losses 7% (losses of Grabbe's detachment 7%, S XI, 234) or 71,750.

Russo-Turkish War, 1828–1829, 2 years. 100,000 (a simultaneous war with Turkey on European and Caucasian theaters is taken into consideration, in the Balkans 100,000, in Caucasus 30,000, E VII, 1–9; Akhalzik 22–27/VIII, 1828, 10,000, B 494; Siege of Brailow 11/V–18/VI, 1828, 17,000, B 495; Kulevcha 11/VI, 1829, 28,000, B 496) gives 200,000 and losses 18% (Akhalzik 16%, B 494; Varna 30%, B 495; Kulevcha 9%, B 496) or 36,000.

Polish Insurrection, 1830–1831, 2 years. 80,000 (Grochow 25/II, 1831, 80,000, B 497; Warsaw 6–7/IX, 1831, 78,000, B 498) or 160,000 or losses 13% (Grochow 12.5%, B 497; Ostrolenka 26/V, 1831, 13.9%, Z 59) or 20,800.

Expedition of Gen. Perovsky to Khiva, 1839–1840, 2 years. 4000 (E VIII, 219) gives 8000 and losses 1% (less than 1%, E VIII, 219) or 80.

War in Central Asia, 1842–1850, 9 years. 7000 gives 63,000 and 3% or 1890 (the figures are averages of the army and losses during the whole war in the central part of Asia, 1851–1875 and 1876–1884).

Hungarian War, 1849, 1 year. 30,000 (Komorn 2/VII, 1849, 51,000 Austrians and Russians, B 509) gives 30,000 and losses 2% (Komorn 1.8%, B 509) or 600.

Totals for the period: 1,576,000 and 138,320.

1851–1875.

————— Central Asian War, 1851–1875, 25 years. 7000 (expedition to Kokand, 1875–1876, 1400, detachment of Trotzky, 2800, detachment of Scobeleff at Andijan, E IV, 295–296; expedition to Khiva, 1873, 17,500, E VIII, 213) gives 175,000. Losses 1% (Kokand expedition, 1875–

1876, losses less than 1%, E IV, 295–296; Khiva expedition, 1873, losses less than 1%, E VIII, 217) or 1750.

Caucasian War, 1851–1864, 14 years. 60,000 (detachments of Gen. Evdokimov, 1860, up to 80,000, S XI, 240; Gunib, against Shamil in 1859 up to 40,000, S XI, 239–240) gives 840,000 and losses 7% or 58,800.

"Eastern War," 1853–1856, 4 years. 200,000 (four fronts, 120,000 in Crimea, up to 90,000 in Moldavia, 39,000 in Caucasus, E II, 300–322; Silistria, 1854, up to 90,000, E II, 305; Crimea, 1854, up to 50,000, E II, 311; Crimea IX, 1854, 64,000, E II, 315; all together, 1855, in Crimea, 120,000, E II, 316–317; on the Caucasian front, 1854, up to 40,000, E II, 320) gives 800,000 and losses 18% (Alma 17.3%, Z 61; Inkerman 24.4%, Z 61; Chernaia River 13.1%, Z 61; general losses 128,000, E II, 319) gives 144,000.

Polish Insurrection, 1863–1864, 2 years. 45,000 (all together up to 195,000, E VI, 100–110; average strength of the army 45,000, E VI, 102) gives 90,000 and losses 2.3% (general losses 4500, E VI, 100–110) or 2070.

Totals for the period: 1,905,000 and 206,620.

1876–1900.

———— Russo-Turkish War, 1877–1878, 2 years. 300,000 (two fronts, 310,000 in Bulgaria, 50,000 in Caucasus, E VI, 29 and 49; average strength of the army IV, 1877, 135,000; 1/VIII, 1877, 220,000; 2/XII, 1877, 340,000, Z 41) gives 600,000 and losses 11% (Kars 8.3%, B 577; third Plevna 16.7%, B 575; Sheinovo 9%, B 579) or 66,000.

Central Asiatic War, 1876–1884, 9 years. 8000 (Akhal-Teke's Expedition, 1877–1879, up to 10,600, S III, 382–386; Akhal-Teke's Expedition, 1880–1881, 7000, S III, 283–286) gives 72,000 total and losses 5% (assault of Geok-Tepe 20/XII, 1880, 5%, S III, 283–286) or 3600.

Boxers' Revolt, 1900, 1 year. 60,000 (12/X, 1900, 13,000 in China and up to 100,000 in Manchuria, S IV, 614–622) and total losses 2000

(S IV, 614–622, and general losses not more than 2000, S IV, 614–622).

Totals for the period: 732,000 and 71,600.

1901–1925.

———— Boxers' insurrection, 1901–1902, 2 years. 60,000 gives 120,000 (1 to 2% losses, 1000 in 1901).

Russo-Japanese War, 1904–1905, 2 years. 250,000 (Liauyang 25/VIII–3/IX, 1904, 150,000, B 597; Mukden 1–10/III, 1905, 310,000, B 599; Tsushima, naval, 27–28/V, 1905, 16,000, B 600) gives 500,000 and losses 170,000, at 34% (Liauyang 11%, B 597; Mukden 23%, B 599; Tsushima, naval, 70%, B 600).

World War, 1914–1919, 4 years. Average for the army, 4,000,000 and total 15,000,000 (see USSR Central Statistical Bureau, Department of Military Statistics, *Russia in the World War* (Moscow, 1925); general strength of the army 1/X, 1914, 2,700,000; 15/V, 1915, 3,900,000; 1/II, 1916, 6,200,000; 1/IX, 1917, 6,000,000, G 107–112). Total losses 5,500,000 (mobilized 15,500,000, G 94–97, *i.e.*, per cent of losses 35). See also Russian Historical Commission, *La grand guerre. Relation de l'État-Major Russe* (French trans. Paris, 1927). Here again the discrepancies between various official data are very considerable, but do not change appreciably the results, whichever of the variants is taken.

(Civil) Internal war of 1918–1920, 3 years. Average strength for both sides was 700,000 and the total for both sides 2,000,000 (Red Army in I, 1919, 800,000, in 1920, 5,500,000, of these in reality on the fighting front were not more than 581,000, Gr I; White Army strength on the average about 300,000). Total losses for both sides 700,000 (the percentage of losses, about 35, because of entire absence of statistics, cannot be exactly estimated; most of the casualties were from sickness; average figure of the losses in the World War is taken because the losses of Russia during the civil war were very high).

Totals for the period: 17,620,000 and 6,371,000.

ENGLAND [1]

1051–1075.

———— Conquest by the Normans (William the Conqueror), 1066, 1 year. 5000 (Hastings 14/X, 1066, 4000–7000, D III, 153) and losses — unusually high — 10% or 500.

War with France, 1068, 1 year. 1000 strength and losses 5% or 50.

Totals for the period: 6000 and 550.

1076–1100.

———— No important wars recorded.

[1] Meaning of abbreviations in the tables:
CO — C. W. Oman, *Wellington's Army* (London, 1912).
D — as before.
F — J. W. Fortescue, *History of the British Army* (London, 1899).
En — as before.
S — as before.
B — G. Bodart, *Militär-historisches Kriegslexikon*.
M — J. E. Morris, *The Welsh Wars of Edward I* (Oxford, 1901).
Z — as before.
L — G. Bodart, *Losses*.
GB — G. E. Bertin, *L'effort britannique de 1914 à 1918* (Paris, 1924).
R — Sir W. Robertson, *Conduite générale de la Guerre 1914–1918* (Paris, 1929).
E — as before.
MS — T. Mitchell and G. Smith, *Medical Services. Casualties and Medical Statistics of the Great War*, History of the Great War (official) (London, 1931).
Other works cited in this Appendix.

1101–1125.

——————— War with France, 1106–1125, 20 years. 500 (Brémule 500, 20/VIII, 1119, D III, 412) gives 10,000 and losses 1% (less than 1%, D III, 412) or 100.

Totals for the period: 10,000 and 100.

1126–1150.

——————— War with France, 1126–1128, 3 years. 5000 gives 15,000 and 2% losses or 300.

War with Scotland, 1136–1138, 3 years. 10,000 gives 30,000 and losses 2% or 600.

Internal War of Stephen and Mathilda, 1138–1148 and 1149–1150, 13 years. 10,000 for both sides gives 130,000 and 2% or 2600 losses.

Totals for the period: 175,000 and 3500.

1151–1175.

——————— Internal War of Stephen and Mathilda, 1152–1153, 2 years. 10,000 for both sides gives 20,000 and 2% or 400.

First Welsh War, 1158, 1 year. 10,000 for both sides and 2% or 200.

Second Welsh War, 1163, 1 year. 12,000 for both sides and 2% or 240.

Third Welsh War, 1165, 1 year. 15,000 and 2% or 300.

War with Ireland, 1169–1172, 4 years. 10,000 for both sides gives 40,000 and losses 2% gives 800.

Insurrection of Prince Henry, 1173–1174, 2 years. 10,000 or a total strength of 20,000, and 2% losses or 400.

Totals for the period: 117,000 and 2340.

1176–1200.

——————— War with France, 1188–1189, 2 years. 5000 gives 10,000 and 2% or 200.

Third Crusade, Richard the Lion Hearted, 1190–1192, 3 years. 3000 (Ascalon 12/VIII, 1099, up to 10,200 crusaders, D III, 417) gives 9000 and 2% gives 180 losses.

War with France, 1194–1199, 7 years. 5000 gives 35,000 and 2% or 700.

Totals for the period: 54,000 and 1080.

1201–1225.

——————— War with France, 1202–1024, 3 years. 5000 gives 15,000 total and 2% losses or 300.

War with France, 1213–1214, 2 years. 3000 (Bouvines 27/VII, 1214, not more than 8000–10,000 allies, D III, 427) gives 6000 and 2% or 120.

War with France, 1215–1216, 1 year. 5000 and 5% or 250.

War with France, 1216–1217, 2 years. 5000 gives 10,000 and 4% or 400.

War with Wales, 1219–1223, 5 years. 8000 gives 40,000 and 2% or 800.

War with Wales, 1224, 1 year. 10,000 and 2% or 200.

War with France, 1223–1225, 3 years. 8000 gives 24,000 and 2% losses or 480.

Totals for the period: 110,000 and 2550.

1226–1250.

——————— War with Wales, 1228–1231, 4 years. 8000 gives 32,000 and 2% or 640 losses.

War with Wales, 1233–1234, 2 years. 8000 gives 16,000 and 2% or 320 losses.

War with Wales, 1241, 1 year. 10,000 and 2% or 200.

War with France, 1242–1243, 2 years. 7000 gives 14,000 and 2% or 280.

War with France, 1245, 1 year. 7000 and 2% or 140.

Totals for the period: 79,000 and 1580.

1251–1275.

——————— War with Wales, 1257, 1 year. 5000 and 2% or 100.

War with Wales, 1272–1275, 3 years. 10,000 gives 30,000 and 2% or 600.

War with France, 1259, 1 year. 9000 and 3% or 270.

Civil War of Simon de Montfort, 1263–1266, 4 years. 12,000 gives 48,000 and 2% or 960 losses. (The army's strength of 40,000–50,000, indicated by General G. Köhler, *Die Entwickelung des Kriegswesens und der Kriegsführung in der Ritterzeit von Mitte des II. Jahrhundert bis zu den Hussitenkriegen*, 3 pts. in 5 vols., 1886–1889; Oman, *A History of the Art of War*, London, 1893, p. 415, rightly considers "a hopeless exaggeration.")

War of Edward I with Wales, 1272–1275, 4 years. 16,000 (internal) gives 64,000 (army of Edward I had not more than 8000, D III, 404) and losses 5% or 3200.

Totals for the period: 156,000 and 5130.

1276–1300.

——————— War with Wales, 1276–1277, 2 years. 30,000 for both sides gives 60,000 (in 1277, 15,600, D III, 404). Losses at 2% or 1200.

War with France, 1294–1298, 5 years. 8000 gives 40,000 and 3% or 1200.

Subjugation of Scotland, 1296, 1 year. 14,000 (for both sides) and 2% or 280.

Scotch Wars, 1297–1300, 4 years. 25,000 for both sides gives 100,000 (average strength of the army 11,000, M I, 274; Falkirk 22/VII, 1298, 2400–7000, D III, 407–408) and losses 2% or 2000.

War with Wales, 1282–1288, 7 years. 18,000 (for both sides; in 1282, 3000–9400, D III, 404). Total 126,000 and losses 2% or 2520.

War with Wales, 1294–1295, 2 years. 20,000 for both sides makes 40,000 and losses 2% or 800.

Totals for the period: 380,000 and 8000.

1301–1325.

——————— Scotch War, 1301–1304, 4 years. 12,000 for both sides gives 48,000 and 2% losses or 960.

Scotch War, 1306–1307, 2 years. 12,000 for both sides gives 24,000 and losses 2% or 480.

Scotch War, 1310, 1 year. 10,000 for both sides and 2% or 200.

Scotch War, 1311–1323, 13 years. 25,000 for both sides gives 325,000 and losses 2% or 6500. (The strength of the army calculated by contemporaries of being 50,000–60,000, Professor Delbrück rightly considers "evidently exaggerated," D III, 448.)

Insurrection against Edward II, 1321–1322, 2 years. 10,000 for both sides gives 20,000 and 2% or 400.

War with France, 1324–1325, 2 years. 8000 gives 16,000 and 2% gives 320.

Totals for the period: 443,000 and 8860.

1326–1350.

———— War with France, 1326–1327, 2 years. 8000 gives 16,000 and 2% or 320.

Insurrection against Edward II, 1326–1327, 2 years: 10,000 for both sides gives 20,000 and 2% losses or 400.

War with Scotland, 1326–1328, 3 years. 12,000 for both sides gives 36,000 and 3% or 1080.

Hundred Years' War with France, 1339–1347, 9 years. 25,000 (2 fronts, E VII, 301–304; Crecy 26/VIII, 1346, 14,000–20,000, D III, 466; descent of Henry of Lancaster at Bayonne in 1345 with 3000, F 32; descent of Edward III at Cherbourg with 20,000, F 33) gives a total of 225,000 and losses 5% or 11,250.

Totals for the period: 297,000 and 13,050.

1351–1375.

———— Hundred Years' War with France, 1354–1360, 7 years. 20,000 (two fronts, E VII, 301–304) gives 140,000 and 5% or 7000 losses.

Continuation of Hundred Years' War, 1368–1375, 8 years. 20,000 gives 160,000 and 5% or 8000.

Intervention in Castile against France, 1366–1369, 4 years. 30,000 (up to 30,000, F 44) gives 120,000 and 5% or 6000.

Totals for the period: 420,000 and 21,000.

1376–1400.

———— Hundred Years' War with France (and Scotland), 1376–1389, 14 years. 25,000 makes 350,000 and 5% or 17,500 losses.

Great Revolt, 1381, 1 year. 80,000 for both sides and 3% or 2400.

War with Ireland, 1394, 1 year. 10,000 for both sides gives 10,000 total and 3% or 300 losses.

War with Ireland, 1399, 1 year. 10,000 and 3% or 300.

Lancaster Expedition, 1399, 1 year. 10,000 for both sides and 3% or 300.

Insurrection of Richard II, 1400, 1 year. 10,000 for both sides and 3% or 300.

Totals for the period: 470,000 and 21,100.

1401–1425.

———— Welsh Insurrection, 1401–1409, 9 years. 10,000 for both sides makes 90,000 total and 3% losses or 2700.

War with Scotland, 1402–1403, 2 years. 30,000 for both sides gives 60,000 and 5% or 3000.

Percy's uprising, 1403, 1 year. 10,000 for both sides and 3% or 300.

Conspiracy of Scrope, 1405, 1 year. 10,000 for both sides and 3% or 300.

Northumberland's uprising, 1408, 1 year. 10,000 for both sides and 3% or 300.

War with France, Hundred Years' War, 1411–1420, 10 years. 25,000 (two fronts; Agincourt 25/X, 1415, 9000, D III, 480; in 1417 Henry V made a descent in Normandy with an army of 17,000, E VIII, 501) makes 250,000 and 5% losses makes 12,500.

Continuation of the Hundred Years' War, 1421–1422, 2 years. 25,000 gives 50,000 and losses 5% or 2500.

Continuation of the Hundred Years' War, 1423–1425, 3 years. 25,000 gives a total of 75,000 strength and 5% losses gives 3750.

Totals for the period: 555,000 and 25,350.

1426–1450.

———— Hundred Years' War with France, 1426–1439, 14 years. 25,000 gives 350,000 for the war and 5% losses or 17,500.

Continuation of the Hundred Years' War, 1440–1444, 5 years. 25,000 gives 125,000 and 5% losses or 6250.

Continuation of the Hundred Years' War, 1449–1450, 2 years. 25,000 gives 50,000 and 5% gives 2500.

Totals for the period: 525,000 and 26,250.

1451–1475.

———— Hundred Years' War with France, 1451–1453 (end), 3 years. 25,000 gives 75,000 and 5% or 3750.

Wars of the Roses, 1455–1464, 10 years. 30,000 (St. Albans, 1455, 3000 and 2000 for each side, E IX, 558; 30,000 for both sides is taken because the battle at St. Albans is not typical for the whole war, being indicative only of its beginning (1st year) gives 300,000 and 5% losses or 15,000.

Continuation of the Wars of the Roses, 1469–1471, 3 years. 30,000 gives 90,000 and 5% or 4500.

War with France, 1475, 1 year. 15,000 and 5% or 750.

Totals for the period: 480,000 and 24,000.

1476–1500.

———— War with France, 1489–1492, 4 years. 15,000 gives 60,000 and 5% or 3000.

War with Scotland, 1480, 1 year. 30,000 for both sides and 5% or 1500.

War with Scotland, 1482–1484, 3 years. 30,000 gives 90,000 and 5% or 4500.

Campaign of Henry Tudor, 1485, 1 year. 30,000 for both sides and 5% or 1500.

Totals for the period: 210,000 and 10,500.

1501–1525.

———— War with France, 1512–1514, 3 years. 30,000 (army of Henry VIII up to 25,000, E VIII, 501) gives 90,000 and 5% or 4500.

War with France, 1521–1525, 5 years. 30,000 gives 150,000 and 5% or 7500 losses.

War with Scotland, 1513–1515, 3 years. 30,000 for both sides gives 90,000 and 5% or 4500 losses.

War with Scotland, 1522–1523, 2 years. 30,000 for both sides gives 60,000 and 5% gives 3000 for the losses.

Totals for the period: 390,000 and 19,500.

1526–1550.

———— War with Charles V, 1527–1529, 3 years. 30,000 gives 60,000 and 5% or 3000.

War with Scotland, 1532–1534, 3 years. 30,000 for both sides gives 90,000 and 5% losses or 4500.

War with Scotland, 1542–1546, 5 years. 30,000 makes 150,000 and 5% or 7500.

War with Scotland, 1547–1548, 2 years. 35,000 makes 70,000 and 5% or 3500.

War with Scotland, 1548–1550, 3 years. 35,000 gives 125,000 and 5% or 5250.

War with France, 1544–1546, 3 years. 30,000 (up to 30,000, S XI, 155) gives 90,000 and 5% losses or 4500.

War with France, 1548–1550, 3 years. 15,000 gives 45,000 and 5% or 2250.

War with Ireland, 1534–1535, 2 years. 30,000 for both sides gives 60,000 and 5% losses or 3000.

Insurrection in Devonshire, 1549, 1 year. 10,000 for both sides and 5% or 500.

Western Rebellion, 1549, 1 year. 15,000 for both sides and 5% or 750 losses.

Totals for the period: 695,000 and 34,750.

1551–1575.

———— War with France, 1557–1559, 3 years. 8000 (S XI, 156) gives 24,000 and 5% or 1200.

War with Scotland and France, 1559–1560, 2 years. 25,000 (partly internal) gives 50,000 and 7% losses or 3500.

War with France, 1562–1564, 3 years. 15,000 gives 45,000 and 5% or 2250.

Insurrection in Ulster, 1561–1567, 7 years. 10,000 for both sides gives 70,000 and 5% losses or 3500.

Insurrection in Northern England, 1569, 1 year. 10,000 for both sides and 4% or 400 losses.

Insurrection in Munster, 7 years. 10,000 gives 70,000 and 4% or 2800.

Totals for the period: 269,000 and 13,650.

1576–1600.

———— Insurrection in Munster, 1576–1583, 8 years. 10,000 makes 80,000 and 4% or 3200.

War with Spain ("Great Armada"), 1585–1600, 16 years. 20,000 makes 320,000 and 5% or 16,000.

Insurrection in Ulster, 1594–1600, 7 years. 10,000 gives 70,000 and 5% or 3500.

Totals for the period: 470,000 and 22,700.

1601–1625.

———— War with Spain ("Great Armada"), 1601–1604, 4 years. 20,000 gives 80,000 and 5% losses or 4000.

Insurrection in Ulster, 1601–1603, 3 years. 10,000 gives a total of 30,000 and 5% or 1500 losses.

Thirty Years' War (Intervention of England), 1624–1625, 2 years. 15,000 gives 30,000 and 5% losses or 1500.

War with Spain, 1625, 1 year. 20,000 and 5% or 1000.

Totals for the period: 160,000 and 8000.

1626–1650.

———— War with Spain, 1626–1630, 5 years. 20,000 gives 100,000 and 5% or 5000.

First "Bishop's War," 1639, 1 year. 10,000 for both sides and 4% losses or 400.

Second "Bishop's War," 1640, 1 year. 10,000 and 4% or 400.

Uprising of Ireland, 1641–1643, 3 years. 20,000 for both sides gives 60,000 total and 8% or 4800 losses.

Civil War, 1642–1650, 9 years. 50,000 (for both sides; Marston Moor 2/VIII, 1644, 20,000 of Parliamentary forces and 18,000 of the Royalists, B 71; Army of Cromwell not more than 20,000, D IV, 214; Dunbar 3/IX, 1650, 11,000, B 77). Total 450,000 and losses at 10% (Dunbar 9%, B 77) gives 45,000.

Uprising of Ireland, 1649–1650, 2 years. 25,000 for both sides gives 50,000 and 6% gives 3000.

Totals for the period: 680,000 and 58,600.

1651–1675.

———— Civil War, 1651, 1 year. 50,000 (for both sides; Worcester 31/IX, 1651, 28,000 Parliamentary and 16,000 King's, B 78) and losses 11% (Worcester losses of Parliamentary 3.5%, King's army 18.5%, B 78) gives 5500.

Uprising of Ireland, 1651–1652, 2 years. 25,000 for both sides gives 50,000 and 5% or 2500.

War with Netherlands, 1652–1655, 4 years. 15,000 (Scheveningen, naval, 1653, 17,000, B 82; La Hougue, 1653, 13,000, B 80) gives 60,000, and losses at 14% (Scheveningen 12%, B 82; La Hougue 15.5%, B 80) gives 8400.

War with Spain, 1655–1659, 5 years. 15,000 gives 75,000 and 10% losses gives 7500.

War with Netherlands, 1665–1667, 3 years. 30,000 (Lowestoff, 1665, 28,200, B 89; Lowestoff, naval, 1666, 23,000, B 89) gives 90,000 and losses 10% (Lowestoff 5.5%, naval, B 89; Lowestoff, naval, 14%, B 89) gives 9000.

War with Netherlands, 1672–1674, 3 years. 18,000 (Solebay, naval, 1672, 35,000 English and French, B 91) gives 54,000. Losses at 16% (Solebay 15.7%, B 92) gives 8640.

Totals for the period: 379,000 and 39,540.

1676–1700.

———— Third war with Louis XIV, 1688–1697, 10 years. 30,000 (2 fronts, E V, 365; La Hougue, naval, 1692, 40,000 English and Dutch, B 116; Cap Sao Vicente, naval, 1693, 15,000 English and Dutch, B 117; Neerwinden 29/VII, 1693, 50,000 English, Austrians, and Dutch, B 118) gives 300,000 and losses 18% (La Hougue, naval, 12.5%, B 116; Cap Sao Vicente 16%, B 117; Neerwinden 24%, B 118) or 54,000.

Totals for the period: 300,000 and 54,000.

1701–1725.

———— War for the Spanish Succession, 1701–1713, 13 years. 90,000 (4 fronts, E III, 402–404; Velez Malaga, naval, 1704, 18,000 English and Dutch, B 138; Ramillies 23/V, 1706, 60,000 English and Dutch, B 147; Almanza, 16,000 English, Dutch, and Portuguese, B 151; Oudenarde 11/VII, 1708, 90,000 English, Dutch, and Emperor's, B 154; Malplaquet 11/IX, 1709, 93,000 English, Dutch, and Emperor's, B 160) gives 1,170,000. Losses at 18% (Velez-Malaga 15.5%, B 138; Ramillies 8.4%, B 147; Almanza 25/IV, 1707, 31%, B 151; Oudenarde 6.7%, B 154; Malplaquet 27%, B 170) gives 210,600.

War of the "Quadruple Alliance," 1718–1720, 3 years. 20,000 gives 60,000 and 10% or 6000.

Great Northern War, 1720–1721, 2 years. 10,000 gives 20,000 and 5% losses or 1000.

War with the Pretender, 1715–1716, 2 years. 10,000 gives 20,000 and 5% or 1000.

Naval war with Sweden, 1715–1719, 5 years. 10,000 gives 50,000 and 5% or 2500.

Totals for the period: 1,320,000 and 226,000.

1726–1750.

—————— War for the Austrian Succession, 1743–1748, 6 years. 40,000 (two fronts, E I, 45–48; Lawfeldt 2/VII, 1747, 82,000 English and Austrians, B 211; Dettingen 27/VI, 1743, 35,000 English, Hannoverians, and Austrians, B 194) gives 240,000. Losses at 11% gives 26,400 (Lawfeldt 11%, B 211).

War with the Younger Pretender, 1745–1746, 2 years. 25,000 for both sides gives 50,000 (Culloden-Moor 27/IV, 1746, 10,000 English and 6000 Scots, B 200–250). Losses 5% gives 2500.

Totals for the period: 290,000 and 28,900.

1751–1775.

—————— Seven Years' War, 1755–1763, 8 years. 50,000 (four fronts, 40,000 in Germany, 14,000 in America, then in Africa and India, E VII, 142–147; Quiberon, naval, 1759, 14,000, B 236; Minden, 1759, 38,000 English and allies, B 231; Vellinghausen 15–16/VIII, 1761, 52,000 English and German allies, B 203–250) gives 400,000. Losses at 5% (Minden, 1759, 7.1%, B 231; Quiberon, naval, 1758, 2.2%, B 236) gives 20,000.

War in India, 1763–1765, 3 years. 15,000 gives 45,000 and 5% or 2250.

Sepoy Mutiny of 1764, 1 year. 15,000 and 5% or 750.

North American War, 1775, 1 year. 2000 (Bunker Hill, 1775, 2000, B 254) and 55% (Bunker Hill 55%, B 254) losses or 1100.

Totals for the period: 462,000 and 24,100.

1776–1800.

—————— First Mahratta War, 1778–1781, 3 years. 15,000 gives 45,000 and 5% or 2250.

North American (and with France), 1776–1783, 8 years. 17,000 (Long Island 27/VIII, 1776, 25,000, B 254; Dominica, naval, 1782, 21,000, B 261; Yorktown 19/X, 1781, 6000, B 255–263) gives 136,000 and losses at 3% (Long Island, 1.3%, B 254; Dominica, naval, 5.3%, B 261) gives 4080.

War with Netherlands, 1780–1784, 5 years. 15,000 gives 75,000 and 5% losses or 3750.

Revolutionary, with France, 1793–1800, 8 years. 25,000 (3 fronts, 15,000 in the Netherlands, 8000 in Ireland, E VI, 270–284; Bergen 19/IX, 1799, 23,000 English and Russians, B 339; Quessant, naval, 1794, 17,000, B 290; Kamperdouin, naval, 2/X, 1797, 9400, B 322) gives 200,000.

Losses 9% (Bergen 9.5%, B 339; Quessant, naval, 7%, B 290; Aboukir, naval, 1–2/VIII, 1789, 10.6%, L 108; Kamperdouin, naval, 10.6%, B 322) gives 18,000.

First Mysore War, 1782–1784, 3 years. 15,000 gives 45,000 and 5% or 2250 losses.

Second Mysore War, 1790–1792, 3 years. 15,000 gives 45,000 and 5% or 2250.

Totals for the period: 446,000 and 32,580.

1801–1825.

—————— Revolutionary War, with France, 1801–1802, 2 years. 13,000 gives 26,000 and 9% or 2340.

War with France, 1803–1814, 12 years. 35,000 (2 fronts, E III, 393; La Coruna 16/I, 1809, 15,000, B 393; Talavera de la Reina 27–28/VIII, 1809, 54,000 English and Spaniards, B 410; Albuera 16/V, 1811, 32,000 English, Spaniards, and Portuguese, B 425; Salamanca 22/VII, 1812, 46,000 English and Portuguese, B 432; Vittoria 21/VI, 1813, 80,000 English, Spaniards, and Portuguese, Z 53. In 1809 the English Army in Spain 21,000, CO 164. On the Spanish theater up to 2/5 of the English Army under Wellington consisted of Portuguese, CO 229; Trafalgar 21/X, 1805, naval, 16,000, B 366) gives 420,000. Losses at 12% (La Coruna 6.6%, B 393; Talavera de la Reina 11.1%, B 393; Albuera 21.9%, B 425; Salamanca 11.3%, B 432; Trafalgar, naval, 10.7%, B 366; general losses of the English Army in 1813, 25,000, and in 1814, 15,000, L 46–47) or 50,400.

"One Hundred Days' War," 1815, 1 year. 35,000 (Waterloo 18/VI, 1815, 35,300 from which 11,300 were Hannoverian, B 487) and losses 30% (Waterloo 29.9%, B 487) or 10,500.

War with Denmark, 1801, 1 year. 8000 (Copenhagen, naval, 1808, 8000, B 360) and losses 15% (Copenhagen, naval, 15%, B 360) or 1200.

War with Sweden, 1810–1812. There was no real fighting.

War with Russia, 1807–1812. There was no real fighting.

United States of America, 1812–1815, 4 years. 5000 (Lundy's Lane 25/VII, 1814, 5000, B 484) gives 20,000, and losses 18% (Lundy's Lane 18%, B 484) gives 3600.

Second Mahratta War, 1802–1806, 5 years. 15,000 gives 75,000 and 5% or 3750.

Sepoy Revolt, 1806, 1 year. 15,000 and 5% or 750.

Goorkha War, 1814–1817, 4 years. 15,000 gives 60,000 and 5% or 3000.

Third Mahratta War, 1817–1818, 2 years. 15,000 gives 30,000 and losses 5% or 1500.

First Burma War, 1824–1825, 2 years. 15,000 gives 30,000 and 5% or 1500.

Ashanti War, 1824–1825, 2 years. 500 (Essamako 21/I, 1824, 500, E II, 505) gives 1000 and 5% or 50.

Totals for the period: 720,000 and 78,590.

1826–1850.

—————— First Burma War, 1826, 1 year. 15,000 and 5% or 750.

Intervention in Portugal, 1826, 1 year. 10,000 and 2% or 200.

War with Turkey, 1827, 1 year. 3000 (Navarin 20/X, 1827, 8000 English, French, and Russians, B 492) and 9% losses (Navarin 8.8%, B 492) gives 270.

Intervention in Netherlands, 1832, 1 year. 10,000 and 2% or 200.

War with Afghanistan, 1838–1842, 5 years. 4000 (E XII, 195) and a total of 20,000 with 5% losses or 1000.

War with China, 1840–1842, 3 years. 15,000 gives 45,000 and 5% or 2250.

Egyptian insurrection, 1840–1841, 2 years. 10,000 gives 20,000 and 2% or 400.

Sikh's Wars, 1843–1849, 7 years. 3000 (Miani, 1843, 3000, E XII, 195) gives 21,000 and 5% losses or 1050.

Intervention in Uruguay, 1845, 1 year. 10,000 and 2% or 200.

Intervention in Argentine, 1845–1846, 2 years. 10,000 gives 20,000 and 2% losses or 400.

Totals for the period: 174,000 and 6720.

1851–1875.

———— Kaffir War, 1851–1852, 2 years. 10,000 gives 20,000 and 2% or 400.

Second Burma War, 1852–1853, 2 years. 15,000 gives 30,000 and 5% or 1500.

War with Russia, 1854–1856, 3 years. 50,000 (2 fronts, 22,000 on the Baltic, 22,000 on the Black Sea, plus other regions, E II, 300–322; Inkerman 5/XI, 1856, 16,000, B 516; average strength of the English Army IX, 1854, 26,000; XI, 1854, 23,000; V, 1855, 32,000, Z 35) gives 150,000. Losses at 18.3% (Inkerman 23%, L 141; general total number of fighters in the English Army 98,000, L 142; general losses 18,000, Z 35, i.e., 18.3%) gives 27,450.

War with Persia, 1856–1857, 2 years. 10,000 gives 20,000 and 2% or 400.

War with China, 1856–1860, 5 years. 15,000 gives 75,000 and 5% or 3750.

Mutiny of the Sepoys in India, 1857–1858, 2 years. 15,000 gives 30,000 and 5% or 1500.

Ashanti War, 1863–1864, 2 years. 10,000 gives 20,000 and 2% or 400.

Maori War, 1863–1869, 7 years. 10,000 gives 70,000 and 2% or 1400.

War with Abyssinia, 1867–1868, 2 years. 10,000 gives 20,000 total strength and 2% losses or 400.

Ashanti War, 1874, 1 year. 2400 (2400, E II, 505) and 2% or 48.

Totals for the period: 437,400 and 37,248.

1876–1900.

———— War with Afghanistan, 1878–1880, 3 years. 15,000 gives 45,000 and 5% or 2250.

Zulu War, 1879, 1 year. 13,000 (13,200, En XXIII, 992) and 2% losses (White Umfolosi 2%, En XXIII, 993) gives 260.

War in Transvaal, 1880–1881, 2 years. 1700 (1881, 1400–2000, En XXII, 425) gives 3400 and 50% losses (Majuba 27/II, 1881, up to 50%, En XXII, 425) or 1700.

War of the Sudan, 1881–1885, 5 years. 30,000 and 5% or 1500.

Occupation of Egypt, 1882–1884, 3 years. 15,000 gives 45,000 and 5% or 2250.

Third Burma War, 1885–1889, 5 years. 15,000 gives 75,000 and 5% or 3750.

Ashanti War, 1895–1896, 2 years. 10,000 gives 20,000 and 2% or 400.

War of the Sudan, 1896–1899, 4 years. 15,000 gives 60,000 and 5% or 3000.

Intervention in Crete, 1897–1898, 2 years. 10,000 gives 20,000 and 2% or 400.

Boer War, 1899–1900, 2 years. 10,000 (Lady Smith 30/X, 1899, 9500, B 586; Maggersfontein 11/XII, 1899, 11,500, B 586) gives 20,000 and losses 11% (Lady Smith 13.9%, B 586; Maggersfontein 8.9%, B 586) or 2200.

Boxers' insurrection, 1900, 1 year. 8000 (IX, 1900, 8300, S IV, 614–622) and 1% (losses less than 1%) or 80.

Totals for the period: 339,400 and 17,790.

1901–1925.

———— Boer War, 1901–1902 (continuation), 2 years. 100,000 (up to 100,000) gives 200,000 and 11% losses or 22,000.

Tibet Expedition, 1903–1904, 2 years. 10,000 gives 20,000 and 1% or 200.

Somali War, 1901–1902, 2 years. 15,000 gives 30,000 and 2% or 600.

On the Northwestern boundary of India, 1908, 1 year. 15,000 (about 15,000, S II, 429) and 5% or 750.

World War, 1914–1918, 5 years. Average 1,500,000; French-Balkan front 1,400,000, Palestine 240,000, Mesopotamia 200,000, and Africa, naval, and other fronts, R. Total strength, 7,500,000 (1914, 160,000, En XXIII, 750; XI, 1916, 1,200,000, En XXIII, 766; 11/XI, 1918, 2,100,000 on the fronts, En X, 681) Total losses 3,070,000 (altogether 9,490,000 entered into army and fleet; general losses 3,070,000 or 32.3%, GB 29, with reference to the written statement by the Honorable S. Baldwin. MS as an official volume, gives similar though not identical data, pp. 2–7 and 12. Similar but not quite the same figures are given in *War Office Statistics of the Military Effort of the British Empire*, 1914–1920 (London, 1922). For my purposes any of these figures, however, can be accepted. The gross results will be the same.

Afghan War, 1919, 1 year. 50,000 and 2% or 1000.

Totals for the period: 7,815,000 and 3,094,550.

AUSTRIA–HUNGARY [1]

951–975.
———————— Uprising of Henry II, Bavarian, 974, 1 year. 6000 (the figure is doubled for the internal character of the war) was the total strength, and the losses at 5% gives 300.
Totals for the period: 6000 and 300.

976–1000.
———————— Expedition against Lothaire, 978, 1 year. 2000 (981 strength of the imperial army not more than 2080–2090 fighters, D III, 98) and losses at 5% gives 100.
Struggle with Saracens and Greeks in Italy, 982, 1 year. 3000 and losses at 5% gives 150.
Totals for the period: 5000 and 250.

1001–1025.
———————— No trustworthy data are available.

1026–1050.
———————— No trustworthy data are available.

1051–1075.
———————— Struggle of Henry IV with the Saxons, 1073–1075, 3 years. 3000 gives a total of 9000 for the war, and losses 5% or 450.
Struggle with Rudolf of Sweden, 1080, 1 year. 6000 and 5% losses or 300.
Conquest of Rome by Henry IV, 1084, 1 year. 3000 and 5% or 150.
Totals for the period: 18,000 and 900.

1076–1100.
———————— No data.

1101–1125.
———————— Struggle of Henry IV with his sons, Conrad and Henry, 1105, 1 year. 6000 (doubled because internal) and 5% losses or 300.
Uprising of the Saxons, 1120, 1 year. 3000 and 5% or 150.
Totals for the period: 9000 and 450.

1126–1150.
———————— Struggle of Conrad III with Henry the Proud and Henry the Lion, 1138–1142, 5 years. 6000 (internal; wars were not simultaneous) gives 30,000 and 5% or 1500 losses.
Second Crusade of Emperor Conrad III, 1147–1149, 3 years. 3000 gives 9000 and 5% or 450.
Totals for the period: 39,000 and 1950.

1151–1175.
———————— Expeditions of Frederic I Barbarossa: First Italian Expedition, 1154, 1 year. 3000 and 5% or 150.
Expedition to Poland, 1175, 1 year. 3000 and 5% or 150.
Second Italian Expedition, 1158–1162, 5 years. 3000 gives a total of 15,000 and 5% losses gives 750.

(Third Italian Expedition was without battles and losses.)
Fourth Italian Expedition, 1166–1168, 3 years. 3000 gives 9000 and 5% or 450.
Fifth Italian Expedition, 1174–1175, 2 years. 3000 gives 6000 and 5% or 300.
Totals for the period: 36,000 and 1800.

1176–1200.
———————— Fifth Italian Expedition, 1176–1178, 3 years. 3000 (Legnano, 1176, 3000–3500, D III, 357) gives 9000 and 5% or 450.
Third Crusade of Frederic Barbarossa, 1189–1191, 3 years. 3000 gives 9000 and 5% or 450.
Wars of Henry VI in Sicily and with Henry the Lion, 1190–1197, 8 years. 6000 (doubled, internal) gives 48,000 and 5% losses or 2400.
Totals for the period: 66,000 and 3300.

1201–1225.
———————— War with France, 1214, 1 year. 9000 (Bouvines 27/VII, 1214, 8000–10,000, D III, 427–428) and 5% losses or 450.
Crusade of the Hungarian King Andreas, 1217, 1 year. 3000 and 5% losses or 150.
Totals for the period: 12,000 and 600.

1226–1250.
———————— Fifth Crusade of Frederic II, 1228–1229, 2 years. 3000 gives 6000 and 5% or 300 losses.
Struggle of Frederic II Hogenstaufen with the Guelfs in Italy, 1237–1294, 13 years. 8000 (Cortenuova 27/XI, 1237, 10,000, D III, 362–363; Siege of Parma, 1247–1248, up to 5000, D III, 365) gives 104,000 and 5% or 5200.
Invasion of Batyi into Silesia, Moravia, and Hungary, 1240–1241, 2 years. 5000 gives 10,000 and 5% or 500.
Struggle of Conrad IV with Naples, 1250, 1 year. 3000 and 5% losses or 150.
Totals for the period: 123,000 and 6150.

1251–1275.
———————— War of Conrad IV with Naples, 1251–1254, 4 years. 3000 gives 12,000 and 5% or 600.
Expedition of Conrad into Lower Italy, 1268, 1 year. 5000 and 5% losses or 250.
Totals for the period: 17,000 and 850.

1276–1300.
———————— German–Bohemian, 1276–1278, Rudolf of Hapsburg with Ottocar of Bohemia, 3 years. 20,000 (doubled because internal; usually accepted figures: Marchfelde 2/VIII, 1278, up to 32,300 with Rudolf of Hapsburg and up to 30,000 with Ottocar of Bohemia; trustworthy are, however, participation on Rudolf's side 2300 and some number of Hungarians, while Ottocar has

[1] Abbreviated references in the tables mean:
D — as before.
B — G. Bodart, *Militär-historisches Kriegslexikon*, quoted.
L — G. Bodart, *Losses*.
S — as before.
E — as before.
Other sources indicated in the detailed data throughout this Appendix.

c. 6500 plus some amount of militia, D III, 433) gives 60,000 and 5% or 3000.

War of Emperor Rudolf of Hapsburg with Eberhardt of Wurtemberg, 1286, 1 year. 6000 (doubled, internal) and 5% or 300.

Totals for the period: 66,000 and 3300.

1301–1325.

———— Swiss-Austrian War, 1308–1318, 10 years. 2000 (Morgarten, 1315, 2000, D III, 572) gives 20,000 and 10% or 2000.

Bavarian-Austrian War, 1322, 1 year. 6000 (doubled, internal) and 10% or 600.

Totals for the period: 26,000 and 2600.

1326–1350.

———— Swiss-Austrian War, 1339, 1 year. 2000 and 10% or 200.

Totals for the period: 2000 and 200.

1351–1375.

———— No data.

1376–1400.

———— Swiss-Austrian War, 1386, 1 year. 3500 (Sempach, 1386, 3000–4000, D III, 591) and 5% or 175.

South-German Municipal War, 1377–1389, 13 years. 5000 (doubled, internal; Doffingen, 1388, 2000–3000 on each side, D III, 603) gives 65,000 and 5% losses or 3250.

Hungarian-Turkish War, 1396, 1 year. 7000 (Nikopol 25/IX, 1396, about 6500–7500, D III, 492) and 5% or 350.

Totals for the period: 75,500 and 3775.

1401–1425.

———— Hussite Wars, 1419–1425, 7 years. 2000 gives 14,000 and 10% or 1400.

The Templars with Poland and Lithuania, 1410, 1 year. 11,000 (Tannenberg 15/VII, 1410, 11,000, D III, 539) and 10% or 1100.

Totals for the period: 25,000 and 2500.

1426–1450.

———— Hussite Wars, 1426–1436, 11 years. 20,000 (Aussig, 1426, 12,000 Hussites, D III, 513; Glatz, 1428, 15,000 on each side, D III, 513) gives 220,000 and 10% or 22,000.

Turkish-Greek-Hungarian Wars, Hunyadi, 1444, 1 year. 11,000 and 10% or 1000.

Turkish-Hungarian War, Hunyadi, 1448, 1 year. 10,000 and 10% or 1000.

Totals for the period: 240,000 and 24,000.

1451–1475.

———— War with Turkey, 1454–1456, 10,000, 3 years. 30,000 and 10% or 3000.

Wars of Hunyadi, 1462–1464, 3 years. 10,000 gives 30,000 and 10% or 3000.

Wars of Hunyadi, 1468–1469, 2 years. 20,000 gives 40,000 and 10% or 4000.

War of Podiebrad of Bohemia, 1462, 1 year. 20,000 and 10% or 2000.

War with Turkey, 1469–1475, 6 years. 10,000 gives 60,000 and 10% or 6000.

Bohemian-Hungarian (half-Hussite, internal), 1470–1475, 6 years. 20,000 for both sides gives 120,000 and 10% or 12,000 losses.

Totals for the period: 300,000 and 30,000.

1476–1500.

———— Bohemian-Hungarian War (half Hussite), 1476–1478, 3 years. 20,000 (doubled, internal) gives 60,000 and 10% or 6000.

Hungarian War, 1477–1478, 2 years. 20,000 (doubled, internal) gives 40,000 and 10% or 4000.

Hungarian War, 1480–1491, 11 years. 20,000 (doubled, internal) gives 220,000 and 10% or 22,000.

Turkish-Hungarian War, 1482–1483, 2 years. 20,000 total, at 10,000 average strength and losses at 10% or 2000.

Turkish-Hungarian War, 1490–1495, 6 years. 10,000 gives 60,000 and 10% or 6000.

War with France, 1495–1497, 3 years. 10,000 gives 30,000 and 10% or 3000.

Totals for the period: 430,000 and 43,000.

1501–1525.

———— War with Venice (Cambrian League), 1508–1512, 4 years. 10,000 gives 40,000 and 10% or 4000.

War with Turkey, 1512–1519, 8 years. 10,000 gives 80,000 and 10% or 8000.

War with France, 1512–1514, 3 years. 10,000 gives 30,000 and 10% or 3000.

War with France, 1515, 1 year. 10,000 and 10% or 1000.

War with Venice, 1513–1518, 6 years. 10,000 (11,000, S XI, 149) and 10% or 6000 with a total strength of 60,000.

Peasant War in Hungary, 1514, 1 year. 20,000 (doubled, internal) and 5% or 1000.

Peasant War in Austria, 1515, 1 year. 20,000 (doubled, internal) and 5% or 1000.

Knight War, 1522–1523, 2 years. 20,000 (doubled, internal) gives 40,000 and 5% or 2000.

War with Turkey and Hungary, 1521–1525, 5 years. 10,000 gives 50,000 and 10% or 5000.

Peasant War in Saxony, 1524–1525, 2 years. 20,000 (doubled, internal) gives 40,000 and 5% or 2000.

War with France and Venice (first war of Charles V), 1521–1525, 4 years. 20,000 (Bicocca 27/IV, 1522, 20,000, D IV, 103; Pavia 24/II, 1525, 20,000, D IV, 110–111) gives 80,000. Losses 15% (Biocca, 3000 killed, which according to accepted proportion of 1 killed per 3 or 4 wounded gives 50% losses) gives 12,000. (The per cent of losses in the battle at Bicocca cannot be the intensity of the struggle; for this reason the coefficient is increased to 15%.)

Totals for the period: 470,000 and 45,000.

1526–1550.

———— War with France (second war of Charles V), 1527–1529, 3 years. 20,000 gives 60,000 and 10% losses or 6000.

War with France (third war of Charles V), 1536–1538, 3 years. 60,000 (up to 62,000, S XI, 154) gives 180,000 and 10% or 18,000 losses.

War with France (fourth war of Charles V), 1542–1544, 3 years. 90,000 (the figure is increased in view of three different fronts of the war, L III, 556; 60,000, S XI, 155) gives 270,000 and 10% or 27,000 losses.

War with Turkey and Hungary, 1526–1532, 7 years. 20,000 gives 140,000 and 10% or 14,000.

War with Turkey and Hungary, 1532–1534, 3 years. 20,000 gives 60,000 and 10% or 6000.

War between Württemberg and Hessen, 1534, 1 year. 20,000 (doubled, internal) and 5% or 1000.

Tunis Expedition, 1535, 1 year. 10,000 and 10% or 1000.

Ghent's Insurrection, 1537–1540, 3 years. 20,000 (doubled, internal) gives 60,000 and 5% or 3000.

Insurrection in Hungary, Zapolya, 1537–1538, 2 years. 40,000 (doubled, internal) gives 80,000 and 10% or 8000.

War with Turkey, 1537–1547, 11 years. 20,000 gives 220,000 and 10% or 22,000.

Expedition to Algeria, 1541, 1 year. 20,000 and 10% or 2000.

War with Schmalkaldic League, 1546–1547, 2 years. 40,000 (doubled internal) gives 80,000 and 10% or 8000.

Totals for the period: 1,200,000 and 116,000.

1551–1575.
——————— War with France, 1552–1556, 5 years. 60,000 (the figure is increased in view of the two fronts of the war; 56,000, S XI, 155) gives 300,000 and 10% or 30,000.

War with Turkey, 1551–1562, 12 years. 20,000 gives 240,000 and 10% or 24,000.

War with Turkey, 1565–1568, 4 years. 20,000 gives 80,000 and 10% or 8000.

Totals for the period: 620,000 and 62,000.

1576–1600.
——————— War with Turks in Hungary, 1576–1583, 8 years. 20,000 gives 160,000 and 10% or 16,000 losses.

War with Poland, 1587–1588, 2 years. 20,000 gives 40,000 and 10% or 4000.

Totals for the period: 340,000 and 34,000.

1601–1625.
——————— War with Turkey, 1601–1606, 6 years. 20,000 gives 120,000 and 10% or 12,000.

With Bethlen-Gabor, 1623–1625, 3 years. 20,000 gives 60,000 and 10% or 6000.

The Thirty Years' War, 1618–1626, 8 years. 125,000 (the general strength of the Austrian Army during the Thirty Years' War was about 100,000 on the average, 100,000 in 1627, 102,000 in 1633, and 74,000 in 1648; it is raised on account of the partly internal nature of the war; Prague, Weissen-Berge, 8/XI, 1620, 28,000, L 22) gives 1,000,000. Losses 25% (Wimpfen 5/V, 1622, 25%, B 50) gives 250,000.

Uskok War with Venice, 1615–1617, 3 years. 20,000 gives 60,000 and 10% or 6000 losses.

Totals for the period: 1,240,000 and 274,000.

1626–1650.
——————— War with Bethlen-Gabor, 1626–1627, 2 years. 20,000 gives 40,000 and 10% or 4000.

Mantuan War, 1630–1631, 2 years. 10,000 (the principal adversary in the war against France was Spain, and therefore the military effort of Austria was insignificant, L 23) gives 20,000 and 5% or 1000 losses.

The Thirty Years' War, 1626–1628, 22 years. 125,000 (see the preceding remark about this war; Breitenfeld 7/IX, 1631, 34,000, B 55; Lutzen 16/XI, 1632, 25,000, L 23) gives 2,750,000 and losses 30% (Breitenfeld, 1631, 24%, B 55; 1642, 33%, B 69) gives 825,000.

Totals for the period: 2,810,000 and 830,000.

1651–1675.
——————— First Northern War, 1658–1660, 3 years. 10,000 (the participation of Austria in this war was insignificant, L 23) gives 30,000 and 5% or 1500.

Transylvanian War, 1661–1664, 4 years. 24,000 (Lewencz 20/VII, 1664, 12,000, B 87; Parkany 7/VIII, 1633, 5000, L 24; St. Gothard, 1664, 30,000, L 24) gives 96,000 and losses 23% (Parkany 40%, L 24; St. Gothard 7%, L 24) gives 22,080.

Insurrection of Hungarian Magnates, 1670, 1 year. 20,000 (intensity of military effort insignificant, L 24), and 5% losses or 1000 (doubled, internal).

"Kuruzen" War, 1672–1675, 4 years. (Doubled, internal; see above remark) 20,000 gives 80,000 and 5% losses or 4000.

Second war of Louis XIV, 1673–1675, 3 years. 100,000 (Turkheim 5/I, 1675, 30,000, B 96; Seneffe 11/VIII, 1674, 70,000, L 28; the figure is raised on account of two different fronts of the war, E V, 364–365) gives 300,000 and 12% losses (Seneffe 12.2%, L 28) gives 36,000.

Totals for the period: 526,000 and 64,580.

1676–1700.
——————— Great Turkish War, 1683–1699, 16 years. 60,000 (Kahlenberg 12/IX, 1683, 76,000, L 25; Szlankamen 19/VIII, 1691, 50,000, B 115) gives 960,000. Losses 10% (Szlankamen 16%, B 115; Vienna 12/IX, 1683, 6.5%, B 104; Zenta 11/IX, 1697, 4%, B 122) gives 96,000.

"Kuruzen" War, 1676–1682, 7 years. 20,000 (doubled, internal) gives 140,000 and 5% or 7000.

Second war of Louis XIV, 1676–1679, 4 years. 100,000 (figure raised, two different fronts, E V, 354–365) gives 400,000 and 12% losses or 48,000.

Third war of Louis XIV, 1688–1697, 10 years. 88,000 (figure raised, two different fronts; Fleurus 1/VII, 1690, 38,000, L 29; Neerwinden 29/VII, 1693, 50,000, L 29) gives 880,000. Losses 27% (Fleurus 29% and Neerwinden 24%, L 29) gives 237,600.

Austrian-Sardinian War, 1696–1697, 2 years. 20,000 gives 40,000 and 10% or 4000.

Totals for the period: 2,420,000 and 392,600.

1701–1725.
——————— Austrian-Sardinian War, 1701–1703, 3 years. 20,000 gives 60,000 and 10% or 6000 losses.

Austrian-Venetian War, 1716–1718, 3 years. 57,000 (Belgrade 16/VIII, 1717, 50,000, B 175; Peterwardein 5/VIII, 1716, 63,000, B 173) gives 171,000. Losses 6% (Belgrade 10.8%, B 175; Peterwardein 6.1%, B 173) gives 10,260.

Hungarian Insurrection War, 1703–1711, 9 years. 30,000 (doubled, internal; Szibo 11/XI, 1705, 13,000 against 24,000 Hungarians, B 144; Pata 8/X, 1704, 3000 against 12,000 Hungarians, B 139) gives 270,000. Losses 16% (Szibo 25% of the Hungarians, while 4% with the Austrians, B 144; Pata 33% Hungarians and 3.5% Austrians, B 139) gives 43,200.

War for the Spanish Succession, 1701–1714, 13 years. 250,000 (Hochstadt 13/VIII, 1704, 50,000, L 30; Malplaquet 11/IX, 1709, 93,000, L 30; the figure is raised because the war was fought on four different fronts, E III, 402–404) gives a total of 3,250,000 for the war. Losses 19% (Ramiellies 23/V, 1706, 8.4%, L 30; Malplaquet 27%, L 30; Villaviciosa 10/XI, 1710, 22.3%, L 30) gives 617,500.

War of the "Quadruple Alliance," 1718–1720, 3 years. 25,000 (Francavilla 20/VI, 1719, 21,000, L 32) gives 75,000 and losses 15% (Francavilla 14.5%, L 32) gives 11,250.

Totals for the period: 3,826,000 and 688,210.

1726–1750.

———————— Russian-Austrian War with Turkey, 1736–1739, 4 years. 40,000 (Grocka 23/VII, 1739, 40,000, L 33) gives 160,000 and losses 14% (Grocka 14%, L 33) gives 22,400.

First Silesian War, 1740–1742, 3 years. 30,000 (Czaslau 17/V, 1742, 28,000, B 183–189) gives 90,000 and 11% losses (Chotusitz 17/V, 1742, 4%, L 35) gives 9900.

War for the Polish Succession, 1733–1738, 5 years. 40,000 (Parma 29/VI, 1734, 37,000, B 180) gives 200,000 and losses 16% (Parma 16.2%, B 180) gives 32,000.

Second Silesian War, 1744–1745, 2 years. 70,000 (Hohenfriedenberg 4/VI, 1745, 75,000, L 35) gives 140,000 and losses 13% (Hohenfriedenberg 12.8%, L 35) or 18,200.

War for the Austrian Succession, 1741–1748, 8 years. 150,000 (Piacenza 16/VI, 1746, 40,000, B 200–250; Campo Santo 8/VI, 1743, 11,000, L 35) gives 1,200,000 and losses 10% (Campo Santo 15%, L 35; Piacenza 7.6%, L 35) gives 120,000. (Taking into consideration that the general Austria-Hungarian losses during the War for the Polish Succession were not more than 30,000, and during the War for the Austrian Succession were up to 120,000, and considering that the war was fought on four different fronts, the figures are raised.)

Totals for the period: 1,790,000 and 202,500.

1751–1775.

———————— Seven Years' War 1756–1763, 7 years. 170,000 (1757, Kolin, 54,000, B 217; 1757, Leuthen, 65,000, B 222; 1760, Torgau, 66,000, L 37) gives 1,190,000 and losses 400,000 (Kolin 12%, B 217; Leuthen 15.4%, B 222; Torgau 13.6%, L 37). (Having in view that general losses during this war reached for Austria up to 400,000, L 36, i.e., were three times more than the losses during the war for the Austrian Succession, that Austria fought on two different fronts, and that

the total fighting force was 170,000, this figure is taken, E VII, 142–167.)

Totals for the period: 1,190,000 and 400,000.

1776–1800.

———————— War for the Bavarian Succession, 1778–1779, 2 years. 11,000 (Habelschwerdt 18/I, 1779, 11,000, B 255–263) gives 22,000 and 1% (losses small, L 37) or 220.

Second Russo-Austrian War with Turkey, 1788–1791, 4 years. 100,000 (general strength of the Austrian armies reached 264,000, L 38) gives 400,000. Total losses 10,000 (L 38).

First Coalitional War, 1792–1797, 6 years. 200,000 (Neerwinden 18/III, 1793, 43,000, B 271–283; Castiglione 5/VIII, 1796, 25,000, B 301–317; Rivoli 14–15/I, 1797, 28,000, B 318) gives 1,200,000. Losses 10% (Neerwinden 6.2%, L 40; Jemappes 6/XI, 1792, 8%, L 40; Castiglione 8%, L 41; Rivoli 14.3%, B 318) gives 120,000. (The figures for the size of the armies and of the losses are enlarged because the war was conducted simultaneously on several fronts; in the Netherlands the army's size was 100,000, on Rhine 85,000–180,000; in Italy 38,000–50,000, E III, 525–536 and VI, 270–281.)

Second Coalitional War, 1799–1800, 2 years. 240,000 (Marengo 14/VI, 1800, 35,000, B 355; Trebbia 17–19/VI, 1799, 20,000, L 42; Novi 15/VIII, 1799, 35,000, L 42; Hohenlinden 3/XII, 1800, 52,000, L 42) gives 480,000. Losses 16% (Marengo 22.4%, B 355; Trebbia 13.5%, L 42; Novi 14.3%, L 42; Hohenlinden 10%, L 42) or 76,800. (See the preceding remark; E VI, 282; VIII, 339; V, 58.)

Insurrection in Transylvania, 1784–1785, 2 years. 20,000 (doubled, internal) gives 40,000 and losses for both sides 2000 (less than 2000, L 39).

War with Holland (Scheldt), 1784–1785, 2 years. 40,000 (doubled, internal) gives 80,000 and 5% or 4000.

Insurrection in the Austrian Netherlands, 1789–1790, 2 years. 20,000 gives 40,000 and losses for both sides 1000.

Totals for the period: 2,262,000 and 214,020.

1801–1825.

———————— Second Coalitional War, 1801, 1 year. 100,000 and 5% or 5000.

Third Coalitional War, 1805, 1 year. 180,000 (Caldiero 30–31/X, 1805, 49,000, L 43; Austerlitz 2/XII, 1805, 16,000, L 43) gives 180,000 and losses 15% (Caldiero 12%, L 43; Austerlitz 25%, L 43) gives 27,000. (Taking into consideration that the war was on several fronts, and losses at Ulm where the whole of the Mack's army was imprisoned, the figures are raised, E I, 60–65; in South Germany and Bohemia 156,000 and in Italy 55,000.)

War with France, 1809, 1 year. 200,000 (in Austria-Bavaria up to 120,000, in Italy 50,000, in Poland 30,000, Dalmatia 8000, E I, 65–70; Aspern 21–22/V, 1809, 99,000, L 44; Vagram 5–6/VII, 1809, 136,000, L 44) gives 200,000 total and losses 25% (Aspern 20.2% and Vagram 14%, L 43) gives 50,000.

War with Russia, 1812, 1 year. 40,000 (33,000, L 45) and losses 5500 (L 45).

War of 1813–1814, 2 years. 160,000 (in Germany and France 110,000, Italy 75,000, E V, 405–417; Dresden 26–27/VII, 1813, 120,000, L 47; Leipzig 16–19/X, 1813, 105,000, L 47; La Rothiere, 45,000, L 48) gives 320,000. Losses 20% (Leipzig 17%, L 47; Dresden 5.8%, L 47; Arcy sur Aube 6.5%, L 48) gives 64,000.

"One Hundred Days' War," 1815, 1 year. 50,000 and losses 3000 (not more than 3000 during the whole war, L 48).

War with Naples, 1815, 1 year. 30,000 (L 49; Tolentino, 11,000, L 49) and 6% (Tolentino 6.3%, L 49) gives 1800 losses.

Insurrection in Italy, 1821, 1 year. 30,000 and 1% or 300.

Totals for the period: 950,000 and 156,600.

1826–1850.

————— Austrian-Sardinian War, 1848–1849, 2 years. 40,000 (Custozza 25/VII, 1848, 55,000, L 52; Novara 23/III, 1849, 41,000, L 53) gives 80,000 and losses 4% (Custozza 2.7%, L 52; Novara 8%, L 53) gives 3200.

Hungarian Insurrection, 1848–1849, 2 years. 80,000 (internal; Komern 2/VII, 1849, 50,000 on each side, L 54; with part of Russian Army) gives 160,000 and losses 2% (Komern 1.8%, L 54) gives 3200.

Occupation of Modena and Parma, 1831, 1 year. 10,000 and 1% (losses slight, L 50) gives 100.

Expedition against Bosnia, 1835–1846, 11 years. 10,000 gives 110,000 and 1% or 1100.

Expedition against Montenegro, 1838, 1 year. 10,000 and 1% or 100.

War with Egypt, 1840, 1 year. 10,000 and 1% or 100.

Totals for the period: 380,000 and 7800.

1851–1875.

————— Austrian-Sardinian War, 1859, 1 year. 130,000 (Solferino 24/VI, 1859, 130,000, L 55) and 10% (Solferino 10.1%, L 55) or 13,000.

Austrian-Prussian War, 1866, 1 year. 350,000 (in Bohemia 225,000, Italy 138,000, West Germany 10,000, E I, 43–60; army 407,000, L 57; Koniggratz 3/VII, 1866, 215,000, L 64; Custozza 24/VI, 1866, 75,000, L 64) gives 350,000 and losses 12% (losses of Austrians for the whole war 12.1%, L 63) gives 42,000.

War with Denmark, 1864, 1 year. 20,000 (21,000, L 56) and the losses were 1000 (L 56).

Totals for the period: 500,000 and 56,000.

1876–1900.

————— Insurrection in Bosnia and Herzegovina, 1878, 1 year. 100,000 (75–145,000, L 64) and 5000 losses (L 64).

Insurrection in Southern Dalmatia, 1882, 1 year. 100,000 (internal; 63,000, L 65) and losses 2000 for both sides (330 Austrians, L 65).

Totals for the period: 200,000 and 7000

1901–1925.

————— World War, 5 years. Average 1,800,-000. Total 7,000,000 (VIII, 1914, 1,800,000; X, 1918, 2,640,000, Major General Kerchnawe's data in "Oesterreichische Wehrzeitung," 17/IV (Wien, 1925); Russian front 490,000 to 1,230,000 and 2108 cannons; Italian front 271,000 to 681,000 and 2300 cannons; Serbian front 123,000 to 309,000 and 500 cannons; given with reservations by the Austrian Kriegsarchiv, in 1933). Losses 3,000,000 (in the whole there were mobilized 7,500,000; losses 4,810,000, "Oesterreichische Wehrzeitung," 24/IV; losses 2,290,000, incomplete figures given with reservations by the Austrian Kriegsarchiv, in 1933). (Because the figures given by Major General Kerchnawe and the official figures given by the Austrian Kriegsarchiv differ, an intermediary for the losses of the two is taken, i.e., 4,810,000–2,290,000 or 3,000,000; see also Oesterreichs-Ungarns letzter Krieg, 1914–1918, Wien, 1931, Vol. III, pp. 15–48.) Here also there are no official figures perfectly identical and free from discrepancies.

GERMANY [1]

1651–1675.

————— War with Poland, 1656–1657, 2 years. 9000 (Warsaw 28–30/VII, 1656, 9000, B 83) gives a total strength of 18,000 for the war, and the losses at 3% gives 540.

First Northern War, 1658–1660, 3 years. 20,000 gives 60,000 and 3% losses or 1800.

Second War of Louis XIV, 1672–1673, 2 years. 20,000 gives 40,000 and 4% or 1600.

Continuation of the Second War of Louis XIV, 1674–1675, 2 years. 20,000 gives 40,000 and 4% or 1600.

Totals for the period: 158,000 and 5540.

1676–1700.

————— Second War with Louis XIV, 1676–1679, 4 years. 20,000 gives 80,000 and 4% or 3200 losses.

[1] Abbreviations in the references mean:
B — G. Bodart, Militär-historisches Kriegslexikon.
Z — as before.
D — as before.
L — G. Bodart, Losses.
S — as before.
Sh — Schwarte, Der Grosse Krieg 1914–1918. Die Organisationen der Kriegsführung, 10 vols. (Leipzig, 1921 and 1936), esp. Vols. I and III.
G — L. Gehre, Die Deutsche Kräftverteilung während der Weltkriege (Berlin, 1928).
E — as before.
Other works cited in this Appendix.

Third War with Louis XIV, 1689–1697, 9 years. 20,000 gives 180,000 and 4% or 10,400.

Totals for the period: 260,000 and 10,400.

1701–1725.

—————— War for Spanish Succession, 1702–1713, 12 years. 20,000 (Hochstadt 13/VIII, 1704, 102,000, British, Dutch, Austrians, and Prussians, B 137) gives 240,000 and 25% (Hochstadt 25%, B 137) gives 60,000 losses.

Great Northern War, 1715–1720, 6 years. 20,000 gives 120,000 and 3% losses gives 3600.

Totals for the period: 360,000 and 63,600.

1726–1750.

—————— War for Polish Succession, 1733–1735, 3 years. 20,000 gives 60,000 and 3% or 1800.

First Silesian War, 1740–1742, 3 years. 25,000 (Mollwitz 10/IV, 1741, 21,600, B 189; Czaslau, Chotusitz, 17/V, 1742, 28,000, B 192) gives 75,000 and 18% losses (Mollwitz 18.2%, B 189) gives 13,500.

Second Silesian War, 1744 1745, 2 years. 80,000 (Hohenfriedberg 4/VI, 1745, 77,000, Z 64; Siege of Prague 6–16/IX, 1744, 80,000, B 198) gives 160,000. Losses 6% (Hohenfriedberg 6.2%, Z 64) gives 9600.

Totals for the period: 295,000 and 24,900.

1751–1775.

—————— Seven Years' War, 1756–1763, 7 years. 150,000 (at the time of the death of Frederic the Great, 1786, Prussia had an army of 200,000, D IV, 304. In this war the Prussian Army in Bohemia was about 100,000, in East Prussia 30,500, Pomerania 6000, West Germany up to 50,000, E VII, 142–166. For these reasons the figure 150,000 is taken. Prague 6/V, 1757, 64,000, Z 64; Rossbach 5/XI, 1757, 22,000, B 220; Zorndorf Kunersdorf 12/VIII, 1759, 48,000, B 232; Torgau 3/XI, 1760, 44,000, B 243) gives 1,050,000. Losses 25% (Prague 20.8%, Z 64; Rossbach 2.4%, B 220; Zorndorf Kunersdorf 39%, B 232; Torgau 29.8%, B 243) gives 262,500.

Totals for the period: 1,050,000 and 262,500.

1776–1800.

—————— War for Bavarian Succession, 1778–1779, 2 years. 3000 (Habelschwerdt 18/I, 1779, 3000, B 254–263). Total 6000. 2% losses (the war was of an entirely negligible strain, so-called "potato war") gives 120.

First Coalitional War, 1792–1795, 4 years. 45,000 (Valmy 20/IX, 1792, 35,000, B 269; Wattignies 15–16/X, 1793, 30,000 allies, B 284; Cateau Cambresis 26/IV, 1794, 90,000 allies, B 285–289) gives a total of 180,000. Losses 5% (Valmy 57%, B 269; the battle at Valmy cannot be considered typical, the rest of the battles seem to have been of an average strain; the army's strength is raised on account of the two different fronts of the war) gives 9000.

Totals for the period: 186,000 and 9120.

1801–1825.

—————— War with France, 1806–1807, 2 years. 60,000 (Jena 14/X, 1806, 54,000 and at the same day Auerstedt 50,000, B 372; Preussisch-Eylau 8/II, 1807, 8500, B 380) gives 120,000. Losses 27% (Jena 22.3%, B 372; Preussisch-Eylau 27.7%, B 380) gives 32,400 losses.

War of 1813–1814, 2 years. 200,000 (Bautzen 20–21/V, 1813, 31,000, B 450; Leipzig 16–19/X, 1813, 80,000, B 461; Laon 9–10/III, 1814, 52,000, Z 58) gives 400,000. Losses 30% (Bautzen 11.3%, B 450; Leipzig 27.7%, B 461; Laon 8.2%, Z 58) gives 120,000. (General losses of Prussia and its German allies were: for 1813, 75,000, and 1814, 31,000, or a total of 106,000. General losses of German contingents which fought on the side of France in 1813 were 18,000–20,000, L 46. Having in view that German contingents which fought on the side of Napoleon were about 1/5, judging after losses, of the Prussian contingents and its German allies, the army's strength and the losses are increased.)

"One Hundred Days' War," 1815, 1 year. 75,000 (Waterloo 18/VI, 1815, 75,000, Z 59) and 10% losses (Waterloo 9.3%, Z 59) gives 7500.

Totals for the period: 595,000 and 159,900.

1826–1850.

—————— War with Denmark, 1848–1849, 2 years. 14,000 (Fredericia 6/VII, 1849, 14,000, B 509) gives 28,000 and 10% losses (Fredericia 9.6%, B 509) gives 2800.

Totals for the period: 28,000 and 2800.

1851–1875.

—————— War with Denmark, 1864, 1 year. 37,000 (Duppeler Schanzen 18/VI, 1864, 37,000, B 534) and 3% losses (Duppeler Schanzen 3.3%, B 534) gives 1110.

Austrian-Prussian War, 1866, 1 year. 574,000 (Prussian Army 437,000 plus German contingents which fought against Prussia 137,000, or a total of 574,000, L 57) and losses 4.7% (losses of Prussia 4.6% and losses of German contingents which fought against Prussia 4.7%, L 61–63) gives 25,978.

Franco-Prussian War, 1870–1871, 2 years. 887,000 (German Army 887,000, L 148) gives 1,774,000. Losses of Germany 15.1% (L 149) gives 267,874.

Totals for the period: 2,385,000 and 295,962.

1876–1900.

—————— Boxers' insurrection in China, 1900, 1 year. 20,000 (end of 1900 up to 20,000, S IV, 614–622) and 1% (less than 1%, S IV, 614–622) gives 200.

Totals for the period: 20,000 and 200.

1901–1925.

—————— Insurrection of Herrero in Southwestern Africa, 1904, 1 year. 10,000 and 1% or 100.

World War, 1914–1918, 5 years. Average 3,000,000. Total 13,000,000 for the war and so many were called to the colors (VIII, 1914, 3,840,000, Sh I, 17–27, III, 552). Eastern front ninety divisions, VIII, 1917; French front 200 divisions VI, 1918; Italian front seven divisions XI, 1917; Serbian front eight divisions, X, 1915; Rumanian front thirteen divisions XI, 1916; naval front. G (table "*Steindruckkarte*"). General losses 6,060,000 or 46.6% of the 13,000,000

(Sh I, 17). Many details and data are given in the *Reichsarchiv: Der Weltkrieg, 1914–1918*, 10 vols. so far. It is the official history of the war. But here also there are discrepancies, as far as figures are concerned.

Totals for the period: 13,010,000 and 6,060,100.

ITALY [1]

1551–1575.

——————— War with Turkey, 1570–1573, 4 years. 10,000 gives a total strength of 40,000 for the war and 3% losses or 1200.

Totals for the period: 40,000 and 1200.

1576–1600.

——————— War with Geneva, 1580–1600, 21 years. 10,000 gives 210,000 and 3% or 6300 losses.

War with France, 1589, 1 year. 10,000 and 4% or 400.

War with France, 1600, 1 year. 10,000 and 4% or 400.

Totals for the period: 230,000 and 7100.

1601–1625.

——————— War with Geneva, 1601–1603, 3 years. 10,000 gives 30,000 and 3% or 900.

War with France, 1601, 1 year. 10,000 and 4% or 400.

War with Spain, 1613–1617, 5 years. 10,000 gives 50,000 and 4% or 2000.

Totals for the period: 90,000 and 3300.

1626–1650.

——————— War with Spain, 1626, 1 year. 10,000 and 4% or 400 losses.

War for the Mantuan Succession, 1630–1631, 2 years. 10,000 gives 20,000 and 4% or 800.

War with Spain, on the side of France (Thirty Years' War of France with Spain), 1635–1650, 16 years. 10,000 gives 160,000 and 3% or 4800.

Totals for the period: 190,000 and 6000.

1651–1675.

——————— The same (continuation of war with Spain), 1650–1659, 10 years. 10,000 gives 100,000 and 3% or 3000 losses.

War with Genoa, 1672–1673, 2 years. 20,000 (internal, doubled) gives 40,000 and 3% or 1200.

Totals for the period: 140,000 and 4200.

1676–1700.

——————— Third War of Louis XIV, 1690–1696, 7 years. 10,000 gives 70,000 and 4% or 2800.

Austria-Sardinian War, 1696–1697, 2 years. 10,000 gives 20,000 and 4% or 800.

Totals for the period: 90,000 and 3600.

1701–1725.

——————— Austria-Sardinian War, 1701–1703, 3 years. 10,000 gives 30,000 and 4% or 1200.

War for the Spanish Succession, 1703–1713, 10 years. 30,000 (Turin 7/IX, 1706, 30,000 Austrians and Sardinians, B 143–150; 1703, 11,500 Sardinians, S XI, 61–73; 1704 up to 30,000 Sardinians, S XI, 61–73) gives 300,000 and 5% losses or 15,000.

War of the "Quadruple Alliance," 1718–1720, 3 years. 15,000 gives 45,000 and 5% or 2250.

Totals for the period: 375,000 and 18,450.

1726–1750.

——————— War for the Polish Succession, 1733–1738, 6 years. 15,000 (Siege of Milan 11/XIII–29/XII, 1733, 17,000 French and Sardinians, B 160–179; Parma 29/VI, 1734, 53,000 French and Sardinians, B 180) gives 90,000 and losses 8% (Parma 7.6%, B 180) gives 7200. (Russia and Prussia were only juridically in a state of war with Sardinia, but no real fighting took place between them.)

War for the Austrian Succession, 1743–1748, 7 years. 8000 (Coni 30/IX, 1744, 25,000 Austrians and Sardinians, B 199; Rotofreno 10/VIII, 1746, 25,000 Austrians and Sardinians, B 200–250) gives 56,000 and losses 14% (Coni 14.4%, B 199) gives 7840.

Totals for the period: 146,500 and 15,040.

1751–1775.

——————— No data.

1776–1800.

——————— First Coalitional War, 1792–1796, 5 years. 7000 (Levens 28/II, 1793, 7000 Sardinians, B 272; Siege of Toulon 18/IX–18/XII, 1793, 18,000 allies; English, Spaniards, Neapolitans, and Sardinians, B 284) gives 35,000 and losses 22% (Siege of Toulon 22%, B 284) or 7700.

Totals for the period: 35,000 and 7700.

1801–1825.

——————— Participation in wars of French armies from 1805–1814, 9 years. 12,000 gives 108,000 and 20% of 21,600.

"One Hundred Days' War," 1815, 1 year. 10,000 (Sardinia did not take any important part in serious fighting) and 3% or 300.

Totals for the period: 118,000 and 21,900.

---

[1] Meaning of the abbreviations:
B — G. Bodart, *Militär-historisches Kriegslexikon.*
L — G. Bodart, *Losses.*
Z — as before.
En — as before.
S — as before.
Other works cited in this Appendix.

1826–1850.

——————— Austrian-Sardinian War, 1848–1849, 2 years. 75,000 (end of May, 1848, general size of the army 50,000; 20/VII, 75,000; middle of March, 1849, up to 100,000, Z 34) gives 150,000 and total losses 7000 (general losses for the whole war 7000, L 53; St. Lucia 6/VI, 1848, 4.8%, Z 60; Navara 23/III, 1849, 13.8, Z 60; Custozza 25/VI, 1848, 1.5%).

Totals for the period: 150,000 and 7000.

1851–1875.

——————— War with Russia, 1855–1856, 2 years. 21,000 (general strength of the army 21,000, L 142) and total 42,000 and losses 8% (general losses during the siege of Sebastopol 8.1%, L 141-142) or 3360.

War with Austria-Hungary, 1859, 1 year. 60,000 (average size of the army 60,000, L 143) and 10% (L 143) or 6000.

War with Naples and the Papal State, 1860-1861, 2 years. 20,000 gives 40,000 and 3% or 1100.

Expedition of Garibaldi in Calabria, 1862, 1 year. 10,000. Losses 4% or 400.

War with Austria-Hungary, 1866. 1 year. 200,000 (166,000 regulars and 34,000 volunteers, L 57) and a total loss of 11,000 (L 57).

Attack of Garibaldi upon the Papal State, 1867, 1 year. 10,000 and 3% or 300.

Occupation of Papal State, 1870, 1 year. 20,000 and 3% or 600.

Totals for the period: 382,000 and 22,860.

1876–1900.

——————— War with Abyssinia, 1895–1896, 2 years. 21,000 gives 42,000 and 5% or 2100. (The figures are taken for Abyssinia in accordance with an analogous war of Italy with Turkey, 1911–1912, but because Abyssinia as an adversary is weaker than Turkey they are lowered by one-third.)

Totals for the period: 42,000 and 2100.

1901–1925.

——————— Italo-Turkish War, 1911–1912, 2 years. 30,000 (up to 30,000, En XII, 752) gives 60,000 and 5% or 3000.

World War, 1915–1918, 3.5 years. Total 5,000,000 (average size of the army 1/I, 1916, 1,010,000; 1/I, 1917, 1,750,000; 1/I, 1918, 1,890,000; X, 1918, 2,180,000, E XII, 786; average 1,700,000). Total loss 1,780,000 (general number of the mobilized 5,180,000, general losses 1,780,000, i.e., 34.3%, En XII, 786). See also A. Tosti, *La guerra Italo-Austriaca, 1915–1918* (Roma, 1925). Previous note on discrepancy of the data given by different sources applies here, too. However, for our results it does not have any appreciable importance.

Totals for the period: 5,060,000 and 1,783,000.

SPAIN [1]

1476–1500.

——————— War with Portugal, 1476–1479, 4 years. The strength of the army was 10,000 giving a total of 40,000 for the period of the war; and 5% or 2000 for the total casualties.

War with the Moors (Mauritanian War) 1482–1492, 10 years. 20,000, total 200,000 and 5% or 10,000 for the losses.

War with France (The Holy League), 1495-1497, 3 years. 10,000 (6000, S XI, 148); total 30,000 and at 5% there were 1500 casualties.

Totals for the period: 270,000 and 13,500.

1501–1525.

——————— Insurrection of Morisco, 1501, 1 year, 10,000 and 5% or 500.

War with France, 1502–1504, 3 years. 15,000 (S XI, 146–148). Total 45,000 and 5% or 2250.

War with Venice (Cambrian League), 1508-1509, 2 years. 15,000, total 30,000 and 5% or 1500 losses.

African War, 1508–1511, 4 years. 15,000, total 60,000 and 5% or 3000.

War with France (The Holy League), 1511-1513, 3 years. 20,000 (Ravenna 11/IV, 1512, 16,000, D IV, 82–89; in France, 6500, E III, 550). Total 60,000 and 5% or 3000.

War with France, 1515, 1 year. 13,000 (13,000, S XI, 146–148). Total 13,000 and 5% or 650 for the losses.

Conquest of Mexico, 1519–1521, 3 years. 1000 (700, Ba, 171). Total 3000 and 5% or 150.

Insurrection of "Comuneros" in Castile and of "Germanias" in Barcelona, 1520–1522, 3 years. 10,000 strength of the army gives 30,000 for the period of the war and 5% or 1500 losses.

War with France, the Pope, and Venice (first war of Charles V), 1521–1525, 5 years. 23,000 (up to 23,000, S XI, 152). Total 115,000 and 5% losses or 5750.

Totals for the period: 396,000 and 18,300.

1526–1550.

——————— Second war of Charles V, 1526–1529, 4 years. 25,000 giving a total of 100,000 and 5% or 5000 losses.

[1] Abbreviations in the tables on Spain mean:
E — as before.
S — as before.
D — as before.
Ba — R. Ballester, *Histoire de l'Espagne* (Paris, 1928).
W — K. Wenzelburger, *Geschichte der Niederlande* (Gotha, 1886), Vol. II.
B — G. Bodart, *Militär-historisches Kriegslexikon*, quoted.
En — as before.
M — A. Mousset, *L'Espagne dans la politique mondiale* (Paris, 1928).

War with Peru, 1531–1535, 5 years. 500 (200, Ba, 173). Total 2500 and 5% or 125.

War with Turkey (Tunis), 1535, 1 year. 30,000 (a maximum coefficient is taken because this expedition of Charles V was his principal Turkish expedition). Total 30,000 and 5% or 1500.

War with France (third war of Charles V), 1536–1538, 3 years. 50,000 (up to 50,000, S XI, 152; E III, 556). Total 150,000 and 5% or 7500 casualties.

War with Peru, 1526–1541, 6 years. 500 gives a total of 3000 and 5% or 150 as the losses.

War with Turkey (Algir), 1541, 1 year. 20,000 and 5% or 1000.

War with France (fourth war of Charles V), 1542–1544, 3 years. 60,000 (Luxembourg 16,000–30,000, Italy 30,000, E III, 556). Total 180,000 and 5% or 9000 losses.

Totals for the period: 485,500 and 24,275.

1551–1575.

———— War of Charles V with France, 1552–1556, 5 years. 60,000 (Lotharingia 56,000, Italy 17,000, E III, 557). Total strength for the war 300,000 and 5% losses or 15,000.

War with France, 1556–1559, 4 years. 63,000 (St. Quentin, 1557, 53,000, D IV, 221. In Italy 22,000, in Flanders 47,000, E III, 558). Total 252,000 and 5% or 12,600.

War with Turkey, 1559–1564, 6 years. 20,000 gives a total strength of 120,000 and 5% or 6000 casualties.

Insurrection of the "Beggars" in the Netherlands, 1566–1567, 2 years. 900 (900, W II, 194). Total 1800 and 5% or 90.

War with Turkey, 1569–1575, 7 years. 20,000 makes a total of 140,000 and 5% or 7000.

Insurrection of the Moriscoes, 1569–1571, 3 years. 10,000 makes a total of 30,000 and 5% or 1500.

Insurrection in the Netherlands, 1568–1575, 8 years. 29,000 (20,000, W II, 217; 37,000, W II, 265). Total 232,000 and 5% or 11,600.

Totals for the period: 1,075,800 and 53,790.

1576–1600.

———— War with Turkey, 1576–1580, 5 years. 20,000 gives a total of 100,000 for the war and 5% or 5000.

Insurrection in the Netherlands, 1579–1600, 21 years. 30,000 (two fronts, E V, 363). Total 630,000 and 5% or 31,500.

War with Portugal, 1579–1581, 3 years. 24,000 (24,000 in 1580, S XI, 57). Total strength for the war 72,000 and 5% losses or 3600.

War with England (Armada), 1585–1600, 16 years. 30,000 (30,000 in 1587, "Armada," Ba 191). Total 480,000 and 5% or 24,000.

Totals for the period: 1,282,000 and 64,100.

1601–1625.

———— Insurrection in the Netherlands, 1601–1609, 9 years. 20,000 gives 180,000 and 5% or 9000.

War with England, 1601–1605, 4 years. 20,000 gives 80,000 and 5% or 4000.

Thirty Years' War, 1620–1625, 6 years. 12,000 (Wimpfen 6/V, 1622, imperials and Spaniards 20,000, B 50). Total 72,000. 25% (Wimpfen 25%, B 50) or 18,000 for the losses.

War with Turkey, 1604, 1 year. 20,000 or 1000 losses at 5%.

War with Turkey, 1610–1614, 5 years. 20,000 gives 100,000 and 5% or 5000.

War with Savoy, 1615–1617, 3 years. 15,000 gives 45,000 and 5% or 2250.

War with Venice, 1617–1621, 5 years. 20,000 gives 100,000 and 5% or 5000.

War with Turkey, 1618–1619, 2 years. 20,000 gives 40,000 and 5% or 2000.

Totals for the period: 637,000 and 46,250.

1626–1650.

———— Thirty Years' War, 1626–1648, 22 years. 40,000 (Rocroi 19/V, 1643, 25,000, B 70; Dunkirchen, naval, 20,000, 1693, B 65; Barcelona, naval, 1642, 15,000, B 68). Total 880,000 and the losses at 30% makes 264,000. (There were four different fronts, E II, 22–24 and VII, 546–555.)

Mantuan War, 1629–1631, 3 years. 30,000 (see the note about this war in the data for Austria-Hungary). Total 90,000 and 5% or 4500.

War with France, 1648–1650, 3 years. 15,000 gives 45,000 and 5% or 2250.

War with Portugal (for independence), 1642–1650, 9 years. 15,000 gives 135,000 and 5% or 6750.

Totals for the period: 1,150,000 and 277,500.

1651–1675.

———— War with France, 1651–1659, 9 years. 20,000 (Arras 24/VII, 1654, Spaniards and Fronds up to 25,000, B 32). Total 180,000 and 8% (Arras 8%, B 82) gives 14,400.

Devolutionary War, 1667–1668, 2 years. 20,000 gives 40,000 and 5% or 2000.

Second war of Louis XIV, 1672–1675, 4 years. 72,000 (Seneffe 11/VIII, 1674, 70,000 allies: Dutch, Spaniards, Imperials, B 117). Total 288,000 and 5% or 14,400. (There were three different fronts, E V, 364–365.)

War with Portugal (for independence), 1651–1668, 18 years. 17,000 (Almexial 8/VI, 1663, 16,000, B 87; Villa Viciosa 17/VI, 1665, 18,000, B 89). Total 306,000. (Almexial 25%, B 87; Villa Viciosa 22.5%, B 89). Total losses, 73,440.

War in Africa, 1661–1667, 2 years. 15,000 gives 30,000 and 5% or 1500.

War in Africa, 1672–1673, 2 years. 15,000 gives 30,000 and 5% or 1500.

Totals for the period: 874,000 and 107,240.

1676–1700.

———— Second war of Louis XIV, 1676–1678, 3 years. 35,000 (Agosta, 1676, 12,000 Spaniards and Dutch, B 98; Mont Cassel 11/IV, 1677, 30,000 Spaniards and Dutch, B 101). Total 105,000. 20% (Agosta 17%, B 98; Mont Cassel 23.5%, B 101). (There were three different fronts, E V, 364–365.) Total losses 21,000.

Third war of Louis XIV, 1688–1697, 10 years. 50,000 (Steenkerke 3/VIII, 1692, 63,000 allies: English, Imperials, Spaniards, and Dutch, B 117; Fleurus 1/VII, 1690, 38,000 allies: Dutch, Imperials, and Spaniards, B 112). Total 500,000. 20% (Steinkirke 10.5%, B 117; Fleurus 29%, B 112) or 100,000 losses. (There were three different fronts.) (E V, 365.)

"Reunion" War, 1683–1684, 2 years. 15,000 gives 30,000 and losses at 10% or 3000.

War in Africa, 1681, 1688–1689, 1693–1694, 5 years. 15,000 gives a total of 75,000 and losses at 5% or 3750.

Totals for the period: 710,000 and 127,750.

1701–1725.

——————— War for the Spanish Succession, 1701–1713, 13 years. 35,000 (Caparocca 20/VII, 1710, 20,000 French and Spaniards, B 161; Ramillies 23/V, 1706, 62,000 French, Spaniards, and Bavarians, B 147; Turin 7/IX, 1706, 42,000 French and Spaniards, B 149; Almanza 25/IV, 1707, 21,000 French and Spaniards, B 151; Oudenarde 11/VII, 1708, 80,000 French and Spaniards, B 154). The losses at 10% (Caparocca 25%, B 161; Ramillies 3.3%, B 147; Turin 3.8%, B 149; Almanza 9.5%, B 151, Oudenarde 7.5%, B 154) gives a total of 45,500. (There were three fronts, E III, 402–404.)

War with the Quadruple Alliance, 1718–1720, 3 years. 29,000 (Francavilla 20/VI, 1719, 29,000, B 159–160). Total strength was 87,000 and the losses at 5% were 4350.

Totals for the period: 542,000 and 49,850.

1726–1750.

——————— War for the Polish Succession, 1733–1738, 6 years. 10,000 (Siege of Capua 9/VI–20/XI, 1734, 10,000, B 181). Total 60,000 and 5% or 3000.

War for the Austrian Succession, 1744–1748, 6 years. 21,000 (Coni 30/IX, 1744, 26,000 French and Spaniards, B 199; Piacenza 16/VI, 1746, 44,000 French and Spaniards, B 203. Total 126,000 and losses at 15% (Coni 15.4%, B 199) or 3000.

Totals for the period: 186,000 and 21,000.

1751–1775.

——————— Seven Years' War, 1761–1763, 3 years. 20,000 gives a total of 60,000 and losses at 5% or 3000.

War with Portugal, 1762, 1 year. Total strength 20,000 and the losses at 5% were 1000.

War with England (mostly in America), 1779–1783, 5 years. 20,000 gives a total of 100,000 and losses at 5% or 5000.

Totals for the period: 180,000 and 9000.

1776–1800.

——————— First Coalitional War, 1793–1795, 3 years. 50,000 (Siege of Bellegarde 23/VI, 1793, 6000, B 270–284; Campmany 17–20/XI, 1794, 50,000, B 300). Total 150,000, and the losses at 5% or 7500. (There were two fronts, E VI, 270–284.)

War with England, 1795–1800, 6 years. 20,000 gives 120,000, and 5% or 6000.

Totals for the period: 270,000 and 13,500

1801–1825.

——————— War with England, 1801, 1 year. 20,000 and 5% or 1000.

War with England, 1803–1808, 6 years. 20,000 gives 120,000 and 5% or 6000.

War with France, 1808–1814, 7 years. 37,000 (Telavera de la Reine 27–28/VII, 1809, 54,000 English and Spaniards, B 410; Albuero 16/V, 1811, 32,000 English and Portuguese, B 425; Bailen 19/VII, 1808, 32,000, B 355–390; Siege of Saragossa 19/XII, 1808, 20/III, 1809, 30,000, B 394). Total 259,000. Losses at 16% (Telavera 11.1%, B 40; Albuero 21.9%, B 425) or a total of 43,440.

War in South and in Central America, 1808–1823, 17 years. 25,000 (Araura 5/XII, 1813, 5000; La Puerta 15/VI, 1815, 8000–10,000; in 1819, 5000; in 1823, 9000, En III, 810–812). Total 425,000 and 5% or 21,250. (There were four different fronts, En II, 328; III, 810–812; V, 126–127; XV, 388–389.)

War with France, 1823, 1 year. 70,000 (70,000, S XI, 73) and losses at 5% or 3500.

Totals for the period: 794,000 and 75,190.

1826–1850.

——————— In Southern and Central America, 1826–1829, 4 years. 15,000 (Cabo-Roina 27/VII, 1829, S XI, 60). Total 60,000 and 5% or 3000. (There were four fronts.)

First Carlist War, 1833–1840, 8 years. 20,000 and 40,000 for both sides, it being an internal war, gives 320,000 and losses 5% or 16,000.

Intervention in Portugal, 1834, 1 year. 10,000 and losses 5% or 500.

Continuation of the Carlist War, 1847–1849, 3 years. 40,000 (internal) gives 120,000 and 5% or 6000 losses. Totals 510,000 and 25,500 for the period.

1851–1875.

——————— War with Morocco, 1859–1860, 1 year. 42,000 (41,600, S XI, 57). Total 42,000 and 5% or 2100.

Second Carlist War, 1868–1874, 7 years. 40,000 (internal) gives 280,000 and 5% or 14,000.

Insurrection on the Island of S. Domingo, 1863–1865, 2 years. 20,000 gives 40,000 and 5% or 2000.

Totals for the period: 362,000 and 18,100.

1876–1900.

——————— War with Morocco, 1893–1894, 2 years. 25,000 (25,000, E XV, 816). Total 50,000 and 5% or 2500.

With United States of America, 1898, 1 year. 100,000 (El Caney 1/VII, 1896, 1300, B 583; S. Yago, naval, 1898, 4000, B 584. General strength of the Spanish land army on the islands of Cuba, Puerto Rico, and the Philippines reached 150,000, S XI, 51). The losses at 25% (El Caney 50%, B 583; S. Yago 21.5%, B 584) gives 25,000.

(There were two fronts, S XI, 51.) (Remark: the number of real fighters was less and therefore the figure is lowered from the total strength of the army.)

Third Carlist War, 1876–1885, 10 years. 40,000 gives 400,000 and 5% or 20,000.

Totals for the period: 550,000 and 47,500.

1901–1925.

———— War with Morocco, 1909, 1 year. 50,000 (50,000, M 149) and losses at 5% or 2500. War with Morocco, 1919–1925, 6 years. 140,000 (1923 up to 160,000, M 253). Total 840,000 and 5% or 42,000.

Totals for the period: 890,000 and 44,500.

HOLLAND [1]

1551–1575.

———— Insurrection of the "Beggars," 1566–1567, 2 years. 3000 (Antwerp 13/III, 1567, 3000, W II, 194) gives a total strength of 6000 and the losses 5% or 300.

War for Independence from Spain, 1568–1575, 8 years. 3000 (1568, 3000, W II, 267) gives 24,000 and 5% or 1200.

Totals for the period: 30,000 and 1500.

1576–1600.

———— War for Independence from Spain, 1576–1600, 25 years. 50,000 (figure is raised because the war was fought on two different fronts, E V, 363) gives 1,250,000 and 5% losses or 62,500.

Totals for the period: 1,250,000 and 62,500.

1601–1625.

———— War for Independence from Spain, 1601–1609, 9 years. 30,000 gives 270,000 and 5% or 13,500.

War with Spain, 1621–1625, 5 years. 55,000 (size of the army raised in view of the two different fronts of the war, E VII, 546–555; in 1620, 33,600, D IV, 190) gives 275,000 and losses 10% (this figure is the average of the losses in the naval battle at Dunkirchen, 16%, and the typical rate of losses for the territorial wars, 5%) or 27,500.

Totals for the period: 545,000 and 41,000.

1626–1650.

———— War with Spain, 1626–1648, 23 years. 50,000 (Dunkirchen, naval, 1639, 28,000, B 65, E VII, 540–555) gives 1,150,000. Losses 10% (Dunkirchen 16%, B 65; see the preceding remark) gives 115,000.

War with Portugal, 1648–1650, 3 years. 20,000 gives 60,000 and 5% or 3000.

Totals for the period: 1,210,000 and 118,000.

1651–1675.

———— War with Portugal, 1651–1661, 11 years. 20,000 gives 220,000 and 5% or 11,000.

War with Portugal, 1663–1669, 7 years. 20,000 gives 140,000 and 5% or 7000.

War with Sweden, 1657–1660, 4 years. 30,000 (Copenhagen, 1658, 40,000 Danes and Dutch, B 792–794) gives 120,000 and 5% or 6000. (Considering the greater strength of the Dutch Navy

as compared with the Danish of the same epoch, the figure for the strength is taken.)

War with England, 1652–1655, 4 years. 13,000 (Scheveningen, 1653, naval, 15,000, B 82; La Hougue, 1653, naval, 10,000, B 80) gives 52,000 and losses 32% (Scheveningen 33%, B 82; La Hougue 30%, B 82) or 17,640.

War with England, 1665–1667, 3 years. 21,000 (Lowestoff, 1666, naval, 21,000, B 89) gives 63 000. Losses 30% (Lowestoff 30%, B 89) or 18,900.

War with England, 1672–1674, 3 years. 21,000 (Solebay, 1672, naval, 21,000, B 92) gives 63,000 and losses 12% (Solebay 12%, B 92) or 7560.

Second war with Louis XIV, 1673–1675, 3 years. 10,000 (the figure is raised in view of two different fronts of the war, E V, 365; Siege of Maestricht 5–30/VI, 1673, 6000, B 93) gives 30,000 and losses 5% or 1500.

Totals for the period: 688,000 and 59,600.

1676–1700.

———— Second war with Louis XIV, 1676–1679, 4 years. 25,000 (a figure of equal participation of Spanish and Dutch contingents is accepted, but the figure is raised due to two different fronts of the war, E V, 365; Mont-Cassel 11/IV, 1677, 30,000 Spanish and Dutch, B 101) gives 100,000 and 23.5% losses (Mont-Cassel 23.5%, B 101) or 23,500.

Third war with Louis XIV, 1688–1697, 10 years. 28,000 (see the previous remark) (Neerwinden 29/VII, 1693, 50,000 English, Dutch, and Imperials, B 118; Steinkirke 3/VIII, 1692, 63,000 English, Dutch, and Imperials, B 117) gives 280,000. Losses 17% (Neerwinden 24%, B 118; Steinkirke 10.5%, B 117) or 47,600.

Totals for the period: 380,000 and 71,100.

1701–1725.

———— War for the Spanish Succession, 1701–1713, 13 years. 50,000 (figure is raised in view of three different fronts of the war, E III, 402–404; Ramillies 23/V, 1706, 60,000 English and Dutch, B 147; Almansa 25/IV, 1701, 16,000 English, Dutch, and Portuguese, B 151; Malplaquet 11/IX, 1709, 93,000 English, Dutch, and Imperials, B 160; Velez-Malaga, naval, 1704, 46,000 English and Dutch, B 138) gives 650,000

---

[1] Abbreviations of the references in the tables on Holland mean:
W — K. Wenzelburger, *Geschichte der Niederlande* (Gotha, 1886), Vol. II.
B — G. Bodart, *Militär-historisches Kriegslexikon*.
D — as before.
E — as before.
En — as before.

total and losses 20.4% (Ramillies 8.4%, B 147; Almansa 31%, B 151; Malplaquet 27%, B 160; Velez-Malaga 15.5%, B 138) or 132,600.

War of the "Quadruple Alliance," 1718–1720, 3 years. 10,000 gives 30,000 and 5% or 1500.

Totals for the period: 680,000 and 134,100.

1726–1750.

———— War for the Austrian Succession, 1742–1748, 7 years. 19,000 (Rocoux 11/X, 1746, 75 000 English, Imperial, and Dutch, B 201–250; Lawfeldt 2/VII, 1747, 82,000 English, Dutch, and Austrians, B 211) gives 133,000 total strength. Losses 11% (Lawfeldt 11%, B 211) gives 14,630.

Totals for the period: 133,000 and 14,630.

1751–1775.

———— No important war.

1776–1800.

———— War with England, 1780–1784, 5 years. 20,000 gives 100,000 and 5% or 5000 losses.

First Coalitional War, 1792–1795, 4 years. 15,000 (Fleurus 26/VI, 1794, 46,000 Austrians and Dutch, B 293; Famars 23/V, 1793, 53,000, Austrians, English, and Dutch, B 271–283) gives 60,000. Losses 11% (Fleurus 11%, B 293) gives 6600.

War of Batavian Republic on the side of France, 1795–1800, 6 years. 25,000 (figure is increased in view of two different fronts of the war, VI, 270–284; Kamperduin 11/X, 1797, naval, 10,600, B 322; Groet-Keeten 27/VIII, 1799, 11,000 French and Dutch, B 340; Bergen 19/IX, 1799, 22,000 French and Dutch, B 340) gives 150,000 and losses 8% (Kamperduin 11%, B 322; Bergen 4.5%, B 340) or 12,000.

Totals for the period: 310,000 and 21,000.

1801–1825.

———— War of Batavian Republic on the side of France, 1801–1812, 12 years. 15,000 gives 180,000 and 10% or 18,000.

War of 1813–1814, 2 years. 15,000 gives 30,000 and 10% or 3000.

War of 1815, 1 year. 18,000 (Waterloo, 1815, 17,800, B 487) and 15.8% (Waterloo, B 487) or 2844.

Totals for the period: 228,000 and 23,844.

1826–1850.

———— War with Belgium, 1830–1833, 4 years. 50,000 gives 200,000 and 5% losses or 10,000.

Totals for the period: 200,000 and 10,000.

1851–1875.

———— Peace.

1876–1900.

———— Peace.

1901–1925.

———— Peace.

POLAND AND LITHUANIA [1]

1386–1400.

———— War with Teutonic Order, 1392, 1 year. Total strength 20,000 and the losses 4% or 800.

Russian-Lithuanian War, 1395–1396, 2 years. The strength at 20,000 gives a total of 40,000 and the losses at 4% or 1600.

War with Tartars (Edigey), 1399, 1 year. 20,000 and 4% or 800.

Totals for the period: 80,000 and 3200.

1401–1425.

———— Russian-Lithuanian War, 1401–1408, 8 years. 20,000 gives 160,000 and 4% or 6400 losses.

War with Teutonic Order, 1409–1410, 2 years. (Tannenberg, Grünwald, 10/VII, 1410, 11,000 to 15,000. D III, 539.) 15,000 gives 30,000 and 4% or 1200 losses.

War with Teutonic Order, 1413–1422, 10 years. 15,000 gives 150,000 and 4% or 6000.

Totals for the period: 340,000 and 13,600.

1426–1450.

———— Russian-Lithuanian War, 1426–1428, 3 years. 20,000 gives 60,000 and 4% or 2400.

Internal, of Swidrigail and the Teutonic Order, 1430–1434, 5 years. 40,000 gives 200,000 and 4% or 8000.

War with Turkey, 1443–1444, 2 years. 20,000 gives 40,000 and 4% or 1600.

Russian-Lithuanian War, 1445, 1 year. 20,000 and 4% or 800.

Totals for the period: 320,000 and 12,800.

1451–1475.

———— War with Teutonic Order, 1454–1466, 13 years. 20,000 gives a total of 260,000 and losses 4% or 10,400.

Hunyadi War, 1471–1475, 5 years. 20,000 gives 100,000 and 4% or 4000.

Totals for the period: 360,000 and 14,400.

1476–1500.

———— Hunyadi War, 1476–1478, 3 years. 20,000 gives 60,000 and losses 4% or 2400.

War with Russia, 1482–1500, 19 years. 20,000 gives a total of 380,000 and 4% or 15,200.

War with Turkey, 1486–1489, 4 years. 20,000 gives 80,000 and 4% or 3200.

Jahn Albrecht with Moldavia, 1497–1498, 3 years. 20,000 gives 60,000 and 4% or 2400 losses.

---

[1] Abbreviations of the references on Poland and Lithuania mean:
B — G. Bodart, *Militär-historisches Kriegslexikon.*
E — as before.
D — as before.

War with Turkey, 1499–1500, 2 years. 20,000
gives 40,000 and 4% or 1600.
Totals for the period: 620,000 and 24,800.

1501–1525.
——————— War with Russia, 1501–1503, 3 years.
30,000 gives 90,000 and 4% or 3600.
War with Moldavia, 1501–1506, 6 years.
30,000 gives 180,000 and 4% or 7200.
War with Crimea, 1506, 1 year. 15,000 and
4% or 600.
War with Russia, 1507–1508, 2 years. 30,000
gives 60,000 and 4% or 2400.
War with Russia, 1512–1522, 11 years. 30,000
gives 330,000 and 4% or 13,200.
War with Crimea, 1512–1515, 4 years. 15,000
gives 60,000 and 4% or 2400.
War with Teutonic Order, 1519–1520, 2 years.
30,000 gives 60,000 and 4% or 2400.
Totals for the period: 795,000 and 31,800.

1526–1550.
——————— War with Crimea, 1526–1528, 3 years.
15,000 gives a total of 45,000 and 4% losses or
1800.
War with Moldavia, 1530–1531, 2 years.
30,000 gives 60,000 and 4% or 2400.
Russian-Lithuanian War, 1534–1537, 4 years.
30,000 gives 120,000 and 4% or 4800.
War with Crimea (Khmelnitzky), 1534, 1 year.
15,000 and 4% or 600.
Totals for the period: 240,000 and 9600.

1551–1575.
——————— Intervention in Valakhia, 1552, 1
year. 15,000 and 2% gives 300 (the war was
of small intensity).
Intervention in the Livonic Order, 1556–1557,
2 years. 15,000 gives 30,000 and 2% or 600.
Livonian War with Russia, 1563–1575, 13 years.
30,000 (40,000 of Radzivill army, plus 70,000
army of Kurbski given in E VI, 81 and IV, 585,
appear little probable) gives 390,000 and losses
4% or 15,600.
War with Crimea, 1569, 1 year. 15,000 and
4% or 600.
War with Crimea, 1575, 1 year. 15,000 and
4% or 600.
Totals for the period: 460,000 and 17,700.

1576–1600.
——————— War with Crimea, 1576, 1 year.
15,000 and 4% or 600.
War with Russia, 1576–1582, 7 years. 40,000
(100,000 Polish army at Pskov appears little
probable, given in E VI, 222) gives 280,000 and
5% or 14,000.
War with Turkey, 1582, 1 year. 30,000 and
4% or 1200.
Civil war between Maximilian and Vasa, 1587–
1588, 2 years. 50,000 (for both sides) gives 100,-
000 and 4% or 4000.
Confederation and Sapolski, 1590, 1 year.
60,000 (for both sides) and 4% or 2500.
War with Cossacks of Nalivaiko, 1596, 1 year.
40,000 (for both sides) and 5% or 2000.

War with Turkey, 1 year. 30,000 and 4% or
1200.
War with Cossacks of Sagaidatchny, 1598–1600,
3 years. 40,000 (for both sides) gives 120,000
and 5% or 6000.
Totals for the period: 675,000 and 31,400.

1601–1625.
——————— War with Sweden, 1601–1609, 9 years.
50,000 gives 450,000 and 5% or 22,500.
War with Crimea, 1605, 1 year. 15,000 and
5% or 750 losses.
War with Cossacks of Sagaidatchny, 1605,
1 year. 45,000 (for both sides) and 5% or 2250.
Revolt of Zybrzidowski, 1606–1609, 4 years.
55,000 (for both sides) gives 225,000 and 5% or
12,250.
Intervention in Russia, 1609–1613, 5 years.
40,000 gives 200,000 and 5% or 10,000.
War with Russia, 1617–1618, 2 years. 40,000
gives 80,000 and 5% or 4000.
War with Turkey and Crimea, 1619–1621,
3 years. 50,000 gives 150,000 (50,000 Chotin
6/IX, 1621, B 49) and 5% losses or 7500.
Totals for the period: 1,065,000 and 59,250.

1626–1650.
——————— War with Sweden, 1626–1629, 4 years.
15,000 (7/I, 1626, 15,000, B 52, Wallhof) gives
60,000 and 15% or 9000.
War with Crimea, 1626–1628, 3 years. 15,000
gives 45,000 and 4% or 1800.
War with Cossacks of Taras, 1628, 1 year.
45,000 (for both sides) and 5% or 2250.
War with Russia, 1632–1634, 3 years. 40,000
gives 120,000 and 5% or 6000.
War with Cossacks of Pavluk, 1637, 1 year.
45,000 (for both sides) and 5% or 2250.
War with Cossacks of Ostraniitza, 1638, 1 year.
45,000 and 5% or 2250.
War with Cossacks of Khmelnitzky and Crimea,
1647–1649, 3 years. 90,000 (for both sides; at
Zcorow 15–16/VIII, 1649, 20,000–30,000 Poles
and 70,000 Cossacks and Tartars; at Zcarage,
1649, 12,000 Poles and 70,000 Cossacks, E III,
245) gives 270,000 and 20% or 54,000.
Totals for the period: 630,000 and 77,550.

1651–1675.
——————— War with Cossacks of Khmelnitzky
and Crimea, 1651–1654, 4 years. 100,000 (for
both sides) gives 400,000 and 20% losses or
80,000.
First Russian-Polish for Ukraine, 1654–1655,
2 years. 40,000 gives 80,000 and 5% or 4000.
First Northern War, 1655–1660, 6 years.
40,000 (all at Warsaw 28–30/VII, 1656, 70,000,
but of these 30,000–40,000 Tartars) gives 240,000
and 4% or 9600.
With Transylvania, 1657–1662, 6 years. 40,000
gives 240,000 and 4% or 9600.
Second Russian-Polish War, 1658–1667, 10
years. 40,000 gives 400,000 and 5% or 20,000.
Revolt of Lubomirsky, 1664–1666, 3 years.
40,000 (for both sides; at Montwy 13/VII, 1666,
Lubomirsky's 18,000 and 26,000 of king's army,

B 90; Montwy 23% losses) gives 120,000 and 23% or 27,600.

Turkish-Polish (Doroshenko) War, 1666–1667, 2 years. 12,000 (at Podgaiz, E VII, 583, 15/X, 1667) gives 24,000 and 5% or 1200.

War with Turkey, 1672–1675, 4 years. 31,000 (Chotin 11/XI, 1673, 50,000, B 94; Lemberg 15/VIII, 1675, 12,000, B 97) gives 124,000 and 2% (Chotin, B 94) or 2480.

Totals for the period: 1,124,000 and 154,480.

1676–1700.
——————— War with Turkey, 1683–1699, 17 years. 24,000 (Wiena 12/IX, 1683, 24,000, B 104) gives 408,000 and 14% (Wiena, 1683, 6.5%, B 104; Parkany 7/X, 1683, 22%, B 105) gives 57,120.

Totals for the period: 408,000 and 57,120.

1701–1725.
——————— Great Northern War, first period, 1701–1706, 6 years. 14,000 (Pultusk 1/V, 1708, 12,000, B 131) gives 84,000 and 16% (Pultusk 17%, B 131) gives 13,440. (Strength continued: Schagarin 27/III, 1708, 8700, B 130; Klissow 19/VII, 1702, 22,000, B 126.) (Losses continued: Riga 18/VII, 1701, 14%, B 124; Klissow 18%, B 126.)

Great Northern War, second period, 1709–1721, 13 years. 20,000 (two fronts for a short time) gives 260,000 and 16% or 41,600.

Tarnograd Confederation, 1715–1717, 2 years. 25,000 (for both sides) gives 50,000 and 11% or 5500.

Totals for the period: 394,000 and 60,540.

1726–1750.
——————— War for the Polish Succession, 1733–1735, 3 years. 20,000 gives 60,000 and 2% or 1200.

Totals for the period: 60,000 and 1200.

1751–1775.
——————— War with Russia, 1768–1772, 5 years. 10,000 (E VI, 608,613) gives 50,000 and 23% or 11,500.

Revolt of Gaidamacks, 1768, 1 year. 2000 (for both sides, E II, 374) and 23% or 460.

Totals for the period: 52,000 and 11,960.

1776–1800.
——————— Insurrectional, 1792–1794, 3 years. 30,000 (Dubienka 17/VII, 1792, 6000, B 268; Rawka 6/VI, 1794, 26,000, B 292; Brest Litowski 10/VI, 1794, 12,000, B 297; Maciejowice 10/X, 1794, 10,000, B 298; Praga 4/XI, 1794, 28,000, B 300) gives a total of 90,000 and losses 30% (Dubienka 16%, B 268; Rawka 12%, B 292; Brest Litowski 33%, B 297; Maciejowice 60%, B 298; Praga 28%, B 300) gives 27,000.

Totals for the period: 90,000 and 27,000.

FLUCTUATION OF INTERNAL DISTURBANCES IN INTRA-GROUP RELATIONSHIPS

ANCIENT GREECE

NUMBER	YEAR	SPECIFICATION OF THE INTERNAL DISTURBANCE	MEASURES OF:							SOURCES [2]
			Social Area	Duration	Size of the Masses Involved	Intensity	Masses and Intensity Combined	Nature [1]	Geometric Average	
1	2	3	4	5	6	7	8	9	10	11
1	B.C. 600	Insurrection of Panaetios at Leontine (Sicily) . . .	5	3	3	4	35	A	8.07	B I, 318
2	594	Disorders at Athens before Solon's reforms	40	3	2	2	10	B	10.63	G VII, 219
3	584–3	Riots at Athens	40	15	3	2	15	AB	20.80	B I, 188 Gl I, 443
4	582	Putting down the oligarchy at Corinth	10	1	3	4	35	A	7.05	Gl I, 323
5	561	Seizure of power by Pisistratus at Athens . . .	40	3	2	5	30	A	15.43	Bu 192
6	556	Rebellion against Pisistratus; his expulsion .	40	1	2	5	30	A	10.63	Bu 193
7	550	Return of Pisistratus . .	40	1	2	5	30	A	10.63	Bu 194
8	549	Second expulsion of Pisistratus	40	1	2	5	30	A	10.63	Bu 194
9	540	Polycrates puts down the oligarchy on the Samos; Pisistratus again at Athens	60	3	2	5	30	A	17.54	Bu 194 B I, 137
10	514	Riots at Athens; murder of Hipparchus	40	1	1	2	3	F	4.93	D I, 452
11	510	Deposition of Hippias at Athens and of the tyrant Aeschines in Sicyon . .	60	3	3	5	50	A	20.80	Bu 207 Gl I, 333

[1] See the text, p. 403, for a key to this column.
[2] Sources in the order of their appearance in the text. In the first item B I, 318, read as Julius Beloch, *Griechische Geschichte*, Vol. I, p. 318.

B —Julius Beloch. *Griechische Geschichte*, 2 vols. Strassburg, 1904.
G — George Grote. *History of Greece*, 12 vols. London, 1847–1856.
Gl — Gustave Glotz. *Histoire grecque*, 2 vols. Paris, 1925–1928.
Bu — J. B. Bury. *A History of Greece to the Death of Alexander the Great*. London, 1924.
D — Victor Duruy. *Histoire des Grecs*, 3 vols. Paris, 1888–1889.
C — Eugene Cavaignac. *Histoire de l'antiquité*, Vols. II and III. Paris, 1914.
R — Pierre Roussel. *La Grèce et l'Orient des guerres médiques à la conquête romaine*. Paris, 1928.
F — William S. Ferguson. *Hellenistic Athens*. London, 1911.
W — Ulrich Wilcken. *Griechische Geschichte in Rahmen der Altertumsgeschichte*. München, 1924.
En — *Encyclopaedia Britannica*, 14th ed.
Also: J. Bury, E. Barber, E. Bevan, and W. Tarn. *The Hellenistic Age*. Cambridge, 1923.
Corrado Barbagallo. *Le déclin d'une civilisation*. Paris, 1927.
M. Rostovtzeff. *History of the Ancient World*, Vol. I, of *The Orient and Greece*. Oxford, 1926.

ANCIENT GREECE — *Continued*

1	2	3	4	5	6	7	8	9	10	11
12	B.C. 508	Insurrection at Athens in favor of Alcmoenidae . .	40	3	3	2	15	F	12.16	B I, 333
13	491	Seizure of power by Gelon at Syracuse	10	3	2	5	30	A	9.66	Bu 299
14	489	Conspiracy and deposition of Cleomenes at Sparta .	40	3	2	4	20	A	13.39	B I, 367
15	488	Insurrection at Aegina . .	10	3	3	3	25	B	9.09	B I, 363
16	480	Insurrection in Arcadia . .	20	5	2	3	15	A	11.45	B I, 433
17	479	Revolution at Thebes . .	20	3	2	3	15	B	9.06	B I, 451
18	475	Revolt of Naxos against Athens	10	5	2	3	15	C	9.09	B I, 384
19	473	Revolution at Tarentum .	10	3	2	3	15	A	7.66	B I, 446
20	470	Conspiracy of Pausanias at Sparta	40	3	1	2	3	D	7.11	Bu 325
21	467	Anarchy in Sicily after the death of Gelon	40	10	4	4	50	A	27.14	B I, 445 / G V, 312
22	465–3	Insurrection of Thasos against Athens	10	20	2	3	15	B	14.42	G V, 417
23	464–55	Insurrection of helots in Sparta and Messenia . .	40	50	4	3	35	BC	41.21	B I, 457 / G V, 424
24	460–40	Insurrection of Sicily's natives against Greeks . .	40	85	3	3	25	C	49.19	G VII, 167
25	454	Insurrection of Tintaridas in Syracuse	40	3	3	2	15	F	12.16	B I, 446
26	445	Insurrection at Euboea . .	20	3	2	3	15	A	9.66	G V, 468
27	440	Revolt of Samos against Athens	20	5	3	4	35	C	15.18	Bu 383
28	428–7	Revolt of Lesbos against Athens	10	15	3	4	35	C	17.38	G VI, 298
29	427–5	Civil war at Corinth . . .	20	20	3	4	35	AB	24.10	Bu 419 / G VI, 514
30	424	Revolt of several cities against Athens and Sparta; revolution in Megara	40	5	3	4	35	CA	19.13	Bu 447 / G VI, 514
31	422	Insurrection of allies against Athens	40	3	3	3	25	C	14.42	G VI, 551–94
32	418	Revolution at Argos . . .	20	1	3	5	50	A	10.00	G VII, 130
33	417	Revolution at Argos and Sicyon	40	3	3	4	35	A	16.13	G VII, 133
34	412	Social revolution on Samos; insurrection on Chios and at Miletus against Athens	40	5	1	4	30	BC	21.54	B II, 65 / Bu 487
35	411	Revolution in the Athenian Navy; oligarchical revolution at Athens; an attempt at insurrection on Samos	60	3	2	5	30	A	17.54	Bu 494 / B II, 65 / G VIII, 36
36	410	Revolution in Salamis . .	10	3	3	4	35	A	10.16	G VIII, 22
37	406	Disturbances at Miletus .	10	1	2	2	10	A	4.64	G VIII, 289
38	405	Seizure of power by Dionysius at Syracuse . . .	40	3	2	5	30	A	15.43	B II, 90
39	404	" 30 tyrants " in Athens .	40	3	2	5	30	A	15.43	Bu 511
40	403	Deposition of " 30 tyrants " in Athens; uprising at Syracuse	80	5	3	5	50	A	27.14	Bu 513 / G X, 626
41	401	Oligarchical revolution at Elis	20	3	2	3	15	A	9.66	G IX, 313
42	397	Conspiracy of Kinadon at Sparta	20	1	3	2	15	A	6.69	G IX, 344
43	395	Insurrection of Sicilians against Dionysius; uprising of Rhodes against Sparta	40	5	4	3	35	C	19.13	G IX, 375 / G X, 687
44	383	Revolution in Thebes (oligarchical)	20	1	2	4	20	A	7.37	G X, 81
45	379	Revolution in Thebes against Sparta .	20	1	2	4	20	AC	7.37	G X, 113
46	376	Insurrection on Delos against Athens	20	3	2	3	15	C	9.66	Bu 568

ANCIENT GREECE — *Continued*

1	2	3	4	5	6	7	8	9	10	11
	B.C.									
47	371	Massacre at Argos; revolution at Tegea	40	3	4	4	50	A	18.17	G X, 271, 285
48	370	Revolution against the oligarchs in Middle Greece and Peloponnesus after Leuctra	60	3	3	4	35	A	18.47	B II, 259
49	369	Insurrection at Messenia; conspiracy at Corinth	20	5	4	3	35	AC	15.18	B II, 264, 278
50	366	Insurrection at Achaea and Sicyon	40	3	3	4	35	A	16.13	B II, 272
51	357-6	Civil war in Sicily (Dion.) .	40	15	2	3	15	F	20.80	G XI, 117
52	357	Revolt of the islands against Athens (" Union war ") .	20	5	3	3	25	C	13.57	G XI, 310
53	354	Revolution at Phocaea (Onomarchus)	10	3	2	3	15	A	7.66	B II, 324
54	352	Rebellion of Hipparinos at Syracuse	40	1	3	2	15	F	12.16	B II, 334
55	349	Uprising of Euboea against Athens	20	3	3	3	25	C	11.45	G XI, 473
56	345	Revolt at Elis	20	3	2	3	15	A	9.66	C II, 409
57	343	Dethroning of Dionysius the Younger at Syracuse .	40	3	2	5	30	A	15.43	D III, 586
58	337	Overthrow of the oligarchs in Sicily	40	3	3	5	50	A	18.17	B II, 586
59	335	Uprising of Thebes against Macedonia	20	3	3	4	35	C	12.81	G XII, 39
60	330	Uprising of Sparta (Agis) against Macedonia . .	40	5	3	4	35	C	19.13	G XII, 381
61	323	Uprising of Athens against Macedonia	40	5	3	3	25	C	17.10	R 385
62	318	Disturbances at Athens .	40	3	3	2	15	A	12.16	C III, 21
63	317	Seizure of power in Sicily by Agathocles	40	3	2	5	30	A	15.43	G XII, 541
64	303	Uprising in Athens . .	40	3	3	3	25	A	14.42	F 95, 122
65	295	Uprising in Athens . . .	40	3	3	3	25	A	14.42	F 95, 122
66	289	Civil war in Sicily; uprising in Athens	40	5	4	4	50	A	21.54	G XII, 607
67	287-6	Uprising in Athens . . .	40	3	3	3	25	A	14.42	F 95, 122, 151
68	281-0	Uprising of the Achaeans against Macedonia . .	40	10	3	3	25	C	21.54	D III, 414
69	275	Insurrection of Aegina against Macedonia . .	40	3	3	3	25	C	14.42	D III, 414
70	270	Murder of the tyrant Aristoaemus at Elis . . .	20	1	3	4	35	A	8.88	C III, 155
71	265-1	Insurrection of Athens, Sparta, and others against Macedonia . .	80	30	2	3	15	C	33.02	F 176 ff. C III, 156
72	251	Revolution at Sicyon .	20	3	2	4	20	AC	10.63	W 197
73	238	Dethroning of Agis in Sparta	40	3	2	4	20	A	16.13	D III, 435
74	227	Revolt of Cleomenes at Sparta	40	1	3	4	35	A	11.19	C III, 268
75	220	Disturbances in Messenia; civil war in Crete . . .	40	3	3	3	25	A	14.42	C III, 270 R 436
76	219	Uprising at Sparta . . .	40	1	3	2	15	A	8.43	C III, 271
77	218	Revolution at Sparta . .	40	3	3	4	35	A	16.13	C III, 271
78	217	Return of Lycurgus in Sparta	40	1	2	5	30	A	10.63	C III, 271
79	208	Seizure of power at Sparta by the tyrant Machanidos	40	1	3	5	50	A	12.60	C III, 305
80	207	Tyranny of Nabis at Sparta; social-revolutionary measures	40	5	3	5	50	AB	21.54	C III, 330
81	202	Insurrection in Messenia .	20	3	2	3	15	A	9.66	En XVII, 742
82	189	Insurrection in Messenia .	20	3	2	3	15	A	9.66	En XVII, 742
83	184	Insurrection in Messenia, death of Philopoemen .	20	3	2	3	15	A	9.66	En XVII, 742
84	147-6	Insurrection of Corinth against Romans; the end of the autonomy of the Greek cities	20	10	3	3	25	C	17.10	C III, 391

ANCIENT ROME

NUMBER	YEAR	SPECIFICATION OF THE INTERNAL DISTURBANCE	MEASURES OF:							SOURCES[2]
			Social Area	Duration	Size of the Masses Involved	Intensity	Masses and Intensity Combined	Nature[1]	Geometric Average	
1	2	3	4	5	6	7	8	9	10	11
	B.C.									
1	509	Dethroning of the Etruscan dynasty	100	3	3	5	50	A	24.66	P 81
2	493	First exit of the plebeians on the Aventine	80	3	4	2	20	AB	16.87	M I, 269
3	486	Conspiracy of Spurius Cassius	40	1	2	2	10	B	7.37	M I, 279
4	479–7	Disturbances in connection with the expulsion of the Fabii	80	20	3	2	15	F	28.84	D I, 164
5	460	Insurrection of Cacson . .	40	3	2	2	10	A	10.63	D I, 193
6	449	Deposition of the decemviri	100	3	3	5	50	A	24.66	S II, 5
7	444	Disturbances before proclaiming the " lex connubii "	60	3	2	2	10	B	12.16	S II, 5
8	439	Conspiracy of Maelius . .	60	3	2	2	10	A	12.16	S II, 15
9	438	Uprising of Fidenae . . .	20	3	2	3	15	F	9.66	S II, 136
10	414	Mutiny in the army . . .	40	1	2	3	15	F	8.43	D I, 225
11	385	Conspiracy and execution of Manlius	60	3	2	2	10	B	12.16	S II, 195
12	342	A new exit of the plebeians .	80	3	4	2	20	AB	16.87	Bl 91
13	287	Disturbances before " lex Hortensia "	80	3	3	3	25	AB	18.17	S II, 195
14	198	Rebellions of the slaves at Setia and Praeneste . .	20	3	3	3	25	B	11.45	M I, 859
15	196	Struggle against the slaves in Etruria	10	3	3	3	25	B	9.09	M I, 859
16	185	Conspiracy of the slaves in Apulia	10	3	3	2	15	B	9.09	M I, 859
17	180	Mutiny in the legions in Spain	40	3	2	3	15	F	12.16	Bl 148
18	171	Mutiny in the legions in Spain	40	0	1	3	15	F	12.16	Bl 148
19	134–3	Insurrection in Lusitania . .	20	15	3	3	25	C	19.57	M II, 4
20	134–2	Insurrection of the slaves in Sicily	20	20	4	3	35	B	24.10	M II, 78
21	133	Insurrection of the slaves at Rome, Minturnae, etc.; murder of Tiberius Gracchus	40	5	3	3	25	AB	17.10	M II, 77, 90
22	125	Insurrection at Fregellae .	10	3	2	3	15	C	7.66	Ro 106
23	121	Insurrection and murder of Caius Gracchus . . .	40	1	3	3	25	AB	10.00	M II, 123
24	104–1	Insurrection of the slaves in Sicily	20	25	4	3	35	B	25.96	M II, 136

[1] See the text, p. 403, for a key to this column.
[2] Sources in the order of their appearance in the text:

P   —A. Piganiol. *La conquête romaine.* Paris, 1927.
M   —T. Mommsen. *Römische Geschichte,* 8th ed., 3 vols. Berlin, 1888–1889.
D   —V. Duruy. *Histoire des romains,* 7 vols. Paris, 1888–1889.
S   —G. de Sanctis. *Storia dei Romani,* 4 vols. Rome, 1907–1923.
Bl —G. Bloch. *La république Romaine.* Paris, 1913.
Ro —M. Rostovtzeff. *Rome.* Oxford, 1925.
R-H —T. Rice-Holmes. *The Roman Republic,* 3 vols. Oxford, 1923.
J   —H. Stuart Jones. *The Roman Empire.* London, 1923.
Go —G. Goyau. *Chronologie de l'empire Romain.* Paris, 1891.
Bu —J. Bury. *The Later Roman Empire,* Vol. I. London, 1923.
J En —*Jewish Encyclopaedia.* New York and London, 1901–1905.
Also:
      Eugene Albertini. *L'empire Romain.* Paris, 1928.
      L. Homo. *L'Italie primitive et les débuts de l'impérialisme.* Paris, 1925.
      Ettore Pais. *Histoire de l'Italie antique.* Paris, 1928.
      O. Seeck. *Untergang der antiken Welt,* 2 vols. Berlin, 1901.

ANCIENT ROME — *Continued*

1	2	3	4	5	6	7	8	9	10	11
25	B.C. 100	Disturbances in connection with the "lex Saturnia".	40	3	3	2	15	B	12.16	M II, 207
26	91–89	War of the Allies	80	20	4	4	50	C	43.09	M II, 246
27	88	Disturbance in connection with the leges Sulpiciae .	40	3	3	2	15	B	12.16	M II, 253
28	87	Civil war (victory of Marius)	80	5	4	5	70	AB	30.37	M II, 311
29	84	Rebellion at Ancona . . .	10	3	2	3	15	A	7.66	M 318
30	83–2	Civil war (victory of Sulla)	80	5	4	5	70	AB	30.37	M 324
31	80–79	Conquest of Samnium . .	60	15	4	4	50	AB	35.57	M 331
32	78	Insurrection of Lepidus . .	20	3	2	2	10	F	8.43	R-H I, 135
33	77	Second insurrection and the death of Lepidus . . .	20	3	2	3	15	F	9.66	R-H I, 137
34	80–72	War with Sertorius in Spain	40	46	3	3	25	AC	35.83	M III, 20
35	73–1	Insurrection of the slaves in southern Italy (Spartacus)	60	20	4	3	35	B	34.76	M III, 84
36	66	First conspiracy of Catiline	40	3	2	2	10	A	10.63	M III, 109
37	63–2	Insurrection of Catiline . .	60	5	3	3	25	A	19.57	M III, 184
38	52	Street battles at Rome (Clodius and Milo) . .	40	3	2	2	15	F	12.16	M III, 337
39	49–6	Civil war (Caesar-Pompeius)	100	25	3	5	50	A	50.00	M III, 374
40	45	Struggle in Spain . . .	40	5	3	4	35	A	19.13	D III, 386
41	44	Disturbances after the murder of Caesar . . .	40	3	4	3	35	A	16.13	D III, 426
42	43	Struggle of the Senate with Antonius	40	5	2	3	15	A	14.42	Ro 150
43	42	Civil war (Antonius-Brutus)	60	10	3	3	25	A	24.66	D III, 484
44	41–0	Perusian war	40	15	3	3	25	F	24.66	D III, 500
45	37–6	War with Sextus Pompeius	20	15	2	3	15	F	14.42	D III, 518
46	31	War between Octavianus and Antonius . . .	60	10	3	3	25	F	28.23	D III, 549
47	27–5	Disturbances in Spain . .	40	15	3	2	15	C	12.16	J 19
48	22	Revolt at Rome	40	3	3	2	15	B	14.42	J 21
49	19	Disturbances in Spain . .	40	5	3	2	15	C	12.16	Go 18
50	13	Insurrection at Pannonia .	20	3	3	2	15	F	9.66	D IV, 111
51	10	Insurrection of the Hatts .	20	3	3	2	15	C	9.66	Go 29
52	4	Disturbances at Jerusalem	10	1	2	2	10	C	4.64	Go 35
53	A.D. 1	Uprising in Germany . .	20	3	3	2	15	C	9.66	Go 39
54	6	Uprising in Africa and Macedonia	40	3	2	3	15	F	12.16	Go 44
55	8	Uprising in Pannonia . .	20	3	2	3	15	F	9.66	Ro 196
56	14	Mutiny in armies on the Rhine and Danube . .	40	5	2	3	15	F	14.42	J 44
57	15	Disturbances at Rome . .	20	1	2	2	10	F	5.85	Go 54
58	24	Rebellion of the slaves in South Italy	40	5	3	3	25	B	17.10	Go 69
59	25	Uprising in Thracia . .	20	3	2	3	15	C	9.66	Go 70
60	28	Disturbances on the lower Rhine (Frisians) . .	10	5	3	2	15	C	9.09	Go 72
61	36	Disturbances in Asia Minor	20	3	2	2	10	C	8.43	Go 80
62	38	Jewish disturbances in Alexandria	10	3	2	2	10	C	6.69	J En I, 304
63	41	Murder of Caligula; proclamation of Claudius .	100	1	1	5	10	F	10.00	
64	42	Conspiracy at Rome (Scribonianus) . . .	40	1	2	2	10	F	7.37	J 60
65	44	Disturbances in Palestine .	20	3	2	2	10	CD	8.43	Go 95
66	59	Disturbances at Pompeii .	5	1	2	2	10	AB	3.68	Ro 270
67	61	Uprising in Britain . .	20	5	3	3	25	C	13.57	J 124
68	64	Fire of Rome and disturbances	40	3	4	2	20	D	13.39	J 79
69	65	Conspiracy at Rome . .	20	1	2	1	3	D	3.91	J 80
70	66–8	Uprising in Palestine . .	20	20	3	3	25	C	21.54	J 109
71	68	Uprising against Nero . .	100	3	2	5	30	D	20.80	J 84
72	69	"Year of the three Emperors"	100	10	3	5	30	F	36.84	J 84
73	69–70	Revolt of the Batavians .	20	10	3	3	25	C	17.10	J 121
74	70	Conquest of Palestine; rebellions in Gallia . . .	60	5	4	3	35	C	21.90	J 102 D IV, 604
75	73	Jewish rebellions in Egypt and Cyrene	20	3	3	3	25	C	11.45	Go 153
76	88	Mutiny of legions in Germania	20	3	2	3	15	F	9.66	J 137
77	95	Conspiracy at Rome . .	40	1	2	1	3	F	4.93	D IV, 722

ANCIENT ROME — *Continued*

1	2	3	4	5	6	7	8	9	10	11
	A.D.									
78	96	Murder of Domitianus; Nerva	100	3	2	5	30	D	20.80	J 148
79	97	Mutinies of armies on Rhine and Danube	40	5	2	3	15	F	14.42	D IV, 736
80	115–7	Jewish uprising in Egypt, Cyrene, and Cyprus	40	20	3	3	25	C	27.14	J En I, 365 / II, 400
81	117	Uprising in Britain	20	3	2	2	10	C	8.43	J 178
82	131–5	Uprising in Palestine (Bar-Kohba)	20	30	3	4	35	C	27.59	J En II, 507
83	141	Rebellion of Celsius	40	1	2	2	10	F	7.37	D V, 160
84	147–8	Uprising in Egypt	20	15	3	2	15	F	16.51	D V, 161
85	155	Jewish uprising in Palestine	20	3	3	3	25	C	11.45	Go 211
86	160	Uprising in Africa	20	3	2	3	15	F	9.66	Go 213
87	161	Disturbances in Gallia and Britain	60	5	3	3	25	F	19.57	D V, 179
88	170	Uprising in Egypt	40	3	2	3	15	F	12.16	D V, 202
89	175	Rebellion of Avidius Cassius	40	5	2	3	15	F	14.42	J 226
90	182	Conspiracy at Rome	40	3	2	2	10	F	10.63	J 230
91	186	Disturbances in Gallia and Spain	60	5	2	2	10	C	14.42	D VI, 20
92	189	Famine Revolution at Rome	40	1	3	2	15	B	8.43	J 232
93	193	Murder of Commodus; civil war	100	5	2	5	30	F	24.66	J 235
94	194	Struggle with Niger	80	10	2	3	15	F	22.89	J 237
95	194–6	Siege of Byzantium	20	20	2	3	15	F	18.17	J 240
96	197	Struggle with Albinus	40	5	2	3	15	F	14.42	J 240
97	212	Civil war (Caracalla)	40	3	2	3	15	F	12.16	J 225
98	217	Murder of Caracalla; Macrinus	100	1	2	5	30	F	14.42	J 262
99	218	Civil war (against Macrinus)	100	5	2	5	30	F	24.66	J 265
100	221	Mutiny of army near Rome	20	3	2	2	10	F	8.43	D VI, 282
101	222	Deposition of Heliogabalus	100	3	2	5	30	F	20.80	J 268
102	228	Disturbances in armies in Rome and Mesopotamia	40	3	2	3	15	F	12.16	J 271
103	231	Disturbances at Antiochia	10	1	2	2	10	C	4.64	Go 279
104	235	Deposition of Alexander Severus	100	1	2	5	30	F	14.42	J 278
105	238	Civil war (several emperors)	60	5	2	4	20	F	18.17	J 280
106	240	Rebellion at Carthage	10	3	2	3	15	F	7.66	J 287
107	244	Military rebellion (in Asia)	60	3	2	5	30	F	17.54	J 289
108	248–9	Revolts in Syria, Egypt, and at Rome	80	10	2	3	15	F	22.80	J 290
109	251	Civil war (at Rome and on the Danube)	60	5	2	4	20	F	18.17	D VI, 403
110	253–4	Civil war (battle at Terni)	60	10	2	4	20	F	22.89	J 303
111	257–68	Separate empire in Gallia	40	50	2	4	20	FC	35.93	D VI, 431
112	258–61	Civil war (Valerianus-Postumus)	60	20	2	4	20	F	28.84	J 303
113	268	Civil war (several emperors)	60	10	2	5	30	F	26.21	J 310
114	269	Revolt at Bologna and other cities	10	3	3	2	15	F	7.06	Go 322 / D VI, 487
115	270	Civil war (Quintilianus-Aurelianus)	100	3	2	5	30	F	20.80	J 316
116	273	Rebellion in Egypt and Palmyra	20	3	2	3	15	F	9.66	J 316
117	274	Revolt at Rome (monetarii)	20	1	3	3	25	F	7.94	J 325
118	275	Disturbances at Rome after the assassination of Aurelianus	100	3	2	5	30	F	20.80	J 347
119	276	Deposition of Tacitus; Probus	100	1	2	5	30	F	14.42	J 347
120	282	Military revolt; murder of Probus	100	1	2	5	30	F	14.42	J 350
121	284	Civil war (Diocletian-Carinus)	40	3	2	3	15	F	12.16	J 351
122	285	Disturbances in several provinces	40	3	3	3	25	FB	14.42	J 355
123	286	Rebellion in Britain	20	3	2	4	20	F	10.63	J 355
124	289	Rebellion in Mauritania	20	3	2	3	15	F	9.66	Go 342
125	291	Agitation in Africa	20	3	2	3	15	F	9.66	Go 345
126	295–6	Siege of Alexandria	10	10	3	3	25	F	13.57	D VI, 551
127	303	Commotion in Seleucia	5	1	2	2	10	F	3.60	Go 365
128	307	Civil war (Maxentius-Flavius Severus)	40	3	2	3	15	F	12.16	Go 375
129	308	Civil war (Maximianus-Maxentius)	80	3	2	4	20	F	16.87	J 380

ANCIENT ROME — *Continued*

1	2	3	4	5	6	7	8	9	10	11
	A.D.									
130	311–2	Civil war (Maxentius-Constantine)	80	10	2	4	20	F	25.20	J 382
131	313	Civil war (Licinius-Maximin Daia)	80	3	2	4	20	FD	16.87	J 383
132	314	Civil war (Licinius-Constantine)	80	3	2	3	15	DF	15.36	J 384
133	323	Civil war (Licinius-Constantine)	80	3	2	5	30	DF	19.31	J 386
134	335	Rebellion in Cairo . . .	10	3	2	3	15	F	7.66	J 391
135	337	Soldiers' mutinies (assassination of the members of the dynasty)	20	1	2	3	15	F	6.69	J 399
136	340	Civil war (Constantine the younger — Constantius)	80	3	2	3	15	F	15.36	J 400
137	342	Disturbances at Constantinople	5	3	3	2	15	D	6.08	Go 439
138	350	Revolt in Gallia (Magnentius)	40	3	2	4	20	F	13.39	J 401
139	351–2	Civil war (Constantius-Magnentius)	40	3	2	4	20	F	13.39	D VII, 227
140	352	Rebellion in Palestine . .	10	3	2	3	15	F	7.66	Go 455
141	354	Disturbances in Antiochia .	10	1	2	2	10	B	4.64	D VII, 234
142	355	Rebellion in Gallia; in Alexandria	60	3	3	3	25	DF	16.51	Go 462
143	361	Civil war (Julianus-Magnentius)	60	5	2	5	30	F	20.80	Go 486
144	362	Fights between Christians and Heathens	40	3	3	2	15	D	12.16	Go 495
145	363	Commotion in Antiochia . .	10	1	2	2	10	D	4.64	D VII, 392
146	365	Disturbances at Nicaea and Chalcedon	5	3	3	2	15	F	6.08	Go 513
147	366	Civil war (Procopius); commotion at Rome . . .	60	5	2	3	15	D	16.51	Go 518, 519
148	368	Rebellion in Britain . . .	20	3	2	3	15	F	9.66	D VII, 413
149	369	Conspiracy of Valentinianus	40	1	2	2	10	F	7.37	Go 529
150	383	Rebellion in Britain . . .	20	3	2	3	15	F	9.66	J 424
151	384	Famine riots in Britain . .	20	1	3	3	25	B	7.94	Go 582
152	387–8	Civil war (Theodosius-Maximus)	60	3	2	3	15	F	13.92	J 424
153	390	Rebellion at Saloniki . .	5	1	3	2	15	F	4.22	Go 603
154	391	Heathen rebellion in Alexandria	5	3	3	3	25	D	7.21	D VII, 461
155	392	Rebellion of Arbogastes .	60	3	2	4	20	D	15.36	J 425
156	394	Civil war (Theodosius-Arbogastes)	60	5	2	4	20	D	18.17	J 426
157	397–8	Rebellion in Africa . . .	20	10	2	3	15	F	14.42	Bu I, 122
158	407	Military rebellion in Britain	20	3	2	3	15	F	9.66	Bu I, 188
159	408	Rebels occupy Gallia and Spain	40	5	2	4	20	F	15.87	Bu I, 190
160	411	Civil war (Honorius-Constantine)	40	3	2	3	15	F	12.16	J 434
161	412	Rebellion of Jovianus . .	20	3	2	3	15	F	9.66	Bu I, 194
162	413	Rebellion of Heraclius (Africa)	40	5	2	3	15	F	14.42	Bu I, 196
163	422	Rebellion of Bonifacius (Africa); commotion at Ravenna	40	5	2	3	15	F	14.42	J 436 Bu I, 210
164	432	Civil war in Italy (Aetius-Bonifacius)	60	5	2	3	15	F	16.51	Bu I, 248
165	443	Peasant rebellion at Baetica	10	3	3	3	25	B	9.09	Bu I, 252
166	449	Conspiracy at Rome (Eugenius)	20	1	1	2	3	F	3.91	Bu I, 289
167	454	Assassination of Aetius and Valentinian III	40	1	2	4	20	F	9.28	J 443
168	456	Deposition of Avitus . .	80	1	1	5	10	F	9.28	Bu I, 328
169	475	Deposition of Julius Nepos	80	1	1	5	10	F	9.28	J 445
170	476	Dethroning of Romulus Augustulus	80	1	1	5	10	F	9.28	Bu I, 405

BYZANTIUM

NUMBER	YEAR	SPECIFICATION OF THE INTERNAL DISTURBANCE	MEASURES OF:							SOURCES[2]
			Social Area	Duration	Size of the Masses Involved	Intensity	Masses and Intensity Combined	Nature[1]	Geometric Average	
1	2	3	4	5	6	7	8	9	10	11
	A.D.									
1	532	Revolt of the "Nika" .	40	3	4	3	35	ABF	16.14	V I, 205
2	599–602	Revolt against Maurice, civil war	60	20	3	4	35	F	34.74	Bu II, 86–92
3	603–10	Revolt in Syria and Egypt; disturbances at Constantinople	60	42	3	4	35	F	44.46	Bu II, 199–206
4	641	Change of three emperors	40	10	2	4	20	F	20.00	Bu II, 284–86
5	668	Assassination of Constantine II; interregnum .	20	3	2	3	15	F	9.66	Bu II, 302–3
6	695	Dethroning of Justinian II	20	1	2	4	20	F	7.36	Bu II, 327–8
7	698	Dethroning of Leontius .	20	5	2	4	20	F	12.59	Bu II, 354
8	705	Dethroning of Tiberius III	20	1	2	4	20	F	7.36	Bu II, 360
9	711–7	Civil war	80	38	3	4	35	F	42.36	V I, 256–7, 303
10	726	Revolt in Greece . . .	20	3	3	3	25	D	11.45	V 342–3
11	741–3	Insurrection of Artavasdas	40	20	3	4	35	D	30.34	V 344
12	783	Revolt of Slovenians . .	20	5	4	3	35	C	15.17	Bu II, 484
13	786	Dispersing of the conclave by mutineer soldiers .	20	1	2	2	10	D	5.86	V II, 349
14	790–3	"Insurrection of the Caesars"	40	25	2	3	15	F	24.66	Bu II, 485–6
15	797	Dethroning of Constantine VI	20	1	2	4	20	F	7.36	Bu II, 488
16	802	The fall of Irene . . .	20	1	2	4	20	F	7.36	Bu II, 490
17	811	The fall of Stauracius . .	20	3	2	4	20	F	10.06	Bu III, 16–17
18	813	The fall of Michael I . .	20	3	2	4	20	F	10.06	Bu III, 26–28
19	820	The fall of Leo II . . .	20	3	2	4	20	F	10.06	Bu III, 48–56
20	821–3	Rebellion of Thomas the Slavonian	40	20	2	3	15	CF	22.91	Bu III, 84–100
21	867	Dethroning of Michael III	20	1	2	4	20	F	7.36	Bu III, 177–180
22	944–5	Anarchy	40	15	3	4	35	F	27.61	V I, 399
23	969	Assassination of Emperor Nicephorus Phoca . .	20	1	1	1	?	F	5.18	V I, 400
24	971	Rebellion of Bardas Phoca	60	3	3	4	35	F	18.46	Sc I, 59–74
25	976–80	Rebellion of Bardas Skleros	60	30	3	4	35	F	39.81	Sc I, 355–435
26	987–9	Rebellion of both Bardases	60	20	3	4	35	F	34.74	Sc I, 676–743
27	1022	Rebellion of Nicephorus Kaphias and Nicephorus Phoca	40	3	2	3	15	F	12.16	CMH 95
28	1031	Rebellion of Prusianus and Constantine Diogenes .	20	3	1	1	1	F	3.91	CMH 100
29	1042	People's rebellion at Constantinople	40	1	4	3	35	F	11.29	CMH 106–107
30	1043	Rebellion of Maniaces . .	20	3	3	3	25	F	11.45	CMH 110
31	1047	Rebellion of Tornicius . .	20	3	3	4	35	F	12.79	CMH 110–111
32	1057	Dethroning of Michael VI .	20	3	2	4	20	F	10.06	V I, 465
33	1078	Rebellion of Nicephorus Barangetus	20	3	2	4	20	F	10.06	V I, 465–6
34	1081	Deposition of Nicephorus .	20	3	2	4	20	F	10.06	V I, 466
35	1118	Conspiracy of Princess Anna	20	3	1	1	1	F	3.91	V II, 2
36	1182–3	Rebellion of Andronicus .	40	3	3	4	35	F	16.14	V II, 6
37	1185	Deposition of Andronicus .	40	3	2	4	20	F	13.40	V II, 7, 82–3
38	1186	Bulgarian rebellion . . .	20	5	4	4	50	C	17.10	V II, 87
39	1195	Deposition of Isaac Comnenus	20	3	3	4	35	F	12.79	V II, 84

[1] See the text, p. 403, for a key to this column.
[2] Sources in the order of their appearance in the text:

V — A. A. Vasiliev. *Histoire de l'empire byzantin.* Paris, 1932.
Bu II — J. B. Bury. *A History of the Later Roman Empire*, Vol. II. London, 1889.
Bu III — J. B. Bury. *A History of the Eastern Roman Empire, 809–867.* London, 1912.
Sc — G. Schlumberger. *L'épopée byzantine à la fin du X siècle.* Paris, 1896.
CMH — *The Cambridge Mediaeval History*, Vol. IV. Cambridge, 1923.

BYZANTIUM — *Continued*

1	2	3	4	5	6	7	8	9	10	11
40	c. 1200	Rebellion at Constantino-ple	40	3	3	3	25	F	14.66	V II, 85
41	1204	Rebellion at Constantino-ple	40	3	3	4	35	F	16.14	V II, 85
42	1205	Greek-Bulgarian rebellion	40	5	4	4	50	C	21.53	V II, 179
43	1261	Overthrow in favor of Michael Paleologue . .	20	1	1	4	7	F	5.18	V II, 213
44	1348	Rebellion of Andreas the Younger	40	3	3	4	35	F	16.14	V II, 258
45	1341–7	Civil war	60	38	3	4	35	F	43.05	V II, 259–60
46	1354	Deposition of Cantacuzene	20	3	2	4	20	F	10.06	V II, 260
47	1376	Dethroning of John V . .	20	3	1	4	7	F	7.48	V II, 261
48	1379	Armed reinstatement of John V	40	3	2	4	20	F	13.60	V II, 261
49	1390	Overthrow in favor of John VI	40	3	2	4	20	F	13.40	V II, 261

FRANCE

NUMBER	YEAR	SPECIFICATION OF THE INTERNAL DISTURBANCE	MEASURES OF:							SOURCES [2]
			Social Area	Duration	Size of the Masses Involved	Intensity	Masses and Intensity Combined	Nature [1]	Geometric Average	
1	2	3	4	5	6	7	8	9	10	11
1	531	Insurrection in Auvergne under the leadership of Arcadius	10	15	4	3	35	F	17.38	B 119
2	534	An attempt of Childebert and Chlotair to take away the succession from Theodobert	20	3	1	2	3	F	5.64	B 119–20
3	556	Insurrection of Chramn in Aquitaine	10	5	2	3	15	F	9.08	B 120
4	558–60	Second insurrection of Chramn	10	20	2	4	20	F	15.85	B 120–1
5	583	Murder of King Chilperic	20	1	1	4	7	F	5.18	B 142
6	584–5	Insurrection of Gondovald (Austrasia and the South)	40	15	3	3	25	F	24.66	B 143–4
7	587	Conspiracy of Austrasian nobles against Childebert	20	5	2	1	3	F	6.70	B 144
8	after 600	Conspiracy of Austrasian nobles against Brunhildis	20	5	2	2	10	F	10.00	B 147
9	605	Insurrection of Burgundian nobles	20	5	2	3	15	F	11.45	B 147
10	after 613	Insurrection of Burgundian nobles	10	5	2	3	15	F	9.08	B 157
11	673	Insurrection in Burgundy (for relative autonomy)	20	10	3	3	25	FC	17.10	B 166
12	678–86	Civil war between the mayors of the palace .	80	46	2	3	15	F	38.28	B 166–7
13	715	Civil war of Neustria against Austrasia and Aquitaine	60	5	3	4	35	F	21.88	H 206

[1] See the text, p. 403, for a key to this column. Statements like 14/T mean day and month (January 14).
[2] Sources in the order of their appearance in the text:

B   —C. Bayet, C. Pfister, and A. Kleinclauss. *Le christianisme, les barbares, mérovingiens et carolingiens.* (H. F., Vol. II, pt. i).[3] Paris, 1903.
H   —L. Halphen. *Les barbares,* Paris, 1926. (*Peuples et civilisations,* Vol. V.)
L   —A. Luchaire. *Histoire des institutions monarchiques de la France,* Paris, 1891. Vols. I and II.
He   —K. Hegel. *Städte und Gilden der germanischen Völker im Mittelalter,* Vol II. Leipzig, 1891.
G   —Guizot. *Histoire de la civilisation en France,* 2d ed., Vol. III, Paris, 1869.
Lu   —A. Luchaire. *Les premiers capétiens,* Paris, 1903 (H. F., Vol. II, pt. ii.)
Luc   —A. Luchaire. *Louis VII, Philippe Auguste, Louis VIII,* Paris, 1901. (H. F., Vol. III, pt. i.)
Luch   —A. Luchaire. *Les communes française,* Paris, 1911.
Be   —E. Berger. *Histoire de la reine Blanche de Castille,* Paris, 1895.
La   —C. Langlois. *Les derniers capétiens,* Paris, 1901. (H. F., Vol. III, pt. ii.)
C   —A. Coville. *Les premiers Valois,* Paris, 1902. (H. F., Vol. IV, pt. i.)
P   —C. Petit-Dutaillis. *Charles VII, Louis IX et les premières années de Charles VIII,* Paris, 1902. (H. F., Vol. IV, pt. ii.)
Le I, II   —H. Lemonnier. *Les guerres d'Italie, la lutte contre la maison d'Autriche,* Paris, 1903–1904. (H. F., Vol. V, pts. i–ii.)
M I, II   —H. Mariéjol. *La réforme et la ligue. Henri IV et Louis XIII,* Paris, 1904. (H. F., Vol. VI, pts. i–ii.)
Lav I, II   —E. Lavisse. *Le règne de Louis XIV,* Paris, 1907. (H. F., Vol. VII, pts. i–ii.)
C I   —H. Carré. *Le règne de Louis XV,* Paris, 1909. (H. F., Vol. VIII, pt. ii.)
C II   —H. Carré et P. Sagnac. *Le règne de Louis XVI,* Paris, 1910. (H. F., Vol. IX.)
Sa   —P. Sagnac et G. Parizet. *La révolution,* Paris, 1920. (H. F. cont.[3] Vols. I and II.)
Ch I   —S. Charléty. *Le restauration,* Paris, 1921. (H. F. cont., Vol. IV.)
Ch II   —S. Charléty. *La monarchie de juillet,* Paris, 1921. (H. F. cont., Vol. V.)
Ha   —E. Hamel. *Histoire de Louis-Philippe,* Vol. II, Paris, 1890.
S I   —C. Seignobos. *Révolution de 1848 et second empire,* Paris, 1921. (H. F. cont., Vol. VI.)
S II   —C. Seignobos. *Le déclin de l'empire,* Paris, 1921. (H. F. cont., Vol. VII.)
S III   —C. Seignobos. *L'évolution de la 3e république,* Paris, 1921. (H. F. cont., Vol. VIII.)
Also: G. Parizet. *Le consulat et l'empire,* Paris, 1920. (H. F. cont., Vol. III.)

[3] Abbreviations:

H. F.   —*Histoire de France,* ed. by E. Lavisse.
H. F. cont. —*Histoire de France contemporaine,* ed. by E. Lavisse.

FRANCE — *Continued*

1	2	3	4	5	6	7	8	9	10	11
14	717	Civil war of Neustria against Austrasia and Aquitaine	60	5	3	4	35	F	21.88	H 206
15	719	The same	60	5	3	4	35	F	21.88	H 206
16	720	Insurrection of Aquitanians for independence . . .	20	5	3	4	35	C	15.17	H 207
17	760–7	The same	20	42	4	4	50	C	34.74	B 277
18	769	The same	20	5	4	4	50	C	17.10	B 277
19	830–1	Insurrection against Emperor Louis by his sons .	60	15	2	4	20	FD	26.18	B 362–3
20	832–4	Second insurrection of the sons of Louis	60	15	2	4	20	F	26.18	B 364–5
21	840	Insurrection of Aquitanians in favor of Pepin II .	20	5	3	4	35	C	15.17	B 366
22	844–5	Insurrection in Bretagne and Aquitaine. . . .	40	15	4	6	50	C	31.05	B 377
23	848–52	Insurrection in Aquitaine.	20	30	4	4	50	C	31.05	B 377–8
24	887	Dethroning of Charles the Stout	20	1	1	4	7	F	5.18	L I, 6
25	922–3	Struggle of Charles the Simple and Robert . .	40	5	2	4	20	F	15.85	B 403
26	945	Capture of Louis the Simple by the inhabitants of Rouen	5	1	4	2	20	F	4.64	B 406–8
27	960	First insurrection at Cambrai against the bishop .	5	3	4	2	35	F	8.07	He II, 33
28	997	Peasant insurrection in Normandy	3	3	3	3	25	B	6.08	G 200
29	1030	Insurrection in Burgundy	20	5	2	4	20	F	12.59	Lu 156
30	1031–9	Insurrection of feudal barons against Henry I	40	46	2	3	15	F	30.02	Lu 161
31	1034	Peasant insurrection in Bretagne	3	3	3	3	25	B	6.08	G 200–1
32	1048–53	Insurrection of barons in Normandy	20	34	2	3	15	F	21.08	Lu 162
33	1060–2	Civil war during the infancy of Philip I	40	15	3	3	25	F	24.66	L I, 82
34	1064–8	Civil war in Anjou . . .	20	30	2	3	15	F	20.80	Lu 296
35	1069	Communal revolution at Le Mans	15	3	4	4	50	AB	9.08	Lu 348
36	1076	Communal revolution at Cambrai	5	3	4	4	50	AB	9.08	Lu 348
37	1099	Communal revolution at Beauvais	5	3	4	4	50	AB	9.08	Lu 349
38	1101–3	Second communal revolution at Cambrai	5	20	4	4	50	AB	17.10	Lu 349
39	1103	Feudal insurrection in Anjou	20	5	2	4	20	F	12.59	Lu 297
40	1106	Communal revolution at Vézélui	3	3	4	4	50	AB	6.08	Lu 354
41	1109	Insurrection of Norman, Aquitanian, and Burgundian dukes	40	5	2	3	15	F	14.66	L I, 83
42	1111–4	Communal revolution at Laon	3	25	4	3	35	AB	14.42	Lu 351–2
43	1113–7	Communal revolution at Amiens	5	30	4	4	50	AB	19.59	Lu 352
44	1120	Insurrection in Aquitaine against the duke by his son	20	5	2	3	15	F	11.45	Lu 309
45	1130	Communal revolution at Abbeville	3	5	4	4	50	AB	9.08	Lu 352
46	1131	Feudal coalition	40	3	2	3	15	F	12.16	L I, 83
47	1132	Communal revolution at Orléans (unsuccessful) .	5	3	4	3	35	AB	8.07	L 354
48	1137	Communal revolution at Poitiers and neighboring cities	10	3	4	3	35	AB	10.02	Lu 354–5
49	1139	Communal revolution at Reims (unsuccessful) .	5	5	4	3	35	AB	9.52	Lu 353–4
50	1140	Communal revolution at Sens (unsuccessful) . .	3	5	4	3	35	AB	8.07	Lu 354
51	1153	Communal revolution at Chateauneuf la Tour .	3	5	4	3	35	AB	8.07	L II, 172
52	1164	Communal revolution at Chateauneuf la Tour .	3	5	4	3	35	AB	8.07	L II, 172
53	1173–5	General insurrection of nobles in Anjou, Bretagne, Touraine, Poitou, and Normandy . . .	40	10	2	3	15	F	18.15	Luc 70

FRANCE — *Continued*

1	2	3	4	5	6	7	8	9	10	11
54	1177	Peasant insurrection near Laon	3	5	3	3	25	BF	7.21	Luc 81
55	1178	Communal revolution at Valence	3	5	4	4	35	AB	8.07	Luc 406
56	1181–4	Feudal coalition	40	25	2	3	15	A	24.66	Luc 86–9
57	1181	Insurrection at Aurillac .	3	5	4	3	35	AB	8.07	Luc 406
58	1185	Insurrection at Soissons .	3	5	4	3	35	AB	8.07	Luc 405
59	1189	Civil war at Toulouse . .	5	5	4	3	35	F	9.52	Luc 407
60	1194	Insurrection at Mende . .	3	3	4	4	50	F	7.65	Luc 407
61	1194	Insurrection at Rouen . .	5	3	4	3	35	F	8.07	Luc 405
62	1197	Second feudal coalition (as in 1181)	40	15	7	3	15	A	20.80	Luc 116
63	1203	Communal revolution at Limoges (unsuccessful) .	3	3	4	3	35	AB	6.76	Luc 406
64	1207–9	Civil war at Nimes . . .	5	20	4	3	35	AB	15.17	Luc 407
65	1207–21	Peasant insurrection in the Orléans episcopate . .	3	66	3	3	25	B	17.06	Luc 293–4
66	1208	Communal revolution at Avignon	5	3	4	3	35	AB	8.07	Luc 407
67	1208	Communal revolution at Lyon (unsuccessful) . .	5	3	4	3	35	AB	8.07	Luc 406
68	1209	Communal revolution at Metz	3	3	4	3	35	AB	6.76	Luch 253
69	1209	Communal revolution at Verdun	3	3	4	4	50	AB	7.65	Luch 253
70	1210–9	Armed struggle at Le Puy	3	50	4	3	35	AB	17.38	Luc 406
71	1210	Insurrection at Aurillac .	3	3	4	4	35	AB	7.21	Luc 406
72	1217	Insurrection at Toulouse .	5	5	4	3	35	F	9.52	Luc 278
73	1217–8	Communal revolution at Marseilles	5	15	4	3	35	AB	14.42	Luc 407
74	1219	Peasant disturbances near Corbie and Chables . .	3	5	3	2	15	BF	6.08	Luc 394
75	1222	Communal revolution at Noyon	3	5	4	4	50	AB	9.08	Luch 284
76	1225	Civil war at Avignon . .	5	3	4	4	50	AB	9.08	Luc 409
77	1226	Feudal coalition against Louis IX	40	10	2	2	10	F	15.85	Be 80–3
78	1228–9	Second feudal coalition . .	40	15	2	2	10	F	18.15	Be 123–5
79	1230	Third feudal coalition . .	40	10	2	2	10	F	15.85	Be 153–5
80	1238	Insurrection at Corbie . .	3	5	4	3	35	AB	8.07	Luch 259
81	1241	Fourth feudal coalition .	40	10	2	2	10	F	15.85	Be 350–1
82	1251	The " Pastourneaux " at Paris	20	5	2	3	15	D	11.45	La 80
83	1280–1	Insurrection at Douai, Tournai, Provins, and Rouen	10	15	4	3	35	AD	17.38	La 71
84	1305	Insurrection at Beauvais .	3	5	4	3	35	AB	8.07	Luch 259
85	1314	" Disturbances of the barons "	80	5	2	1	3	F	10.06	La 265–6
86	1334	Insurrection at St. Pigiers	3	3	4	3	35	F	6.76	Luch 261–7
87	1357 (14/I)	Disturbances at Paris . .	20	1	3	1	5	A	4.64	C 118
88	1358 (22/II)	The same	20	1	3	3	25	A	7.92	C 128
89	1358	" Jacquerie "	60	3	3	3	25	AB	16.52	C 133–7
90	1378–79	Disturbances at Puy, Montpellier, Clermont, and Alain	10	10	3	2	15	F	11.45	C 270
91	1379	Insurrection of Bretagnian barons against the duke	20	3	2	2	10	F	8.43	C 249–50
92	1380	Disturbances at Paris, Normandy, and Picardy .	60	5	3	2	15	F	16.52	C 272
93	1381	Insurrection at Béziers .	3	5	3	3	25	FD	7.21	C 277
94	1382	Disturbances at Paris and Rouen	60	5	3	3	25	AF	19.59	C 275–6
95	1413	Disturbances at Paris . .	20	5	3	2	15	AF	11.45	C 343–50
96	1418	Disturbances at Paris and Burgundy	60	5	3	3	25	AF	19.59	C 377
97	1438	Feudal coalition " La Praguerie "	40	3	2	1	3	F	7.12	P 281
98	1440	Feudal coalition " La Praguerie " — 2d time . .	40	5	2	2	10	F	12.59	P 281–2
99	1444	Disturbances at Toulouse	5	3	3	1	5	A	4.21	P 277
100	1446	Conspiracy of the dauphin	20	5	1	1	1	F	4.64	P 288–9
101	1455	" Guerre du bien public "	40	5	2	1	3	F	8.43	P 345
102	1467	Feudal coalition	40	5	2	1	3	F	8.43	P 355
103	1471–2	Feudal coalition	40	10	2	1	3	F	10.06	P 366–8

FRANCE — *Continued*

1	2	3	4	5	6	7	8	9	10	11
104	1485	"La guerre folle" (Foolish war)	40	10	2	1	3	F	8.43	P 431–2
105	1539	Armed conflict at Paris and Lyon	60	3	2	2	10	BF	12.16	Le I, 273
106	1542	Insurrection at La Rochelle, Libourne, and Bordelais	10	3	3	2	15	F	7.65	Le II, 119–20
107	1548	Insurrection at Pays de Blois et de Saintonge	10	5	3	3	25	F	10.76	Le II, 137
108	1560	An attempt to seize the king at Amboise	3	1	2	1	3	F	2.08	M I, 177
109	1562–3	First religious war	40	10	3	3	25	D	10.00	M I, 62–74
110	1566–8	Second religious war	40	15	3	3	25	D	11.45	M I, 93–100
111	1568–70	Third religious war	40	15	3	4	35	D	27.61	M I, 106–113
112	1572–7	Fourth religious war	60	30	3	4	35	D	39.81	M I, 129–30
113	1585–93	Fifth religious war	60	42	3	4	35	D	44.46	M I, 254–380
114	1579–80	Insurrection of peasants in Dauphiné	3	10	3	3	25	BF	9.08	M II 4
115	1590	Insurrection of peasants in Normandy	5	5	3	3	25	BF	8.55	M II, 4
116	1592	Insurrection of peasants at Comminges	1	5	3	3	25	BF	4.86	M II, 4
117	1594–5	Insurrection of peasants at Périgord, Limousin, Agenois, and Quercy	5	5	3	3	25	BF	8.55	M II, 4
118	1601	Insurrection at Poitiers	3	3	3	2	15	F	5.13	M II, 41
119	1615	Protestant uprising in Languedoc	20	5	3	2	15	D	11.45	M II, 183
120	1620	Protestant uprising in three provinces	40	3	3	2	15	D	12.16	M II, 203
121	1625–8	Protestant uprising in La Rochelle and Ile de Ré	10	20	3	4	35	D	19.14	M II, 234–69
122	1630	Insurrection at Dijon	5	1	3	3	25	F	4.86	M II, 431
123	1631	Insurrection at Paris	40	1	3	3	25	F	10.00	M II, 286
124	1631	Insurrection in Provence	20	1	3	3	25	F	7.92	M II, 431
125	1632	Insurrection at Lyon	5	1	3	3	25	F	4.86	M II, 431
126	1635–7	Insurrection at Limousin, Poitou, Gascogne, Normandy, Bordeaux, Perigueux, Monferrand, Cannes, Rouen, etc.	60	15	3	3	25	F	28.25	M II, 431–3
127	1649	First attack of the Fronde (around Paris)	20	5	2	2	10	F	10.00	Lav I, 43
128	1650	Second attack of the Fronde at Guyenne	20	10	2	2	10	F	12.59	Lav I, 47
129	1651	Third attack of the Fronde in different provinces	40	10	2	2	10	F	10.06	Lav I, 47
130	1662–4	Insurrection at Laval, Clermont, Poitou, Burgundy, Boulonnais, Béarn, and Bigorre	40	15	3	3	25	F	24.66	Lav I, 345–9
131	1669	Insurrection at Lyon	5	1	2	2	10	F	3.68	Lav I, 346
132	1670	Insurrection of peasants at Vivarrais	1	5	3	2	15	F	4.21	Lav I, 349
133	1675	Insurrection in Poitou, Bordeaux, and Bretagne	40	5	3	3	25	F	17.10	Lav I, 350–53
134	1680	Insurrection of peasants near Crossé in Champagne	1	3	3	2	10	F	3.15	Lav I, 346
135	1685	Insurrection of unemployed in Normandy	20	3	3	2	15	F	9.66	Lav II, 275
136	1702–10	Protestant insurrection in the Cevennes	20	42	3	2	15	D	23.28	Lav II, 378–9
137	1703	"Grande Peur"	40	3	4	1	7	F	9.44	Lav II, 276
138	1706–9	Insurrections at Paris, Rouen, Perigord, and Quercy	60	25	2	2	10	F	24.66	Lav II, 275 383, 485
139	1719	An attempt at insurrection in Bretagne	20	5	2	1	3	F	4.70	C I, 55–6
140	1720	Riot in front of the Bank Law at Paris	20	1	2	2	10	F	5.84	C I, 37
141	1740	Famine revolution at Paris	20	3	3	2	15	F	9.66	C I, 110
142	1744 (6/VIII)	Disturbances at Lyon	3	1	2	2	10	B	3.15	C I, 104–5
143	1774 (VIII)	Disturbances at Paris in connection with a conflict at Parliament	20	1	2	2	10	BF	7.36	C II, 12

FRANCE — *Continued*

1	2	3	4	5	6	7	8	9	10	11
144	1775–6	Disturbances of peasants in Picardy and Ile de France	3	5	3	2	15	BF	6.08	C II, 32–3
145	1776	Disturbances of peasants in Bretagne	3	5	3	2	15	B	6.08	C II, 45
146	1787 (12/VIII)	Seizure of the Palais de Justice by a mob . .	20	1	3	2	15	AF	6.70	C II, 337–8
147	1788	Insurrection of peasants in different provinces . .	10	5	3	3	25	F	10.47	C II, 372–3
148	1789–99	The great revolution . .	100	50	5	5	100	A	79.43	Sa I, 27–II 426
149	1803	Conspiracy of Pichegru and Moreau	20	3	1	1	1	F	3.91	Pa 204
150	1803	Disturbances in Vendée .	10	3	2	2	10	A	6.70	Pa 201–2
151	1812	Conspiracy of Mallet . .	20	3	1	1	1	F	3.91	Pa 128–9
152	1815 (March)	Military insurrection of Napoleon	60	3	4	5	70	A	23.28	Ch I, 46–8
153	1815 (VI/VIII)	Civil war in the south . .	60	5	3	3	25	F	19.59	Ch I, 77–8
154	1816	Insurrection at Grenoble .	5	1	2	2	10	A	3.68	Ch I, 173
155	1820	Disturbances at Paris . .	20	1	3	1	5	A	4.64	Ch I, 174
156	1821–2	Conspiracy of the Carbonarii	20	3	2	1	3	A	5.64	Ch I, 178–9
157	1830	Revolution of July . .	40	3	4	5	70	A	20.32	Ch I, 372–89
158	1831	Insurrection at Lyon . .	5	3	4	3	35	AB	8.07	Ch II, 65–6
159	1832	Insurrection at Paris . .	20	1	4	3	35	A	8.87	Ch II, 78
160	1834	Armed insurrection at Paris, Lyon, and Marseilles.	60	3	4	3	35	AB	18.46	Ch II, 104–17
161	1836	An attempt of Louis Napoleon at Strasbourg .	5	1	1	2	3	A	2.46	Ch II, 142
162	1839	Barricades at Paris . . .	20	1	1	2	3	A	5.84	Ch II, 158
163	1840	Second attempt of Louis Napoleon	5	1	1	2	3	A	2.46	Ha II, 149–53
164	1848	Revolution of February .	40	3	4	5	70	AB	20.32	Ch II, 383–99
165	1848	Insurrection of June . .	20	3	3	3	25	AB	11.45	S I, 245–8
166	1849	Disturbances at Lyon . .	5	3	3	3	25	AB	8.07	S I, 139
167	1851	Coup d'état by Louis Napoleon	20	3	2	5	30	A	12.16	S I, 201–21
168	1858	Insurrection at Chalon s. Saone	5	1	2	2	10	AB	3.68	S I, 267
169	1870	Deposition of the empire .	20	1	3	5	50	A	10.00	S II, 245–8
170	1871	Commune at Paris . . .	40	5	4	4	50	AB	21.53	S II, 293, 317
171	1899	Strikes, ended by armed conflicts	10	3	3	3	25	B	9.68	S III, 213
172	1901	Conflicts in connection with dissolutions of the congregations . . .	40	5	3	2	15	AD	14.66	S III, 229
173	1908	Disturbances in the vineyard departments . .	40	5	3	2	15	B	14.66	S III, 261–2

GERMANY AND AUSTRIA

NUMBER	YEAR	SPECIFICATION OF THE INTERNAL DISTURBANCE	MEASURES OF:							SOURCES[2]
			Social Area	Duration	Size of the Masses Involved	Intensity	Masses and Intensity Combined	Nature[1]	Geometric Average	
1	2	3	4	5	6	7	8	9	10	11
1	709	Uprising of the Allemanni	20					C		G I, 168
2	724	Uprising in Bavaria	20	5	3	2	15		7.65	B 52
3	725	Expedition of C. Martel against the uprising in Bavaria	20	5	3	3	25	C	13.58	B 53
4	727-8	Uprising in Allemannia and Bavaria	40	15	3	2	15	C	20.80	B 56
5	730	Uprising of the Allemannian Duke Winifred	20	3	3	3	25	C	11.45	B 59
6	742	Uprising of the Allemannian Duke Theotbald	20	3	3	3	25	C	11.45	H 23-4
7	745-6	Uprising in Allemannia	20	15	3	2	15	C	16.52	H 83
8	748	Uprising of Grifo in North Schwaben	10	5	2	3	15	F	9.08	H 93
9	749	Uprising of Grifo in Bavaria	20	5	3	3	25	F	13.58	H 115-6
10	774	First uprising of Saxons	20	5	4	4	50	C	17.10	M 119
11	776	Second uprising of Saxons	20	5	4	4	50	C	17.10	M 121
12	779	Third uprising of Saxons	20	5	4	4	50	C	17.10	M 122
13	782	Fourth uprising of Saxons	20	5	4	4	50	C	17.10	M 129
14	784-5	Fifth uprising of Saxons	20	15	4	4	50	C	24.66	M 133
15	786	Uprising of nobles in Thuringia	10	5	2	3	10	F	7.92	M 135
16	792-4	Uprising of Saxons	20	20	4	4	50	C	27.16	M 136
17	830	Uprising against Ludwig the Pious of his sons	40	10	2	4	20	F	20.00	M 372
18	832	Uprising of nobles in Bavaria	20	5	2	3	10	F	10.00	M 382
19	833-5	Second uprising of the sons of Ludwig the Pious	40	20	2	4	20	F	25.12	G I, 208
20	861	Uprising of Karloman against Ludwig the German	20	5	1	3	5	F	7.92	R 613
21	865	Uprising of Ludwig against Ludwig the German	20	5	1	3	5	F	7.92	R 619
22	870	Uprising of Charles	20	3	1	2	3	F	5.64	R 626
23	871	Uprising of Ludwig and Charles	40	5	2	3	15	F	14.66	M 553-4
24	882	Civil war in Ostmark	10	5	3	3	25	F	10.76	M 604
25	887	Uprising against Charles the Stout; his deposition	40	1	3	4	35	F	11.29	M 617
26	890	Attempt at uprising in Allemannia	20	1	2	1	3	F	3.91	M 627

[1] See the text, p. 403, for a key to this column.
[2] Sources in the order of their appearance in the text:

G   — B. Gebhardt. *Handbuch der deutscher Geschichte*, 2 vols.   Stuttgart, 1891.
B   — T. Breysig.   *Die Zeit Karl Martells*.   Leipzig, 1869.
H   — H. Hahn.   *Jahrbücher des frankischen Rechts*.   Berlin, 1863.
M   — E. Mühlbacher.   *Deutsche Geschichte unter den Karolingen*.   Stuttgart, 1896.
R   — *Die Regenten der Kaiserzeit unter den Karolingen*.   Innsbruck, 1908.
K   — R. Köpke and S. Dummler.   *Kaiser Otto der Grosse*.   Leipzig, 1876.
Gi — W. Giesebrecht.   *Geschichte der deutschen Kaiserzeit*, 4 vols.   Braunschweig, 1875-1895.
L   — O. Lorenz.   *Deutsche Geschichte in 13 und 14 Jahrhunderts*.   Wien, 1883.
He — K. Hegel.   *Städte und Gilden in deutschen Mittelalter*.   Leipzig, 1891.
Li — T. Lindner.   *Deutsche Geschichte unter den Habsburgern und Luxemburgern*, Vol. III.   Stuttgart, 1893.
J   — J. Janssen.   *Geschichte des deutschen Volks seit dem Ausgange des Mittelalters*.   Freiburg im Breisgau, 1897-1899.
Ha — L. Hausser.   *Deutsche Geschichte vom Tode Friedrich des Grossen bis zur Gründung des deutschen Bundes*, Vol. III.   Berlin, 1863.
Bi — V. Bibl. *Der Zerfall Oesterreichs*.   Wein, 1924.
S   — E. Strauss.   *Die Entstehung der Tchecho-Slovakischen Republik*.   Prag, 1934.
En — *Encyclopaedia Britannica*, supp. vols. to 13th ed.

GERMANY AND AUSTRIA — *Continued*

1	2	3	4	5	6	7	8	9	10	11
27	895	Disturbances in northern Bavaria	10	3	3	2	15	F	7.65	M 627
28	912	Expedition of Conrad against Lorraine . . .	20	5	3	3	25	F	13.58	G I, 243
29	915	Struggle of the king with the Duke of Saxony . .	20	3	2	3	20	F	10.06	G I, 243
30	915	Expedition of the king against rebel dukes of Bavaria and Swabia. . .	40	5	2	3	20	F	15.85	G I, 243
31	929	Insurrection of Slavonic tribes	10	5	4	3	35	C	12.05	G I, 249
32	930	The same	10	5	4	3	35	C	12.05	G I, 251
33	939	The same	10	5	4	4	50	C	13.58	K 85–6
34	939	Feudal uprising in Franconia, Bavaria, and Saxony	40	5	2	3	15	F	14.66	K 71–80
35	941	Conspiracy of Henry . .	20	3	1	2	3	F	5.64	K 117
36	953–4	Uprising of Ludolf . . .	20	10	1	2	3	F	8.43	K 211–2
37	954	Insurrection of Slavonic tribes	10	3	4	3	35	C	10.02	K 250–1
38	973	Disturbances in Lorraine .	20	3	2	2	10	F	8.43	G I, 264
39	974–6	Feudal uprising in Bavaria and Swabia	40	15	2	3	15	F	20.80	G I, 264
40	977	Feudal uprising in Bavaria	20	5	2	3	15	F	11.45	G I, 265
41	983	Insurrection of Slavonic tribes	10	5	4	4	50	C	13.58	G I, 266–7
42	985	Dynastic uprising after the death of Otto II . . .	40	1	1	4	7	F	6.54	G I, 267
43	1002	Expedition of Henry II against Swabia . . .	20	5	2	3	15	F	11.45	Gi II, 23–4
44	1003	Conspiracy of Margrave Henry	20	3	1	1	1	F	3.91	Gi II, 34–6
45	1005	Uprising in Western Franconia	10	3	2	2	10	F	6.70	Gi II, 49
46	1008	Disturbances in Lorraine .	20	3	2	2	10	F	8.43	Gi II, 103
47	1012	Disturbances at Metz . .	5	3	3	3	25	F	7.21	Gi II, 162–3
48	1018–9	Insurrection of Slavonic tribes	10	3	4	4	50	C	11.45	Gi II, 165–6
49	1019	Uprising of Conrad of Franconia and feudal barons of Saxony . .	40	3	2	3	15	F	12.16	Gi II, 162–3
50	1025	Feudal coalition	40	3	2	2	10	F	10.06	Gi II, 236–7
51	1027	Second uprising of Conrad of Franconia	40	3	2	2	10	F	10.06	Gi II, 253–5
52	1044–5	Uprising in Lorraine . .	20	5	2	4	20	F	12.59	Gi II, 391–3
53	1048–9	Feudal war in Lorraine .	20	10	2	3	15	F	14.66	Gi II, 474 f
54	1053	Uprising of Conrad of Bavaria	20	5	2	3	15	F	11.45	Gi II, 485–8
55	1055	Feudal conspiracy in different parts of the Empire	60	5	1	1	1	F	6.76	Gi II, 523
56	1056	Feudal uprising in northern Saxony	10	3	2	3	5	F	5.31	Gi II, 529
57	1062	Deposition of the Regent Agnes	20	1	1	4	7	F	5.18	Gi III, 81–2
58	1066	Insurrection of Slavonic tribes	10	3	4	4	50	C	11.45	Gi III, 136–7
59	1069	Uprising of Margrave Dedi	10	1	2	2	10	F	4.64	Gi III, 146–7
60	1071	Uprising of the Bavarian Otto	20	3	2	3	15	F	9.66	Gi III, 159–62
61	1073	Uprising in Saxony and Thuringia	40	5	3	4	35	F	19.14	G I, 311
62	1073	Movement in the Rhine cities against the bishops	10	5	4	3	35	AF	12.05	G I, 311
63	1075	Uprising in Saxony . . .	20	5	4	4	50	F	17.10	G I, 314
64	1077–80	Struggle of Henry IV with Rudolph	60	20	3	3	25	F	31.05	G I, 316–7
65	1105	Deposition of Henry IV .	20	3	2	4	20	F	10.06	Gi III, 753–761
66	1106	Local uprising in Alsace .	5	3	3	3	25	F	7.21	Gi III, 751
67	1112	Uprising in Saxony . . .	20	3	3	3	25	F	11.45	Gi III, 838–42
68	1115	Uprising at Köln and Mainz	10	3	3	3	25	F	10.02	Gi III, 850–61
69	1126–30	Disturbances in Swabia, Lorraine, Saxony, and Bavaria	60	30	3	2	15	F	13.90	Gi IV, 176–96
70	1138–42	First struggle of the Staufens with the Guelfs .	20	30	2	3	15	F	20.80	Gi IV, 176–96
71	1143	Disturbances in Bavaria and Lorraine	40	5	3	2	15	F	14.66	Gi IV, 257

GERMANY AND AUSTRIA — *Continued*

1	2	3	4	5	6	7	8	9	10	11
72	1150	A new uprising of the Guelf	20	5	2	3	15	F	11.45	Gi IV, 333
73	1155	Conspiracy of the feudal barons in Bavaria and Saxony	40	5	1	1	1	F	5.84	Gi V, 74–5
74	1158–9	Uprising at Mainz against the bishop	5	15	4	4	50	AF	15.52	Gi V, 362–70
75	1166–8	Uprising of Saxon barons against Henry the Lion	20	15	2	3	15	F	16.52	Gi V, 612–3
76	1175–8	Uprising of Bernhard against Henry the Lion	20	25	1	3	5	F	13.58	Gi V, 782–3
77	1178–81	Struggle of the Emperor with Henry the Lion .	40	20	2	3	15	F	22.91	Gi V, 926–43
78	1189–90	Uprising of Henry the Lion	20	15	2	3	15	F	16.52	G I, 394
79	1190–9	Feudal uprising in Saxony and Thuringia . . .	40	50	2	2	10	F	27.16	G I, 395
80	1192–4	"Conspiracy of the princes"	40	20	2	1	3	F	15.31	G I, 394
81	1211	Uprising of the Sicilian Frederic against Otto .	40	5	1	3	5	F	10.00	G I, 426
82	1232	Expedition of Henry VII against insurgent Bavaria	20	5	2	3	15	F	11.45	G I, 441
83	1241–73	Great interregnum . . .	80	124	3	4	35	F	70.31	G I, 444–6
84	1267	Uprising at Köln against the bishop	10	10	4	3	35	AF	15.17	L II, 103
85	1276	Feudal uprising at Carinthia	10	3	2	3	15	F	7.65	L II, 138–9
86	1278	Feudal uprising in Austria	20	3	2	2	15	F	9.66	L II, 221
87	1285	Disturbances at Aachen, Wurzburg, Köln, Frankfurt, and other places .	20	5	4	2	20	AF	12.59	L II, 382–400
88	1285	Uprising of the pseudo Frederic at Neiss . . .	5	3	1	3	5	F	4.21	L II, 395
89	1285–6	Feudal uprising in Swabia	20	10	2	3	15	F	14.66	L II, 413
90	1291–3	Uprising of the barons in Styria	10	15	2	2	10	F	11.45	L II, 588–94
91	1294	Civil war in Thuringia .	10	5	3	4	35	F	12.05	G I, 506
92	1298	Deposition of Adolph of Nassau	20	1	1	4	7	F	5.18	G I, 508
93	1300–2	Uprising of the Rhine archbishops	20	20	2	3	15	F	18.15	G I, 513
94	1308	Murder of Emperor Albrecht	20	1	2	3	15	F	6.70	G I, 515
95	1327	Municipal uprising at Spires	10	3	4	3	35	AB	10.02	G I, 582
96	1330	Municipal uprising at Lübeck and Magdeburg .	10	3	4	3	35	AB	10.02	He 443, 469
97	1337	Municipal uprising at Strassburg	10	3	4	3	35	AB	10.02	G I, 582
98	1346–7	Civil war of Charles IV with the antiking Ludwig the Bavarian . .	40	15	3	3	25	F	24.66	G I, 536
99	1348	Municipal uprising at Nürnberg	10	3	4	3	35	AB	10.02	G I, 583
100	1349	Civil war of Charles IV with antiking Gunther .	40	5	3	3	25	F	17.10	Li 24
101	1349–50	Uprising at Brandenburg .	20	10	2	3	15	F	14.66	G I, 557–8
102	1365	Municipal uprising at Lübeck	10	3	4	3	35	AB	10.02	He 419
103	1370	The same at Köln . . .	10	3	4	3	35	AB	10.02	G I, 583
104	1374	The same at Braunschweig	10	3	4	4	50	AB	11.45	He 420–1
105	1375	The same at Hamburg, Lübeck, and Stade . .	20	3	4	3	35	AB	12.79	G I, 583
106	1388–9	Uprising in the Swabian and Rhine cities . . .	20	10	4	4	50	AB	21.53	G I, 577–8
107	1393–4	Uprising of the Bohemian princes against King Wenceslas	20	10	2	4	20	F	15.85	Li 168
108	1400	Deposition of King Wenceslas	20	1	1	4	7	F	5.18	G I, 580
109	1419–20	Uprising of the Hussites in Bohemia	20	15	3	4	35	D	21.88	Li 326–7
110	1426–7	First Hussite war . . .	20	15	3	4	35	D	21.88	Li 343–7
111	1430–1	Second Hussite war . .	20	15	3	4	35	D	21.88	Li 358–63
112	1434	Internal war between the Hussites	20	10	3	4	35	D	19.14	Li 371
113	1439	Civil war in Bohemia . .	20	10	2	4	20	F	15.85	G I, 618

GERMANY AND AUSTRIA — *Continued*

1	2	3	4	5	6	7	8	9	10	11
114	1474	Municipal uprising at Lüneburg	10	3	4	3	35	AB	10.02	He 428
115	1478	The same at Halle . . .	10	3	4	3	35	AB	10.02	H 447
116	1488	Uprising in the cities of Altmark against the margrave	20	5	4	3	35	AF	15.17	H 487
117	c. 1490	Peasant uprising in different parts of the Empire	40	10	3	3	25	BF	21.53	G I, 641
118	1521	Disturbances at Erfurt .	3	1	3	3	25	D	4.21	J II, 223
119	1522	Disturbances at Wittenberg	3	1	3	3	25	D	4.21	J II, 224
120	1522–3	Uprising of Franz von Sickingen	10	10	3	3	25	AD	13.58	J II, 253–4
121	1524–5	Great peasant war . .	60	10	3	4	35	B	27.61	J II, 508–92
122	1534–5	Uprising at Münster . .	5	10	4	4	50	D	13.58	G II, 50
123	1546–7	Schmalkaldic war . .	20	10	2	4	20	D	15.85	J II, 626–71
124	1552	Conspiracy of the princes against the emperor . .	40	3	2	1	3	F	7.12	G II, 77
125	1559	Disturbances at Trier . .	5	1	3	2	15	D	4.21	J IV, 121
126	1567	Soldiers' mutiny at Gotha	5	1	2	3	15	F	4.21	J IV, 252
127	1618	Uprising at Prague . . .	10	3	4	4	50	AC	11.45	G II, 138–9
128	1634	Uprising of Wallenstein .	20	3	1	3	5	F	6.70	G II, 168–9
129	1713	Noblemen's disturbances at Mecklenburg . . .	10	5	2	1	3	F	5.31	G II, 239
130	1793	Revolution at Mainz and in the Rhine cities . .	10	5	3	4	35	A	12.05	G II, 367
131	1794	Uprising in "southern Prussia"	10	5	3	3	25	C	10.76	G II, 371
132	1795	Revolutionary attempts in different parts of Austria	20	5	2	2	10	A	10.00	G II, 376
133	1806	Uprising in "southern Prussia"	10	5	3	3	25	C	10.76	G II, 410
134	1809	Uprising in Tyrol and Kurhessen	40	3	2	3	15	C	12.16	Ha III, 291–307
135	1830	Revolution in Braunschweig, Hannover, and Saxony	40	5	3	3	25	A	17.10	G II, 525
136	1833	Disorders of students at Frankfurt	10	3	2	2	10	A	6.70	G II, 527
137	1837	Coup d'état at Hannover	20	1	2	4	20	A	7.36	G II, 529
138	1847–9	"March revolution" . .	80	15	4	5	70	AB	22.91	G II, 589
139	1868	Disturbances in Prague .	10	1	2	2	10	C	4.64	Bi 333
140	1893	Disturbances in Prague .	10	3	3	2	15	C	7.66	Bi 378
141	1897	Disturbances in Vienna .	20	3	3	2	15	A	9.66	Bi 382
142	1904	Disturbances in Innsbruck	10	1	2	2	10	C	4.64	Bi 437
143	1907	Disturbances in Prague .	10	3	3	2	15	C	7.66	S 50
144	1908	Disturbances in Prague .	10	5	3	2	15	C	9.09	S 50
145	1918–9	"November and October revolutions" in Germany and Austria in Berlin, Vienna	100	5	5	5	100	A	36.73	En II, 210–1
146	1919	Soviet republic in Bavaria	20	3	3	4	35	AB	12.79	En II, 212
147	1920	Kapp's uprising in Middle Germany	20	5	3	4	35	AB	15.17	En II, 212–3
148	1921	Communistic uprising at Hamburg, Halle, and other cities	10	5	3	3	25	B	10.76	En II, 213
149	1923	München's "Putsch" . .	5	1	2	3	15	A	4.21	En II, 215
150	1923–4	Separatism in the Rhine provinces	20	5	2	1	3	A	6.70	En II, 215

ENGLAND

NUMBER	YEAR	SPECIFICATION OF THE INTERNAL DISTURBANCE	MEASURES OF:							SOURCES[2]
			Social Area	Duration	Size of the Masses Involved	Intensity	Masses and Intensity Combined	Nature[1]	Geometric Average	
1	2	3	4	5	6	7	8	9	10	11
1	656	Conspiracy and murder of the King at South Mercia	20	1	1	4	7	F	5.13	O I, 286
2	659	Insurrection at Mercia against Northumberlandish supremacy . .	20	3	4	4	50	C	14.66	O I, 287
3	671–2	Insurrection of the Picts against Northumberland king Egfrith . .	10	15	4	3	35	C	17.38	O I, 298
4	685	Second insurrection of the Picts.	10	10	4	3	35	C	15.17	O I, 308
5	687	Insurrection in Kent . .	20	3	4	4	50	F	14.66	O I, 312
6	692–4	Civil war in Kent . . .	20	20	4	4	50	F	27.16	O I, 313
7	697	Palace overthrow at Mercia	20	1	1	4	7	F	5.18	O I, 314
8	705	Disturbances in Northumberland after the death of Aldfrid	20	3	3	3	25	F	11.48	O I, 316
9	716	Insurrection at the same place against Osred . .	20	3	3	4	35	F	12.79	O I, 325
10	716	Civil war in Mercia . . .	20	3	3	4	35	F	12.79	O I, 329
11	718	Deposition of King Coetwulf at Northumberland	20	3	2	4	20	F	10.00	O I, 325
12	721–2	Insurrection of yeomanry in Wessex	20	15	3	1	15	F	16.52	O I, 330
13	725	The same.	20	3	3	2	15	F	2.66	O I, 330
14	728–30	Civil war in Wessex . .	20	20	3	3	25	F	21.53	O I, 330
15	731	Deposition of the King in Northumberland . .	20	1	1	4	7	F	5.13	O I, 320–1
16	750–2	Insurrection at Wessex against the supremacy of Mercia	20	20	3	4	35	C	24.10	O I, 334, 344
17	756–7	Disturbances at Wessex	20	15	3	3	25	F	19.59	O I, 335–6
18	757	Murder of the King Aethebald at Mercia . . .	20	1	1	4	7	F	5.13	O I, 335
19	758	Expulsion of the King Beornred at Mercia . .	20	3	2	4	20	F	10.06	O I, 335
20	759	Palatial overthrow at Northumberland . .	20	2	2	4	20	F	4.35	O I, 334
21	760–1	Civil war at Northumberland	20	15	3	4	35	F	21.88	O I, 344
22	765	Dethroning of the King in Northumberland . .	20	1	2	4	20	F	7.36	O I, 345
23	774	The same.	20	3	2	4	20	F	10.06	O I, 345
24	778	The same	20	1	3	4	35	F	8.87	O I, 346

[1] See the text, p. 403, for a key to this column.
[2] Sources in the order of their appearance in the text:

O I —C. Oman. *England before the Norman Conquest.* London, 1913.
A   —G. B. Adams. *History of England from the Norman Conquest to the Death of John.* London, 1905.
T   —T. F. Tout. *History of England from the Accession of Henry III to the Death of Edward III.* London, 1905.
O II —C. Oman. *History of England from the Accession of Richard II to the Death of Richard III.* London, 1918.
F   —H. A. Fisher. *History of England from the Accession of Henry VII to the Death of Henry VIII.* London, 1913.
P   —R. S. Poole. *History of England from the Accession of Edward VI to the Death of Elizabeth.* London, 1915.
M   —F. C. Montague. *History of England from the Accession of James I to the Restoration.* London, 1916.
L   —R. Lodge. *History of England from the Restoration to the Death of William III.* London, 1918.
Le —J. S. Leadam. *History of England from the Accession of Anne to the Death of George II.* London, 1909.
H   —W. Hunt. *History of England from the Accession of George III to 1800.* London, 1905.
B   —G. C. Brodrick and J. K. Fotheringhan. *History of England from 1801 to the Close of William IV's Reign.* London, 1911.
Lo —S. Low. *History of England during the Reign of Victoria.* London, 1913.
En — *Encyclopaedia Britannica,* 14th ed.

ENGLAND — *Continued*

1	2	3	4	5	6	7	8	9	10	11
25	786	Murder of King Cynewulf at Wessex	20	1	1	4	7	F	5.18	O I, 338
26	788	Murder of King Aelfwald at Northumberland	20	1	1	4	7	F	5.18	O I, 346
27	790	Deposition of King Osred at Northumberland	20	1	1	4	7	F	5.18	O I, 347
28	792	An attempt of Osred to return the throne	20	3	1	3	5	F	6.70	O I, 347
29	796	Deposition of the King Acthelred at Northumberland	20	5	1	4	7	F	8.87	O I, 348–9
30	796–8	Insurrection in Kent against the supremacy of Mercia	20	20	4	3	35	C	24.10	O I, 384
31	796–803	Disturbances in Northumberland	20	42	4	4	50	F	34.74	O I, 397
32	803	Expulsion of Eardwulf from Northumberland	20	3	2	4	20	F	11.45	O I, 422
33	821–3	Civil war in Mercia	20	20	3	3	25	F	21.53	O I, 391
34	822–3	Insurrection in East Anglia against the supremacy of Mercia	20	15	4	4	50	C	24.66	O I, 394
35	825	Liberation of Wessex from dependency to Mercia	20	3	3	4	35	C	12.79	O I, 397
36	844	Civil war in Northumberland	20	5	4	4	50	F	17.10	O I, 422
37	844	Deposition of the King at Northumberland	20	1	1	4	7	F	5.18	O I, 435
38	848	The same	20	1	1	4	7	F	5.18	O I, 435
39	856	Uprising against Aethelwulf of his son Aethelbald	20	3	1	3	5	F	6.70	O I, 431
40	861–6	Civil war in Northumberland	20	30	3	3	25	F	24.66	O I, 436
41	878	Disturbances after the expulsion of Halfdenc, King of York	20	10	4	4	50	F	21.53	O I, 482
42	900	Insurrection of Aethelwald against Edward	20	3	2	2	10	F	8.43	O I, 492
43	900	Disturbances in the Kingdom of York	20	3	2	3	15	F	9.66	O I, 492
44	933	Insurrection of the Picts and Scots	10	5	4	3	35	C	12.05	O I, 518–9
45	937	The same	10	5	4	3	35	C	14.42	O I, 520–1
46	941–2	Insurrection in Northumberland	20	15	3	3	25	F	19.59	O I, 524–5
47	943	Insurrection in Northern Wales	10	3	4	3	35	C	10.02	O I, 529
48	944	Deposition of the King at Northumberland	20	1	1	4	7	F	5.18	O I, 527
49	947–8	Insurrection of the Danes in Northumberland	20	3	3	3	25	C	11.45	O I, 530
50	952	Deposition of the King at Northumberland	20	3	2	4	20	F	10.06	O I, 532
51	954	Expulsion of Eric the Bloody	20	3	3	4	35	F	12.79	O I, 533
52	957	Uprising in the north against Eadwig	20	5	4	3	35	F	15.17	O I, 540
53	966	Insurrection in Westmoreland	10	3	3	2	15	F	7.65	O I, 543
54	968	Insurrection in Thanet	5	3	3	3	25	F	7.21	O I, 543
55	975	Disturbances at the time of the enthroning of Edward	60	3	3	2	15	F	12.16	O I, 549
56	1015	Insurrection of Edmund against Aethelred	40	5	2	3	15	F	14.66	O I, 576
57	1016	Insurrection of Aedwig against Knut	60	3	3	3	25	F	16.52	O I, 583
58	1036	Struggle for the succession of Knut	40	5	2	3	15	F	14.66	O I, 603
59	1042	Insurrection at Worcester	5	3	3	3	25	F	7.21	O I, 607
60	1051	Civil war with Godwin	20	3	3	2	15	F	9.66	O I, 618
61	1052	Return of Godwin	20	3	3	2	15	F	9.66	O I, 620
62	1058	Disturbances in Mercia	20	3	3	3	25	F	11.45	O I, 627
63	1064	Disturbances in Northumberland	20	3	3	3	25	F	11.45	O I, 632
64	1066–70	Conquest by the Normans and subsequent disturbances	80	30	4	5	70	F	55.22	A 1–38

ENGLAND — *Continued*

1	2	3	4	5	6	7	8	9	10	11
65	1075	First feudal uprising	40	5	2	2	10	F	12.59	A 60-3
66	1088	Feudal uprising in favor of Robert	40	3	2	2	10	F	10.06	A 72-5
67	1095	Feudal uprising	20	3	2	2	10	F	8.43	A 79
68	1101	An attempt to seize the throne by Robert	10	3	1	1	1	F	3.15	A 128
69	1102	Revolt of Robert of Belleme	10	5	1	2	3	F	5.31	A 129
70	1136	Revolt of Robert of Bampton and Baldwin of Revers	10	5	1	2	3	F	5.31	A 206
71	1136	Insurrection in southern Wales	10	5	4	2	20	C	10.00	A 208-9
72	1138-53	Civil war (Stephen and Matilda, later Henry)	80	73	2	4	20	F	49.20	A 214-52
73	1155	Insurrection of Roger of Hereford	10	3	1	2	3	F	4.47	A 261
74	1173-4	Uprising of Henry the Younger	60	15	2	3	15	F	23.82	A 308-13
75	1215-7	Civil war	100	20	3	4	35	AF	41.21	A 440-46 T 1-12
76	1222	Uprising of the Earl of Albermele and Fitzathulf	20	5	3	3	25	F	13.58	T 21-2
77	1224	Baron's war	40	3	2	2	10	F	10.06	T 24-5
78	1232	Revolt against the papal collectors	3	3	3	2	15	F	5.13	T 39
79	1233-4	Marshal's revolt	10	10	3	4	35	F	15.17	T 44-9
80	1263-4	Baron's war	40	10	2	4	20	F	15.17	T 114-9
81	1265-7	Second Baron's war	40	15	2	4	20	F	22.91	T 127-32
82	1284	Uprising in Wales	10	5	4	4	50	C	13.58	T 161-5
83	1287	Uprising in Wales	10	5	4	3	35	C	12.05	T 168
84	1294-5	The same	10	5	4	3	35	C	12.05	T 189-90
85	1297-1300	Insurrection in Scotland	20	25	4	3	35	C	25.94	T 206-18
86	1306	The same	20	5	4	4	50	C	17.10	T 233
87	1315	Private wars in several counties in the south	60	5	2	3	15	F	17.06	T 267
88	1315-6	Disturbances in Bristol	5	15	4	3	35	F	14.42	T 268-9
89	1320	Insurrection in southern Wales	10	5	4	3	35	F	12.05	T 280
90	1322	Uprising of the barons in the western counties	60	5	2	3	15	F	16.52	T 284
91	1326-7	Rebellion of Queen Isabella and Mortimer against Edward II	20	5	2	4	20	F	12.59	T 298-302
92	1330	Downfall of Mortimer	20	1	1	4	7	F	5.18	T 308-9
93	1381	"Great rebellion"	80	5	3	4	35	AB	24.10	O II, 33-60
94	1387-8	Insurrection of the "Lords Appellants"	40	5	2	3	15	AF	14.66	O II, 106-16
95	1391	Coup d'état of Richard II	20	1	1	4	7	F	5.13	O II, 134
96	1399	Deposition of Richard II	40	5	3	4	35	F	19.14	O II, 147-51
97	1400-8	Insurrection in Northern Wales	20	46	3	3	25	B	28.44	O II, 168-213
98	1403	Revolt in Ost Shrewsbury	10	5	2	3	15	F	9.08	O II, 180-4
99	1406	Conspiracy of the lady Despenser	10	3	2	3	15	F	7.65	O II, 193
100	1406	Conspiracy of the archbishop Scrope	20	3	2	3	15	F	9.66	O II, 194-7
101	1414	Uprising of Sir J. Oldkop	20	3	2	2	10	FD	8.43	O II, 236-7
102	1415	Conspiracy of the Earl of Cambridge	20	5	1	1	1	F	4.64	O II, 248
103	1450	Uprising of Jack Cade	40	5	3	3	25	AF	17.10	O II, 347-90
104	1455-6	First stage of the Wars of the Roses	80	15	3	4	35	F	34.74	O II, 368-9
105	1460-4	Second stage	80	30	3	4	35	F	43.75	O II, 380-419
106	1467-71	Third stage	80	30	3	4	35	F	43.75	O II, 431-50
107	1483-5	Fourth stage	80	20	3	4	35	F	38.28	O II, 473-95
108	1489	Disturbances in Northumberland	10	3	4	3	35	F	10.02	F 34-5
109	1495	Attempts of Perkin Warbeck	10	3	2	3	15	F	7.65	F 58
110	1497	Insurrection in Cornwallis	20	5	3	3	25	F	13.58	F 69-71
111	1497	New attempt of Perkin Warbeck	10	3	2	3	15	F	7.65	F 73-4
112	1499	Conspiracy of Warwick	20	5	1	1	1	F	4.64	F 82-6
113	1517	Disturbances at London's City	20	1	3	2	15	DF	6.70	F 218-9
114	1534-5	Uprising of H. Fitzgerald	10	5	2	2	10	F	7.92	F 366-7
115	1536	Uprising in Lincolnshire and Yorkshire	40	5	3	3	25	FD	17.10	F 397-407

ENGLAND — *Continued*

1	2	3	4	5	6	7	8	9	10	11
116	1536–7	Hallom's rebellion . . .	20	5	3	2	15	FD	11.65	F 414–5
117	1540	Catholic conspiracy in Yorkshire	20	3	2	1	3	AD	5.64	F 450–1
118	1549	Disturbances on the social-economic ground . .	40	10	3	2	15	B	18.15	P 26–33
119	1553	Coup d'état in favor of Mary	20	1	2	4	20	F	7.36	P 89–94
120	1554	Wyatt's rebellion . . .	20	3	2	2	10	FD	8.43	P 107–10
121	1557	Attempt to seize power by Stafford	5	3	1	2	3	F	3.55	P 164
122	1569–70	Disturbances in connection with Mary Stuart	20	3	2	2	10	FD	8.43	P 293–5
123	1579–80	Insurrection in Ireland .	20	10	3	3	25	C	17.10	P 430
124	1598–1600	The same . . .	20	15	4	3	35	C	17.38	P 436–8
125	1601	Rising of Essex	20	1	1	2	3	FD	3.91	P 471–2
126	1603	Conspiracy against James I	20	3	2	1	3	F	5.64	M 7–8
127	1605	"Gunpowder plot" . .	20	3	2	1	3	F	5.64	M 25–31
128	1637	Disturbances at Edinburgh	5	1	3	1	5	D	2.92	M 205
129	1639	First bishops' war . .	20	3	2	1	3	D	5.64	M 211
130	1640	Second bishops' war . .	20	5	2	2	10	D	10.00	M 223
131	1641–9	Great revolution . .	100	46	5	5	100	AD	77.27	M 268–350
132	1650–2	Disturbances in Scotland and Ireland . . .	40	20	3	3	25	AD	27.16	M 356–77
133	1655	Uprising of royalists in Salisbury	10	3	2	1	3	AF	4.43	M 428
134	1659	Uprising of royalists in Chester,Lancashire,and other counties . . .	20	3	2	2	10	A	8.43	M 469–70
135	1666	Disturbances in Scotland	10	3	2	3	15	F	7.65	L 187–8
136	1679	The same	10	3	3	3	25	FD	9.08	L 201–3
137	1683	"Rye House" plot . . .	10	3	2	1	3	A	4.47	L 224
138	1685	Uprising of Argyle and Monmouth	10	3	2	2	10	F	6.70	L 248–51
139	1688	Second revolution . . .	80	3	4	5	70	A	25.59	L 288–307
140	1691	Jacobite plot	10	3	2	1	3	AF	4.47	L 373
141	1705	Conspiracy in Scotland .	10	3	2	1	3	F	4.47	Le 38–9
142	1715–6	Attempt of the Pretender	40	5	3	3	25	F	17.10	Le 245–65
143	1736	Disturbances in Edinburgh and other cities .	10	3	2	2	10	F	6.70	Le 352
144	1745–6	Attempt of the Pretender	40	5	3	4	35	F	19.14	Le 391–408
145	1765	Disturbances amongst the weavers	10	1	2	2	10	B	4.64	H 66
146	1761	Disturbances of the White Boys in Ireland . . .	20	5	3	1	5	BD	7.92	H 92
147	1780	Disturbances at Edinburgh, Glasgow, and near London	20	3	3	3	25	D	11.45	H 205–7
148	1795	"Bread" disturbances in different counties . .	20	3	3	2	15	F	9.66	H 378
149	1797	Mutiny in the navy . .	10	3	2	3	15	F	7.65	H 391–6
150	1798	Insurrection in Ireland .	20	3	3	4	35	DC	12.79	H 408–16
151	1803	Disturbances in Ireland .	20	1	2	2	10	DC	5.84	B 23
152	1811–2	Luddite riots.	5	5	2	?	10	BF	6.29	D 83, 85
153	1816	Spa Fields riots . . .	3	1	3	2	15	BF	3.58	B 175
154	1820	Conspiracy of Cato Street	20	3	1	1	1	A	3.91	B 192–3
155	1831	Reform Bill riots . . .	40	3	2	2	10	A	10.06	B 296–8
156	1831–2	"Tithe war" in Ireland .	20	15	3	2	15	BF	16.52	B 314–5
157	1839	Disturbances in connection with Chartist movement	20	3	3	2	15	A	9.66	Lo 24
158	1848	Young Ireland rebellion .	10	1	2	2	10	C	4.69	Lo 86
159	1867	Uprising at Dublin and Kerry	10	3	2	2	10	C	6.70	Lo 223–7
160	1886	Disturbances in Ireland .	10	5	3	2	15	C	9.08	Lo 384
161	1916	Irish rebellion	20	3	3	4	35	C	12.79	En XII, 614
162	1919–21	"Anglo-Irish war" . .	20	15	3	2	15	C	16.52	En 614

ITALY

NUMBER	YEAR	SPECIFICATION OF THE INTERNAL DISTURBANCE	MEASURES OF:							SOURCES[2]
			Social Area	Duration	Size of the Masses Involved	Intensity	Masses and Intensity Combined	Nature[1]	Geometric Average	
1	2	3	4	5	6	7	8	9	10	11
1	526	Disturbances at the death of Theodoric	60	3	3	2	15	F	13.90	R 182
2	536	Insurrection against Theodat	40	1	2	4	20	F	9.29	R 191
3	541	Murder of Ildabad	20	1	2	4	20	F	7.36	R 204
4	566–7	Uprising of Sinduald against the Byzantines	60	10	4	4	50	C	31.05	R 213
5	572	Murder of Alboin	20	1	2	4	20	F	7.36	R 237
6	590–1	Disturbances after the death of Autaris	60	15	3	4	35	F	31.55	R 246, 258
7	619	Insurrection at Ravenna and Naples	10	3	3	3	25	F	9.08	R 264
8	626	Deposition of Duke Adaloa	20	1	2	4	20	F	7.36	R 264
9	between 642–6	Insurrection at Rome	20	3	3	3	25	F	11.45	R 302
10	652	Deposition of Prince Rodoald	20	1	2	4	20	F	7.36	R 266
11	661–2	Civil war after the death of Prince Aripert	40	10	3	4	35	F	24.10	R 306–8
12	671	Deposition of King Grimoald	20	1	2	4	20	F	7.36	R 311
13	688	Uprising of the Duke of Frioul	10	5	3	3	25	F	10.76	R 319
14	c. 690	Uprising of Ansfried from Ragogna	10	3	2	3	15	F	7.65	R 319
15	between 692–4	Mutiny of the Byzantine armies at Rome	20	3	2	3	15	F	9.66	R 324
16	701–2	Civil war after the death of Cunipert	40	10	3	4	35	F	24.70	R 320
17	703	Insurrection at Rome and Ravenna against Byzantium	40	5	3	3	25	C	17.10	R 325
18	710	Insurrection at Ravenna and other cities against Byzantium	20	5	3	3	25	C	13.58	R 327
19	712	Deposition of Aripert II	20	3	2	4	20	F	10.06	R 320–1
20	713	Insurrection at Rome	20	3	3	3	25	F	11.45	R 328
21	714	New insurrection at Rome	20	5	2	3	15	F	11.45	R 341
22	720–32	Disturbances in the Duchy of Benevento	20	58	3	3	25	F	30.69	R 346
23	727	Uprising at Ravenna	10	3	2	3	15	C	7.65	R 342
24	730	Uprising of Tiberio Petasio near Rome	3	3	2	3	15	F	5.13	R 344
25	739–42	Uprising in the Duchy of Spoleto	20	20	2	3	15	F	18.15	R 346
26	744–56	Civil war at Venice	10	58	2	3	15	F	20.56	R 441
27	745	Deposition of King Hildebrand	20	1	2	4	20	F	7.36	R 349

[1] See the text, p. 403, for a key to this column.
[2] Sources in the order of their appearance in the text:

R   —G. Romano. *Le dominatione barbariche in Italia.* Milano, n.d.
B   —C. Bayet, C. Pfister, and A. Kleinclauss. *Le christianisme les barbares, mérovingiens et carolingiens.* Paris, 1903.
H   —L. M. Hartmann. *Geschichte Italiens in Mittelalter*, Vol. III. Gotha, 1911.
G   —F. Gianani. *I communi.* Milano, n.d.
L   —F. Lanzani. *Storia dei communi italiani.* Milano, 1882.
O I —P. Orsi. *Signorie e principati.* Milano, n.d.
C   —C. Cipolla. *Storia delle signorie italiane.* Milano, 1881.
Co —A. Cosci. *L'Italia durante le preponderanze straniere.* Milano, n.d.
O II—P. Orsi. *Histoire de l'Italie moderne.* Paris, 1911.
En —*Encyclopaedia Britannica*, 14th ed., Vol. XII.

ITALY — *Continued*

1	2	3	4	5	6	7	8	9	10	11
28	749	Deposition of King Rachis	20	1	2	4	20	F	7.36	R 349
29	756	Disturbances after the death of Astolf . . .	40	3	2	2	10	F	10.06	R 362
30	767	Uprising of the nobles at Rome	20	3	2	3	15	F	9.66	R 365
31	768	Disturbances at Rome .	20	3	3	2	15	F	9.66	R 366
32	775–6	Insurrection of the Friouls against Charles the Great	10	10	4	3	35	C	15.17	R 399–400
33	782	Insurrection in Sicily against Byzantium . .	20	5	4	4	50	C	17.10	R 405–6
34	792	Uprising at Benevento against the Franks . .	10	5	4	4	50	C	13.58	R 413–4
35	799	Uprising at Rome against the Pope	20	3	3	4	35	F	12.79	R 419–20
36	800–40	Civil war at Naples . .	10	145	2	2	10	F	24.88	R 470
37	815	Conspiracy at Rome against the Pope . . .	20	1	2	1	3	F	3.91	R 449–50
38	817	Insurrection of Bernardo against Ludwig the Pious	40	5	2	4	20	C	15.85	R 453–4
39	823	Disturbances at Rome .	20	3	2	2	10	F	8.43	R 456
40	827	Insurrection in Sicily against Byzantium . .	20	5	4	3	35	C	15.17	R 475–6
41	830–1	Uprising of the sons of Emperor Ludwig . . .	40	10	1	4	7	F	14.09	B 362–3
42	832	Murder of the Duke of Benevento	20	1	2	4	20	F	7.36	R 473
43	832–4	Second insurrection . .	40	15	1	4	7	F	16.14	B 364–5
44	836	Deposition of the Doge in Venice	10	1	1	4	7	F	4.12	R 646
45	839–40	Civil war at Benevento .	20	10	3	3	25	F	17.10	R 478
46	849	Dynastic coup d'état at Salerno	10	3	2	4	20	F	8.43	R 513
47	850	Insurrection of the Duke of Spoleto	10	3	2	3	15	C	7.65	R 515
48	864	Deposition of the Doge at Venice	10	1	1	4	7	F	4.12	R 646
49	871	Uprising at Benevento against the Emperor .	10	3	3	4	35	C	10.02	R 521
50	877	Uprising of Karlmann against Charles the Bald	40	5	2	3	15	F	14.66	R 528
51	878	Coup d'état at Benevento	10	1	2	4	20	F	5.84	H III, 4
52	878	Coup d'état at Naples . .	10	1	2	4	20	F	5.84	H III, 49
53	884	Insurrection of the Duke of Spoleto against the Emperor	10	5	2	3	15	C	9.08	R 535
54	886	Insurrection of Berengar .	20	5	2	3	15	C	11.45	R 541
55	887	Deposition of Charles the Fat	40	1	1	4	7	F	6.54	R 611
56	897	Murder of the Marquis of Spoleto	10	1	1	4	7	F	4.12	R 634
57	898	Insurrection of the Marquis of Tuscany against the Emperor	10	3	2	3	15	F	7.65	R 620
58	899	Deposition of the Prince of Capua	10	1	1	4	7	F	4.12	R 635
59	900	General insurrection against King Berengar .	80	3	3	4	35	F	20.32	R 622
60	902	Deposition of King Ludwig	20	1	2	4	20	F	7.36	R 624
61	905	Civil war between King Ludwig and Berengar .	60	5	2	4	20	F	18.15	R 624–5
62	916	Deposition of the Doge at Venice	10	1	1	4	7	F	4.12	R 653
63	920–1	Uprising in Calabria and Apulia against Byzantium	10	10	4	3	35	C	15.17	R 636
64	922–3	Feudal insurrection against Emperor Berengar . .	40	10	2	4	20	F	9.29	R 629–30
65	926	Civil war of Ugo and Rodolfo for the crown . .	40	5	2	3	15	F	14.66	R 655
66	929–34	Insurrection at Salerno and Capua against Byzantium	10	30	3	3	25	C	19.59	R 637
67	929	Deposition of Pope John X	10	1	2	4	20	F	5.84	R 660
68	930	Murder of Berengar by conspirators	20	1	1	4	7	F	5.18	R 630
69	932	Uprising of Alberico at Rome	20	1	2	4	20	F	7.36	R 661–2
70	935	Uprising at Verona . . .	10	3	3	4	35	F	10.02	R 665–6

ITALY — *Continued*

1	2	3	4	5	6	7	8	9	10	11
71	946	Uprising at Apulia against Byzantium	10	5	4	3	35	C	12.05	R 638
72	958–9	Disturbances at Venice .	10	10	2	3	15	F	11.45	R 650
73	962	Insurrection against the Arabs at Taormina . .	3	3	3	3	25	C	6.08	R 706
74	964	Disturbances at Rome . .	20	1	4	2	20	F	7.36	R 692
75	965	Disturbances at Rome . .	20	1	3	3	25	F	7.92	R 695
76	972	Deposition of Pope Benedict VII	20	1	2	4	15	F	6.70	R 716
77	973–4	Civil war in the princedom of Salerno	10	10	2	4	20	F	12.59	R 719
78	976–9	Disturbances at Venice .	10	20	2	3	15	F	14.66	R 723–4
79	c. 980	Disturbances at Salerno, Amalfi, and Benevento .	20	3	3	3	25	F	11.45	R 721
80	983	Revolution at Salerno . .	10	3	3	4	35	F	10.02	R 727
81	985	Revolution at Rome . .	20	5	4	4	50	F	17.10	R 732
82	993	Murder of the prince at Capua	10	1	1	4	7	F	4.12	R 727
83	995	Revolution at Capua . .	10	1	2	4	20	F	5.84	R 736
84	997	Uprising at Rome . . .	20	3	3	4	35	F	12.79	R 739
85	1000	Uprising at Capua . . .	10	3	3	4	35	F	10.02	R 746
86	1001	Uprising at Rome against the Emperor	20	1	4	3	35	F	8.87	R 746
87	1002	The same	20	3	4	3	35	F	12.79	R 751
88	1004	Uprising at Pavia during the coronation . . .	20	3	4	3	35	F	12.79	R 763
89	1004–12	Civil war in northern and middle Italy	60	42	2	3	15	F	33.57	R 764–6
90	1009	Uprising at Apulia against Byzantium	10	5	4	3	35	C	12.05	R 773
91	1016	Conspiracy at Lombardy .	20	3	1	1	1	F	3.91	R 768
92	1026	Uprising at Pavia against King Conrad	20	1	3	3	25	F	7.92	G 26
93	1026	Disturbances at Rome . .	20	1	3	2	15	F	6.70	G 28
94	1030	Expulsion of Pandolfo from Naples	10	3	3	3	25	F	9.08	G 30
95	1035–45	Revolution at Milan . .	10	50	2	3	15	AC	19.59	G 36–49
96	1038	Deposition of Pope Benedict IX	20	1	4	4	50	F	10.00	G 50
97	1043	Uprising at Apulia against Byzantium	10	5	3	3	25	C	10.76	G 57
98	1047	Disturbances at Benevento	10	1	4	3	35	F	7.04	G 59
99	1051	Murder of Drogone, Prince of Apulia	10	1	1	4	7	F	4.12	G 65–6
100	1061	Uprising at Apulia against the Normans . . .	10	5	3	4	35	C	12.05	G 99
101	1062	Civil war in Calabria . .	10	5	3	4	35	F	12.05	G 101
102	1064	Disturbances at Mantua and Milan	10	3	3	3	25	F	9.08	G 87
103	1082	Insurrection at Calabria and Apulia against the Normans	20	3	3	4	35	C	12.79	G 133
104	1086	Civil war in the Norman duchy	10	5	3	3	25	F	10.76	G 148
105	1093	Insurrection of the Lombardian cities against Henry IV	20	5	4	3	35	F	15.17	G 154–5
106	1117–8	Anarchy at Rome . . .	20	10	4	2	20	F	15.85	G 182–3
107	1118–20	Civil war at Como . . .	10	15	3	4	35	F	17.38	L 200
108	1141	Revolution at Rome . .	20	1	4	4	50	A	10.00	G 231
109	1154	Disturbances at Rome . .	20	1	3	2	15	F	6.70	G 248
110	1155	The same	20	1	3	2	15	F	6.70	G 253–4
111	1156	Insurrection in Apulia against the Normans .	10	5	3	3	25	C	10.76	G 255
112	1158–62	Insurrection of the Lombardian cities	20	25	4	4	50	A	28.84	G 266–74
113	1160–6	Disturbances at Palermo .	5	34	2	2	10	F	11.94	G 278–80
114	1174–8	Second insurrection of the Lombardian cities . .	20	25	4	4	50	A	28.84	G 294–302
115	1191–4	Civil war in Sicily . . .	20	25	3	3	25	F	23.23	G 396
116	1221	Civil war at Milan . . .	10	5	2	2	10	F	7.92	L 310
117	1223	Uprising of Saracens in Sicily	20	3	3	3	25	C	11.45	G 396
118	1234–41	Civil war in northern Italy	40	38	3	3	25	F	33.65	L 358–86
119	1243	Insurrection at Viterbo against the Emperor .	5	3	2	3	15	F	6.08	G 452
120	1247	Insurrection at Parma against the Emperor .	5	3	3	3	25	F	7.21	G 459

ITALY — *Continued*

1	2	3	4	5	6	7	8	9	10	11
121	1247–8	Conspiracy at Naples . .	10	3	2	1	3	F	4.47	G 462–4
122	1250	Revolution at Florence .	10	1	3	4	35	AB	7.04	G 493
123	1252	Insurrection at Rome . .	20	3	3	2	15	F	9.66	G 479
124	1254	Coup d'état at Piacenza .	5	3	3	4	35	A	8.07	L 674
125	1256	Democratic coup d'état at Bologna	5	3	4	4	50	AB	9.08	L 697
126	1257	Coup d'état at Piacenza .	5	3	3	4	35	F	8.07	L 674
127	1257	Insurrection at Milan . .	10	3	3	4	35	AB	10.02	L 658
128	1258	Seizure of the Sicilian throne by Manfred . .	20	1	1	4	7	F	5.18	G 486
129	1258–9	Crusade against Ezzelino .	40	10	2	3	15	F	18.15	G 487–92
130	1259	Coup d'état at Lodi . .	5	1	3	4	35	A	5.60	L 673
131	1260	Coup d'état at Florence .	10	1	3	4	35	A	7.04	G 495
132	1261	Coup d'état at Piacenza .	5	1	3	4	35	A	5.60	L 675
133	1263	Coup d'état at Verona .	10	1	3	4	35	A	7.04	L 678
134	1265	Coup d'état at Reggio .	5	1	3	4	35	A	5.60	L 681
135	1266	Civil war at Florence . .	10	3	4	4	50	F	11.45	G 522
136	1267–8	Expedition of Conradin .	80	10	2	4	20	F	25.12	G 530–7
137	1272	Coup d'état at Mantua .	5	1	3	4	35	A	5.60	L 679
138	1274	Insurrection at Bologna .	5	1	3	3	25	F	4.86	L 699–700
139	1277	Civil war in Lombardy .	20	3	3	3	25	F	11.45	G 533
140	1282	Sicilian "vespers" . .	20	3	3	4	35	F	12.79	G 568–75
141	1284–7	Civil war at Modena . .	5	20	3	3	25	F	13.58	L 681
142	1290	Coup d'état at Pavia . .	5	1	3	4	35	A	5.60	L 674
143	1290	Coup d'état at Piacenza .	5	1	3	4	35	A	5.60	L 675
144	1295	Coup d'état at Parma . .	5	1	3	4	35	A	5.60	L 683–4
145	1296	Coup d'état at Bergamo .	5	1	3	4	35	A	5.60	L 673
146	1296	Coup d'état at Rimini . .	5	1	3	4	35	A	5.60	L 688
147	1300–4	Civil war at Florence . .	10	25	3	3	25	F	18.41	L 759–68
148	1301	Coup d'état at Bergamo .	5	1	3	4	35	F	5.60	L 673
149	1302	Insurrection at Milan . .	10	3	3	3	25	F	9.08	L 670–1
150	1302	Coup d'état at Navarre .	5	1	3	4	35	A	5.60	L 673
151	1303	Armed attack of Pope .	20	1	1	2	3	F	3.91	O I, 15–6
152	1304	Coup d'état at Piacenza .	5	1	3	4	35	A	5.60	L 675
153	1306–7	Civil war at Montferrat .	5	10	3	3	25	F	10.76	O I, 24
154	1308	Civil war at Ferrara, Modena, and Reggio . .	10	5	3	4	35	F	12.05	O I, 22
155	1309	Coup d'état at Piacenza .	5	1	3	4	35	A	5.60	L 675
156	1310	Insurrection at Venice . .	10	1	3	3	25	F	6.29	O I, 23
157	1311	Movement in northern Italy against Henry VII	20	5	3	2	15	F	11.48	L 797–8
158	1312	Civil war at Parma and Reggio	10	5	3	3	25	F	10.76	O I, 30
159	1315–6	Insurrection of Lucca and Pisa against Florence .	10	5	3	3	25	C	10.76	O I, 33
160	1316	Coup d'état at Brescia .	5	1	3	4	35	A	5.60	O I, 34
161	1317	Insurrection at Ferrara .	5	1	3	4	35	A	5.60	O I, 36
162	1317–8	Civil war at Genoa . .	5	10	3	3	25	F	10.76	O I, 37
163	1327	Revolution at Rome . .	20	1	3	3	25	F	7.92	O I, 45
164	1328	Coup d'état at Mantua .	5	1	3	3	25	F	4.86	O I, 49
165	1332	Disturbances at Bologna .	10	1	4	2	20	F	5.84	C 53
166	1339	Disturbances at Genoa .	10	5	3	3	25	F	10.76	O I, 65
167	1343	General insurrection at Florence	10	3	4	4	50	A	11.45	O I, 68
168	1345	Murder of the King at Naples; disturbances .	20	3	3	4	35	F	12.79	O I, 72
169	1349	Roman revolution (Cola di Rienzi)	20	3	4	5	70	A	16.14	O I, 79–81
170	1350	Civil war at Naples . .	10	5	3	3	25	F	10.76	O I, 75
171	1353	Insurrection at Messina .	5	3	4	2	20	F	6.70	O I, 98
172	1354	Conspiracy at Venice . .	10	3	2	1	3	F	4.47	O I, 94
173	1356	Insurrection at Genoa against Milan . . .	10	3	3	4	35	C	10.02	O I, 117
174	1358	Coup d'état at Florence .	10	1	3	4	35	F	7.04	O I, 126
175	1363	People's disturbances at Genoa	10	1	4	2	20	F	5.84	O I, 122
176	1367	Uprising of Prince Philip at Piedmont . . .	20	5	2	2	10	F	10.00	O I, 143
177	1369	Uprising of Como against Milan	5	5	3	3	25	C	8.55	O I, 144
178	1369	Uprising of the Venetian cities	20	5	4	3	35	C	15.17	O I, 146
179	1375–8	Uprising in the Pope's province	20	20	4	3	35	C	24.10	O I, 155–9
180	1378	Revolution at Florence .	10	5	4	4	50	A	13.58	O I, 169–71
181	1378	Deposition of the Doge at Genoa	10	1	2	4	20	A	5.84	O I, 175
182	1382	Civil war at Naples . .	20	5	2	4	20	F	12.59	O I, 180–1

ITALY — *Continued*

1	2	3	4	5	6	7	8	9	10	11
183	1383	Civil war at Naples . .	20	5	2	4	20	F	12.59	O I, 184
184	1385	Disturbances at Milan .	10	3	4	2	20	F	8.43	O I, 188
185	1385	Revolution at Genoa . .	10	3	4	3	35	F	10.02	O I, 194–5
186	1390–4	Civil war at Genoa . . .	10	25	3	3	25	F	18.41	O I, 209
187	1393–4	Civil war at Ferrara . .	5	15	3	3	25	F	15.52	O I, 193
188	1393	Disturbances at Viterbo and Perugia . .	10	5	3	2	15	F	9.08	O I, 214
189	1394–6	Civil war at Piedmont .	20	15	3	3	25	F	19.59	O I, 209
190	1403	Disturbances at Milan .	10	5	4	2	20	F	10.00	O I, 220
191	1405	Insurrection at Pisa against Florence . . .	5	1	4	3	36	C	5.60	C 217
192	1405	Disturbances at Rome .	20	3	3	2	15	F	9.66	O I, 226
193	1409	Insurrection at Genoa against France . . .	10	3	3	4	35	C	10.02	O I, 233
194	1410–2	Civil war at Bologna . .	10	15	3	3	25	F	15.52	C 305
195	1410–1	Civil war at Sicily . . .	20	10	3	3	25	F	17.10	O I, 259
196	1416	Insurrection at Bologna .	10	1	4	3	35	F	15.17	C 310
197	1416	Insurrection of the barons at Naples	20	5	2	3	15	F	11.45	O I, 248
198	1427	Insurrection of Volterra against Florence . .	5	5	3	4	35	C	9.52	O I, 275
199	1434	Insurrection at Florence .	10	1	3	2	15	F	5.31	O I, 283
200	1434	Republican insurrection at Rome	20	5	4	4	50	A	17.10	O I, 300–1
201	1435	Uprising at Genoa against Milan	10	3	4	4	50	C	11.45	O I, 295
202	1461	Uprising at Genoa against France	10	3	4	4	50	C	11.45	O I, 343
203	1462	Uprising of Prince Philip at Piedmont . . .	20	3	2	3	15	F	9.66	O I, 337
204	1466	Conspiracy of Neroni at Florence	10	1	2	1	3	F	3.15	O I, 378
205	1472	Insurrection of Volterra against Florence . . .	5	3	3	4	35	C	8.07	O I, 398
206	1476–8	Insurrection at Genoa against Milan . . .	10	15	3	3	25	C	15.52	O I, 391–5
207	1476	Murder of the Duke at Milan	10	1	1	4	7	F	4.12	O I, 393
208	1478	Conspiracy at Florence .	10	3	2	2	10	F	6.70	O I, 403
209	1485–6	Insurrection of the barons at Naples	20	10	2	3	15	F	14.66	O I, 415–17
210	1488	Murder of the tyrant at Forli-Fachino	5	1	2	4	20	F	4.54	O I, 420–1
211	1494	Republican uprising at Pisa and Florence	20	3	4	4	50	A	14.66	O I, 444–5
212	1495	Uprising of Montepulchiano against Florence	5	3	3	4	35	C	8.07	O I, 458
213	1498	Disturbances at Florence .	10	1	4	2	20	D	5.84	C 752–7
214	1502	Uprising of the condottieri in Romagna	10	5	2	3	15	F	9.06	O I, 477–9
215	1507	Uprising of Genoa against France	10	3	3	4	35	C	10.02	O I, 495
216	1511	Disturbances at Rome . .	20	3	3	2	15	F	9.66	C 823
217	1527	Republican insurrection at Florence	10	1	4	4	50	A	7.92	O I, 550
218	1531	Revolution at Lucca . .	5	1	4	4	50	A	6.29	Co 126–7
219	1537	Murder of the Duke at Florence	10	1	1	4	7	F	4.12	Co 39
220	1548	Conspiracy at Florence and Venice	20	3	1	1	1	F	3.91	Co 54–5
221	1564–7	Insurrection of Corsica against Genoa . . .	10	20	4	3	35	C	19.14	Co 123–4
222	1575–6	Revolution at Genoa . .	10	10	3	4	35	A	15.17	Co 125–6
223	1576	Conspiracy at Florence .	10	3	1	1	1	F	3.15	Co 107
224	1598	Conspiracy at Naples against Spaniards . .	10	3	2	1	3	C	4.47	Co 196
225	1612	Conspiracy at Parma . .	5	1	2	1	3	F	2.46	Co 210
226	1619	Conspiracy at Naples against Spaniards . .	10	3	1	1	1	C	3.15	Co 226–7
227	1628	Conspiracy at Genoa . .	10	1	1	1	1	F	2.15	Co 240
228	1639–40	Civil war at Piedmont .	20	15	3	3	35	F	21.88	Co 254–60
229	1672	Conspiracy at Genoa . .	10	3	1	1	1	F	3.15	Co 296–7
230	1678	Disturbances at Messina .	5	1	4	2	20	F	4.64	Co 300
231	1680	Disturbances at Mondovi	5	3	4	2	20	F	6.70	Co 313–4
232	1701	Conspiracy at Naples . .	10	3	1	1	1	F	3.15	Co 366
233	1723–4	Insurrection of Corsica against Genoa . . .	10	10	3	4	35	C	15.17	Co 424–5

ITALY — *Continued*

1	2	3	4	5	6	7	8	9	10	11
234	1737–8	Insurrection of Corsica against Genoa	10	10	3	3	25	C	13.58	Co 505–6
235	1755–6	Insurrection of Corsica against Genoa	10	10	3	4	35	C	15.17	Co 582
236	1796–7	Republican insurrection in middle Italy	20	5	3	4	35	A	15.17	O II, 36
237	1806	Peasant insurrection in southern Italy	10	3	3	3	25	F	9.08	En 800
238	1814	Insurrection at Milan against France	5	1	4	4	50	C	6.29	O II, 58
239	1820–1	Revolution at Naples and Piedmont	20	10	3	4	35	A	19.14	O II, 73–85
240	1831	Revolution at Romagna, Parma, and Modena	20	5	4	3	35	A	15.17	O II, 94–101
241	1833–4	Conspiracy of Mazzini-Ruffini	20	5	1	2	3	A	6.70	O II, 107
242	1848–9	Revolution at Naples, Piedmont, Tuscany, Rome, and Venice	60	10	4	5	70	AC	34.74	O II, 143–201
243	1859–60	Revolution in middle Italy and Naples	60	10	4	4	50	A	14.66	O II, 253–73
244	1893–4	Peasant disturbances in Sicily	5	5	3	2	15	B	7.21	O II, 328
245	1898	Disturbances in Lombardy and southern Italy	20	3	2	2	10	B	8.43	O II, 330
246	1900	Murder of King Humbert	20	1	1	4	7	A	5.18	O II, 333
247	1904	Disturbances in Lombardy, Sicily, and Sardinia	40	3	2	2	10	B	10.06	En 815
248	1905	Peasant disturbances near Ferrara and Ravenna	5	3	2	2	10	B	5.31	En 815
249	1917	Disturbances at Turin	5	1	3	2	15	F	4.21	En 816
250	1920–2	Disturbances in different provinces	60	15	3	2	15	B	23.82	En 820
251	1922	Fascisti revolution	100	3	2	5	30	A	20.80	En 822–3

SPAIN

NUMBER	YEAR	SPECIFICATION OF THE INTERNAL DISTURBANCE	MEASURES OF:							SOURCES [2]
			Social Area	Duration	Size of the Masses Involved	Intensity	Masses and Intensity Combined	Nature [1]	Geometric Average	
1	2	3	4	5	6	7	8	9	10	11
1	467 [3]	Foundation of independent Visigoth Kingdom .								
2	531	Mutiny in armies; murder of Amalaric . . .	80	1	2	5	30	F	13.39	A I, 182
3	549	Dethroning of Theodicelus	80	1	2	5	30	F	13.39	L II, 339
4	550	Insurrection at Baetica .	40	1	3	3	25	F	10.00	Enc XXI, 903
5	551–4	Struggle for the throne (Agila — Athanagild) .	80	25	3	5	50	F	46.42	L II, 339
6	567	Disturbances during the interregnum	80	10	2	2	15	F	22.89	L II, 342
7	570	Insurrection of Cantabrians (against Visigoths)	20	30	4	3	35	C	19.13	L II, 346
8	573–8	Struggle of Leovigildo with the vassals . . .	80	15	2	4	20	A	36.34	A I, 185
9	580–1	Rebellion of Basques . .	20	15	3	3	25	C	19.57	A I, 187
10	581–2	Struggle of Leovigildo with Hermenegildo . .	60	15	3	4	35	CD	31.58	L II, 349
11	585 [3]	Uniting of Spain (Conquest of Suevia) . . .								
12	586	Insurrection of Aryans against Reccared . .	60	5	2	3	15	CD	16.51	L II, 360
13	603	Deposition of Liuva . .	100	1	2	3	15	F	11.45	L II, 403
14	609	Deposition of Witheric .	100	1	2	3	15	F	11.45	L II, 404
15	616	Prosecution of the Jews during the reign of Sicebuto	60	5	3	2	15	B	16.51	L II, 407
16	631	Deposition of Svintila .	100	3	3	4	35	F	21.90	A I, 193
17	642	Deposition of Tulga . .	100	1	2	4	20	F	12.60	L II, 418
18	650–1	Riot against Recceswinto	60	15	3	3	25	F	28.23	L II, 421
19	672	Insurrection at Toledo and in the Province of the Basques	60	5	3	3	25	C	19.57	A I, 195 L II, 428
20	692	Conspiracy against Egica	60	1	1	2	3	F	5.65	L II, 450
21	694	Conspiracy of Jews; prosecution	40	3	3	2	15	C	12.16	L II, 451
22	709–10	Disturbances; deposition of Witiza	100	15	2	4	20	F	31.07	A I, 197
23	711–3 [3]	Conquest of Spain by the Arabs								
24	728–9	Moslem internal disturbances (Caisites — Kelbites)	40	5	3	3	25	C	17.10	D I, 219
25	740	Insurrection of Berbers against the Arabs . .	60	5	3	4	35	C	21.90	D I, 240
26	742–3	Struggle of Berbers with the Syrians	60	15	3	4	35	C	31.58	D I, 245
27	745	Moslem disturbances (Maodites — Caisites) .	40	5	3	4	35	C	19.13	D I, 280
28	747	Moslem disturbances (Caisites — Yemenites)	40	5	3	4	35	C	19.13	D I, 284

[1] See the text, p. 403, for a key to this column.

[2] Sources in the order of their appearance in the text:

A   —R. Altamira. *Historia de Espana*, 4 vols. 1909–1911.
L   —Lafuente y Zamallon. *Historia general de Espana*, 30 vols. 1861.
Enc —*Encyclopedia Universal*, 70 vols. Barcelona. (Vol. XXI, *Espana*, appeared in 1923.)
D   —C. Dozy. *Histoire des musulmans en Espagne*, 4 vols. Leyde, 1861. (Revised edition in 2 volumes, 1932.)
B   —R. Ballester. *Histoire d'Espagne*. Paris, 1928.
A (fr.) —R. Altamira. *Histoire d'Espagne*, ed. by Armand Colin. Paris, 1931.
M   —De Mazade. *Les révolutions d'Espagne*. Paris, 1868.
En   —*Encyclopaedia Britannica*, 14th ed.

[3] War rather than internal disturbances; for this reason it is listed but not included among disturbances.

SPAIN — *Continued*

1	2	3	4	5	6	7	8	9	10	11
29	750	Disturbances of the Ko-reishites	40	5	3	3	25	C	17.10	D I, 290
30	753-4	Moslem disturbances; siege of Saragossa	40	15	3	4	35	F	27.59	D I, 292
31	756	Seizure of power by Ab-durrahman I	80	3	3	5	50	A	22.89	D I, 355
32	759	Insurrection of Basques against Froila	10	3	3	3	25	C	9.09	L III, 121
33	763-4	Rebellion of Yemenites at Toledo	10	15	3	4	35	C	17.38	D I, 365
34	765	Uprising in Galicia	20	3	3	3	25	F	11.45	L III, 123
35	766	Uprising in Seville	10	3	3	3	25	F	9.09	D I, 369
36	770	Disturbances of the slaves in northern Spain	20	3	3	3	25	B	11.45	L II, 125
37	767-77	Insurrection of Berbers; civil war	60	54	3	4	35	C	48.40	D I, 373
38	780	Insurrection in Galicia	20	3	3	3	25	F	11.45	L III, 126
39	788	Struggle for the throne of Asturias; conspiracy of the brothers of Hicham I	40	3	1	2	3	F	9.44	L III, 127 A I, 239
40	789	Struggle for the throne of Asturias	20	3	1	2	3	F	7.49	L III, 129
41	805	Commotion at Cordova	20	1	2	3	15	F	6.69	D II, 59
42	806	Insurrection at Cordova	20	1	3	3	25	F	7.94	D II, 61
43	814	Insurrection and massacre at Cordova	20	1	3	3	25	F	7.94	D II, 69
44	822	Conspiracy at Toledo; executions	20	1	1	3	5	F	4.64	D II, 94
45	829	Insurrection at Toledo	20	5	3	3	25	C	13.57	D II, 97
46	834-7	Siege and conquest of Toledo	20	25	3	4	35	C	25.96	D II, 98
47	842	Struggle for the throne of Asturias (Ramiro I)	60	3	2	3	15	F	13.92	L III, 289
48	844-50	Insurrections at Merida and Murcia	20	38	2	4	20	F	24.77	A I, 240
49	850	Insurrection of Basques	20	3	2	3	15	C	9.66	L III, 306
50	853-8	Insurrection at Toledo	20	30	3	4	35	F	27.59	D II, 161
51	862	Disturbances in the valley of the Ebro	20	5	2	3	15	F	11.45	B 49
52	866	Insurrection of Count Fruela	40	3	1	4	7	F	9.44	L III, 319
53	867	Insurrection of Alaves	20	3	2	3	15	C	9.66	L III, 320
54	872	Insurrection of Beni-Casi in the valley of the Ebro	20	5	2	3	15	F	11.45	D II, 183
55	875	Insurrection of Ibn-Mervan	20	3	2	3	15	F	9.66	D II, 185
56	879	Insurrection in southern Spain	10	3	2	3	15	F	7.66	D II, 188
57	880	Seizure of Bobastro by Ibn-Hafsun	3	3	1	4	7	F	3.98	A I, 245
58	883	Struggle of the Caliph with Beni-Casi	20	5	2	4	20	F	12.60	D II, 197
59	884	Insurrection in Galicia	10	3	2	3	15	F	7.66	L III, 322
60	884-901	Struggle with Ibn-Hafsun	5	76	1	4	7	F	13.86	D II, 200
61	885	Insurrection in Galicia	10	5	2	3	15	F	9.09	L III, 322
62	889	Insurrection in Seville	10	5	2	3	15	F	9.09	D II, 240
63	889-91	Insurrection at Elvira; anarchy	10	20	3	3	25	F	17.10	D II, 213
64	895	Civil war near Seville	10	5	2	3	15	F	9.09	D II, 288
65	902	Struggle with Ibn-Hafsun (Ronda)	5	5	1	4	7	F	5.59	D II, 308
66	909-10	Struggle for the throne of Alphonso III	40	15	2	4	20	F	22.89	L III, 351
67	913-4	Struggle with Ibn-Hafsun (Ronda)	10	15	2	3	15	F	13.10	D II, 329
68	919-28	Struggle with Ibn-Hafsun (Ronda)	5	50	2	4	20	F	17.10	D II, 340
69	923	Insurrection in Navarre	5	3	2	3	15	F	6.08	L III, 414
70	924	Civil war in Valencia	10	3	2	3	15	A	7.66	D II, 346
71	926-8	Civil war (Sancho — Alphonso IV)	40	20	2	3	15	F	22.89	L III, 422
72	928	Insurrection at Tadmir	10	3	2	3	15	A	7.66	D II, 346
73	930	Disturbances at Badajoz	5	10	4	2	20	A	10.00	D II, 346
74	931-2	Uprising in favor of Alphonso IV	40	15	2	2	10	F	18.17	A I, 255
75	940	Insurrection in Castile	10	3	2	3	15	A	7.66	L III, 435

SPAIN — *Continued*

1	2	3	4	5	6	7	8	9	10	11
76	951–2	Civil war (Sancho-Ordonio)	40	15	2	3	15	F	20.80	L III, 452
77	955	Insurrection in Galicia	20	3	2	3	15	F	9.66	L III, 488
78	956	Insurrection in Castile (Gonzales)	20	5	2	3	15	F	11.45	L III, 454
79	958	Deposition of King Sancho	40	3	2	4	20	F	13.39	L III, 455
80	960	Reinstatement of Sancho	40	3	2	4	20	F	13.39	L III, 456
81	966	Insurrection in Galicia	20	3	2	3	15	F	9.66	L III, 488
82	967	Struggle with Count Gonzalva	5	5	2	3	15	F	7.21	L III, 489
83	980–2	Insurrection in Galicia; civil war	20	20	2	3	15	F	18.17	L IV, 35
84	981	Uprising of Ghalib	40	3	3	3	25	A	14.42	D III, 189
85	989	Conspiracy against Almanzor	60	1	2	2	10	A	8.43	D III, 210
86	997–8	Uprising of Ziri	40	10	2	3	15	A	18.17	D III, 222
87	1002	Insurrection at Cordova	20	1	3	1	5	F	4.64	D III, 259
88	1006	Conspiracy at Cordova	20	3	3	1	5	F	6.69	D III, 259
89	1009	Coup d'état at Cordova (Makhdi)	60	10	2	5	30	F	26.21	D III, 271
90	1010	Uprising of Berbers	60	5	3	4	35	C	21.90	D III, 304
91	1011	Disturbances at Cordova	20	3	2	3	15	F	9.66	D III, 307
92	1013	Civil war; seizure of Cordova	40	3	3	4	35	F	16.13	D III, 308
93	1016	Deposition of Solaiman	60	1	2	4	20	F	10.63	D III, 318
94	1017–8	Struggle of Ali for power	60	15	2	4	20	F	26.21	D III, 325
95	1021	Deposition of Casim	60	1	2	4	20	F	10.63	Enc XXI, 912 A I, 250
96	1023	Reinstatement of Casim	60	1	2	4	20	F	10.63	Enc XXI, 913 A I, 250
97	1028	Uprising of vassals in northern Spain	20	5	2	3	15	F	11.45	Enc XXI, 930
98	1029	Overthrow at Cordova (Hicham III)	60	1	2	4	20	F	10.63	Enc XXI, 913 A I, 250
99	1031	Deposition of Hicham III	60	1	2	4	20	F	10.63	D III, 368
100	1035	Struggle in Catalonia	20	5	2	3	15	F	11.45	A I, 400
101	1035–7	Struggle of Leo for the throne	20	20	2	3	15	F	18.17	L IV, 151
102	1039	Conspiracy in Granada	10	3	2	2	10	F	6.69	D IV, 48
103	1043	Internal disturbances in Malaga	10	1	2	3	15	F	5.31	D IV, 60
104	1046–7	Insurrection of Negroes in Malaga	10	3	2	3	15	C	7.66	D IV, 64
105	1054	Civil war in Castile	40	5	2	4	20	F	15.87	L IV, 193
106	1063	Mutiny at Seville	10	1	2	3	15	F	5.31	D IV, 104
107	1064	Insurrection of Arabs in Malaga	10	1	2	3	15	C	5.31	D IV, 108
108	1066	"War of the three Sanchoes"; prosecution of Jews	40	5	2	3	15	CD	14.42	D IV, 117 L IV, 215
109	1068	Internal disturbances in Castile (Sancho-Alphonso)	40	3	1	3	5	F	8.43	L IV, 216
110	1071	Deposition of Alphonso	40	3	1	4	7	F	9.44	L IV, 217
111	1072	Civil war (Sancho-Urraca)	20	5	1	3	5	F	7.94	L IV, 222
112	1090	Mutiny at Seville	10	1	2	3	15	F	5.31	D IV, 239
113	1092	Insurrection and Arabian republic in Valence	10	5	3	4	20	A	10.00	D IV, 304
114	1095–7	Insurrection near Alyesiras	10	20	2	3	15	F	14.42	D IV, 279
115	1111–3	Disturbances in Castile; insurrection in Galicia	60	20	2	3	15	F	26.21	L IV, 272
116	1115–6	Internal disturbances in Castile	40	15	2	3	15	F	20.80	L IV, 482
117	1117	Uprising in Santiago	10	1	2	2	10	F	4.64	L IV, 484
118	1120	The same	10	1	2	2	10	F	4.64	L IV, 492
119	1121	Mutiny at Cordova against the Arabs	10	5	3	3	25	C	10.77	D IV, 266
120	1122–6	Civil war in Castile (Urraca)	40	25	2	3	15	F	24.66	A I, 374
121	1127	Uprising of vassals in Castile	20	3	2	3	15	A	9.66	L IV, 521
122	1133	Civil war in Castile	40	10	2	3	15	A	18.17	Enc XXI, 939
123	1136	Insurrection at Santiago	10	3	3	4	35	F	10.16	A I, 420
124	1143–5	Uprising of Arabs against Almoravids	40	20	3	3	25	C	27.14	L V, 64

SPAIN — *Continued*

1	2	3	4	5	6	7	8	9	10	11
125	1157–8	Internal troubles in Castile	40	15	2	2	10	F	18.17	A I, 377
126	1160	Internal troubles in Castile (Laras and Castras)	40	5	2	3	15	F	14.42	L V, 129
127	1162	Insurrection in Salamanca at Toledo	10	5	2	3	15	F	9.09	A I, 379
128	1164	Internal troubles in Castile (Laras and Castras)	40	5	2	3	15	F	14.42	L V, 130
129	1166	The same	20	5	2	2	15	F	11.45	L V, 131
130	1174	Justice of the King on Laras	40	3	2	3	15	F	12.16	L V, 132
131	1180	Last battles of Laras and Castras	40	5	2	2	10	F	12.60	A I, 379
132	1204	Insurrection in Aragon	20	5	2	3	25	A	13.58	L V, 191
133	1214	Commotion in Castile	40	3	2	2	10	F	10.63	L V, 241
134	1217	Insurrection in Castile	40	3	2	3	15	F	12.16	A I, 382
135	1219–27	Internal troubles in Aragon	20	42	2	3	15	F	23.27	L V, 389
136	1224	Insurrection in Arabian Spain	60	5	2	3	15	F	16.51	Enc XXI, 918
137	1226	Disturbances in Huesca	5	1	2	3	15	F	4.22	L V, 393
138	1230³	Union of Leon and Castile								
139	1245³	Decline of Arabian Kingdom								
140	1254	Internal trouble in Castile	40	5	1	3	5	F	10.00	L VI, 18
141	1254–7	Uprising of the Moors against the Spaniards	20	25	3	3	25	C	23.21	L VI, 30
142	1270–1	Uprising of nobles in Castile	40	15	2	3	15	A	20.80	L VI, 30
143	1272–5	Insurrection in Aragon	20	25	2	3	15	AC	19.57	L VI, 67
144	1276	Insurrection in Valence	20	6	2	3	15	F	11.45	L VI, 73
145	1280	Insurrection in Catalonia	20	5	2	3	15	F	11.45	A I, 618
146	1282–4	Internal troubles in Castile	40	20	2	3	15	F	22.89	L VI, 90
147	1287	Uprising of nobles in Castile	40	1	2	3	15	A	8.43	L VI, 206
148	1288	Intervention of the Union in Aragon	20	5	3	3	25	A	13.57	L VI, 236
149	1288–91	Civil war in Castile	40	25	2	3	15	AC	24.66	L VI, 210
150	1293	Uprising of Infant Juan in Castile	20	3	1	3	5	F	6.69	L VI, 223
151	1295–1303	Disturbances during the minority of Ferdinand IV (Castile)	40	46	2	2	10	F	26.40	L VI, 356 A I, 623
152	1301	New "Union" in Aragon	20	5	2	2	10	A	10.00	L VI, 410
153	1310	Coup d'état at Granada	40	3	2	4	20	F	13.39	L VI, 376
154	1312–9	Internal trouble in Castile	40	42	2	3	15	F	29.32	L VI, 457
155	1313	Internal trouble in Granada	40	3	1	4	7	F	9.44	L VI, 460
156	1321–5	Insurrection in Castile	40	30	2	3	15	F	26.21	L VI, 468
157	1326	Insurrection in Castile	20	3	2	2	10	F	8.43	L VI, 471
158	1333–8	Civil war in Castile	40	34	2	3	15	F	27.32	L VI, 485
159	1334	Commotion in Valence	20	1	2	2	10	A	5.85	L VI, 448
160	1335–8	Struggle for power in Aragon	20	25	2	3	15	A	19.57	L VII, 60
161	1347–8	Insurrections in Valence and Aragon	40	15	3	3	25	A	24.66	A I, 630
162	1350	Resistance of Pedro I at Algeciras	5	3	2	2	10	F	5.31	L VII, 150
163	1352–3	Insurrection in Ashlar	5	15	2	3	15	F	10.40	L VII, 167
164	1354–6	Civil war in Castile	40	25	2	3	15	F	24.66	L VII, 188
165	1365–9	Civil war in Castile	40	20	2	3	15	F	22.89	A I, 604
166	1370–1	Struggle with the allies of Pedro I	20	15	2	3	15	F	16.51	L VII, 324
167	1386	Disturbances in Aragon	20	5	2	2	10	F	10.00	L VII, 139
168	1390–1	Commotion in Castile	40	15	2	3	15	F	20.80	L VIII, 32
169	1391	"Pogroms" of the Jews in Aragon	20	3	2	3	15	F	9.66	A I, 608
170	1394	Struggle of Henry III with the vassals	20	3	2	2	10	A	8.43	L VIII, 46
171	1395	Insurrection in Aragon (Count Foix)	20	3	2	2	10	F	8.43	L VII, 423
172	1410–2	Struggle for the throne in Aragon	20	20	2	3	15	F	18.17	L VIII, 115
173	1413	Insurrection in Aragon (Count Urgel)	10	5	2	2	10	F	7.94	L VIII, 139

³ War rather than internal disturbances; for this reason it is listed but not included among disturbances.

SPAIN — *Continued*

1	2	3	4	5	6	7	8	9	10	11
174	1420–2	Internal troubles in Castile (Infant Henry) . .	40	5	1	2	3	F	8.43	L VIII, 171
175	1423	Coup d'état at Granada .	40	3	2	3	15	F	12.16	L VIII, 195
176	1429	Commotion in Castile .	20	3	2	2	10	F	8.43	L VIII, 191
177	1431–2	Disturbances at Granada	40	15	2	3	15	F	20.80	L VIII, 205
178	1438–40	Commotion in Castile (feudal)	20	20	2	3	15	A	18.17	L VIII, 216
179	1441	Civil war (feudal barons against the King) in Castile	40	5	2	3	15	A	14.42	L VIII, 224
180	1442	The same	40	5	2	3	15	A	14.42	L VIII, 227
181	1445	Internal troubles in Castile; insurrection at Granada	60	5	2	3	15	A	16.51	L VIII, 234, 238
182	1452	Civil war in Navarre . .	20	5	2	3	15	F	11.45	L VIII, 362
183	1461	Insurrection in Castile and Aragon	60	3	2	3	15	F	13.92	L VIII, 376
184	1461–72	Struggle in Catalonia . .	20	58	3	3	25	C	30.72	L VIII, 379–409
185	1465–8	Internal troubles in Castile	40	25	2	4	20	F	27.14	A I, 616
186	1474–7	Struggle for the throne in Castile	40	25	2	4	20	F	27.14	L IX, 124
187	1476	Mutiny at Segovia . . .	5	3	2	3	15	F	6.08	L IX, 145
188	1479[3]	Union of Aragon and Castile								
189	1482–3	Insurrection at Granada .	20	5	2	3	15	F	11.45	L IX, 262
190	1485	Coup d'état at Granada .	40	1	1	4	7	F	6.54	L IX, 298
191	1491	Mutiny at Granada . . .	20	1	3	3	25	C	7.94	L IX, 393
192	1492[3]	Conquest of Granada . . .								
193	1499–1501	Uprising of the Moors against the Spaniards .	40	20	3	3	25	C	27.41	L IX, 116
194	1508	Uprising of feudal barons in Andalusia	20	5	2	3	15	F	11.45	L X, 336, 345
195	1516–7	Uprising against Cardinal Cisneros	60	15	2	3	15	A	23.81	L X, 458
196	1520–2	Insurrection against absolutism ("communeros")	80	20	3	3	25	A	34.20	A III, 14
197	1523–4	Insurrection on Majorca .	10	20	3	3	25	A	17.10	A III, 205
198	1548	Insurrection at Alicante and other cities . . .	20	3	2	3	15	F	9.66	A III, 196
199	1568–71	Uprising of the Moors in Granada	20	25	3	4	35	C	25.96	A III, 78
200	1591	Insurrection at Saragossa (Perez)	5	3	2	3	15	F	6.08	A III, 117
201	1592	Insurrection at Aragon .	20	3	2	3	15	F	9.66	A III, 117
202	1618	Conspiracy against Count Lerma	20	1	1	2	3	F	3.91	L XV, 461
203	1620–1	Disturbances near Gerona	5	3	2	3	15	F	6.08	A III, 200
204	1631	Disturbances in Basque provinces	20	5	2	2	10	C	10.00	A III, 158
205	1640–52	Insurrection in Catalonia	20	62	2	3	15	C	26.50	A III, 146
206	1654	Conquest of Barcelona .	10	15	2	3	15	C	13.10	A III, 151
207	1666	Uprising of Infant Juan .	10	1	1	2	3	F	3.11	A III, 165
208	1667	Overthrow; Infant Juan regent	100	1	1	4	7	F	8.88	A III, 166
209	1704–15	Civil war in Catalonia .	20	58	2	3	15	C	25.91	A IV, 9
210	1766	Rebellions at Madrid and other cities	20	3	3	2	15	AB	9.66	A IV, 55
211	1807	Conspiracy at Escurial .	10	1	2	2	10	F	4.64	A IV, 96
212	1808	Insurrection at Aranjuez	100	1	2	5	30	F	14.42	A IV, 100
213	1815	Conspiracy in Galicia . .	20	1	1	2	3	A	3.91	L XXVII, 59
214	1817	Conspiracy in Catalonia .	20	1	1	2	3	A	3.91	L XXVII, 85
215	1820–3	Revolution and civil war	100	25	3	5	50	A	50.00	L XXVII, 115 ff.
216	1824	Insurrection in Tarifa . .	10	3	2	3	15	A	7.66	L XXVIII, 381
217	1827	Commotion in Catalonia .	20	3	2	2	10	A	8.43	L XXVIII, 454
218	1830–1	Commotion in Pyrenees .	20	5	2	2	10	A	10.00	L XXVIII, 72
219	1833–40	Insurrection of the Carlists; civil war; coup d'état of Espartero . .	100	42	4	4	70	A	66.49	L XXIX, 150 Enc XXI, 1029
220	1842	Insurrection at Barcelona	10	3	2	3	15	A	7.66	Enc XXI, 1032
221	1843	Insurrection at Malaga .	5	3	2	2	10	A	5.31	Enc XXI, 1032

[3] War rather than internal disturbances; for this reason it is listed but not included among disturbances.

SPAIN — *Continued*

1	2	3	4	5	6	7	8	9	10	11
222	1844	Military riot at Madrid .	10	1	2	3	15	F	5.31	Enc XXI, 1032
223	1846	Military riot at Galicia .	20	1	2	3	15	F	6.69	Enc XXI, 1033
224	1847–9	Carlist movement in northern Spain . . .	40	20	2	3	15	A	22.89	A (fr.), 202
225	1854	Pronunciamento (Vicalvaro)	100	1	2	2	10	A	10.00	M 23
226	1856	New pronunciamento . .	100	1	2	2	10	F	10.00	M 119
227	1859	Republican movement at Estramadura	20	3	2	2	10	A	8.43	Enc XXI, 1034
228	1863	Peasant insurrection at Loja	10	3	3	2	15	B	7.66	Enc XXI, 1034
229	1866	Military rebellion at Aranjuez; insurrection in Madrid	10	3	2	3	15	A	7.66	M 341
230	1868–70	Coup d'état; provisional government of Primo .	100	30	2	5	30	A	39.15	M 390 Enc XXI, 1035
231	1872–6	Anarchy and civil war	100	30	5	5	100	AB	66.94	Enc XXI, 1035
232	1883	Republican movement at Badajoz	10	3	2	2	10	A	6.69	Enc XXI, 1037
233	1884	Conspiracies at Madrid .	10	3	2	2	10	F	6.69	Enc XXI, 1037
234	1887	Military rebellion at Madrid	10	1	2	3	15	F	5.31	Enc XXI, 1038
235	1892	Insurrection at Xeres . .	5	1	2	3	15	F	4.22	Enc XXI, 1039
236	1899	Commotion in Catalonia and in Basque provinces	20	3	2	2	10	C	8.43	Enc XXI, 1040
237	1902	Commotion in Barcelona	10	3	2	2	10	AB	6.69	Enc XXI, 1040
238	1906	Commotion in Barcelona	10	1	2	2	10	AB	4.64	Enc XXI, 1041
239	1909	Insurrection at Barcelona	20	1	4	3	35	AB	8.68	Enc XXI, 1042
240	1917	General strike; unrest in the army	80	5	3	3	25	AB	21.54	En XXI, 143
241	1920	Rebellion at Saragossa and Santander . . .	10	1	2	3	15	AB	5.31	En XXI, 143
242	1923	Coup d'état of Primo de Rivera	100	1	1	5	10	A	10.00	En XXI, 144

THE NETHERLANDS

NUMBER	YEAR	SPECIFICATION OF THE INTERNAL DISTURBANCE	MEASURES OF:							SOURCES [2]
			Social Area	Duration	Size of the Masses Involved	Intensity	Masses and Intensity Combined	Nature [1]	Geometric Average	
1	2	3	4	5	6	7	8	9	10	11
1	678–86	Civil war between the mayors of the Palace .	100	46	2	3	15	F	41.02	B 166–7
2	697	Insurrection of Frisians .	20	3	3	3	25	C	11.45	J I, 83
3	715	Civil war of Neustria against Austrasia . .	80	5	3	3	25	F	21.53	B 206
4	717	The same	80	5	3	3	25	F	21.53	B 206
5	719	The same	80	5	3	3	25	F	21.53	B 206
6	737	Insurrection of Frisians .	20	3	3	3	25	C	11.45	J I, 87
7	754	The same	20	3	3	3	25	C	11.45	Bl I, 84
8	755	The same	20	3	3	3	25	C	11.45	Bl I, 84
9	785	The same	20	3	3	3	25	C	11.45	Bl I, 85
10	790	The same	20	3	3	3	25	C	11.45	Bl I, 99
11	830–1	Insurrection of the sons of Emperor Louis . . .	80	15	2	4	20	F	28.84	B 362–3
12	832–4	Second insurrection . .	80	15	2	4	20	F	28.84	B 364–5
13	892–5	Civil war in lower Lorraine	20	25	3	4	35	F	25.94	J I, 111
14	900	Civil war in lower Lorraine	20	5	3	4	35	F	15.17	J I, 111
15	921	Insurrection of Gislebert against the French king	20	5	2	3	15	F	11.45	J I, 113
16	922–3	Struggle between Charles the Simple and Robert	60	5	2	4	20	F	18.15	B 403
17	936	A new insurrection of Gislebert	20	5	2	3	15	F	11.45	J I, 114
18	953–4	Insurrection of Ludolf against Otton	20	10	1	2	3	F	8.43	K 211–2
19	973–7	Disturbances in Lorraine	20	30	3	3	25	F	19.59	G I, 264
20	1000	Insurrection of Frisians .	20	3	3	3	25	C	9.08	Bl I,156
21	1005	Civil war in lower Lorraine	20	5	3	3	25	F	13.58	J I, 131
22	1014–6	Civil war in Holland . .	20	20	3	3	25	F	21.53	Bl I, 160–1
23	1047	Civil war in lower Lorraine	20	5	3	3	25	F	13.58	J I, 136
24	1051	Pretender in Holland . .	20	5	2	3	15	F	11.45	Bl I, 170
25	1061	Civil war in Holland . .	20	5	3	3	25	F	13.58	Bl I, 172
26	1070–2	Civil war in Flanders . .	20	20	3	3	25	F	21.53	Bl I, 176–7
27	1085	Insurrection in Holland against Utrecht . . .	20	5	3	4	35	F	15.17	Bl I, 181
28	1105	Struggle between Henry IV and Henry V . . .	60	5	2	4	20	F	18.15	Gi III, 753–61
29	1109	Civil war at Liège . . .	20	5	3	3	25	F	13.58	Bl I, 188
30	1126–8	Civil war in Flanders . .	20	20	3	3	25	F	21.53	Bl I, 232
31	1128	Disturbances in lower Lorraine	20	3	3	3	25	F	11.45	J I, 167
32	1130–59	Civil war in Limburg . .	20	115	3	3	25	F	38.64	Bl I, 185
33	1142	Feudal conspiracy at Brabant	20	3	2	2	10	F	8.43	J I, 168
34	1147	Communal revolution at Poperinghe	3	3	3	4	35	AB	6.76	J I, 209

[1] See the text, p. 403, for a key to this column.
[2] Sources in the order of their appearance in the text:

B — C. Bayet, C. Pfister, and A. Kleinclauss. *Le christianisme, les barbares, mérovingiens et carolingiens.* Paris, 1903.
J — T. Juste. *Histoire de Belgique.* Bruxelles, 1898.
Bl — P. J. Blok. *Geschichte der Niederlande.* Gotha, 1902–1907.
K — R. Köpke and S. Dummler. *Kaiser Otto der Grosse.* Leipzig, 1876.
G — B. Gebhardt. *Handbuch der deutschen Geschichte.* Stuttgart, 1896.
Gi — W. Giesebrecht. *Geschichte der deutschen Kaiserzeit.* Braunschweig, 1875–1895.
W — K. Wenzelburger. *Geschichte der Niederlande.* B. I. Gotha, 1879.
P — H. Pirenne. *Histoire de Belgique.* Bruxelles, 1900–1907.
E — G. Edmundson. *History of Holland.* Cambridge, 1922.
En — *Encyclopaedia Britannica,* 14th ed., Vol. III.

THE NETHERLANDS — *Continued*

1	2	3	4	5	6	7	8	9	10	11
35	1157	Insurrection of Frisians .	20	3	3	3	25	C	11.45	W 119
36	1192	Disturbances at Liège .	10	3	3	3	25	F	9.08	J I, 219
37	1201–5	Civil war in Holland . .	20	30	3	3	25	F	24.66	Bl I, 276–8
38	1204–5	Disturbances in Flanders	20	15	3	2	15	F	16.52	J I, 293
39	1220–45	Civil war at Utrecht . .	20	103	3	3	25	F	37.24	Bl I, 280–3
40	1225	Insurrection of the pseudo Baldwin in Flanders .	20	5	2	3	15	F	11.45	J I, 238–9
41	1252	Civil war at Liège . . .	10	5	3	3	25	F	10.76	J I, 252
42	1253–6	Civil war in Flanders . .	20	25	3	3	25	F	23.49	J I, 244–5
43	1267	Peasant rebellion in Holland	5	5	3	3	25	BF	8.55	Bl I, 285
44	1275	Insurrection of Frisians .	20	5	3	3	25	C	13.58	W 181
45	1296	Conspiracy and civil war in Holland	20	5	3	3	25	F	13.58	Bl I, 246–7
46	1297–1315	Civil war in a part of Liège	10	82	3	3	25	F	34.59	Bl II, 59–62
47	1299	Insurrection at Delft . .	5	3	3	4	35	F	8.07	Bl I, 247
48	1302	Insurrection at Brugge and towns of Brabant .	10	5	3	3	25	AB	10.76	P II, 45
49	1306	Insurrection at towns of Brabant	10	5	3	3	25	AB	10.76	Bl II, 43
50	1312–3	Democratic insurrection at Brugge and other provinces	40	15	4	3	35	AB	27.61	P II, 29–35
51	1316–8	Civil war at Helder . .	5	20	3	3	25	F	13.58	Bl II, 257–8
52	1323–8	Insurrection in maritime Flanders	10	34	3	4	35	AB	22.86	P II, 76–90
53	1325	Insurrection at Dordrecht	5	3	3	2	15	F	6.08	Bl II, 94
54	1325	Insurrection of nobles in Zeeland	10	3	2	2	10	F	6.70	Bl II, 94
55	1337	Disturbances at Ghent .	5	3	4	3	35	AB	8.07	P II, 101–10
56	1345	The same	5	1	3	2	15	F	4.21	P II, 119
57	1345	Disturbances at Friesland	20	5	3	2	15	F	11.45	Bl II, 306
58	1347	Disturbances at Helder .	5	10	3	3	25	F	10.76	Bl II, 266–7
59	1348–9	Civil war in Flanders . .	20	15	3	4	35	F	10.02	P II, 122
60	1350–9	Disturbances at Helder .	5	50	3	4	35	F	20.61	Bl II, 266–7
61	1358–9	Disturbances in Holland .	20	15	3	3	25	F	19.59	Bl II, 115
62	1358	Civil war at Hainaut . .	10	3	3	3	25	F	9.08	Bl II, 115
63	1359–61	Disturbances at Brugge and Ypern	10	20	3	3	25	AB	17.10	P II, 188–9
64	1360	Insurrection of gilds at Löwen	5	3	2	4	20	AB	6.70	Bl II, 49
65	1361	Disturbances at Helder .	5	3	3	4	35	F	8.07	Bl II, 270
66	1362	Disturbances at Löwen .	5	3	3	3	25	F	7.21	Bl II, 50
67	1373	Insurrection of gilds at Dordrecht	5	3	2	3	15	AB	6.08	Bl II, 123
68	1378	Disturbances at Löwen .	5	3	2	3	15	F	6.08	Bl II, 50
69	1379 00	Civil war at Ghent . .	3	23	3	3	25	ABF	14.63	P II, 189–94
70	1379–80	Insurrection at Utrecht .	5	10	3	4	35	F	12.08	Bl II, 207
71	1388	Disturbances at Brugge and Antwerp	10	3	3	2	15	F	7.65	Bl II, 52
72	1392–3	Civil war in Holland . .	20	15	3	4	35	F	21.88	Bl II, 127–8
73	1413–5	Disturbances in Friesland	20	20	3	2	15	F	18.15	Bl II, 312
74	1420–1	Revolution in Brabant .	20	15	3	4	35	F	21.88	Bl II, 155–191
75	1424	Insurrection in Hainaut .	10	3	3	4	35	F	10.02	Bl II, 159
76	1425–8	Civil war in Holland and Hainaut	40	25	3	3	25	F	29.24	Bl II, 162–72
77	1425–7	Civil war in Utrecht . .	20	15	3	4	35	F	21.88	Bl II, 247
78	1428–31	Civil war in Helder. . .	10	20	3	3	25	F	17.10	Bl II, 286–7
79	1447	The same	10	5	3	3	25	F	10.76	Bl II, 291
80	1459	The same	10	5	3	3	25	F	10.76	Bl II, 293–4
81	1461	Insurrection of Cluppelslagers	3	5	2	3	15	BF	6.08	P II, 274
82	1465	Disturbances at Liège . .	5	5	3	3	25	F	8.55	Bl II, 487
83	1476	Insurrection at Helder against Burgundy . .	10	3	3	2	15	C	7.65	P II, 310
84	1566	Disturbances at Utrecht .	10	3	2	3	15	D	7.65	Bl III, 58–60
85	1567	Calvinistic disturbances in different provinces . . .	40	5	3	3	25	D	17.10	Bl III, 68–70
86	1572–1609	Great revolution	80	139	4	5	70	ACD	91.83	E 51–109
87	1622	Conspiracy against Staatshalter	20	3	2	2	10	F	8.43	E 140
88	1632	Conspiracy of the nobility in Belgium	40	3	2	1	3	F	7.12	En III, 357
89	1650	Insurrection at Amsterdam	5	3	3	3	25	F	7.21	E 207–8
90	1672	People's insurrection in Holland	20	3	3	2	10	F	8.43	E 255–6
91	1683–4	Disturbances at Liège .	5	10	3	3	25	F	10.76	P V, 147

THE NETHERLANDS — *Continued*

1	2	3	4	5	6	7	8	9	10	11
92	1698	Disturbances at Brussels .	5	3	3	2	10	F	5.31	P V, 68
93	1717	The same	5	3	3	2	10	F	5.31	P V, 187
94	1747	Antirepublican revolution in the United Provinces	60	3	2	5	30	A	17.54	E 311–2
95	1785–7	Civil war in the United Provinces	80	20	3	2	15	F	28.84	E 333–4
96	1788–90	Revolution at Brabant and Liège	40	20	4	4	50	AC	34.20	P V, 458–541
97	1795	Republican insurrection .	80	3	3	5	50	A	22.91	E 342–3
98	1798	Peasants' insurrection in Flanders	20	3	3	2	15	C	9.66	J III, 117
99	1798	Revolution at Hague . .	5	3	3	5	50	A	9.08	E 350
100	1813	National coup d'état . .	80	1	3	5	50	C	15.85	E 365
101	1830	Belgian revolution . . .	60	10	4	5	70	C	34.74	E 389
102	1852	Disturbances at Brussels and other cities . . .	10	3	3	1	5	BF	5.31	En III, 361
103	1886	Disturbances at Liège .	5	3	3	2	15	BF	6.08	En III, 361

RUSSIA

NUMBER	YEAR	SPECIFICATION OF THE INTERNAL DISTURBANCE	MEASURES OF:							SOURCES[2]
			Social Area	Duration	Size of the Masses Involved	Intensity	Masses and Intensity Combined	Nature[1]	Geometric Average	
1	2	3	4	5	6	7	8	9	10	11
1	946	Uprising of Drevlians	20	3	4	2	20	C	10.62	S I, 128, 131
2	972	Internal war for Kiev throne	60	3	3	2	15	AF	13.03	S I, 152
3	977	The same	60	5	3	3	25	AF	19.59	S I, 153-6
4	981	Uprising of Viatichis	10	3	4	2	20	C	8.43	S I, 174
5	982	The same	10	3	4	2	20	C	8.43	S I, 174
6	986	Uprising of Radimichis	10	3	4	2	20	C	8.43	S I, 174
7	1014-9	Internal war for Kiev throne	80	34	3	4	35	C	45.71	S I, 193-9
8	1023-5	The same	60	20	3	4	35	C	34.75	S I, 200-3
9	1064	Deposition of the Prince at Tmutarakan	10	3	2	4	20	C	8.43	S I, 290-1
10	1068	People's uprising at Kiev	40	1	4	4	50	C	12.59	S I, 293
11	1078	Internal mutiny in Kiev and Chernigov princedoms	60	5	3	2	15	C	16.52	S I, 302
12	1081	Deposition of the Prince at Tmutarakan	10	3	2	4	20	C	8.43	S I, 306
13	1083	The same	10	3	2	4	20	C	8.43	S I, 306
14	1084-6	Mutiny in the Princedom of Volyn	20	20	3	2	15	C	18.16	S I, 306-10
15	1094	Civil war for Chernigov throne	20	3	3	2	15	A	9.66	S I, 320
16	1095	Civil war for Smolensk throne	20	3	3	2	15	A	9.66	S I, 322
17	1097-1100	Internal war for Kiev throne	60	25	3	3	25	A	33.50	S I, 3
18	1104	Internal mutiny in Polotzk Princedom	20	3	3	2	15	F	11.46	S I, 330-41
19	1117-8	Disturbances in Novgorod	20	15	4	2	20	F	18.16	S I, 373
20	1123	Disturbances in Volyn	20	3	3	2	15	F	9.66	S I, 353-4
21	1127	Internal mutiny in Chernigov Princedom	20	3	3	2	15	F	9.66	S I, 361-2
22	1134	Internal mutiny in Polotzk and Smolensk princedoms	40	3	3	2	15	F	12.16	S I, 363
23	1135-62	Great internal war for the Kiev throne	60	106	3	4	35	F	67.61	S I, 367-470
24	1136-7	Disturbances at Novgorod	20	15	4	2	20	F	18.46	S I, 389-91
25	1151	Uprising in Polotzk Princedom	20	1	4	3	35	F	8.67	S I, 452
26	1156	Internal mutiny in Chernigov Princedom	20	5	3	2	15	F	11.45	S I, 450
27	1159	Uprising in Polotzk Princedom	20	3	4	2	20	F	10.62	S I, 478-9

[1] See the text, p. 403, for a key to this column.
[2] Sources in the order of their appearance in the text:

S —Soloviev. *History of Russia from Ancient Times* (in Russian [3]). St. Petersburg, 1911.
E —A. V. Exemplarsky. *Great and Appanage Princes in Northern Russia* (in Russian). St. Petersburg, 1889-1891.
B —A Brückner. *Katherina II*. Berlin, 1883.
Sh —N. K. Shilder. *Emperor Paul I* (in Russian). St. Petersburg, 1902.
K —A. Korniloff. *Modern Russian History*. 1916.
Sc —Th. Schiemann. *Geschichte Russlands unter Kaiser Nikolaus I*. Berlin, 1908-1919.
Se —V. I. Semevsky. *Peasant Question in Russia*, Vol. II (in Russian). St. Petersburg, 1888.
T —S. S. Tatitchev. *Emperor Alexander II* (in Russian). St. Petersburg, 1903.
Ba —M. Balabanov. *Sketches of the History of the Revolutionary Movement in Russia* (in Russian). Leningrad, 1929.
B E —*Encyclopedic Dictionary of Brokhaus-Efron*, 1st supp. vol. (in Russian). St. Petersburg, 1905.
En —*Encyclopaedia Britannica*, 14th ed. Vol. XIX.
V —G. Vernadsky. *The Russian Revolution*, 1917-31. New York, 1932.

[3] Analyzing the facts given in Vol. I of Soloviev's History, N. Pogodin's *Studies, Notes and Lectures in Russian History* (in Russian). Moscow, 1857, Vol. V, was also consulted.

RUSSIA — *Continued*

1	2	3	4	5	6	7	8	9	10	11
28	1164	Internal mutiny in Chernigov Princedom . .	20	3	3	2	15	F	9.66	S I, 470–1
29	1169–70	Internal war for Kiev throne	80	15	3	4	35	F	34.76	S I, 473–7
30	1174–5	Internal war for Vladimir's throne and in the southern princedoms .	80	15	3	4	35	F	34.76	S I, 512–23, 525–31
31	1176	Disturbances at Novgorod	20	3	4	2	20	F	9.66	S I, 574
32	1185–6	Mutiny in Riazan Province	20	5	3	3	25	F	13.58	S I, 564
33	1192	Expulsion of the Prince at Novgorod	20	1	4	2	20	F	7.36	S I, 574
34	1196–7	Internal war in the southern princedoms . . .	60	15	3	3	25	F	28.23	S I, 544–6
35	1197	Expulsion of the Prince at Novgorod	20	1	4	2	20	F	7.36	S I, 577
36	1202–3	Internal war in Kiev Princedom	20	15	3	3	25	F	16.71	S I, 557
37	1204	Disturbances at Novgorod	20	3	4	2	20	F	10.62	S I, 576
38	1207	Internal war in the southern princedoms . . .	60	5	3	3	25	F	13.49	S I, 565–6
39	1210–1	Disturbances at Novgorod	20	15	4	2	20	F	18.03	S I, 577–9
40	1214–6	Internal war for the Great Princedom's throne . .	60	20	3	3	25	F	24.66	S I, 581–94
41	1217	Massacre of the princes at Riazan	10	1	2	3	15	F	5.39	S I, 595
42	1218	Disturbances at Novgorod	20	3	4	2	20	F	10.62	S I, 595–6
43	1220	The same	20	3	4	2	20	F	10.62	S I, 597
44	1228	The same	20	2	4	2	20	F	10.62	S I, 599
45	1228–9	Uprising of Mordva against Suzdal . . .	3	15	4	2	20	C	9.66	E II, 356–7
46	1230	Disturbances at Novgorod	20	3	4	2	20	F	10.62	E I, 13
47	1230–2	Mutiny at Smolensk . .	10	20	3	3	25	F	17.10	S I, 807
48	1234–5	Internal war for Kiev throne	20	15	3	3	25	F	19.59	E I, 15
49	1239	The same	20	3	3	3	25	F	11.45	S I, 814
50	1248	Internal war for the throne of Vladimir	40	3	3	4	35	F	16.14	E I, 23–4
51	1255	Expulsion of the Prince at Novgorod	20	1	3	4	35	F	8.67	E I, 35–6
52	1259	Disturbances at Novgorod against the Tartars . .	20	3	4	2	20	C	10.62	S I, 841
53	1262	Uprising against Tartars in many cities . . .	40	5	4	3	35	C	19.14	E I, 38
54	1263	Expulsion of the Prince at Novgorod	20	1	4	2	20	F	7.36	E I, 45
55	1269–70	Disturbances at Novgorod	20	15	4	3	35	F	21.88	E I, 41
56	1281	Internal war for the throne of Vladimir	40	5	3	3	25	F	16.98	E I, 47
57	1283	The same	40	5	3	3	25	F	16.98	E I, 48
58	1289	Disturbances at Novgorod	20	3	4	2	20	F	10.62	S I, 870
59	1289–94	Internal war for the throne of Vladimir . . .	40	34	3	3	25	F	31.84	S I, 880
60	1290	Uprising at Rostov against the Tartars	5	1	4	3	35	C	5.47	E II, 32
61	1293	Disturbances at Novgorod	20	3	4	2	20	F	10.62	E I, 51–6
62	1298	Internal war in Smolensk Princedom	20	3	3	2	15	F	9.66	S I, 883
63	1302	The same	20	3	3	2	15	F	9.66	S I, 884
64	1304	Mutiny at Kostroma against the boyars . .	5	1	4	2	20	B	4.64	S I, 912
65	1304	Internal war for the throne of Vladimir . . .	40	5	3	3	25	F	16.98	E I, 58–60
66	1305	Mutiny at Nijni-Novgorod against the boyars	5	1	4	2	20	B	4.64	S I, 912
67	1313–4	Uprising of Korels against Novgorod . . .	3	15	4	3	35	C	11.56	S I, 914
68	1314–7	Internal war for the throne of Vladimir . . .	40	25	3	3	25	F	29.24	E I, 63
69	1315–8	Internal war in Tver Princedom	20	25	3	2	15	F	19.59	E II, 423–8
70	1323	Uprising in Ustushna against Novgorod . .	3	3	4	2	20	C	6.70	S I, 916
71	1327	Massacre of Tartars at Tver	10	1	4	3	35	C	6.88	E I, 70, 73
72	1332	Disturbances at Novgorod	10	3	4	2	20	F	8.43	E I, 383
73	1340	The same	10	3	3	2	15	F	7.65	E I, 83

RUSSIA — *Continued*

1	2	3	4	5	6	7	8	9	10	11
74	1340	Mutiny at Briansk (murder of the Prince) . .	5	1	4	3	35	F	6.04	S I, 936
75	1341	Disturbances at Novoi-Torjok against Novgorod	3	1	4	2	20	C	3.91	S I, 938
76	1342	Disturbances at Novgorod	10	3	4	2	20	F	8.43	E I, 356
77	1345	Internal troubles in the Princedom of Tver . .	20	5	3	2	15	F	11.46	E II, 480
78	1348	The same	20	5	3	2	15	F	11.46	E II, 481
79	1348	Disturbances at Novgorod	20	3	3	2	15	F	9.66	S I, 940
80	1350	The same	20	3	3	2	15	F	9.66	S I, 946
81	1354	Mutiny in the Princedom of Murom	10	3	3	3	25	F	9.07	S I, 952
82	1357	Disturbances at Moscow .	20	1	4	2	20	F	7.36	E I, 90
83	1359	Disturbances at Novgorod	20	3	4	3	35	F	12.89	E I, 360
84	1362–3	Mutiny in the Princedom of Rostov	10	15	3	2	15	F	13.09	E I, 93
85	1363	Mutiny in the Princedom of Tver	20	3	3	2	15	F	9.66	S I, 960
86	1366	The same	20	3	3	2	15	F	9.66	S I, 960
87	1375	Uprising at Kashin against Tver	3	3	4	2	20	F	5.64	E II, 529
88	1388	Internal war in Nijni-Novgorod	20	3	3	2	15	F	9.66	S I, 985
89	1388	Disturbances at Novgorod	20	3	4	2	20	F	10.62	S I, 992
90	1392	Disturbances at Torjok .	3	1	3	2	15	F	3.56	E II, 223
91	1403	Mutiny in the Princedom of Tver	20	3	3	2	15	F	9.66	S I, 1026
92	1408	The same	20	3	3	2	15	F	9.66	S I, 1027
93	1411	Mutiny in the Princedom of Suzdal	10	3	3	2	15	F	7.65	S I, 1012
94	1411	Mutiny in the Princedom of Nijni-Novgorod . .	10	5	3	2	15	F	9.07	E II, 432
95	1412	Mutiny in the Princedom of Tver	20	3	3	2	15	F	9.66	S I, 1027
96	1418	Disturbances at Novgorod	20	3	4	2	20	F	10.62	E I, 430
97	1425–40	Internal war for Moscow throne	80	70	3	4	35	F	58.08	E I, 157–60
98	1446–62	The same	80	76	3	4	35	F	59.07	E I, 169–80
99	1462	Conspiracy in favor of Prince Borovsky . . .	20	3	1	1	1	F	3.91	E I, 187
100	1462	Expulsion of the Prince at Pskov	10	3	3	4	35	F	10.02	S I, 1381
101	1477	Conspiracy at Novgorod .	20	1	3	1	5	F	4.64	S I, 1376
102	1477	Disturbances at Pskov .	10	3	4	2	20	F	8.43	E I, 239
103	1483	Disturbances at Pskov .	10	3	4	2	20	F	8.43	S I, 1385
104	1534	Disturbances in the Great Princedom of Moscow .	40	5	3	1	5	F	10.00	S II, 3–8
105	1538–40	Boyars' mutiny	40	20	3	1	5	F	15.89	S II, 29–37
106	1547	People's uprising in Moscow against Prince Glinsky	40	1	4	3	35	F	11.16	S II, 41–2
107	1578	Disturbances of Tcheremis	3	5	4	2	20	F	6.74	S II, 304
108	1589	Disturbances after the death of Ivan the Terrible	60	5	4	2	20	F	8.43	S II, 538–9
109	1591	Disturbances at Uglich .	3	1	4	2	20	F	3.91	S II, 668
110	1604–13	"Time of trouble" . . .	100	50	5	5	100	F	79.44	S II, 760–1038
111	1627	Murder of the "Woyewod" (governor of province) by rebels on the Don	10	1	4	3	35	F	6.88	S II, 1245
112	1648	Mutiny at Moscow, Ustug, and Solvichegodsk	60	3	4	2	20	F	15.31	S II, 1515, 1520, 1522
113	1650	Rebellions at Novgorod and Pskov	40	5	4	3	20	F	15.89	S II, 1526–50
114	1662	"Copper rebellion" at Moscow	40	1	4	3	20	F	9.29	S III, 192–4
115	1666–75	Rebellion at Solovetsky Monastery.	3	50	2	2	10	D	11.46	S III, 288–90, 407, 324–31
116	1667–71	Revolt of Stephen Razin .	40	30	4	3	35	BD	34.75	S III, 294–324
117	1668	Disturbances in Little Russia	20	10	4	2	20	F	15.89	S III, 357–68
118	1675	Disturbances on the Don	10	3	3	2	15	F	7.65	S III, 492
119	1679–81	Insurrection of Bashkirs .	3	20	4	2	20	C	10.62	S III, 861
120	1682	Disturbances at Moscow .	20	3	3	2	15	F	9.66	S III, 893–932

RUSSIA — *Continued*

1	2	3	4	5	6	7	8	9	10	11
121	1689	Mutiny of "Streltzi"	20	3	3	3	25	F	11.46	S III, 1070-81
122	1698	The same	20	5	3	3	25	F	13.58	S III, 1177-91
123	1705	Rebellion at Astrakhan and other cities	10	3	4	2	20	F	8.43	S III, 1377-82
124	1707-8	Rebellion of Bashkirs	3	15	4	2	20	C	9.66	S III, 1446-9
125	1707-8	Rebellion of Bulavin	10	15	3	2	15	F	13.09	S III, 1452-67
126	1723	Uprising of Kalmyks	3	10	4	2	20	C	8.43	S IV, 653-4
127	1735	Rebellion of Bashkirs	3	5	4	2	20	C	6.70	S IV, 1533
128	1740	Deposition of Byron	20	1	1	4	7	F	5.18	S V, 20
129	1741	Deposition of Ivan VI	20	1	1	5	10	F	5.84	S V, 121-9
130	1742	Rebellion of Mordva	3	3	4	2	20	C	5.64	S V, 209
131	1749	Uprising of fugitive peasants at Briansk	3	3	3	2	15	B	5.12	S V, 604
132	1751-3	Uprising of peasants in different provinces	10	20	3	2	15	B	14.42	S V, 688-90, 758-9
133	1755	Rebellion of Bashkirs	3	10	4	2	20	C	8.43	S V, 526-7
134	1756	Rebellion of peasants of Shatsk	1	3	3	2	15	B	3.55	S V, 966
135	1757	Disturbances of peasants in different provinces	10	3	3	2	15	B	7.83	S V, 1025
136	1760	Peasant rebellion at Shuvalov works	1	3	3	2	15	B	3.55	S V, 1178
137	1762	Dethroning of Emperor Peter III	20	1	2	5	30	F	8.43	S V, 1330-43
138	1762	Rebellion of peasants in Kazan and Ohrenburg provinces	3	3	3	2	15	B	5.12	S V, 1361-2
139	1763	The same in Ufa and Novgorod provinces	3	3	3	2	15	B	5.12	S V, 1474
140	1764	Plot of Mirovich	20	1	1	2	3	C	3.91	B 152-4
141	1766	Peasant disturbances at Lipsky works	1	3	3	2	15	B	3.55	S VI, 331-2
142	1771	"Black plague mutiny" at Moscow	20	3	4	3	35	F	12.89	S VI, 1032-52
143	1773-4	Pugachev's mutiny	60	15	4	4	50	BF	35.56	B 190-205
144	1797	Disturbances of peasants	3	3	3	1	5	B	3.55	Sh 327-30
145	1801	Murder of Paul I	20	1	1	5	10	F	5.84	Sh 491
146	1820	Mutiny of Semenovsky regiment	20	1	2	2	10	F	5.84	K I, 202-3
147	1825	Mutiny of Decembrists	20	1	3	3	25	A	7.94	K 227-8
148	1830	Mutiny at Sebastopol	5	3	4	2	20	F	6.71	Sc II, 409-10
149	1830-1	Polish revolution	20	15	5	4	20	AB	27.51	Sc III, 85-141
150	1831	"Cholera mutiny" at St. Petersburg	20	1	3	2.	15	F	5.84	Sc III, 145-9
151	1831	Mutiny at military settlements	3	3	2	3	15	F	5.12	Sc III, 150-1
152	1833	Peasant disturbances	5	5	3	2	15	B	7.21	Sc III, 229
153	1840-53	The same	5	66	3	2	15	B	17.05	Se 587-95
154	1846	Disturbances in Poland	20	3	3	1	5	C	6.71	Sc IV, 85
155	1854-5	Disturbances of reserve soldiers	20	5	3	2	15	F	7.65	K I, 308
156	1861	Peasant disturbances at the time of their liberation	40	3	3	2	15	BF	10.62	K II, 66
157	1863	Polish revolution	20	10	4	4	50	C	21.53	T I, 459-72
158	1877	Mutiny at Chiguirin	1	1	3	2	15	BF	2.46	T I, 594
159	1878-80	Years of revolutionary terror	60	20	2	3	10	A	22.91	Ba 94-104
160	1881	Murder of Alexander II	20	1	1	5	10	A	5.84	T II, 656
161	1898	Mutiny at Andijan	3	1	3	2	15	C	3.56	B E 112
162	1901-4	Attempts, student and workmen's disorders	60	25	3	2	15	AB	28.25	Ba 161-75
163	1902	Peasant disturbances in provinces of Poltava and Kharkov	3	3	3	2	15	B	5.12	Ba 170-2
164	1905-6	"First revolution"	80	15	4	4	50	AB	39.17	Ba 200-30
165	1910-1	Disturbances during the agrarian reform	5	15	3	1	5	BD	7.21	Ba 230
166	1914	Political strikes and disturbances at St Petersburg	20	3	3	1	5	BF	6.71	Ba 267-8
167	1917-21	Second revolution and civil war (NOTE: Only first four years of it are considered, because in 1921 the Soviet regime was established and the civil war was ended.)	100	25	5	5	100	AB	63.08	V pt. iii

POLAND AND LITHUANIA

NUMBER	YEAR	SPECIFICATION OF THE INTERNAL DISTURBANCE	MEASURES OF:							SOURCES[2]
			Social Area	Duration	Size of the Masses Involved	Intensity	Masses and Intensity Combined	Nature[1]	Geometric Average	
1	2	3	4	5	6	7	8	9	10	11
1	1031	Uprising of Otto against Meczyslaw	40	3	2	3	15	F	12.16	R I, 168–9
2	1032	Murder of Otto	20	1	1	4	7	F	5.18	R I, 169
3	1034–43	Peasant uprising, anarchy	80	50	4	4	50	BF	58.48	R I, 175–81
4	1080	Dethroning of Boleslaw	20	1	2	4	20	F	7.36	R I, 204
5	1092	Uprising against Wladislaw II	40	3	2	3	15	F	12.16	R I, 215
6	1102–8	Civil war	60	38	2	3	15	F	32.43	R I, 229
7	1118–9	Uprising in the West, Pomerania	10	15	4	3	35	C	17.38	R I, 263
8	1139–42	Civil war of Wladislaw II with brothers	60	25	2	3	15	F	28.25	R I, 349–50
9	1146	Dethronement and banishment of Wladislaw	20	1	2	4	20	F	7.36	H 36
10	1163	Civil war in Silesia	10	5	2	2	10	F	7.92	R I, 363
11	1172	War of Kasimier with Meczyslaw III	40	5	2	3	15	F	14.66	R I, 366–7
12	1181	Uprising of Meczyslaw	20	3	1	3	7	F	7.48	R I, 370
13	1190	Second attempt of Meczislaw	20	3	1	3	7	F	7.48	R I, 382
14	1194–206	Civil war	80	62	4	4	50	F	62.81	R I, 386–403
15	1216	Civil war of the Wladislaws	40	5	2	3	15	F	14.66	R I, 422
16	1227–31	Second civil war	40	30	2	3	15	F	26.18	R I, 124–6
17	1234–5	Civil war between Heirich and Konrad	40	15	2	3	15	F	20.80	R I, 455–7
18	1244–52	Civil war between Heirich and Konrad	40	15	2	3	15	F	20.80	R I, 471–7
19	1254	Civil war in the Great Poland	20	5	3	3	25	F	13.58	R I, 477
20	1255	Civil war in Masovia	10	5	3	3	25	F	10.76	R I, 495
21	1257	Civil war in Great Poland	20	5	3	3	25	F	13.58	R I, 477
22	1258	Civil war in Masovia	10	5	3	3	25	F	10.76	R I, 498
23	1263	Civil war in Litva	20	5	3	3	25	F	13.58	L 14
24	1268	Uprising of the Shliachta	10	5	3	3	15	F	9.08	R I, 497
25	1271	Civil war	10	5	3	3	25	F	9.08	R I, 498
26	1277	Civil war in Great Poland	20	5	3	3	25	F	13.58	R I, 482
27	1285	Uprising against Leszek	60	3	4	4	50	F	20.80	R I, 540
28	1286	Murder of the Princes in Lithuania	40	3	4	4	50	F	18.13	L 13
29	1288–91	Civil war	40	3	3	3	25	F	14.66	G 27
30	1296	Civil war after Przemyslaw	40	3	3	3	25	F	14.66	R I, 557–8
31	1305–14	Civil war after Wenceslaw	40	50	3	3	25	F	36.73	H 64
32	1311	Uprising of German Colonists	20	3	3	3	15	C	11.45	R II, 57
33	1340	Murder of Boleslaw of Galicia	10	1	2	4	20	F	5.84	L 28
34	1341	Dethroning of the Grand Duke in Lithuania	40	1	2	4	20	F	9.29	L 39
35	1376	Uprising in Cracow	20	1	3	3	25	FB	7.92	R II, 403
36	1377–82	Civil war in Lithuania	40	34	3	3	25	F	32.42	H 86
37	1383	Civil war in Masovia	40	5	3	3	25	F	17.10	G 47

[1] See the text, p. 403, for a key to this column.
[2] Sources in the order of their appearance in the text:

R —R. Röpell and J. Caro. *Geschichte Polens*, 5 vols. Berlin, 1840–1883.
H —O. Halecki. *Histoire de la Pologne.* Paris, 1933.
L —M. Lubavsky. *History of the Lithuanian-Russian State* (in Russian). Moscow, 1910.
G —H. Grappin. *Histoire de la Pologne.* Paris, 1922.
Gr—M. Grushevsky. *History of the Ukrainian People* (in Russian). St. Petersburg, 1914.
Lè—L. Léger. "*La Pologne*" in "*Histoire générale par Lavisse et Rambaud,*" Vols. IV, V, and VI. Paris 1894–1895.
E —A. Efimenko. *History of the Ukrainian People* (in Russian). St. Petersburg, 1906.

POLAND AND LITHUANIA — *Continued*

1	2	3	4	5	6	7	8	9	10	11
38	1389	Attempt of Waclaw . .	20	1	1	2	3	F	3.91	R III, 119
39	1392	Revolt of the Princes . .	10	3	2	3	15	F	7.65	L 81
40	1396	Revolt of the Duke of Oppeln	10	3	2	3	15	F	7.65	R III, 139
41	1401	Murder of the governor in Smolensk	5	1	3	4	35	F	5.60	L 31
42	1408	Revolt of Swiedrigaillo .	40	5	3	2	15	F	14.66	R III, 284
43	1409	Uprising in Samostie . .	10	5	3	3	25	C	9.08	R III, 288
44	1431	Civil war after Vitovt . .	80	5	2	3	15	F	18.15	R IV, 14–15
45	1434	Sigismund's enthronement	40	1	1	4	7	F	6.54	R IV, 55
46	1437	Attack of Kiev and Lutzk	40	3	2	3	15	F	12.16	R IV, 157
47	1439	Uprising of Spytek . . .	20	1	1	3	5	F	4.64	R IV, 197
48	1440	Disturbances in Lithuania	40	3	3	3	25	F	14.66	R IV, 246
49	1441	Uprising in Smolensk . .	5	3	3	3	25	C	7.21	R IV, 257
50	1451–3	Civil war in upper Silesia	10	20	2	3	15	F	14.66	R IV, 294–5
51	1460–4	Civil war in lower Silesia .	10	30	2	3	15	F	16.52	R IV, 290–3
52	1481	Plot of the Princes . . .	20	2	2	1	3	C	5.64	Gr 152
53	1508	Glinsky's plot	20	3	2	1	3	C	5.64	Gr 153–4
54	1575	Plot against Heinrich Valois	20	3	2	1	3	F	5.64	G 97
55	1581	Civil war in Volyn . . .	10	3	2	1	3	F	5.64	Gr 226
56	1584	Attempt of S. Zborowsky	10	3	1	1	1	F	3.15	Lè IV, 713
57	1587	Civil war after S. Bathorius	40	5	2	3	15	F	14.66	Lè IV, 713
58	1592–3	Cossacks' uprising . . .	10	15	3	3	25	CD	15.52	Gr 226
59	1596–7	Civil religious war . . .	20	15	3	3	25	D	19.59	Gr 227
60	1599	Cossacks' uprising . . .	10	5	3	3	25	CD	10.76	Lè IV, 721
61	1606–7	Rokosz Schrydomski . .	40	15	2	3	15	F	20.80	Lè IV, 717
62	1623	Uprising in Vitebsk . . .	5	3	3	3	25	C	8.55	Lè IV, 720
63	1625	Cossacks' uprising . . .	20	5	3	3	25	CD	13.58	Gr 235
64	1630	Cossacks' uprising . . .	20	5	3	3	25	CD	13.58	Gr 238
65	1637–8	Cossacks' uprising . . .	20	15	3	3	25	CD	19.59	Gr 243
66	1648–9	Cossacks' uprising . . .	20	15	3	4	35	CD	21.88	Gr 249–50
67	1651–4	Cossacks' uprising . . .	20	15	3	3	25	CD	23.26	Gr 252–3
68	1662–6	Uprising of Schliachta . .	40	25	2	2	10	F	21.53	G 116
69	1672	Disturbances on Ukraina .	10	5	3	3	25	F	10.76	Gr 264
70	1674	Civil war	40	5	2	3	15	F	14.66	G 119
71	1696	Civil war after J. Sobessky	40	5	2	3	15	F	14.66	Lè VI, 644–6
72	1699	Peasant uprising in Lithuania	20	5	3	3	25	BD	13.58	Lè VI, 647
73	1704	Overthrow of Auguste II .	20	1	2	4	20	F	7.36	H 229
74	1715	Confederation in Tarnograd	40	3	2	1	3	F	7.12	G 129
75	1734	Cossacks' uprising of Ukraina	20	3	3	3	25	CD	11.45	E 348
76	1768	Uman massacre . . .	20	3	3	3	25	CD	11.45	E 348–9
77	1770	Dethronement of Stanislaw Auguste	20	1	2	4	20	F	7.36	G 146
78	1794	Uprising against Russian army of occupation . .	20	3	3	3	25	C	11.45	G 156

INDEXES

Index of Authors

All names not included in the Index of Authors will be found in the Index of Subjects or the Appendixes.

Achner, L., 243
Afanassief, 203
Akraskranianz, A., 203
Alcuin, 52
Altamira y Crevea, D. R., 326, 327
Amira, K. von. See Von Amira, K.
Ardasheff, P. H., 237
Aristotle, 24, 25–26, 144, 146, 177, 178, 186
Arndt, A., 243
Arnold, T., 186
Ashley, W. J., 243
Augé-Laribé, M., 237
Aurelius, M., 166
Avenel, G. d'. See D'Avenel, G.

Baltzly, A., 264, 293–94, 316
Barthélémy, H., 112
Baudin, L., 186
Baudry-Lacantinière, G., 110
Beaumanoir, P., 83, 89
Beloch, J., 290, 291, 295, 303
Below, G. von. See Von Below, G.
Benedict, R., 144
Berardinis, L., 340
Berkut, L. N., 243
Berndt, O., 264, 291, 325
Beutin, L., 243
Bilimowitsch, A., 243
Blache, Vidal de la. See De la Blache, Vidal.
Block, M., 237
Böckh, A., 201–2
Bodart, G., 264, 294, 306, 316, 325
Boissonade, P., 70, 88, 91, 237
Boldrini, M., 340
Boldyreff, J. W., 509, 517, 526–27
Bondois, P. M., 237
Bonnecasse, J., 110
Borchardt, J., 243
Bornhak, C., 105, 107, 109, 112, 169
Botero, G., 159
Bothe, F., 243
Bouglé, C., 141, 194
Boutaric, E., 83, 85, 89
Brauer, T., 243
Breasted, J. H., 186, 200
Brentano, L., 186
Brissand, J., 186
Brissaud, J., 65–66
Brück, H., 243
Brunialti, A., 169
Bücher, K., 243
Busold, G., 202

Calmette, J., 37, 53, 54–56, 73, 75, 76, 77–78
Campanella, 159

Cantalupi, P., 296
Carlyle, A. J., 55, 62, 83, 134, 148, 220
Carlyle, R. W., 55, 62, 83, 134, 148, 220
Cavaignac, E., 232
Chang, C. H., 186, 201
Chénon, E., 53, 59, 65, 66–68, 70, 73, 74, 75, 77, 94, 95, 148, 374
Cicero, 26
Cohen, A., 243
Corda, H., 350
Cossio, C., 505
Coulanges, F. de. See De Coulanges, F.
Coulton, G. G., 55
Cournot, A., 6
Coville, A., 237
Crew, H., 161
Cunow, H., 243
Curschmann, F., 203, 218, 243

Daenell, E., 243
Dalin, V., 237
Danz, 146
Darmstaedter, L., 294
D'Avenel, G., 237
Davy, G., 30
De Beaumanoir, P. See Beaumanoir, P. de.
De Coulanges, F., 144, 146, 255
De la Blache, Vidal, 321, 324
De la Mazallière, 186
De Lamothe, de N., 168
De la Rivière, M., 30
De la Tour, I., 148
Delbrück, H., 264, 290, 296, 299, 300, 305, 313, 317, 318, 321, 332
De Maistre, J., 367
Denis, E., 186
De Ribbe, C., 64, 70, 87, 148
De Tocqueville, A. See Tocqueville, A. de.
Diamond, A. S., 157–58
Diehl, C., 186
Dill, S., 203
Dopsch, A., 243
Du Bourg, 237
Duchesne, L., 62
Duguit, L., 106–7, 108, 109, 113–14, 116, 168
Dujarric, G., 305, 313
Dumas, S., 306
Dungern, O. von. See Von Dungern, O.
Dunning, W. A., 134
Dupréel, E., 15
Durkheim, É., 500
Duruy, 203

Ebengreuth, A. Luschin von. See Luschin von Ebengreuth, A.

Eberstadt, R., 70
Ehrenberg, R., 243
Engelmann, A., 110
Epictetus, 165–66
Epstein, R. C., 218
Erman, A., 186
Espinas, A., 256

Fehr, H., 67, 87
Ferguson, W. S., 290, 413
Ferrari, F. L., 169
Ferrari, G., 483–85
Festenberg-Packish, H. V., 243
Fevre, L. le.   See Le Fevre, L.
Flick, A. C., 83, 148
Foakes-Jackson, F. J., 62
Fortescue, J. W., 313
Frampton, M., 29, 111
Francotte, 202
Frank, T., 232
Freiberg, N. P., 237
Fulbert, 74
Funk, F. X., 243

Galpin, C., 8, 45, 71, 186
Gand, N., 105
Geiger, T., 243
Gennep, A. van.   See Van Gennep, A.
Gierke, O. von.   See Von Gierke, O.
Gini, C., 340
Ginsberg, M., 264
Glasson, E. D., 53, 83, 85, 87, 88, 93–94, 95, 97–98, 99, 102
Glotz, G., 231
Godart, L., 237
Golovine, N. N., 259, 291
Goltz, T. von der.   See Von der Goltz, T.
Granet, M., 48–49, 186
Graziansky, N. P., 237
Green, J. R., 305, 313
Grinevitch, V., 243
Grousset, R., 186
Guéttée, R. F. W., 63
Guiraud, P., 202
Günther, A., 243
Gurvitch, G., 29

Halecki, O., 331
Hanefeld, K., 243
Hannan, I. C., 62
Hannay, J. O., 62
Hansen, A. H., 495
Harnack, A., 62
Hartmann, M., 186
Hasebroek, J., 231–32
Hatschek, J., 106–7
Hauck, A., 243
Hearnshaw, F. J. C., 148
Hegel, E., 69, 70, 71, 89
Heichelheim, F., 232
Herkner, H., 243
Heussler, A., 67, 70, 77, 88
Hincmar, I., 51–52, 69
Hinschius, P., 63
Hirschfeld, O., 202

Hobhouse, L., 264
Holland, F. M., 167
Hötsch, O., 243
Hrdlička, Ă., 176
Hue, O., 243
Hume, D., 159

Ibn-Khaldun, 159
Inama-Sternegg, K. T. von.   See Von Inama-Sternegg, K. T.
Ivanoff, 186

Jager, J. N., 108
Janet, P., 98, 134
Janssen, J., 243
Jarrett, B., 65, 83
Jastrow, J., 243
Jellineck, G., 104, 168–69
Jöhlinger, O., 169

Kant, I., 510
Kareef, N., 237
Karsavin, L., 65
Kaser, K., 243
Kaskel, W., 115
Kautsky, K., 186
Kawan, L., 206, 218
Kidd, B. J., 61–62
Kistiakowsky, B., 29
Knapp, G. F., 243
Kondratieff, N. D., 217
Kötzschke, R., 243, 344
Kovalevsky, M., 237
Kropotkin, P., 71
Kuczynski, R., 243
Kulemann, W., 115
Kulisher, J., 237, 243
Künstle, F. X., 243
Kuske, B., 243
Kuznets, S. S., 217

Laband, P., 105, 107
Labrousse, C. E., 237
Lair, M., 237
Lamothe, De N. de.   See De Lamothe, de N.
Lamprecht, C. G., 115, 344
Lamprecht, K., 237
Langlois, C. V., 237
Lao-tse, 167
Latouche, R., 237
Laum, B., 256
Lavisse, E., 104, 111, 113, 237
Lee, J. S., 357
Lee, M. P. H., 186, 201
Leer, Gen., 309
Lefebvre, G., 237
Le Fevre, L., 175–76
Lemonnier, H., 237
Levasseur, E., 101, 237
Levitski, V. F., 237
Lewinski-Corwin, E., 332
Lippert, J., 243
Löning, E., 115
Lot, F., 237
Loutchisky, J. L., 88, 91, 237

Lowie, R. H., 186
Luchaire, A., 58–59, 60, 61, 63–65, 72, 73, 74, 75, 76, 85, 90, 148, 237
Luschin von Ebengreuth, A., 243

Machiavelli, N., 159
Madelin, L., 104
Maine, H. S., 157
Maistre, J. de. See De Maistre, J.
Makarewicz, 29
Malcolm, J., 186
Mannheim, K., 485
Marcus Aurelius. See Aurelius.
Mariéjol, H., 237
Marion, H., 237
Marion, M., 93, 95–96, 99–100, 101, 103
Maritain, J., 164
Martin, G., 237
Mathieu, F. D., 108
Maximovitch, E. F., 217, 237
Mazallière, de la. See De la Mazallière.
Mazzarella, 194.
McGarry, E. D., 218
McIlwain, C. H., 83, 134, 148
McIver, R., 160
Means, P. A., 186
Meerwarth, R., 243
Meinecke, F., 96
Meissner, P., 37
Mentré, F., 485
Menzel, A., 26
Mewes, K., 353–55, 357
Meyer, E., 295
Meyer, G., 115
Mickwitz, G., 217, 232
Mitchell, T. J., 350
Mitchell, W. C., 217
Molschanowski, N., 243
Mommsen, T., 146, 400
Monod, G., 237
Müller, J., 243
Munsterberg, E., 65
Murray, G., 144

Nast, A., 116
Nickerson, H., 337
Niese, B., 202
Nikiforoff, N., 237
Novosadsky, 201–2

Oberascher, L., 243
Ogburn, W. F., 183
Oldenburg, S., 383
Olorinus, J., 159
Olovianishnikova, E. V., 237
Ono, T., 186
Orlando, V., 169
Ostrouchov, P. A., 217
Otto, E., 243

Pareto, V., 186
Pariset, E, 237
Pavlov, I. P., 174
Petit-Dutaillis, C., 237
Petrajitsky, L. 19

Petrushevski, D. M., 237
Philipovich, E. von. See Von Philipovitch, E.
Pigou, A. C., 217
Pirenne, H., 237
Plato, 145, 177
Plutarch, 145
Podhorsky, A., 332
Pöhlmann, R., 62, 186, 201–2, 295
Pokrovski, M. N., 237
Pöschl, A., 243
Potemkin, F., 237
Pott, W. S. A., 167
Potulicki, M., 169
Poviña, A., 505
Prince, S. H., 207
Pushkareff, S. G., 217, 243

Ratzinger, G., 65
Raveau, P., 237
Ribbe, C. de. See De Ribbe, C.
Richard, G., 29
Rivers, W. H. R., 175
Rivière, M. de la. See De la Rivière, M.
Roguin, E., 87
Rostovtzeff, M. I., 186, 201, 202, 232

Sagnac, P., 110
Saint-Léon, E. M., 68–69, 89–90, 100–1, 113
Saitzoff, A. A., 259
Salvioli, G., 203
Sander, P., 243
Sarkar, B. K., 167
Sartorius von Waltershousen, A., 243
Savitsky, P., 217
Sayous, A. E., 237
Schäfer, D., 243
Scharnagl, A., 243
Scheffel, P. A., 237
Schmoller, G., 344
Schnapper-Arndt, G., 243
Schnürer, G., 243
Schröder, R., 52, 61, 67, 68, 73, 75, 76, 77, 84, 85, 89, 91, 96, 102, 103
Schubert, H. von, 243
Schulgin, A., 237
Schumpeter, P., 243
Schutiakow, P., 243
Sée, H., 77, 88, 91, 237
Segré, A., 232
Seignobos, C., 237
Sénart, M., 141
Seneca, 166–67
Seridg, M., 243
Sieveking, H., 243
Simiand, F., 237
Simmel, G., 3
Smith, G. M., 350
Smith, K. K., 161
Sombart, W., 243, 255, 344
Sommerlad, T., 243
Sorokin, P. A., 3, 6–7, 15, 20, 29, 38, 45–46, 71, 111, 147, 186, 204, 214, 218–19, 222, 256, 259, 264, 361, 366, 370, 371, 393, 485, 495, 500
Spaulding, C. L., 337
Spencer, H., 186, 196

Stein, E., 232
Steinmetz, S. R., 264, 370-71
Stier-Somló, F., 106
Suchov, A. A., 237

Taine, H., 94, 95, 96-97, 99, 104-5
Tarlé, E., 237
Thurnwald, R., 144, 158, 186
Timasheff, N. S., 43, 81, 383
Tocqueville, A. de, 93, 95, 99
Tombaro, J., 169
Tönnies, F., 3, 29
Tour, I. de la. See De la Tour, I.
Tschuproff, A. A., 6
Tyszka, K. von. See Von Tyszka, K.

Van Gennep, A., 50
Vedel-Petersen, K., 306
Veit, L. A., 243
Verriest, L., 237
Vico, G. B., 154
Vidal de la Blache. See De la Blache, Vidal.
Vierkandt, A., 3
Vinogradoff, P., 186
Viollet, P., 49
Virgil, 55
Vivier, R., 237
Vladimirsky-Budanoff, M., 65-66
Volters, F., 237
Von Amira, K., 59, 60, 65, 67, 69, 75
Von Below, G., 37, 54, 58, 77, 89, 243
Von der Goltz, T., 243
Von Dungern, O., 243
Von Gierke, O., 62, 83, 134, 148
Von Inama-Sternegg, K. T., 243
Von Philipovich, E., 243

Von Schubert, H. See Schubert, H. von.
Von Tyszka, K., 237
Von Wiese, L., 3

Wagemann, E., 217
Wagner, A., 243
Waitz, G., 51-52, 53, 59, 71, 85
Waltershousen, A. Sartorius von. See Sartorius von Waltershousen, A.
Waltzing, J. P., 186, 189, 202-3
Weber, A., 160, 243
Weber, M., 224, 243, 255
Weil, D. G., 116
Weill, G., 107
Wernicke, J., 243
Westergaard, H., 306
Wheeler, G., 264
Wiebe, G., 237, 243
Wiese, L. von. See Von Wiese, L.
Wilda, W. E., 69
Woblyi, K., 243
Wood, M. M., 29, 50
Woods, F. A., 264, 293-94, 316
Woytinski, W., 243
Wright, J. W., 337
Wright, Q., 264, 276, 339, 357, 371

Zahn, F., 243
Zeidler, H., 115
Zeumer, K., 60
Ziebarth, E., 232
Zimmerman, C. C., 8, 29, 45, 71, 111, 186, 225, 393, 500
Zimmerman, W., 243
Zingali, G., 340
Zoepfl, F., 243

Index of Subjects

Aberration in estimation of economic conditions, 225–27; of magnitude of revolutions, 404–5; of wars, 287–88

Absolute, magnitude of war activities by countries, 348–49; monarchy, growth of, 82–84, 93–97; values and self-control, 539

Absolute indicators of war movement, 287–88; in Ancient Greece, 290–95; Ancient Rome, 296–303; Austria-Hungary, 319–20; England, 314–17; Europe, 335–44; France, 306–9; Germany, 322; Holland, 331; Italy, 325; Poland and Lithuania, 333; Russia, 310–11; Spain, 328

Absolutism, political, and totalitarianism, 82–84, 93–97, 188–89, 195–98, 204–7

Acceleration in change of Sensate political leaders, 153

Accidental factors in history, 221–22, 235, 239, 244, 247–48

Accomplishers, generation of, 484

Action and counteraction in revolution, 481

Actual (overt) behavior, and mentality and culture, 221–22, 254–56, 510–29

Adaptation, type of, among all historical persons, 519; English, French, Hapsburg, and Russian kings, 524; Roman Catholic popes, 522

Adjacency in physical and social space, 509

Adulescentuli, 55, 73

Adventurers, percentage of, among Roman emperors, 147

Affrairements, 68. See also *Bruderschaften*

Age of gods, heroes, men, and forms of government, 154

Agricultural. See Rural

All-embracing social relationship, 6–8, 16, 27. See also Familistic

Allgemeines Landrecht, 96, 98, 101

Alternation. See Crises, Cycles, Fluctuation

Altruism, and familistic relationships, 24–27; and friendship, 25–27; and solidary relationships, 15–16

Amount, of violence in internal disturbances, 395–96; of bloody and bloodless revolutions, 476–78

Amplitude of change, from order to disorder, 481; in the nature of social relationships, 125–26

Anarchy, and *laissez faire*, 181–84, 208; ideal of, and trend of history, 191–92

Anomie, and crime, disturbances, and suicide, 500–1

Antagonistic interaction, 15; and organized interaction, 21–23; forms of, 16–18

Antiliberal trend, in postwar period, 115, 118–21, 127–32, 150–53, 169–70, 191–92, 204–8. See also Communism, Fascism, Hitlerism, Totalitarianism

Antrustiones, 55, 73

Area, social, of revolution, 393–94

Aristocracy, economic conditions of, in Ancient Greece, 233; Ancient Rome, 235–37; France, 240–41; Germany, 245; Ideational and Sensate, 140–43, 249–50; in the cycle of political regimes, 155, 158–60. See also Leadership

Aristotle, on friendship, 25–26; on immanent change of political regimes, 177

Armaments, increase of, 361

Army, foreigners in, 281, 304, 321; growth of casualties and growth of, 336–37, 346–47; in Carlovingian state, 55–56; feudal state, 85; modern times, 95–96, 107; nature of bonds in, 39–40, 196–99; per unit of population, in Ancient Greece, 295; Ancient Rome, 303–4; Europe, 345–46; strength of, by countries, 348; uncertainties as to the exact size of, 265–67, 273; variable size in the Middle Ages, 281. See also Absolute indicators.

Art and science, associated with types of culture, 254

Artistic concoctions, and contemporary governments, 151

Arts, blossoming of, and war, 364–69. See also Blossoming

Association, of forms of liberty and revolts, 177–79; of war, and internal disturbances, 487–93

Association of totalitarianism, and emergency, 196, 206–8; and impoverishment, 198–206; and war, 196–98

Association of transitional periods, and crime, 500–1; and disturbances, 177–79, 487–505; and forms of liberty, 177–79; and war, 370–80

Association of types of culture, and economic well-being, 220–24, 232–34, 238–48, 253; and forms of liberty, 163, 169–77; and political regimes, 140–56, 160; and forms of social relationships, 132–38; and totalitarianism, 192–96; and war, 370–77

Associations and communities, forms of, 48–49, 181–82; nature of social relationships in specified, 48, 68–70, 89, 100–1, 112–17. See also *Bruderschaften*, Communities, Guild

Assyria, theocracy in, 141

Astrological theory of war periodicity, 352–56

Atomism, and contractualism, 113–15; and individualism and singularism, 136

Atomization, of labor, 113; of values, 128–30, 150–55

Atrophy of contractual relationships, 115, 118–21; reasons for, 127–32, 150–53, 169–70, 191–92, 204–8. See also Crises, Decline

Attic landlords, economic conditions of, 235; peasants, 232–33

Attributive-imperative character of law, 19

Auspicia publica, 146

Austria-Hungary, disturbances in, 399, 430–35, 474, 476, 478; wars of, 317–20, 348–52. See also Germany

Austrian kings, percentage of Ideational and Sensate types among, 524

Autocracy and democracy, and internal disturbances, 504–5; and wars, 371; rhythm of, as political regimes, 154–55, 158–59. See also Cycles, Disturbances, Freedom, Government, Totalitarianism, War.

Automobile firms, duration of life of, 218

Barbarism in revolutions, 477

Barometer of economic well-being, 225–30

Battles, frequency of, in long wars, 265–66, 338–40

Beautification, mental, of our actions, 3–6, 510–13

Behavior, overt, and mentality, 221–24, 254–56, 510–14; mentality as, 513–14

Behavioristic criteria, inadequacy of, in defining forms of interaction and social relationships, 23–28, 35; intensity of interaction, 10–11, 15; of liberty, 161–62; what is and is not internal disturbance and war, 279–80, 406–7

Belligerency, and blooming of arts, culture, economic conditions, political power, and sciences, 363–69

Bellum omnium contra omnes, 177

Beneficium, 73, 75

Benevolence as purpose of association, 70

Bestial behavior in revolutions, 477

Biography, debunking, 152, 155; subjectivity of historical, 515

Biological, factors of continuity of interaction, 14; molding derivations, 510–12; necessity, freedom as, 173–76; needs common to all types of culture, 511

Blank character of familistic relationships, 27

Bloodless revolutions, percentage of, 477–78

Bloody festivals of history, 532–35

Blossoming of arts, culture, economic conditions, political power, sciences, and disturbances, 412, 419, 422, 493–96; and war, 363–69

Bonds, social, compulsory, 35–38; contractual, 30–32; familistic, 25–26; nature of, in the relationships, between free classes, 72–77, 90–91, 102–3, 117–18; of Church, 39, 61–65, 85–86, 97–98, 108–9, 120; of communes and communities, 70–72, 88–89, 99–100, 111–12; of family, 65–68, 86–88, 98–99, 109–11, 120; of guilds, 68–69, 89, 100–2, 112–15; of serfdom, 76–78, 91–92; of the State, 49–61, 82–85, 93–97, 104–8, 118–21

Bourgeois prejudice, liberty as, 169

Bourgeoisie, and secular intelligentsia, 250–51; as bearers of and leaders in Sensate culture, 140, 146, 150, 153, 249–51; economic situation of, in Ancient Greece, 233–34; Ancient Rome, 235–36; France, 241–42; Germany, 245–47; Middle Ages, 72

Brahmans, as aristocracy, bearers, and leaders of Ideational culture, 140–41, 142–44

Breakdown of system of social relationships and values, and disturbances, 260–64, 496–503; and wars, 260–64, 370–80

Britannica, Encyclopaedia, as source, 313, 517, 521, 526

Broken reed, population as, 211

Bruderschaften, companionship, confraternities, *Schwurbruderschaften,* 39, 68–69, 89, 100–2, 112–15. See also Guilds

Buddhist theocracy, 140–41

Bundbruderschaften. See *Bruderschaften*

Burden of war, comparative by countries, 348–49; shift from country to country of, 350–51

Bureaucracy, and private business, 189–90, 213; totalitarian in, Ancient Greece, 185, 201–2; Ancient Rome, 188–89, 194, 202–3; China, 185, 201; contemporary, 190–92, 204–7; Egypt, 185, 200; Europe, 186, 189, 195–96, 203–4; Incas, 185; India, 193–94; Lipara, Persia, Peru, Sparta, 185. See also Communism, Fascism, Hitlerism, New Deal, Socialism, Totalitarianism.

Business, per cent of historical persons in, 527

Byzantium, internal disturbances in, 420–23, 474, 476, 478; totalitarianism in, 185

Capitalism, and contractualism, 30–35, 44, 57, 79–80, 85, 104–8; and disturbances, 486–87; and war, 364–69; decline of, 115, 118–21, 127–32, 150–53, 169–71, 184–85, 191–92, 204–8

Capitalist class. See Bourgeoisie

Carolingian state, nature of social relationships in, 49–55

Carthage, theocracy in, 141–43

Casualty of war, absolute figures of, in Ancient Greece, 293; Ancient Rome, 301–2; Austria, 319; England, 315–16; Europe, 335–37; France, 307; Holland, 331; Italy, 325; Poland and Lithuania, 333; Russia, 311–12; Spain, 328; as per cent of the army, 337–39, 346–47; burden by countries, 348–49; defined, 282, 307, 338, 553; faster growth of, compared with that of the army, 337; ratio of the killed per wounded, 291; reasons for high, in modern wars, 338–43; relative, per population, in Ancient Greece, 295; Ancient Rome, 303; Europe, 342–46

Catastrophe and totalitarianism, 196, 206–7. See also Crises, Disturbances, War

Catholic, Church, economic conditions of, in France and Germany, 241–43, 245–47, see also Christian Church, Clergy, Religion, Sacerdotal; popes, percentage of Ideational and Sensate types among Roman, 523

Causa sive ratio, 185

Causal relationships between types of culture, and disturbances, 177–79, 487–505; and economic well-being, 220–24, 232–34, 238–48, 253; and forms of liberty, 163, 169–77; and forms of social relationships, 132–38; and political regimes, 140–55, 160; and totalitarianism, 192–96; and war, 370–77. See also Association

Causes, accidental, 221–22, 235, 239, 244, 247; immanent, in change of economic conditions, 220–25; of forms of government, 158–60; of forms of social relationships, 125–31; of disturbances, 177–79, 487–505; of *laissez faire* and totalitarianism, 196–208; of war, 370–80

Chance factors. See Accidental factors; Causes, accidental

Change, acceleration of, in Sensate governments, 153; accidental, see Accidental factors; immanent, see Causes, immanent. See also Crises, Cycles, Evolution, Fluctuation, Progress

Changing rhythm and tempo of order-disorder, 481; of social relationships, 125–26

Chef d'œuvre in guilds, 89

China, disturbances in, 357–59; Taoist theocracy in, 141; totalitarianism of, 201

Chivalry as factor in casualty, 341

Christian Church, as corpus mysticum, 62, 64; as familistic group, 39–40, 61–65; as Ideational institution, 523; economic conditions of, 241–43, 245–47; nature of social relationships in, 61–65, 85–86, 97–99, 108–9; relationship to serfdom and compulsion, 134–35. See also Catholic, Clergy, Sacerdotal, Theocracy

Cicero on friendship, 26

Citizen, contractual rights of man and, 104–8, 163, 167–70; decline of rights of man and, 115, 118–21, 127–32, 150–53, 169–70, 191–92, 204–8

City. See Municipalities, Rural

Classes, social, economic conditions of main, in Ancient Greece, 230–33, Ancient Rome, 234–37; France, 237–43; Germany, 241–47; nature of social relationship between free and unfree, 72–78, 90–92, 102–3, 117–18; types of culture and the integrating and leading, 140–43, 249–50. See also Aristocracy, Bourgeoisie, Clergy, Government, Labor, Leadership

Classification of, forms of freedom, 161–64; forms of government, 140–44; forms of social groups and systems of interaction, 22–23; forms of social relationships, 23–41; modalities of interaction, 5–22; qualitative nature of disturbances, 403; types of personality, 511–29

Clear-cut definition of nebulous phenomena, 227

Clergy, as bearer and leader in Ideational culture, 140–45, 147–49; economic position of, in France, 241–43; in Germany, 245–47. See also Christian Church, Sacerdotal, Theocracy

Coercion. See Compulsory

Collectivism, 57. See also Communism, Familistic, Socialist

Coloni, 91

Comitatus, 61

Commercial exploitation of liberty, 172–73

Common property in Church, 62–65

Communis omnium possessio, 62–65

Communis, vita, in Church, 62–64; in sects, 65

Communism, and emergency, 196, 206–7; and impoverishment, 199–207; and liberty and totalitarianism, 57, 119–20, 128, 138, 150, 152–53, 169, 182–87, 191, 204, 213; and militarism, 196–98; cynical ideologies of, 151; military and starving, 205; violence of, 477. See also Fascism, Socialist, Totalitarian

Communities, rural and urban, nature of social relationship in, 70–72, 88–89, 99–100, 111–12

Companies, duration of life of joint stock and business, 218

Companionship. See Bruderschaften

Compulsory relationships, 35–37; and antagonism and conflict, 36; and disturbances, 261–63; and freedom of the parties, 36–37; and mutual disdain, 37–38; and stranger, 37–38; and totalitarianism, 208–11; and war, 261–63; in relationship of free and unfree classes, 76–78, 91–92; increase of, in disorganization of social relationships, 260–63; proportion in various social groups, 123–24

Condensation and rarefaction of social relationships, 181–82; and governmental regimentation, 182–85; and laissez faire and totalitarianism, 182–85; factors of, 192–208

Conditioned reflex and liberty, 176

Conduct, and mentality, 511–13; and types of culture, 511–12; types of, among all historical persons, 513–21; kings, 524; Roman Catholic popes, 522

Confarreatio, 146

Conflict. See Antagonistic, Compulsory, Disturbances, War

Confraternities. See Bruderschaften, Guild

Conjugal fidelity, 99

Connubii, jus, 177

Consent of the parents and parties in marriage, 64, 67, 87, 99, 100

Consequences immanent, 222–24, 250–51

Conservative and liberal nations, and war, 371, 503–5

Consortium omnis vitae in familistic relationships, 28–29, 55

Continuity and discontinuity of interaction, 11–14; factors of, 14–15

Continuous trend, lack of, in movement of disturbances, 481–82; of fluctuation of social relationships, 123–31; of war, 336–47. See also Linear

Contraction and expansion of governmental regimentation, 181–85; factors of, 192–208. See also Laissez faire, Totalitarianism

Contractual emancipation of children, 87

Contractual relationships, 30–35; and capitalism, 30–35, 44, 57, 79–80, 85, 104–8; and egotism, 31; and freedom of the parties, 34, 106, 126, 129; and Gesellschaft, 29; and laissez faire, 181–84; and liberalism, 184–85; and pacta sunt servanda, 106, 126, 129; and rights of man and citizen, 104–8, 167–70; and stranger, 32; and totalitarianism, 118–20, 181; decline and degeneration of, 115, 118–21, 127–32, 150–53, 169, 191–92, 204–8; difference in nature and mode of origin of, 40–41; governments as underminers of, 128–30; growth of theories of, 84, 145, 148–49; marriage and, 33, 87, 99, 109, 120; proportion of, in various groups, 123–24; pseudo, 34, 127–31. See also Freedom, Laissez faire, Totalitarianism

Convivium. See Bruderschaften, Corporations, Guild

Corporations, nature of social relationships in various, 48, 68–70, 89, 100–1, 112–17, 181–82. See also Associations, Bruderschaften, Guild

Corps, l'ésprit de, in knighthood, 91

Correlations. See Association, Causal, Causes

Coutumes, 68

Crafts. See *Bruderschaften*, Corporations, Guild
Crime, and revolution, 500; factors of, 500–1
Crises, social, and *anomie*, 500–1; and breakdown
of social relationships and values, 260–64;
and crime, 500–1; and decay of society, 537–
38; and disturbances, 496–503; and war, 370–
80; contemporary, of capitalism, democracy,
economic well-being, individualism, liberalism,
liberties, parliamentarism, religion, science,
128, 531–39; of capitalism and contractualism, 115, 118–21, 123–32, 150–52, 168–70, 190–
92, 204–8; of compulsory relationships, 65–68,
76–78, 91–93, 99, 104, 123–24; of economic
well-being, in Ancient Greece, 231–34; Ancient
Rome, 235–37; France, 239–43; Germany,
243–47; of familism, 74–76, 78–81, 85, 87, 89,
93, 94, 97–99, 103–4, 109, 119–20, 123–24; of
Sensate culture, 531–35; of Sensate government, 151–52; of Sensate liberty, 169–70
Criteria, of antagonism and solidarity of interaction, 15; of continuity and duration of inter-
action-process, 11–14; of economic well-being,
225–30; of intensity of interaction, 10–11; of
magnitude of disturbances, 385, 389–97; of
magnitude of war, 282. See also Behavioristic
Crystallization of social relationships and values,
18–21; and crime, 500–1; and disturbances and
war, 177–79, 370–80, 487–505; and law, 19–20;
and organized group, 18–19; and social differentiation and stratification, 19–20; and solidarity, 21–23; symptoms of, 19–23
Culture, relation to behavior and personality.
See Behavior, Personality
Cycles of, condensation and rarefaction of social
relationships, 185–92; contraction and expansion of governmental control, 185–92; culture,
537–38; forms of political regime, 139–54,
158–60, 177; four generations, 159, 482–85;
Ideational and Sensate liberty, 164–70; internal
disturbances, 357–60; peace and war, 352–57;
secular and theocratic government, 139–54.
See also Crises, Fluctuation, Periodicity
Cynicism of contemporary political ideologies,
151–53

Debasement of man and culture in Sensate
theories, 152–53, 539
Debunking biographies and mentality of social
sewers, 152–53
Decay of culture, 537–39; and disturbances, 412,
419, 422, 493–96; and war, 363–69. See also
Crises
Decay of nation. See Decay of culture
Decline of spiritual power and church, 97–98, 108,
148–49. See also Atrophy, Crises, Decay
Degen, 73
Degeneration, of liberty, 170–77; of social rela-
tionships, 125–31. See also Atrophy, Crises
Democracy, and cycles of political regimes, 158–
60; crisis of, 115, 118–21, 123–32, 150–52, 168–
70, 190–92, 204–8, 531–35; and historical trend,
191–92. See also Contractual relationships,
Crises, Dictatorship, Freedom, Rights, Totali-
tarianism
Demoralization. See Crises, Disintegration

Depression, economic, and expansion of govern-
mental control, 198–205
Derivations, and actual behavior, 3–5, 510–12.
See also Actual behavior, Conduct, Mentality
Desires, in definition of liberty, 162
Deus non homo facit heredes, 65, 87
Dharma, 142–43
Diagnosis of contemporary crisis, 531–39
Dictatorship, contemporary, as a sign of decline
of Sensate contractualism and freedom, 115,
118–21, 127–32, 150–53, 169–70, 191–92, 204–8;
as wrecking company, 121; factors of, 192–98
Dies nefasti, 146
Difference between nature and mode of origin of
social relationship, 40–41
Differentiation of population, and social stratifi-
cation, as a sign of organization, 19–20; multi-
linear, 45
Difficulties in study of, disturbances, 384–85;
economic conditions, 225–29; social relationships, 43–47; wars, 215–83
Diffusion of disturbances, 505–6, 533–37
Directions of interaction, as modality, 15–18
Disaster, and governmental control, 196, 206–7;
as accidental factor, 221–22, 235, 239, 244
Discrepancy between overt behavior and men-
tality, 3–6, 150–53, 213, 221–22, 254–55, 510–
30
Disdain of the parties in compulsory relationships,
37
Disintegrated and unintegrated minds, 537
Disintegration of system of social relationships
and values; and crime, 500–1; and disturb-
ances, 260–64, 496–503; and revolutionaries,
537–8; of war, 260–64, 370–80. See also
Crises, Disturbances, War
Disorder. See Disturbances
Disorderly and orderly nations, 475–77
Disorganization. See Disintegration
Disruption of crystallized bonds, and disturbances
and war, 371. See also *Anomie*, Crises, Disintegration
Distribution of Ideational and Sensate types of
personality among, all historical persons, 518–
20; kings, 524; Roman Catholic popes, 522
Disturbances, internal; and blossoming of culture,
412, 419, 422, 493–96; and breakdown of social
relationships and values, 260–64; and capitalism, 487; and economic conditions, 238; and
education, 504–5; and forms of government,
504–5; and liberty, 177–79; and urban or rural
conditions, 504; and war, 488–92; causes of,
496–503; comparative violence by nations, 476–
78; criteria of magnitude, 385, 389–97; duration,
478–79; frequency by countries, 473–76; important, 385; impossibility of provision, 485;
movement, in Ancient Greece, 409–13; Ancient
Rome, 414–20; Austria and Germany, 430–35;
Byzantium, 420–23; China, 357–59; England,
435–40; Europe, 470–71; France, 423–29;
Holland, 457–59; Italy, 441–48; Poland and
Lithuania, 467–69; Russia, 461–66; Spain,
449–55; organico-proportional method of study
of, 386–89; periodicity, 481–86; qualitative
nature of, 403; rhythm of, 481; synchronous

in various countries, 505–6; trendless fluctuation of, 481–82

Divorce, 66–67, 87, 99, 109, 120

Divus, emperor as, 147

Domestici, 55

Domination, of Christian Church, 63–64, 147–48; of compulsory, contractual, and familistic relationships, 123–24; of forms of liberty, 178–80; of Sensate and theocratic government, 139–52

Dura lex sed lex, 129

Duration of interaction, 11–13; factors of, 12–14

Duration, of disturbances, 478–79; of life of business organizations, 218; of peace and war periods, 351–52

Duration of wars, actual and arithmetical, 265–66, 275–76, 338–39

Economic, factor, varying efficiency of, 374; impoverishment and government control, 196–208; interdependence of bourgeoisie and secular intelligentsia, 250–51; interpretation of history, 219–20; organizations, duration of life, 217–18; value, different estimation of in different cultures, 248–49

Economic conditions, accidental factors of, 235, 244, 247; immanent factors of, 222–24; in Ancient Greece, 230–33; Ancient Rome, 234–37; France, 237–43; Germany, 243–47; long-time and short-time waves in, 217–18; of main social classes in these countries, 232–47; related to types of culture, 220–23, 247–55; wider amplitude of fluctuation of leading classes, 251–52

Economic situation; and disturbances, 238–39, 359, 371–73, 500; and noneconomic cultural values, 220–23, 247–56; and war, 372–80

Economic standard of living, complexity of concept of, 225–27; inadequacy of dollar measured, 225–27

Economic well-being, barometer of, 225, 229–30; concept of, 226–27; dependent upon type of culture, 220–22

Economics, contemporary, as Sensate, 256

Education, and disturbances, 504; and war, 372–80

Efficiency, varying, of the same factor, 374

Egotism, in compulsory and contractual relationships, 31–32, 35–38; in pseudo-friendship, 25–26; of contemporary governments, 150–53

Egypt, impoverishment and totalitarianism in, 200–1; theocracy in, 141

Election, as an element of contractual relationship, 31–32, 104–8, 163, 167–70

Elements of compulsory relationship, 35; contractual, 30; familistic, 24

Elite. See Aristocracy, Leadership

Emancipation, of children in the family, 66–67, 87, 99, 110; of serfs, 77, 91–92, 103, 117

Emergency, social, and expansion of governmental control, 192, 207–8

Encyclopaedia Britannica. See *Britannica*

Engineering, social, limited possibility of, 485

England, disturbances in, 397, 435–40, 474, 476; 478; wars of, 312–17, 335, 345, 348–49, 352

English kings, percentage of Ideational and Sensate types among, 524

Europe, disturbances in, 469–71; population of, 340–45; wars of, 297, 335–48

Evolution of war, 360–63

Evolutionary delusions, 535–37

Expansion of governmental regimentation, and emergency, 196, 206–7; and impoverishment, 198–206; and liberty, 205–11; and type of culture, 192–96; and war, 196–98; contemporary, 118–21, 187, 205–11; factors of, 192–208; long-time waves in, 185–92; short-time waves, 192. See also Contraction, *Laissez faire*, Totalitarianism

Expectations, deductive, and inductive corroborations, 156

Expediency, as principle of contemporary politics, 128–29, 150–55; generating coercion, egotism, force, and self-destruction, 129–31, 153–54

Exploitation, commercial, of liberty, 172–73

Extensity of interaction, 6–9, 24–27, 30–32

External factors. See Accidental factors

Externalistic standpoint and liberty, 27–28, 187. See Behavioristic

Factors, accidental and externalistic, 221–22, 235, 239, 244, 247–48; immanent and internal, 125–31, 158–60, 170–77, 220–25; of crime, 500–1; disturbances, 177–79, 487–505; economic conditions, 220–25; expansion and contraction of governmental interference, 196–208; suicide, 500–1; totalitarianism, 196–208; war, 370–80. See also Causes

Fall of man, and government, as least evil, 207

Familistic relationships, 24–25; all-embracing character of, 27; and freedom, 27–28; and friendship, 25–26; and fusion of parties, 27–28; and *Gemeinschaft*, 29; and governmental regime, 153–54; and stranger, 28–29; and totalitarianism, 209–11; and type of culture, 132–38; fluctuation of proportion of, in main social groups of Europe, 123–24; pseudo-, 26, 36

Family, as all-embracing union, 27, 40; nature of social relationships in, 65–68, 86–88, 98–99, 109–11, 120–21. See also Consent, Divorce, Familistic

Famines, and expansion of governmental control, 198–205

Fas, 146

Fascism, 57, 119–20, 128, 138, 150, 152–53, 169, 182, 187, 191, 204

Feudal society, nature of social bonds, between free and unfree classes, 72–78; in Church, 61–65; family, 65–68; guilds, 68–70; rural and urban communes, 70–72; social strata in, 73

Feudalism, nature of social relationship in, 72–73

Fideles, 51–57

Fidelitas, as central category of medieval social relationship, 48–49; as a form of social relationship, 48; duties of the parties bound by, 55–56; role in main social groups, 49–137

Fidelitatis, sacramentum, 50, 53–57, 74, 78–79

Fluctuation, trendless, of, contraction and expansion of regimentation, 185–92; disturbances, 481–82; economic conditions, 230–47;

forms of government, 139–54, 158–60, 177; forms of liberty, 164–70; forms of social relationships, 123–31; *laissez faire* and totalitarianism, 208–11; war, 336–47, 352–57

Force, and compulsory relationships, 35–37; and contemporary politics, 128–29, 150–55; and expediency, 130–31, 153–54; as a result of disintegration of social relationships, 260–63

Foreigners in armies, 287, 306, 321

France, disturbances in, 397, 423–28, 374, 376, 378; economic conditions in, 237–43; social relationships in, 49–123; wars of, 304–9, 335–36, 345, 348–52, 367

Fraternities. See *Bruderschaften*

Free classes, nature of relationship between, 72–77, 90–91, 102–3, 117–18; unfree classes, 76–78, 91–92

Freedom, and genius, 176; and revolutions, 177–79; and types of culture, 170–71; as biological necessity, 173–74; behavioristic conception of, 161–62; decline of Senate form of, 168–70; factors of fluctuation of, 170–77; fluctuation of forms, 164–70; forms of, 163–64; formula of, 162–63; in relationships, compulsory, 35–37; contractual, 34; familistic, 27–28; pseudo, 172; reflex of, 176

Frequency of disturbances, 473–74; of war, 351–52

Friendship, Aristotle and Cicero on, 25–26; as a form of familistic relationship, 25–26; pseudo, 26

Fusion of parties in familistic relationships, 24–30

Future of Western culture and society, 532–39

General States, 83

Generations of predecessors, revolutionaries, reactionaries, accomplishers, cycle of, 482–85

Genius, and disturbances, 412, 419, 422, 493–96; and freedom, 176; and war, 364–69

Germany, disturbances in (with Austria), 430–35, 474, 476, 478; economic conditions of, 243–47; social relationships in, 49–137; totalitarianism in, 57, 119–20, 128, 138, 150, 152–53, 169–70, 182, 187, 191, 204; wars of, 321–23, 348–52

Gesellschaft and *Gemeinschaft*, 29

Globus, 55

God, age of, 154; and contemporary governments, 149–52; and theocracy, 140–45, 147–49

Government, as the least evil, 207; cycles of, 158–60, 177; fluctuation of, 140–54; forms of, 139; immanent change of forms of, 158, 177. See also Leadership

Governmental regimes, and disturbances, 504–5; and types of culture, 139–46; and war, 351, 370–71; compulsory, 93–97, 205–11; contractual, 82–85, 104–8; familistic, 47–61, 82–85; secular and theocratic, 139–40

Governmental regulation, and emergency, 196, 206–7; and impoverishment, 198–206; and liberty, 205–11; and war, 196–98; contemporary, 119–21, 187, 205–11; contraction and expansion of, 181–85; factors of, 192–208

Gradation of social relationships, 38

Greece, Ancient, disturbances in, 385, 409–13, 474, 476, 478; economic conditions of, 230–34; governmental regimes and poverty in, 201–2;

theocracy in, 144–45; totalitarianism, 185, 201–2; wars of, 290–95

Group, social, as a system of interaction, 5–6; antagonistic, 15–18; compulsory, 35–38; contractual, 30–35; familistic, 23–30; important, 46; modalities of, 6–21; organized, 18–21

Groups, social, nature of relationships in, associations, communes, guilds, labor unions, 68–69, 89, 100–2, 112–15; Church, 39, 61–65, 85–86, 97–98, 108–9, 120; family, 65–68, 86–88, 98–99, 109–11, 120; State, 49–61, 82–85, 93–97, 104–8, 118–21. See also Army, Associations, *Bruderschaften*, Christian, Classes, Communities, Family, Guild, Municipalities

Guarantees of Sensate liberty, 104–8, 163, 167–70; decline of, 115, 118–21, 127–32, 150–53, 169, 191–92, 204–8

Guild, forms of social relationships in, 68–69, 89, 100–1, 112–15

Hammurabi, code of, 155

Hapsburg kings, percentage of Ideational and Sensate types among, 524

Heredes, Deus non homo facit, 65–66, 86–87

Heroes, age of, 154

Heuristic value of logico-meaningful method, 156

Hierarchical bonds between free strata of medieval society, 70–78, 90–92

Hierarchy of social ranks in medieval society, 73

Hindu theocracy, 140–43. See also Brahmans

Historical persons, percentage of businessmen and religious leaders among, 526–28; percentage of Ideational and Sensate types among, 517–20

Historical process as a good little boy, 535–36

Historical tendency, and economic conditions, 247–48; and liberty, 164–79; and orderly progress, 481–82, 535–36; and peace, 346–47, 360–69; and political regimes, 140–60; and revolutionary progress, 536–37; and social relationships, 123–24. See also Cycles, Fluctuation, Progress

Hitlerism, 57, 119–20, 128, 138, 150–53, 169, 182, 187, 191, 204

Hittite code of law, 158

Holland, disturbances in, 457–60, 474, 476, 478; wars of, 329–31, 348–52, 365–66

Homage, 76, 102

Hominium ligium and *planum*, 75–76

Hungary. See Austria-Hungary

Husbandmen in Ancient Greece, 145

Idealistic culture, and economic well-being, 233, 238, 244, 247

Ideational culture, and disturbances, 498–503; and economic well-being, 232, 253–54; and forms of liberty, 162–67; and forms of political regimes, 139–53; and forms of social relationships, 132–37; and the future, 537–39; and war, 370–75; main bearers of, 223–24, 235–36, 241–42, 245

Ideational type of personality, percentage of, among all historical persons, 519; kings, 523; Roman Catholic popes, 522

Ideologies, and actual behavior, 221–22, 254–55,

510-29; Sensate, 145-50; theocratic, 140-45, 147-48, 155-56

Immanent causes and self-regulation of social processes. See Causes, immanent

Impoverishment and governmental regimentation, 198-205

Incas, theocracy of, 141; totalitarianism among, 186

Inch and continental maps, errors of, 273-75

Individual liberties. See Contractual relationships, Freedom, Rights

Individualism, and contractualism, egotism, and singularism, 33, 113-15, 136; and familism, 24-30; and freedom, 163-64, 168-70, 177-79; and relativism and utilitarianism, 151-53

Industrial strikes, and economic situation, 495

Inherently disorderly and orderly nations, fallacy of, 475-77

Inhibition, and Ideational culture, 253-55, 515

Institutiones pacis, 70

Integrating social classes, 223-53

Intelligentsia and bourgeoisie, as twins, 250-51

Intensity, of interaction, 9-10; of violence in revolutions by countries, 395-96, 476

Interaction, social, 5; antagonistic and solidary, 15-18, 21-23; continuous and discontinuous, 11-12; direction of, 15-18; duration of, 11-15; extensity of, 6-9; intensity of, 9-10; inter- and intragroup, 259-60; one-sided and two-sided, 6; organized and nonorganized, 18-22; tangible, 5-6

Intergroup relationship, and war, 260-64

Intermittent interaction, 11-12

Internal disturbances. See Disturbances, internal

Intimacy in compulsory relationships, 35-38; contractual, 30-35; familistic, 24-30

Intragroup relationship and disturbances, 260-64

Isolation. See Stranger

Italy, disturbances in, 441-48, 474, 476, 478; wars of, 323-26, 348-52

Japan, totalitarianism in, 186

Judgment of God, 154-55

Jus, connubii, 177; *divinum*, 146-47; *pontificum*, 146-47; *sacrum*, 146

Key principles, 529

Kings, nature of relationships to army, officials, and subjects, 49-61, 82-85, 93-97, 104-8, 118-21; proportion of Ideational and Sensate types among Austrian, English, French, and German, 524; proportion of upstarts among Roman, 147

Kinship and Germanic family, 65

Knighthood, as a class, 91; as vassal, 73, 91; economic conditions of, 241, 243-44; social rank of, 90-91;

Labor classes, economic conditions of, in Ancient Greece, 230-34; Ancient Rome, 234-37; Germany, 243-47; France, 237-47; social relationships among free and unfree, 68-69, 70-72, 76-78, 88-89, 91-92, 99-101, 111-15; unions of, 68-69, 89, 100-1, 112-15

Lag of immaterial culture from material, fallacy of, 495; of war from disturbances, 376-77, 498-99

Laissez faire versus totalitarianism, 181; and anarchism, 184; and contractualism, 184-85; and liberalism, 184-85; and liberty, 208-11; as a decrease of governmental regimentation, 182-85; as rarefaction of network of group, 182-85; factors and fluctuation of, 185-208. See also Freedom, Totalitarianism

Lamas, as theocracy, 141

Law, and contemporary governments, 150; of diminishing returns in wishes and means of their satisfaction, 171-72; theory of religious origin of, 156-58; undermined by expediency, 129-31, 153-54

Lawful, category of, in organized group, 19

Laws, expanding liberty of individuals, 104-9, 112-15, 168-69; limiting it, 115-16, 118-21, 169-70; prohibiting associations, 100-2, 112-14, 116-17

Leadership, and types of culture, 140-43; of the mighty and rich, 145-46, 148-58; of the sacerdotal class, 140-44, 147-49; secular and theocratic, 140-43

Leading and integrating classes, 223-53

League of Nations as homeopathic doctor, 534

Lex Burgundiorum, 65; *Wisigothorum*, 66

Liberalism, and contractual theories, 84, 145, 148-49; as contractualism, 34, 104-8, 167-70; decline of, 57, 115, 118-21, 127-33, 150-53, 169-70, 182, 187, 191-92, 204-8. See also Contractual relationships, Freedom, Democracy, Individualism, Totalitarianism

Liberty. See Freedom

Life, grim and stern in transitory periods, 532-35

Limit, principle of, 115-31, 158-60, 170-77, 220-25. See also Causes, immanent

Limited extensity of interaction, 7; in contractual relationships, 30-33

Linear, orderly progress, as Victorian utopia, 535-36; trend, lack of, 123-31, 139-54, 158, 160, 164-70, 177, 185-92, 336-47, 352-57, 481-82. See also Cycles, Fluctuation, Historical tendency

Lithuania. See Poland

Livre de justice et de plet, 73

Logico-meaningful method, heuristic value of, 156

Long- and short-time waves in historical process. See also Cycles, Fluctuation, Historical tendency, Linear

Love, in familistic relationship, 24-27; lack of, in compulsory and contractual, 30-31, 35-38

Loyalty, limited and unlimited in feudal relationships, 55-56, 68-69, 75-76, 89, 100-2. See also *Fidelitas*

Lupus, faction to faction as, 152

Magnitude of disturbances, see Disturbances; of war, see War

Man, debased and reviled in Sensate culture, 151-53, 539

Manus, 49, 73; *immixtio*, 73

Marriage, and consent of parents and parties, 64, 67, 87, 99, 110; as contract, 40-41; as unlimited familistic relationship, 28-29, 40-41. See also Contractual relationships, Divorce, Familistic, Family, *Manus*, *Mundium*, *Munt*

Masses with unintegrated minds, 537

Material culture, lag of immaterial from, 495. See also Economic

Mechanical periodicity, lack of, in disturbances, 482–86; in war, 351–60

Mechanistic conception of freedom, 161

Memory, and continuity of interaction, 14

Men, age of, 155

Mentality, and actual behavior, 221–23, 510–29; discrepancy between overt behavior and, 3–6 150–53, 213, 221–22, 254–55, 510–30; disintegrated and unintegrated, 537; of social sewers, 151–53. See also Mind

Merry-go-round of Sensate governments, 153

Method, heuristic value of logico-meaningful, 156; organico-proportional, 387–89; quantitative, numerically and verbally, 399–401

Might is right, and contemporary politics, 147, 151

Migration of social relationships, 211–16; and types of culture, 214–16

Militarism and totalitarianism, 196–98. See also War

Military leaders as totalitarianists, 197

Milites in privato obsequio, 55

Mind, disintegrated and unintegrated, 537; and crime, 500–1; and disturbances, 177–79, 487–505; and war, 177–79, 370–80. See also Mentality

Mir, 71

Missi dominici, 53

Mixed, forms of liberty, 167; modality of interaction, 15–17

Mob rule, in cycle of governments, 146, 159. See also Masses

Modalities of interaction and process, 5–23. See also Interaction

Moment, overestimation of the present, 151

Momentary values, overestimated, 151

Monarchy, and republic, 154; Aristotle, Botero, Ibn-Khaldun, Plato, Polybius on, 158–60; compulsory, 93–94; contractual, 104–8; familistic-patriarchal, 49–61; nature of social relationships in, 49–61, 82–85, 93–97, 104–8, 118–21; theocratic, 140–47; totalitarian, 93–97. See also Aristocracy, Democracy, Government, Totalitarianism

Mundium, 49

Municipalities, nature of social relationships in, 99–100, 111–12

Munt, 67, 73

Narrow utilitarianism of contemporary governments, 151

Nation, curve of war in history of, 363–68

Nationalistic disturbances, 403

Nations, disorderly and orderly, 475–77; militaristic and pacifistic, 348–51

Nazi. See Hitlerism

Necessity, freedom as biological, 173–77

Needs, biological, 511

Netherlands, the. See Holland

New and old Deal, ideologies of, 150–52, 199

Nominalism, conditionally assumed, 5

Nonmaterial culture, alleged lag of, 495

Numerical and verbal quantitativism, 399–400

Oath of fidelity. See *Fidelitas*

Obsequium, 55, 61

Oligarchy, in cycle of government, 159

One-sided interaction, 6

Opposition, and contemporary governments, 149–51

Optimism concerning the future, 536–39

Oracles in theocratic regime, 155

Ordeal in theocratic regime, 154–55

Organico-proportional method, 387–89

Organized group and interaction, solidary, 21–23; criteria of, 18–21

Oscillations. See Cycles, Fluctuation

Outlawing war, contemporary magic for, 363, 531–32

Overripe Sensate stage of contemporary culture, 532

Ownership, limitation of, in emergency, famine, war, 196–220. See also Communism, Contractual relationships, Familistic, Fascism, Hitlerism, Socialism, Totalitarianism

Pacta sunt servanda, as a condition of contractual relationships, 106, 126, 129

Pater familias, 49–50, 53, 73, 83

Patriarchal monarchy. See Monarchy

Pax romana, efficiency of, 304, 364

Peace. See War

Peaks of disturbances, 496–97

Percentage, of Ideational and Sensate types among all historical persons, 519–20; kings, 524; popes, 522–23; of persons historical through business and religious activity, 527; of years with and without disturbances, 473–74; of years with and without war, 351–52

Periodicity, lack of, in disturbances, 482–86; in wars, 293, 303, 309, 317, 320, 322, 325–26, 329, 330, 351–60; of socially established dates, 483; of wars, 352–56; theories of periodicity of disturbances, 482–84. See also Cycles, Fluctuation

Personality, definition of, 512–13; percentage of Ideational and Sensate types. See also Percentage

Perspective, narrow and shortsighted, of governments, 150–51

Pessimism, 536–39

Phenomena, clear-cut definition of nebulous. See Clear-cut

Placita, 51, 60

Planning, social, 485

Pluralistic differentiation of population, 45

Poland and Lithuania, disturbances in, 397, 466–69, 474, 476; wars of, 331–34, 348–52

Political, ideologies, see Ideologies; regimes, see Government; revolutions, 403–4

Polynesian tribes, theocracy of, 143–44

Pontifex maximus, 146–47

Popes, Roman Catholic, fluctuation of power of, 147–49; percentage of Ideational and Sensate types among, 522–23. See also Christian Church, Clergy, Sacerdotal class, Theocracy

Population, of Ancient Greece, 295; Ancient Rome, 296, 303; Europe, 340–45; Holland, 329; Italy, 324; Prussia, 321; Spain, 327

Position, social, in organized group, 18–19
Poverty. See Economic, Impoverishment
Predecessors, generation of, 483
Predictability and logico-meaningful method, 156; uncertainty of, 485
Priesthood as integrating class, 140–45, 147–49. See also Clergy, Sacerdotal, Theocracy
Princeps legibus solutus est, 189
Principles of immanent self-regulation and limit, 115–31, 158–60, 170–77, 220–25; of nebulous definitions, 227; of varying efficiency of a given factor, 374
Progress, of war, 360–63; utopia of orderly and revolutionary, 481–82, 535–37. See also Crises, Cycles, Fluctuation, Linear
Progressives, 536
Prohibited actions in organized groups, 19
Property. See Capitalism, Ownership
Prophets in theocratic regimes, 154–55
Prosperity, and governmental regimentation, 198–205; periods of, in Ancient Greece, 230–33; Ancient Rome, 234–37; France, 237–43; Germany, 243–47. See also Economic
Prussia, foreigners in army of, 321–22; population of, 321; wars of, 320–23. See also Germany
Psychoanalytical debasement of man, 152–53, 539
Pueri vel vassali, 55, 73
Punishment in theocratic regimes, ideology of, 155–56

Qualifications and reservations in study of, disturbances, 384–85; economic conditions, 225–29; social relationships, 43–47; wars, 265–83
Qualitative nature of disturbances, 403
Quantitative method, numerical and verbal, 399–401

Ranks social in medieval society, 70, 73–78, 90–92; and types of culture, 149–60.
Rapport, social, 37–38. See also Relationships
Reaction and counterreaction in revolutions, 481
Reactionaries, generation of, 484
Rebellion. See Disturbances
Recommended actions in organized group, 19
Recurrence. See Cycles, Fluctuation
Reflex of freedom, 176
Relationships, social, and crime, 500–1; and disturbances, 260–64, 496–503; and war, 260–64, 370–80; antagonistic, 21–23; compulsory, 35–39; contractual, 30–35; familistic, 23–30; fluctuation of, in Church, 39, 61–65, 85–86, 97–98, 108–9, 120; communes and guilds, 68–69, 89, 100–2, 112–15; family, 65–68, 86–88, 98–99, 109–11, 120; free and unfree classes, 72–78, 90–92, 102–3, 117–18; State, 49–61, 82–85, 93–97, 104–8, 118–21; migration of, 211–16; mode of origin and nature of, 40–41; organized, 18–21; solidary, 21–23. See also Compulsory, Contractual, Familistic, Interaction
Relative indicators of war magnitude, in Ancient Greece, 295, 297; Ancient Rome, 297, 303; Europe, 342–46
Relativism in politics, 128–29, 130–31, 150–55. See also Expediency
Religio, Cujus regio ejus, 86

Religion, and disturbances, 504; and social relationships, 39, 131–38; and theocracy, 139–54; and war, 373–76. See also Catholic, Christian, Clergy, Priesthood, Ideational, Theocracy
Religious, activity, percentage of persons historical through, 527; disturbances, 403; origin of law, 156–58
Repression of biological needs, and types of culture, 253–55, 515
Reservations. See Qualifications
Revolt against, contractualism, democracy, liberalism, 128–29; Sensate freedom, 168–70
Revolts. See Disturbances
Revolutionaries, generation of, 483–84
Revolutionary progress, 536–37
Revolutions. See Disturbances
Rex sacrificulus, 146
Rhythm, varying, in disturbances, 476–78
Rights of man and citizen, declaration of, 104–8, 163, 167–70; decline of, 115, 118–21, 123–32, 150–53, 169, 191–92, 204–8
Riots. See Disturbances
Rites of passage, 50
Rome, Ancient, disturbances in, 414–20, 474, 476, 478; government, secular and theocratic, 144–48; population of, 296, 303; totalitarianism, 188–89, 194, 202–3; wars of, 296–304, 352–53
Rural and urban communities, nature of social relationships in, 70–72, 88–89, 99–100, 111–12
Russia, disturbances in, 397, 460–66, 474, 476, 478; wars of, 309–12, 348–52

Sacer esto, 146
Sacerdotal, class, as leaders and rulers, 140–45, 147–48, 223, 231–52; monarchy, in Greece, 144–45; Rome, 146–47, see Monarchy
Sacramentum fidelitatis. See *Fidelitas*
Sacrosanctus, 146–47
Sacrum jus, 146
Satellites, 73
Scholae and *scholares*, 55
Schwurbruderschaften. See *Bruderschaften*
Secular government, contemporary, 149–54; in Ancient Greece, 145–46; Ancient Rome, 147; Europe, 148–49. See also Government
Self-regulation of social processes. See also Causes, immanent; Principle of limit
Sensate government, and freedom, 149–53, 163–64, 168–70, 177–79
Sensate mentality, and actual behavior, 3–5, 150–53, 213, 221–23, 254, 510–29; and atomism, individualism, 113–15, 136; and cynicism, expediency, and utilitarianism, 151–53; and disturbances, 498–504; and economic conditions, 221–23, 231–56; and efficiency of economic factors, 374; and egotism, 31–32; and force, 31–35, 129–31, 153–54; and forms of freedom, 163–65; and forms of government, 139–45, 149–54; and war, 373–77; percentage, of historical persons with, 519–20; kings with, 524; popes with, 522–23
Separatistic disturbances, 403
Singularism and contractualism, 113–15, 136
Social, and cultural, as two inseparable aspects,

3–6; bond, see Bond; classes, see Classes; differentiation and stratification, 19–20; group, see Group; etc.

Socialism, and freedom, 36–37; and impoverishment, 199–207; and militarism, 196–98; and totalitarianism, 184–85, 191–92, 213. See also Communism, Fascism, Hitlerism, Totalitarianism.

Socialist derivations and reality, 151, 213

Society. See Group, Interaction

Socioeconomic disturbances, 403

Solidary relationship, 15–18; different from organized, 21–23. See also Familistic

Sophists, theory of government and law of, 145

Spain, disturbances in, 397, 448–55, 474, 476, 478; wars of, 327–29, 348–53

Spectrum sociorelational, 47

Standard of living, criteria of, 225–31. See also Economic

Stoic freedom, 165–66

Stranger, as social category, in compulsory relationships, 37–38, 50; contractual, 32–33; familistic, 28–30, 50

Stratification of organized group, 19–20; and types of culture, 140–60; in Middle Ages, 70, 73, 78, 90–92

Taille abonnée, 77–78

Taoism, and liberty, 167; theocracy of, 141, 143

Tempo, varying in disturbances and wars, 476–78

Theocracy, and political leadership, 139; and types of culture, 139–40; fluctuation of, 140–54, 158, 223, 231–52; in Ancient Greece, 144–45; Ancient Egypt, 141; Ancient Rome, 146–47; Carthage, 141; China, 141, 143; Europe, 147–48; Incas, 141; India, 140–41; Islamic countries, 141, 143; Polynesian tribes, 143; Tibet, 141, 143; Zuñi, 143; satellites of, 154–56

Tibet, theocracy of, 141, 143

Totalitarianism, and anarchism, 184; and communism, 184–87, 191–92, 213; and emergency, 196, 207; and fascism, Hitlerism, 184–87, 191–92, 213; and freedom, 208–11; and impoverishment, 199–207; and laissez faire, 181; and liberalism, 184–85, 189–90; and militarism, 196–98; and New Deal, 184–87, 191–92, 213; and socialism, 184–87, 191–92, 213; and types of culture, 192–96; as increase of governmental regimentation, 182–85; contemporary, 190–92, 204–7; factors of, 192–208; fluctuation of, 185–92; in Ancient Egypt, 185, 200; Ancient Greece, 185, 201–2; Ancient Rome, 188–89, 194, 202–3; China, 185, 201; Europe, 186, 189, 195–96, 203–4; Inca, 186; India, 193–94; Islamic countries, Lipara, Persia, Peru, Sparta, 186

Transference of social relationships. See Migration

Transitional periods, and crime, 500–1; and disturbances, 177–79, 487–505; and forms of liberty, 177–79; and migration of social relationships, 211–16; and war, 370–80; contemporary, 535. See also Crises

Turkey, theocracy in, 141, 143

Type of personality. See Personality

Unam sanctam, 148–49

Unemployment relief in Ancient Egypt, Greece, Rome, China, India, Persia, Europe, 199–200

Unintegrated mentality. See Mentality

United States, crisis in, 534–35; depression and regimentation and totalitarianism, 149–52, 190–92, 203–4, 206; overripe Sensate freedom, 172

Universal suffrage, limitation of, 169–70

Unorganized group. See Group

Upstarts among Roman kings, percentage of, 147

Urban. See Municipalities, Rural

Utilitarianism, and Sensate leadership, 140, 144–46; narrow, of contemporary governments. 149–53

Value, of contemporary freedom, decline of, 168–70; of contractualism, decline of, 115, 118–21

Variable size of medieval military forces, 281

Variables, association between. See Association

Varying rhythm and tempo of social processes. See Periodicity, Rhythm, Tempo

Vassali, 55, 73

Villein, 77

Violence, and breakdown of network of social relationships, 260–64; and compulsory relationships, 35–37; and contemporary governments, 149–53; and freedom, 36–37; and totalitarianism, 208–11; in revolutions, 395–96; revolutionary, by countries and percentages, 476–78. See also Compulsory, Force

Vision, shortsighted, of governments, 149–53

Vita communis, in church, 62–64; in sects, 65

War, absolute indicators of, 287–88; and blossoming of nation, 363–69; and breakdown of social relationships, 259–64; and decline of nation, 363–69; and disturbances, 487–93; and economic conditions, 238–39; and forms of government, 196–98, 351; and sun spots and other cosmic conditions, 352–57; and types of culture, 370–76; as ultima ratio of conflict, 261; difficulties in study of, 265–83; duration of, 265–66, 275–76, 338–39; factors of, 375–80; lag from disturbances, 376–77, 498–99; movement of, in Ancient Greece, 290–95; Ancient Rome, 295–304; Austria-Hungary, 317–20, 348–53; England, 312–17, 348–53; Europe, 335–48; France, 304–9, 348–53; Germany, 320–23, 348–53; Holland, 329–31, 348–53; Italy, 323–26, 348–53; Poland and Lithuania, 331–34, 348–53; Russia, 309–12, 348–53; Spain, 326–29, 348–53; percentage of years with and without, 351–52; periodicity in, 352–60; relative indicators of magnitude of, 295; trendless fluctuation of, 360–63. See also Army, Casualty, Disturbances

Wealth, and freedom, 162–64, 167–68, 170–73; and leadership, 139–54; different estimation in Ideational and Sensate cultures, 220–29, 247–49. See also Economic

Weber-Fechner law and liberty, 171–72

Weltanschauung of person and type of culture, 509–10

Zuñi, theocracy of, 143